D1745612

9781734497304

Advanced Analytical Models
in ROV Modeling Toolkit

Second Edition

Advanced Analytical Models in ROV Modeling Toolkit

Second Edition

Over 800 Models and
300 Applications from the
Basel Accords to Wall Street
and Beyond

Johnathan Mun, Ph.D.

California, USA

WILEY

First Edition

John Wiley & Sons, Inc.

Second Edition

THOMSON-SHORE

For Jayden, Emma, and Penny.

In a world where risk and uncertainty abound,
you are the only constants in my life.

.

Dedicated in loving memory of my mom.

Delight yourself in the Lord and He will
give you the desires of your heart.

Psalm 37:4

PREFACE

Advanced Analytical Models is a large collection of advanced models with a multitude of industry and domain applications. The book is based on years of academic research and practical consulting experience, coupled with industry and problem-specific applications. The Modeling Toolkit software that holds all the models, Risk Simulator software, and Real Options SLS software were all developed by the author, with over 1,000 functions, tools, and model templates in these software applications. Trial versions are included with the book and can be downloaded online.

The applications covered are vast. Included are Basel II/III banking risk requirements (credit risk, credit spreads, default risk, market risk, value at risk, etc.) and financial analysis (exotic options and valuation), risk analysis (stochastic forecasting, risk-based Monte Carlo simulation, optimization), real options analysis (strategic options and decision analysis), Six Sigma and quality initiatives, management science and statistical applications, and everything in between, such as applied statistics, manufacturing decision analysis, operations research, optimization, forecasting, and econometrics.

This book is targeted at practitioners who require the algorithms, examples, models, and insights in solving more advanced and even esoteric problems. This book does not only talk about modeling or illustrate basic concepts and examples; it directs you to the author's company's website is filled with sample modeling videos, case studies, and software applications to help you get started immediately. It dispenses with all the theoretical discussions and mathematical models that are extremely hard to decipher and apply in the real business world. Instead, these theoretical models have been coded up into user-friendly and powerful software, and this book shows the reader how to start applying advanced modeling techniques almost immediately. The trial software applications allow you to access the approximately 300 model templates and 800 functions and tools, understand the concepts, and use embedded functions and algorithms in their own models. In addition, you can run risk-based Monte Carlo simulations and advanced forecasting methods, and perform optimization on a myriad of situations as well as structure and solve customized real options and financial options problems.

Each model template that comes in the Modeling Toolkit software is described in this book. Descriptions are provided in as much detail as the applications warrant. Some of the more fundamental concepts in risk analysis and real options are covered in the author's other books. It is suggested that these books, *Modeling Risk: Applying Monte Carlo Risk Simulation, Strategic Real Options, Stochastic Forecasting, and Portfolio Optimization,* Third Edition (2015) and *Real Options Analysis,* Third Edition (2016), both published by Thomson-Shore and ROV Press, be used as references for some of the models in this book. Those modeling issues that are, in the author's opinion, critical, whether they are basic issues or more advanced analytical ones, are presented in detail. As software applications change continually, it is recommended that you check the author's website (www.realoptionsvaluation.com) frequently for any analytical updates, software upgrades, and revised or new models.

This book covers the following software applications:

Modeling Toolkit

- Over 800 functions, models, and tools and over 300 Excel and SLS templates
- Covering the following applications:
  - Business analytics and statistics (CDF, ICDF, PDF, data analysis, integration)
  - Credit and Debt Analysis (credit default swap, credit spread options, credit rating, debt options and pricing)
  - Decision Analysis (decision tree, Minimax, utility functions)
  - Exotic Options (over 100 types of financial and exotic options)
  - Forecasting (ARIMA, econometrics, EWMA, GARCH, nonlinear extrapolation, spline, time-series)
  - Industry Applications (banking, biotech, insurance, IT, real estate, utility)
  - Operations Research and Portfolio Optimization (continuous, discrete, integer, static, dynamic, and stochastic)
  - Options Analysis (BDT interest lattices, debt options, options trading strategies)
  - Portfolio Models (investment allocations, optimization, risk and return profiles)
  - Probability of Default and Banking Credit Risk (private, public and retail debt, credit derivatives and swaps)
  - Real Options Analysis (over 100 types: abandon, barrier, contract, customized, dual asset, expand, multi-asset, multi-phased, pentanomials, quadranomials, sequential, switch, and trinomials)
  - Risk Hedging (delta and delta-gamma hedges, foreign exchange and interest rate risk)
  - Risk Simulation (correlated simulation, data fitting, Monte Carlo simulation, risk-simulation)
  - Six Sigma (capability measures, control charts, hypothesis tests, measurement systems, precision, sample size)
  - Statistical Tools (ANOVA, Two-Way ANOVA, nonparametric hypotheses tests, parametric tests, principal components, variance-covariance)
  - Valuation (APT, buy versus lease, CAPM, caps and floors, convertibles, financial ratios, valuation models)
  - Value at Risk (static covariance and simulation-based VaR)
  - Volatility (EWMA, GARCH, implied volatility, Log Returns, Real Options Volatility, probability to volatility)
  - Yield Curve (BIS, Cox, Merton, NS, spline, Vasicek)

Risk Simulator

- Over 50 statistical probability distributions
- Covering the following applications:
  - Applied Business Statistics (descriptive statistics, CDF/ICDF/PDF probabilities, stochastic parameter calibration)
  - Bootstrap Nonparametric Simulation and Hypothesis Testing (testing empirical and theoretical moments)
  - Correlated Simulations (simulation copulas and Monte Carlo)
  - Data Analysis and Regression Diagnostics (heteroskedasticity, multicollinearity, nonlinearity, outliers)
  - Forecasting (ARIMA, Auto-ARIMA, J-S curves, GARCH, Markov chains, multivariate regressions, stochastic processes)
  - Optimization (static, dynamic, stochastic)
  - Sensitivity Analysis (correlated sensitivity, scenario, spider, tornado)

Real Options SLS

- Customizable Binomial, Trinomial, Quadranomial, and Pentanomial Lattices
- Lattice Makers (lattices with Monte Carlo simulation)
- Super-fast super lattice algorithms (running thousands of lattice steps in seconds)
- Covering the following applications:
  - Exotic Options Models (barriers, benchmarked, multiple assets, portfolio options)
  - Financial Options Models (3D dual asset exchange, single and double barriers)
  - Real Options Models (abandon, barrier, contract, expand, sequential compound, switching)
  - Specialized Options (mean-reverting, jump-diffusion, dual asset rainbows)

Employee Stock Options Valuation Toolkit

- Applied by the U.S. Financial Accounting Standards Board for FAS 123R 2004
- Binomial and closed-form models
- Covering the following applications:
  - Blackout Periods, Changing Volatility, Forfeiture Rates, Suboptimal Exercise Multiple, and Vesting

ABOUT THE AUTHOR

Dr. Johnathan C. Mun is the founder, chairman, and CEO of Real Options Valuation, Inc. (ROV), a consulting, training, and software development firm specializing in strategic real options, financial valuation, Monte Carlo risk simulation, stochastic forecasting, optimization, decision analytics, business intelligence, healthcare analytics, enterprise risk management, project risk management, and risk analysis located in northern Silicon Valley, California. ROV has partners around the world including Argentina, Beijing, Chicago, China, Colombia, Hong Kong, India, Italy, Japan, Malaysia, Mexico City, New York, Nigeria, Peru, Puerto Rico, Russia, Saudi Arabia, Shanghai, Singapore, Slovenia, South Korea, Spain, Venezuela, Zurich, and others. ROV also has a local office in Shanghai.

Dr. Mun is also the chairman of the International Institute of Professional Education and Research (IIPER), an accredited global organization staffed by professors from named universities from around the world that provides the Certified Quantitative Risk Management (CQRM) and Certified Risk Management (CRM) designations, among others. He is the creator of many different powerful software tools including Risk Simulator, Real Options SLS Super Lattice Solver, Modeling Toolkit, Project Economics Analysis Tool (PEAT), Credit Market Operational Liquidity Risk (CMOL), Employee Stock Options Valuation, ROV BizStats, ROV Modeler Suite (Basel Credit Modeler, Risk Modeler, Optimizer, and Valuator), ROV Compiler, ROV Extractor and Evaluator, ROV Dashboard, ROV Quantitative Data Miner, other software applications, and the risk-analysis training DVD. He holds public seminars on risk analysis and CQRM programs. He has over 21 registered patents and patents pending globally. Dr. Mun has authored 13 books published by John Wiley & Sons, Elsevier Science, Thomson–Shore, and ROV Press, including *Modeling Risk: Applying Monte Carlo Simulation, Real Options, Optimization, and Forecasting,* First Edition (Wiley, 2006), Second Edition (Wiley, 2010), and Third Edition (Thomson–Shore, 2015); *Real Options Analysis: Tools and Techniques for Making Decisions Under Uncertainty,* First Edition (Wiley, 2006), Second Edition (Wiley, 2010), and Third Edition (Thomson–Shore, 2016); *The Banker's Handbook on Credit Risk* (2008); *Advanced Analytical Models: Over 800 Models and 300 Applications from the Basel Accords to Wall Street and Beyond,* First Edition (Wiley, 2008) and Second Edition (ROV Press, 2016); *Real Options Analysis: Tools and Techniques,* First Edition (Wiley, 2003), Second Edition (Wiley, 2005), and Third Edition (Thomson–Shore, 2016); *Real Options Analysis Course: Business Cases* (Wiley, 2003); *Applied Risk Analysis: Moving Beyond Uncertainty* (Wiley, 2004); and *Valuing Employee Stock Options* (Wiley, 2004). His books and software are being used at over 350 top universities around the world, including the Bern Institute in Germany, Chung-Ang University in South Korea, Georgetown University, ITESM in Mexico, Massachusetts Institute of Technology, U.S. Naval Postgraduate School, New York University, Stockholm University in Sweden, University of the Andes in Chile, University of Chile, University of Pennsylvania Wharton School, University of York in the United Kingdom, and Edinburgh University in Scotland, among others.

Currently a risk, finance, and economics professor, Dr. Mun has taught courses in financial management, investments, real options, economics, and statistics at the undergraduate and the graduate MBA levels. He teaches and has taught at universities all over the world, from the U.S. Naval Postgraduate School (Monterey, California) and University of Applied Sciences (Switzerland and Germany) as full professor, to Golden Gate University (California) and St. Mary's College (California), and has chaired many graduate research MBA thesis and Ph.D. dissertation committees. He also teaches weeklong Risk Analysis, Real Options Analysis, and Risk Analysis for Managers public courses where participants can obtain the CRM and CQRM designations on completion. He is a senior fellow at the Magellan Center and sits on the board of standards at the American Academy of Financial Management.

He was formerly the Vice President of Analytics at Decisioneering, Inc., where he headed the development of options and financial analytics software products, analytical consulting, training, and technical support, and where he was the creator of the Real Options Analysis Toolkit software, the older and much less powerful predecessor of the Real Options Super Lattice software. Prior to joining Decisioneering, he was a Consulting Manager and Financial Economist in the Valuation Services and Global Financial Services practice of KPMG Consulting and a Manager with the Economic Consulting Services practice at KPMG LLP.

He has extensive experience in econometric modeling, financial analysis, real options, economic analysis, and statistics. During his tenure at Real Options Valuation, Inc., Decisioneering, and KPMG Consulting, he taught and consulted on a variety of real options, risk analysis, financial forecasting, project management, and financial valuation issues for more than 100 multinational firms (current and former clients include 3M, Airbus, Boeing, BP, Chevron Texaco, Financial Accounting Standards Board, Fujitsu, GE, Goodyear, Microsoft, Motorola, Pfizer, Timken, U.S. Department of Defense, U.S. Navy, Veritas, and many others). His experience prior to joining KPMG includes being department head of financial planning and analysis at Viking Inc. of FedEx, performing financial forecasting, economic analysis, and market research. Prior to that, he did financial planning and freelance financial consulting work.

Dr. Mun received a Ph.D. in finance and economics from Lehigh University, where his research and academic interests were in the areas of investment finance, econometric modeling, financial options, corporate finance, and microeconomic theory. He also has an M.B.A. in business administration, an M.S. in management science, and a B.S. in biology and physics. He is Certified in Financial Risk Management, Certified in Financial Consulting, and Certified in Quantitative Risk Management. He is a member of the American Mensa, Phi Beta Kappa Honor Society, and Golden Key Honor Society as well as several other professional organizations, including the Eastern and Southern Finance Associations, American Economic Association, and Global Association of Risk Professionals.

In addition, he has written many academic articles published in the *Journal of Expert Systems with Applications; Defense Acquisition Research Journal; American Institute of Physics Proceedings; Acquisitions Research (U.S. Department of Defense); Journal of the Advances in Quantitative Accounting and Finance; Global Finance Journal; International Financial Review; Journal of Financial Analysis; Journal of Applied Financial Economics; Journal of International Financial Markets, Institutions and Money; Financial Engineering News;* and *Journal of the Society of Petroleum Engineers.* Finally, he has contributed chapters in dozens of books and written over a hundred technical whitepapers, newsletters, case studies, and research papers for Real Options Valuation, Inc.

JohnathanMun@cs.com

San Francisco, California

CONTENTS

PART I: MODELING TOOLKIT AND RISK SIMULATOR

APPLICATIONS 19

PART II: REAL OPTIONS SLS APPLICATIONS **533**

PART III: REAL OPTIONS STRATEGIC CASE STUDIES –

FRAMING THE OPTIONS.. 607

PART I: MODELING TOOLKIT AND RISK SIMULATOR APPLICATIONS

This book covers about 300 different analytical model templates that apply up to 800 modeling functions and tools from a variety of software applications. Trial versions of Risk Simulator and Real Options SLS are downloadable at www.realoptionsvaluation.com by clicking on **Download | Software.** The Modeling Toolkit software can be downloaded directly from the website at www.realoptionsvaluation.com/attachments/mt2016.exe.

Part I of the book deals with models using the Modeling Toolkit and Risk Simulator software applications, while Part II deals with real options and financial option models using the Real Options SLS software. Readers who are currently expert users of the Modeling Toolkit software and Risk Simulator software may skip this section and dive directly into the models. The Modeling Toolkit software incorporates about 800 different advanced analytical models, functions, and tools, applicable in a variety of industries and applications. Appendix A lists the models available in the software as of this book's publication date. These three software applications work on Windows 8/10 and require Excel 2013/2016/365 to run.

After installing the ROV Modeling Toolkit software, you will be prompted for a license key. Please write down the *Hardware Fingerprint* when the message appears. Then, in order to use the software immediately, enter the user name and license key provided below. This key will activate the software for 3 days. In the meantime, please send an e-mail request to admin@realoptionsvaluation.com with your *Hardware Fingerprint* as well as your full name, company you work for, and contact information (telephone and e-mail) so that you will be registered in the system and an extended 30-day trial license can be e-mailed to you.

Name: Temporary License   Key: 4B9A-FDF2-CMT7-DC98

To start the software, double click on the desktop icon for **Modeling Toolkit**. This action will start Excel. Inside Excel, you will notice a new menu item called *Modeling Toolkit*. This menu is self-explanatory as the models are categorized by application domain, and each model is described in more detail in this book. Please note that this software uses Excel macros. If you receive an error message on macros, it is because your system is set to a high security level. You need to fix this by starting Excel 2013/2016/365 and clicking on **File | Excel Options | Trust Center | Trust Center Settings | Macro Settings | Enable All Macros.**

In addition, please make sure to also install Risk Simulator and the Real Options SLS applications. After installation, start the Risk Simulator software by double clicking on its icon on the desktop. Excel will start. Inside Excel, click on the Risk Simulator ribbon and then click on **Risk Simulator | License.** E-mail admin@realoptionsvaluation.com your Hardware ID and we will issue you extended 90-day trial licenses for Risk Simulator and Real Options SLS. When sending the e-mail, please include the code: *AAM2E* for reference.

Note that the trial version of Modeling Toolkit will expire in 30 days. To obtain a full corporate license, please contact the author's firm, Real Options Valuation, Inc., at admin@realoptionsvaluation.com or visit the company's website. Notice that after the software expiration date, some of the models that depend on Risk Simulator or Real Options SLS software still will function, until their respective expiration dates. In addition, after the expiration date, these worksheets still will be visible, but the analytical results and functions will return null values. Finally, software versions continually change and improve, and the best recommendation is to visit the company's website for any new versions or details on installation and licensing. The appendixes provide detailed lists of all the functions, tools, and models, and the glossary describes the required variable inputs in this software.

1. Analytics – Central Limit Theorem

File Name: Analytics – Central Limit Theorem

Location: Modeling Toolkit | Analytics | Central Limit Theorem

Brief Description: Illustrates the concept of the Central Limit Theorem and the Law of Large Numbers using Risk Simulator's set assumptions functionality, where many distributions, at the limit, are shown to approach normality

Requirements: Modeling Toolkit, Risk Simulator

This example shows how the Central Limit Theorem works by using Risk Simulator and without the applications of any mathematical derivations. Specifically, we look at how the *normal* distribution sometimes can be used to approximate other distributions and how some distributions can be made to be highly flexible, as in the case of the beta distribution.

The Central Limit Theorem contains a set of weak-convergence results in probability theory. Intuitively, they all express the fact that any sum of many independent and identically distributed random variables will tend to be distributed according to a particular attractor distribution. The most important and famous result is called the Central Limit Theorem, which states that if the sum of the variables has a finite variance, then it will be approximately normally distributed. As many real processes yield distributions with finite variance, this theorem explains the ubiquity of the normal distribution. Also, the distribution of an average tends to be normal, even when the distribution from which the average is computed is decidedly not normal.

Discrete Uniform Distribution

In this model, we look at various distributions and see that over a large sample size and various parameters, they approach normality. We start off with a highly unlikely candidate, the *discrete uniform* distribution, also known as the equally likely outcomes distribution, where the distribution has a set of N elements, and each element has the same probability (Figure 1.1). This distribution is related to the *uniform* distribution but its elements are discrete instead of continuous. The input requirement is such that minimum < maximum and both values must be integers. An example would be tossing a single die with 6 sides. The probability of hitting 1, 2, 3, 4, 5, or 6 is exactly the same: 1/6. So, how can a distribution like this be converted into a normal distribution?

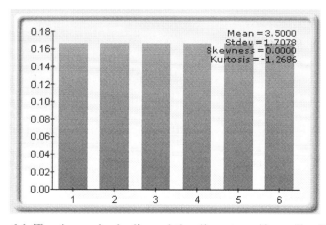

Figure 1.1: Tossing a single die and the discrete uniform distribution

The idea lies in the combination of multiple distributions. Suppose you now take a pair of dice and toss them. You would have 36 possible outcomes, that is, the first single die can be 1 and the second die can be 1, or perhaps 1-2, or 1-3, and so forth, until 6-6, with 36 outcomes as shown in Figure 1.2.

	1	2	3	4	5	6
1	1,1	2,1	3,1	4,1	5,1	6,1
2	1,2	2,2	3,2	4,2	5,2	6,2
3	1,3	2,3	3,3	4,3	5,3	6,3
4	1,4	2,4	3,4	4,4	5,4	6,4
5	1,5	2,5	3,5	4,5	5,5	6,5
6	1,6	2,6	3,6	4,6	5,6	6,6

Figure 1.2: Tossing two dice

Now, summing up the two dice, you get an interesting set of results (Figure 1.3).

	1	2	3	4	5	6
1	2	3	4	5	6	7
2	3	4	5	6	7	8
3	4	5	6	7	8	9
4	5	6	7	8	9	10
5	6	7	8	9	10	11
6	7	8	9	10	11	12

Figure 1.3: Summation of two dice

If you then plotted out these sums, you get an approximation of a normal distribution (Figure 1.4).

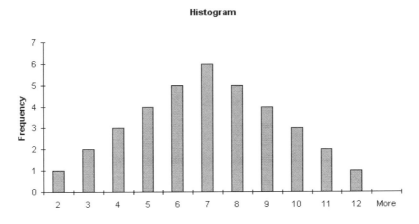

Figure 1.4: Approximation to a normal distribution

In fact, if you threw 12 dice together and added up their values, and repeated the process many times, you get an extremely close discrete normal distribution. If you add 12 continuous uniform distributions, where the results can, say, take on any continuous value between 1 and 6, you obtain a perfectly normal distribution.

Poisson, Binomial, and Hypergeometric Distributions

Continuing with the examples, we show that for higher values of the distributional parameters (where many trials exist), these three distributions also tend to normality. For instance, in the *Other Discrete* worksheet in the model, notice that as the number of trials (N) in a *binomial* distribution increases, the distribution tends to normal. Even with a small probability (P) value, as the number of trials N increases, normality again reigns (Figure 1.5). In fact, as $N \times P$ exceeds about 30, you can use the normal distribution to approximate the binomial distribution. Also, this is important, as at high N values, it is very difficult to compute the exact binomial distribution value, and the normal distribution is a lot easier to use.

We can test this approximation by using the *Distribution Analysis* tool (**Risk Simulator | Distribution Analysis**). As an example, we test a binomial distribution with $N = 5000$ and $P = 0.50$. We then compute the mean of the distribution, $NP = 2500$, and the standard deviation of the binomial distribution, $\sqrt{NP(1-P)} = \sqrt{5000(0.5)(1-0.5)} = 35.3553$. We then enter these values in the normal distribution and look at the *Cumulative Distribution Function* (CDF) of some random range. Sure enough, the probabilities we obtain are close although not precisely the same (Figure 1.6).

The normal distribution does in fact approximate the binomial distribution when $N \times P$ is large (compare the results in Figures 1.6 and 1.7).

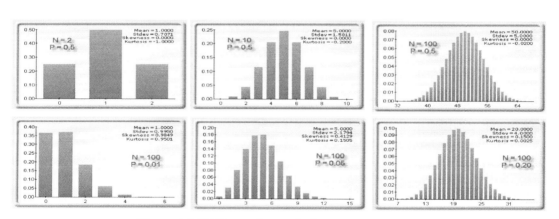

Figure 1.5: Different faces of a binomial distribution

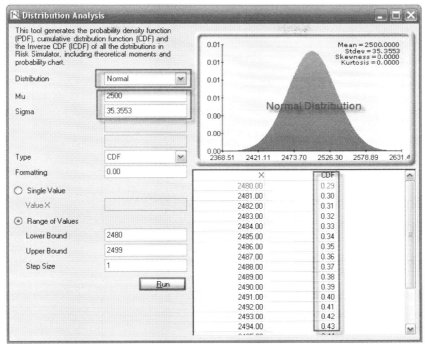

Figure 1.6: Normal approximation of the binomial

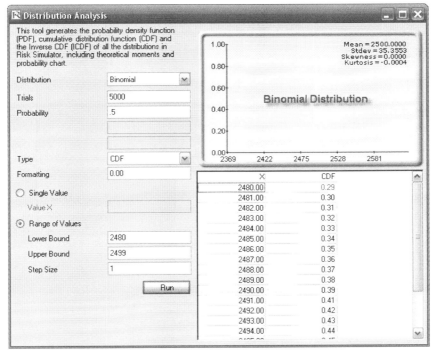

Figure 1.7: Binomial approximation of the normal

23

The examples also examine the *hypergeometric* and *Poisson* distributions. A similar phenomenon occurs: When the input parameters are large, they revert to the normal approximation. In fact, the normal distribution also can be used to approximate the Poisson and hypergeometric distributions. Clearly there will be slight differences in value as the normal is a continuous distribution whereas the binomial, Poisson, and hypergeometric are discrete distributions. Therefore, slight variations will obviously exist.

Beta Distribution

Finally, the *Beta* worksheet illustrates an interesting distribution, the beta distribution. Beta is a highly flexible and malleable distribution and can be made to approximate multiple distributions. If the two input parameters, *alpha* and *beta*, are equal, the distribution is symmetrical. If either parameter is 1 while the other parameter is greater than 1, the distribution is triangular or J-shaped. If alpha is less than beta, the distribution is said to be positively skewed (most of the values are near the minimum value). If alpha is greater than beta, the distribution is negatively skewed (most of the values are near the maximum value).

2. Analytics – Central Limit Theorem – Winning Lottery Numbers

File Name: Analytics – Central Limit Theorem (Winning Lottery Numbers)

Location: Modeling Toolkit | Analytics | Central Limit Theorem – Winning Lottery Numbers

Brief Description: Uses distributional fitting on past winning lottery numbers and illustrates the Central Limit Theorem and the Law of Large Numbers

Requirements: Modeling Toolkit, Risk Simulator

This fun model is used to illustrate the behavior of seemingly random events. For the best results, first review the *Central Limit Theorem* model in Chapter 1 before going over this example model. As in the *Central Limit Theorem* model, tossing a single six-sided die will yield a discrete uniform distribution with equal probabilities (1/6) for each side of the die. In contrast, when a pair of dice is tossed, there are 36 permutations of outcomes, and the sum of each of the 36 outcomes actually follows a discrete normal distribution. When more dice are tossed, the resulting sums are normally distributed. The same concept applies here.

Suppose that in a lottery there are 6 numbers you have to choose. First, you choose 5 numbers ranging from 1 to 47, without repetition, and then, you choose the sixth special number, from 1 to 27. You need to hit all 6 numbers to win the lottery jackpot. Clearly, assuming that the lottery balls selected at random are truly random and fair (i.e., the State Lottery Commission actually does a good job), then over many trials and many lottery games, the distribution of each value selected follows a discrete uniform distribution. That is, the probability of the number 1 being chosen is 1/47, and the probability of the number 2 being chosen is also 1/47, and so forth.

However, if all of the 5 balls that are randomly chosen between 1 and 47 are summed, an interesting phenomenon occurs. The *Historical* worksheet in the model shows the actual biweekly historical lottery winning numbers for several past years. Summing up the 5 values and performing a distributional fitting routine using Risk Simulator reveals that the distribution is indeed normal.

The probability of hitting the jackpot is clearly very small. In fact, this can be computed using a combinatorial equation. The probability of selecting the 5 exact numbers out of 47 is 1 out of 1,533,939 chances. That is, we have:

$$C_x^n = \frac{n!}{x!(n-x)!} = \frac{47!}{5!(47-5)!} = \frac{47!}{5!42!} = \frac{47 \times 46 \times 45 \, x...x \, 1}{(5 \times 4 \, x...x \, 1)(42 \times 43 \, x...x \, 1)} = 1,533,939$$

where C represents the number of possible combinations, n is the total number of balls in the population, and x represents the total number of balls chosen at a time.

The chances of choosing the sixth special number are 1 out of 27, hence, the probability is $1/27$. Therefore, the chance of choosing the correct 5 numbers and the special number is $1,533,939 \times 27 = 41,416,353$. So, the odds are 1 in 41,416,353 or 0.000002415% probability of hitting the jackpot. In fact, from the State Lottery Commission, we see that the published odds are exactly as computed (Figure 2.1).

SuperLotto Plus Prize Categories and Odds:

Match	Odds 1 in	Prizes
All 5 of 5 and Mega	41,416,353	Jackpot Pari-mutuel**
All 5 of 5	1,592,937	Pari-mutuel**
Any 4 of 5 and Mega	197,221	Pari-mutuel**
Any 4 of 5	7,585	Pari-mutuel**
Any 3 of 5 and Mega	4,810	Pari-mutuel**
Any 3 of 5	185	Pari-mutuel**
Any 2 of 5 and Mega	361	Pari-mutuel**
Any 1 of 5 and Mega	74	Pari-mutuel**
None of 5, Only Mega	49	Pari-mutuel**
Overall odds of winning	**23**	

Figure 2.1: Lottery winnings and payoffs

Also as expected, performing a data-fitting routine to the raw numbers (the first 5 values between 1 and 47), we have a discrete uniform distribution (see Figure 2.2 or the *Report 2* worksheet in the model).

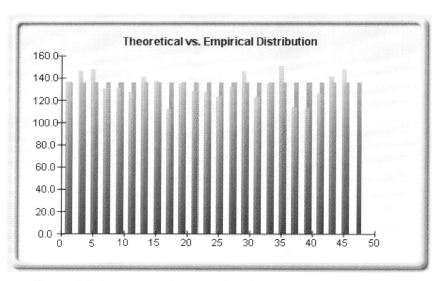

Figure 2.2: Lottery numbers and the discrete uniform distribution

However, when we performed a data fitting on the *sum* of the 5 values, we obtain an interesting result. The distribution is, as expected, normal (see Figure 2.3 or the *Report* worksheet in the model). In fact, running the simulation 10,000 trials using the fitted normal assumption, we obtain the forecast results seen in Figure 2.4.

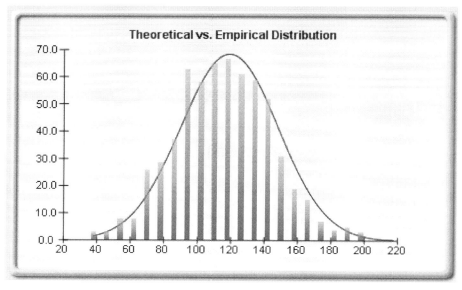

Figure 2.3: Sum of the lottery numbers are normally distributed

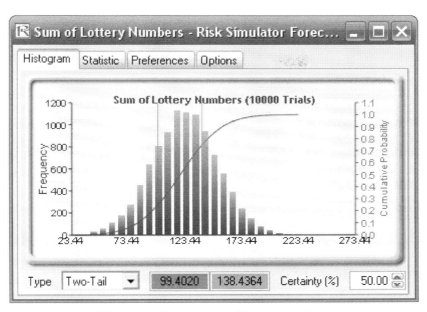

Figure 2.4: Simulation of lottery numbers

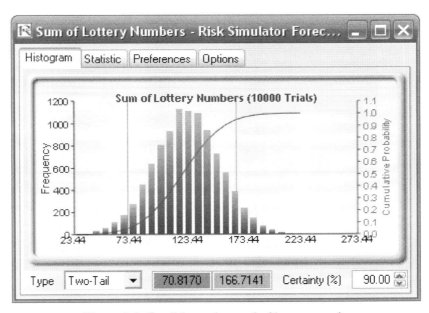

Figure 2.5: Confidence interval of lottery results

The theoretical distribution predicts that 90% of the time, the sum of the first five winning lottery numbers will be between 71 and 167 (rounded), and 50% of the time, they will be between 99 and 138 (rounded), as seen in Figures 2.4 and 2.5. We then looked at the raw historical winning numbers and computed the percentage of winning sequences that fall within this range, and the actual statistics are shown in Figure 2.6.

Actual Statistics

Minimum of Numbers 1-5	1
Maximum of Numbers 1-5	47
Minimum of Special Numbers	1
Maximum of Special Numbers	27
Between 71 and 167	90.38%
Between 99 and 138	50.48%

Figure 2.6: Actual empirical statistics of lottery drawings

Sure enough, the empirical statistics of actual winning numbers are very close to the theoretically predicted values. This means that, if you followed the statistics and picked the first 5 numbers such that the sum of the 5 values is within 71 and 167, your odds will have significantly improved! This is, of course, only an academic example and does not guarantee any results. So, don't go rushing out to buy any lottery tickets!

3. Analytics – Flaw of Averages

File Name: Analytics – Flaw of Averages

Location: Modeling Toolkit | Analytics | Flaw of Averages

Brief Description: Illustrates the concept of the Flaw of Averages (where using the simple average sometimes yields incorrect answers) through the introductions of harmonic averages, geometric averages, medians, and skew

Requirements: Modeling Toolkit

This model does not require any simulations or sophisticated modeling. It is simply an illustration of various ways to look at the first moment of a distribution (measuring the central tendency and location of a distribution), that is, the mean or average value of a distribution or data points. This model shows how a simple arithmetic average can be wrong in certain cases and how *harmonic averages*, *geometric averages*, and *medians* are sometimes more appropriate.

Flaw of Averages: Geometric Average

Suppose you purchased a stock at some time period (call it time zero) for $100. Then, after one period (e.g., a day, a month, a year), the stock price goes up to $200 (period one), at which point you should sell and cash in the profits, but you do not, and hold it for another period. Further suppose that at the end of period two, the stock price drops back down to $100, and then you decide to sell. Assuming there are no transaction costs or hidden fees for the sake of simplicity, what is your average return for these two periods?

Period	Stock Price
0	$100
1	$200
2	$100

First, let's compute it the incorrect way, using arithmetic averages:

Absolute Return from Period 0 to Period 1:   100%
Absolute Return from Period 1 to Period 2:   -50%
Average Return for both periods: 25%

That is, the return for the first holding period is (New – Old)/Old or ($200 – $100)/$100 = 100%, which makes sense as you started with $100 and it then became $200, or returned 100%. Next, the second holding period return is ($100 – $200)/$200 = –50%, which also makes sense as you started with $200 and ended up with $100, or lost half the value. So, the arithmetic average of 100% and –50% is (100% + [–50%])/2 = 25%.

Well, clearly you did not make 25% in returns. You started with $100 and ended up with $100. How can you have a 25% average return? So, this simple arithmetic mean approach is incorrect. The correct methodology is to use geometric average returns, applying something called *relative returns*:

Period	Stock Price	Relative Returns
0	$100	
1	$200	2.00
2	$100	0.50

Absolute returns are similar to relative returns, less one. For instance, going from $10 to $11 implies an absolute return of ($11–$10)/$10 = 10%. However, using relative returns, we have $11/$10 = 1.10. If you take 1 off this value, you obtain the absolute returns. Also, 1.1 means a 10% return and 0.9 means a –10% return, and so forth. The preceding table shows the computations of the two relative returns for the two periods. We then compute the geometric average where we have:

$$Geometric\ Average = \sqrt[N]{\left(\frac{X_1}{X_0}\right)\left(\frac{X_2}{X_1}\right)\cdots\left(\frac{X_N}{X_{N-1}}\right)} - 1$$

That is, we take the root of the total number of periods N of the multiplications of the relative returns. We then obtain a geometric average of 0.00%.

Alternatively, we can use Excel's equation of "=POWER(2.00*0.50,1/2)–1" to obtain 0%. Note that the *POWER* function in Excel takes X to some power Y in "POWER (X,Y)"; the root of 2 (N is 2 periods in this case, not including period 0) is the same as taking it to the power of 1/2.

This 0% return on average for the periods make a lot more sense. Be careful when you see large stock or fund returns as some may actually be computed using arithmetic averages. Where there is an element of time series in the data and fluctuations of the data are high in value, be careful when computing the series' average as the geometric average might be more appropriate.

Note: For simplicity, you can also use Excel's *GEOMEAN* function on the relative returns and deduct one from it. Note that you have to take the GEOMEAN of the relative returns: =GEOMEAN(2,0.5)-1 and minus one, not the raw stock prices themselves.

Say there are three people, Larry, Curly, and Moe, who happen to be cycling enthusiasts, apart from being movie stars and close friends. Further, suppose each one has a different level of physical fitness and they ride their bikes at a constant speed of 10 miles per hour (mph), 20 mph, and 30 mph, respectively.

Biker	Constant Miles/Hour
Larry	10
Curly	20
Moe	30

The question is, how long will it take on average for all three cyclists to complete a 10-mile course? Well, let's first solve this problem the incorrect way, in order to understand why it is so easy to commit the Flaw of Averages. First, computing it the wrong way, we obtain the average speed of all three bikers, that is, $(10 + 20 + 30)/3 = 20$ mph. So, according to that calculation, it would take 10 miles/20 miles per hour = 0.5 hours to complete the trek on average.

Biker	Constant Miles/Hour
Larry	10
Curly	20
Moe	30
Average	20 miles/hour
Distance	10 miles
Time to complete the 10-mile trek	**0.5 hours**

By doing this, we are committing a serious mistake. The average time is not the 0.5 hours figured by using the simple arithmetic average. Let us prove why this is the case. First let's show the time it takes for each biker to complete 10 miles. Then we simply take the average of these times.

Biker	Constant Miles/Hour	Time to Complete 10 miles
Larry	10	1.00 hours
Curly	20	0.50 hours
Moe	30	0.33 hours
Average		**0.6111 hours**

So, the true average is actually 0.6111 hours or **36.67** minutes, not 30 minutes or 0.5 hours. How do we compute the true average?

The answer lies in the computation of harmonic averages, where we define the harmonic average as $\dfrac{N}{\sum (1/X_i)}$ where N is the total number of elements, in this case, 3; and X_i are values of the individual elements. That is, we have the following computations:

Biker	Constant Miles/Hour
Larry	10
Curly	20
Moe	30
N	3.0000
SUM (1/X)	0.1833
Harmonic	16.3636
Arithmetic	20.0000

Therefore, the harmonic average speed of 16.3636 mph would mean that a 10-mile trek would take 10/16.3636 or 0.6111 hours (36.67 minutes). Using a simple arithmetic average would yield wrong results when you have rates and ratios that depend on time.

Flaw of Averages: Skewed Average

Assume that you are in a room with 10 colleagues and you are tasked with figuring out the average salary of the group. You start to ask around the room to obtain 10 salary data points, and then quantify the group's average:

Person	Salary
1	$75,000
2	$120,000
3	$95,000
4	$69,800
5	$72,000
6	$75,000
7	$108,000
8	$115,000
9	$135,000
10	$100,000
Average	$96,480

This average is, of course, the arithmetic average or the sum of all the individual salaries divided by the number of people present.

Suddenly, a senior executive enters the room and participates in the little exercise. His salary, with all the executive bonuses and perks came to $20 million last year. What happens to your new computed average?

Person	Salary
1	$75,000
2	$120,000
3	$95,000
4	$69,800
5	$72,000
6	$75,000
7	$108,000
8	$115,000
9	$135,000
10	$100,000
11	$20,000,000
Average	$1,905,891

The average now becomes $1.9 million. This value is clearly not representative of the central tendency and the "true average" of the distribution. Looking at the raw data, to say that the average salary of the group is $96,480 per person makes more sense than $1.9 million per person.

What happened? The issue was that an outlier existed. The $20 million is an outlier in the distribution, skewing the distribution to the right. When there is such an obvious skew, the *median* would be a better measure as the median is less susceptible to outliers than the simple arithmetic average.

Median for 10 people:	$97,500
Median for 11 people:	$100,000

Thus, $100,000 is a much better representative of the group's "true average."

Other approaches exist to find the "true" or "truncated" mean. They include performing a single variable statistical hypothesis t-test on the sample raw data or simply removing the outliers. However, be careful when dealing with outliers; sometimes outliers are very important data points. For instance, extreme stock price movements actually may yield significant information. These extreme price movements may not be outliers but, in fact, are part of doing business, as extreme situations exist (i.e., the distribution is leptokurtic, with a high kurtosis) and should be modeled if the true risk profile is to be constructed.

Another approach to spot an outlier is to compare the mean with the median. If they are very close, the distribution is probably symmetrically distributed. If the mean and median are far apart, the distribution is skewed, and a skewed mean is typically a bad approximation of the true mean of the distribution. Care should be taken when you spot a high positive or negative skew. You can use Excel's SKEW function to compute the skew:

Skew for 10 people:	0.28
Skew for 11 people:	3.32

As expected, the skew is high for the 11-person group as there is an outlier and the difference between the mean and median is significant.

4. Analytics – Mathematical Integration Approximation Model

File Name: Analytics – Mathematical Integration Approximation Model

Location: Modeling Toolkit | Analytics | Mathematical Integration Approximation Model

Brief Description: Applies simulation to estimate the area under a curve without the use of any calculus-based mathematical integration

Requirements: Modeling Toolkit, Risk Simulator

Theoretical Background

There are several ways to compute the area under a curve. The best approach is mathematical integration of a function or equation. For instance, if you have the equation:

$$f(x) = x^3$$

then the area under the curve between 1 and 10 is found through the integral:

$$\int_{1}^{10} x^3 dx = \left[\frac{x^4}{4} \right]_{1}^{10} = 2499.75$$

Similarly, any function *f(x)* can be solved and found this way. However, for complex functions, applying mathematical integration might be somewhat cumbersome. This is where simulation comes in. To illustrate, how would you solve a seemingly simple problem like the following?

$$\int_{A}^{B} \frac{1}{x^4 - \sin(1 - x^4)} dx$$

Well, dust off those old advanced calculus books and get the solution:

$$\int_{A}^{B} \frac{1}{x^4 - Sin(1 - x^4)} dx = \frac{Log\left(Sin(x)^{1/4} - x(1 + Sin(x))^{1/4}\right) - Log\left(Sin(x)^{1/4} - x(1 + Sin(x))^{1/4}\right) - 2ArcTan\left(x\left(\frac{Sin(x)}{1 + Sin(x)}\right)^{-1/4}\right)}{4Sin(x)^{3/4}(1 + Sin(x))^{1/4}} \Bigg|_{A}^{B}$$

The point is, sometimes simple-looking functions get really complicated. Using Monte Carlo simulation, we can *approximate* the value under the curve. Note that this approach yields only approximations, not exact values. Let's see how this approach works…

The area under a curve can be seen as the shaded area (A.T.R.U.B) in Figure 4.1, between the x-axis values of A and B, and the *y = f(x)* curve.

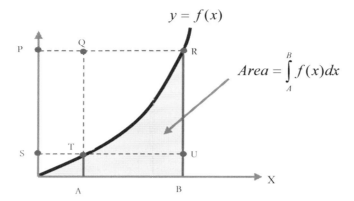

$$y = f(x)$$

$$Area = \int_{A}^{B} f(x)dx$$

Figure 4.1: Graphical representation of a mathematical integration

Looking closely at the graph, one can actually imagine two boxes. Specifically, if the area of interest is the shaded region or A.T.R.U.B, then we can draw two imaginary boxes, A.T.U.B and T.Q.R.U. Computing the area of the first box is simple, where we have a simple rectangle. Computing the second box is trickier, as part of the area in the box is below the curve and part of it is above the curve. In order to obtain the area under the curve that is within the T.Q.R.U box, we run a simulation with a uniform distribution between the values A and B, and compute the corresponding values on the y-axis using the *f(x)* function, while at the same time, simulate a uniform distribution between *f(A)* and *f(B)* on the y-axis. Then we find the average number of times the simulated values on the y-axis are at or below the curve or *f(x)* value. Using this average value, we multiply it by the area in the box to approximate the value under the curve in the box. Summing this value with the smaller box of A.T.U.B provides the entire area under the curve.

Model Background

The analysis in the *Model* worksheet illustrates an approximation of a simple equation; namely, we have the following equation to value:

$$\int_{1}^{10} x^3 dx$$

Solving this integration, we obtain the value under the curve of:

$$\int_{1}^{10} x^3 dx = \left[\frac{x^4}{4}\right]_{1}^{10} = 2499.75$$

Now, we attempt to solve this using simulation through the model shown in Figure 4.2.

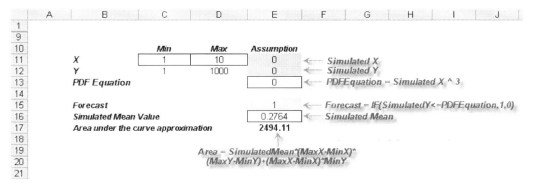

Figure 4.2: Simulation model for mathematical integration

Procedure

1. We first enter the minimum and maximum values on the x-axis. In this case, they are 1 and 10 (cells **C11** and **D11** in Figure 4.2). This represents the range on the x-axis we are interested in.

2. Next, compute the corresponding y-axis values (cells **C12** and **D12**). For instance, in this example we have $y = f(x) = x^3$, which means that for $x = 1$, we have $y = 1^3 = 1$ and for $x = 10$, we have $y = 10^3 = 1000$.

3. Set two uniform distribution assumptions between the minimum and maximum values, one for x and one for y (cells **E11** and **E12**).

4. Compute the PDF equation, in this example, it is $y = f(x) = x^3$ in cell **E13**, linking the x value in the equation to the simulated x value.

5. Create a dummy **0,1** variable and set it as **IF(SimulatedY <= PDFEquation, 1, 0)** in cell **E15** and set it as a forecast cell. This means that if the simulated y value is under the curve on the graph, the cell returns the value 1, or the value 0 if it is above the curve.

6. Run the simulation and manually type in the simulated mean value into cell **E16**.

7. Compute the approximate value under the curve using:

   SimulatedMean*(MaxX–MinX)*(MaxY–MinY)+(MaxX–MinX)*MinY,
   that is, the area T.Q.R.U plus the area under the curve of A.T.U.B.

The result is 2494.11, a close approximation to 2499.75, with an error of about 0.23%. Again, this is a fairly decent result but still an approximation. This approach relieves the analyst from having to apply advanced calculus to solve difficult integration problems.

5. Analytics – Projectile Motion

File Name: Analytics – Projectile Motion

Location: Modeling Toolkit | Analytics | Projectile Motion

Brief Description: Uses simulation to compute the probabilistic distance a missile will travel given the angle of attack, initial velocity, and probability of midflight failure

Requirements: Modeling Toolkit, Risk Simulator

This example illustrates how a physics model can be built in Excel and simulated, to account for the uncertainty in inputs. This model shows the motion of a projectile (e.g., a missile) launched from the ground with a particular initial velocity, at a specific angle. The model computes the height and distance of the missile at various points in time, and maps the motion in a graph. Further, we model the missile's probability of failure (i.e., we assume that the missile can fail midflight and is a crude projectile, rather than a smart bomb, where there is no capability for any midcourse corrections and no onboard navigational and propulsion controls).

We know from physics that the location of the projectile can be mapped on an x-axis and y-axis chart, representing the distance and height of the projectile at various points in time, and those x-axis and y-axis values are determined by:

$$\text{Location on x-axis}: X_t = V_0 t Cos(\theta)$$

$$\text{Location on y-axis}: Y_t = V_0 t Sin(\theta) - \frac{1}{2} g t^2$$

t = time, V_0 = initial velocity, g = gravitational acceleration, θ = angle of attack

In addition, we can compute the following assuming that there is no midflight failure:

$$\text{Time to reach Max height} = \frac{V_0 Sin(\theta)}{g}$$

$$\text{Max height} = \frac{V_0^2 [Sin(\theta)]^2}{2g}$$

$$\text{Time to impact} = \frac{2 V_0 Sin(\theta)}{g}$$

$$\text{Max range} = \frac{V_0^2}{g} Sin(2\theta)$$

The inputs are initial velocity, angle, time step, and failure rate (Figure 5.1). Time step (delta *t*) is any positive value representing how granular you wish the distance and height computations to be, in terms of time. For instance, if you enter 0.10 for time steps, the time period will step 0.1 hours each period.

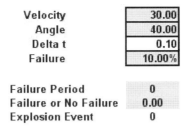

Velocity	30.00
Angle	40.00
Delta t	0.10
Failure	10.00%

Failure Period	0
Failure or No Failure	0.00
Explosion Event	0

Figure 5.1: Assumptions in the missile trajectory model

Velocity, angle, and failure rate can be uncertain and hence subject to simulation. The results are shown as a table and graphical representation. Failure rate is simulated using a Bernoulli distribution (yes-no or 0-1 distribution, with 1 representing failure, and 0 representing no failure), as seen in Figure 5.2. Figure 5.3 illustrates the sample flight path or trajectory of the missile.

		Position		
Period	time	x	y	Failure
0	0.00	0.0000	0.0000	0
1	0.10	2.2981	1.8794	0
2	0.20	4.5963	3.6607	0
3	0.30	6.8944	5.3441	0
4	0.40	9.1925	6.9295	0
5	0.50	11.4907	8.4168	0
6	0.60	13.7888	9.8062	0
7	0.70	16.0869	11.0975	0
8	0.80	18.3851	12.2909	0
9	0.90	20.6832	13.3863	0
10	1.00	22.9813	14.3836	0
11	1.10	25.2795	15.2830	0
12	1.20	27.5776	16.0844	0

Figure 5.2: Missile coordinates midflight and probability of missile failure

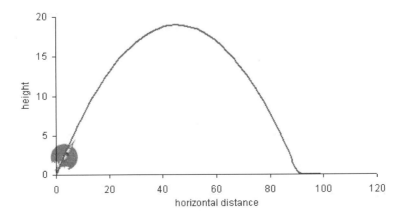

Figure 5.3 Graphical representation of the missile flight path

Procedure

This model has preset assumptions and forecasts, and is ready to be run by following these steps:

1. Go to the *Model* worksheet and click on **Risk Simulator | Change Profile,** and select the *Projectile Motion* profile.

2. Run the simulation by clicking the **RUN** icon or **Risk Simulator | Run Simulation**.

3. On the forecast chart, select **Right-Tail**, type in **110**, and hit **TAB** on your keyboard. The results indicate that there is only 6.80% chance that you will be hit by the missile if you lived 110 miles away, assuming all the inputs are valid (Figure 5.4).

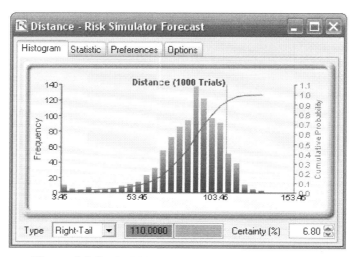

Figure 5.4: Probabilistic forecast of projectile range

Alternatively, you can recreate the model assumptions and forecast by following these steps:

1. Go to the *Model* worksheet and click on **Risk Simulator | Change Profile** and select the *Projectile Motion* profile.

2. Select cell **E4** and define it as an input assumption (**Risk Simulator | Set Input Assumption**) and choose a distribution of your choice (e.g., *Normal*) and click **OK**. Repeat for cells **E5** and **E7**, one at a time. Then, select cell **E9** and make it a *Discrete Uniform* distribution between **0** and **44**; make cell **E10** a *Bernoulli* distribution and click on the **link** icon and link it to cell **E7**; and make sure to check the *Enable Dynamic Simulations* check box and click **OK** (Figure 5.5).

3. Select cell **D60** and make it a forecast (**Risk Simulator | Set Output Forecast**).

4. Run the simulation by clicking the **RUN** icon or **Risk Simulator | Run Simulation**.

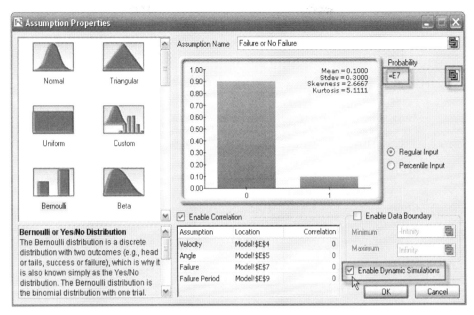

Figure 5.5: Simulating midflight failures

6. Analytics – Regression Diagnostics

File Name: Analytics – Regression Diagnostics

Location: Modeling Toolkit | Analytics | Regression Diagnostics

Brief Description: Shows how to run a Diagnostic Analysis on your data before generating forecast models.

Requirements: Modeling Toolkit, Risk Simulator

Most forecast models (e.g., time-series, extrapolation, ARIMA, regression, and others) suffer from model errors because analysts neglect to check the data for the correct model assumptions (autocorrelation, heteroskedasticity, micronumerosity, multicollinearity, nonlinearity, outliers, seasonality, sphericity, stationarity, structural breaks, and others). This model provides a sample dataset on which we can run Risk Simulator's *Diagnostic* tool in order to determine the econometric properties of the data. The diagnostics include checking the data for heteroskedasticity, nonlinearity, outliers, specification errors, micronumerosity, stationarity and stochastic properties, normality and sphericity of the errors, and multicollinearity. Each test is described in more detail in its respective report in the model.

Procedure

To run the analysis, follow the instructions below:

1. Go to the *Time-Series Data* worksheet and select the data including the variable names (cells **C5:H55**).

2. Click on **Risk Simulator | Analytical Tools | Diagnostic Tool**.

3. Check the data and select the **Dependent Variable Y** from the drop-down menu. Click **OK** when finished (Figure 6.1).

Spend some time reading through the reports generated from this diagnostic tool.

A common violation in forecasting and regression analysis is *heteroskedasticity*, that is, the variance of the errors increases over time (see Figure 6.2 for test results using the *Diagnostic* tool). Visually, the width of the vertical data fluctuations increases or fans out over time, and the coefficient of determination (R-squared coefficient) typically drops significantly when heteroskedasticity exists. If the variance of the dependent variable is not constant, then the error's variance will not be constant. Unless the heteroskedasticity of the dependent variable is pronounced, its effect will not be severe: The least-squares estimates will still be unbiased, and the estimates of the slope and intercept will be either normally distributed if the errors are normally distributed, or at least normally distributed asymptotically (as the number of data points becomes large) if the errors are not normally distributed. The estimate for the variance of the slope and overall variance will be inaccurate, but the inaccuracy is not likely to be substantial if the independent-variable values are symmetric about their mean.

Multiple Regression Analysis Data Set

Aggravated Assault	Bachelor's Degree	Police Expenditure Per Capita	Population in Millions	Population Density (Persons/Sq Mile)	Unemployment Rate
521	18308	185	4.041	79.6	7.2
367	1148	600	0.55	1	8.5
443	18068	372	3.665	32.3	5.7
365	7729	142	2.351	45.1	7.3
614	100484	432	29.76	190.8	7.5
385	16728	290	3.294	31.8	5
286	14630				
397	4008				
764	38927				
427	22322				
153	3711				
231	3136				
524	50508				
328	28886				
240	16996				
286	13035				
285	12973				
569	16309				
96	5227				
498	19235				
481	44487				
468	44213				
177	23619				
198	9106				
458	24917				
108	3872				
246	8945				
291	2373				
68	7128				
311	23624				
606	5242				
512	92629				
426	28795				
47	4487	143	0.639	9.3	4.1

Figure 6.1: Running the data diagnostic tool

Diagnostic Results

	Heteroskedasticity		Micronumerosity	Outliers			Nonlinearity	
Variable	W-Test p-value	Hypothesis Test result	Approximation result	Natural Lower Bound	Natural Upper Bound	Number of Potential Outliers	Nonlinear Test p-value	Hypothesis Test result
Y			no problems	-7.86	671.70	2		
Variable X1	0.2543	Homoskedastic	no problems	-21377.95	64713.03	3	0.2458	linear
Variable X2	0.3371	Homoskedastic	no problems	77.47	445.93	2	0.0335	nonlinear
Variable X3	0.3649	Homoskedastic	no problems	-5.77	15.69	3	0.0305	nonlinear
Variable X4	0.3066	Homoskedastic	no problems	-295.96	628.21	4	0.9298	linear
Variable X5	0.2495	Homoskedastic	no problems	3.35	9.38	3	0.2727	linear

Figure 6.2: Results from tests of outliers, heteroskedasticity, micronumerosity, and nonlinearity

If the number of data points is small (*micronumerosity*), it may be difficult to detect assumption violations. With small sample sizes, assumption violations such as non-normality or heteroskedasticity of variances are difficult to detect even when they are present. With a small number of data points, linear regression offers less protection against violation of assumptions. With few data points, it may be hard to determine how well the fitted line matches the data, or whether a nonlinear function would be more appropriate. Even if none of the test assumptions is violated, a linear regression on a small number of data points may not have sufficient power to detect a significant difference between the slope and zero, even if the slope is nonzero. The power depends on the residual error, the observed variation in the independent variable, the selected significance alpha level of the test, and the number of data points. Power decreases as the residual variance increases, decreases as the significance level is decreased (i.e., as the test is made more stringent), increases as the variation in observed independent variable increases, and increases as the number of data points increases.

Values may not be identically distributed because of the presence of outliers. *Outliers* are anomalous values in the data. They may have a strong influence over the fitted slope and intercept, giving a poor fit to the bulk of the data points. Outliers tend to increase the estimate of residual variance, lowering the chance of rejecting the null hypothesis, that is, creating higher prediction errors. They may be due to recording errors, which may be correctable, or they may be due to not all of the dependent-variable values being sampled from the same population. Apparent outliers may also be due to the dependent-variable values being from the same, but non-normal, population. However, a point may be an unusual value in either an independent or dependent variable without necessarily being an outlier in the scatter plot. In regression analysis, the fitted line can be highly sensitive to outliers. In other words, least squares regression is not resistant to outliers, thus, neither is the fitted-slope estimate. A point vertically removed from the other points can cause the fitted line to pass close to it, instead of following the general linear trend of the rest of the data, especially if the point is relatively far horizontally from the center of the data.

However, great care should be taken when deciding if the outliers should be removed. Although in most cases the regression results look better when outliers are removed, a priori justification must first exist. For instance, if one is regressing the performance of a particular firm's stock returns, outliers caused by downturns in the stock market should be included; these are not truly outliers. Rather they are inevitabilities in the business cycle. Forgoing these outliers and using the regression equation to forecast one's retirement fund based on the firm's stocks will yield incorrect results at best. In contrast, suppose the outliers are caused by a single nonrecurring business condition (e.g., merger and acquisition) and such business structural changes are not forecast to recur. Then these outliers should be removed and the data cleansed prior to running a regression analysis. The analysis here only identifies outliers; it is up to the user to determine if they should remain or be excluded.

Sometimes a *nonlinear* relationship between the dependent and independent variables is more appropriate than a linear relationship. In such cases, running a linear regression will not be optimal. If the linear model is not the correct form, then the slope and intercept estimates and the fitted values from the linear regression will be biased, and the fitted slope and intercept estimates will not be meaningful. Over a restricted range of independent or dependent variables, nonlinear models may be well approximated by linear models (this is, in fact, the basis of linear interpolation), but for accurate prediction, a model appropriate to the data should be selected. A nonlinear transformation should be applied to the data first before running a regression. One simple approach is to take the natural logarithm of the independent variable (other approaches include taking the square root or raising the independent variable to the second or third power) and run a regression or forecast using the nonlinearly transformed data.

Another typical issue when forecasting time-series data is whether the independent-variable values are truly independent of each other or whether they are dependent. Dependent-variable values collected over a time series may be *autocorrelated*. For serially correlated dependent-variable values, the estimates of the slope and intercept will be unbiased, but the estimates of their forecast and variances will not be reliable; hence the validity of certain statistical goodness-of-fit tests will be flawed. For instance, interest rates, inflation rates, sales, revenues, and many other time-series data typically are autocorrelated, where the value in the current period is related to the value in a previous period, and so forth (clearly, the inflation rate in March is related to February's level, which, in turn, is related to January's level, and so forth). Ignoring such blatant relationships will yield biased and less accurate forecasts. In such events, an autocorrelated regression model or an ARIMA model may be better suited (**Risk Simulator | Forecasting | ARIMA**). Finally, the autocorrelation functions of a series that is nonstationary tend to decay slowly (see the Nonstationary report in the model).

If autocorrelation AC(*1*) is nonzero, it means that the series is first-order serially correlated. If AC(*k*) dies off more or less geometrically with increasing lag, it implies that the series follows a low-order autoregressive process. If AC(*k*) drops to zero after a small number of lags, it implies that the series follows a low-order moving-average process. Partial correlation PAC(*k*) measures the correlation of values that are *k* periods apart after removing the correlation from the intervening lags. If the pattern of autocorrelation can be captured by an autoregression of order less than *k*, then the partial autocorrelation at lag *k* will be close to zero. Ljung-Box Q-statistics and their p-values at lag *k* have the null hypothesis that there is no autocorrelation up to order *k*. The dotted lines in the plots of the autocorrelations are the approximate two standard error bounds. If the autocorrelation is within these bounds, it is not significantly different from zero at the 5% significance level.

Autocorrelation measures the relationship to the past of the dependent *Y* variable to itself. Distributive lags, in contrast, are time-lag relationships between the dependent *Y* variable and different independent *X* variables. For instance, the movement and direction of mortgage rates tend to follow the Federal Funds Rate but at a time lag (typically 1 to 3 months). Sometimes, time lags follow cycles and seasonality (e.g., ice cream sales tend to peak during the summer months and hence are related to last summer's sales, 12 months in the past). The distributive lag analysis (Figure 6.3) shows how the dependent variable is related to each of the independent variables at various time lags, when all lags are considered simultaneously, to determine which time lags are statistically significant and should be considered.

Autocorrelation

Time Lag	AC	PAC	Lower Bound	Upper Bound	Q-Stat	Prob
1	0.0580	0.0580	-0.2828	0.2828	0.1786	0.6726
2	-0.1213	-0.1251	-0.2828	0.2828	0.9754	0.6140
3	0.0590	0.0756	-0.2828	0.2828	1.1679	0.7607
4	0.2423	0.2232	-0.2828	0.2828	4.4865	0.3442
5	0.0067	-0.0078	-0.2828	0.2828	4.4890	0.4814
6	-0.2654	-0.2345	-0.2828	0.2828	8.6516	0.1941
7	0.0814	0.0939	-0.2828	0.2828	9.0524	0.2489
8	0.0634	-0.0442	-0.2828	0.2828	9.3012	0.3175
9	0.0204	0.0673	-0.2828	0.2828	9.3276	0.4076
10	-0.0190	0.0865	-0.2828	0.2828	9.3512	0.4991
11	0.1035	0.0790	-0.2828	0.2828	10.0648	0.5246
12	0.1658	0.0978	-0.2828	0.2828	11.9466	0.4500
13	-0.0524	-0.0430	-0.2828	0.2828	12.1394	0.5162
14	-0.2050	-0.2523	-0.2828	0.2828	15.1738	0.3664
15	0.1782	0.2089	-0.2828	0.2828	17.5315	0.2881
16	-0.1022	-0.2591	-0.2828	0.2828	18.3296	0.3050
17	-0.0861	0.0808	-0.2828	0.2828	18.9141	0.3335
18	0.0418	0.1987	-0.2828	0.2828	19.0559	0.3884
19	0.0869	-0.0821	-0.2828	0.2828	19.6894	0.4135
20	-0.0091	-0.0269	-0.2828	0.2828	19.6966	0.4770

Distributive Lags

P-Values of Distributive Lag Periods of Each Independent Variable

Variable	1	2	3	4	5	6	7	8	9	10	11	12
X1	0.8467	0.2045	0.3336	0.9105	0.9757	0.1020	0.9205	0.1267	0.5431	0.9110	0.7495	0.4016
X2	0.6077	0.9900	0.8422	0.2851	0.0638	0.0032	0.8007	0.1551	0.4823	0.1126	0.0519	0.4383
X3	0.7394	0.2396	0.2741	0.8372	0.9808	0.0464	0.8355	0.0545	0.6828	0.7354	0.5093	0.3500
X4	0.0061	0.6739	0.7932	0.7719	0.6748	0.8627	0.5586	0.9046	0.5726	0.6304	0.4812	0.5707
X5	0.1591	0.2032	0.4123	0.5599	0.6416	0.3447	0.9190	0.9740	0.5185	0.2856	0.1489	0.7794

Figure 6.3: Autocorrelation and distributive lag results

Another requirement in running a regression model is the assumption of *normality* and *sphericity* of the error term. If the assumption of normality is violated or if outliers are present, then the linear regression goodness-of-fit test may not be the most powerful or informative test available, and this could mean the difference between detecting a linear fit or not. If the errors are not independent and not normally distributed, it may indicate that the data might be autocorrelated or suffer from nonlinearities or other more destructive errors. Independence of the errors can also be detected in the heteroskedasticity tests (Figure 6.4).

Test Result

		Errors	Relative Frequency	Observed	Expected	O-E
Regression Error Average	0.00	-219.04	0.02	0.02	0.0612	-0.0412
Standard Deviation of Errors	141.83	-202.53	0.02	0.04	0.0766	-0.0366
D Statistic	0.1036	-186.04	0.02	0.06	0.0948	-0.0348
D Critical at 1%	0.1138	-174.17	0.02	0.08	0.1097	-0.0297
D Critical at 5%	0.1225	-162.13	0.02	0.10	0.1265	-0.0265
D Critical at 10%	0.1458	-161.62	0.02	0.12	0.1272	-0.0072
Null Hypothesis: The errors are normally distributed.		-160.39	0.02	0.14	0.1291	0.0109
		-145.40	0.02	0.16	0.1526	0.0074
Conclusion: The errors are normally distributed at the		-138.92	0.02	0.18	0.1637	0.0163
1% alpha level.		-133.81	0.02	0.20	0.1727	0.0273
		-120.76	0.02	0.22	0.1973	0.0227
		-120.12	0.02	0.24	0.1985	0.0415

Figure 6.4: Test for normality of errors

The Normality test performed on the errors is a nonparametric test, which makes no assumptions about the specific shape of the population from which the sample is drawn, thus allowing for smaller sample datasets to be analyzed. This test evaluates the null hypothesis of whether the sample errors were drawn from a normally distributed population, versus an alternate hypothesis that the data sample is not normally distributed. If the calculated D-Statistic is greater than or equal to the D-Critical values at various significance values, then reject the null hypothesis and accept the alternate hypothesis (the errors are not normally distributed). Otherwise, if the D-Statistic is less than the D-Critical value, do not reject the null hypothesis (the errors are normally distributed). This test relies on two cumulative frequencies: one derived from the sample dataset and the second, from a theoretical distribution based on the mean and standard deviation of the sample data.

Sometimes, certain types of time-series data cannot be modeled using any other methods except for a stochastic process, because the underlying events are stochastic in nature. For instance, you cannot adequately model and forecast stock prices, interest rates, price of oil, and other commodity prices using a simple regression model because these variables are highly uncertain and volatile, and do not follow a predefined static rule of behavior; in other words, the process is not stationary. *Stationarity* is checked here using the Runs Test while another visual clue is found in the Autocorrelation report (the ACF or autocorrelation function tends to decay slowly). A stochastic process is a sequence of events or paths generated by probabilistic laws. That is, random events can occur over time but are governed by specific statistical and probabilistic rules. The main stochastic processes include Random Walk or Brownian Motion, Mean-Reversion, and Jump-Diffusion. These processes can be used to forecast a multitude of variables that seemingly follow random trends but are restricted by probabilistic laws. The process-generating equation is known in advance but the actual results generated are unknown (Figure 6.5).

The Random Walk Brownian Motion process can be used to forecast stock prices, prices of commodities, and other stochastic time-series data given a drift or growth rate and volatility around the drift path. The Mean-Reversion process can be used to reduce the fluctuations of the Random Walk process by allowing the path to target a long-term value, making it useful for forecasting time-series variables that have a long-term rate such as interest rates and inflation rates (these are long-term target rates by regulatory authorities or the market). The Jump-Diffusion process is useful for forecasting time-series data when the variable occasionally can exhibit random jumps, such as oil prices or price of electricity (discrete exogenous event shocks can make prices jump up or down). These processes also can be mixed and matched as required.

Multicollinearity exists when there is a linear relationship between the independent variables. When this occurs, the regression equation cannot be estimated at all. In near collinearity situations, the estimated regression equation will be biased and provide inaccurate results. This situation is especially true when a step-wise regression approach is used, where the statistically significant independent variables will be thrown out of the regression mix earlier than expected, resulting in a regression equation that is neither efficient nor accurate. One quick test of the presence of multicollinearity in a multiple regression equation is that the R-squared value is relatively high while the t-statistics are relatively low.

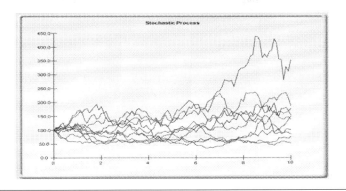

Figure 6.5: Stochastic process parameter estimation

Another quick test is to create a correlation matrix between the independent variables. A high cross-correlation indicates a potential for autocorrelation. The rule of thumb is that a correlation with an absolute value greater than 0.75 is indicative of severe multicollinearity. Another test for multicollinearity is the use of the Variance Inflation Factor (VIF), obtained by regressing each independent variable to all the other independent variables, obtaining the R-squared value and calculating the VIF. A VIF exceeding 2.0 can be considered as severe multicollinearity. A VIF exceeding 10.0 indicates destructive multicollinearity (Figure 6.6).

The Correlation Matrix lists the Pearson's Product Moment Correlations (commonly referred to as the Pearson's R) between variable pairs. The correlation coefficient ranges between −1.0 and +1.0 inclusive. The sign indicates the direction of association between the variables, while the coefficient indicates the magnitude or strength of association. The Pearson's R only measures a linear relationship and is less effective in measuring nonlinear relationships.

Correlation Matrix

CORRELATION	X2	X3	X4	X5
X1	0.333	0.959	0.242	0.237
X2	1.000	0.349	0.319	0.120
X3		1.000	0.196	0.227
X4			1.000	0.290

Variance Inflation Factor

VIF	X2	X3	X4	X5
X1	1.12	12.46	1.06	1.06
X2	N/A	1.14	1.11	1.01
X3		N/A	1.04	1.05
X4			N/A	1.09

Figure 6.6: Multicollinearity errors

To test whether the correlations are significant, a two-tailed hypothesis test is performed and the resulting p-values are computed. P-values less than 0.10, 0.05, and 0.01 are highlighted in blue to indicate statistical significance. In other words, a p-value for a correlation pair that is less than a given significance value is statistically significantly different from zero, indicating that there is significant a linear relationship between the two variables.

The Pearson's Product Moment Correlation Coefficient (R) between two variables (x and y) is related to the covariance (cov) measure where $R_{x,y} = \dfrac{COV_{x,y}}{s_x s_y}$. The benefit of dividing the covariance by the product of the two variables' standard deviations (s) is that the resulting correlation coefficient is bounded between -1.0 and $+1.0$ inclusive. This makes the correlation a good relative measure to compare among different variables (particularly with different units and magnitude). The Spearman rank-based nonparametric correlation is also included. The Spearman's R is related to the Pearson's R in that the data are first ranked and then correlated. Rank correlations provide a better estimate of the relationship between two variables when one or both of them is nonlinear.

It must be stressed that a significant correlation does not imply causation. Associations between variables in no way imply that the change of one variable causes another variable to change. Two variables that are moving independently of each other but in a related path may be correlated, but their relationship might be spurious (e.g., a correlation between sunspots and the stock market might be strong, but one can surmise that there is no causality and that this relationship is purely spurious).

7. Analytics – Ships in the Night

File Name: Analytics – Ships in the Night

Location: Modeling Toolkit | Analytics | Ships in the Night

Brief Description: Simulates arrival and meeting times and calculates the probability that two individuals will meet given a meeting time window

Requirements: Modeling Toolkit, Risk Simulator

This chapter models the arrival of two people at a prespecified location at a prespecified time and figures out the probability of whether they will meet. For instance, we can simulate the probability that two people will meet if they have a prespecified time window to meet (e.g., if the time to meet is between 1:30 PM and 2:00 PM, then the time window to meet is 30 minutes) and time to wait (e.g., when each person arrives, the person will wait up to, say, 5 minutes before leaving).

Time window to meet (minutes)	30
Time waiting at agreed location (minutes)	5
Arrival time for first person (lateness in minutes)	0.00
Arrival time for second person (lateness in minutes)	0.00
Meeting?	1

Figure 7.1: Meeting time model

The arrival times of both people are simulated assumptions using a uniform distribution between 0 and the time window to meet (i.e., if the time window is between 1:30 PM and 2:00 PM, then the person can arrive exactly at 1:30 PM, defined as 0 minutes arrival time, 1:31 PM, defined as 1 minute arrive time, and so forth) as seen in Figure 7.1. Therefore, both people meet if the absolute value of the difference between these arrival times defined as "Absolute value of (Second Person's Arrival Time minus the First Person's Arrival Time)" is less than or equal to the Waiting Time, then they meet; otherwise they do not meet. We simulate both arrival times without any correlations. You can add in correlations to account for any co-experiences upon arrival (e.g., traffic congestion is felt by both parties and they can potentially arrive late together if they take the same route).

After running the simulation, the forecast chart is typically bimodal, one for zero (not meeting), and the other for one (meeting). The table and forecast chart (Figures 7.2 and 7.3) show the results of a 1,000-trial simulation run with a seed value. The left-tail probability less than or equal to 0.9990 is 68.50%. This means that 68.50% of the time, the two parties do not meet, while they meet 31.50% of the time. Figure 7.2 shows various combinations of outcomes to test the sensitivity of the results of whether or not the two meet.

Time Window to Meet	30	30	60	60	10	10
Time Agreed to Wait	5	10	5	10	5	10
Probability of Meeting	31.50%	51.60%	16.90%	31.50%	50.00%	100.00%

Figure 7.2: Summary results of probability of meeting

The sample results in Figure 7.2 make perfect sense. For instance, if they agree on a 30-minute window, the longer they agree to wait when they each arrive, the higher the probability of meeting up (i.e., 31.50% increases to 51 60% but notice that the probability is not doubled). In contrast, the wider the time to meet window (e.g., 60 minutes), the smaller the probability of meeting given the same agreed time to meet. One interesting fact is that as long as the proportion of waiting time to time window is the same, the probability of meeting is the same (e.g., 10 minutes waiting to 60-minute window is the same as 5 minutes waiting to a 30-minute window).

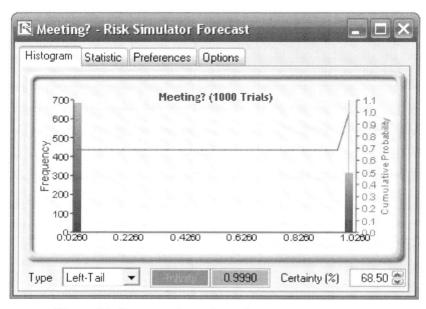

Figure 7.3: Forecast chart of meeting versus not meeting

Procedure

To run the predefined simulation, simply:

1. Go to the *Model* worksheet and click on **Risk Simulator | Change Profile** and select the *Ships in the Night* profile.

2. Click on the **RUN** icon or click on **Risk Simulator | Run Simulation.**

3. Once the simulation has been completed, in the forecast chart, select **Left-Tail** or **Right-Tail** and enter in **0.999** in the *Value* box and hit **TAB** on the keyboard to obtain the certainty value.

To recreate the simulation model, simply:

1. Go to the *Model* worksheet and click on **Risk Simulator | New Profile** and give it a name.

2. Go to cell **G8** and set an *assumption* (click on **Risk Simulator | Set Input Assumption** and select *Uniform Distribution* and type in **0** for the *minimum* value). Click on the **link** icon beside the maximum input parameter and link it to cell **G5**, and click **OK**. Repeat for cell **G9**.

3. Select cell **G11** and make it a *forecast* (click on **Risk Simulator | Set Output Forecast**) and click **OK**.

4. Click on the **RUN** icon or click on **Risk Simulator | Run Simulation.**

5. Once the simulation has been completed, in the forecast chart, select **Left-Tail** or **Right-Tail** and enter in **0.999** in the *Value* box and hit **TAB** on the keyboard, to obtain the certainty value.

8. Analytics – Statistical Analysis

File Name: Analytics – Statistical Analysis

Location: Modeling Toolkit | Analytics | Statistical Analysis

Brief Description: Applies the *Statistical Analysis* tool to determine the key statistical characteristics of your dataset, including linearity, nonlinearity, normality, distributional fit, distributional moments, forecastability, trends, and the stochastic nature of the data

Requirements: Modeling Toolkit, Risk Simulator

This model provides a sample dataset on which to run the *Statistical Analysis* tool in order to determine the statistical properties of the data. The diagnostics run include checking the data for various statistical properties.

Procedure

To run the analysis, follow the instructions below:

1. Go to the *Data* worksheet and select the data including the variable names (cells **D5:F55**).

2. Click on **Risk Simulator | Analytical Tools | Statistical Analysis** (Figure 8.1).

3. Check the data type: whether the data selected are from a single variable or multiple variables arranged in columns. In our example, we assume that the data areas selected are from multiple variables. Click **OK** when finished.

4. Choose the statistical tests you wish performed. The suggestion (and by default) is to choose all the tests. Click **OK** when finished (Figure 8.2).

Spend some time going through the reports generated to get a better understanding of the statistical tests performed.

Data Set

Variable X1	Variable X2	Variable X3
521	18308	185
367	1148	600
443	18068	372
365	7729	
614	100484	
385	16728	
286	14630	
397	4008	
764	38927	
427	22322	
153	3711	
231	3136	
524	50508	
328	28886	
240	16996	
286	13035	
285	12973	
569	16309	
96	5227	
498	19235	
481	44487	
468	44213	
177	23619	
198	9106	
458	24917	
108	3872	196

Statistical Analysis

This tool is used to describe and find statistical relationships in a set of raw data.

Selected Data

Variable X1	Variable X2	Variable X3
521	18308	185
367	1148	600
443	18068	372
365	7729	142
614	100484	432
385	16728	290
286	14630	346
397	4008	328
764	38927	354
427	22322	266
153	3711	320
231	3136	197

○ Data is from a single variable

● Data comprises multiple variables in columns

OK   Cancel

Figure 8.1: Running the Statistical Analysis tool

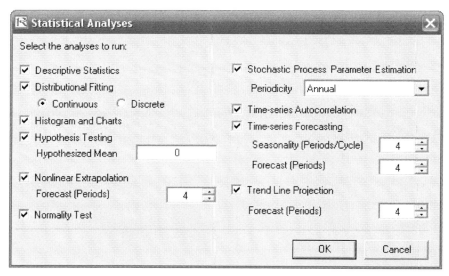

Statistical Analyses

Select the analyses to run:

☑ Descriptive Statistics

☑ Distributional Fitting
　● Continuous　○ Discrete

☑ Histogram and Charts

☑ Hypothesis Testing
　Hypothesized Mean　[0]

☑ Nonlinear Extrapolation
　Forecast (Periods)　[4]

☑ Normality Test

☑ Stochastic Process Parameter Estimation
　Periodicity　[Annual ▼]

☑ Time-series Autocorrelation

☑ Time-series Forecasting
　Seasonality (Periods/Cycle)　[4]
　Forecast (Periods)　[4]

☑ Trend Line Projection
　Forecast (Periods)　[4]

OK   Cancel

Figure 8.2: Statistical tests

The analysis reports include the following statistical results:

- Descriptive Statistics: Arithmetic and geometric mean, trimmed mean (statistical outliers are excluded in computing its mean value), standard error and its corresponding statistical confidence intervals for the mean, median (the 50th percentile value), mode (most frequently occurring value), range (maximum less minimum), standard deviation and variance of the sample and population, confidence interval for the population standard deviation, coefficient of variability (sample standard deviation divided by the mean), first and third quartiles (25th and 75th percentile value), skewness, and excess kurtosis.

- Distributional Fit: Fitting the data to all 24 discrete and continuous distributions in Risk Simulator to determine which theoretical distribution best fits the raw data, and proving it with statistical goodness-of-fit results (Kolmogorov-Smirnov and Chi-Square tests' p-value results).

- Hypothesis Tests: Single variable one-tail and two-tail tests to see if the raw data is statistically similar or different from a hypothesized mean value.

- Nonlinear Extrapolation: Tests for nonlinear time-series properties of the raw data, to determine if the data can be fitted to a nonlinear curve.

- Normality Test: Fits the data to a normal distribution using a theoretical fitting hypothesis test to see if the data is statistically close to a normal distribution.

- Stochastic Calibration: Using the raw data, various stochastic processes are fitted (Brownian motion, jump-diffusion, mean-reversion, and random walk processes) and the levels of fit as well as the input assumptions are automatically determined.

- Autocorrelation and Partial Autocorrelation: The raw dataset is tested to see if it is correlated to itself in the past by applying some econometric estimations and tests of autocorrelation and partial autocorrelation coefficients.

- Time-Series Forecasting: Eight most-commonly used time-series decomposition models are applied to determine if the raw dataset follows any trend and seasonality, and whether the time-series is predictable.

- Trend Analysis: A linear time-trend is tested to see if the data has any appreciable trend, using a linear regression approach.

Figure 8.3 shows a sample report generated by Risk Simulator that analyzes the statistical characteristics of your dataset, providing all the requisite distributional moments and statistics to help you determine the specifics of your data, including the skewness and extreme events (kurtosis and outliers). The descriptions of these statistics are listed in the report for your review. Each variable will have its own set of reports.

Analysis of Statistics

Almost all distributions can be described within 4 moments (some distributions require one moment, while others require two moments, and so forth). Descriptive statistics quantitatively capture these moments. The first moment describes the location of a distribution (i.e., mean, median, and mode) and is interpreted as the expected value, expected returns, or the average value of occurrences.

The Arithmetic Mean calculates the average of all occurrences by summing up all of the data points and dividing them by the number of points. The Geometric Mean is calculated by taking the power root of the products of all the data points and requires them to all be positive. The Geometric Mean is more accurate for percentages or rates that fluctuate significantly. For example, you can use Geometric Mean to calculate average growth rate given compound interest with variable rates. The Trimmed Mean calculates the arithmetic average of the data set after the extreme outliers have been trimmed. As averages are prone to significant bias when outliers exist, the Trimmed Mean reduces such bias in skewed distributions.

The Standard Error of the Mean calculates the error surrounding the sample mean. The larger the sample size, the smaller the error such that for an infinitely large sample size, the error approaches zero, indicating that the population parameter has been estimated. Due to sampling errors, the 95% Confidence Interval for the Mean is provided. Based on an analysis of the sample data points, the actual population mean should fall between these Lower and Upper Intervals for the Mean.

Median is the data point where 50% of all data points fall above this value and 50% below this value. Among the three first moment statistics, the median is least susceptible to outliers. A symmetrical distribution has the Median equal to the Arithmetic Mean. A skewed distribution exists when the Median is far away from the Mean. The Mode measures the most frequently occurring data point.

Minimum is the smallest value in the data set while Maximum is the largest value. Range is the difference between the Maximum and Minimum values.

The second moment measures a distribution's spread or width, and is frequently described using measures such as Standard Deviations, Variances, Quartiles, and Inter-Quartile Ranges. Standard Deviation indicates the average deviation of all data points from their mean. It is a popular measure as is associated with risk (higher standard deviations mean a wider distribution, higher risk, or wider dispersion of data points around the mean) and its units are identical to original data sets. The Sample Standard Deviation differs from the Population Standard Deviation in that the former uses a degree of freedom correction to account for small sample sizes. Also, Lower and Upper Confidence Intervals are provided for the Standard Deviation and the true population standard deviation falls within this interval. If your data set covers every element of the population, use the Population Standard Deviation instead. The two Variance measures are simply the squared values of the standard deviations.

The Coefficient of Variability is the standard deviation of the sample divided by the sample mean, proving a unit-free measure of dispersion that can be compared across different distributions (you can now compare distributions of values denominated in millions of dollars with one in billions of dollars, or meters and kilograms, etc.). The First Quartile measures the 25th percentile of the data points when arranged from its smallest to largest value. The Third Quartile is the value of the 75th percentile data point. Sometimes quartiles are used as the upper and lower ranges of a distribution as it truncates the data set to ignore outliers. The Inter-Quartile Range is the difference between the third and first quartiles, and is often used to measure the width of the center of a distribution.

Skewness is the third moment in a distribution. Skewness characterizes the degree of asymmetry of a distribution around its mean. Positive skewness indicates a distribution with an asymmetric tail extending toward more positive values. Negative skewness indicates a distribution with an asymmetric tail extending toward more negative values.

Kurtosis characterizes the relative peakedness or flatness of a distribution compared to the normal distribution. It is the fourth moment in a distribution. A positive Kurtosis value indicates a relatively peaked distribution. A negative kurtosis indicates a relatively flat distribution. The Kurtosis measured here has been centered to zero (certain other kurtosis measures are centered around 3.0). While both are equally valid, centering across zero makes the interpretation simpler. A high positive Kurtosis indicates a peaked distribution around its center and leptokurtic or fat tails. This indicates a higher probability of extreme events (e.g., catastrophic events, terrorist attacks, stock market crashes) than is predicted in a normal distribution.

Summary Statistics

Statistics	Variable X1		
Observations	50.0000	Standard Deviation (Sample)	172.9140
Arithmetic Mean	331.9200	Standard Deviation (Population)	171.1761
Geometric Mean	281.3247	Lower Confidence Interval for Standard Deviation	148.6090
Trimmed Mean	325.1739	Upper Confidence Interval for Standard Deviation	207.7947
Standard Error of Arithmetic Mean	24.4537	Variance (Sample)	29899.2588
Lower Confidence Interval for Mean	283.0125	Variance (Population)	29301.2736
Upper Confidence Interval for Mean	380.8275	Coefficient of Variability	0.5210
Median	307.0000	First Quartile (Q1)	204.0000
Mode	47.0000	Third Quartile (Q3)	441.0000
Minimum	764.0000	Inter-Quartile Range	237.0000
Maximum	717.0000	Skewness	0.4838
Range		Kurtosis	-0.0952

Figure 8.3: Sample report on descriptive statistics

Figure 8.4 shows the results of taking your existing dataset and creating a distributional fit on 24 distributions. The best-fitting distribution (after Risk Simulator goes through multiple iterations of internal optimization routines and statistical analyses) is shown in the report, including the test statistics and requisite p-values indicating the level of fit. For instance, Figure 8.4's example dataset shows a 99.54% fit to a normal distribution with a mean of 319.58 and a standard deviation of 172.91. In addition, the actual statistics from your dataset are compared to the theoretical statistics of the fitted distribution, providing yet another layer of comparison. Using this methodology, you can take a large dataset and collapse it into a few simple distributional assumptions that can be simulated, thereby vastly reducing the complexity of your model or database while at the same time adding an added element of analytical prowess to your model by including risk analysis.

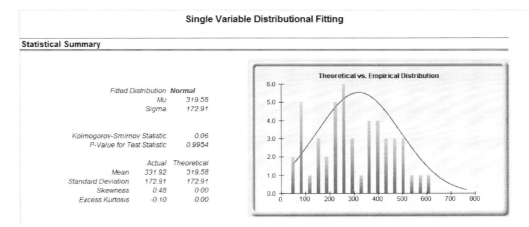

Figure 8.4: Sample report on distributional fitting

Sometimes, you might need to determine if the dataset's statistics are significantly different than a specific value. For instance, if the mean of your dataset is 0.15, is this statistically significantly different than, say, zero? What about if the mean was 0.5 or 10.5? How far enough away does the mean have to be from this hypothesized population value to be deemed statistically significantly different? Figure 8.5 shows a sample report of such a hypothesis test.

Hypothesis Test (t-Test on the Population Mean of One Variable)

Statistical Summary

Statistics from Dataset:		Calculated Statistics:	
Observations	50	t-Statistic	13.5734
Sample Mean	331.92	P-Value (right-tail)	0.0000
Sample Standard Deviation	172.91	P-Value (left-tailed)	1.0000
		P-Value (two-tailed)	0.0000
User Provided Statistics:			
		Null Hypothesis (Ho):	μ = Hypothesized Mean
Hypothesized Mean	0.00	Alternate Hypothesis (Ha):	μ < > Hypothesized Mean

Notes: "<>" denotes "greater than" for right-tail, "less than" for left-tail, or "not equal to" for two-tail hypothesis tests.

Hypothesis Testing Summary

The one-variable t-test is appropriate when the population standard deviation is not known but the sampling distribution is assumed to be approximately normal (the t-test is used when the sample size is less than 30 but is also appropriate and in fact, provides more conservative results with larger data sets). This t-test can be applied to three types of hypothesis tests: a two-tailed test, a right-tailed test, and a left-tailed test. All three tests and their respective results are listed below for your reference.

Two-Tailed Hypothesis Test

A two-tailed hypothesis tests the null hypothesis Ho such that the population mean is statistically identical to the hypothesized mean. The alternative hypothesis is that the real population mean is statistically different from the hypothesized mean when tested using the sample dataset. Using a t-test, if the computed p-value is less than a specified significance amount (typically 0.10, 0.05, or 0.01), this means that the population mean is statistically significantly different than the hypothesized mean at 10%, 5% and 1% significance value (or at the 90%, 95%, and 99% statistical confidence). Conversely, if the p-value is higher than 0.10, 0.05, or 0.01, the population mean is statistically identical to the hypothesized mean and any differences are due to random chance.

Right-Tailed Hypothesis Test

A right-tailed hypothesis tests the null hypothesis Ho such that the population mean is statistically less than or equal to the hypothesized mean. The alternative hypothesis is that the real population mean is statistically greater than the hypothesized mean when tested using the sample dataset. Using a t-test, if the p-value is less than a specified significance amount (typically 0.10, 0.05, or 0.01), this means that the population mean is statistically significantly greater than the hypothesized mean at 10%, 5% and 1% significance value (or 90%, 95%, and 99% statistical confidence). Conversely, if the p-value is higher than 0.10, 0.05, or 0.01, the population mean is statistically similar or less than the hypothesized mean.

Left-Tailed Hypothesis Test

A left-tailed hypothesis tests the null hypothesis Ho such that the population mean is statistically greater than or equal to the hypothesized mean. The alternative hypothesis is that the real population mean is statistically less than the hypothesized mean when tested using the sample dataset. Using a t-test, if the p-value is less than a specified significance amount (typically 0.10, 0.05, or 0.01), this means that the population mean is statistically significantly less than the hypothesized mean at 10%, 5%, and 1% significance value (or 90%, 95%, and 99% statistical confidence). Conversely, if the p-value is higher than 0.10, 0.05, or 0.01, the population mean is statistically similar or greater than the hypothesized mean and any differences are due ti random chance.

Because the t-test is more conservative and does not require a known population standard deviation as in the Z-test, we only use this t-test.

Figure 8.5: Sample report on theoretical hypothesis tests

Figure 8.6 shows the test for normality. In certain financial and business statistics, there is a heavy dependence on normality (e.g., asset distributions of option pricing models, normality of errors in a regression analysis, hypothesis tests using t-tests, Z-tests, analysis of variance, and so forth). This theoretical test for normality is automatically computed as part of the *Statistical Analysis* tool.

Test for Normality

The Normality test is a form of nonparametric test, which makes no assumptions about the specific shape of the population from which the sample is drawn, allowing for smaller sample data sets to be analyzed. This test evaluates the null hypothesis of whether the data sample was drawn from a normally distributed population, versus an alternate hypothesis that the data sample is not normally distributed. If the calculated p-value is less than or equal to the alpha significance value then reject the null hypothesis and accept the alternate hypothesis. Otherwise, if the p-value is higher than the alpha significance value, do not reject the null hypothesis. This test relies on two cumulative frequencies: one derived from the sample data set, the second from a theoretical distribution based on the mean and standard deviation of the sample data. An alternative to this test is the Chi-Square test for normality. The Chi-Square test requires more data points to run compared to the Normality test used here.

Test Result

		Data	Relative Frequency	Observed	Expected	O-E
Data Average	331.92					
Standard Deviation	172.91	47.00	0.02	0.02	0.0497	-0.0297
D Statistic	0.0859	68.00	0.02	0.04	0.0635	-0.0235
D Critical at 1%	0.1150	87.00	0.02	0.06	0.0783	-0.0183
D Critical at 5%	0.1237	96.00	0.02	0.08	0.0862	-0.0062
D Critical at 10%	0.1473	102.00	0.02	0.10	0.0918	0.0082
Null Hypothesis: The data is normally distributed.		108.00	0.02	0.12	0.0977	0.0223
		114.00	0.02	0.14	0.1038	0.0362
Conclusion: The sample data is normally distributed at		127.00	0.02	0.16	0.1180	0.0420
the 1% alpha level.		153.00	0.02	0.18	0.1504	0.0296
		177.00	0.02	0.20	0.1851	0.0149
		186.00	0.02	0.22	0.1994	0.0206
		188.00	0.02	0.24	0.2026	0.0374
		198.00	0.02	0.26	0.2193	0.0407
		222.00	0.02	0.28	0.2625	0.0175
		231.00	0.02	0.30	0.2797	0.0203
		240.00	0.02	0.32	0.2975	0.0225
		246.00	0.02	0.34	0.3096	0.0304
		251.00	0.02	0.36	0.3199	0.0401
		265.00	0.02	0.38	0.3494	0.0306
		280.00	0.02	0.40	0.3820	0.0180

Figure 8.6: Sample report on testing for normality

If your dataset is a time-series variable (i.e., data that has an element of time attached to them, such as interest rates, inflation rates, revenues, and so forth, that are time-dependent) then the Risk Simulator data analysis reports shown in Figures 8.7 to 8.11 will help in identifying the characteristics of this time-series behavior, including the identification of nonlinearity (Figure 8.7) versus linear trends (Figure 8.8), or a combination of both where there might be some trend and nonlinear seasonality effects (Figure 8.9). Sometimes, a time-series variable may exhibit relationship to the past (autocorrelation). The report shown in Figure 8.10 analyzes if these autocorrelations are significant and useful in future forecasts, that is, to see if the past can truly predict the future. Finally, Figure 8.11 illustrates the report on nonstationarity to test if the variable can or cannot be readily forecasted with conventional means (e.g., stock prices, interest rates, foreign exchange rates are very difficult to forecast with conventional approaches and require stochastic process simulations) and identifies the best-fitting stochastic models such as a Brownian motion random walk, mean-reversion and jump-diffusion processes, and provides the estimated input parameters for these forecast processes.

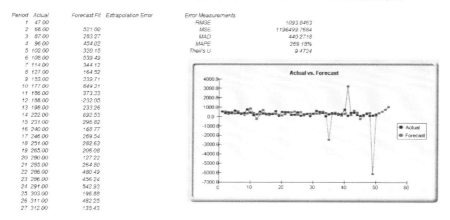

Figure 8.7: Sample report on nonlinear extrapolation forecast
(nonlinear trend detection)

Linear Trend Line Projection

Regression Statistics

R-Squared (Coefficient of Determination)	0.1193
Adjusted R-Squared	0.1009
Multiple R (Multiple Correlation Coefficient)	0.3454

The R-Squared or Coefficient of Determination indicates the percent variation in the data set that can be explained and accounted for by the linear trend line alone, whereas the Adjusted R-Squared takes into account the limited data set and exogenous variables and adjusts this R-Squared value to a more accurate view of the explanatory power of the trend line in isolation.

The Multiple Correlation Coefficient (Multiple R) measures the correlation between the actual data and the fitted forecast of using a trend line. This is also the square root of the Coefficient of Determination (R-Squared).

Linear Trend Line Analysis Results

	Intercept	Trend
Coefficients	436.3910	-4.0969
Standard Error	47.0778	1.6067
t-Statistic	9.2696	-2.5498
p-Value	0.0000	**0.0140**
Lower 5%	341.7347	-7.3275
Upper 95%	531.0473	-0.8663

The Trend Line coefficients provide the estimated intercept and trend. The Standard Error measures how accurate the predicted Coefficients are, and the t-Statistics are the ratios of each predicted Coefficient to its Standard Error.

The t-Statistic is used in hypothesis testing, where we set the null hypothesis (Ho) such that the real mean of the Coefficient = 0, and the alternate hypothesis (Ha) such that the real mean of the Coefficient is not equal to 0. A t-test is is performed and the calculated t-Statistic is compared to the critical values at the relevant Degrees of Freedom for Residual. The t-test is very important as it calculates if the trend line is statistically significant.

The Linear Trend Line is statistically significant and correct if its calculated t-Statistic exceeds the Critical t-Statistic at the relevant degrees of freedom (df). The three main confidence levels used to test for significance are 99%, 95% and 90%. If a Coefficient's t-Statistic exceeds the Critical level, it is considered statistically significant. Alternatively, the p-Value calculates each t-Statistic's probability of occurrence, which means that the smaller the p-Value, the more significant the Coefficient. The usual significant levels for the p-Value are 0.01, 0.05, and 0.10, corresponding to the 99%, 95%, and 90% confidence levels.

The Coefficients with their p-Values highlighted in blue indicate that they are statistically significant at the 90% confidence or 0.10 alpha level, while those highlighted in red indicate that they are not statistically significant at any other alpha levels.

Forecasting

Period	Actual (Y)	Forecast (F)	Error (E)
1	521	432.2941	88.7059
2	367	428.1972	(61.1972)
3	443	424.1003	18.8997
4	365	420.0034	(55.0034)
5	614	415.9065	198.0935
6	385	411.8096	(26.8096)
7	286	407.7127	(121.7127)
8	397	403.6158	(6.6153)
9	764	399.5189	364.4811
10	427	395.4220	31.5780
11	153	391.3251	(238.3251)
12	231	387.2282	(156.2282)
13	524	383.1313	140.8687
14	328	379.0344	(51.0344)
15	240	374.9375	(134.9375)
16	286	370.8406	(84.8406)
17	285	366.7437	(81.7437)
18	569	362.6468	206.3532
19	96	358.5499	(262.5499)
20	498	354.4530	143.5470
21	481	350.3561	130.6439

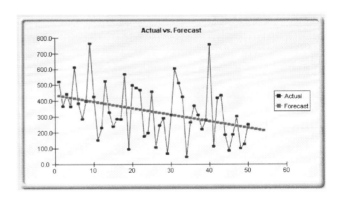

Figure 8.8: Sample report on trend-line forecasts (linear trend detection)

Time-Series Analysis Summary

Time-series forecasting is used to forecast the future based on historical data, through the decompositon of the historical data into the baseline. The best-fitting test for the moving average forecast uses the root mean squared errors (RMSE). The RMSE calculates the square root of the average squared deviations of the fitted values versus the actual data points.

Mean Squared Error (MSE) is an absolute error measure that squares the errors (the difference between the actual historical data and the forecast-fitted data predicted by the model) to keep the positive and negative errors from canceling each other out. This measure also tends to exaggerate large errors by weighting the large errors more heavily than smaller errors by squaring them, which can help when comparing different time-series models. Root Mean Square Error (RMSE) is the square root of MSE and is the most popular error measure, also known as the quadratic loss function. RMSE can be defined as the average of the absolute values of the forecast errors and is highly appropriate when the cost of the forecast errors is proportional to the absolute size of the forecast error. The RMSE is used as the selection criteria for the best-fitting time-series model.

Mean Absolute Percentage Error (MAPE) is a relative error statistic measured as an average percent error of the historical data points and is most appropriate when the cost of the forecast error is more closely related to the percentage error than the numerical size of the error. Finally, an associated measure is the Theil's U statistic, which measures the naivety of the model's forecast. That is, if the Theil's U statistic is less than 1.0, then the forecast method used provides an estimate that is statistically better than guessing.

The analysis was run with periodicity = 12

Period	Actual	Forecast Fit		Error Measurements	
1	47.00			RMSE	169.4315
2	68.00			MSE	28707.0345
3	87.00			MAD	138.4189
4	96.00			MAPE	85.13%
5	102.00			Theil's U	0.4781
6	108.00				
7	114.00				
8	127.00				
9	153.00				
10	177.00				
11	186.00				
12	188.00				
13	198.00	412.75			
14	222.00	413.00			
15	231.00	409.75			
16	240.00	392.83			
17	246.00	386.25			
18	251.00	358.83			
19	265.00	374.17			
20	280.00	358.33			
21	285.00	366.75			
22	286.00	343.17			
23	286.00	346.58			
24	291.00	348.58			
25	303.00	345.83			
26	311.00	340.33			
27	312.00	322.00			
28	328.00	322.50			
29	365.00	322.92			
30	367.00	304.83			

Figure 8.9: Sample report on time-series forecasting (seasonality and trend detection)

Autocorrelation

If autocorrelation $AC(1)$ is nonzero, it means that the series is first order serially correlated. If $AC(k)$ dies off more or less geometrically with increasing lag , it implies that the series follows a low-order autoregressive process. If $AC(k)$ drops to zero after a small number of lags, it implies that the series follows a low-order moving-average process. Partial Autocorrelation $PAC(k)$ measures the correlation of values that are k periods apart after removing the correlation from the intervening lags. If the pattern of autocorrelation can be captured by an autoregression of order less than k, then the partial autocorrelation at lag k will be close to zero. Ljung-Box Q-statistics and their p-values at lag k has the null hypothesis that there is no autocorrelation up to order k. The dotted lines in the plots of the autocorrelations are the approximate two standard error bounds. If the autocorrelation is within these bounds, it is not significantly different from zero at the 5% significance level.

Time Lag	AC	PAC	Lower Bound	Upper Bound	Q-Stat	Prob
1	0.0580	0.0580	-0.2828	0.2828	0.1752	0.6755
2	-0.1213	-0.1251	-0.2828	0.2828	0.9574	0.6196
3	0.0590	0.0756	-0.2828	0.2828	1.1464	0.7659
4	0.2423	0.2232	-0.2828	0.2828	4.4070	0.3537
5	0.0067	-0.0078	-0.2828	0.2828	4.4095	0.4921
6	-0.2654	-0.2345	-0.2828	0.2828	8.5034	0.2035
7	0.0814	0.0939	-0.2828	0.2828	8.8978	0.2601
8	0.0634	-0.0442	-0.2828	0.2828	9.1427	0.3304
9	0.0204	0.0673	-0.2828	0.2828	9.1688	0.4218
10	-0.0190	0.0865	-0.2828	0.2828	9.1920	0.5140
11	0.1035	0.0790	-0.2828	0.2828	9.8960	0.5398
12	0.1658	0.0978	-0.2828	0.2828	11.7535	0.4657
13	-0.0524	-0.0430	-0.2828	0.2828	11.9440	0.5322
14	-0.2050	-0.2523	-0.2828	0.2828	14.9439	0.3820
15	0.1782	0.2089	-0.2828	0.2828	17.2766	0.3026
16	-0.1022	-0.2591	-0.2828	0.2828	18.0670	0.3200
17	-0.0861	0.0808	-0.2828	0.2828	18.6463	0.3492
18	0.0418	0.1987	-0.2828	0.2828	18.7870	0.4050
19	0.0869	-0.0821	-0.2828	0.2828	19.4161	0.4304
20	-0.0091	-0.0269	-0.2828	0.2828	19.4233	0.4945

Figure 8.10: Sample report on autocorrelation (past relationship and correlation detection)

Stochastic Process - Parameter Estimations

Statistical Summary

A stochastic process is a sequence of events or paths generated by probabilistic laws. That is, random events can occur over time but are governed by specific statistical and probabilistic rules. The main stochastic processes include Random Walk or Brownian Motion, Mean-Reversion, and Jump-Diffusion. These processes can be used to forecast a multitude of variables that seemingly follow random trends but yet are restricted by probabilistic laws. The process-generating equation is known in advance but the actual results generated is unknown.

The Random Walk Brownian Motion process can be used to forecast stock prices, prices of commodities, and other stochastic time-series data given a drift or growth rate and a volatility around the drift path. The Mean-Reversion process can be used to reduce the fluctuations of the Random Walk process by allowing the path to target a long-term value, making it useful for forecasting time-series variables that have a long-term rate such as interest rates and inflation rates (these are long-term target rates by regulatory authorities or the market). The Jump-Diffusion process is useful for forecasting time-series data when the variable can occasionally exhibit random jumps, such as oil prices or price of electricity (discrete exogenous event shocks can make prices jump up or down). Finally, these three stochastic processes can be mixed and matched as required.

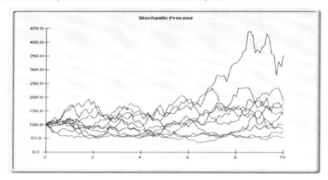

Statistical Summary

The following are the estimated parameters for a stochastic process given the data provided. It is up to you to determine if the probability of fit (similar to a goodness-of-fit computation) is sufficient to warrant the use of a stochastic process forecast, and if so, whether it is a random walk, mean-reversion, or a jump-diffusion model, or combinations thereof. In choosing the right stochastic process model, you will have to rely on past experiences and a priori economic and financial expectations of what the underlying data set is best represented by. These parameters can be entered into a stochastic process forecast (**Simulation | Forecasting | Stochastic Processes**).

(Annualized)

Drift Rate	-1.48%	Reversion Rate	283.89%	Jump Rate	20.41%
Volatility	88.84%	Long-Term Value	327.72	Jump Size	237.89

Probability of stochastic model fit: 46.48%

Figure 8.11: Sample report on stochastic parameter calibration (nonstationarity detection)

9. Analytics – Weighting of Ratios

File Name: Analytics – Weighting of Ratios

Location: Modeling Toolkit | Analytics | Weighting of Ratios

Brief Description: Illustrates how weighted averages are computed and how sometimes picking the wrong weighting factor results in wrong answers

Requirements: Modeling Toolkit

This is a simple example model illustrating how choosing the weighting factor is critical in obtaining the correct answer to a weighted average approach. In Example 1, we see a portfolio of 8 projects, each with its own revenue, cost, and return on investment (ROI) values (Figure 9.1). The idea is to compute the total portfolio ROI given these various projects. This first example illustrates that given a simple identical allocation of cost, revenues, and ROI, you can just compute the average of the total ROI, and this yields the correct ROI for the portfolio. However, in Example 2, we have a set of very different projects, which is oftentimes the case in real life, with different costs, revenues, and individual ROIs.

Using a simple sum or simple average will yield grossly misleading results. For instance, a grossly inflated sum yields a value of 3,900% ROI, while the average per project yields a value of 487.59%, which are both incorrect. The correct ROI for the total portfolio should be 288.08% (as confirmed by summing the total costs and total revenues for all projects in the portfolio and then computing the ROI for this portfolio level), as seen in Figure 9.1.

EXAMPLE 1:

Projects	Revenue	Cost	ROI
A	$100	$50	100%
B	$100	$50	100%
C	$100	$50	100%
D	$100	$50	100%
E	$100	$50	100%
F	$100	$50	100%
G	$100	$50	100%
H	$100	$50	100%

Simple Sum of all ROI			**800.00%**
Simple Average of Sum of all ROI			**100.00%**
Sum	$800	$400	**100.00%**

EXAMPLE 2:

Projects	Revenue	Cost	ROI
A	$100	$25	300%
B	$200	$16	1150%
C	$150	$35	329%
D	$162	$48	238%
E	$135	$99	36%
F	$187	$56	234%
G	$265	$74	258%
H	$233	$16	1356%

Simple Sum of all ROI			**3900.72%**
Simple Average of Sum of all ROI			**487.59%**
Sum	$1,432	$369	**288.08%**

Figure 9.1: Weighting of ratios

The same result can be obtained through a weighted average of the ROI. However, choosing the right weighting factor is critical. For instance, in the examples provided, we wanted to determine the total portfolio ROI, which is computed as (Returns − Cost)/Cost, which means that the denominator in this case is Cost. If we choose cost as the weighting factor, we get the correct answer of 288.08%. Had we chosen revenues as the weighting factor, we get an incorrect answer (Figure 9.2). Therefore, weighted averages and weighting factors are important when determining portfolio totals. This is a simple concept but its importance and potentials for error are often overlooked.

Correct way is to use a weighted average:

Weighted ROI by Cost	12.50%
Weighted ROI by Cost	12.50%
Weighted ROI by Cost	12.50%
Weighted ROI by Cost	12.50%
Weighted ROI by Cost	12.50%
Weighted ROI by Cost	12.50%
Weighted ROI by Cost	12.50%
Weighted ROI by Cost	12.50%
Sum of Weighted Avgs:	**100.00%**

Correct way is to use a weighted average. For simple identical weights, the choice of a factor is irrelevant.

Weighted ROI by Revenue	12.50%
Weighted ROI by Revenue	12.50%
Weighted ROI by Revenue	12.50%
Weighted ROI by Revenue	12.50%
Weighted ROI by Revenue	12.50%
Weighted ROI by Revenue	12.50%
Weighted ROI by Revenue	12.50%
Weighted ROI by Revenue	12.50%
Sum of Weighted Avgs:	**100.00%**

Correct way is to use a weighted average:

Weighted ROI by Cost	20.33%
Weighted ROI by Cost	49.36%
Weighted ROI by Cost	31.17%
Weighted ROI by Cost	30.39%
Weighted ROI by Cost	9.76%
Weighted ROI by Cost	35.50%
Weighted ROI by Cost	51.76%
Weighted ROI by Cost	58.81%
Sum of Weighted Avgs:	**288.08%**

Another Incorrect way using a weighted average of Revenues:

Weighted ROI by Revenue	20.95%
Weighted ROI by Revenue	160.61%
Weighted ROI by Revenue	34.42%
Weighted ROI by Revenue	26.87%
Weighted ROI by Revenue	3.43%
Weighted ROI by Revenue	30.55%
Weighted ROI by Revenue	47.76%
Weighted ROI by Revenue	220.67%
Sum of Weighted Avgs:	**545.26%**

Figure 9.2: Different weighting schemes

10. Credit Analysis – Credit Premium

File Name: Credit Analysis – Credit Premium

Location: Modeling Toolkit | Credit Analysis | Credit Premium

Brief Description: Determines the credit risk premium that should be charged beyond any standard interest rates depending on the default probability of the debt holder

Requirements: Modeling Toolkit

This model is used to determine the credit risk premium that should be charged above the standard interest rate given the default probability of this debt's or credit's anticipated cash flows. Enter the *years* and relevant *cash flows* in the model as well as the *interest rate* and anticipated *default probability* and click **Compute** to determine the credit spread required (Figure 10.1). All values should be positive, and the default probability input can be determined using any of the Modeling Toolkit's default probability models.

For instance, in Figure 10.1, assume a regular 10-year bond with a $1,000 face value paying 10% coupon rate. Where the prevailing interest rate is 5%, a 1% default probability means that the default risk premium spread is 0.14%, making the total interest charge 5.14%.

Credit Risk Premium Based on Default Probability

			Increasing Default Probability Increases Risk Premium				
		Default Probability	1.00%	0.25%	0.50%	2.00%	4.00%
Standard Interest Rate	5.00%						
Default Probability	1.00%	Default Risk Premium	**0.14%**	**0.04%**	**0.07%**	**0.29%**	**0.59%**

	NPV	1386.09						
			Compute!	Adjusted Cash Flows	Adjusted Cash Flows	Adjusted Cash Flows	Adjusted Cash Flows	Adjusted Cash Flows
Year	Cash Flows	PVCF						
1	100.00	95.24		94.42	95.03	94.83	93.59	91.94
2	100.00	90.70		90.04	90.54	90.37	89.38	88.05
3	100.00	86.38		85.87	86.26	86.13	85.36	84.33
4	100.00	82.27		81.90	82.18	82.08	81.52	80.77
5	100.00	78.35		78.11	78.29	78.23	77.86	77.35
6	100.00	74.62		74.49	74.59	74.56	74.36	74.08
7	100.00	71.07		71.04	71.06	71.05	71.01	70.95
8	100.00	67.68		67.75	67.70	67.72	67.82	67.95
9	100.00	64.46		64.61	64.50	64.54	64.77	65.08
10	1100.00	675.30		677.85	675.94	676.57	680.41	685.58

Figure 10.1: A simple credit spread premium computation given default probabilities

The present value of cash flows (PVCF) is the present value of future coupon payments and face value receipt at maturity, discounted at the prevailing interest rate. The sum of these values is the net present value (NPV), which is the price of the bond assuming zero default. By adding a probability of default, the cash flows are adjusted by this default rate and a corresponding default risk premium can be determined whereby the NPV of these risk-adjusted PVCF values will equal the original no-default NPV.

The results indicate that the lower the probability of default on this debt, the lower the additional default spread (interest rate premium), and the higher the probability of default, the higher the required interest rate premium. Using this simple probability-adjusted cash flow model, we can determine the approximate simple credit spread required to obtain the same probability-adjusted cash flow as another debt with no default. This is a simple cash flow model for approximation purposes and does not account for more exotic and real-life conditions such as mean-reverting interest rates, stochastic interest rates (smiles, frowns, and other shapes with localized time-dependent volatilities), credit risk migration, risk-neutral versus empirical probabilities of default adjustments, recovery rate, changing cumulative probabilities of default, and other qualitative factors, which are addressed in later chapters and models. Nonetheless, this model provides a simple and highly intuitive approximation of the default spread required on a risky debt or credit issue, and can use used as a simple benchmark against more advanced models that are discussed in later chapters.

11. Credit Analysis – Credit Default Swaps and Credit Spread Options

File Name: Credit Analysis – Credit Default Swaps and Credit Spread Options

Location: Modeling Toolkit | Credit Analysis | Credit Default Swaps and Credit Spread Options

Brief Description: Examines the basics of credit derivatives

Requirements: Modeling Toolkit, Risk Simulator

A credit default swap (CDS) allows the holder of the instrument to sell a bond or debt at par value when a credit event or default occurs. This model computes the valuation of the CDS spread (Figure 11.1). A CDS does not protect against movements of the credit spread (only a credit spread option can do that), but only protects against defaults. Typically, to hedge against defaults and spread movements, both CDS and credit spread options (CSO) are used. This CDS model assumes a no-arbitrage argument, and the holder of the CDS makes periodic payments to the seller (similar to a periodic insurance premium) until the maturity of the CDS or until a credit event or default occurs. Because the notional amount to be received in the event of a default is the same as the par value of the bond or debt, and time value of money is used to determine the bond yield, this model does not require these two variables as input assumptions.

In contrast, CSOs are another type of exotic debt option where the payoff depends on a credit spread or the price of the underlying asset that is sensitive to interest rate movements such as floating or inverse floating rate notes and debt. A CSO call option provides a return to the holder if the prevailing reference credit spread exceeds the predetermined strike rate, and the duration input variable is used to translate the percentage spread into a notional currency amount. The CSO expires when there is a credit default event. Again, note that a CSO can only protect against any movements in the reference spread and not a default event (only a CDS can do that). Typically, to hedge against both defaults and spread movements, CDS and CSO are used together. In some cases, when the CSO covers a reference entity's underlying asset value and not the spread itself, the credit asset spread options are used instead (Figure 11.1).

CREDIT DEFAULT SWAP (CDS) SPREADS

Input Assumptions

Bond Yield	7.00%
Annual Coupon Rate	10.00%
Coupon Payments Per Year	2
Risk-free Yield	5.00%
Recovery Rate at Default	80.00%

Credit Default Swap Spread   **1.7690%**

Function Used: MTCreditDefaultSwapSpread

CREDIT SPREAD OPTIONS (CSO)

Input Assumptions

Credit Spread	3.00%
Strike Spread	2.90%
Duration (Spread to Currency Conversion Ratio)	1000.00
Probability of Default	2.50%
Maturity	1.00
Riskfree Rate	5.00%
Volatility	25.00%

Credit Spread Call Option   **$3.2102**
Credit Spread Put Option   **$2.2828**

MTCreditSpreadCallOption
MTCreditSpreadPutOption

Forward Asset Price at Maturity	$1,000.00
Strike Price	$900.00
Probability of Default	2.50%
Maturity	1.00
Riskfree Rate	5.00%
Volatility	25.00%

Credit Asset Spread Call Option   **$141.6406**
Credit Asset Spread Put Option   **$48.8957**

Figure 11.1: Credit default swaps and credit spread options

12. Credit Analysis – Credit Risk Analysis and Effects on Prices

File Name: Credit Analysis – Credit Risk and Effects on Prices

Location: Modeling Toolkit | Credit Analysis | Credit Risk and Effects on Prices

Brief Description: Values the effects of credit spreads as applied to bond and debt prices

Requirements: Modeling Toolkit, Risk Simulator

Banks selling or issuing fixed income products and vehicles or issuing debt and credit lines need to understand the effects of interest rate risks. This model is used to analyze the effects of a credit spread as applied to the price of a bond or debt. The worse the credit rating, the higher the required credit spread and the lower the market value of the bond or debt. That is, the lower the credit rating of a debt issue, the higher the probability of default, and the higher the risk to the debt holder. This means that the debt holder will require a higher rate of return or yield on the debt in remuneration of this higher risk level. This additional yield is termed the *credit spread* (the additional interest rate above and beyond a similar debt issue with no default risk). Using a higher yield, the price of the debt is obtained through summing the present values of future coupon payments and principal repayment cash flows, and the higher the yield, the lower the value of the bond or debt. So, risk reduces the value of the bond, which means that assuming the bond does not default, the yield to maturity on the bond is higher for a risky bond than a zero-risk bond (i.e., with the same cash flows in the future, the cheaper the bond, the higher the yield on the bond, holding everything else constant). This model also allows you to determine the effects on the price of debt of a change in credit rating (see Figure 12.1).

The question now is, why do we analyze credit risk based on the bond market as an example? Bonds are, by financial definitions, the same as debt. A bond is issued by a corporation or some government agency (debt is obtained by individuals or companies in need of external funding, that is, a bank provides a loan or credit line to these individuals or corporations). The issuer receives a discounted portion of the face value up front (for debt, the obligor receives the funds up front). A bond is purchased or held by an investor (debt is issued by a bank or financial institution and, so, the holder of the debt). A bond has a face value (for a debt we call this the *principal*). A bond provides periodic payment to the bond holder (the borrower sends periodic payments back to the bank for a debt or credit line). A bond is highly sensitive to the outside market environment (inflation, bond market fluctuations, competition, economic environment) and interest rates (higher prevailing interest rates means lower bond price), and a credit line or debt is susceptible to the same pressures.

However, there are differences between a bond and regular debt or credit. A bond pays back the principal to the bond holder at maturity, whereas a debt's or credit line's principal amount is typically amortized over the life of the debt. However, there are amortizing bonds that provide the same payment as debt, and balloon debt that provides the same payments as bonds. Regardless of the type, both bond and debt have credit risk, prepayment risk, market risk, and other risks (e.g., sovereign and foreign exchange risk for international issues) and the cash flows can be determined up front, and, hence, the valuation approaches are very similar. In addition, for all the models introduced in this book in credit risk modeling, probability of default models, bond valuation, and debt options, we are assuming that these models and techniques are applicable to both regular debt and corporate bonds.

CREDIT RISK ANALYSIS

Face Value	$100.00
Coupon Rate	5.50%
Maturity	10.00
Current Interest Rate	5.00%
Credit Spread	2.39%

Bond Price Original $103.86
Bond Price with Spread $86.96
Reduction in Value   -16.27%

Function Used: MTBondPriceDiscrete

Cash Flow	Interest Rates	Year	Rates with Spread
$5.50	5.00%	1	7.39%
$5.50	5.00%	2	7.39%
$5.50	5.00%	3	7.39%
$5.50	5.00%	4	7.39%
$5.50	5.00%	5	7.39%
$5.50	5.00%	6	7.39%
$5.50	5.00%	7	7.39%
$5.50	5.00%	8	7.39%
$5.50	5.00%	9	7.39%
$105.50	5.00%	10	7.39%

Credit Spreads	
AAA	0.54%
AA	0.64%
A	0.90%
BBB	1.23%
BB	2.39%
B+	2.86%
B	3.40%
B-	4.33%

Figure 12.1: Credit risk analysis

13. Credit Analysis – External Debt Ratings and Spread

File Name: Credit Analysis – External Debt Rating and Spreads

Location: Modeling Toolkit | Credit Analysis | External Debt Rating and Spreads

Brief Description: Simulates and computes the credit risk spread of a particular firm based on industry standards (EBIT and interest expenses of the debt holder) to determine the risk-based spread

Requirements: Modeling Toolkit, Risk Simulator

This model is used to run a simulation on a company's creditworthiness given that the earnings are uncertain. The goal is to determine the credit category this firm is in, given its financial standing and the industry it operates in. Assuming we have a prespecified credit category for various industries (see the various Credit Risk Rating models in the Modeling Toolkit for examples on how to determine the creditworthiness of a customer or company using internal and external risk-based models and how the credit category and scoring table is obtained as well as using Modeling Toolkit's probability of default models to determine the creditworthiness of an obligor), we can then determine what interest rate to charge the company for a new loan.

For instance, Figure 13.1 illustrates a manufacturing firm's earnings before interest and taxes (EBIT) as well as its current interest expenses, and benchmarked against some long-term government bond rate. Using industry standards, the debt is then rated appropriately using a predefined credit ratings table, and the default spread and total interest charge is then computed.

This model is very similar to the examples described in the previous two chapters in that the relevant credit spread is determined for a risky debt. In Chapter 9, given a probability of default (we discuss the applications of probability of default models in detail later in the book), we can determine the relevant credit spread. In Chapter 11, given the credit spread, we can determine the impact in price of a bond or risky debt. In this chapter, we are interested in obtaining the spread on risky debt by looking at industry comparables and using other financial ratios such as a company's interest coverage. This approach is more broad-based and can be used assuming no other financial data are available.

Each of the inputs can be simulated using Risk Simulator to determine the statistical confidence of the cost of debt or interest rate to charge the client (see Figure 13.2). By running a simulation, we can better estimate the relevant credit spread and its confidence interval, rather than relying on a single snapshot value of some financial ratios to determine the credit spread.

Debt Rating and Spreads Analysis Under Uncertainty

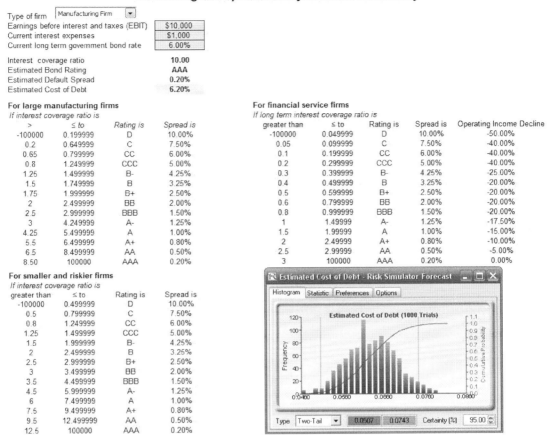

Type of firm: Manufacturing Firm

Earnings before interest and taxes (EBIT)	$10,000
Current interest expenses	$1,000
Current long term government bond rate	6.00%

Interest coverage ratio	10.00
Estimated Bond Rating	AAA
Estimated Default Spread	0.20%
Estimated Cost of Debt	6.20%

For large manufacturing firms
If interest coverage ratio is

>	≤ to	Rating is	Spread is
-100000	0.199999	D	10.00%
0.2	0.649999	C	7.50%
0.65	0.799999	CC	6.00%
0.8	1.249999	CCC	5.00%
1.25	1.499999	B-	4.25%
1.5	1.749999	B	3.25%
1.75	1.999999	B+	2.50%
2	2.499999	BB	2.00%
2.5	2.999999	BBB	1.50%
3	4.249999	A-	1.25%
4.25	5.499999	A	1.00%
5.5	6.499999	A+	0.80%
6.5	8.499999	AA	0.50%
8.50	100000	AAA	0.20%

For financial service firms
If long term interest coverage ratio is

greater than	≤ to	Rating is	Spread is	Operating Income Decline
-100000	0.049999	D	10.00%	-50.00%
0.05	0.099999	C	7.50%	-40.00%
0.1	0.199999	CC	6.00%	-40.00%
0.2	0.299999	CCC	5.00%	-40.00%
0.3	0.399999	B-	4.25%	-25.00%
0.4	0.499999	B	3.25%	-20.00%
0.5	0.599999	B+	2.50%	-20.00%
0.6	0.799999	BB	2.00%	-20.00%
0.8	0.999999	BBB	1.50%	-20.00%
1	1.49999	A-	1.25%	-17.50%
1.5	1.99999	A	1.00%	-15.00%
2	2.49999	A+	0.80%	-10.00%
2.5	2.99999	AA	0.50%	-5.00%
3	100000	AAA	0.20%	0.00%

For smaller and riskier firms
If interest coverage ratio is

greater than	≤ to	Rating is	Spread is
-100000	0.499999	D	10.00%
0.5	0.799999	C	7.50%
0.8	1.249999	CC	6.00%
1.25	1.499999	CCC	5.00%
1.5	1.999999	B-	4.25%
2	2.499999	B	3.25%
2.5	2.999999	B+	2.50%
3	3.499999	BB	2.00%
3.5	4.499999	BBB	1.50%
4.5	5.999999	A-	1.25%
6	7.499999	A	1.00%
7.5	9.499999	A+	0.80%
9.5	12.499999	AA	0.50%
12.5	100000	AAA	0.20%

Figure 13.1: Simulating debt rating and spreads

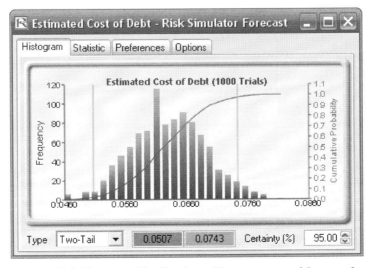

Figure 13.2: Forecast distribution of interest rate with spreads

14. Credit Analysis – Internal Credit Risk Rating Model

File Name: Credit Analysis – Internal Credit Risk Rating Model

Location: Modeling Toolkit | Credit Analysis | Internal Credit Risk Rating Model

Brief Description: Determines the credit shortfall risk and alphabetical risk rating given the probability of default

Requirements: Modeling Toolkit

Modeling Toolkit Functions Used: MTCreditRatingWidth, MTCreditRiskShortfall

This is an internal credit rating model similar to the ones used by Moody's or other rating agencies. Obtain the required *probability of default* input from other probability of default models in the Modeling Toolkit (see the chapters on modeling probability of default later in this book), and use this model to determine the rating of this company or debt holder. To further enhance the model, the category widths of the rating table can be refined and calibrated through additional parameter-width estimates, given actual data. For instance, Figure 14.1 illustrates how a ratings table can be generated. This model shows how the previous model, the *External Ratings and Spreads* example, is generated. That is, by entering the desired number of total categories for the risk ratings table and the base level (which requires calibration with actual data, and typically ranges between 1.1 and 3.0), you can develop the ratings table and determine the risk rating and credit risk shortfall, given some probability of default, recovery rate, and interest charged to a company. In some instances, the base level can be calibrated using a backcasting approach, where several base-level values are tested using various probabilities of default, and the resulting risk rating is used to benchmark against other industry standards.

INTERNAL CREDIT RISK RATING MODEL
RATING OF CREDIT RISK

Probability of Default	1.00%
Recovery Rate	25.00%
Interest Charged	7.00%

Computed Credit Shortfall Risk	0.77%
Computed Risk Rating	B

Function: MTCreditRiskShortfall (Probability of Default, Recovery Rate, Interest)

Assumptions for Creating of a Risk Rating Table

Total Categories	12
Base Level (Requires Calibration)	2.0000

Function: MTCreditRatingWidth (Total Categories, This Category, Base Level)

Example Internal Rating Table

Category	Width	Min	Max	Rating
1	0.0244%	0.0000%	0.0244%	AAA
2	0.0488%	0.0244%	0.0733%	AA
3	0.0977%	0.0733%	0.1709%	A
4	0.1954%	0.1709%	0.3663%	BBB
5	0.3907%	0.3663%	0.7570%	BB
6	0.7814%	0.7570%	1.5385%	B
7	1.5629%	1.5385%	3.1013%	CCC
8	3.1258%	3.1013%	6.2271%	CC
9	6.2515%	6.2271%	12.4786%	C
10	12.5031%	12.4786%	24.9817%	DDD
11	25.0061%	24.9817%	49.9878%	DD
12	50.0122%	49.9878%	100.0000%	D

Figure 14.1: Internal credit risk rating model and risk table generation

15. Credit Analysis – Profit-Cost Analysis of New Credit

File Name: Credit Analysis – Profit Cost Analysis of New Credit

Location: Modeling Toolkit | Credit Analysis | Profit Cost Analysis of New Credit

Brief Description: Analyzes the cost and profit from a potential credit issue based on the possibilities of nonpayment by the debt holder

Requirements: Modeling Toolkit, Risk Simulator

Modeling Toolkit Functions Used: MTCreditAcceptanceCost, MTCreditRejectionCost

This model is used to decide if new credit should be granted to a new applicant based on the requisite costs of opening the new account, as well as other incremental costs. In addition, using the cost of funds and average time to receive payments as well as the probability of nonpayment or default (use the various probability of default models in the Modeling Toolkit, explained in later chapters, to determine this), we can then determine the cost of accepting and the cost of rejecting this new line of credit and the probability of breakeven. By using this model, a bank or credit-issuing firm can decide if it is more profitable to accept or reject the application, as well as compute the probability of breakeven on this line of credit (Figure 15.1).

CREDIT ACCEPTANCE VS. REJECTION PROFIT/COST MODEL

Inputs

Acceptance Costs

Clerical Costs Associated With Opening Account	$30
Credit Investigation Cost	$40
Collection Costs	$130
Dollars Tied Up In Receivables (Sale Price)	$100,000
Probability of Non Payment	3.00%
Incremental Cost of Production and Selling	$60,000
Average Time in Days between Sale and Payment	45
Cost of Funds	15.00%

Rejection Costs

Marginal Profit From Sale	$40,000
Probability of Payment	97.00%

Outputs

Acceptance Cost	$3,849
Rejection Cost	$38,800
Accept/Reject Credit:	ACCEPT CREDIT
Probability B/E	37.98%

Figure 15.1: Credit acceptance and rejection profit and cost model

16. Debt Analysis – Asset-Equity Parity Model

File Name: Debt Analysis – Asset-Equity Parity Model

Location: Modeling Toolkit | Debt Analysis | Asset-Equity Parity Model

Brief Description: Applies the asset-equity parity relationship to determine the market value of risky debt and its required return, as well as the market value of the asset and its volatility

Requirements: Modeling Toolkit

Modeling Toolkit Functions Used: MTAEPMarketValueDebt, MTAEPMarketValueAsset, MTAEPRequiredReturnDebt

This model applies the Asset-Equity Parity assumptions, whereby given the company's book values of debt and asset, and the market value of equity and its corresponding volatility, we can determine the company's market value of risky debt and the required return on the risky debt in the market, and impute the market value of the company's assets and the asset's volatility. Enter the relevant inputs and click on **Compute Implied Volatility** to determine the implied volatility of the asset (Figure 16.1).

This model applies the basic parity assumption that the assets of a company equal any outstanding equity plus its liabilities. In publicly traded companies, the equity value and equity volatility can be computed using available stock prices, while the liabilities of the firm can be readily quantified based on financial records. However, the market value and volatility of the firm's assets are not available or easily quantified (contrary to the book value of asset, which can be readily obtained through financial records). These values are required in certain financial, options, and credit analyses and can be obtained only through this *Asset-Equity Parity* model. In addition, using the equity volatility and book value of debt, we can also impute the market value of debt and the required return on risky debt.

This concept of asset-equity-options parity is revisited later in the chapters on probability of default models. Briefly, equity owners (stockholders) of a firm have the option to pay off the firm's debt to own 100% of the firm's assets. That is, assets in a public company are typically funded by debt and equity, and although debt has a higher priority for repayment (especially at default and bankruptcy situations), only equity holders can cast votes to determine the fate of the company, including the ability and option to pay off all remaining debt and own all of the firm's assets. Therefore, there is an options linkage among debt, equity, and asset levels in a company, and we can take advantage of this linkage (through some simultaneous stochastic equations modeling and optimization) to obtain the firm's market value of asset, asset volatility, market value of debt, and, discussed in later chapters, the probability of default of the firm.

ASSET-EQUITY PARITY MODEL
PRICING DEBT USING AN OPTIONS APPROACH

Input Assumptions

Book Value of Asset	$140.0000
Book Value of Debt	$31.0000
Time to Maturity (Years)	3.0000
Riskfree Rate	5.00%
Volatility of Equity	40.00%
Market Value of Equity	$141.0000

Market Value of Risky Debt	$26.5698
Required Return on Risky Debt	5.1403%
Market Value of Asset	$167.5698
Implied Volatility of Asset	42.8207%

Compute Implied Volatility!

Figure 16.1: Asset-Equity options model

17. Debt Analysis – Cox Model on Price and Yield of Risky Debt with Mean-Reverting Rates

File Name: Debt Analysis – Cox Model on Price and Yield of Risky Debt with Mean-Reverting Rates

Location: Modeling Toolkit | Debt Analysis | Cox Model on Price and Yield of Risky Debt with Mean-Reverting Rates

Brief Description: Applies the Cox model to price risky debt as well as to model the yield curve, assuming that interest rates are stochastic and follow mean-reverting rates

Requirements: Modeling Toolkit, Risk Simulator

Modeling Toolkit Functions Used: MTCIRBondPrice, MTCIRBondYield

The Cox-Ingersoll-Ross (CIR) stochastic model of mean-reverting interest rates is modeled here to determine the value of a zero coupon bond and to reconstruct the yield curve (term structure of interest rates). This model assumes a stochastic and mean-reverting term structure of interest rates with a rate of reversion as well as long-run rate that the interest reverts to in time. A *Yield Curve CIR* model shown in a later chapter is used to generate the yield curve and term structure of interest rates using this CIR model (Figure 17.1).

Such mean-reverting models imply that the underlying asset (bond or debt) is highly susceptible to fluctuations in the prevailing interest rates of the economy. And in order to model the price of these interest-sensitive instruments, the behavior of interest rates will first need to be modeled. Interest rates are assumed to be mean-reverting, that is, there is a long-run mean rate at which short-term interest rates are attracted to, tend to, or revert to, at some rate of mean reversion. For instance, in the United States, the Federal Reserve controls interest rates in the economy (by changing the discount rate at which banks can borrow from the central bank, forcing this rate to permeate throughout to the economy; changing the required reserve ratio of bank holdings; or performing some sale or purchase of Treasury securities by the Federal Open Market Commission) in order to control the general inflation rate and economic growth. This means that there is typically a long-term economic growth rate, inflation rate, and, hence, interest rate that the Federal Reserve targets. When rates are too high, they are reduced, and vice versa, which means that interest rates, although stochastic and unpredictable in nature, are not as volatile as one would expect. This mean-reverting dampening effect is modeled here.

Finally, the interest rate volatility can be easily modeled using the Volatility models in the Modeling Toolkit, and the market price of interest rate risk is the same as the market price of risk for equity. It is the prevailing interest rate for a similar type of bond or debt (with the same credit risk structure), less the risk-free rate of similar maturities.

You may also use Risk Simulator to run simulations on the inputs to determine the price and yield of debt, or to determine the input parameters such as the long-run mean rate and rate of mean reversion. Use Risk Simulator's *Statistical Analysis* tool to determine these stochastic input parameters when calibrated on historical data. The *Forecasting – Data Diagnostics* model has examples on how to calibrate these stochastic input parameters based on historical data).

COX INGERSOLL ROSS MODEL
PRICING RISKY DEBT WITH MEAN-REVERTING INTEREST RATES

Time to Maturity of the Bond or Debt (Years)	1.0000
Risk-free Rate (Short Rate)	3.50%
Long-run Mean Rate	5.00%
Annualized Volatility of Interest Rate	20.00%
Market Price of Interest Rate Risk	5.00%
Rate of Mean Reversion	10.00%

Price of Zero Coupon Bond	$0.9659
Yield of Zero Coupon Bond	3.47%

The Cox-Ingersoll-Ross stochastic model of mean-reverting interest rates is modeled here to determine the value of a zero coupon bond and to reconstruct the yield curve (term structure of interest rates). This model assumes a mean-reverting term structure of interest rates with a rate of reversion as well as long-run rate that the interest reverts to in time. Use the Yield Curve CIR model to generate the yield curve using this model. You may also use Risk Simulator to run simulations on the inputs to determine the price and yield of the debt, or to determine the input parameters such as the long-run mean rate and rate of mean reversion (use Risk Simulator's Statistical Analysis Tool to determine these values).

Function: MTBondCIRBondPrice (Maturity, Riskfree, Longterm Rate, Volatility, Market Price of Risk, Rate of Reversion)
Function: MTBondCIRBondYield (Maturity, Riskfree, Longterm Rate, Volatility, Market Price of Risk, Rate of Reversion)

Sample Monte Carlo risk-simulation results when simulating the rate of mean-reversion:

Type: Two-Tail, Lower: 0.9658, Upper: 0.9660, Certainty: 90.0000%   Type: Two-Tail, Lower: 0.0345, Upper: 0.0348, Certainty: 90.0000%

Figure 17.1: Cox model with underlying mean-reverting interest rates

18. Debt Analysis – Debt Repayment and Amortization

File Name: Debt Analysis – Debt Repayment and Amortization

Location: Modeling Toolkit | Debt Analysis | Debt Repayment and Amortization

Brief Description: Simulates interest rates on a mortgage and amortization schedule to determine the potential savings on interest payments if additional payments are made each period and when the interest rates can become variable and unknown over time

Requirements: Modeling Toolkit, Risk Simulator

This is an amortization model examining a debt repayment schedule. In this example, we look at a 30-year mortgage with a portion of that period based on a fixed interest rate, and a subsequent period of variable rates with minimum and maximum caps. This model illustrates how the mortgage or debt is amortized and paid off over time, resulting in a final value of zero at the end of the debt's maturity (Figure 18.1). Further, this model allows for some additional periodic (monthly, quarterly, semiannually, annually) payment, which will reduce the total amount of payments, the total interest paid, and the length of time it takes to pay off the loan. Notice that initially the principal paid off is low but increases over time. Because of this, the initial interest portion of the loan is high but decreases over time as the principal is paid off.

The required input parameters are highlighted in boxes, and an assumption on the uncertain interest rate is set in cell D9, with a corresponding forecast cell at I12. By entering additional payments per period, you can significantly reduce the term of the mortgage (i.e., pay it off faster), and at a much lower total payment (you end up saving a lot on interest payments). A second forecast cell is set on J12 to find out the number of years it takes to pay off the loan if additional periodic payments are made.

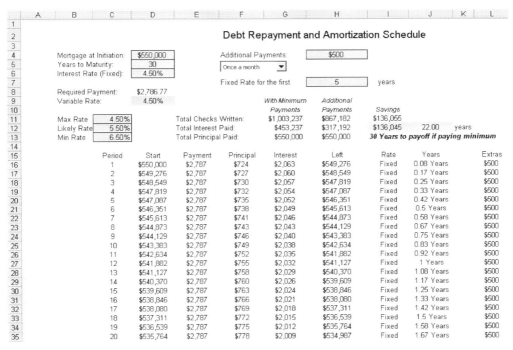

Figure 18.1: Debt amortization table

Procedure

You may either change the assumptions or keep the existing assumptions and run the simulation:

1. Click on **Risk Simulator | Change Profile** and select the *Debt Repayment and Amortization* profile and click **OK**.

2. Run the simulation by clicking on **Risk Simulator | Run Simulation**.

Interpretation

The resulting forecast chart on the example inputs indicates that paying an additional $500 per month can potentially save the mortgage holder $136,985 (minimum) and at most $200,406 (maximum), given the assumed uncertainty fluctuations of interest rates during the variable rate period. The 90% confidence level also can be obtained, meaning that 90% of the time, the total interest saved is between $145,749 and $191,192 (Figures 18.2 and 18.3).

In addition, the Payoff Year with Extra Payment forecast chart shows that given the expected fluctuations of interest rates and the additional payments made per period, there is a 90% chance that the mortgage will be paid off between 20.9 and 21.8 years, with an average of 21.37 years (mean value). The quickest payoff is 20.67 years (minimum). If interest rates are on the high end, payoff may take up to 22 years (maximum), as seen in Figures 18.4 and 18.5.

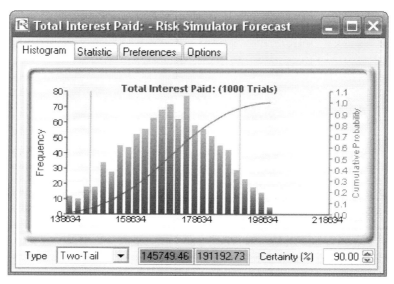

Figure 18.2: Forecast of total interest paid

Total Interest Paid: - Risk Simulator Forecast

Histogram | Statistic | Preferences | Options

Statistics	Result
Number of Trials	1000
Mean	1.690514E+005
Median	1.692578E+005
Standard Deviation	1.359216E+004
Variance	1.847468E+008
Average Deviation	1.114806E+004
Maximum	2.004062E+005
Minimum	1.369855E+005
Range	6.342076E+004
Skewness	-0.0645
Kurtosis	-0.6164
25% Percentile	1.592768E+005
75% Percentile	1.787881E+005
Percentage Error Precision at 95% Confidence	0.4983%

Figure 18.3: Forecast statistics of total interest paid

Figure 18.4: Forecast of payoff year

Statistics	Result
Number of Trials	1000
Mean	21.3694
Median	21.3333
Standard Deviation	0.2818
Variance	0.0794
Average Deviation	0.2317
Maximum	22.0000
Minimum	20.6667
Range	1.3333
Skewness	0.0041
Kurtosis	-0.5953
25% Percentile	21.1667
75% Percentile	21.5833
Percentage Error Precision at 95% Confidence	0.0817%

Figure 18.5: Forecast statistics of payoff year

19. Debt Analysis – Debt Sensitivity Models

File Name: Debt Analysis – Debt Sensitivity Models

Location: Modeling Toolkit | Debt Analysis | Debt Sensitivity Models

Brief Description: Models a debt instrument's sensitivity to interest rates using duration and convexity methods, while applying various discrete and continuous discounting measures

Requirements: Modeling Toolkit, Risk Simulator

Modeling Toolkit Functions Used: MTBondPriceDiscrete, MTBondPriceContinuous, MTBondYTMDiscrete, MTBondYTMContinuous, MTDurationDiscrete, MTDurationContinuous, MTMacaulayDuration, MTModifiedDuration, MTConvexityYTMDiscrete, MTConvexityYTMContinuous, MTConvexityDiscrete, MTConvexityContinuous, MTBondPriceChange

This model (Figure 19.1) is used to determine a debt's interest sensitivity while accounting for a series of cash flow payments from the debt over time (e.g., a bond's coupon payments and the final face value repayment) as interest rates are changing over time. The debt's price, yield to maturity, duration, and convexities are computed.

Duration and convexity are sensitivity measures that describe exposure to parallel shifts in the spot interest rate yield curve, applicable to individual fixed income instruments or entire fixed income portfolios. These sensitivities cannot warn of exposure to more complex movements in the spot curve, including tilts and bends, only parallel shifts. The idea behind duration is simple. Suppose a portfolio has a duration measure of 2.5 years. This means that the portfolio's value will decline about 2.5% for each 1% increase in interest rates—or rise about 2.5% for each 1% decrease in interest rates. Typically, a bond's duration is positive, but exotic instruments, such as mortgage-backed securities, may have negative durations, including portfolios that short fixed income instruments or portfolios that pay fixed for floating interest payments on an interest rate swap. Inverse floaters tend to have large positive durations. Their values change significantly for small changes in rates. Highly leveraged fixed income portfolios tend to have very large (positive or negative) durations.

In contrast, convexity summarizes the second-most significant piece of information, or the nonlinear curvature of the yield curve, whereas duration measures the linear or first-approximation sensitivity. Duration and convexity have traditionally been used as tools for immunization or asset-liability management. To avoid exposure to parallel spot curve shifts, an organization (e.g., an insurance company or defined benefit pension plan) with significant fixed income exposures might perform duration matching by structuring assets so that their duration matches the duration of its liabilities so the two offset each other. Even more effective (but less frequently practical) is duration-convexity matching, in which assets are structured so that durations and convexities match.

The standard financial computations for duration, modified duration and convexity are shown below:

- Macaulay Bond Duration $= \sum_{t=1}^{n} \frac{PVCF_t}{V_B} time$

- Modified Duration $= \dfrac{Macaulay}{\left(1 + \dfrac{YTM}{\# coupons}\right)}$

$$\bullet \quad \text{Convexity} = \frac{d^2P}{di^2} = \frac{\sum_{t=1}^{n}\dfrac{CF}{(1+i)^t}(t^2+t)}{(1+i)^2}$$

where $PVCF$ is the present value of cash flows (CF) for individual periods, V is the value of the bond, time (t) is the time period at which the cash flow occurs, YTM is the bond's yield to maturity (internal rate of return on the bond, or identical interest yield by holding the bond to maturity, computed based on the value of the bond at time zero), and i is the interest rate used to discount and price the bond.

DEBT SENSITIVITY MODELS

DURATION AND CONVEXITY ANALYSIS WITH YIELD CURVE ANALYSIS OF INTEREST RATE SENSITIVITIES

Input Assumptions

			Results	Discrete Discounting	Continuous Discounting
Current Interest Rate	7.00%				
Price of Bond or Debt	$1,200.00				
			PV Debt or Bond Price	$1,216.47	$1,210.23

Year	Cash Flow	Interest Rate	Results	Discrete Discounting	Continuous Discounting
			Yield to Maturity (YTM)	0.00%	5.20%
1.00	$100.00	5.00%	Duration	4.2535	4.2514
2.00	$100.00	5.00%	Macaulay Duration	4.2480	4.2480
3.00	$100.00	5.00%	Modified Duration	4.0327	4.0327
4.00	$100.00	5.00%	Convexity	20.8013	20.8013
5.00	$1,100.00	5.00%	Convexity Using YTM	21.6495	19.7743

Figure 19.1: Debt sensitivity models

20. Debt Analysis – Merton Price of Risky Debt with Stochastic Asset and Interest

File Name: Debt Analysis – Merton Price of Risky Debt with Stochastic Asset and Interest

Location: Modeling Toolkit | Debt Analysis | Merton Price of Risky Debt with Stochastic Asset and Interest

Brief Description: Computes the market value of risky debt using the Merton option approach, assuming that interest rates are mean-reverting and volatile, while further assuming that the company's internal assets are also stochastic and changing over time

Requirements: Modeling Toolkit, Risk Simulator

Modeling Toolkit Function Used: MTBondMertonBondPrice

The Merton model for risky debt computes the market value of debt while taking into account the book values of assets and debt in a company as well as the volatility of interest rates and asset value over time. The interest rate is assumed to be stochastic in nature and is mean-reverting, at some rate of reversion, to a long-term value (Figure 20.1). Further, the model also requires as inputs the market price of risk and the correlation of the company's asset value to the market. You can set the correlation and market price of risk to zero for indeterminable conditions, while the rate of reversion and long-run interest rates can be determined and modeled using Risk Simulator's *Statistical Analysis* tool. Simulation on any of the inputs can also be run using Risk Simulator to determine the risk and statistical confidence of the market price of risky debt (Figure 20.2). This model is similar in nature to the Cox mean-reverting model where both assume that the underlying debt instrument is highly sensitive to fluctuations in interest rates. The difference would be that this Merton model accounts for stochastic interest rates as well as stochastic asset movements, and that the market is used to calibrate the movements of the asset value (the correlation between asset and market returns is a required input).

MERTON MODEL OF RISKY DEBT
PRICING DEBT WITH STOCHASTIC ASSET AND STOCHASTIC INTEREST

Input Assumptions

Asset Book Value	$110.0000
Debt Book Value	$36.9940
Time to Maturity	20.00
Riskfree Rate	8.00%
Long-Run Interest Rate	8.00%
Volatility of Interest Rate	16.00%
Volatility of Asset	16.00%
Rate of Reversion of Interest Rate	15.00%
Market Price of Risk	1.00%
Correlation (Market to Asset)	0.00

Price of Debt　　　　　　　　　　**$11.4392**

Figure 20.1: Merton model of risky debt assuming stochastic interest and asset movements

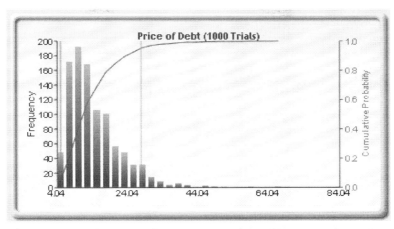

Type: Two-Tail, Lower: 4.9892, Upper: 27.7442, Certainty: 90.0000%

Figure 20.2: Forecast distribution of price of risky debt

21. Debt Analysis – Vasicek Debt Option Valuation

File Name: Debt Analysis – Vasicek Debt Option Valuation

Location: Modeling Toolkit | Debt Analysis | Vasicek Debt Option Valuation

Brief Description: Applies the Vasicek model of debt options assuming that interest rates are stochastic, volatile, and mean-reverting

Requirements: Modeling Toolkit, Risk Simulator

Modeling Toolkit Functions Used: MTBondVasicekBondCallOption, MTBondVasicekBondPutOption

This is the Vasicek model on bond or debt options, where the underlying debt issue changes in value based on the level of prevailing interest rates; that is, the interest rates have a mean-reverting tendency where the interest rate at any future period approaches a long-run mean interest rate with a rate of reversion and volatility around this reversion trend (Figure 21.1). Both options are European and can be executed only at expiration. To determine other types of options such as American and Bermudan options, use the Modeling Toolkit's *Options on Debt* modules to build lattices on mean-reverting interest rates and their respective option values.

A few interesting behaviors can be determined from this model. Typically, a bond call option will have a lower value if the long-run mean interest rate is higher than the current spot risk-free rate and if the rate of reversion is high (this means that the spot interest rates reverts to this long-run rate quickly). The inverse situation is also true, where the bond call option value is higher if the long run rate is lower than the spot rate and if the reversion rate is high. The opposite effects apply to the bond put option. Nonetheless, the reversion effect will be overshadowed by a high volatility of interest rate. Finally, at negligible maturities and interest rates (e.g., bond maturity of 0.01, option maturity of 0.001, spot risk-free rate of 0.001) the bond option values revert to the intrinsic value or Face Value – Strike for bond call option, and Strike – Face Value for put option.

There are also another two models for solving bond call and put options available through the functions:

MTBondHullWhiteBondCallOption

MTBondHullWhiteBondPutOption

These two Hull-White models are slightly different in that they do not require a long-run interest rate. Rather, just the reversion rate will suffice. If we calibrate the long-run rate in the Vasicek model carefully, we will obtain the same results as the Hull-White model. Typically, the Vasicek model is simpler to use.

VASICEK MODEL
PRICING DEBT OPTIONS WITH MEAN-REVERTING INTEREST RATES

Input Assumptions

Face Value of Debt	$100.0000
Strike Price	$90.0000
Time to Bond Maturity (Years)	10.0000
Time to Option Expiration (Years)	5.0000
Risk-free Rate	5.00%
Long-Run Mean Reversion Level	12.00%
Rate of Mean Reversion	25.00%
Annualized Volatility	10.00%
Market Price of Risk	0.00%

Vasicek Call Option Value	$5.3606
Vasicek Put Option Value	$14.9051
Hull-White Call Option Value	$5.9859
Hull-White Put Option Value	$15.4249

Figure 21.1: Vasicek model of pricing debt options and yield with mean-reverting rates

22. Debt Analysis – Vasicek Price and Yield of Risky Debt

File Name: Debt Analysis – Vasicek Price and Yield of Risky Debt

Location: Modeling Toolkit | Debt Analysis | Vasicek Price and Yield of Risky Debt

Brief Description: Uses the Vasicek model to price risky debt and to compute the yield on risky debt, where the underlying interest rate structure is stochastic, volatile, and mean-reverting (this model is also often used to compute and forecast yield curves)

Requirements: Modeling Toolkit, Risk Simulator

Modeling Toolkit Functions Used: MTBondVasicekBondPrice, MTBondVasicekBondYield

The Vasicek stochastic model of mean-reverting interest rates is modeled here to determine the value of a zero coupon bond (Figure 22.1) as well as reconstructing the term structure of interest rates and interest rate yield curve. This model assumes a mean-reverting term structure of interest rates with a rate of reversion as well as long-run rate that the interest reverts to in time. Use the *Yield Curve Vasicek* model to generate the yield curve and term structure of interest rates using this model. You may also use Risk Simulator to run simulations on the inputs to determine the price and yield of the zero coupon debt, or to determine the input parameters such as the long-run mean rate and rate of mean reversion (use Risk Simulator's *Statistical Analysis* tool to determine these values based on historical data).

The previous chapter uses a modification of this Vasicek model to price debt call and put options, versus the models described in this chapter that are used for pricing the risky bond and yield on the bond based on stochastic and mean-reverting interest rates. If multiple maturities and their respective input parameters are obtained, the entire term structure of interest rates and yield curve can be constructed, where the underlying processes of these rates are assumed to be mean reverting.

VASICEK & VAN DEVENTER MODEL
PRICING DEBT AND YIELD WITH MEAN-REVERTING INTEREST RATES

Input Assumptions

Time to Maturity of the Bond or Debt (Years)	1.00
Riskfree Rate (Short Rate)	5.00%
Long-run Mean Rate	8.00%
Annualized Volatility of Interest Rate	10.00%
Market Price of Interest Rate Risk	0.00%
Rate of Mean Reversion	1.00%

Price of Zero Coupon Bond	**$0.9527**
Yield of Zero Coupon Bond	**4.8495%**

Figure 22.1: Price and yield of risky debt

23. Decision Analysis – Decision Tree Basics

File Name: Decision Analysis – Decision Tree Basics

Location: Modeling Toolkit | Decision Analysis | Decision Tree Basics

Brief Description: Shows how to create and value a simple decision tree as well as how to run a Monte Carlo simulation on a decision tree

Requirements: Modeling Toolkit, Risk Simulator

This model provides an illustration on the basics of creating and solving a decision tree. This forms the basis for the more complex model (see the *Decision Tree with EVPI, Minimax and Bayes' Theorem* model presented in the next chapter) with expected value of perfect information, Minimax computations, Bayes' Theorem, and simulation.

Briefly, this example illustrates the modeling of a decision by an oil and gas company of whether Small Drill Bits or Large Drill Bits should be used in an offshore oil exploration project on a secondary well (Figure 23.1). There is a chance (30% probability expected) that this secondary well will become critical (if the primary well does not function properly or when oil prices start to skyrocket). If the large drill bits are used, it will cost more to set up ($20M as opposed to $10M). However, if things do become critical, the project can be completed with less of a delay than if the secondary drill bit is small. The probabilities of occurrence are tabulated in Figure 23.1, showing the weeks to completion or delays and their respective probabilities. The cost of delay per day is $17M. The table also provides the cost to run the drill bits.

Decision Tree Construction and Valuation

	Decision Tree Assumptions			
	Small Drill Bits		Large Drill Bits	
Project Completion Time	Probability of Occurrence	Weeks Delayed	Probability of Occurrence	Weeks Delayed
Fast	30%	16	30%	12
Medium	50%	18	50%	14
Slow	20%	23	20%	18

*Use Large Drill Bits if price and production results in a critical situation (30%)

		Min	Likely	Max	
Probability Critical Level	30%				
Probability Not Critical	70%				
Cost of Small Drill Bits	$1.5	$1.40	$1.50	$1.55	Cost Per Day to Run
Cost of Large Drill Bits	$2.0	$1.80	$2.00	$2.50	Cost Per Day to Run
Initial Setup Costs for Large	$20.0	$18.00	$20.00	$29.00	One-time Cost
Initial Setup Costs for Small	$10.0	$9.00	$10.00	$11.50	One-time Cost
Delayed Cost	$17.0	$15.00	$17.00	$18.00	Cost of Delay Per Day if Critical

Figure 23.1: Decision tree assumptions

Using these assumptions, a simple decision tree can be constructed. The decision tree is a graphical representation of decisions, probabilities of outcomes, and payoffs given certain outcomes, based on a chronological order. The value of each branch on the tree is then computed using backward induction or expected value analysis. The decision tree is constructed as seen in Figure 23.2.

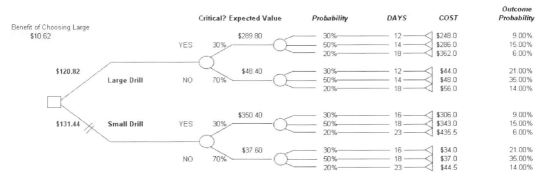

Figure 23.2: Decision tree construction

The payoffs at the terminal nodes of the decision tree are computed based on the path undertaken. For instance, $248M is computed by:

Initial Setup Cost of Large Drill Bit + Number of Days Delayed *

(Cost of Large Drill Bits Per Day + Delay Cost Per Day)

and so forth. Then, the expected values are computed using a backward induction. For instance, $289.80M is computed by:

30% ($248) + 50% ($286) + 20% ($362)

and the expected value at initiation for the Large Bit Drill of $120.82M is computed by:

30% ($289.80) + 70% ($48.40)

The benefit of choosing the large drill bit is the difference between the $120.82M and $131.44M costs, or $10.62M in cost savings. That is, the decision with the lowest cost is to go with the large drill bit. The computations of all remaining nodes on the tree are visible in the model.

Monte Carlo Simulation

The inputs above are single-point estimates and using them as is will reduce the robustness of the model. By adding in input assumptions and probability distributions, the analysis can then be run through a Monte Carlo simulation in Risk Simulator. The highlighted values in Figures 23.1 and 23.2 are set up as simulation input assumptions and the resulting forecast output is the benefit of choosing the large drill bit. To run the simulation, simply:

1. Click on **Risk Simulator | Change Simulation Profile** and select the *Decision Tree Basics* profile.

2. Go to the *Model* worksheet and click on **Risk Simulator | Run Simulation** or click on the **RUN** icon.

The output forecast chart obtained after running the simulation is shown in Figure 23.3. Once the simulation is complete, go to the forecast chart and select **Right Tail** and type in **0** in the right-tail input box and hit **TAB** on the keyboard. The results show that there is a 97.50% probability that choosing Large Drill Bits will be worth more than Small Drill Bits (Figure 23.3), that is, the net benefit exceeds zero.

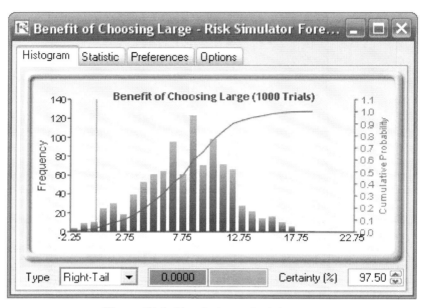

Figure 23.3: Simulating a decision tree

You are now ready to continue on to more sophisticated decision tree analyses. Please refer to the next chapter, *Decision Tree with EVPI, Minimax and Bayes' Theorem*, for an example of more advanced decision tree analytics.

Pros and Cons of Decision Tree Analysis

As you can see, a decision tree analysis can be somewhat cumbersome, with all the associated decision analysis techniques. In creating a decision tree, be careful of its pros and cons. Specifically:

Pros

1. Easy to use, construct, and value. Drawing the decision tree merely requires an understanding of the basics (e.g., chronological sequence of events, payoffs, probabilities, decision nodes, chance nodes, and so forth; the valuation is simply expected values going from right to left on the decision tree).

2. Clear and easy exposition. A decision tree is simple to visualize and understand.

Cons

1. Ambiguous inputs. The analysis requires single-point estimates of many variables (many probabilities and many payoff values), and sometimes it is difficult to obtain objective or valid estimates. In a large decision tree, these errors in estimations compound over time, making the results highly ambiguous. The problem of *garbage-*

in-garbage-out is clearly an issue here. Monte Carlo simulation with Risk Simulator helps by simulating the uncertain input assumptions thousands of times, rather than relying on single-point estimates.

2. Ambiguous outputs. The decision tree results versus *Minimax* and *Maximin* results produce different optimal strategies as illustrated in the next chapter's more complex decision tree example. Using decision trees will not necessarily produce robust and consistent results. Great care should be taken.

3. Difficult and confusing mathematics. To make the decision tree analysis more powerful (rather than simply relying on single-point estimates), we revert to using Bayes' Theorem. From the next chapter's decision tree example, using the Bayes' Theorem to derive implied and posterior probabilities is not an easy task at all. At best it is confusing and at worst, extremely complex to derive.

4. In theory, each payoff value faces a different risk structure on the terminal nodes. Therefore, it is theoretically correct only if the payoff values (which have to be in present values) are discounted at different risk-adjusted discount rates, corresponding to the risk structure at the appropriate nodes. Obtaining a single valid discount rate is difficult enough, let alone multiple discount rates.

5. The conditions, probabilities, and payoffs should be correlated to each other in real life. In a simple decision tree, this is not possible as you cannot correlate two or more probabilities. This is where Monte Carlo simulation comes in because it allows you to correlate pairs of input assumptions in a simulation.

6. Decision trees do not solve real options! Be careful as real options analysis requires binomial and multinomial lattices and trees to solve, not decision trees. Decision trees are great for framing strategic real options pathways but *not* for solving real options values. For instance, decision trees cannot be used to solve a switching option, or barrier option or option to expand, contract, and abandon. The branches on a decision tree are outcomes, while the branches on a lattice in a real option are options, not obligations. They are very different animals, so care should be taken when setting up real options problems versus decision tree problems. See Parts II and III of this book for more advanced cases involving real options problems and models.

24. Decision Analysis – Decision Tree with EVPI, Minimax, and Bayes' Theorem

File Name: Decision Analysis – Decision Tree with EVPI, Minimax and Bayes' Theorem

Location: Modeling Toolkit | Decision Analysis | Decision Tree with EVPI, Minimax and Bayes' Theorem

Brief Description: Creates and solves a decision tree, applies Monte Carlo risk simulation on a decision tree, constructs a risk profile on a decision tree, computes Expected Value of Perfect Information, computes MINIMAX and MAXIMIN analysis, computes a Bayesian analysis on posterior probabilities, and aids in understanding the pros and cons of a decision tree analysis

Requirements: Modeling Toolkit, Risk Simulator

In this model, we create and value a decision tree using backward induction to make a decision on whether a *Large*, *Medium*, or *Small* facility should be built given uncertainties in the market. This model is intentionally set up such that it is generic and can be applied to any industry. For instance, in the oil and gas exploration and production application, "large, medium, and small" refers to the size of the drilling platform to be built, or in the manufacturing industry, these sizes refer to the size of a manufacturing facility to be built; in the real estate business, they refer to the size of the condominiums or quality (expensive, moderate, or low-priced housing), and so forth. In this model, we also determine if there is value in information, whether a market research (the analogy in other industries would include wild cat exploratory wells, proof of concept development, initial research and development, and so forth) is worth anything and if it should be performed. In addition, other approaches are used including the MINIMAX and MAXIMIN computations, together with the application of Bayes' Theorem (posterior updating on probabilities).

The problem is: A real estate developer (oil and gas exploration firm, manufacturing entity, research and development outfit, and others) is faced with the decision on whether to build Small, Medium, or Large condominiums. Clearly the decision depends on how the market will be doing over the next few years, which is an unknown variable that may have significant impact on the decision. The question is whether market research should be performed to obtain valuable information on how the market will be over the next few years as well as what the optimal decisions should be, given that the market research results can return either a *Favorable* or *Unfavorable* outcome. In consultation with marketing professionals and subject matter experts, the information in Figure 24.1 are generated and assumed to hold. For instance, the term *Probability (Strong | Favorable)* is the probability that the true outcome is a strong market given that a favorable rating is obtained through the market research. The same convention is applied to the other probabilities.

Assumed Probability of Outcomes	
Probability (Market Research Returns "Favorable")	77%
Probability (Market Research Returns "Unfavorable")	23%
Probability (Strong | Favorable)	94%
Probability (Weak | Favorable)	6%
Probability (Strong | Unfavorable)	35%
Probability (Weak | Unfavorable)	65%

Payoff Table		
Decision	**Strong**	**Weak**
Small	$8M	$7M
Medium	$14M	$5M
Large	$20M	-$9M

Figure 24.1: Payoff table and assumed probability of outcomes

A decision tree is then constructed using these inputs. That is, the initial decision is whether to invest in market research. If no market research is performed, the next step is to decide if a Small, Medium or Large facility should be built. If a market research is conducted, we wait for the results of the market research before deciding on whether to build the Small, Medium or Large facility.

Decision Tree Construction and Solution

Using the assumptions just presented, a decision tree is built (Figure 24.2), based on a chronological order, starting from the decision (a square box denotes a decision) of whether market research should be conducted or not. If no market research is performed, the next decision (another square box) is whether a Small, Medium or Large facility should be built. Under each decision, the uncertainty of whether a Strong or Weak market exists are modeled (uncertainty outcomes are denoted by a circle), complete with its assumed probability of occurrence and payoff under each state of nature according to the assumptions above.

Next, the same construction is repeated with an intermediate step of performing the market research and waiting on the results (Favorable or Unfavorable). The decision on whether to build the Small, Medium or Large facility now depends on the results of the market research, but all possible outcomes are enumerated, including their probabilities of occurrence and payoff levels according to the assumptions above.

The expected values are then computed on the tree as shown in Figure 24.2 (e.g., 7.94 is computed by taking 94% x 8 + 6% x 7, or 13.46 is computed by taking 94% x 14 + 6% x 5, and 18.26 is computed by taking the MAX [7.94, 13.46, 18.26] to find the optimal decision given a Favorable market research outcome). The optimal path is then listed in bold on the decision tree. The expected value is then worked all the way back to obtain 15.93 for market research (77% x 18.26 + 23% x 8.15) and 14.20 for no market research (computed through MAX [7.80, 12.20, 14.20] to find the optimal decision given no research).

Clearly the higher expected value is 15.93, that is, to perform the market research. Further, if the market research results show a Favorable condition, the optimal decision is to build a Large facility. Conversely, build a Medium facility if an Unfavorable result is obtained.

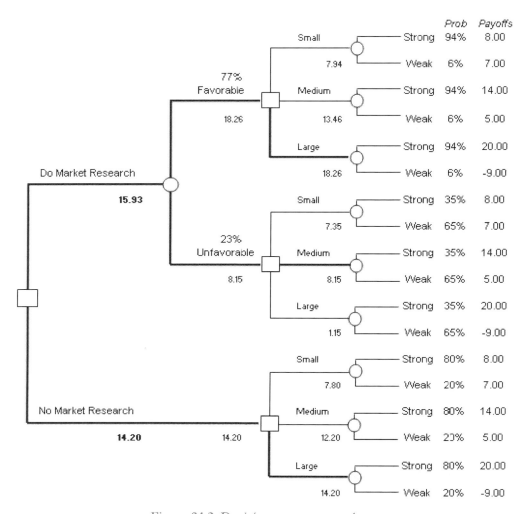

			Prob	Payoffs

Figure 24.2: Decision tree construction

Monte Carlo Simulation on Decision Trees

The assumptions used in a decision tree are single-point estimates and may not be precise. The payoff values and probabilities are simply estimations at best. Hence, these single-point estimates can be enhanced through Risk Simulator's Monte Carlo simulation. For the basic input assumptions, subject matter experts can be tasked with obtaining a most likely single-point estimate result while at the same, time, providing minimum and maximum estimates of each payoff and probability. These estimates are then entered into a Monte Carlo simulation (Figures 24.3, 24.4, and 24.5).

Assumed Probability of Outcomes			Min	Likely	Max
P (B)	Probability (Market Research Returns "Favorable")	77%	70%	77%	80%
P (B')	Probability (Market Research Returns "Unfavorable")	23%			
P (A | B)	Probability (Strong | Favorable)	94%	80%	94%	100%
P (A' | B)	Probability (Weak | Favorable)	6%			
P (A | B')	Probability (Strong | Unfavorable)	35%	30%	35%	40%
P (A' | B')	Probability (Weak | Unfavorable)	65%			
P (A)	Probability (Strong)	80%	75%	80%	85%
P (A')	Probability (Weak)	20%			

Figure 24.3: Probabilistic simulation assumption

Payoff Table				
Decision	Strong	Min	Likely	Max
Small	8.00	6	8	10
Medium	14.00	11	14	15
Large	20.00	18	20	22
Payoff Table				
Decision	Weak	Min	Likely	Max
Small	7.00	6	7	8
Medium	5.00	4.5	5	5.5
Large	-9.00	-10	-9	-8.5

Figure 24.4: Payoff tables

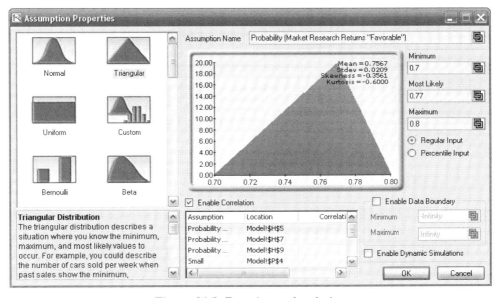

Figure 24.5: Running a simulation

The model already has these assumptions preset. To run the simulation, simply:

1. Click on **Risk Simulator | Change Profile** and select the *Decision Tree EVPI Minimax* profile to open the simulation profile.

2. Go to the *Model* worksheet and click on **Risk Simulator | Run Simulation** or click on the **Run** icon to run the simulation.

The forecast result of the Expected Value of Imperfect Information (cell R30) is shown in Figure 24.6, which is also the value of the difference between the expected value of performing market research and not performing a market research. The forecast chart can be used to determine the probability that performing a market research is better than not having any research. Further, the forecast chart shows that there is a 79.80% probability that doing market research is better than not doing any market research (select **Right Tail** on the forecast chart, enter in **0** on the left tail input box, and hit **TAB** on the keyboard). The expected value or mean of the distribution is 0.9736, indicating that the Expected Value of Imperfect Information is worth $0.9736M, which is the maximum amount of money the firm should spend, on average, to perform the market research. Further, the forecast chart on the Bayesian Posterior Probability (cell H60) indicates that the 95% confidence interval is between 87.83% and 97.69%. This means that on a 95% statistical basis (which means you are 95% sure) the results from the market research provide an accuracy of between 87.83% and 97.69%. That is, if the research results indicate that the market is strong, there is an 87.83% to 97.69% level of accuracy that the market is actually strong in reality. These computations are clearly seen in the Excel model.

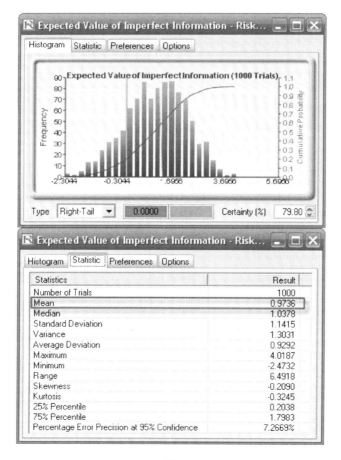

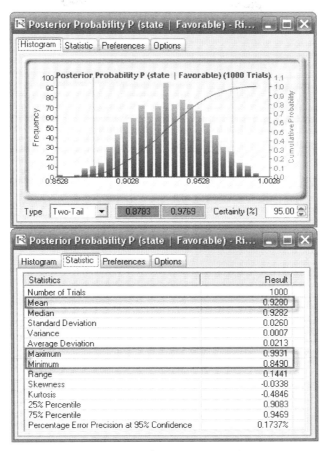

Figure 24.6: Simulation results

Risk Profile and EVPI

A risk profile based on the optimal path in the decision tree can be constructed. Specifically, comparing between not doing any market research versus performing the research, and looking at the optimal decision pathways, we obtain the results shown in Figure 24.7.

Risk Profile			
Do Market Research		**No Market Research**	
Payoff	*Probability*	*Payoff*	*Probability*
20.00	72.38%	20.00	80.00%
-9.00	4.62%	-9.00	20.00%
14.00	8.05%		
5.00	14.95%		
Sum	*100.00%*		*100.00%*
EV	*$15.93*		*$14.20*

Figure 24.7: Risk-return profile

Notice that the expected values (EV) from the risk profile are exactly those in the decision tree (i.e., $15.93M and $14.20M), indicative of the two values from the optimal paths. Further, note that there is an 80% probability of making money ($20M) versus a 20% chance of losing money (-$9M) without the market research. In contrast, the risk profile has changed such that the chance of making a positive payoff is 95.38% (i.e., 72.38% + 8.05% + 14.95%) as compared to 4.62% of possibly losing money. Clearly, doing the research adds positive value to the project.

The difference between these two values, or $1.73M, is the Expected Value of Imperfect Information (EVII), that is, the value of the market research on a single-point estimate basis. This is termed "Imperfect Information" because no market research is perfect or provides the true result 100% of the time. There will clearly be some uncertainty left over.

Further, the Expected Value of Perfect Information (EVPI) can be obtained by computing the expected value of perfect information given the states of nature and the expected value of imperfect information given the states of nature, and taking their differences (Figure 24.8). EVPI assumes that the information from the market research is 100% exact and precise.

Expected Value of Imperfect Information   **$1.73**

The loss profile was reduced from 20% to 5%

Expected Value with Perfect Information of the states of nature	**$17.40**
Expected Value without Perfect Information of the states of nature	**$14.20**
Expected Value of Perfect Information	**$3.20**

There is significant EVPI value, perform the research!

Figure 24.8: Expected value of perfect information

MAXIMIN and MINIMAX Analysis

MAXIMIN means maximizing the minimum outcomes. Specifically, looking at the no research strategy, the minimum payoffs (i.e., in the Weak states of nature), the maximum value is $7M (comparing among $7M, $5M, and -$9M). Therefore, using the MAXIMIN approach, a Small facility should be developed (Figure 24.9).

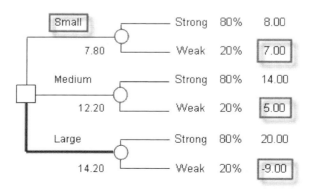

Figure 24.9: Maximin approach

In contrast, using the MINIMAX approach of minimizing the maximum regret, we see that the Medium facility should be built (Figures 24.10 and 24.11). The MINIMAX is computed by first obtaining the opportunity cost or regret matrix. For instance, if we built a Small facility, either a Strong or Weak market can exist. If a Strong market exists, we obtain $8M in payoff, but had we made a Large facility instead, the payoff would have been $20M. Therefore, you regret your decision as you could have made an additional $12M. Continuing with the analysis, a MINIMAX matrix is obtained for each state of nature. The Maximum of these regrets in all states of nature is computed for each decision. The Minimum is then computed. In this case, the result points to $6M or to build the Medium facility.

| *Maximin Conservative Approach Payoff* | | | *$7.00* |
| *Minimax Regret Approach Payoff* | | | *$6.00* |

Minimax Analysis			
Decision	*Strong*	*Weak*	**Max Regret**
Small	12.00	0.00	12.00
Medium	6.00	2.00	6.00
Large	0.00	16.00	16.00
Minimax Payoff	**6**		

Figure 24.10: Minimax approach

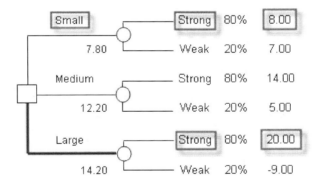

Figure 24.11: Minimax decision tree

Bayesian Analysis

Using the Bayes' Theorem (Figure 24.12) and given that we have the information determined from expert opinions in consultation with the marketing professionals in Figure 24.13, we can derive the posterior probabilities.

According to Probability Rules, we have :

$$P(A \cap B) = P(A).P(B|A)$$

$$P(B \cap A) = P(B).P(A|B)$$

$$P(A \cap B) = P(B \cap A)$$

So, we have :

$$P(A).P(B|A) = P(B).P(A|B)$$

$$P(A|B) = \frac{P(A).P(B|A)}{P(B)}$$

Further, if we have :

$$P(B) = P(A \cap B) + P(A' \cap B)$$

$$P(B) = P(A).P(B|A) + P(A').P(B|A')$$

$$P(A|B) = \frac{P(A).P(B|A)}{P(A).P(B|A) + P(A').P(B|A')} = \frac{P(A).P(B|A)}{\sum_{i=1}^{n} P(A_i).P(B|A_i)}$$

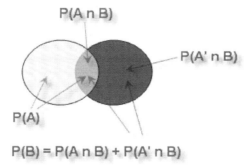

Figure 24.12: Intersection and union rules and graphical representation of probability theory

Notation	Bayesian Analysis	Given
P (B | A)	Probability P(Favorable | Strong)	90%
P (B' | A)	Probability P(Unfavorable | Strong)	10%
P (B | A')	Probability P(Favorable | Weak)	25%
P (B' | A')	Probability P(Unfavorable | Weak)	75%
P (A)	Probability P(Strong)	80%
P (A')	Probability P(Weak)	20%

Figure 24.13: Input assumptions in a Bayes' computation

To simplify, we denote A as the state of nature (A for Strong, and A' for Weak), while we set B as the Favorable (B) or Unfavorable (B') outcomes from the marketing research activities.

Using these rules, we can compute the Joint Probability $P(B \cap A)$ and the Bayes' Posterior Probability $P(A \mid B)$ as seen in Figure 24.14.

		States of Nature		
Notation	Favorable Market Research Outcomes	Strong	Weak	Total
P (A)	Prior Probability P (state)	80%	20%	
P (B | A)	Conditional Probability P (Favorable | state)	90%	25%	
P (B ∩ A)	Joint Probability P (Favorable ∩ state)	72%	5%	77%
P (A | B)	Posterior Probability P (state | Favorable)	94%	6%	100%

Figure 24.14: Bayes' Theorem

That is, we have:

$$P(B \cap A) = P(A \cap B) = P(A).P(B \mid A) = (0.80)(0.90) = 0.72$$

$$P(A \mid B) = \frac{P(A).P(B \mid A)}{\sum_{i=1}^{n} P(A_i).P(B \mid A_i)} = \frac{(0.80)(0.90)}{(0.80)(0.90) + (0.20)(0.25)} = 0.94$$

This means that the market research holds significant value. If the research returns a Favorable judgment, there is a 94% probability of the true state of nature being Strong, and so forth. Using Bayes' Theorem, we can determine this posterior probability, showing that the probabilities of making correct decisions are significantly higher than leaving it to chance. That is, obtain a 94% chance of being right as compared to an 80% chance if no market research is performed. The analysis can be repeated for the Unfavorable market research outcome.

Pros and Cons of Decision Tree Analysis

As you can see, decision tree analysis can be somewhat cumbersome, with all the associated decision analysis techniques. In creating a decision tree, be careful of its pros and cons. Specifically:

Pros

1. Easy to use, construct, and value. Drawing the decision tree merely requires an understanding of the basics (e.g., chronological sequence of events, payoffs, probabilities, decision nodes, chance nodes, and so forth; the valuation is simply expected values going from right to left on the decision tree).

2. Clear and easy exposition. A decision tree is simple to visualize and understand.

Cons

1. Ambiguous inputs. The analysis requires single-point estimates of many variables (many probabilities and many payoff values), and sometimes it is difficult to obtain objective or valid estimates. In a large decision tree, these errors in estimations compound over time, making the results highly ambiguous. The proverbial problem

of *garbage-in-garbage-out* is clearly an issue here. Monte Carlo simulation with Risk Simulator helps by simulating the uncertain input assumptions thousands of times, rather than relying on single-point estimates.

2. Ambiguous outputs. The decision tree results versus MINIMAX and MAXIMIN results produce different optimal strategies as illustrated in this chapter. Using decision trees will not necessarily produce robust and consistent results. Great care should be taken.

3. Difficult and confusing mathematics. To make the decision tree analysis more powerful (rather than simply relying on single-point estimates), we revert to using Bayes' Theorem. From the decision tree example, using the Bayes' Theorem to derive implied and posterior probabilities is not an easy task at all. At best it is confusing and at worst, extremely complex to derive.

4. In theory, each payoff value faces a different risk structure on the terminal nodes. Therefore, it is theoretically correct only if the payoff values (which have to be in present values) are discounted at different risk-adjusted discount rates, corresponding to the risk structure at the appropriate nodes. Obtaining a single valid discount rate is difficult enough, let alone multiple discount rates.

5. The conditions, probabilities, and payoffs should be correlated to each other in real life. In a simple decision tree, this is not possible as you cannot correlate two or more probabilities. This is where Monte Carlo simulation comes in because it allows you to correlate pairs of input assumptions in a simulation.

6. Decision trees do not solve real options problems. Be careful as real options analysis requires binomial and multinomial lattices and trees to solve, not decision trees. Decision trees are great for framing strategic real options pathways but *not* for solving real options values. For instance, decision trees cannot be used to solve a switching option, or barrier option or option to expand, contract, and abandon. The branches on a decision tree are outcomes, while the branches on a lattice in a real option are options, not obligations. They are very different animals, so be extremely careful. In fact, Parts II and III are devoted to solving advanced real options problems, complete with explanations, examples, models, and case studies, clearly indicating that real options analysis is a lot more powerful and correct rather than using decision trees in solving most decisions under uncertainty and risk.

25. Decision Analysis – Economic Order Quantity and Inventory Reorder Point

File Name: Decision Analysis – Economic Order Quantity and Inventory Reorder Point

Location: Modeling Toolkit | Decision Analysis | Economic Order Quantity and Inventory Reorder Point

Brief Description: Computes the optimal order size and optimal inventory units to hold that minimize total cost and maximize profits using the EOQ models

Requirements: Modeling Toolkit, Risk Simulator

Modeling Toolkit Functions Used: MTZEOQ, MTZEOQOrders, MTZEOQProbability, MTZEOQReorderPoint, MTZEOQExcess

This model illustrates the theory of Economic Order Quantity, or EOQ, which is in essence an internal optimization model to determine the best time and the optimal amount to order given levels of demand, uncertainty in demand, the cost of placing new orders, the cost of holding on to obsolete inventory, backorder requirements, and service level requirements. Each of these inputs can be simulated (i.e., set as input assumptions, and the resulting values set as forecasts). The model is fairly self-explanatory. The results obtained tells the store manager how many parts to order the next time an order is placed, the approximate number of orders per year of these many parts, the probability that the part will be out of stock, the reorder point (when inventory on hand hits this point, it is time to reorder) and on average the excess number of parts available (safety level) even with the highest levels of demand (Figure 25.1).

ECONOMIC ORDER QUANTITY AND INVENTORY REORDER POINT

INPUTS	Variable Name	
Annual Average Demand	Demand	1000.00
Standard Deviation of Annual Demand	Stdev Demand	40.80
Cost of Placing an Order	Cost Order	$50.00
Cost of Holding Excess Units Annually	Holding Cost	$10.00
Cost of Lost Sales and Backorder	Lost Sales Cost	$40.00
Average Lead Time on Backorder (Days)	Average Lead	14.00
Standard Deviation of Lead Time on Backorder (Days)	Stdev Lead	0.00

RESULTS	Function Name	
Economic Order Quantity (Order Size on Each Order)	EOQ	100.00
Number of Orders Per Year	EOQ Orders	10.00
Probability of Out of Stock	EOQ Probability	2.44%
Reorder Point	EOQ Reorder Point	54.10
Excess Safety Stock Level	EOQ Excess	15.75

Figure 25.1: EOQ model and inventory controls

26. Decision Analysis – Economic Order Quantity and Optimal Manufacturing

File Name: Decision Analysis – Economic Order Quantity and Optimal Manufacturing

Location: Modeling Toolkit | Decision Analysis | Economic Order Quantity and Optimal Manufacturing

Brief Description: Computes the Economic Order Quantity (EOQ) for inventory purposes and simulates an EOQ model to obtain confidence intervals for optimal quantities to order

Requirements: Modeling Toolkit, Risk Simulator

Modeling Toolkit Functions Used: MTZEOQ, MTZEOQOrders, MTZEOQProbability, MTZEOB, MTZEOBBatch, MTZEOBProductionCost, MTZEOBHoldingCost, MTZEOBTotalCost

Economic Order Quantity (EOQ) models define the optimal quantity to order that minimizes total variable costs required to order and hold in inventory or the optimal quantities to manufacture. EOQ models provide several key insights. The most important one is that the optimal order quantity Q^* varies with the square root of annual demand, and not directly with annual demand. This fact provides an important economy of scale. For instance, if demand doubles, the optimal inventory does not double but goes up by the square root of 2, or approximately 1.4. This also means that inventory rules based on time-supply are not optimal. For example, a simple rule like inventory managers having to maintain a "month's worth" of inventory can lead to dangerously low inventory or inventory shortage situations. If demand doubles, then a month's worth of inventory is twice as large. As noted, this is more quantity than is optimal; a doubling in demand should optimally increase inventory only by the square root of 2, or about 1.4 times.

The EOQ model is a lot more than simple inventory computations, as it computes the optimal quantity to order and the number of orders per year on average, as well as the probability that a product will be out of stock, providing a risk assessment of the probability some items will be out (Figure 26.1). The inputs can be subjected to Monte Carlo simulation using Risk Simulator. For instance, any of the inputs such as demand level or cost of placing an order can be set as input assumptions and the EOQ as the output forecast.

ECONOMIC ORDER QUANTITY (OPTIMAL REORDERING)

INPUTS	Variable Name	
Annual Average Demand	Demand	1000.00
Standard Deviation of Annual Demand	Stdev Demand	40.80
Cost of Placing an Order	Cost Order	$50.00
Cost of Holding Each Excess Units Annually	Holding Cost	$10.00
Cost of Lost Sales and Backorder	Lost Sales Cost	$40.00

RESULTS	Function Name	
Economic Order Quantity (Order Size on Each Order)	EOQ	**100.00**
Number of Orders Per Year	EOQ Orders	**10.00**
Probability of Out of Stock	EOQ Probability	**2.44%**

Figure 26.1: EOQ and optimal reordering

The EOQ model also can be extended to cover manufacturing outputs, specifically, finding the optimal quantities to manufacture given assumed average demand levels, production capacity, cost of setting up production, holding cost of inventory, and so forth (Figure 26.2). These two models are fairly self-explanatory and use preprogrammed functions in the Modeling Toolkit software.

ECONOMIC ORDER QUANTITY (OPTIMAL MANUFACTURING)

INPUTS	Variable Name	
Annual Average Demand	Demand2	10000.00
Annual Production Maximum Capacity	Capacity	25000.00
Cost of Setting Up a Batch for Production	Batch Cost	$200.00
Cost of Holding Each Excess Units Annually	Holding Cost2	$500.00

RESULTS	Function Name	
Economic Order Batch (Manufactured on Each Batch)	EOB	115.47
Number of Batches Manufactured Per Year	EOB Batch	86.60
Cost of Setting Up Production	EOB Production Cost	$17,320.51
Cost of Holding Excess Units	EOB Holding Cost	$17,320.51
Total Costs	EOB Total Cost	$34,641.02

Figure 26.2: EOQ and optimal manufacturing

Procedure

This model already has Monte Carlo simulation predefined using Risk Simulator. To run this model, simply click on **Risk Simulator | Change Simulation Profile** and select the *EOQ Model* profile, then click on **Risk Simulator | Run Simulation**. However, if you wish you can create your own simulation model:

1. Start a new simulation profile and add various assumptions on Demand, Cost of Placing an Order, Holding Cost, and Cost of Lost Sales.

2. Add forecasts to the key outputs, such as EOQ or EOQ Probability.

3. Run the simulation and interpret the resulting forecast charts as usual.

27. Decision Analysis – Expected Utility Analysis

File Name: Decision Analysis – Expected Utility Analysis

Location: Modeling Toolkit | Decision Analysis | Expected Utility Analysis

Brief Description: Constructs a utility function using risk preferences and expected value of payoffs for a decision maker, as an alternative to expected value analysis

Requirements: Modeling Toolkit

This model applies utility theory in decision analysis to determine which projects should be executed given that the projects are risky and carry with them the potential for significant gains as well as significant losses. Using a single-point estimate or expected value given various probabilities of events occurring may not be the best approach. An alternative approach is to determine the risk preferences of the decision maker through the construction of a utility curve. Using the utility curve, we can then determine which project or strategy may best fit the decision-maker's risk preferences.

The first portion of the model looks at the payoff table under three scenarios (high, moderate, and low prices) and their respective payoffs for three strategies (execute Project A, execute Project B, or do nothing). The expected value shows that Project A has the highest payoff. Hence, the best decision is to execute Project A.

However, if the company is a small start-up firm and the owner or decision maker is fairly risk averse (e.g., even a small loss of, say, $30,000 can potentially mean that the business faces bankruptcy). Under such circumstances, executing Project A may not be the best alternative. To analyze this situation, we revert to the use of utility functions. To start off, as an example, suppose we have a project where the maximum payoff on all strategies is $50,000 and the minimum is –$50,000. We construct a graduated set of payoffs from these two values and call them the guaranteed payoff (Figure 27.1). Then the decision maker is to determine the indifference probability (the maximum is always set to 100% whereas the minimum value is always set to 0%). Gradually moving down the payoffs, determine the indifference levels. For instance, say there is a coin toss game where if heads appear, you receive $50,000 versus a loss of –$50,000 if tails appear. This game yields an expected value of $0. In such a scenario, what is the probability you will accept $40,000 guaranteed versus playing the risky game? In the example, the decision maker sets the chances as 97%, and so forth. As another example, the decision maker is willing to accept a sure thing of $10,000 about 85% of the time rather than take the gamble of losing –$50,000 although the upside of $50,000 is still a potential.

From the risk-averse utility function generated, we can then recompute the payoff table by converting the monetary payoffs to utility payoffs. In this example, it is clear that both projects are fairly risky to the owner and the best course of action is to stay away from both projects. For more examples on decision analysis, see the *Decision Analysis – Decision Tree with EVPI, Minimax and Bayes' Theorem* model. In addition, for more advanced decision analysis and strategies, see the real options analysis models and cases in Parts II and III of this book.

Payoff Table	High Prices	Moderate Prices	Low Prices	Expected Value	Decision
Decisions					
Project A	$30,000	$20,000	($50,000)	$9,000	**Execute**
Project B	$50,000	($20,000)	($30,000)	($1,000)	
Neither	$0	$0	$0	$0	
Probability	30%	50%	20%		

Utility Function Construction

Guaranteed Payoff	Indifference	Utility Value	Expected Payoff
$50,000	100%	10.0	$50,000
$40,000	97%	9.7	$48,500
$30,000	95%	9.5	$47,500
$20,000	90%	9.0	$45,000
$10,000	85%	8.5	$42,500
$0	80%	8.0	$40,000
($10,000)	50%	5.0	$25,000
($20,000)	40%	4.0	$20,000
($30,000)	25%	2.5	$12,500
($40,000)	20%	2.0	$10,000
($50,000)	0%	0.0	$0

Utility Table	High Prices	Moderate Prices	High Prices	Expected Utility	Decision
Decisions					
Project A	9.5	9.0	0.0	7.35	
Project B	10.0	4.0	2.5	5.50	
Neither	8.0	8.0	8.0	8.00	**Execute**
Probability	30%	50%	20%		

Figure 27.1: Expected utility analysis

28. Decision Analysis – Inventory Control

File Name: Decision Analysis – Inventory Control

Location: Modeling Toolkit | Decision Analysis | Inventory Control

Brief Description: Creates and simulates a simple inventory control model, which is a precursor to more advanced economic order quantity models

Requirements: Modeling Toolkit, Risk Simulator

This model shows a simple inventory control model, with various inputs such as order cost, carrying or inventory cost, and the projected annual demand, which is deemed to be uncertain and can be simulated. The idea of this model is to allow for the ability to view the various interactions among the input variables and the resulting orders that need to be placed per year. Figures 28.1 and 28.2 illustrate the inventory control model and its output charts. For more advanced and complex inventory control models, see the *Optimization – Inventory Optimization* model, or see the other models dealing with Economic Order Quantity applications (*Decision Analysis – Economic Order Quantity and Inventory Reorder Point* as well as *Decision Analysis – Economic Order Quantity and Optimal Manufacturing*).

Inventory Control and Optimal Order Size

Order Cost	635			Minimum Cost	10,059		
Carrying Cost	71			Orders Per Year	8		
Annual Demand	1122			Order Size	140		

Orders per Year	Order Size	Annual Order Cost	Average Inventory	Annual Carrying Cost	Annual Total Cost	Orders /Year	Order Size
1	1,122	635	561.0	39,831	40,466		
2	561	1,270	280.5	19,916	21,186		
3	374	1,905	187.0	13,277	15,182		
4	281	2,540	140.3	9,958	12,498		
5	224	3,175	112.2	7,966	11,141		
6	187	3,810	93.5	6,639	10,449		
7	160	4,445	80.1	5,690	10,135		
8	140	5,080	70.1	4,979	10,059	8	140.25
9	125	5,715	62.3	4,426	10,141		
10	112	6,350	56.1	3,983	10,333		
11	102	6,985	51.0	3,621	10,606		
12	94	7,620	46.8	3,319	10,939		
13	86	8,255	43.2	3,064	11,319		
14	80	8,890	40.1	2,845	11,735		
15	75	9,525	37.4	2,655	12,180		
16	70	10,160	35.1	2,489	12,649		
17	66	10,795	33.0	2,343	13,138		
18	62	11,430	31.2	2,213	13,643		
19	59	12,065	29.5	2,096	14,161		
20	56	12,700	28.1	1,992	14,692		

Figure 28.1: Inventory control model

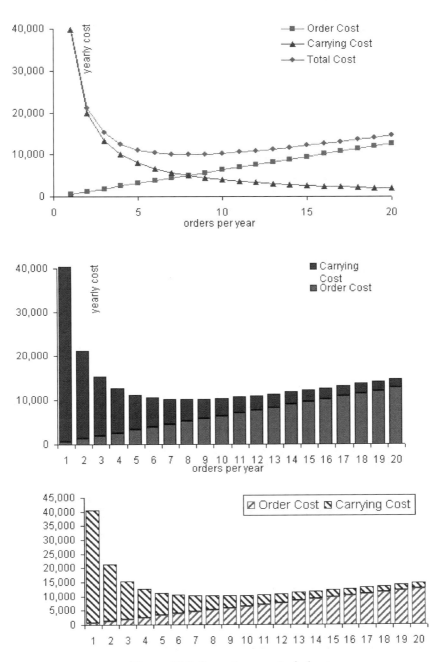

Figure 28.2: Inventory control charts

29. Decision Analysis – Queuing Models

File Name: Decision Analysis – Queuing Models

Location: Modeling Toolkit | Decision Analysis | Queuing Models

Brief Description: Sets up and simulates a queuing model, and interprets the results from a queuing model

Requirements: Modeling Toolkit, Risk Simulator

Think of how queuing models work. Consider a call center, available beds waiting to be occupied in a hospital, or a checkout counter at a McDonald's fast-food restaurant. The *queue* is the line of people waiting to get served. Typically, the arrival rates of patrons follow a Poisson distribution on a per period basis, per hour or per day, and so forth. The number of checkout counters open is the number of *channels* in a queuing model (the rate at which the servers are able to serve the patrons typically follows an Exponential distribution). The questions that a queuing model answers are how many servers or channels should there be if you do not want your patrons to wait more than X minutes, or if we have Y servers, what is the probability that a patron arriving will have to wait and what is the average wait time, and so forth. These types of models are extremely powerful when coupled with simulation, where the arrival rates and service times are variable and simulated. Imagine applications from staffing call centers, customer service lines, and checkout counters to how many hospital beds should exist in a hospital per type of diagnostic-related group, and so forth.

These models are based on operations research queuing models. The *Single Channel Queuing* model and the *Multiple Channel Queuing* model (Figure 29.1 shows the multiple channel model) assume a Poisson distribution of arrival rates and Exponential distribution of service times, with the only difference between them being the number of channels. Both the *MG1 Single Arbitrary* model and *MGK Blocked Queuing* model (Figure 29.2) assume the same Poisson distribution on arrival rates but do not rely on the Exponential distribution for service times. The two main differences between these two general-distribution (G) models are that the MGK uses multiple channels as compared to the single-channel MG1, as well as the fact that the MG1 model assumes the possibility of waiting in line while the MGK model assumes customers will be turned away if the channels are loaded when they arrive. Spend some time in the models to see various interacting effects of each input on the result.

Running a Monte Carlo Simulation

In all of these models, the results are closed-form. Hence, only the input assumptions (arrival rates and service rates) are uncertain and should be simulated. The forecast results should be any of the outputs of interest.

Multiple Channel Queuing Model

This model assumes a Poisson arrival rate with Exponential distribution of service times

Number of Channels (k)	2
Mean Arrival Rate Per Period (λ)	0.75
Mean Service Rate Per Channel Per Period (μ)	1

Cost of waiting	$7,000.00
Adding the single channel	$5,000.00
Total cost per time period	$16,109.09

Probability that no customers are in the system, Po	**45.45%**
Average number of customers in the waiting line, Lq	**0.1227**
Average number of customers in the system, L	**0.8727**
Average time a customer spends in the waiting line, Wq	**0.1636**
Average time a customer spends in the system, W	**1.1636**
Probability an arriving customer has to wait, Pw	**20.45%**

Figure 29.1: Multiple channel queuing model

Queuing Model: M/G/k Blocked Model

This model assumes a Poisson arrival rate with unknown distribution of service times

Number of Channels (k)	15.00
Mean Arrival Rate Per Period (λ)	20.00
Mean Service Rate Per Channel Per Period (μ)	2.00

Cost of losing one demand unit	$7,000.00
Service cost of adding one extra channel	$5,000.00
Total cost per time period	($7,554.79)

Probability demand will be served	**96.35%**
Average number of users in the system (L)	**9.6350**

Number of Channels	Probability Busy	Economic Cost	Probability Served
13	7.66%	$2,445.21	92.34%
14	5.47%	$0.00	94.53%
15	3.65%	$0.00	96.35%
16	2.28%	$0.00	97.72%
17	1.34%	$0.00	98.66%
18	0.75%	$0.00	99.25%
19	0.39%	$0.00	99.61%
20	0.20%	$0.00	99.80%
21	0.09%	$0.00	99.91%
22	0.04%	$0.00	99.96%
23	0.02%	$0.00	99.98%
24	0.01%	$0.00	99.99%
25	0.00%	$0.00	100.00%
26	0.00%	$0.00	100.00%
27	0.00%	$0.00	100.00%
28	0.00%	$0.00	100.00%
29	0.00%	$0.00	100.00%

Figure 29.2: MGK blocked model

30. Exotic Options – Accruals on Basket of Assets

File Name: Exotic Options – Accruals on Basket of Assets

Location: Modeling Toolkit | Real Options Models | Accruals on Basket of Assets

Brief Description: Models the value of an accrual option on a basket or group of underlying assets

Requirements: Modeling Toolkit, Real Options SLS

Accruals on Basket instruments are essentially financial portfolios of multiple underlying assets where the holder of the instrument receives the maximum of the basket of assets or some prespecified guarantee amount. This instrument can be modeled as either an American option which can be executed at any time up to and including maturity; as a European option, which can be exercised only at maturity; or as a Bermudan option (exercisable only at certain times). Using the multiple assets and multiple phased module (MSLS) of the Real Options SLS software, we can model the value of an accrual option (Figure 30.1).

It is highly recommended that at this point, the reader first familiarizes him/herself with the basics of using the **Real Options SLS Software** chapter before attempting to solve any SLS models. Although using the SLS software, this model is listed in the section of Exotic Options because basket accruals are considered exotic options and are solved using similar methodologies as other exotics. The inputs are usual option inputs. The terminal and intermediate equations are shown next.

The Terminal Node Equation is:

Max(FirstAsset,SecondAsset,ThirdAsset,FourthAsset,Guarantee)

while the Intermediate Node Equation is:

Max(FirstAsset,SecondAsset,ThirdAsset,FourthAsset,OptionOpen)

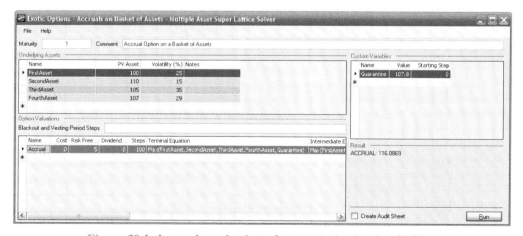

Figure 30.1: Accruals on basket of assets (solved using SLS)

31. Exotic Options – American, Bermudan, and European Options with Sensitivities

File Name: Exotic Options – American, Bermudan, and European Options with Sensitivities

Location: Modeling Toolkit | Exotic Options | American, Bermudan, and European Options

Brief Description: Computes American, Bermudan, and European options with Greek sensitivities

Requirements: Modeling Toolkit

Modeling Toolkit Functions Used: MTBinomialAmericanCall, MTBinomialBermudanCall, MTBinomialEuropeanCall, MTBinomialAmericanPut, MTBinomialBermudanPut, MTBinomialEuropeanPut, MTGeneralizedBlackScholesCall, MTBinomialAmericanPut, MTGeneralizedBlackScholesPut, MTClosedFormAmericanCall, MTClosedFormAmericanPut, MTCallDelta, MTCallGamma, MTCallTheta, MTCallRho, MTPutVega MTPutDelta, MTPutGamma, MTPutTheta, MTPutRho, MTPutVega

American options can be exercised at any time up to and including maturity, European options can only be exercised at maturity, and Bermudan options can be exercised at certain times (exercisable other than during the vesting blackout period). In most cases, American ≥ Bermudan ≥ European options except for one special case: for plain vanilla call options when there are no dividends, American = Bermudan = European call options, as it is never optimal to exercise early in a plain vanilla call option when there are no dividends (Figure 31.1). However, once there is a sufficiently high dividend rate paid by the underlying stock, we clearly see that the relationship where American ≥ Bermudan ≥ European options apply (Figure 31.2).

European options can be solved using the Generalized Black-Scholes-Merton model (a closed-form equation) as well as using binomial lattices and other numerical methods. However, for American options, we cannot use the Black-Scholes model and must revert to using the binomial lattice approach and some closed-form approximation models. Using the binomial lattice requires an additional input variable: lattice steps. The higher the number of lattice steps, the higher the precision of the results. Typically, 100 to 1,000 steps are sufficient to achieve convergence. Use the Real Options SLS software to solve more advanced options vehicles with a fully customizable lattice model. Only binomial lattices can be used to solve Bermudan options. The Real Options SLS software is used to solve more advanced and exotic options vehicles with a fully customizable lattice model in later chapters.

AMERICAN, BERMUDAN AND EUROPEAN OPTIONS WITH SENSITIVITY ANALYSIS

Input Assumptions

Asset Price	$100.00
Strike Price	$100.00
Maturity	5
Riskfree Rate	5.00%
Volatility	25.00%
Dividend Rate	0.00%
Lattice Steps	1000
Vesting Year	4

American Call (Binomial)	$32.50	*MTBinomialAmericanCall*
Bermudan Call (Binomial)	$32.50	*MTROBinomialBermudanCall*
European Call (Binomial)	$32.50	*MTBinomialEuropeanCall*
American Put (Binomial)	$13.50	*MTBinomialAmericanPut*
Bermudan Put (Binomial)	$11.51	*MTROBinomialBermudanPut*
European Put (Binomial)	$10.38	*MTBinomialEuropeanPut*

Generalized Black-Scholes European Call	$32.50	*MTGeneralizedBlackScholesCall*
Generalized Black-Scholes European Put	$10.38	*MTGeneralizedBlackScholesPut*
Closed-Form Approximation American Call	$32.50	*MTClosedFormAmericanCall*
Closed-Form Approximation American Put	$13.40	*MTClosedFormAmericanPut*

Sensitivities on European Options	Call	Put		
Delta (Sensitivity to Stock Price)	0.7663	-0.2337	*MTCallDelta*	*MTPutDelta*
Gamma (Second Order Sensitivity to Delta)	0.0055	0.0055	*MTCallGamma*	*MTPutGamma*
Theta (Sensitivity to Maturity)	-3.9189	-0.0249	*MTCallTheta*	*MTPutTheta*
Rho (Sensitivity to Risk-free Rate)	220.6313	-168.7691	*MTCallRho*	*MTPutRho*
Vega (Sensitivity to Volatility)	68.5037	68.5037	*MTCallVega*	*MTPutVega*

Figure 31.1: American, Bermudan, and European options with Greeks

Input Assumptions

Asset Price	$100.00
Strike Price	$100.00
Maturity	5
Riskfree Rate	5.00%
Volatility	25.00%
Dividend Rate	3.00%
Lattice Steps	1000
Vesting Year	4

Real Options Valuation
www.realoptionsvaluation.com

American Call (Binomial)	$22.77
Bermudan Call (Binomial)	$22.61
European Call (Binomial)	$22.42
American Put (Binomial)	$16.37
Bermudan Put (Binomial)	$15.12
European Put (Binomial)	$14.23

Figure 31.2: American, Bermudan, and European options with Dividends

32. Exotic Options – American Call Option on Foreign Exchange

File Name: Exotic Options – American Call Option on Foreign Exchange

Location: Modeling Toolkit | Real Options Models | American Call Option on Foreign Exchange

Brief Description: Computes American and European options on foreign exchange

Requirements: Modeling Toolkit, Real Options SLS

A Foreign Exchange Option (FX Option or FXO) is a derivative where the owner has the right but not the obligation to exchange money denominated in one currency into another currency at a previously agreed upon exchange rate on a specified date. The FX Options market is the deepest, largest, and most liquid market for options of any kind in the world. The valuation here uses the Garman-Kohlhagen model (Figure 32.1). You can use the *Exotic Options – Currency (Foreign Exchange) Options* model in the Modeling Toolkit software to compare the results of this Real Options SLS model. The exotic options model is used to compute the European version using closed-form models; the Real Options SLS model, the example showcased here, computes the European and American options using a binomial lattice approach. When using the binomial lattice approach in the Real Options SLS software, remember to set the *Dividend Rate* as the foreign country's risk-free rate, *PV Underlying Asset* as the spot exchange rate, and *Implementation Cost* as the strike exchange rate.

As an example of a foreign exchange option, suppose the British pounds (GBP) versus the U.S. dollar (USD) is USD2/GBP1. Then the spot exchange rate is 2.0. Because the exchange rate is denominated in GBP (the denominator), the domestic risk-free rate is the rate in the United Kingdom, and the foreign rate is the rate in the United States. This means that the foreign exchange contract allows the holder the option to call GBP and put USD.

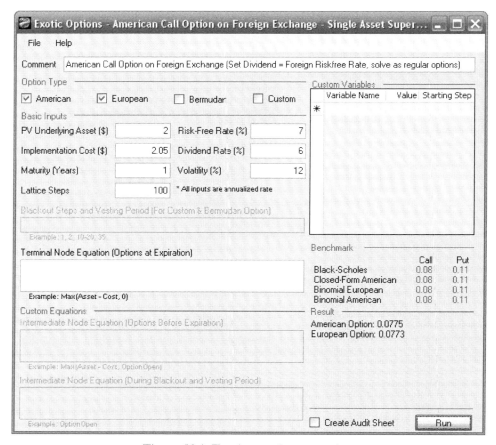

Figure 32.1: Foreign exchange option

To illustrate, suppose a U.K. firm is getting US$1M in six months, and the spot exchange rate is USD2/GBP1. If the GBP currency strengthens, the U.K. firm loses when it has to repatriate USD back to GBP, but gains if the GBP currency weakens. If the firm hedges the foreign exchange exposure with an FXO and gets a call on GBP (put on USD), it hedges itself from any foreign exchange fluctuation risks. For discussion purposes, say the timing is short, interest rates are low, and volatility is low. Getting a call option with a strike of 1.90 yields a call value approximately 0.10 (i.e., the firm can execute the option and gain the difference of 2.00 − 1.90, or 0.10, immediately). This means that the rate now becomes USD1.90/GBP1, and it is cheaper to purchase GBP with the same USD, or the U.K. firm gets a higher GBP payoff. In situations where volatility is nonzero and maturity is higher, there is a significant value in an FXO, which can be modeled using the Real Options SLS approach.

33. Exotic Options – American Call Option on Index Futures

File Name: Exotic Options – American Call Option on Index Futures

Location: Modeling Toolkit | Real Options Models | American Call Option on Index Futures

Brief Description: Computes the value of an Index option using closed-form models and binomial lattices

Requirements: Modeling Toolkit, Real Options SLS

The Index Option is similar to a regular option but the underlying asset is a reference stock index such as the Standard & Poor's 500. The analysis can also be solved using a closed-form Generalized Black-Scholes-Merton model. The model used in this chapter is similar to the closed-form model but applies the binomial lattice instead. The difference here is that Black-Scholes can solve only European options while the binomial lattice model is capable of solving American, European, and Bermudan or mixed and customized options. Instead of using the asset value or current stock price as the input, we use the current Index value. All other inputs remain the same, as in other options models (see Figure 33.1). Index futures are an important investment vehicle as stock indexes cannot be traded directly, so futures based on stock indexes are the primary vehicles for trading indexes. Index futures operate in essentially the same way as other futures, and are traded in the same way. As indexes are based on many separate stocks, index futures are settled in cash rather than stocks. In addition, index futures allow investors to participate in the entire market without the significant cost of purchasing each underlying stock in an index. Index futures are widely used for hedging market movements and applied in portfolios for their diversification effects.

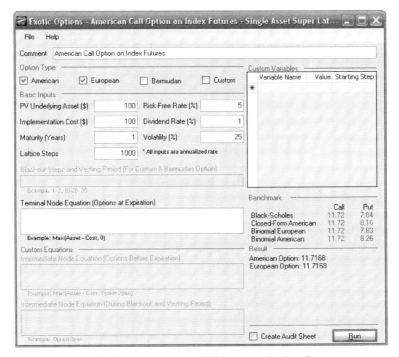

Figure 33.1: American and European index futures

34. Exotic Options – American Call Option with Dividends

File Name: Exotic Options – American Call Option with Dividends

Location: Modeling Toolkit | Real Options Models | American Call Option with Dividends

Brief Description: Solves the American call option using customizable binomial lattices as well as closed-form approximation models

Requirements: Modeling Toolkit, Real Options SLS

The *American Call Option with Dividends* model computes the call option using Real Options SLS software by applying the binomial lattice methodology (Figure 34.1). The results are benchmarked with closed-form approximation models. You can compare the results from this model with the European call option with dividends example. Note that when there are dividends, American options (which can be exercised early) are worth more than Bermudan options (options that can be exercised before termination but not during blackout periods such as vesting or contractual nontrading days), which in turn are worth more than European options (options that can be exercised only at maturity). This value relationship is typically true for most options. In contrast, for plain vanilla basic call options without dividends, American options are worth the same as the Bermudan and European options as they are never optimal to exercise early. This fact is true only for simple plain vanilla call options when no dividends exist. See previous chapters on modeling American, Bermudan, and European options for further details on comparisons of value.

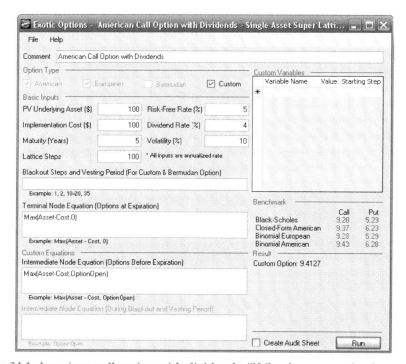

Figure 34.1: American call option with dividends (SLS using customized equations)

35. Exotic Options – Asian Lookback Options Using Arithmetic Averages

File Name: Exotic Options – Asian Arithmetic

Location: Modeling Toolkit | Exotic Options | Asian Arithmetic

Brief Description: Solves an Asian lookback option using closed-form models, where the lookback is linked to the arithmetic average of past prices

Requirements: Modeling Toolkit

Modeling Toolkit Functions Used: MTAsianCallwithArithmeticAverageRate, MTAsianPutwithArithmeticAverageRate

Asian options (also called Average Options) are options whose payoffs are linked to the average value of the underlying asset on a specific set of dates during the life of the option . An average rate option is a cash-settled option whose payoff is based on the difference between the average value of the underlying during the life of the option and a fixed strike. The Arithmetic version means that the prices are simple averages rather than geometric averages (Figure 35.1).

End users of currency, commodities, or energy trading tend to be exposed to average prices over time, so Asian options are attractive for them. Asian options are also popular with corporations and banks with ongoing currency exposures. These options are also attractive because they tend to be less expensive—sell at lower premiums—than comparable vanilla puts or calls. This is because the volatility in the average value of an underlying asset or stock tends to be lower than the volatility of the actual values of the underlying asset or stock. Also, in situations where the underlying asset is thinly traded or there is the potential for its price to be manipulated, an Asian option offers some protection. It is more difficult to manipulate the average value of an underlying asset over an extended period of time than it is to manipulate it just at the expiration of an option.

ASIAN LOOKBACK OPTIONS WITH ARITHMETIC AVERAGES

Input Assumptions

Asset Spot Price	$100.00
Average Asset Price	$100.00
Strike Price	$100.00
Original Maturity	1.00
Time to Maturity	1.00
Riskfree Rate	5.00%
Dividend Rate	0.00%
Volatility	25.00%

Asian Call Option with Geometric Averages   **$6.8831**
Asian Put Option with Geometric Averages   **$4.4649**

Figure 35.1: Computing the Asian lookback option (arithmetic mean)

36. Exotic Options – Asian Lookback Options Using Geometric Averages

File Name: Exotic Options – Asian Geometric

Location: Modeling Toolkit | Exotic Options | Asian Geometric

Brief Description: Solves an Asian lookback option using closed-form models, where the lookback is linked to the geometric average of past prices

Requirements: Modeling Toolkit

Modeling Toolkit Functions Used: MTAsianCallwithGeometricAverageRate, MTAsianPutwithGeometricAverageRate

Asian options (also called Average Options) are options whose payoffs are linked to the average value of the underlying asset on a specific set of dates during the life of the option. An average rate option is a cash-settled option whose payoff is based on the difference between the average value of the underlying during the life of the option and a fixed strike. The Geometric version means that the prices are geometric averages rather than simple arithmetic averages, providing a more conservative measure (Figure 36.1).

End users of currency, commodities or energy trading tend to be exposed to average prices over time, so Asian options are attractive for them. Asian options are also popular with corporations and banks with ongoing currency exposures. These Asian options are attractive because they tend to be less expensive—sell at lower premiums—than comparable vanilla puts or calls. This is because the volatility in the average value of an underlying stock or asset tends to be lower than the volatility of the actual values of the underlying stock or asset. Also, in situations where the underlying asset is thinly traded or there is the potential for its price to be manipulated, an Asian option offers some protection. It is more difficult to manipulate the average value of an underlying asset over an extended period of time than it is to manipulate it just at the expiration of an option.

ASIAN LOOKBACK OPTIONS WITH GEOMETRIC AVERAGES

Input Assumptions

Asset Spot Price	$100.00
Average Asset Price	$100.00
Strike Price	$100.00
Original Maturity	1.00
Time to Maturity	1.00
Riskfree Rate	5.00%
Dividend Rate	0.00%
Volatility	25.00%

Asian Call Option with Geometric Averages	**$6.5298**
Asian Put Option with Geometric Averages	**$4.6284**

Figure 36.1: Computing the Asian lookback option (geometric average)

37. Exotic Options – Asset or Nothing Options

File Name: Exotic Options – Asset or Nothing

Location: Modeling Toolkit | Exotic Options | Asset or Nothing

Brief Description: Computes an Asset or Nothing Option where as long as the asset is above water, the holder will receive the asset at maturity

Requirements: Modeling Toolkit, Real Options SLS

Modeling Toolkit Functions Used: MTAssetOrNothingCall, MTAssetOrNothingPut

An Asset or Nothing Option is exactly what it implies: At expiration, if the option is in the money, regardless of how deep it is in the money, the option holder receives the stock or asset. This means that for a call option, as long as the stock or asset price exceeds the strike at expiration, the stock is received. Conversely, for a put option, the stock is received only if the stock or asset value falls below the strike price. Figure 37.1 shows an example of computing the asset or nothing option.

ASSET OR NOTHING OPTION

Input Assumptions

Stock Price	$100.00
Strike Price	$90.00
Maturity	1.00
Risk-free Rate	5.00%
Dividend Rate	0.00%
Volatility	25.00%

Asset or Nothing Call Option	$77.2300
Asset or Nothing Put Option	$22.7700

Functions:
MTAssetOrNothingCall
MTAssetOrNothingPut

Figure 37.1: Computing the asset or nothing option

38. Exotic Options – Barrier Options

File Name: Exotic Options – Barrier Options

Location: Modeling Toolkit | Exotic Options | Barrier Options

Brief Description: Values various types of barrier options such as up and in, down and in, up and out, and down and out call and put options

Requirements: Modeling Toolkit

Modeling Toolkit Functions Used: MTBarrierDownandInCall, MTBarrierUpandInCall, MTBarrierDownandInPut, MTBarrierUpandInPut, MTBarrierDownandOutCall, MTBarrierUpandOutCall, MTBarrierDownandOutPut, MTBarrierUpandOutPut

Barrier options become valuable or get knocked in the money only if a barrier (upper or lower barrier) is breached (or not), and the payout is in the form of the option on the underlying asset. Sometimes, as remuneration for the risk of not being knocked in, a specified cash rebate is paid at the end of the instrument's maturity (at expiration) assuming that the option has not been knocked in.

As an example, in an Up and In Call option, the instrument pays the specified cash amount at expiration if and only if the asset value does not breach the upper barrier (the asset value does not go above the upper barrier), providing the holder of the instrument with a safety net or a cash insurance. However, if the asset breaches the upper barrier, the option gets knocked in and becomes a live option. An Up and Out option is live only as long as the asset does not breach the upper barrier, and so forth. *Monitoring Periodicities* means how often during the life of the option the asset or stock value will be monitored to see if it breaches a barrier. As an example, entering 12 implies monthly monitoring, 52 means weekly monitoring, 252 indicates monitoring for daily trading, 365 means monitoring daily, and 1,000,000 means continuous monitoring.

In general, barrier options limit the potential of a regular option's profits and hence cost less than regular options without barriers. For instance, in Figure 38.1, if we assume no cash rebates, a Generalized Black-Scholes call option returns $6.50 as opposed to $5.33 for a barrier option (up and in barrier set at $115 with a stock price and strike price value of $100). This is because the call option will only be knocked in if the stock price goes above this $115 barrier, thereby reducing the regular option's profits between $100 and $115. This reduction effect is even more pronounced in the up and out call option, where all the significant upside profits (above the $115 barrier) are completely truncated.

BARRIER OPTIONS

Input Assumptions

Asset Value or Stock Price	$100.00
Strike Price	$100.00
Barrier Price	$115.00
Cash Rebate Value	$3.00
Time to Maturity	0.50
Riskfree Rate	8.00%
Dividend Rate	4.00%
Annualized Volatility	20.00%
Monitoring Periodicities (Per Year)	365.00

Down and In Call Option	**$39.52**
Up and In Call Option	**$7.27**
Down and In Put Option	**$2.16**
Up and In Put Option	**$2.03**
Down and Out Call Option	**$0.00**
Up and Out Call Option	**$2.12**
Down and Out Put Option	**$5.79**
Up and Out Put Option	**$5.42**

Figure 38.1: Computing barrier options

39. Exotic Options – Binary Digital Options

File Name: Exotic Options – Binary Digital Options

Location: Modeling Toolkit | Exotic Options | Binary Digital Options

Brief Description: Computes various binary digital options that either knocked in or out of the money depending if the asset value breaches certain barriers

Requirements: Modeling Toolkit, Real Options SLS

Modeling Toolkit Functions Used:
MTBinaryDownAndInCashAtExpirationOrNothingCall,
MTBinaryUpAndInCashAtExpirationOrNothingCall,
MTBinaryDownAndInAssetAtExpirationOrNothingCall,
MTBinaryUpAndInAssetAtExpirationOrNothingCall,
MTBinaryDownAndOutCashAtExpirationOrNothingCall,
MTBinaryUpAndOutCashAtExpirationOrNothingCall,
MTBinaryDownAndOutAssetAtExpirationOrNothingCall,
MTBinaryUpAndOutAssetAtExpirationOrNothingCall,
MTBinaryDownAndInCashAtExpirationOrNothingPut,
MTBinaryUpAndInCashAtExpirationOrNothingPut,
MTBinaryDownAndInAssetAtExpirationOrNothingPut,
MTBinaryUpAndInAssetAtExpirationOrNothingPut,
MTBinaryDownAndOutCashAtExpirationOrNothingPut,
MTBinaryUpAndOutCashAtExpirationOrNothingPut,
MTBinaryDownAndOutAssetAtExpirationOrNothingPut,
MTBinaryUpAndOutAssetAtExpirationOrNothingPut

Binary exotic options (also known as *Digital*, *Accrual*, or *Fairway* options) become valuable only if a barrier (upper or lower barrier) is breached (or not), and the payout could be in the form of some prespecified cash amount or the underlying asset itself. The cash or asset exchanges hands either at the point when the barrier is breached, or at the end of the instrument's maturity (at expiration) assuming that the barrier is breached at some point prior to maturity.

For instance, in the Down and In Cash at Expiration option, the instruments pay the specified cash amount at expiration if and only if the asset value breaches the lower barrier (the asset value goes below the lower barrier), providing the holder of the instrument a safety net or a cash insurance in case the underlying asset does not perform well. With Up and In options, the cash or asset is provided if the underlying asset goes above the upper barrier threshold. In Up and Out or Down and Out options the asset or cash is paid as long as the upper or lower barrier is not breached. With At Expiration options, cash and assets are paid at maturity, whereas the At Hit instruments are payable at the point when the barrier is breached. Figure 39.1 provides an example of computing binary digital options.

BINARY DIGITAL OPTIONS

Input Assumptions

Asset Value or Stock Price	$10.00
Strike Price	$10.00
Upper Barrier Price	$8.00
Lower Barrier Price	$12.00
Cash Value	$10.00
Time to Maturity	1.00
Risk-free Rate	3.00%
Dividend Rate	0.00%
Annualized Volatility	25.00%
Delta T	0.00

Down and In Cash at Expiration Call Option	$9.96
Up and In Cash at Expiration Call Option	$3.80
Down and In Asset at Expiration Call Option	$14.76
Up and In Asset at Expiration Call Option	$4.87
Down and Out Cash at Expiration Call Option	$0.00
Up and Out Cash at Expiration Call Option	$1.03
Down and Out Asset at Expiration Call Option	$0.00
Up and Out Asset at Expiration Call Option	$1.10

Down and In Cash at Expiration Put Option	$4.87
Up and In Cash at Expiration Put Option	$0.70
Down and In Asset at Expiration Put Option	$4.03
Up and In Asset at Expiration Put Option	$0.63
Down and Out Cash at Expiration Put Option	$0.00
Up and Out Cash at Expiration Put Option	$4.17
Down and Out Asset at Expiration Put Option	$0.00
Up and Out Asset at Expiration Put Option	$3.40

Figure 39.1: Computing binary digital options

40. Exotic Options – Cash or Nothing Options

File Name: Exotic Options – Cash or Nothing

Location: Modeling Toolkit | Exotic Options | Cash or Nothing

Brief Description: Computes the cash or nothing option, where if in the money at expiration, the holder receives some prespecified cash amount

Requirements: Modeling Toolkit, Real Options SLS

Modeling Toolkit Functions Used: MTCashOrNothingCall, MTCashOrNothingPut

A Cash or Nothing Option is exactly what it implies: At expiration, if the option is in the money, regardless of how deep it is in the money, the option holder receives a pre-determined cash payment. This means that for a call option, as long as the stock or asset price exceeds the strike at expiration, cash is received. Conversely, for a put option, cash is received only if the stock or asset value falls below the strike price. An example of computing a cash or nothing option is shown in Figure 40.1.

CASH OR NOTHING OPTION

Input Assumptions

Stock Price	$100.00
Strike Price	$90.00
Cash Payment	$110.00
Maturity	1.00
Risk-free Rate	5.00%
Dividend Rate	0.00%
Volatility	25.00%

Cash or Nothing Call Option	$72.2202
Cash or Nothing Put Option	$32.4151

Functions:
MTCashOrNothingCall
MTCashOrNothingPut

Figure 40.1: Computing cash or nothing options

41. Exotic Options – Chooser Option (Simple Chooser)

File Name: Exotic Options – Simple Chooser

Location: Modeling Toolkit | Exotic Options | Simple Chooser

Brief Description: Computes the value of an option that can become either a call or a put

Requirements: Modeling Toolkit, Real Options SLS

Modeling Toolkit Functions Used: MTChooserBasicOption, MTGeneralizedBlackScholesCall, MTGeneralizedBlackScholesPut

A Simple Chooser Option allows the holder the option to choose if the option is a call or a put within the Chooser Time. Regardless of the choice, the option has the same contractual strike price and maturity. Typically, a chooser option is cheaper than purchasing both a call and a put together, but provides the same level of hedge at a lower cost. The strike prices for both options are identical. The Complex Chooser Option in the next chapter allows for different strike prices and maturities. Figure 41.1 gives an example of computing the value of a simple chooser option.

SIMPLE CHOOSER OPTION

Input Assumptions

Asset Price	$80.00
Strike Price	$90.00
Chooser Time	0.50
Maturity	1.00
Risk-free Rate	10.00%
Dividend Rate	2.00%
Volatility	30.00%

Chooser Option Value	$16.4626
If Purchased as a Call + Put Options	$19.2097

Functions:
MTChooserBasicOption
MTGeneralizedBlackScholesCall
MTGeneralizedBlackScholesPut

Figure 41.1: Computing a simple exotic chooser option

42. Exotic Options – Chooser Option (Complex Chooser)

File Name: Exotic Options – Complex Chooser

Location: Modeling Toolkit | Exotic Options | Complex Chooser

Brief Description: Values the complex chooser option, where the holder has the ability to decide, at a later time, if the option can be a call or a put

Requirements: Modeling Toolkit

Modeling Toolkit Functions Used: MTChooserComplexOption, MTGeneralizedBlackScholesCall, MTGeneralizedBlackScholesPut

The Complex Chooser Option allows the holder to choose if it becomes a call or a put option by a specific chooser time, while the maturity and strike price of the call and put are allowed to be different. Typically, a chooser option is cheaper than purchasing both a call and a put together. It provides the same level of hedge at a lower cost, while the strike price for both options can be different. Figure 21.1 gives an example of computing the value of a complex chooser option.

COMPLEX CHOOSER OPTIONS

Input Assumptions

Asset Price	$80.00
Strike Price for Call	$80.00
Strike Price for Put	$90.00
Chooser Time	0.50
Maturity for Call	1.00
Maturity for Put	1.20
Risk-free Rate	10.00%
Dividend Rate	2.00%
Volatility	30.00%

Complex Chooser Option Value	$19.2269
If Purchased as a Call + Put Options	$23.5087

Functions:
MTChooserBasicOption
MTGeneralizedBlackScholesCall
MTGeneralizedBlackScholesPut

Figure 42.1: Computing a complex chooser option

43. Exotic Options – Commodity Options

File Name: Exotic Options – Commodity Options

Location: Modeling Toolkit | Exotic Options | Commodity Options

Brief Description: Models and values a commodity option where the commodity's spot and future values are used to value the option, while the forward rates and convenience yields are assumed to be mean-reverting and volatile

Requirements: Modeling Toolkit

Modeling Toolkit Functions Used: MTCommodityCallOptionModel, MTCommodityPutOptionModel

This model computes the values of commodity-based European call and put options, where the convenience yield and forward rates are assumed to be mean-reverting, and each has its own volatilities and cross-correlations. This is a complex multifactor model with inter-relationships among all variables. An example of valuing a commodity option is provided in Figure 43.1.

VALUE OF A COMMODITY OPTION

Price of Zero Coupon Bond	$0.9753
Futures Price	$95.0000
Strike Price	$95.0000
Maturity of the Option	0.5000
Maturity of the Futures Contract	1.0000
Volatility of the Spot Commodity Price	26.60%
Volatility of Future Convenience Yield	24.90%
Volatility of the Forward Interest Rate	0.96%
Correlation Commodity Price and Convenience Yield	0.8050
Correlation Commodity Price and Forward Rate	0.0964
Correlation Convenience Yield and Forward Rate	0.1243
Speed of Mean Reversion of the Convenience Yield	104.50%
Speed of Mean Reversion of the Forward Rates	20.00%

Commodity Call Option Value	**$4.7245**
Commodity Put Option Value	**$4.7262**

Figure 43.1: Computing the commodity option

44. Exotic Options – Currency (Foreign Exchange) Options

File Name: Exotic Options – Currency Options

Location: Modeling Toolkit | Exotic Options | Currency Options

Brief Description: Values a foreign exchange currency option, typically used in hedging foreign exchange fluctuations, where the key inputs are the spot exchange rate and the contractual purchase or sale price of the foreign exchange currency for delivery in the future

Requirements: Modeling Toolkit

Modeling Toolkit Functions Used: MTCurrencyCallOption, MTCurrencyPutOption

A Foreign Exchange Option (FX Option or FXO) is a derivative where the owner has the right but not the obligation to exchange money denominated in one currency into another currency at a previously agreed upon exchange rate on a specified date. The FX Options market is the deepest, largest, and most liquid market for options of any kind in the world. The sample valuation here (Figure 44.1) uses the Garman-Kohlhagen model.

Input Assumptions	
Spot Exchange Rate	2.00
Strike Exchange Rate	2.05
Maturity	1.00
Domestic Riskfree Rate	7.00%
Foreign Riskfree Rate	6.00%
Volatility	12.00%

Foreign Currency Call Option	**$0.0775**
Foreign Currency Put Option	**$0.1054**

Figure 44.1: Computing the foreign exchange option

As an example, suppose the British pounds (GBP) versus the U.S. dollar (USD) is USD2/GBP1, then the spot exchange rate is 2.0, and because the exchange rate is denominated in GBP (the denominator), then the domestic risk-free rate is the rate in the United Kingdom, and the foreign rate is the rate in the United States. This means that the foreign exchange contract allows the holder the option to call GBP and put USD.

To illustrate, suppose a U.K. firm is getting US$1M in six months, and the spot exchange rate is USD2/GBP1. If the GBP strengthens, the U.K. firm loses if it has to repatriate USD back to GBP; it gains if the GBP currency weakens. If the firm hedges the foreign exchange exposure with an FXO and gets a call on GBP (put on USD), it hedges itself from any foreign exchange fluctuation risks. For discussion purposes, say the timing is short, interest rates are low, and volatility is low. Getting a call option with a strike of 1.90 yields a call value approximately 0.10 (i.e., the firm can execute the option and gain the difference of 2.00 – 1.90, or 0.10, immediately). This means that the rate now becomes USD1.90/GBP1, and it is cheaper to purchase GBP with the same USD, or the U.K. firm gets a higher GBP payoff.

45. Exotic Options – Double Barrier Options

File Name: Exotic Options – Double Barrier Options

Location: Modeling Toolkit | Exotic Options | Double Barriers

Brief Description: Values various double barrier options, including up and in, up and out, with down and in, and down and out combinations, where a call or put option is knocked in or out of the money depending if it breaches an upper or lower barrier

Requirements: Modeling Toolkit

Modeling Toolkit Functions Used: MTBarrierDoubleUpOutDownOutCall, MTBarrierDoubleUpOutDownOutPut, MTBarrierDoubleUpInDownInCall, MTBarrierDoubleUpInDownInPut

Barrier options become valuable or get knocked in the money only if a barrier (upper or lower barrier) is breached (or not), and the payout is in the form of the option on the underlying asset. Double barrier options have two barriers, one above the current asset value (upper barrier) and one below it (lower barrier). Either barrier has to be breached for a knock-in or knock-out event to occur. In general, barrier options limit the potential of a regular option's profits and hence cost less than regular options without barriers. Figure 45.1 gives an example of valuing double barrier options.

DOUBLE BARRIER OPTIONS

Input Assumptions	
Asset Value or Stock Price	$100.00
Strike Price	$100.00
Lower Barrier	$90.00
Upper Barrier	$110.00
Time to Maturity	1.00
Risk-free Rate	10.00%
Dividend Rate	0.00%
Annualized Volatility	25.00%
Upper Delta Curvature	0.00
Lower Delta Curvature	0.00
Monitoring Periodicities (Per Year)	365.00

		Functions:
Up and Out, Down and Out Call Option	$0.0027	MTBarrierDoubleUpOutDownOutCall
Up and Out, Down and Out Put Option	$0.0030	MTBarrierDoubleUpOutDownOutPut
Down and In, Up and In Call Option	$14.9731	MTBarrierDoubleUpInDownInCall
Down and In, Up and In Put Option	$5.4565	MTBarrierDoubleUpInDownInPut

Figure 45.1: Computing double barrier options

As an example, in the Up and Out, Down and Out Call Option, the instrument is knocked out if the asset breaches either the upper or lower barriers, but remains in effect and the option is live at the end of maturity if the asset prices remain between these two barriers. *Monitoring Periodicities* means how often during the life of the option the asset or stock value will be monitored to see if it breaches a barrier. For example, entering 12 implies monthly monitoring, 52 means weekly monitoring, 252 indicates monitoring for daily trading, 365 means monitoring daily, and 1,000,000 is used for continuous monitoring. The delta curvature can also be entered for the upper and lower barrier asset prices if using barrier options as a delta or gamma hedge; otherwise, set these as zero.

46. Exotic Options – European Call Option with Dividends

File Name: Exotic Options – European Call Option with Dividends

Location: Modeling Toolkit | Real Options Models | European Call Option with Dividends

Brief Description: Uses the customized binomial lattice approach to solve a European call option with dividends, where the holder of the option can exercise only at maturity and not before

Requirements: Modeling Toolkit, Real Options SLS

A European call option allows the holder to exercise the option only at maturity. An American option can be exercised at any time before as well as up to and including maturity. A Bermudan option is like an American and European option mixed—at certain vesting and blackout periods, the option cannot be executed until the end of the blackout period, when it then becomes exercisable at any time until its maturity. In a simple plain vanilla call option, all three varieties have the same value, as it is never optimal to exercise early, making all three options revert to the value of a simple European option. However, this does not hold true when dividends exist. When dividends are high enough, it is typically optimal to exercise a call option early, particularly before the ex-dividend date hits, reducing the value of the asset and, consequently, the value of the call option. The American call option typically is worth more than a Bermudan option, which is typically worth more than a European option, except in the special case of a simple plain vanilla call option.

Figure 46.1 illustrates how a simple European call option with dividends can be modeled using the binomial lattice with 100 steps. The terminal equation is simply set as *Max (Asset – Cost, 0)* indicative of the ability to execute the option at the terminal nodes at maturity if it is in the money or expire worthless otherwise. The intermediate equation is set as *OptionOpen,* which indicates that at any time before expiration, the only thing the owner can do is to keep the option open and wait until maturity to decide if the option should be executed. You can refer to Part II in this book on using the Real Options SLS software for more details on using the software in more sophisticated and customized options with changing inputs and real options applications.

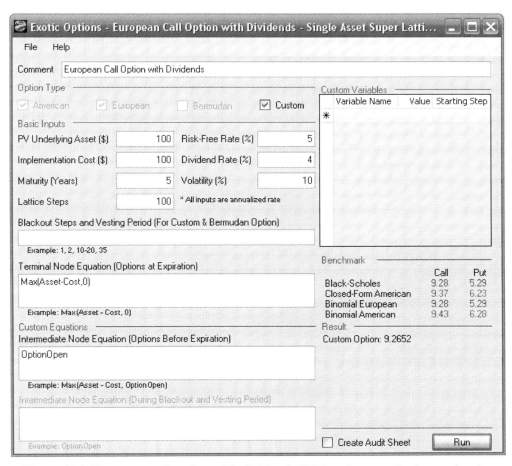

Figure 46.1: European call option with dividends (SLS and customized equations)

47. Exotic Options – Exchange Assets Option

File Name: Exotic Options – Exchange Assets

Location: Modeling Toolkit | Exotic Options | Exchange Assets

Brief Description: Values the asset exchange option, where the holder has the ability to swap one asset with another

Requirements: Modeling Toolkit

Modeling Toolkit Functions Used: MTAssetExchangeAmericanOption, MTAssetExchangeEuropeanOption

The Exchange of Assets Option provides the option holder the right at expiration (European version) to swap and give *Asset 2* away and, in return, receive *Asset 1*, with predetermined quantities of the first and second assets (Figure 47.1). The American option allows the swap to occur at any time before as well as up to and including maturity. Clearly, the more negative the correlation between the assets, the larger the risk reduction and diversification effects and hence the higher the value of the option. Sometimes in a real options world, where the assets swapped are not financial instruments but real physical assets, this option is called a switching option. We discuss switching options in later chapters when dealing with real options applications.

EXCHANGE OF ONE ASSET FOR ANOTHER

Input Assumptions

Asset 1 Price	$80.00
Asset 2 Price	$70.00
Quantity of Asset 1	10
Quantity of Asset 2	10
Maturity	1.00
Risk-free Rate	5.00%
Dividend Rate Asset 1	2.00%
Dividend Rate Asset 2	3.00%
Volatility Asset 1	25.00%
Volatility Asset 2	30.00%
Correlation Between Assets	0.50

Exchange of Asset American Option $143.8997
Exchange of Asset European Option $143.8731

Functions:
MTAssetExchangeAmericanOption
MTAssetExchangeEuropeanOption

Figure 47.1: Exchange assets options

48. Exotic Options – Extreme Spreads Option

File Name: Exotic Options – Extreme Spreads

Location: Modeling Toolkit | Exotic Options | Extreme Spreads

Brief Description: Computes extreme spread option values, where the vehicle is divided into two segments, and the option pays off the difference between the extreme values (min or max) of the asset during the two time segments

Requirements: Modeling Toolkit

Modeling Toolkit Functions Used: MTExtremeSpreadCallOption, MTExtremeSpreadPutOption, MTExtremeSpreadReverseCallOption, MTExtremeSpreadReversePutOption

Extreme Spread Options (Figure 48.1) have their maturities divided into two segments, starting from time zero to the *First Time Period* (first segment) and from the *First Time Period* to *Maturity* (second segment). An extreme spread call option pays the difference between the maximum asset value from the second segment and the maximum value of the first segment. Conversely, the put pays the difference between the minimum of the second segment's asset value and the minimum of the first segment's asset value. A reverse call pays the minimum from the first less the minimum of the second segment, whereas a reverse put pays the maximum of the first less the maximum of the second segments.

EXTREME SPREAD OPTIONS

Input Assumptions

Asset Price	$100.00
Observed Minimum	$90.00
Observed Maximum	$110.00
First Time Period	0.25
Maturity	1.00
Risk-free Rate	5.00%
Dividend Rate	0.00%
Volatility	30.00%

Extreme Spread Call	$14.4021
Extreme Spread Put	$7.3515
Reverse Extreme Spread Call	$4.4490
Reverse Extreme Spread Put	$4.2039

Functions:
MTExtremeSpreadCallOption
MTExtremeSpreadPutOption
MTExtremeSpreadReverseCallOption
MTExtremeSpreadReversePutOption

Figure 48.1: Extreme spreads options

49. Exotic Options – Foreign Equity-Linked Foreign Exchange Options in Domestic Currency

File Name: Exotic Options – Foreign Equity Linked Forex Options

Location: Modeling Toolkit | Exotic Options | Foreign Equity Linked Forex

Brief Description: Computes the option where the underlying asset is in a foreign market, the exchange rate is fixed in advance to hedge the exposure risk, and the strike price is set as a foreign exchange rate rather than a price

Requirements: Modeling Toolkit

Modeling Toolkit Functions Used: MTEquityLinkedFXCallOptionDomesticValue, MTEquityLinkedFXPutOptionDomesticValue

Equity-Linked Foreign Exchange Options are options (see Figure 49.1) whose underlying asset is in a foreign equity market. The option holder can hedge the fluctuations of the foreign exchange risk by having a strike price on the foreign exchange rate. The resulting valuation is in the domestic currency. There are three closely related models in this chapter and the following two chapters (foreign equity–linked foreign exchange option, foreign equity struck in domestic currency, and foreign equity with fixed exchange rate in domestic currency). Their similarities and differences can be summarized as follow:

- The underlying asset is denominated in a foreign currency.

- The foreign exchange rate is domestic currency to foreign currency.

- The option is valued in domestic currency.

- The strike prices are different where:

    o The exchange rate is the strike for the foreign equity–linked foreign exchange option.

    o The domestic currency is the strike for the foreign equity struck in domestic currency option.

    o The foreign currency is the strike for the foreign equity with fixed exchange rate in domestic currency option.

EQUITY LINKED FOREIGN EXCHANGE OPTIONS IN DOMESTIC CURRENCY

Input Assumptions

Fixed Exchange Rate	1.50
Asset Price	$70.00
Strike Price	1.25
Maturity	0.50
Domestic Risk-free Rate	5.00%
Foreign Risk-free Rate	6.00%
Dividend Rate	1.00%
Volatility of Asset	25.00%
Volatility of Currency	15.00%
Correlation	0.25

Foreign Equity Linked Call Option   **$17.5633**
Foreign Equity Linked Put Option   **$0.1777**

Functions:
MTEquityLinkedFXCallOptionDomesticValue
MTEquityLinkedFXPutOptionDomesticValue

Figure 49.1: Equity-linked options

50. Exotic Options – Foreign Equity Struck in Domestic Currency

File Name: Exotic Options – Foreign Equity Struck in Domestic Currency

Location: Modeling Toolkit | Exotic Options | Foreign Equity Domestic Currency

Brief Description: Values the options on foreign equities denominated in foreign exchange currency while the strike price is in domestic currency

Requirements: Modeling Toolkit

Modeling Toolkit Functions Used: MTForeignEquityDomesticCurrencyCall, MTForeignEquityDomesticCurrencyPut

Foreign Equity Options Struck in Domestic Currency is an option on foreign equities in a foreign currency but the strike price is in domestic currency (see Figure 50.1). At expiration, assuming the option is in the money, its value will be translated back into the domestic currency. The Exchange Rate is the spot rate for domestic currency to foreign currency, the asset price is denominated in a foreign currency, and the strike price is in domestic currency.

FOREIGN EQUITY OPTIONS STRUCK IN DOMESTIC CURRENCY

Input Assumptions

Exchange Rate (Domestic/Foreign)	1.50
Asset Price in Foreign Currency	70.00
Strike Price in Domestic Currency	80.00
Maturity	0.50
Domestic Risk-free Rate	5.00%
Dividend Rate	1.00%
Volatility of Asset	25.00%
Volatility of Currency	15.00%
Correlation (Asset and Currency)	0.25

Foreign Equity Struck in Domestic Currency Call	$27.4203
Foreign Equity Struck in Domestic Currency Put	$0.9688

Functions:
MTForeignEquityDomesticCurrencyCall
MTForeignEquityDomesticCurrencyPut

Figure 50.1: Foreign equity with the strike in domestic currency

51. Exotic Options – Foreign Equity with Fixed Exchange Rate

File Name: Exotic Options – Foreign Equity with Fixed Exchange Rates

Location: Modeling Toolkit | Exotic Options | Foreign Equity Fixed Forex

Brief Description: Values foreign equity options where the option is in a currency foreign to that of the underlying asset but with a risk hedging on the exchange rate

Requirements: Modeling Toolkit

Modeling Toolkit Functions Used:
MTForeignEquityFixedFXRateDomesticValueQuantoCall,
MTForeignEquityFixedFXRateDomesticValueQuantoPut

Quanto options, also known as Foreign Equity Options, are traded on exchanges around the world. The options are denominated in a currency different from that of the underlying asset. The option has an expanding or contracting coverage of the foreign exchange value of the underlying asset. The valuation of these options depends on the volatilities of the underlying assets and the currency exchange rate, as well as the correlation between the currency and the asset value (Figure 51.1).

FOREIGN EQUITY QUANTO OPTIONS WITH FIXED EXCHANGE RATES VALUED IN DOMESTIC CURRENCY

Input Assumptions

Fixed Exchange Rate	1.50
Asset Price	70.00
Strike Price	80.00
Maturity	0.50
Domestic Risk-free Rate	5.00%
Foreign Risk-free Rate	6.00%
Dividend Rate	1.00%
Volatility of Asset	25.00%
Volatility of Currency	15.00%
Correlation	0.25

Quanto Call Option	**$3.0794**
Quanto Put Option	**$15.6076**

Functions:
MTForeignEquityFixedFXRateDomesticValueQuantoCall
MTForeignEquityFixedFXRateDomesticValueQuantoPut

Figure 51.1: Foreign equity with fixed forex in domestic currency

52. Exotic Options –
Foreign Takeover Options

File Name: Exotic Options – Foreign Takeover Options

Location: Modeling Toolkit | Exotic Options | Foreign Takeover Options

Brief Description: Computes a foreign takeover option, where the holder has the right to purchase some foreign exchange at a prespecified rate for the purposes of a takeover or acquisition of a foreign firm

Requirements: Modeling Toolkit

Modeling Toolkit Function Used: MTTakeoverFXOption

In a Foreign Takeover Option with a Foreign Exchange element, if a successful takeover ensues (if the value of the foreign firm denominated in foreign currency is less than the foreign currency units required), the option holder has the right to purchase the number of foreign units at the predetermined strike price (denominated in exchange rates of the domestic currency to the foreign currency), at the option expiration date (Figure 52.1).

FOREIGN TAKEOVER OPTIONS

Input Assumptions

Value of Foreign Firm (Foreign Currency)	200.00
Currency Units Required	260.00
Exchange Rate (Domestic/Foreign)	1.50
Strike Price (Domestic/Foreign)	1.45
Maturity	0.50
Domestic Risk Free	6.00%
Foreign Risk Free	5.00%
Volatility of Asset	25.00%
Volatility of Currency	15.00%
Correlation	0.25

Foreign Takeover Option　　　　　　　　　　$21.3089

Figure 52.1: Foreign exchange–based takeover options

53. Exotic Options – Forward Start Options

File Name: Exotic Options – Forward Start

Location: Modeling Toolkit | Exotic Options | Forward Start

Brief Description: Computes the value of an option that technically starts in the future, and its strike price is a percentage of the asset price in the future when the option starts

Requirements: Modeling Toolkit

Modeling Toolkit Functions Used: MTForwardStartCallOption, MTForwardStartPutOption

Forward Start Options start at the money or proportionally in or out of the money after some time in the future (the time to forward start). These options sometimes are used in employee stock options, where a grant is provided now but the strike price depends on the asset or stock price at some time in the future and is proportional to the stock price. The *Alpha* variable measures the proportionality of the option being in or out of the money. *Alpha = 1* means the option starts at the money or that the strike is set exactly as the asset price at the end of the time to forward start. *Alpha < 1* means that the call option starts (*1 – Alpha*) percent in the money, or (*1 – Alpha*) out of the money for puts. Conversely, for *Alpha > 1*, the call option starts (*Alpha – 1*) out of the money and puts start (*Alpha – 1*) in the money. Figure 53.1 shows an example of valuing Forward Start options.

FORWARD START OPTIONS

Input Assumptions

Asset Price	$100.00
Alpha	1.10
Time to Forward Start	0.50
Maturity	1.00
Risk-free Rate	5.00%
Dividend Rate	1.00%
Volatility	25.00%

Forward Start Call	$4.0195
Forward Start Put	$11.7635

Functions:
MTForwardStartCallOption
MTForwardStartPutOption

Figure 53.1: Forward start options

54. Exotic Options – Futures and Forward Options

File Name: Exotic Options – Futures Options

Location: Modeling Toolkit | Exotic Options | Futures and Forward Options

Brief Description: Applies the same generalities as the Black-Scholes model but the underlying asset is a futures or forward contract, not a stock

Requirements: Modeling Toolkit

Modeling Toolkit Functions Used: MTFuturesForwardsCallOption, MTFuturesForwardsPutOption

The Futures Option (Figure 54.1) is similar to a regular option, but the underlying asset is a futures or forward contract. Be careful here as the analysis cannot be solved using a Generalized Black-Scholes-Merton model. In many cases, options are traded on futures. A put is the option to sell a futures contract, and a call is the option to buy a futures contract. For both, the option strike price is the specified futures price at which the future is traded if the option is exercised.

FUTURES OPTIONS

Input Assumptions

Futures Price	$100.00
Strike Price	$100.00
Maturity	1.00
Risk-free Rate	5.00%
Volatility	25.00%

Futures Call Option	$9.4625
Futures Put Option	$9.4625

Functions:
MTFuturesForwardsCallOption
MTFuturesForwardsPutOption

Figure 54.1: Futures options

A futures contract is a standardized contract, typically traded on a futures exchange, to buy or sell a certain underlying instrument at a certain date in the future, at a prespecified price. The future date is called the delivery date or final settlement date. The preset price is called the futures price. The price of the underlying asset on the delivery date is called the settlement price. The settlement price normally converges toward the futures price on the delivery date.

A futures contract gives the holder the obligation to buy or sell, which differs from an options contract, which gives the holder the right but not the obligation to buy or sell. In other words, the owner of an options contract may exercise the contract. If it is an American-style option, it can be exercised on or before the expiration date; a European option can be exercised only at expiration. Thus, a Futures contract is more like a European option. Both parties of a "futures contract" must fulfill the contract on the settlement date. The seller delivers the commodity to the buyer, or, if it is a cash-settled future, cash is transferred from the futures trader who sustained a loss to the one who made a profit. To exit the commitment prior to the settlement date, the holder of a futures position has to offset the position either by selling a long position or by buying back a short position, effectively closing out the futures position and its contract obligations.

55. Exotic Options – Gap Options

File Name: Exotic Options – Gap Options

Location: Modeling Toolkit | Exotic Options | Gap Options

Brief Description: Values Gap options, where there are two strike prices with respect to one underlying asset, and where the first strike acts like a barrier that, when breached, triggers the second strike price to come into play

Requirements: Modeling Toolkit

Modeling Toolkit Functions Used: MTGapCallOption, MTGapPutOption

Gap Options are similar to Barrier Options and Two-Asset Correlated Options in the sense that the call option is knocked in when the underlying asset exceeds the reference *Strike Price 1*, making the option payoff the asset price less *Strike Price 2* for the underlying. Similarly, the put option is knocked in only if the underlying asset is less than the reference *Strike Price 1*, providing a payoff of *Strike Price 2* less the underlying asset. See Figure 55.1.

GAP OPTIONS

Input Assumptions

Stock Price	$100.00
Strike Price 1 (Reference)	$100.00
Strike Price 2 (Underlying)	$100.00
Maturity	1.00
Risk-free Rate	5.00%
Dividend Rate	1.00%
Volatility	25.00%

Gap Call Options   **$11.7193**
Gap Put Options   **$7.8372**

Functions:
MTGapCallOption
MTGapPutOption

Figure 55.1: Gap options

56. Exotic Options –
Graduated Barrier Options

File Name: Exotic Options – Graduated Barriers

Location: Modeling Toolkit | Exotic Options | Graduated Barriers

Brief Description: Values barrier options with flexible and graduated payoffs, depending on how far above or below a barrier the asset ends up at maturity

Requirements: Modeling Toolkit

Modeling Toolkit Functions Used: MTGraduatedBarrierDownandInCall, MTGraduatedBarrierDownandOutCall, MTGraduatedBarrierUpandInPut, MTGraduatedBarrierUpandOutPut

Graduated or Soft Barrier options are similar to standard Barrier options except that the barriers are no longer static values but a graduated range between the lower and upper barriers. The option is knocked in or out of the money proportionally. Both *Upper* and *Lower Barriers* should be either above (for *Up and In* or *Up and Out* options) or below (for *Down and In* or *Down and Out* options) the starting stock price or asset value. See Figure 56.1 for a sample valuation of Graduated Barrier options.

For instance, in the *Down and In* call option, the instruments become knocked-in or live at expiration if and only if the asset or stock value breaches the lower barrier (asset value goes below the barriers). If the option to be valued is a *Down and In* call, then both the *Upper Barrier* and the *Lower Barrier* should be lower than the starting stock price or asset value, providing a collar of graduated prices. For instance, if the upper and lower barriers are $90 and $80, and if the asset price ends up being $89, a down and out option will be knocked out 10% of its value. Standard barrier options are more difficult to delta hedge when the asset values and barriers are close to each other. Graduated barrier options are more appropriate for delta hedges, providing less delta risk and gamma risk.

GRADUATED BARRIER OPTIONS

Input Assumptions

Asset Value or Stock Price	$100.00
Strike Price	$100.00
Lower Barrier Price	$90.00
Upper Barrier Price	$95.00
Time to Maturity	0.50
Risk-free Rate	10.00%
Dividend Rate	5.00%
Annualized Volatility	30.00%

Graduated Barrier Down and In Call Option	$3.1374
Graduated Barrier Down and Out Call Option	$6.2595
Graduated Barrier Up and In Put Option	$14.6850
Graduated Barrier Up and Out Put Option	$0.0000

Figure 56.1: Graduated barrier options

57. Exotic Options – Index Options

File Name: Exotic Options – Index Options

Location: Modeling Toolkit | Exotic Options | Index Options

Brief Description: Solves Index options using the Black-Scholes model

Requirements: Modeling Toolkit

Modeling Toolkit Functions Used: MTStockIndexCallOption, MTStockIndexPutOption, MTGeneralizedBlackScholesCall, MTGeneralizedBlackScholesPut

The Index Option is similar to a regular plain vanilla option, but the underlying asset is not a stock but a reference stock index such as the Standard & Poor's 500 (Figure 57.1). The analysis can be solved using a Generalized Black-Scholes-Merton model as well.

INDEX OPTIONS

Input Assumptions

Index Price	$100.00
Strike Price	$100.00
Maturity	1.00
Risk-free Rate	5.00%
Dividend Rate	1.00%
Volatility	25.00%

Call Option on a Stock Index	$11.7193
Put Option on a Stock Index	$7.8372

Call Option on a Stock Index	$11.7193
Put Option on a Stock Index	$7.8372

Functions:
MTStockIndexCallOption
MTStockIndexPutOption
MTGeneralizedBlackScholesCall
MTGeneralizedBlackScholesPut

Figure 57.1: Index options

58. Exotic Options – Inverse Gamma Out-of-the-Money Options

File Name: Exotic Options – Inverse Gamma Out-of-the-money Options

Location: Modeling Toolkit | Exotic Options | Inverse Gamma Out-of-the-money Options

Brief Description: Analyzes options using an inverse gamma distribution rather than the typical normal-lognormal assumptions; this type of analysis is important for valuing extreme in- or out-of-the-money options

Requirements: Modeling Toolkit

Modeling Toolkit Functions Used: MTInverseGammaCallOption, MTInverseGammaPutOption

This model computes the value of European call and put options using an Inverse Gamma distribution, as opposed to the standard normal distribution (Figure 58.1). This distribution accounts for the peaked distributions of asset returns and provides better estimates for deep out-of-the-money options. The traditional Generalized Black-Scholes-Merton model is also provided as benchmark.

INVERSE GAMMA OPTION VALUES FOR DEEP OUT-OF-THE-MONEY OPTIONS

Asset	$80.00
Strike	$100.00
Maturity	0.50
Risk-free	8.00%
Volatility	20.00%
DividendRate	3.00%

Inverse Gamma Call Option	$0.5001
Inverse Gamma Put Option	$17.7701
Black-Scholes Call Option	$0.4494
Black-Scholes Put Option	$17.7194

MTInverseGammaCallOption(Asset,Strike,Maturity,Riskfree,Volatility,DividendRate)
MTInverseGammaPutOption(Asset,Strike,Maturity,Riskfree,Volatility,DividendRate)

Figure 58.1: Inverse gamma options

59. Exotic Options – Jump-Diffusion Options

File Name: Exotic Options – Jump Diffusion

Location: Modeling Toolkit | Exotic Options | Jump Diffusion

Brief Description: Values an option whose underlying asset follows a stochastic jump-diffusion process

Requirements: Modeling Toolkit

Modeling Toolkit Functions Used: MTMertonJumpDiffusionCall, MTMertonJumpDiffusionPut

A Jump-Diffusion Option is similar to a regular option except that instead of assuming that the underlying asset follows a lognormal Brownian Motion process, the process here follows a Poisson jump-diffusion process. That is, stock or asset prices follow jumps, which occur several times per year (observed from history). Cumulatively, these jumps explain a certain percentage of the total volatility of the asset. See Figure 59.1.

JUMP-DIFFUSION OPTIONS

Input Assumptions

Asset Price	$100.00
Strike Price	$100.00
Maturity	1.00
Risk-free Rate	5.00%
Volatility	30.00%
Jumps Per Year	1
Percent of Volatility	30.00%

Jump Diffusion Call	$14.1131
Jump Diffusion Put	$9.2360

Functions:
MTMertonJumpDiffusionCall
MTMertonJumpDiffusionPut

Figure 59.1: Jump-diffusion options

60. Exotic Options – Leptokurtic and Skewed Options

File Name: Exotic Options – Leptokurtic and Skewed Options

Location: Modeling Toolkit | Exotic Options | Leptokurtic and Skewed Options

Brief Description: Computes options where the underlying assets are assumed to have returns that are skewed and leptokurtic or have fat tails and are leaning on one end of the distribution rather than having symmetrical returns

Requirements: Modeling Toolkit

Modeling Toolkit Functions Used: MTAltDistributionCallOption, MTAltDistributionPutOption

This model is used to compute the European call and put options using the binomial lattice approach when the underlying distribution of stock returns is not normally distributed, is not symmetrical, and has additional slight kurtosis and skew (Figure 60.1). Be careful when using this model to account for a high or low skew and kurtosis. Certain combinations of these two coefficients actually yield unsolvable results. The Black-Scholes results are also included to benchmark the effects of a high kurtosis and positive or negatively skewed distributions compared to the normal distribution assumptions on asset returns.

PEAKED AND FAT-TAILED DISTRIBUTION OPTIONS

Asset	$100.00
Strike	$100.00
Maturity	0.50
Risk-free Rate	8.00%
Volatility	20.00%
Dividend Rate	0.00%
Skewness Coefficient	0.00
Kurtosis (Excess) Coefficient	0.00
Lattice Steps	100

Alternative Distribution Call Option	$7.6990
Alternative Distribution Put Option	$3.7779
Black-Scholes Call Option	$7.7064
Black-Scholes Put Option	$3.7854

Function: MTAltDistributionCallOption
Function: MTAltDistributionPutOption

Figure 60.1: Leptokurtic options

61. Exotic Options – Lookback with Fixed Strike (Partial Time)

File Name: Exotic Options – Lookback with Fixed Strike Partial Time

Location: Modeling Toolkit | Exotic Options | Lookback Fixed Strike Partial Time

Brief Description: Computes an option where the strike price is predetermined but the payoff on the option is the difference between the highest or the lowest attained asset price against the strike

Requirements: Modeling Toolkit

Modeling Toolkit Functions Used: MTFixedStrikePartialLookbackCall, MTFixedStrikePartialLookbackPut

In a Fixed Strike Option with Lookback Feature (Partial Time), the strike price is predetermined, while at expiration, the payoff on the call option is the difference between the maximum asset price less the strike price during the time between the starting period of the lookback to the maturity of the option (Figure 61.1). Conversely, the put will pay the maximum difference between the lowest observed asset price less the strike price during the time between the starting period of the lookback to the maturity of the option.

Input Assumptions	
Asset Price	$100.00
Strike Price	$105.00
Lookback Starting Time	0.25
Time to Maturity	0.50
Risk-free Rate	10.00%
Dividend Rate	0.00%
Annualized Volatility	20.00%

Fixed Strike Partial Lookback Call Option	**$9.2064**
Fixed Strike Partial Lookback Put Option	**$10.0566**

Figure 61.1: Lookback options with fixed strike (partial lookback time)

62. Exotic Options – Lookback with Fixed Strike

File Name: Exotic Options – Lookback with Fixed Strike

Location: Modeling Toolkit | Exotic Options | Lookback Fixed Strike

Brief Description: Computes the value of an option where the strike price is fixed but the value at expiration is based on the value of the underlying asset's maximum and minimum values during the option's lifetime

Requirements: Modeling Toolkit

Modeling Toolkit Functions Used: MTFixedStrikeLookbackCall, MTFixedStrikeLookbackPut

In a Fixed Strike Option with Lookback Feature, the strike price is predetermined, while at expiration, the payoff on the call option is the difference between the maximum asset price less the strike price during the lifetime of the option. Conversely, the put will pay the maximum difference between the lowest observed asset price less the strike price during the lifetime of the option (Figure 62.1).

Input Assumptions

Asset Price	$100.00
Observed Minimum Asset Price	$95.00
Observed Maximum Asset Price	$130.00
Strike Price	$105.00
Time to Maturity	0.50
Risk-free Rate	10.00%
Dividend Rate	0.00%
Annualized Volatility	20.00%

Fixed Strike Lookback Call Option	$24.6152
Fixed Strike Lookback Put Option	$13.9571

Figure 62.1: Lookback options with fixed strike

63. Exotic Options – Lookback with Floating Strike (Partial Time)

File Name: Exotic Options – Lookback with Floating Strike Partial Time

Location: Modeling Toolkit | Exotic Options | Lookback Floating Strike Partial Time

Brief Description: Computes the value of an option where the strike price is not fixed but floating, and the value at expiration is based on the value of the underlying asset's maximum and minimum values starting from the lookback inception time to maturity, as the purchase or sale price

Requirements: Modeling Toolkit

Modeling Toolkit Functions Used: MTFloatingStrikePartialLookbackCallonMin, MTFloatingStrikePartialLookbackPutonMax

In a Floating Strike Option with Lookback Feature (Partial Time), the strike price is floating. At expiration, the payoff on the call option is being able to purchase the underlying asset at the minimum observed price from inception to the end of the lookback time. Conversely, the put will allow the option holder to sell at the maximum observed asset price from inception to the end of the lookback time (Figure 63.1).

Input Assumptions

Asset Price	$100.00
Observed Minimum Asset Price	$95.00
Observed Maximum Asset Price	$130.00
Time to Lookback	0.25
Time to Maturity	0.50
Risk-free Rate	10.00%
Dividend Rate	0.00%
Annualized Volatility	20.00%
Above or Below Extremum	1.00

Floating Strike Lookback Call on Min Option (Partial Time)	$13.1069
Floating Strike Lookback Put on Max Option (Partial Time)	$24.1436

Figure 63.1: Lookback options with floating strike (partial lookback)

64. Exotic Options – Lookback with Floating Strike

File Name: Exotic Options – Lookback with Floating Strike

Location: Modeling Toolkit | Exotic Options | Lookback Floating Strike

Brief Description: Computes the value of an option where the strike price is not fixed but floating, and the value at expiration is based on the value of the underlying asset's maximum and minimum values during the option's lifetime as the purchase or sale price

Requirements: Modeling Toolkit

Modeling Toolkit Functions Used: MTFloatingStrikeLookbackCallonMin, MTFloatingStrikeLookbackPutonMax

In a Floating Strike Option with Lookback Feature, the strike price is floating. At expiration, the payoff on the call option is being able to purchase the underlying asset at the minimum observed price during the life of the option. Conversely, the put will allow the option holder to sell at the maximum observed asset price during the life of the option (Figure 64.1).

Input Assumptions

Asset Price	$100.00
Observed Minimum Asset Price	$95.00
Observed Maximum Asset Price	$130.00
Time to Maturity	0.50
Risk-free Rate	10.00%
Dividend Rate	0.00%
Annualized Volatility	20.00%

Floating Strike Lookback Call on Min Option	**$14.0780**
Floating Strike Lookback Put on Max Option	**$24.4943**

Figure 64.1: Lookback options with floating strike

65. Exotic Options – Min and Max of Two Assets

File Name: Exotic Options – Min and Max of Two Assets

Location: Modeling Toolkit | Exotic Options | Min and Max of Two Assets

Brief Description: Computes the value of an option where there are two underlying assets that are correlated with different volatilities, and the differences between the assets' values are used as the benchmark for determining the value of the payoff at expiration

Requirements: Modeling Toolkit

Modeling Toolkit Functions Used: MTCallOptionOnTheMin, MTCallOptionOnTheMax, MTPutOptionOnTheMin, MTPutOptionOnTheMax

Options on Minimum or Maximum are used when there are two assets with different volatilities. Either the maximum or the minimum value at expiration of both assets is used in option exercise. For instance, a call option on the minimum implies that the payoff at expiration is such that the minimum price between Asset 1 and Asset 2 is used against the strike price of the option (Figure 65.1).

OPTIONS ON THE MINIMUM OR MAXIMUM OF TWO ASSETS

Input Assumptions

Asset 1 Price	$80.00
Asset 2 Price	$70.00
Strike Price	$75.00
Maturity	1.00
Risk-free Rate	5.00%
Dividend Rate Asset 1	2.00%
Dividend Rate Asset 2	3.00%
Volatility Asset 1	25.00%
Volatility Asset 2	30.00%
Correlation Between Assets	0.50

Call Option on the Minimum	**$4.0114**
Call Option on the Maximum	**$14.2045**
Put Option on the Minimum	**$11.3250**
Put Option on the Maximum	**$3.2282**

Functions:
MTCallOptionOnTheMin
MTCallOptionOnTheMax
MTPutOptionOnTheMin
MTPutOptionOnTheMax

Figure 65.1: Options on the min and max between two assets

66. Exotic Options – Options on Options

File Name: Exotic Options – Options on Options

Location: Modeling Toolkit | Exotic Options | Options on Options

Brief Description: Computes the value of an option on another option, or a compound option, where the option provides the holder the right to buy or sell a subsequent option at the expiration of the first option

Requirements: Modeling Toolkit

Modeling Toolkit Functions Used: MTCompoundOptionsCallonCall, MTCompoundOptionsCallonPut, MTCompoundOptionsPutonCall, MTCompoundOptionsPutonPut, MTGeneralizedBlackScholesCall, MTGeneralizedBlackScholesPut

Options on Options, sometimes known as Compound Options, allow the holder to call or buy versus put or sell an option in the future. For instance, a *Put on Call* option means that the holder has the right to sell a call option in some future period for a specified strike price (*Strike Price for the Option on Option*). The time for this right to sell is called the *Maturity of the Option on Option*. The *Maturity of the Underlying* means the maturity of the option to be bought or sold in the future, starting from now (Figure 66.1).

OPTIONS ON OPTIONS (COMPOUND OPTIONS)

Input Assumptions

Asset Price	$100.00
Strike Price Underlying	$120.00
Strike Price Option on Option	$10.00
Maturity Option on Option	0.25
Maturity Underlying	0.50
Risk-free Rate	5.00%
Dividend Rate	1.00%
Volatility	25.00%

Compound Call on Call	$0.1834
Compound Call on Put	$10.2677
Compound Put on Call	$8.2109
Compound Put on Put	$0.7592

Functions:
MTCompoundOptionsCallonCall
MTCompoundOptionsCallonPut
MTCompoundOptionsPutonCall
MTCompoundOptionsPutonPut

Figure 66.1: Compound options on options

67. Exotic Options – Option Collar

File Name: Exotic Options – Option Collar

Location: Modeling Toolkit | Exotic Options | Options Collar

Brief Description: Computes the call-put collar strategy, that is, to short a call and long a put at different strike prices such that the hedge is costless and effective

Requirements: Modeling Toolkit

The call and put collar strategy requires that one stock be purchased, one call be sold, and one put be purchased (Figure 67.1). The idea is that the proceeds from the call sold are sufficient to cover the proceeds of the put bought. Therefore, given a specific set of stock price, option maturity, risk-free rate, volatility, and dividend of a stock, you can impute the require strike price of a call if you know what put to purchase (and its relevant strike price) or the strike price of a put if you know what call to sell (and its relevant strike price).

CALL AND PUT COLLAR STRATEGY

Stock Price	$100.00		Stock Price	$100.00
Strike Price (Put)	$100.00		Strike Price (Call)	$100.00
Maturity	1.00		Maturity	1.00
Risk-free Rate	5.00%		Risk-free Rate	5.00%
Volatility	10.00%		Volatility	10.00%
Dividend Rate	0.00%		Dividend Rate	0.00%
Short Call Value	$1.9288		Short Call Value	$1.9279
Long Put Value	$1.9279		Long Put Value	$1.9279
Call Strike Required	**$110.8775**		**Put Strike Required**	**$110.8811**
Additional Cost	$0.00		Additional Cost	$0.00

Figure 67.1: Creating a call and put collar strategy

68. Exotic Options – Perpetual Options

File Name: Exotic Options – Perpetual Options

Location: Modeling Toolkit | Exotic Options | Perpetual Options

Brief Description: Computes the value of an American option that has a perpetual life where the underlying is a dividend-paying asset

Requirements: Modeling Toolkit

Modeling Toolkit Functions Used: MTPerpetualCallOption, MTPerpetualPutOption

The perpetual call and put options are American options with continuous dividends that can be executed at any time but have an infinite life. Clearly, a European option (only exercisable at termination) has a zero value, hence only American options are viable perpetual options. American closed-form approximations with 100-year maturities are also provided in the model to benchmark the results. See Figure 68.1.

PERPETUAL AMERICAN OPTION

Asset Price	$110.0000
Strike Price	$100.0000
Risk-free Rate	5.00%
Volatility	20.00%
Dividend Rate	5.00%

Perpetual Call Option	$27.6787
Perpetual Put Option	$20.1772
American Call Option	$27.6748
American Put Option	$20.1725

Figure 68.1: Perpetual American options

69. Exotic Options – Range Accruals (Fairway Options)

File Name: Real Options Models – Range Accruals

Location: Modeling Toolkit | Real Options Models | Range Accruals

Brief Description: Computes the value of Fairway options or Range Accrual options, where the option pays a specified return if the underlying asset is within a range, but pays something else if it is outside the range, at any time during its maturity

Requirements: Modeling Toolkit and Real Options SLS

A Range Accrual option is also called a Fairway option. Here, the option pays a certain return if the asset value stays within a certain range (between the upper and lower barriers) but pays a different amount or return if the asset value falls outside this range during any time before and up to maturity. The name *Fairway option* sometimes is used because the option is similar to the game of golf where if the ball stays within the fairway (a narrow path), it is in play, and if it goes outside, a penalty might be imposed (in this case, a lower return). Such options and instruments can be solved using the Real Options SLS software as seen in Figure 69.1, using the Custom Option approach, where we enter the terminal equation as:

    If(Asset>=LowerBarrier & Asset<=UpperBarrier,
    Asset*(1+InsideReturn),Asset*(1+OutsideReturn))

If we wish to solve a European option, we enter the following as the intermediate equation:

    OptionOpen

If we are solving an American option, the intermediate equation is:

    If(Asset>=LowerBarrier & Asset<=UpperBarrier,
    Max(Asset*(1+InsideReturn),OptionOpen),Max(Asset*(1+OutsideReturn),
        OptionOpen))

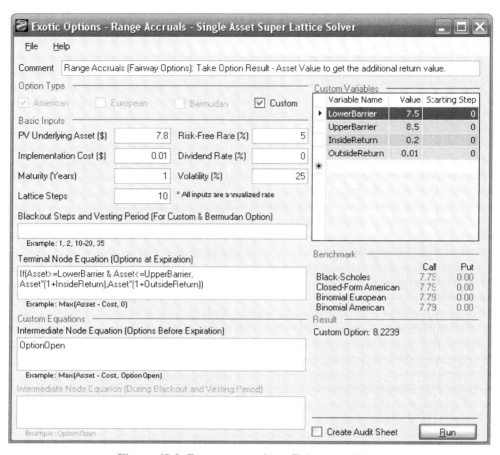

Figure 69.1: Range accruals or Fairway options

70. Exotic Options – Simple Chooser

File Name: Exotic Options – Simple Chooser

Location: Modeling Toolkit | Exotic Options | Simple Chooser

Brief Description: Computes the value of an option where the holder has the ability to decide if it is a call or a put at some future time period, where this option is similar to purchasing a call and a put together but costs less as a single chooser option

Requirements: Modeling Toolkit

Modeling Toolkit Functions Used: MTChooserBasicOption, MTGeneralizedBlackScholesCall, MTGeneralizedBlackScholesPut

A Simple Chooser Option allows the holder the ability to choose if the option is a call or a put within the Chooser Time (Figure 70.1). Regardless of the choice, the option has the same contractual strike price and maturity. Typically, a chooser option is cheaper than purchasing both a call and a put together, and provides the same level of hedge at a lower cost, but the strike prices for both options are identical. The Complex Chooser Option allows for different strike prices and maturities.

SIMPLE CHOOSER OPTION

Input Assumptions

Asset Price	$80.00
Strike Price	$90.00
Chooser Time	0.50
Maturity	1.00
Risk-free Rate	10.00%
Dividend Rate	2.00%
Volatility	30.00%

Chooser Option Value	**$16.4626**
If Purchased as a Call + Put Options	**$19.2097**

Functions:
MTChooserBasicOption
MTGeneralizedBlackScholesCall
MTGeneralizedBlackScholesPut

Figure 70.1: Simple chooser option

71. Exotic Options – Spread on Futures

File Name: Exotic Options – Spread on Futures

Location: Modeling Toolkit | Exotic Options | Spread on Futures

Brief Description: Computes the value of an option where the underlying assets are two different futures contracts, and their spreads (the difference between the futures) are used as a benchmark to determine the value of the option

Requirements: Modeling Toolkit

Modeling Toolkit Functions Used: MTFuturesSpreadCall, MTFuturesSpreadPut

A Spread on Futures Options is an option where the payoff is the difference between the two futures values at expiration (Figure 71.1). That is, the spread is *Futures 1 – Futures 2*, while the *call* payoff is the value *Spread – Strike*, and the *put* payoff is *Strike – Spread*.

SPREAD ON FUTURES OPTIONS

Input Assumptions

Futures 1	25.00
Futures 2	28.00
Strike	10.00
Maturity	1.00
Risk-free Rate	5.00%
Volatility 1	30.00%
Volatility 2	25.00%
Correlation	0.50

Futures Spread Call	**$0.1784**
Futures Spread Put	**$12.5443**

Functions:
MTFuturesSpreadCall
MTFuturesSpreadPut

Figure 71.1: Spread on futures options

72. Exotic Options – Supershare Options

File Name: Exotic Options – Supershare Options

Location: Modeling Toolkit | Exotic Options | Supershares

Brief Description: Computes the value of an option where it is a hybrid of a double barrier Fairway option that pays a percentage proportional to the level it is in the money within the barriers

Requirements: Modeling Toolkit

Modeling Toolkit Function Used: MTSuperShareOptions

Typically, Supershare Options are traded or embedded in supershare funds. These options are related to *Down and Out, Up and Out* double barrier options, where the option has value only if the stock or asset price is between the upper and lower barriers, and at expiration, the option provides a payoff equivalent to the stock or asset price divided by the lower strike price (S/X Lower). See Figure 72.1.

SUPERSHARE OPTIONS

Input Assumptions

Stock Price	$100.00
Lower Strike	$90.00
Upper Strike	$110.00
Maturity	1.00
Risk-free Rate	5.00%
Dividend Rate	0.00%
Volatility	25.00%

Supershare Options $0.3275

Functions:
MTSuperShareOptions

Figure 72.1: Supershare options

73. Exotic Options – Time Switch Options

File Name: Exotic Options – Time Switch Options

Location: Modeling Toolkit | Exotic Options | Time Switch

Brief Description: Computes the value of an option where its value is dependent on how many times a barrier is breached during the life of the option

Requirements: Modeling Toolkit

Modeling Toolkit Functions Used: MTTimeSwitchOptionCall, MTTimeSwitchOptionPut

In a Time Switch Option, the holder receives the *Accumulated Amount* x *Time Steps* each time the asset price exceeds the strike price for a call option (or falls below the strike price for a put option), as seen in Figure 73.1. The time steps are how often the asset price is checked if the strike threshold has been breached (typically, for a one-year option with 252 trading days, set *DT* as 1/252). Sometimes, the option has already accumulated past amounts, or as agreed to in the option as a minimum guaranteed payment, as measured by the number of time units fulfilled (which is typically set as 0).

TIME SWITCH OPTIONS

Input Assumptions

Asset Price	$100.00
Strike Price	$100.00
Accumulated Amount	$5.00
Maturity	1.00
Number of Time Units Fulfilled	0
Time Steps (DT)	0.0027
Risk-free Rate	5.00%
Dividend Rate	0.00%
Volatility	30.00%

Time Switch Call	$2.3992
Time Switch Put	$2.3569

Functions:
MTTimeSwitchOptionCall
MTTimeSwitchOptionPut

Figure 73.1: Time switch options

74. Exotic Options – Trading-Day Corrections

File Name: Exotic Options – Trading Day Corrections

Location: Modeling Toolkit | Exotic Options | Trading Day Corrections

Brief Description: Computes the value of plain vanilla call and put options corrected for the number of trading days and calendar days left in their maturity

Requirements: Modeling Toolkit

Modeling Toolkit Functions Used: MTTradingDayAdjustedCall, MTTradingDayAdjustedPut, MTGeneralizedBlackScholesCall, MTGeneralizedBlackScholesPut

An Option with a Trading-Day Correction uses a typical option and corrects it for the varying volatilities (Figure 74.1). Specifically, volatility tends to be higher on trading days than on nontrading days. The *Trading Days Ratio* is simply the number of trading days left until maturity divided by the total number of trading days per year (typically between 250 and 252). The *Calendar Days Ratio* is the number of calendar days left until maturity divided by the total number of days per year (365).

Typically, with the adjustments, the option value is lower. In addition, if the trading-days ratio and calendar-days ratio are identical, the result of the adjustment is zero and the option value reverts back to the generalized Black-Scholes results. This is because the number of days left is assumed to be all fully trading.

OPTIONS WITH TRADING DAY CORRECTIONS

Input Assumptions

Asset Price	$100.00
Strike Price	$100.00
Trading Days Ratio	0.75
Calendar Days Ratio	0.90
Risk-free Rate	5.00%
Volatility	25.00%
Dividend Rate	0.00%

Call Option Value Adjusted for Trading Days	$10.8117
Put Option Value Adjusted for Trading Days	$6.4114
Call Option Value (Black-Scholes) Unadjusted	$11.5969
Put Option Value (Black-Scholes) Unadjusted	$7.1967

Figure 74.1: Options with trading-day corrections

75. Exotic Options – Two-Asset Barrier Options

File Name: Exotic Options – Two Asset Barrier

Location: Modeling Toolkit | Exotic Options | Two Asset Barrier

Brief Description: Computes the value of an option with two underlying assets, one of which is a reference benchmark, with the second asset being used to compute the value of the option payoff

Requirements: Modeling Toolkit

Modeling Toolkit Functions Used: MTTwoAssetBarrierDownandInCall, MTTwoAssetBarrierUpandInCall, MTTwoAssetBarrierDownandInPut, MTTwoAssetBarrierUpandInPut, MTTwoAssetBarrierDownandOutCall, MTTwoAssetBarrierUpandOutCall, MTTwoAssetBarrierDownandOutPut, MTTwoAssetBarrierUpandOutPut

Two-Asset Barrier Options become valuable or get knocked in the money only if a barrier (upper or lower barrier) is breached (or not), and the payout is in the form of the option on the first underlying asset. In general, a barrier option limits the potential of a regular option's profits and hence costs less than regular options without barriers. A barrier option thus is a better bet for companies trying to hedge a specific price movement as it tends to be cheaper. See Figure 75.1.

As an example, in the *Up and In Call Option,* the instrument is knocked in if the asset breaches the upper barrier but is worthless if this barrier is not breached. The payoff on this option is based on the value of the first underlying asset (*Asset 1*) less the *Strike* price, while whether the barrier is breached or not depends on whether the second reference asset (*Asset 2*) breaches the *Barrier. Monitoring Periodicities* refers to how often during the life of the option the asset or stock value will be monitored to see if it breaches a barrier. As an example, entering 12 implies monthly monitoring, 52 for weekly, 252 for daily trading, 365 for daily calendar, and 1,000,000 for continuous monitoring.

TWO ASSET BARRIER OPTIONS

Input Assumptions

Asset 1 (Underlying Asset)	$100.00
Asset 2 (Barrier Reference Asset)	$100.00
Strike	$95.00
Barrier	$90.00
Time to Maturity (Underlying Asset)	1.00
Risk-free Rate	5.00%
Dividend Rate 1 (Reference Asset)	1.00%
Dividend Rate 2 (Underlying Asset)	1.00%
Volatility 1 (Reference Asset)	25.00%
Volatility 2 (Underlying Asset)	20.00%
Correlation (Reference and Underlying Assets)	0.50
Periodicities (Per Year)	365

Down and In Call Option	**$5.1155**
Up and In Call Option	**$15.3525**
Down and In Put Option	**$4.3929**
Up and In Put Option	**$11.2278**
Down and Out Call Option	**$9.2399**
Up and Out Call Option	**$0.0000**
Down and Out Put Option	**$1.3244**
Up and Out Put Option	**$0.0000**

Figure 75.1: Two-asset barrier options

76. Exotic Options – Two-Asset Cash or Nothing

File Name: Exotic Options – Two Asset Cash or Nothing

Location: Modeling Toolkit | Exotic Options | Two Asset Cash

Brief Description: Computes the value of an option that pays a prespecified amount of cash as long as the option stays in the money at expiration, regardless of how valuable the intrinsic value is at maturity

Requirements: Modeling Toolkit

Modeling Toolkit Functions Used: MTTwoAssetCashOrNothingCall, MTTwoAssetCashOrNothingPut, MTTwoAssetCashOrNothingUpDown, MTTwoAssetCashOrNothingDownUp

Cash or Nothing Options pay out a prespecified amount of cash at expiration as long as the option is in the money, without regard to how much it is in the money (Figure 76.1). The Two-Asset Cash or Nothing Option means that both assets must be in the money before cash is paid out (for call options, both asset values must be above their respective strike prices, and for puts, both assets must be below their respective strike prices). For the Up-Down Option, this implies that the first asset must be above the first strike price, and the second asset must be below the second strike price. Conversely, the Down-Up Option implies that cash will be paid out only if, at expiration, the first asset is below the first strike and the second asset is above the second strike.

TWO ASSET CASH OR NOTHING OPTIONS

Input Assumptions

Asset 1 Price	$80.00
Asset 2 Price	$70.00
Strike Price 1	$80.00
Strike Price 2	$80.00
Cash Payment	$10.00
Maturity	0.50
Riskfree Rate	5.00%
Dividend Rate Asset 1	1.00%
Dividend Rate Asset 2	1.00%
Volatility Asset 1	25.00%
Volatility Asset 2	30.00%
Correlation Between Assets	0.25

Cash or Nothing Call Option	$1.6135
Cash or Nothing Put Option	$3.8513
Cash or Nothing Up Down	$3.3594
Cash or Nothing Down Up	$0.9290

Figure 76.1: Two-asset cash or nothing options

77. Exotic Options – Two Correlated Assets Option

File Name: Exotic Options – Two Correlated Assets

Location: Modeling Toolkit | Exotic Options | Two Asset Correlated

Brief Description: Computes the value of an option that depends on two assets: a benchmark asset that determines if the option is in the money and a second asset that determines the payoff on the option at expiration

Requirements: Modeling Toolkit

Modeling Toolkit Functions Used: MTTwoAssetCorrelationCall, MTTwoAssetCorrelationPut

The Two Correlated Asset Options use two underlying assets, Asset 1 and Asset 2 (Figure 77.1). Typically, Asset 1 is the benchmark asset (e.g., a stock index or market comparable stock), whereby if at expiration Asset 1's values exceed Strike 1's value, then the option is knocked in the money, meaning that the payoff on the call option is *Asset 2 – Strike 2* and *Strike 2 – Asset 2* for the put option (for the put, Asset 1 must be less than Strike 1).

A higher positive correlation between the reference and the underlying asset implies that the option value increases as the comovement of both assets is highly positive, meaning that the higher the price movement of the reference asset, the higher the chances of it being in the money and, similarly, the higher the chances of the underlying asset's payoff being in the money. Negative correlations reduce the option value even if the reference asset is in the money and the value of the option of the underlying is very little in the money or completely out of the money. Correlation is typically restricted between -0.9999 and +0.9999. If there is a perfect correlation (either positive or negative), then there is no point in issuing such an asset, as a regular option model will suffice.

Two Correlated Asset Options sometimes are used as a performance-based payoff option. For instance, the first or reference asset can be a company's revenues or profit margin; an external index such as the Standard & Poor's 500; or some reference price in the market such as the price of gold. Therefore, the option is live only if the benchmark value exceeds a prespecified threshold. This European option is exercisable only at expiration. To model an American (exercisable at any time up to and including expiration) or Bermudan option (exercisable at specific periods only, with blackout and vesting periods where the option cannot be exercised), use the Real Options SLS software.

TWO CORRELATED ASSET OPTIONS

Input Assumptions

Asset 1 (Reference Asset)	$100.00
Asset 2 (Underlying Asset)	$10.00
Strike 1 (Reference Asset's Strike)	$110.00
Strike 2 (Underlying Asset's Strike)	$12.00
Time to Maturity (Underlying Asset)	1.00
Risk-free Rate	10.00%
Dividend Rate 1 (Reference Asset)	0.00%
Dividend Rate 2 (Underlying Asset)	0.00%
Volatility 1 (Reference Asset)	20.00%
Volatility 2 (Underlying Asset)	30.00%
Correlation (Reference and Underlying Assets)	0.75

Two Asset Correlation Call Option   **$0.7891**
Two Asset Correlation Put Option   **$1.4219**

Functions:
MTTwoAssetCorrelationCall
MTTwoAssetCorrelationPut

Figure 77.1: Two correlated asset options

78. Exotic Options – Uneven Dividend Payments Option

File Name: Exotic Options – Uneven Dividend Payments

Location: Modeling Toolkit | Exotic Options | Uneven Dividends

Brief Description: Computes the value of plain vanilla call and put options when the dividend stream of the underlying asset comes in uneven payments over time

Requirements: Modeling Toolkit

Modeling Toolkit Functions Used: MTGeneralizedBlackScholesCallCashDividends, MTGeneralizedBlackScholesPutCashDividends, MTGeneralizedBlackScholesCall, MTGeneralizedBlackScholesPut

Sometimes dividends are paid in various lump sums, and sometimes these values are not consistent throughout the life of the option. Accounting for the average dividend yield and not the uneven cash flows will yield incorrect valuations in the Black-Scholes paradigm. See Figure 78.1.

OPTIONS WITH UNEVEN DIVIDEND PAYMENTS

Input Assumptions		Dividend Payments	
Asset Price	$100.00		
Strike Price	$100.00	**Payments**	**Time**
Maturity	1.00	$2.00	0.25
Risk-free Rate	5.00%	$2.00	0.50
Volatility	25.00%	$2.00	0.75
		$2.00	1.00

Call Option Value (Dividend Payments)	$7.9505	
Put Option Value (Dividend Payments)	$10.8280	
Call Option Value (Black-Scholes) Unadjusted	$12.3360	
Put Option Value (Black-Scholes) Unadjusted	$7.4589	

Functions:
MTGeneralizedBlackScholesCallCashDividends
MTGeneralizedBlackScholesPutCashDividends
MTGeneralizedBlackScholesCall
MTGeneralizedBlackScholesPut

Figure 78.1: Options with uneven dividend payments

79. Exotic Options – Writer Extendible Option

File Name: Exotic Options – Writer Extendible

Location: Modeling Toolkit | Exotic Options | Writer Extendible

Brief Description: Computes the value of various options that can be extended beyond the original maturity date if the option is out of the money, providing an insurance policy for the option holder, and thereby typically costing more than conventional options

Requirements: Modeling Toolkit

Modeling Toolkit Functions Used: MTWriterExtendibleCallOption, MTWriterExtendiblePutOption

Writer Extendible Options can be seen as insurance policies in case the option becomes worthless at maturity (Figure 79.1). Specifically, the call or put option can be extended automatically beyond the initial maturity date to an extended date with a new extended strike price assuming that, at maturity, the option is out of the money and worthless. This extendibility provides a safety net of time for the holder of the option.

WRITER EXTENDIBLE OPTIONS

Input Assumptions

Asset Price	$80.00
Initial Strike Price	$90.00
Extended Strike Price	$82.00
Initial Maturity	0.50
Extended Maturity	0.75
Riskfree Rate	10.00%
Dividend Rate	2.00%
Volatility	30.00%

Extendible Call	**$6.4042**
Extendible Put	**$10.7880**

Figure 79.1: Writer Extendible options

80. Forecasting – Data Diagnostics

File Name: Forecasting – Data Diagnostics

Location: Modeling Toolkit | Forecasting | Data Diagnostics

Brief Description: Illustrates how to use Risk Simulator for running diagnostics on your data before generating forecast models, including checking for heteroskedasticity, nonlinearity, outliers, specification errors, micronumerosity, stationarity and stochastic properties, normality and sphericity of the errors, and multicollinearity

Requirements: Modeling Toolkit, Risk Simulator

This example model provides a sample dataset on which we can run Risk Simulator's *Diagnostic* tool so that we can determine the econometric properties of the data. The diagnostics run include checking the data for heteroskedasticity, nonlinearity, outliers, specification errors, micronumerosity, stationarity and stochastic properties, normality and sphericity of the errors, and multicollinearity. Each test is described in more detail in its respective report.

Procedure

To run the analysis, follow the instructions below:

1. Go to the *Time-Series Data* worksheet and select the data including the variable names (cells **C5:H55**) as seen in Figure 80.1.

2. Click on **Risk Simulator | Analytical Tools | Diagnostic Tool**.

3. Check the data and select the **dependent variable** from the drop-down menu. Click **OK** when finished.

Spend some time reading through the reports generated from this *Diagnostic* tool.

Multiple Regression Analysis Data Set

Aggravated Assault	Bachelor's Degree	Police Expenditure Per Capita	Population in Millions	Population Density (Persons/Sq Mile)	Unemployment Rate
521	18308	185	4.041	79.6	7.2
367	1148	600	0.55	1	8.5
443	18068	372	3.665	32.3	5.7
365	7729	142	2.351	45.1	7.3
614	100484				
385	16728				
286	14630				
397	4008				
764	38927				
427	22322				
153	3711				
231	3136				
524	50508				
328	28886				
240	16996				
286	13035				
285	12973				
569	16309				
96	5227				
498	19235				
481	44487				
468	44213				
177	23619				
198	9106				
458	24917				
108	3872	196	0.799	5.5	6.9

Diagnostic Tool — □ ×

This tool is used to test and diagnose your data (dependent and independent variables) for assumption violations and potential forecasting problems such as outliers, multicollinearity, autocorrelation, heteroskedasticity, nonlinearity, normality of the errors, and other potential issues.

Dependent Variable: Aggravated Assault ▼

Aggravated Assault	Bachelor's Degree	Police Expenditure
521	18308	185
367	1148	600
443	18068	372
365	7729	142
614	100484	432
385	16728	290
286	14630	346
397	4008	328
764	38927	354
427	22322	266

OK   Cancel

Figure 80.1: Running a diagnostic analysis on your dataset

A common violation in forecasting and regression analysis is *heteroskedasticity*, that is, the variance of the errors increases over time. Visually, the width of the vertical data fluctuations increases or fans out over time, and, typically, the coefficient of determination (R-squared coefficient) drops significantly when heteroskedasticity exists. If the variance of the dependent variable is not constant, then the error's variance will not be constant. Unless the heteroskedasticity of the dependent variable is pronounced, its effect will not be severe: The least-squares estimates will still be unbiased, and the estimates of the slope and intercept will be either normally distributed if the errors are normally distributed, or at least normally distributed asymptotically (as the number of data points becomes large) if the errors are not normally distributed. The estimate for the variance of the slope and overall variance will be inaccurate, but the inaccuracy is not likely to be substantial if the independent-variable values are symmetric about their mean.

If the number of data points is small (*micronumerosity*), it may be difficult to detect assumption violations. With small samples, assumption violations such as non-normality or heteroskedasticity of variances are difficult to detect even when they are present. With a small number of data points, linear regression offers less protection against violation of assumptions. With few data points, it may be hard to determine how well the fitted line matches the data or whether a nonlinear function would be more appropriate. Even if none of the test assumptions is violated, a linear regression on a small number of data points may not have sufficient power to detect a significant difference between the slope and zero, even if the slope is nonzero. The power depends on the residual error, the observed variation in the independent variable, the selected significance alpha level of the test, and the number of data points. Power decreases as the residual variance increases, decreases as the significance level is decreased (i.e., as the test is made more stringent), increases as the variation in observed independent variable increases, and increases as the number of data points increases.

Values may not be identically distributed because of the presence of outliers. *Outliers* are anomalous values in the data. They may have a strong influence over the fitted slope and intercept, giving a poor fit to the bulk of the data points. Outliers tend to increase the estimate of residual variance, lowering the chance of rejecting the null hypothesis, that is, creating higher prediction errors. They may be due to recording errors, which may be correctable, or they may be due to the dependent-variable values not all being sampled from the same population. Apparent outliers may also be due to the dependent-variable values being from the same, but non-normal, population. However, a point may be an unusual value in either an independent or dependent variable without necessarily being an outlier in the scatter plot. In regression analysis, the fitted line can be highly sensitive to outliers. In other words, least-squares regression is not resistant to outliers, thus, neither is the fitted-slope estimate. A point vertically removed from the other points can cause the fitted line to pass close to it instead of following the general linear trend of the rest of the data, especially if the point is relatively far horizontally from the center of the data.

However, great care should be taken when deciding if the outliers should be removed. Although in most cases the regression results look better when outliers are removed, a priori justification must first exist. For instance, if you regress the performance of a particular firm's stock returns, outliers caused by downturns in the stock market should be included; these are not truly outliers as they are inevitabilities in the business cycle. Forgoing these outliers and using the regression equation to forecast your retirement fund based on the firm's stocks will yield incorrect results at best. In contrast, suppose the outliers are caused by a single nonrecurring business condition (e.g., merger and acquisition), and such business structural changes are not forecast to recur. Then these outliers should be removed and the data cleansed prior to running a regression analysis. The analysis here only identifies outliers; it is up to the user to determine if they should remain or be excluded.

Sometimes a *nonlinear* relationship between the dependent and independent variables is more appropriate than a linear relationship. In such cases, running a linear regression will not be optimal. If the linear model is not the correct form, then the slope and intercept estimates and the fitted values from the linear regression will be biased, and the fitted slope and intercept estimates will not be meaningful. Over a restricted range of independent or dependent variables, nonlinear models may be well approximated by linear models (this is in fact the basis of linear interpolation), but for accurate prediction, a model appropriate to the data should be selected. A nonlinear transformation should be applied to the data first, before running a regression. One simple approach is to take the natural logarithm of the independent variable (other approaches include taking the square root or raising the independent variable to the second or third power) and run a regression or forecast using the nonlinearly transformed data.

The results from running these tests are seen in Figure 80.2.

Diagnostic Results

Variable	Heteroskedasticity W-Test p-value	Heteroskedasticity Hypothesis Test result	Micronumerosity Approximation result	Outliers Natural Lower Bound	Outliers Natural Upper Bound	Outliers Number of Potential Outliers	Nonlinearity Nonlinear Test p-value	Nonlinearity Hypothesis Test result
Variable Y			no problems	-7.86	671.70	2		
Variable X1	0.2543	Homoskedastic	no problems	-21377.95	64713.03	3	0.2458	linear
Variable X2	0.3371	Homoskedastic	no problems	77.47	445.93	2	0.0335	nonlinear
Variable X3	0.3649	Homoskedastic	no problems	-5.77	15.69	3	0.0305	nonlinear
Variable X4	0.3066	Homoskedastic	no problems	-295.96	628.21	4	0.9298	linear
Variable X5	0.2495	Homoskedastic	no problems	3.35	9.38	3	0.2727	linear

Figure 80.2: Heteroskedasticity, micronumerosity, outliers, and nonlinearity results

Another typical issue when forecasting time-series data is whether the independent-variable values are truly independent of each other or whether they are dependent. Dependent-variable values collected over a time series may be *autocorrelated*. For serially correlated dependent variable values, the estimates of the slope and intercept will be unbiased, but the estimates of their forecast and variances will not be reliable. Hence the validity of certain statistical goodness-of-fit tests will be flawed. For instance, interest rates, inflation rates, sales, revenues, and many other time-series data typically are autocorrelated, where the value in the current period is related to the value in a previous period, and so forth. Clearly, the inflation rate in March is related to February's level, which, in turn, is related to January's level, and so forth. Ignoring such blatant relationships will yield biased and less accurate forecasts. In such events, an autocorrelated regression model or an ARIMA model may be better suited (**Risk Simulator | Forecasting | ARIMA**). Finally, the autocorrelation functions of a series that is nonstationary tend to decay slowly (see Nonstationary report).

If autocorrelation AC(1) is nonzero, the series is first-order serially correlated. If AC(k) dies off more or less geometrically with increasing lag, the series follows a low-order autoregressive process. If AC(k) drops to zero after a small number of lags, the series follows a low-order moving-average process. Partial correlation PAC(k) measures the correlation of values that are k periods apart after removing the correlation from the intervening lags. If the pattern of autocorrelation can be captured by an autoregression of order less than k, then the partial autocorrelation at lag k will be close to zero. Ljung-Box Q-statistics and their p-values at lag k have the null hypothesis that there is no autocorrelation up to order k. The dotted lines in the plots of the autocorrelations are the approximate two standard error bounds. If the autocorrelation is within these bounds, it is not significantly different from zero at the 5% significance level.

Autocorrelation measures the relationship to the past of the dependent Y variable to itself. Distributive Lags, in contrast, are time-lag relationships between the dependent Y variable and different independent X variables. For instance, the movement and direction of mortgage rates tend to follow the Federal Funds Rate but at a time lag (typically 1 to 3 months). Sometimes, time lags follow cycles and seasonality (e.g., ice cream sales tend to peak during the summer months and hence are related to last summer's sales, 12 months in the past). The distributive lag analysis in Figure 80.3 show how the dependent variable is related to each of the independent variables at various time lags, when all lags are considered simultaneously, to determine which time lags are statistically significant and should be considered.

Autocorrelation

Time Lag	AC	PAC	Lower Bound	Upper Bound	Q-Stat	Prob
1	0.0580	0.0580	-0.2828	0.2828	0.1786	0.6726
2	-0.1213	-0.1251	-0.2828	0.2828	0.9754	0.6140
3	0.0590	0.0756	-0.2828	0.2828	1.1679	0.7607
4	0.2423	0.2232	-0.2828	0.2828	4.4865	0.3442
5	0.0067	-0.0078	-0.2828	0.2828	4.4890	0.4814
6	-0.2654	-0.2345	-0.2828	0.2828	8.6516	0.1941
7	0.0814	0.0939	-0.2828	0.2828	9.0524	0.2489
8	0.0634	-0.0442	-0.2828	0.2828	9.3012	0.3175
9	0.0204	0.0673	-0.2828	0.2828	9.3276	0.4076
10	-0.0190	0.0865	-0.2828	0.2828	9.3512	0.4991
11	0.1035	0.0790	-0.2828	0.2828	10.0648	0.5246
12	0.1658	0.0978	-0.2828	0.2828	11.9466	0.4500
13	-0.0524	-0.0430	-0.2828	0.2828	12.1394	0.5162
14	-0.2050	-0.2523	-0.2828	0.2828	15.1738	0.3664
15	0.1782	0.2089	-0.2828	0.2828	17.5315	0.2881
16	-0.1022	-0.2591	-0.2828	0.2828	18.3296	0.3050
17	-0.0861	0.0808	-0.2828	0.2828	18.9141	0.3335
18	0.0418	0.1987	-0.2828	0.2828	19.0559	0.3884
19	0.0869	-0.0821	-0.2828	0.2828	19.6894	0.4135
20	-0.0091	-0.0269	-0.2828	0.2828	19.6966	0.4770

Distributive Lags

P-Values of Distributive Lag Periods of Each Independent Variable

Variable	1	2	3	4	5	6	7	8	9	10	11	12
X1	0.8467	0.2045	0.3336	0.9105	0.9757	0.1020	0.9205	0.1267	0.5431	0.9110	0.7495	0.4016
X2	0.6077	0.9900	0.8422	0.2851	0.0638	0.0032	0.8007	0.1551	0.4823	0.1126	0.0519	0.4383
X3	0.7394	0.2396	0.2741	0.8372	0.9808	0.0464	0.8355	0.0545	0.6828	0.7354	0.5093	0.3500
X4	0.0061	0.6739	0.7932	0.7719	0.6748	0.8627	0.5586	0.9046	0.5726	0.6304	0.4812	0.5707
X5	0.1591	0.2032	0.4123	0.5599	0.6416	0.3447	0.9190	0.9740	0.5185	0.2856	0.1489	0.7794

Figure 80.3: Autocorrelation and distributive lags

Another requirement in running a regression model is the assumption of *normality* and *sphericity* of the error term. If the assumption of normality is violated or outliers are present, then the linear regression goodness-of-fit test may not be the most powerful or informative test available, and this could mean the difference between detecting a linear fit or not. If the errors are not independent and not normally distributed, the data might be autocorrelated or suffer from nonlinearities or other more destructive errors. Independence of the errors can also be detected in the heteroskedasticity tests.

The Normality test on the errors performed is a nonparametric test that makes no assumptions about the specific shape of the population from which the sample is drawn, allowing for smaller sample datasets to be analyzed. This test evaluates the null hypothesis of whether the sample errors were drawn from a normally distributed population versus an alternate hypothesis that the data sample is not normally distributed (Figure 80.4). If the calculated D-Statistic is greater than or equal to the D-Critical values at various significance values, reject the null hypothesis and accept the alternate hypothesis (the errors are not normally distributed). Otherwise, if the D-Statistic is less than the D-Critical value, do not reject the null hypothesis (the errors are normally distributed). This test relies on two cumulative frequencies: one derived from the sample dataset and the second derived from a theoretical distribution based on the mean and standard deviation of the sample data.

Test Result

		Errors	Relative Frequency	Observed	Expected	O-E
Regression Error Average	0.00	-219.04	0.02	0.02	0.0612	-0.0412
Standard Deviation of Errors	141.83	-202.53	0.02	0.04	0.0766	-0.0366
D Statistic	0.1036	-186.04	0.02	0.06	0.0948	-0.0348
D Critical at 1%	0.1138	-174.17	0.02	0.08	0.1097	-0.0297
D Critical at 5%	0.1225	-162.13	0.02	0.10	0.1265	-0.0265
D Critical at 10%	0.1458	-161.62	0.02	0.12	0.1272	-0.0072
Null Hypothesis: The errors are normally distributed.		-160.39	0.02	0.14	0.1291	0.0109
Conclusion: The errors are normally distributed at the		-145.40	0.02	0.16	0.1526	0.0074
1% alpha level.		-138.92	0.02	0.18	0.1637	0.0163
		-133.81	0.02	0.20	0.1727	0.0273
		-120.76	0.02	0.22	0.1973	0.0227
		-120.12	0.02	0.24	0.1985	0.0415

Figure 80.4: Normality of errors

Sometimes certain types of time-series data cannot be modeled using any other methods except for a stochastic process, because the underlying events are stochastic in nature. For instance, you cannot adequately model and forecast stock prices, interest rates, price of oil, and other commodity prices using a simple regression model because these variables are highly uncertain and volatile, and do not follow a predefined static rule of behavior. In other words, the processes are not stationary. Stationarity is checked here using the Runs Test while another visual clue is found in the Autocorrelation report (the ACF tends to decay slowly). A stochastic process is a sequence of events or paths generated by probabilistic laws. That is, random events can occur over time but are governed by specific statistical and probabilistic rules. The main stochastic processes include Random Walk or Brownian Motion, Mean-Reversion, and Jump-Diffusion. These processes can be used to forecast a multitude of variables that seemingly follow random trends but are restricted by probabilistic laws. The process-generating equation is known in advance, but the actual results generated are unknown.

The Random Walk Brownian Motion process can be used to forecast stock prices, prices of commodities, and other stochastic time-series data given a drift or growth rate and volatility around the drift path. The Mean-Reversion process can be used to reduce the fluctuations of the Random Walk process by allowing the path to target a long-term value, making it useful for forecasting time-series variables that have a long-term rate, such as interest rates and inflation rates (these are long-term target rates by regulatory authorities or the market). The Jump-Diffusion process is useful for forecasting time-series data when the variable occasionally can exhibit random jumps, such as oil prices or price of electricity (discrete exogenous event shocks can make prices jump up or down). These processes can also be mixed and matched as required. Figure 80.5 illustrates the results from Risk Simulator's data *Diagnostic* tool, to determine the stochastic parameters of the dataset. It shows the probability of a stochastic fit as opposed to conventional models, and the relevant input parameters in these stochastic models. It is up to the user to determine if the probability of fit is significant enough to use these stochastic processes.

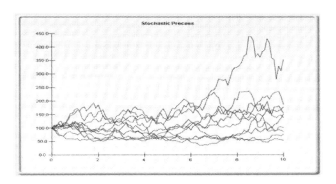

Figure 80.5: Stochastic processes

Multicollinearity exists when there is a linear relationship between the independent variables. When this occurs, the regression equation cannot be estimated at all. In near-collinearity situations, the estimated regression equation will be biased and provide inaccurate results. This situation is especially true when a step-wise regression approach is used, where the statistically significant independent variables will be thrown out of the regression mix earlier than expected, resulting in a regression equation that is neither efficient nor accurate. One quick test of the presence of multicollinearity in a multiple regression equation is that the R-squared value is relatively high while the t-statistics are relatively low.

Another quick test is to create a correlation matrix between the independent variables. A high cross-correlation indicates a potential for autocorrelation. The rule of thumb is that a correlation with an absolute value greater than 0.75 is indicative of severe multicollinearity. Another test for multicollinearity is the use of the Variance Inflation Factor (VIF), obtained by regressing each independent variable to all the other independent variables, obtaining the R-squared value, and calculating the VIF (Figure 80.6). A VIF exceeding 2.0 can be considered as severe multicollinearity. A VIF exceeding 10.0 indicates destructive multicollinearity.

Correlation Matrix

CORRELATION	X2	X3	X4	X5
X1	0.333	0.959	0.242	0.237
X2	1.000	0.349	0.319	0.120
X3		1.000	0.196	0.227
X4			1.000	0.290

Variance Inflation Factor

VIF	X2	X3	X4	X5
X1	1.12	12.46	1.06	1.06
X2	N/A	1.14	1.11	1.01
X3		N/A	1.04	1.05
X4			N/A	1.09

Figure 80.6: Correlation and variance inflation factors

The Correlation Matrix lists the Pearson's Product Moment Correlations (commonly referred to as the Pearson's R) between variable pairs. The correlation coefficient ranges between –1.0 and +1.0 inclusive. The sign indicates the direction of association between the variables while the coefficient indicates the magnitude or strength of association. The Pearson's R only measures a linear relationship and is less effective in measuring nonlinear relationships.

To test whether the correlations are significant, a two-tailed hypothesis test is performed and the resulting p-values are listed as shown in Figure 80.6. P-values less than 0.10, 0.05, and 0.01 are highlighted in blue to indicate statistical significance. In other words, a p-value for a correlation pair that is less than a given significance value is statistically significantly different from zero, indicating that there is a significant linear relationship between the two variables.

The Pearson's Product Moment Correlation Coefficient (R) between two variables (x and y) is related to the covariance (cov) measure where $R_{x,y} = \dfrac{COV_{x,y}}{s_x s_y}$. The benefit of dividing the covariance by the product of the two variables' standard deviation (s) is that the resulting correlation coefficient is bounded between –1 0 and +1.0 inclusive. This makes the correlation a good relative measure to compare among different variables (particularly with different units and magnitude). The Spearman rank-based nonparametric correlation is also included in the report. The Spearman's R is related to the Pearson's R in that the data is first ranked and then correlated. The rank correlations provide a better estimate of the relationship between two variables when one or both of them is nonlinear.

It must be stressed that a significant correlation does not imply causation. Associations between variables in no way imply that the change of one variable causes another variable to change. When two variables are moving independently of each other but in a related path, they may be correlated, but their relationship might be spurious (e.g., a correlation between sunspots and the stock market might be strong but one can surmise that there is no causality and that this relationship is purely spurious).

81. Forecasting – Econometric, Correlations, and Multiple Regression Modeling

File Name: Forecasting – Econometric, Correlations and Multiple Regression Modeling

Location: Modeling Toolkit | Forecasting | Econometric, Correlations and Multiple Regression Modeling

Brief Description: Illustrates how to use Risk Simulator for running a multiple regression analysis and econometric modeling

Requirements: Modeling Toolkit, Risk Simulator

This example shows how a multiple regression can be run using Risk Simulator. The raw data are arranged in the *Cross-Sectional Data* worksheet, which contains cross-sectional data on 50 months of a bank's *key risk indicators* as they pertain to Basel II/III's Operational Risk analysis guidance. The idea is to see if there is a relationship between the *Impact Losses ($M)* per month and these explanatory variables using multiple regression, econometric modeling, and correlation analysis.

Procedure

To run this model, simply:

1. In the *Cross Sectional Data* worksheet, select the area **C5:H55** (Figure 81.1).

2. Select **Risk Simulator | Forecasting | Multiple Regression.**

3. Choose *Impact Losses* as the dependent variable in the regression and click on **OK** to run the regression (Figure 81.2).

Multiple Regression and Econometric Analysis Data Set

Impact Losses ($M)	Cycle Time and Timeliness of Transactions	Transaction Volume	Hiring and Training Costs	Customer Satisfaction Index	IT Network Downtime
521	18308	185	4.041	79.6	7.2
367	1148	600	0.55	1	8.5
443	18068	372	3.665	32.3	5.7
365	7729	142	2.351	45.1	7.3
614	100484	432	29.76	190.8	7.5
385	16728	290	3.294	31.8	5
286	14630	346	3.287	678.4	6.7
397	4008	328	0.666	340.8	6.2
764	38927	354	12.938	239.6	7.3
427	22322	266	6.478	111.9	5
153	3711	320	1.108	172.5	2.8
231	3136	197	1.007	12.2	6.1
524	50508	266	11.431	205.6	7.1
328	28886	173	5.544	154.6	5.9
240	16996	190	2.777	49.7	4.6
286	13035	239	2.478	30.3	4.4
285	12973	190	3.685	92.8	7.4
569	16309	241	4.22	96.9	7.1
96	5227	189	1.228	39.8	7.5
498	19235	358	4.781	489.2	5.9
481	44487	315	6.016	767.6	9
468	44213	303	9.295	163.6	9.2
177	23619	228	4.375	55	5.1
198	9106	134	2.573	54.9	8.6
458	24917	189	5.117	74.3	6.6
108	3872	196	0.799	5.5	6.9
246	8945	183	1.578	20.5	2.7
291	2373	417	1.202	10.9	5.5
68	7128	233	1.109	123.7	7.2
311	23624	349	7.73	1042	6.6
606	5242	284	1.515	12.5	6.9
512	92629	499	17.99	381	7.2

Figure 81.1: Econometric dataset

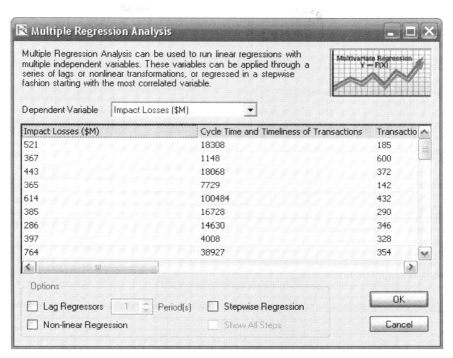

Figure 81.2: Running a multiple regression

Model Results Analysis

Note that more advanced regressions such as lag regressors, stepwise regression, and nonlinear regressions can also be run using Risk Simulator. For more details on running such regressions as well as the interpretation of the regression report, refer to *Modeling Risk*, Third Edition (Thomson–Shore, 2015) by Dr. Johnathan Mun.

Results Summary

Refer to the *Report* worksheet for details on the regression output. The report has more details on the interpretation of specific statistical results. It provides these elements: multiple regression and analysis of variance output, including coefficients of determination; hypothesis test results (single variable t-test and multiple variable F-test); computed coefficients for each regressor; fitted chart; and much more.

Additional econometric analyses can be performed. For instance, a nonlinear relationship is appropriate here. Simply follow the three-step procedure described, but remember to check the **Nonlinear Regression** box before hitting **OK**. Also, interactions between variables might exist in this model, and a modification of the data variables can be done before further regression models are run. In such instances, combine various independent variables to create new variables (e.g., $X_1, X_2, \ldots X_n$, and X_1X_2, X_1X_3, X_1X_4, and so forth, and then run a **Stepwise Regression**). In addition, the *Basic Econometrics* tool in Risk Simulator can be used to first modify these dependent and independent variables on-the-fly, before a regression is run.

Finally, the previous chapter, *Forecasting – Data Diagnostics,* provides the critical modeling prerequisites before running any multivariate regression analysis, to make sure that all the required assumptions have not been violated in the dataset and to check the modeling and predictive quality of the data.

Sometimes, the variables themselves require tweaking before a multiple regression is run. This is the basics of econometrics. Using Risk Simulator, this process can be applied quickly and the variables can be manipulated (log, addition, subtraction, multiplication, lagged, and so forth, using the *Basic Econometrics* tool) and modeled. The procedure is described next.

Procedure

To run a basic econometrics model, simply:

1. In the *Cross Sectional Data* worksheet, select the area **C5:H55** (Figure 81.1).

2. Select **Risk Simulator | Forecasting | Basic Econometrics.**

3. Type in the required single dependent variable and multiple independent variables with the required modifications but separated by a semicolon (Figure 81.3). Click **Show Results** to view the results of this model, and make additional modifications as required, and when done, click on **OK** to generate the full model report as seen in Figure 81.4.

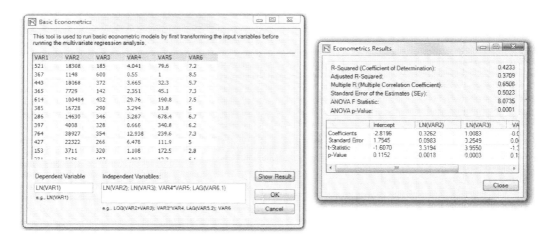

Figure 81.3: Basic econometrics results

Basic Econometrics Analysis Report

Regression Statistics

R-Squared (Coefficient of Determination)	0.4233
Adjusted R-Squared	0.3709
Multiple R (Multiple Correlation Coefficient)	0.6506
Standard Error of the Estimates (SEy)	0.5023
Number of Observations	49

The R-Squared or Coefficient of Determination indicates that 0.42 of the variation in the dependent variable can be explained and accounted for by the independent variables in this regression analysis. However, in a multiple regression, the Adjusted R-Squared takes into account the existence of additional independent variables or regressors and adjusts this R-Squared value to a more accurate view of the regression's explanatory power. Hence, only 0.37 of the variation in the dependent variable can be explained by the regressors.

The Multiple Correlation Coefficient (Multiple R) measures the correlation between the actual dependent variable (Y) and the estimated or fitted (Y) based on the regression equation. This is also the square root of the Coefficient of Determination (R-Squared).

The Standard Error of the Estimates (SEy) describes the dispersion of data points above and below the regression line or plane. This value is used as part of the calculation to obtain the confidence interval of the estimates later.

Regression Results

	Intercept	LN(VAR2)	LN(VAR3)	VAR4*VAR5	LAG(VAR6,1)
Coefficients	-2.8196	0.3262	1.0083	-0.0001	-0.0209
Standard Error	1.7545	0.0983	0.2549	0.0001	0.0516
t-Statistic	-1.6070	3.3194	3.9550	-1.3271	-0.4055
p-Value	0.1152	0.0018	0.0003	0.1913	0.6871
Lower 5%	-6.3556	0.1282	0.4945	-0.0002	-0.1248
Upper 95%	0.7165	0.5243	1.5221	0.0000	0.0830

Degrees of Freedom		Hypothesis Test	
Degrees of Freedom for Regression	4	Critical t-Statistic (99% confidence with df of 44)	2.6923
Degrees of Freedom for Residual	44	Critical t-Statistic (95% confidence with df of 44)	2.0154
Total Degrees of Freedom	48	Critical t-Statistic (90% confidence with df of 44)	1.6802

The Coefficients provide the estimated regression intercept and slopes. For instance, the coefficients are estimates of the true; population b values in the following regression equation $Y = \beta 0 + \beta 1X1 + \beta 2X2 + ... + \beta nXn$. The Standard Error measures how accurate the predicted Coefficients are, and the t-Statistics are the ratios of each predicted Coefficient to its Standard Error.

The t-Statistic is used in hypothesis testing, where we set the null hypothesis (Ho) such that the real mean of the Coefficient = 0, and the alternate hypothesis (Ha) such that the real mean of the Coefficient is not equal to 0. A t-test is is performed and the calculated t-Statistic is compared to the critical values at the relevant Degrees of Freedom for Residual. The t-test is very important as it calculates if each of the coefficients is statistically significant in the presence of the other regressors. This means that the t-test statistically verifies whether a regressor or independent variable should remain in the regression or it should be dropped.

The Coefficient is statistically significant if its calculated t-Statistic exceeds the Critical t-Statistic at the relevant degrees of freedom (df). The three main confidence levels used to test for significance are 90%, 95% and 99%. If a Coefficient's t-Statistic exceeds the Critical level, it is considered statistically significant. Alternatively, the p-Value calculates each t-Statistic's probability of occurrence, which means that the smaller the p-Value, the more significant the Coefficient. The usual significant levels for the p-Value are 0.01, 0.05, and 0.10, corresponding to the 99%, 95%, and 99% confidence levels.

The Coefficients with their p-Values highlighted in blue indicate that they are statistically significant at the 90% confidence or 0.10 alpha level, while those highlighted in red indicate that they are not statistically significant at any other alpha levels.

Figure 81.4: Basic econometrics report

Analysis of Variance

	Sums of Squares	Mean of Squares	F-Statistic	p-Value	Hypothesis Test	
Regression	8.15	2.04	8.07	0.0001	Critical F-statistic (99% confidence with df of 4 and 44)	3.7784
Residual	11.10	0.25			Critical F-statistic (95% confidence with df of 4 and 44)	2.5837
Total	19.25				Critical F-statistic (90% confidence with df of 4 and 44)	2.0772

The Analysis of Variance (ANOVA) table provides an F-test of the regression model's overall statistical significance. Instead of looking at individual regressors as in the t-test, the F-test looks at all the estimated Coefficients' statistical properties. The F-Statistic is calculated as the ratio of the Regression's Mean of Squares to the Residual's Mean of Squares. The numerator measures how much of the regression is explained, while the denominator measures how much is unexplained. Hence, the larger the F-Statistic, the more significant the model. The corresponding p-Value is calculated to test the null hypothesis (Ho) where all the Coefficients are simultaneously equal to zero, versus the alternate hypothesis (Ha) that they are all simultaneously different from zero, indicating a significant overall regression model. If the p-Value is smaller than the 0.01, 0.05, or 0.10 alpha significance, then the regression is significant. The same approach can be applied to the F-Statistic by comparing the calculated F-Statistic with the critical F values at various significance levels.

Forecasting

Period	Actual (Y)	Forecast (F)	Error (E)
1	5.9053618	5.7783	0.1270
2	6.0935698	6.1590	(0.0654)
3	5.8998974	4.9704	0.9295
4	6.4199949	6.4560	(0.0360)
5	5.9532433	5.9047	0.0485
6	5.6559918	5.9237	(0.2677)
7	5.9839363	5.5699	0.4141
8	6.6385678	6.1722	0.4663
9	6.056784	5.8670	0.1898
10	5.0304379	5.5582	(0.5278)
11	5.4424177	5.0743	0.3682
12	6.2614917	6.0303	0.2312
13	5.7930138	5.5111	0.2819
14	5.4806389	5.5144	(0.0337)
15	5.6559918	5.6913	(0.0353)
16	5.6524892	5.4415	0.2110
17	6.3438804	5.6879	0.6559
18	4.5643482	5.1063	(0.5420)
19	6.2106001	5.9865	0.2241
20	6.1758673	5.9846	0.1912
21	6.1484683	6.1230	0.0255
22	5.1761497	5.7285	(0.5523)
23	5.288267	4.9752	0.3131
24	6.1268692	5.5583	0.5686
25	4.6821312	5.0591	(0.3769)
26	5.5053315	5.2546	0.2508
27	5.6733233	5.7414	(0.0681)
28	4.2195077	5.4450	(1.2255)

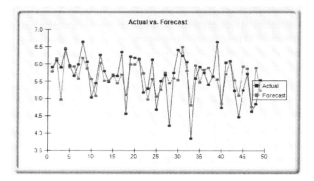

Figure 81.4: Basic econometrics report *(continued)*

82. Forecasting – Exponential J-Growth Curves

File Name: Forecasting – Exponential J-Growth Curves

Location: Modeling Toolkit | Forecasting | Exponential J-Growth Curves

Brief Description: Illustrates how to use Risk Simulator for running a simulation model on the Exponential J-growth curve where the growth rate is uncertain over time, to determine the probabilistic outcomes at some point in the future

Requirements: Modeling Toolkit, Risk Simulator

In mathematics, a quantity that grows exponentially is one whose growth rate is always proportional to its current size. Such growth is said to follow an exponential law. This implies that for any exponentially growing quantity, the larger the quantity gets, the faster it grows. But it also implies that the relationship between the size of the dependent variable and its rate of growth is governed by a strict law, of the simplest kind: direct proportion. The general principle behind exponential growth is that the larger a number gets, the faster it grows. Any exponentially growing number will eventually grow larger than any other number that grows at only a constant rate for the same amount of time. Figure 82.1 shows an exponential growth curve.

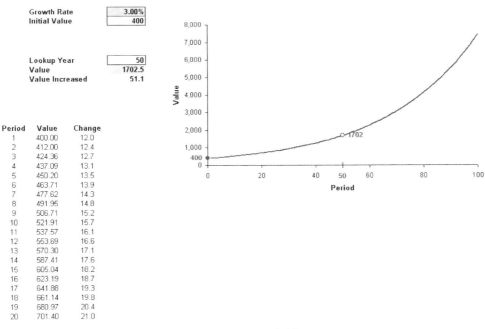

Figure 82.1: Exponential J curve

Procedure

You can run the preset simulation by clicking on **Risk Simulator | Change Profile** and selecting the *J Curve* profile, then run the simulation by going to **Risk Simulator | Run Simulation**. Alternatively, you can set your own or change the underlying simulation assumption as well as the input parameters. The *Growth Rate* and *Initial Value* are the input values in the model to determine the characteristics of the J curve. In addition, you can also enter in the *Lookup Year* to determine the value for that particular year, where the corresponding value for that year is set as a forecast.

Using the initial model inputs and running the simulation yields the forecast charts shown in Figure 82.2. The expected value of Year 50 is 1717.63 units.

An alternative approach is to go to **Risk Simulator | Forecasting | J-S Curves** to generate forecasts of exponential J curves.

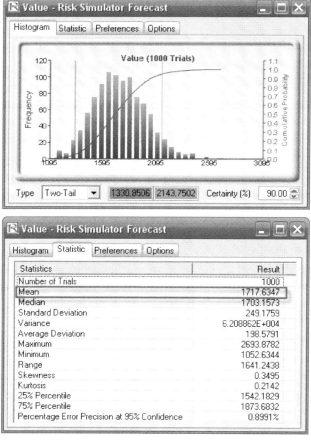

Figure 82.2: Simulated results of a J curve

83. Forecasting – Forecasting Manual Computations

File Name: Forecasting – Forecasting Manual Computations

Location: Modeling Toolkit | Forecasting | Forecasting Manual Computations

Brief Description: Illustrates how to use Risk Simulator for running optimization to determine the optimal forecasting parameters in several time-series decomposition models

Requirements: Modeling Toolkit, Risk Simulator

This example model shows the manual computations of the eight time-series decomposition and forecasting techniques in Risk Simulator and how the computations are done. We illustrate the step-by-step computations of backcast and forecast values, plus use Risk Simulator's optimization routines to find the best and optimal forecast parameters (e.g., *Alpha*, *Beta*, and *Gamma*) that yield the lowest error. The eight methods covered in this model are shown in Figure 83.1.

	NO SEASONALITY	WITH SEASONALITY
WITHOUT TREND	Single Moving Average	Seasonal Additive
WITHOUT TREND	Single Exponential Smoothing	Seasonal Multiplicative
WITH TREND	Double Moving Average	Holt–Winters Additive
WITH TREND	Double Exponential Smoothing	Holt–Winters Multiplicative

Figure 83.1: The eight time-series forecasting models

Procedure

The manual computations are shown in each of the worksheets in the model. In some of the methods, optimization is required to find the best input parameters to backcast-fit and forecast-fit the data going forward. In each method requiring optimization (six of the eight methods, excluding the *Single Moving Average* and *Double Moving Average* approaches), a new profile has already been created and the relevant objectives and decision variables have been set up. To run the model, follow these steps:

1. Go to the relevant worksheet and change the profile to match the worksheet (**Risk Simulator | Change Profile**), and find the matching profile for the model.

2. You can change the decision variables (*Alpha, Beta,* and *Gamma*) in the model to some starting point (e.g., *0.1*) so that you can tell whether anything had changed at the end of the optimization procedure. Then run the optimization (**Risk Simulator | Optimization | Run Optimization**).

To recreate the optimization, follow these steps instead:

1. Go to the relevant worksheet, create a new simulation profile (**Risk Simulator | New Profile**) and give it a name.

2. Select the **RMSE** or *Root Mean Squared Error* cell, make it an objective (**Risk Simulator | Optimization | Set Objective**), and set to **Minimize**.

3. Select the input parameter one at a time (e.g., *Alpha, Beta,* or *Gamma*), make it a decision variable (**Risk Simulator | Set Decision**), and make it a **Continuous Variable** between **0** and **1** (the input parameters Alpha, Beta and Gamma can take values only between 0 and 1, inclusive).

4. Run the optimization (**Risk Simulator | Optimization | Run Optimization**), and choose **Static Optimization**.

84. Forecasting – Linear Interpolation and Nonlinear Spline Extrapolation

File Name: Forecasting – Linear Interpolation

Location: Modeling Toolkit | Forecasting | Linear Interpolation and Modeling Toolkit | Yield Curve |Spline Interpolation and Extrapolation

Brief Description: Illustrates how to compute a linear and nonlinear interpolation and extrapolation of missing values in a time-series forecast model and for forecasting

Requirements: Modeling Toolkit, Risk Simulator

Modeling Toolkit Functions Used: MTInterpolationLinear, MTCubicSpline

Sometimes interest rates or any type of time-dependent rates may have missing values. For instance, the Treasury rates for Years 1, 2, and 3 exist, and then jump to Year 5, skipping Year 4. We can, using linear interpolation (i.e., we assume the rates during the missing periods are linearly related), determine and "fill in" or interpolate their values. This model illustrates how to use this function (Figure 84.1).

In contrast, the cubic spline polynomial interpolation and extrapolation model is used to "fill in the gaps" of missing values (interpolation) and forecasting outside of the known values (extrapolation) when the underlying structure is nonlinear. For example, we can apply this approach to spot yields and term structure of interest rates whereby the model can be used to both interpolate missing data points within a time series of interest rates (as well as other macroeconomic variables such as inflation rates and commodity prices or market returns) and also used to extrapolate outside of the given or known range, useful for forecasting purposes. Figure 84.2 illustrates the cubic spline model.

The cubic spline extrapolation approach can be applied either by using the Modeling Toolkit function or Risk Simulator's *Cubic Spline* module as seen in Figure 84.3. The example file using this module can be accessed through **Risk Simulator | Examples | Advanced Forecasting Models** and going to the *Cubic Spline* worksheet. Figure 84.4 shows the results of running the *Cubic Spline* module.

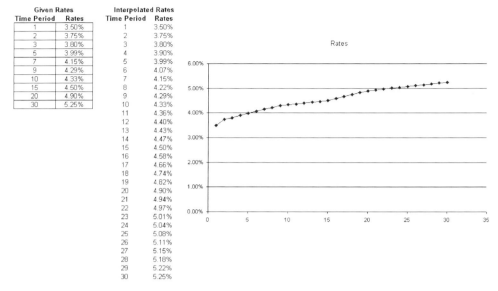

Figure 84.1: Interpolating missing values in a linear time series

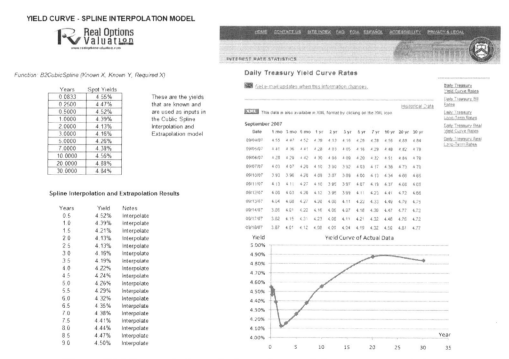

Figure 84.2 Interpolating missing values and forecast extrapolation
in a nonlinear time series

Cubic Spline Interpolation and Extrapolation

The cubic spline polynomial interpolation and extrapolation model is used to "fill in the gaps" of missing spot yields and term structure of interest rates whereby the model can be used to both interpolate missing data points within a time series of interest rates (as well as other macroeconomic variables such as inflation rates and commodity prices or market returns) and also used to extrapolate outside of the given or known range, useful for forecasting purposes

Years	Spot Yields	
0.0833	4.55%	These are the yields
0.2500	4.47%	that are known and
0.5000	4.52%	are used as inputs in
1.0000	4.39%	the Cubic Spline
2.0000	4.13%	Interpolation and
3.0000	4.16%	Extrapolation model
5.0000	4.26%	
7.0000	4.38%	
10.0000	4.56%	
20.0000	4.88%	
30.0000	4.84%	

To run the Cubic Spline forecast, click on **Risk Simulator | Forecasting | Cubic Spline** and then click on the link icon and select C15:C25 as the Known X values (values on the x-axis of a time-series chart) and D15:D25 as the Known Y values (make sure the length of Known X and Y values are the same). Enter the desired forecast periods (e.g., Starting 1, Ending 50, Step Size 0.5). Click OK and review the generated forecasts and chart

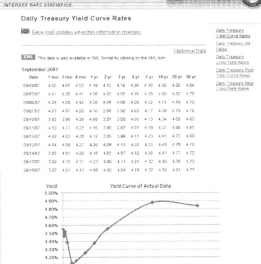

Figure 84.3 Cubic Spline module in Risk Simulator

Cubic Spline Forecasts

The cubic spline polynomial interpolation and extrapolation model is used to "fill in the gaps" of missing values and for forecasting time-series data, whereby the model can be used to both interpolate missing data points within a time series of data (e.g., yield curve, interest rates, macroeconomic variables like inflation rates and commodity prices or market returns) and also used to extrapolate outside of the given or known range, making it useful

Spline Interpolation and Extrapolation Results

X	Fitted Y	Notes
1.0	4.39%	Interpolate
1.5	4.21%	Interpolate
2.0	4.13%	Interpolate
2.5	4.13%	Interpolate
3.0	4.16%	Interpolate
3.5	4.19%	Interpolate
4.0	4.22%	Interpolate
4.5	4.24%	Interpolate
5.0	4.26%	Interpolate
5.5	4.29%	Interpolate
6.0	4.32%	Interpolate
6.5	4.35%	Interpolate
7.0	4.38%	Interpolate
7.5	4.41%	Interpolate
8.0	4.44%	Interpolate
8.5	4.47%	Interpolate
9.0	4.50%	Interpolate
9.5	4.53%	Interpolate
10.0	4.56%	Interpolate
10.5	4.59%	Interpolate
11.0	4.61%	Interpolate
11.5	4.64%	Interpolate
45.0	4.91%	Extrapolate
45.5	4.93%	Extrapolate
46.0	4.95%	Extrapolate
46.5	4.98%	Extrapolate
47.0	5.00%	Extrapolate
47.5	5.03%	Extrapolate
48.0	5.05%	Extrapolate
48.5	5.08%	Extrapolate
49.0	5.12%	Extrapolate
49.5	5.15%	Extrapolate
50.0	5.19%	Extrapolate

These are the known value inputs in the Cubic Spline Interpolation and Extrapolation model:

Observation	Known X	Known Y
1	0.0833	4.55%
2	0.2500	4.47%
3	0.5000	4.52%
4	1.0000	4.39%
5	2.0000	4.13%
6	3.0000	4.16%
7	5.0000	4.26%
8	7.0000	4.38%
9	10.0000	4.56%
10	20.0000	4.88%
11	30.0000	4.84%

Figure 84.4 Cubic Spline results

85. Forecasting – Logistic S-Growth Curves

File Name: Forecasting – Logistic S-Growth Curves

Location: Modeling Toolkit | Forecasting | Logistic S-Growth Curves

Brief Description: Illustrates how to run a simulation model on the logistic S-growth curve where the growth rate is uncertain over time, to determine the probabilistic outcomes at some point in the future

Requirements: Modeling Toolkit, Risk Simulator

A logistic function or logistic curve models the S curve of growth of some variable. The initial stage of growth is approximately exponential; then, as competition arises, growth slows, and at maturity, growth stops (Figure 85.1). These functions find applications in a range of fields, from biology to economics. For example, in the development of an embryo, a fertilized ovum splits, and the cell count grows: 1, 2, 4, 8, 16, 32, 64, etc. This is exponential growth. But the fetus can grow only as large as the uterus can hold; thus other factors start slowing down the increase in the cell count, and the rate of growth slows (but the baby is still growing, of course). After a suitable time, the child is born and keeps growing. Ultimately, the cell count is stable; the person's height is constant; the growth has stopped, at maturity. The same principles can be applied to population growth of animals or humans, and the market penetration and revenues of a product, where there is an initial growth spurt in market penetration, but over time, the growth slows due to competition and eventually the market declines and matures.

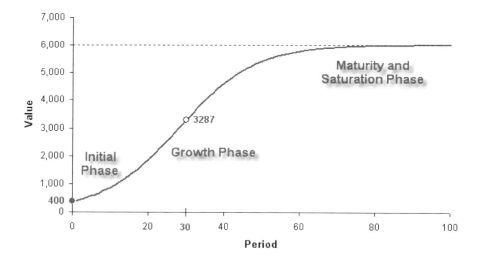

Figure 85.1: Logistic S curve

Procedure

You can run the preset simulation by clicking on **Risk Simulator | Change Profile** and selecting the *S Curve* profile, then run the simulation by going to **Risk Simulator | Run Simulation**. Alternatively, you can set your own or change the underlying simulation assumption as well as the input parameters. The *Growth Rate*, *Maximum Capacity*, and *Initial Value* are the input values in the model to determine the characteristics of the S curve. In addition, you can also enter in the *Lookup Year* to determine the value for that particular year, where the corresponding value for that year is set as a forecast. Using the initial model inputs and running the simulation yields the forecast charts seen in Figure 85.2, where the expected value of Year 30 is 2054.88 units.

Alternatively, you can use Risk Simulator's *S-curve* forecasting module to automatically generate forecast values (**Risk Simulator | Forecasting | JS Curves**).

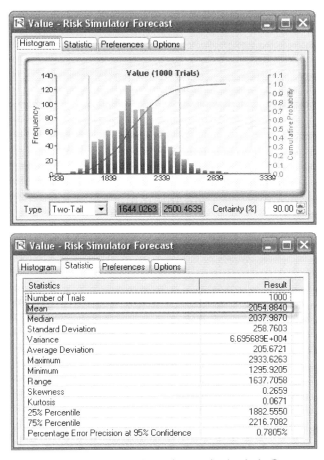

Figure 85.2: Simulated results on the logistic S curve

86. Forecasting – Markov Chains and Market Share

File Name: Forecasting – Markov Chains and Market Share

Location: Modeling Toolkit | Forecasting | Markov Chains and Market Share

Brief Description: Illustrates how to run a simulation model on Markov chains to determine path-dependent movements of market share and the long-term steady-state effects of market share

Requirements: Modeling Toolkit, Risk Simulator

The Markov Process is useful for studying the evolution of systems over multiple and repeated trials in successive time periods. The system's state at a particular time is unknown, and we are interested in knowing the probability that a particular state exists. For instance, Markov Chains are used to compute the probability that a particular machine or equipment will continue to function in the next time period or whether a consumer purchasing Product A will continue to purchase Product A in the next period or switch to a competitive brand B.

Procedure

1. When opening this model, make sure to select **Enable Macros** when prompted (you will get this prompt if your security settings are set to Medium, i.e., click on **Tools | Macros | Security | Medium** when in Excel). The *Model* worksheet shows the Markov Process and is presented as a chain of events, also known as a Markov Chain.

2. Enter the required inputs (i.e., values in blue: probabilities of switching or transition probabilities, the initial store location, and number of periods to forecast using the Markov Process). Click **Compute** when ready.

    Note: The probabilities are typically between 5% and 95%, and the *Checksum* total probabilities must be equal to 100%. These transition probabilities represent the probabilities that a customer will visit another store in the next period. For instance, 90% indicates that the customer is currently a patron of Store A and there is a 90% probability that s/he will stay at Store A the next period, and 10% probability that s/he will be visiting another store (Store B) the next period. Therefore, the total probability must be equal to 100% (Figure 86.1).

3. Further, select the location of the customer at time zero or right now, whether it is Store A or Store B.

4. Finally, enter the number of periods to forecast, typically between 5 and 50 periods. You cannot enter a value less than 1 or more than 1000.

Current Period	Next Period		Checksum
	Store A	Store B	
Store A	90.00%	10.00%	100.00%
Store B	20.00%	80.00%	100.00%

At initiation, which store is the customer at?

Store A ▾

How many periods to forecast?

Figure 86.1: Markov chain input assumptions

Results

The results from a Markov Process include a chain of events, indicating the transition from one store to the next. For instance, if there are 1,000 customers total, at Period 5, there will be 723 customers, on average, in Store A versus 277 in Store B, and so forth. Over time, a steady state occurs, and the *Steady State Probability* results indicate what would happen if the analysis is performed over a much longer period. These steady-state probabilities are also indicative of the respective market shares. In other words, over time and at equilibrium, Store A has a 66.67% market share as compared to 33.33% market share (Figure 86.2).

Alternatively, you can use Risk Simulator's *Markov Chain* forecasting module to automatically generate forecast values (**Risk Simulator | Forecasting | Markov Chain**).

How many periods to forecast? 20 Compute!

Period	Store A	Store B
0	100.00%	0.00%
1	90.00%	10.00%
2	83.00%	17.00%
3	78.10%	21.90%
4	74.67%	25.33%
5	72.27%	27.73%
6	70.59%	29.41%
7	69.41%	30.59%
8	68.59%	31.41%
9	68.01%	31.99%
10	67.61%	32.39%
11	67.33%	32.67%
12	67.13%	32.87%
13	66.99%	33.01%
14	66.89%	33.11%
15	66.82%	33.18%
16	66.78%	33.22%
17	66.74%	33.26%
18	66.72%	33.28%
19	66.70%	33.30%
20	66.69%	33.31%

Steady State Probability

	Store A	Store B
Market Share:	66.67%	33.33%

Figure 86.2: Markov chain results with steady-state effects

This analysis can be extended to, say, a machine functioning over time. In the example given, say the probability of a machine functioning in the current state will continue to function the next period about 90% of the time. Then the probability that the machine will still be functioning in 5 periods is 72.27% or 66.67% in the long run.

87. Forecasting – Multiple Regression

File Name: Forecasting – Multiple Regression

Location: Modeling Toolkit | Forecasting | Multiple Regression

Brief Description: Illustrates how to run a multiple or multivariate regression analysis

Requirements: Modeling Toolkit, Risk Simulator

This example shows how a multiple regression can be run using Risk Simulator. The raw data are arranged in the *Cross-Sectional Data* worksheet, which contains cross-sectional data on all 50 U.S. states on the number of aggravated assaults (in thousands) per year, the number of bachelor's degrees awarded per year, police expenditure per capita population, population size in millions, population density (person per square mile), and unemployment rate. The idea is to use multiple regression analysis to see if there is a relationship between the number of aggravated assaults per year and these explanatory variables.

Multiple Regression Analysis

To run this model, simply:

1. In the *Cross Sectional Data* worksheet, select the area **C5:H55**.

2. Select **Risk Simulator | Forecasting | Multiple Regression**.

3. Choose **Aggravated Assault** as the dependent variable in the regression and click on **OK** (Figure 87.1).

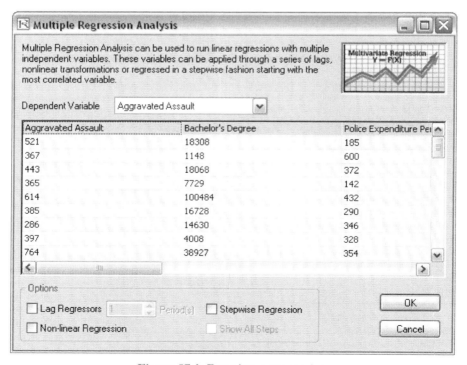

Figure 87.1: Running a regression

Note that more advanced regressions such as lag regressors, stepwise regression, and nonlinear regressions can also be run using Risk Simulator. For details on running such regressions as well as the results interpretation, refer to *Modeling Risk,* Third Edition (Thomson–Shore 2015) by Dr. Johnathan Mun.

Results Summary

Refer to the *Report* worksheet for details on the regression output. The worksheet has more details on the interpretation of specific statistical results. It provides these elements: multiple regression and analysis of variance output, including coefficients of determination; hypothesis test results (single variable *t-test* and multiple variable *F-test*); computed coefficients for each regressor; fitted chart; and much more. Also, remember to look at the *Forecasting – Data Diagnostics* models chapter for running analytical and econometric diagnostics such as multicollinearity, autocorrelation, micronumerosity, distributive lags, and other technical regression issues before running a regression analysis.

The dataset was set up intentionally in such a way that some of the independent variables are significant while others are not statistically significant (you can tell this from the t-test computed p-values in the report), and some of the variables are nonlinearly related to the dependent variable. Therefore, try out several variations of your model to find the best fit. Finally, do not forget to put the dataset through the data diagnostics tool in Risk Simulator. See the *Forecasting – Data Diagnostics* chapter for how to do this.

88. Forecasting – Nonlinear Extrapolation and Forecasting

File Name: Forecasting – Nonlinear Extrapolation

Location: Modeling Toolkit | Forecasting | Nonlinear Extrapolation

Brief Description: Illustrates how to forecast with a nonlinear extrapolation as well as compare the results using more conventional time-series decomposition forecasts with trends and seasonality effects

Requirements: Modeling Toolkit, Risk Simulator

This model provides some historical data on sales revenues for a firm. The goal of this exercise is to use Risk Simulator to run the *Nonlinear Extrapolation* tool and forecast the revenues for the next several periods. The data are located in the *Time-Series Data* worksheet and are arranged by months, from January 2004 to December 2004. As the data are time series in nature, we can apply extrapolation to forecast the results.

Nonlinear Extrapolation

Note that the Nonlinear Extrapolation methodology involves making statistical projections by using historical trends that are projected for a specified period of time into the future. It is only used for time-series forecasts. Extrapolation is fairly reliable, relatively simple, and inexpensive. However, extrapolation, which assumes that recent and historical trends will continue, produces large forecast errors if discontinuities occur within the projected time period.

To run this model, simply:

1. Go to the *Time-Series Data* worksheet.

2. Select the *Sales Revenue* data series (cells **H11:H22**) and select **Risk Simulator | Forecasting | Nonlinear Extrapolation** (Figure 88.1).

3. Extrapolate for **6 Periods** using the **Automatic Selection** option.

4. Repeat the process by selecting the *Net Income* data series (cells **M11:M22**).

5. Select cells **H11:H22** again but this time run a Time-Series Analysis with forecast period of **6** with seasonality of **6** (**Risk Simulator | Forecasting | Time Series Analysis**).

6. Repeat Step 5's Time-Series Analysis on cells **M11:M22**.

7. Compare the results from Extrapolation and Time-Series Analysis.

Model Results Analysis

For your convenience, the analysis *Report* worksheets are included in the model. A fitted chart and forecast values are provided as well as the error measures and a statistical summary of the methodology. Notice that when the historical data and future expectations are such that growth rates are nonlinear and smooth, extrapolation works better. Similar to the case of the sales revenues, compare the graphs visually and see the corresponding RMSE or root mean squared error values, where the smaller this error, the better the model fits and forecasts the data, but when seasonality occurs, time-series analysis is better.

Historical Sales Revenues Polynomial Growth Rates				Historical Net Income Sinusoidal Growth Rates			
Year	Month	Period	Sales	Year	Month	Period	Income
2014	1	1	$1.00	2014	1	1	$84.15
2014	2	2	$6.73	2014	2	2	$90.93
2014	3	3	$20.52	2014	3	3	$14.11
2014	4	4	$45.25	2014	4	4	($75.68)
2014	5	5	$83.59	2014	5	5	($95.89)
2014	6	6	$138.01	2014	6	6	($27.94)
2014	7	7	$210.87	2014	7	7	$65.70
2014	8	8	$304.44	2014	8	8	$98.94
2014	9	9	$420.89	2014	9	9	$41.21
2014	10	10	$562.34	2014	10	10	($54.40)
2014	11	11	$730.85	2014	11	11	($100.00)
2014	12	12	$928.43	2014	12	12	($53.66)
				2015	1	13	$42.02
				2015	2	14	$99.06
				2015	3	15	$65.03
				2015	4	16	($28.79)
				2015	5	17	($96.14)
				2015	6	18	($75.10)

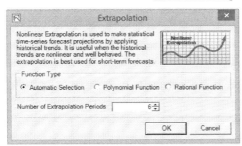

Figure 88.1: Nonlinear extrapolation

89. Forecasting – Stochastic Processes, Brownian Motion, Forecast Distribution at Horizon, Jump-Diffusion, and Mean-Reversion

File Name: Forecasting – Stochastic Processes and others

Location: Modeling Toolkit | Forecasting | Stochastic Processes, as well as various models such as the Brownian Motion, Jump Diffusion, Forecast Distribution at Horizon, and Mean Reverting Stochastic Processes

Brief Description: Illustrates how to simulate Stochastic Processes (Brownian Motion Random Walk, Mean-Reversion, Jump-Diffusion, and Mixed Models)

Requirements: Modeling Toolkit, Risk Simulator

A stochastic process is a sequence of events or paths generated by probabilistic laws. That is, random events can occur over time but are governed by specific statistical and probabilistic rules. The main stochastic processes include Random Walk or Brownian Motion, Mean-Reversion and Jump-Diffusion. These processes can be used to forecast a multitude of variables that seemingly follow random trends but yet are restricted by probabilistic laws. We can use Risk Simulator's *Stochastic Process* module to simulate and create such processes. These processes can be used to forecast a multitude of time-series data including stock prices, interest rates, inflation rates, oil prices, electricity prices, commodity prices, and so forth.

Stochastic Process Forecasting

To run this model, simply:

1. Select **Risk Simulator | Forecasting | Stochastic Processes**.

2. Enter a set of relevant inputs or use the existing inputs as a test case (Figure 89.1).

3. Select the relevant process to simulate.

4. Click on **Update Chart** to view the updated computation of a single path or click **OK** to create the process.

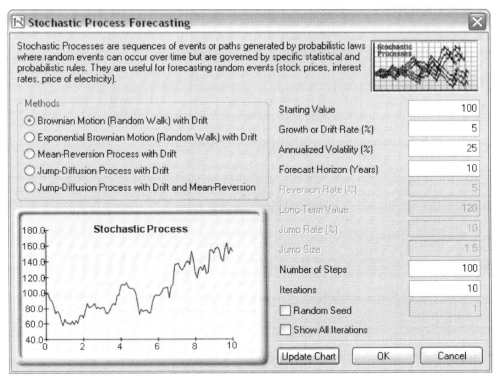

Figure 89.1: Running a stochastic process forecast

Model Results Analysis

For your convenience, the analysis *Report* worksheet is included in the model. A stochastic time-series chart and forecast values are provided in the report as well as each step's time period, mean, and standard deviation of the forecast (Figure 89.2). The mean values can be used as the single-point estimate, or assumptions can be manually generated for the desired time period. That is, after finding the appropriate time period, create an assumption with a normal distribution with the appropriate mean and standard deviation computed. A sample chart with 10 iteration paths is included to graphically illustrate the behavior of the forecasted process.

Clearly, the key is to calibrate the inputs to a stochastic process forecast model. The input parameters can be obtained very easily through some econometric modeling of historical data. The *Data Diagnostic* and *Statistical Analysis* models show how to use Risk Simulator to compute these input parameters. See Dr. Johnathan Mun's *Modeling Risk*, Third Edition (Thomson–Shore, 2015), for the technical details on obtaining these parameters.

The Risk Simulator tool is useful for quickly generating large numbers of stochastic process forecasts. Alternatively, if the inputs are uncertain and need to be simulated, use Modeling Toolkit's examples, *Brownian Motion Stochastic Process, Jump Diffusion Stochastic Process*, or *Mean Reverting Stochastic Process* models (all of these are located in the **Modeling Toolkit | Forecasting** menu item). Finally, a deterministic model on stock price forecast assuming a random walk process is also available (**Modeling Toolkit | Forecasting | Forecast Distribution**) where the stock price forecasts are provided for a future date.

Statistical Summary

A stochastic process is a sequence of events or paths generated by probabilistic laws. That is, random events can occur over time but are governed by specific statistical and probabilistic rules. The main stochastic processes include Random Walk or Brownian Motion, Mean-Reversion, and Jump-Diffusion. These processes can be used to forecast a multitude of variables that seemingly follow random trends but yet are restricted by probabilistic laws.

The Random Walk Brownian Motion process can be used to forecast stock prices, prices of commodities, and other stochastic time-series data given a drift or growth rate and a volatility around the drift path. The Mean-Reversion process can be used to reduce the fluctuations of the Random Walk process by allowing the path to target a long-term value, making it useful for forecasting time-series variables that have a long-term rate such as interest rates and inflation rates (these are long-term target rates by regulatory authorities or the market). The Jump-Diffusion process is useful for forecasting time-series data when the variable can occasionally exhibit random jumps, such as oil prices or price of electricity (discrete exogenous event shocks can make prices jump up or down). Finally, these three stochastic processes can be mixed and matched as required.

The results on the right indicate the mean and standard deviation of all the iterations generated at each time step. If the Show All Iterations option is selected, each iteration pathway will be shown in a separate worksheet. The graph generated below shows a sample set of the iteration pathways.

Stochastic Process: Brownian Motion (Random Walk) with Drift

Start Value	100	Steps	100.00	Jump Rate	N/A	
Drift Rate	5.00%	Iterations	10.00	Jump Size	N/A	
Volatility	25.00%	Reversion Rate	N/A	Random Seed	1431155157	
Horizon	10	Long-Term Value	N/A			

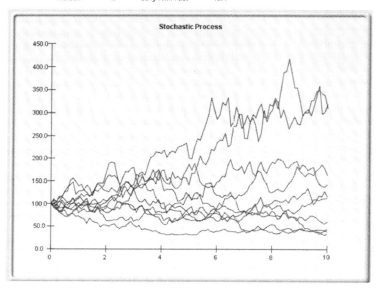

Time	Mean	Stdev
0.0000	100.00	0.00
0.1000	99.10	7.47
0.2000	96.03	7.22
0.3000	94.97	13.59
0.4000	97.39	15.57
0.5000	99.50	17.01
0.6000	97.79	20.92
0.7000	102.23	25.54
0.8000	106.54	26.54
0.9000	102.34	21.16
1.0000	102.77	20.86
1.1000	103.30	22.41
1.2000	103.27	19.23
1.3000	103.02	23.61
1.4000	97.78	19.65
1.5000	96.84	20.53
1.6000	100.92	25.22
1.7000	105.18	26.90
1.8000	100.75	30.33
1.9000	101.20	29.71
2.0000	103.67	36.95
2.1000	108.09	42.76
2.2000	111.58	42.61
2.3000	111.25	41.54
2.4000	108.47	35.22
2.5000	107.13	32.56
2.6000	108.95	32.95
2.7000	114.64	38.78
2.8000	114.13	36.61
2.9000	114.97	35.91
3.0000	114.33	39.90
3.1000	112.69	39.94
3.2000	115.11	39.89
3.3000	117.64	42.82
3.4000	114.70	39.91
3.5000	115.52	43.45
3.6000	117.60	49.89
3.7000	120.21	51.94
3.8000	116.64	53.52
3.9000	118.70	56.12
4.0000	113.19	56.71
4.1000	109.09	58.33
4.2000	103.70	52.23
4.3000	108.41	53.12
4.4000	108.67	56.30
4.5000	105.96	52.42
4.6000	106.12	55.80
4.7000	107.70	55.11
4.8000	109.43	58.43
4.9000	114.50	59.64
5.0000	110.44	53.91

Figure 89.2: Stochastic process forecast results

200

90. Forecasting – Time-Series ARIMA

File Name: Forecasting – Time-Series ARIMA

Location: Modeling Toolkit | Forecasting | Time-Series ARIMA

Brief Description: Illustrates how to run an econometric model called the *Box-Jenkins ARIMA*, which stands for autoregressive integrated moving average, an advanced forecasting technique that takes into account historical fluctuations, trends, seasonality, cycles, prediction errors, and nonstationarity of the data

Requirements: Modeling Toolkit, Risk Simulator

The *Data* worksheet in the model contains some historical time-series data on money supply in the United States, denoted M1, M2, and M3. M1 is the most liquid form of money (cash, coins, savings accounts, etc.); M2 and M3 are less liquid forms of money (bearer bonds, certificates of deposit, etc.). These datasets are useful examples of long-term historical time-series data where ARIMA can be applied.

Briefly, ARIMA econometric modeling takes into account historical data and decomposes it into an *Autoregressive* (AR) process, where there is a memory of past events (e.g., the interest rate this month is related to the interest rate last month, and so forth, with a decreasing memory lag); an *Integrated* (I) process, which accounts for stabilizing or making the data stationary and ergodic, making it easier to forecast; and a *Moving Average* (MA) of the forecast errors, such that the longer the historical data series, the more accurate the forecasts will be, as the model learns over time. ARIMA models therefore have three model parameters: one for the AR(p) process, one for the I(d) process, and one for the MA(q) process, all combined and interacting among each other and recomposed into the ARIMA (p,d,q) model.

There are many reasons why an ARIMA model is superior to ordinary time-series analysis and multivariate regressions. The common finding in time-series analysis and multivariate regression is that the error residuals are correlated with their own lagged values. This serial correlation violates the standard assumption of regression theory that disturbances are not correlated with other disturbances. The primary problems associated with serial correlation are:

- Regression analysis and basic time-series analysis are no longer efficient among the different linear estimators. However, as the error residuals can help to predict current error residuals, we can take advantage of this information to form a better prediction of the dependent variable using ARIMA.

- Standard errors computed using the regression and time-series formula are not correct and are generally understated. If there are lagged dependent variables set as the regressors, regression estimates are biased and inconsistent but can be fixed using ARIMA.

Autoregressive Integrated Moving Average or ARIMA(p,d,q) models are the extension of the AR model that uses three components for modeling the serial correlation in the time-series data. The first component is the autoregressive (AR) term. The AR(p) model uses the p lags of the time series in the equation. An AR(p) model has the form: $y_t = a_1 y_{t-1} + \ldots + a_p y_{t-p} + e_t$. The second component is the integration (d) order term. Each integration order corresponds to differencing the time series. I(1) means differencing the data once. I(d) means differencing the data d times. The third component is the moving average (MA) term. The MA(q) model uses the q lags of the forecast errors to improve the forecast. An MA(q) model has the form: $y_t = e_t + b_1 e_{t-1} + ... + b_q e_{t-q}$. Finally, an ARMA($p,q$) model has the combined form: $y_t = a_1 y_{t-1} + ... + a_p y_{t-p} + e_t + b_1 e_{t-1} + ... + b_q e_{t-q}$.

In interpreting the results of an ARIMA model, most of the specifications are identical to the multivariate regression analysis. However, there are several additional sets of results specific to the ARIMA analysis. The first is the addition of Akaike Information Criterion (AIC) and Schwarz Criterion (SC), which are often used in ARIMA model selection and identification. That is, AIC and SC are used to determine if a particular model with a specific set of p, d, and q parameters is a good statistical fit. SC imposes a greater penalty for additional coefficients than the AIC, but generally the model with the lowest AIC and SC values should be chosen. Finally, an additional set of results called the autocorrelation (AC) and partial autocorrelation (PAC) statistics is provided in the ARIMA report.

For instance, if autocorrelation AC(I) is nonzero, it means that the series is first order serially correlated. If AC dies off more or less geometrically with increasing lags, it implies that the series follows a low-order autoregressive process. If AC drops to zero after a small number of lags, it implies that the series follows a low-order moving-average process. In contrast, PAC measures the correlation of values that are k periods apart after removing the correlation from the intervening lags. If the pattern of autocorrelation can be captured by an autoregression of order less than k, then the partial autocorrelation at lag k will be close to zero. The Ljung-Box Q-statistics and their p-values at lag k are also provided, where the null hypothesis being tested is such that there is no autocorrelation up to order k. The dotted lines in the plots of the autocorrelations are the approximate two standard error bounds. If the autocorrelation is within these bounds, it is not significantly different from zero at approximately the 5% significance level.

Finding the right ARIMA model takes practice and experience. These AC, PAC, SC, and AIC are highly useful diagnostic tools to help identify the correct model specification. Finally, the ARIMA parameter results are obtained using sophisticated optimization and iterative algorithms, which means that although the functional forms look like those of a multivariate regression, they are not the same. ARIMA is a much more computationally intensive and advanced econometric approach.

Running a Monte Carlo Simulation

To run this model, simply:

1. Go to the *Data* worksheet and select **Risk Simulator | Forecasting | ARIMA**.

2. Click on the **link** icon beside the *Time Series Variable* input box, and link in **C7:C442**.

3. Enter in the relevant *P, D, Q* inputs, forecast periods, maximum iterations, and so forth (Figure 90.1) and click **OK**.

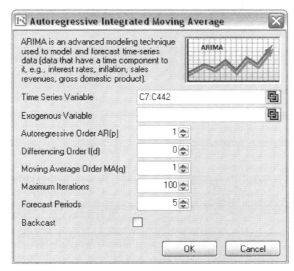

Figure 90.1: Running a Box-Jenkins ARIMA model

The nice thing about using Risk Simulator is the ability to run its *Auto-ARIMA* module. That is, instead of needing advanced econometric knowledge, the *Auto-ARIMA* module can automatically test all most commonly used models and rank them from the best fit to the worst fit. Figure 90.2 illustrates the results generated from an *Auto-ARIMA* module in Risk Simulator and Figure 90.3 shows the best-fitting ARIMA model report. Finally, please note that if the Exogenous Variable input is used, the number of data points in this variable less the number of data points in the Time-Series Variable has to exceed the number of Forecast Periods.

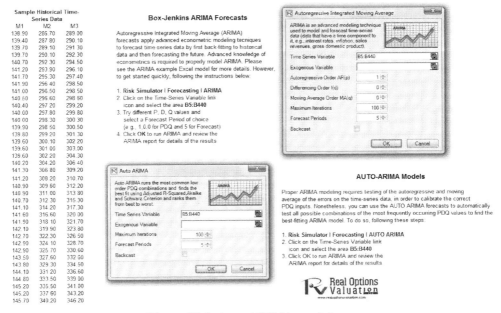

Figure 90.2: Auto-ARIMA model

AUTO-ARIMA (Autoregressive Integrated Moving Average)

Regression Statistics

R-Squared (Coefficient of Determination)	0.9996	Akaike Information Criterion (AIC)	4.5624
Adjusted R-Squared	0.9996	Schwarz Criterion (SC)	4.6044
Multiple R (Multiple Correlation Coefficient)	1.0000	Log Likelihood	-990.04
Standard Error of the Estimates (SEy)	297.93	Durbin-Watson (DW) Statistic	2.1254
Number of Observations	434	Number of Iterations	9

Autoregressive Integrated Moving Average or ARIMA(p,d,q) models are the extension of the AR model that use three components for modeling the serial correlation in the time-series data. The first component is the autoregressive (AR) term. The AR(p) model uses the p lags of the time-series in the equation. An AR(p) model has the form: $x(t)=a1^*x(t-1)+\ldots+ap^*x(t-p)+e(t)$. The second component is the integration (d) order term. Each integration order corresponds to differencing the time series. I(1) means differencing the data once. I(d) means differencing the data d times. The third component is the moving average (MA) term. The MA(q) model uses the q lags of the forecast errors to improve the forecast. An MA(q) model has the form: $y(t)=e(t)+b1^*e(t-1)+\ldots+bq^*e(t-q)$. Finally, an ARIMA(p,d,q) model has the combined form: $x(t)=a1^*x(t-1)+\ldots+ap^*x(t-p)+e(t)+b1^*e(t-1)+\ldots+bq^*e(t-q)$.

The R-Squared, or Coefficient of Determination, indicates the percent variation in the dependent variable that can be explained and accounted for by the independent variables in this regression analysis. However, in a multiple regression, the Adjusted R-Squared takes into account the existence of additional independent variables or regressors and adjusts this R-Squared value to a more accurate view the regression's explanatory power. However, under some ARIMA modeling circumstances (e.g., with nonconvergence models), the R-Squared tends to be unreliable.

The Multiple Correlation Coefficient (Multiple R) measures the correlation between the actual dependent variable (Y) and the estimated or fitted (Y) based on the regression equation. This correlation is also the square root of the Coefficient of Determination (R-Squared).

The Standard Error of the Estimates (SEy) describes the dispersion of data points above and below the regression line or plane. This value is used as part of the calculation to obtain the confidence interval of the estimates later.

The AIC and SC are often used in model selection. SC imposes a greater penalty for additional coefficients. Generally, the user should select a model with the lowest value of the AIC and SC.

The Durbin-Watson statistic measures the serial correlation in the residuals. Generally, DW less than 2 implies positive serial correlation.

Regression Results

	Intercept	AR(1)	AR(2)
Coefficients	-0.0025	1.5404	-0.5429
Standard Error	0.2020	0.0407	0.0410
t-Statistic	-0.0122	37.9479	-13.2551
p-Value	0.9902	0.0000	0.0000
Lower 5%	0.3394	1.6125	-0.4754
Upper 95%	-0.3354	1.4782	-0.6104

Degrees of Freedom

		Hypothesis Test	
Degrees of Freedom for Regression	2	Critical t-Statistic (99% confidence with df of 431)	2.5873
Degrees of Freedom for Residual	431	Critical t-Statistic (95% confidence with df of 431)	1.9655
Total Degrees of Freedom	433	Critical t-Statistic (90% confidence with df of 431)	1.6484

The Coefficients provide the estimated regression intercept and slopes. For instance, the coefficients are estimates of the true, population b values in the following regression equation $Y = b0 + b1X1 + b2X2 + \ldots + bnXn$. The Standard Error measures how accurate the predicted Coefficients are, and the t-Statistics are the ratio of each predicted Coefficient to its Standard Error.

The t-Statistic is used in hypothesis testing, where we set the null hypothesis (Ho) such that the real mean of the Coefficient = 0, and the alternate hypothesis (Ha) such that the real mean of the Coefficient is not equal to 0. A t-test is performed and the calculated t-Statistic is compared to the critical values at the relevant Degrees of Freedom for Residual. The t-test is very important as it calculates if each of the coefficients is statistically significant in the presence of the other regressors. This means that the t-test statistically verifies whether a regressor or independent variable should remain in the regression or it should be dropped.

The Coefficient is statistically significant if its calculated t-Statistic exceeds the Critical t-Statistic at the relevant degrees of freedom (df). The three main confidence levels used to test for significance are 90%, 95% and 99%. If a Coefficient's t-Statistic exceeds the Critical level, it is considered statistically significant. Alternatively, the p-value calculated each t-Statistic's probability of occurrence, which means that the smaller the p-value, the more significant the Coefficient. The usual significant levels for the p-value are 0.01, 0.05, and 0.10, corresponding to the 99%, 95%, and 99% confidence levels.

The Coefficients with their p-Values highlighted in blue indicate that they are statistically significant at the 99% confidence or 0.10 alpha level, while those highlighted in red indicate that they are not statistically significant at any other alpha levels.

Analysis of Variance

	Sums of Squares	Mean of Squares	F-Statistic	p-Value	Hypothesis Test	
Regression	38329216.66	19164607.83	3382629.5	0	Critical F-statistic (99% confidence with df of 2 and 431)	4.6547
Residual	2434.67	5.65			Critical F-statistic (95% confidence with df of 2 and 431)	3.0167
Total	38331650.33	19164613.48			Critical F-statistic (90% confidence with df of 2 and 431)	2.3148

The Analysis of Variance (ANOVA) table provides an F-test of the regression model's overall statistical significance. Instead of looking at individual regressors as in the t-test, the F-test looks at all the estimated Coefficients' statistical properties. The F-Statistic is calculated as the ratio of the Regression's Mean of Squares to the Residual's Mean of Squares. The numerator measures how much of the regression is explained, while the denominator measures how much is unexplained. Hence, the larger the F-Statistic, the more significant the model. The Corresponding p-Value is calculated to test the null hypothesis (Ho) where all the Coefficients are simultaneously equal to zero, versus the alternate hypothesis (Ha) that they are all simultaneously different from zero, indicating a significant overall regression model. If the p-Value is smaller than the 0.01, 0.05, or 0.10 alpha significance, then the regression is significant. The same approach can be applied to the F-Statistic by comparing the calculated F-Statistic with the critical F values at various significance levels.

Autocorrelation

Time Lag	AC	PAC	Lower Bound	Upper Bound	Q-Stat	Prob.
1	0.9921	0.9921	(0.0958)	0.0958	430.1374	-
2	0.9841	(0.0195)	(0.9958)	0.9958	854.3519	-
3	0.9760	(0.0199)	(0.9958)	0.9958	1272.5768	-
4	0.9675	(0.9142)	(0.9956)	0.9956	1684.7063	-
5	0.9594	(0.0098)	(0.9958)	0.9958	2090.7806	-
6	0.9509	(0.0113)	(0.9958)	0.9958	2490.4913	-
7	0.9423	(0.0124)	(0.9998)	0.9998	2884.6858	-
8	0.9336	(0.0147)	(0.9998)	0.9998	3271.1431	-
9	0.9247	(0.0121)	(0.9966)	0.9966	3651.6287	-
10	0.9159	(0.0198)	(0.9958)	0.9958	4020.0018	-
11	0.9066	(0.0048)	(0.9958)	0.9958	4383.8733	-
12	0.8975	(0.0068)	(0.9958)	0.9958	4754.8569	-
13	0.8883	(0.0097)	(0.9958)	0.9958	5105.5387	-
14	0.8791	(0.0087)	(0.9956)	0.9956	5452.6696	-
15	0.8698	(0.0064)	(0.9958)	0.9958	5789.9680	-
16	0.8605	(0.0098)	(0.9958)	0.9958	6136.5714	-
17	0.8512	(0.0062)	(0.9998)	0.9998	6469.3488	-
18	0.8419	(0.0036)	(0.9958)	0.9958	6784.7337	-
19	0.8326	(0.0005)	(0.9956)	0.9956	7106.8567	-
20	0.8235	0.0002	(0.9958)	0.9958	7411.7967	-

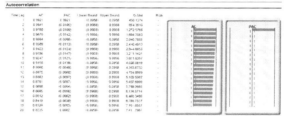

If autocorrelation AC(1) is nonzero, it means that the series is first order serially correlated. If ACF dies off more or less geometrically with increasing lag, it implies that the series follows a low-order autoregressive process. If ACF drops to zero after a small number of lags, it implies that the series follows a low-order moving-average process. Partial correlation PAC(K) measures the correlation of values that are k periods apart after removing the correlation from the intervening lags. If the pattern of autocorrelation can be captured by an autoregression of order less than k, then the partial autocorrelation at lag k will be close to zero. Listing the Q-statistics and their p-values at lag k has the null hypothesis that there is no autocorrelation up to order k. The dotted lines in the plots of the autocorrelations are the approximate two standard error bounds. If the autocorrelation is within these bounds, it is not significantly different from zero at (approximately) the 5% significance level.

Forecasting

Period	Actual (Y)	Forecast (F)	Error (E)
3	139.7600	140.0142	(0.3142)
4	138.7600	140.2063	(5.4063)
5	140.7600	140.0430	0.4050
6	141.2600	141.9868	(0.3968)
7	141.7600	143.3186	(0.1186)
8	141.9800	142.3196	(0.4199)
9	141.0800	142.3675	(1.3575)
10	140.5800	140.8581	(0.5081)
11	140.4000	140.1740	(0.1740)
12	140.0800	140.8969	(0.5809)
13	140.8600	140.1271	(0.1271)
14	138.9800	140.1442	(0.4442)
15	139.8000	140.1897	(0.3897)
16	139.5600	140.0894	(7.4804)
17	139.6600	139.8347	(0.2547)
18	139.6800	139.9432	(0.3432)
19	140.2600	139.9432	0.2966
20	141.5050	140.8764	0.4258
21	141.2800	142.2446	(0.8446)
22	140.9600	141.4979	(0.6929)
23	140.9800	141.0636	(0.1836)
24	140.7000	141.2494	(0.5494)
25	141.1000	140.1074	0.1026
26	141.6600	141.9841	(0.9641)
27	141.9600	142.2196	(0.2196)
28	142.1000	142.4118	(0.3118)
29	142.7000	142.5686	0.1429
30	142.5800	143.3758	(0.4758)
31	142.9800	143.3806	(0.4806)
32	143.9600	143.2514	0.2486
33	142.9800	144.1786	(0.7286)
34	144.1000	144.3805	(0.2785)
35	144.8600	144.6172	0.1628
36	145.2800	145.5361	(0.3361)
37	145.2800	146.2742	(0.1742)
38	146.7800	145.0571	0.1429
39	146.6000	146.1096	(0.1096)
40	146.4000	146.5219	(0.1299)
41	146.8800	146.9772	(0.1772)
42	146.8600	146.3782	(0.7782)

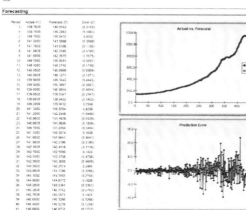

Figure 90.3: Auto-ARIMA results

91. Forecasting – Time-Series Analysis

File Name: Forecasting – Time-Series Analysis

Location: Modeling Toolkit | Forecasting | Time Series Analysis

Brief Description: Illustrates how to run time-series analysis forecasts, which take into account historical base values, trends, and seasonalities to project the future

Requirements: Modeling Toolkit, Risk Simulator

The historical sales revenue data are located in the *Time-series Data* worksheet in the model. The data are quarterly sales revenue from Q1 2000 to Q4 2004. The data exhibit quarterly seasonality, which means that the seasonality is 4 (there are 4 quarters in 1 year or 1 cycle).

Time-series forecasting decomposes the historical data into the baseline, trend, and seasonality, if any. The models then apply an optimization procedure to find the *alpha*, *beta*, and *gamma* parameters for the baseline, trend, and seasonality coefficients, and then recompose them into a forecast. In other words, this methodology first applies a *backcast* to find the best-fitting model and best-fitting parameters of the model that minimizes forecast errors, and then proceeds to *forecast* the future based on the historical data that exist. This, of course, assumes that the same baseline growth, trend, and seasonality hold going forward. Even if they do not—say, when there exists a structural shift (e.g., company goes global, has a merger, spin-off, etc.)—the baseline forecasts can be computed and then the required adjustments can be made to the forecasts.

Procedure

To run this model, simply:

1. Select the historical data (cells **H11:H30**).

2. Select **Risk Simulator | Forecasting | Time-Series Analysis**.

3. Select *Auto Model Selection*, **Forecast 4 Periods** and **Seasonality 4 Periods** (Figure 91.1).

Note that you can select *Create Simulation Assumptions* only if an existing Simulation Profile exists. If not, click on **Simulation | New Simulation Profile**, and then run the time-series forecast per steps 1 to 3 above but remember to check the *Create Simulation Assumptions* box.

Model Results Analysis

For your convenience, the analysis *Report* and *Methodology* worksheets are included in the model. A fitted chart and forecast values are provided in the report as well as the error measures and a statistical summary of the methodology (Figure 91.2). The *Methodology* worksheet provides the statistical results from all eight time-series methodologies.

Several different types of errors can be calculated for time-series forecast methods, including the mean-squared error (MSE), root mean-squared error (RMSE), mean absolute deviation (MAD), and mean absolute percent error (MAPE).

The MSE is an absolute error measure that squares the errors (the difference between the actual historical data and the forecast-fitted data predicted by the model) to keep the positive and negative errors from canceling each other out. This measure also tends to exaggerate large errors by weighting the large errors more heavily than smaller errors by squaring them, which can help when comparing different time-series models. The MSE is calculated by simply taking the average of the $Error^2$. RMSE is the square root of MSE and is the most popular error measure, also known as the *quadratic loss function*. RMSE can be defined as the average of the absolute values of the forecast errors and is highly appropriate when the cost of the forecast errors is proportional to the absolute size of the forecast error.

MAD is an error statistic that averages the distance (absolute value of the difference between the actual historical data and the forecast-fitted data predicted by the model) between each pair of actual and fitted forecast data points. MAD is calculated by taking the average of the $|Error|$, and is most appropriate when the cost of forecast errors is proportional to the absolute size of the forecast errors.

MAPE is a relative error statistic measured as an average percent error of the historical data points and is most appropriate when the cost of the forecast error is more closely related to the percentage error than the numerical size of the error. This error estimate is calculated by taking the average of $\left| \dfrac{Y_t - \hat{Y}_t}{Y_t} \right|$, where Y_t is the historical data at time t, while $\hat{Y}_t$ is the fitted or predicted data point at time t using this time-series method. Finally, an associated measure is the Theil's U statistic, which measures the naivety of the model's forecast. That is, if the Theil's U statistic is less than 1.0, then the forecast method used provides an estimate that is statistically better than guessing. Figure 91.3 provides the mathematical details of each error estimate.

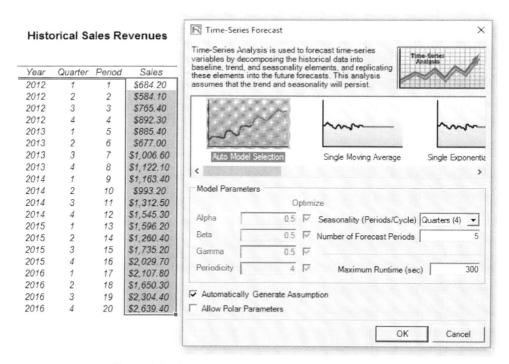

Figure 91.1: Running a time-series analysis forecast

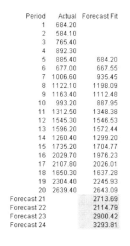

Period	Actual	Forecast Fit
1	684.20	
2	584.10	
3	765.40	
4	892.30	
5	885.40	684.20
6	677.00	667.55
7	1006.60	935.45
8	1122.10	1198.09
9	1163.40	1112.48
10	993.20	887.95
11	1312.50	1348.38
12	1545.30	1546.53
13	1596.20	1572.44
14	1260.40	1299.20
15	1735.20	1704.77
16	2029.70	1976.23
17	2107.80	2026.01
18	1650.30	1637.28
19	2304.40	2245.93
20	2639.40	2643.09
Forecast 21		2713.69
Forecast 22		2114.79
Forecast 23		2900.42
Forecast 24		3293.81

Error Measurements	
RMSE	71.8132
MSE	5157.1348
MAD	53.4071
MAPE	4.50%
Theil's U	0.3054

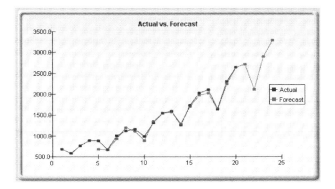

Figure 91.2: Time-series analysis results

RMSE	79.00
MSE	6241.27
MAD	63.00
MAPE	20.80%
Thiel's U	0.80

$$RMSE = \sqrt{\sum_{i=1}^{n} \frac{\left(Error^2\right)_i}{n}} = \sqrt{MSE}$$

$$MSE = \sum_{i=1}^{n} \frac{\left(Error^2\right)_i}{n} = RMSE^2$$

$$MAD = \sum_{i=1}^{n} \frac{\left|Error\right|_i}{n}$$

$$MAPE = \sum_{i=1}^{n} \frac{\left|\dfrac{Y_t - \hat{Y}_t}{Y_t}\right|_i}{n}$$

$$Theil's\,U = \sqrt{\frac{\sum_{i=1}^{n}\left[\dfrac{\hat{Y}_t - Y_t}{Y_{t-1}}\right]_i^2}{\sum_{i=1}^{n}\left[\dfrac{Y_t - Y_{t-1}}{Y_{t-1}}\right]_i^2}}$$

Figure 91.3: Error computations

92. Industry Application – Banking – Integrated Risk Management, Probability of Default, Economic Capital, Value at Risk, and Optimal Bank Portfolios

File Name: Multiple files (see chapter for details of example files used)

Location: Various places in Modeling Toolkit

Brief Description: Illustrates the use of several banking models to develop an integrated risk management paradigm for the Basel II/III Accords

Requirements: Modeling Toolkit, Risk Simulator

Modeling Toolkit Functions Used: MTProbabilityDefaultMertonImputedAssetValue, MTProbabilityDefaultMertonImputedAssetVolatility, MTProbabilityDefaultMertonII, MTProbabilityDefaultMertonDefaultDistance, MTProbabilityDefaultMertonRecoveryRate, MTProbabilityDefaultMertonMVDebt

With the Basel II/III Accords, internationally active banks are now allowed to compute their own risk capital requirements using the internal ratings–based (IRB) approach. Not only is adequate risk capital analysis important as a compliance obligation, it also provides banks the ability to optimize their capital by computing and allocating risks, performing performance measurements, executing strategic decisions, increasing competitiveness, and enhancing profitability. This chapter discusses the various approaches required to implement an IRB method, and the step-by-step models and methodologies in implementing and valuing economic capital, value at risk, probability of default, and loss given default, the key ingredients required in an IRB approach, through the use of advanced analytics such as Monte Carlo and historical risk simulation, portfolio optimization, stochastic forecasting, and options analysis. The use of Risk Simulator and the Modeling Toolkit software in computing and calibrating these critical input parameters is illustrated. Instead of dwelling on theory or revamping what has already been written many times, this chapter focuses solely on the practical modeling applications of the key ingredients to the Basel II/III Accords. Specifically, these topics are addressed:

- Probability of Default (structural and empirical models for commercial versus retail banking)
- Loss Given Default and Expected Losses
- Economic Capital and Portfolio Value at Risk (structural and risk-based simulation)
- Portfolio Optimization
- Hurdle Rates and Required Rates of Return

Please note that several white papers on related topics such as the following are available by request (send an e-mail request to admin@realoptionsvaluation.com):

- Portfolio Optimization, Project Selection, and Optimal Investment Allocation
- Credit Analysis
- Interest Rate Risk, Foreign Exchange Risk, Volatility Estimation, and Risk Hedging
- Exotic Options and Credit Derivatives

To follow along with the analyses in this chapter, we assume that the reader already has Risk Simulator, Real Options SLS, and Modeling Toolkit installed and is somewhat familiar with the basic functions of each software. If not, please refer to www.realoptionsvaluation.com (click on the **Download** link) and watch the getting started videos, read some of the getting started case studies, or to install the latest trial versions of these software programs. Alternatively, refer to the website to obtain a primer on using these software programs. Each topic discussed will start with some basic introduction to the methodologies that are appropriate, followed by some practical hands-on modeling approaches and examples.

Probability of Default

Probability of default measures the degree of likelihood that the borrower of a loan or debt (the obligor) will be unable to make the necessary scheduled repayments on the debt, thereby defaulting on the debt. Should the obligor be unable to pay, the debt is in default, and the lenders of the debt have legal avenues to attempt a recovery of the debt, or at least partial repayment of the entire debt. The higher the default probability a lender estimates a borrower to have, the higher the interest rate the lender will charge the borrower as compensation for bearing the higher default risk.

Probability of default models are categorized as *structural* or *empirical*. Structural models look at a borrower's ability to pay based on market data such as equity prices and market and book values of asset and liabilities, as well as the volatility of these variables. Hence, these structural models are used predominantly to estimate the probability of default of *companies* and *countries*, most applicable within the areas of commercial and industrial banking. In contrast, empirical models or credit scoring models are used to quantitatively determine the probability that a loan or loan holder will default, where the loan holder is an individual, by looking at historical portfolios of loans held and assessing individual characteristics (e.g., age, educational level, debt to income ratio, and so forth). This second approach is more applicable to the retail banking sector.

Structural Models of Probability of Default

Probability of default models are models that assess the likelihood of default by an obligor. They differ from regular credit scoring models in several ways. First of all, credit scoring models usually are applied to smaller credits—individuals or small businesses—whereas default models are applied to larger credits—corporation or countries. Credit scoring models are largely statistical, regressing instances of default against various risk indicators, such as an obligor's income, home renter or owner status, years at a job, educational level, debt to income ratio, and so forth, discussed later in this chapter. Structural default models, in contrast, directly model the default process and typically are calibrated to market variables, such as the obligor's stock price, asset value, debt book value, or the credit spread on its bonds. Default models find many applications within financial institutions. They are used to support credit analysis and determine the probability that a firm will default, to value counterparty credit risk limits, or to apply financial engineering techniques in developing credit derivatives or other credit instruments.

The model illustrated in this chapter is used to solve the probability of default of a publicly traded company with equity and debt holdings, and accounting for its volatilities in the market (Figure 92.1). This model is currently used by KMV and Moody's to perform credit risk analysis. This approach assumes that the book value of asset and asset volatility are unknown and solved in the model; that the company is relatively stable; and that the growth rate of the company's assets is stable over time (e.g., not in start-up mode). The model uses several simultaneous equations in options valuation coupled with optimization to obtain the implied underlying asset's market value and volatility of the asset in order to compute the probability of default and distance to default for the firm.

Illustrative Example: Structural Probability of Default Models on Public Firms

It is assumed that the reader is well versed in running simulations and optimizations in Risk Simulator. The example model used is the *Probability of Default – External Options Model* and can be accessed through **Modeling Toolkit | Prob of Default | External Options Model (Public Company)**.

To run this model (Figure 92.1), enter in the required inputs:

- Market value of equity (obtained from market data on the firm's capitalization, i.e., stock price times number of stocks outstanding)

- Market equity volatility (computed in the *Volatility* or *LPVA* worksheets in the model)

- Book value of debt and liabilities (the firm's book value of all debt and liabilities)

- Risk-free rate (the prevailing country's risk-free interest rate for the same maturity)

- Anticipated growth rate of the company (the expected annualized cumulative growth rate of the firm's assets, which can be estimated using historical data over a long period of time, making this approach more applicable to mature companies rather than start-ups)

- Debt maturity (the debt maturity to be analyzed, or enter **1** for the annual default probability)

The comparable option parameters are shown in cells G18 to G23. All these comparable inputs are computed except for Asset Value (the market value of asset) and the Volatility of Asset. You will need to input some rough estimates as a starting point so that the analysis can be run. The rule of thumb is to set the volatility of the asset in G22 to be one-fifth to half of the volatility of equity computed in G10, and the market value of asset (G19) to be approximately the sum of the market value of equity and book value of liabilities and debt (G9 and G11).

Then, an optimization needs to be run in Risk Simulator in order to obtain the desired outputs. To do this, set Asset Value and Volatility of Asset as the decision variables (make them continuous variables with a lower limit of 1% for volatility and $1 for asset, as both these inputs can only take on positive values). Set cell G29 as the objective to minimize as this is the absolute error value. Finally, the constraint is such that cell H33, the implied volatility in the default model, is set to exactly equal the numerical value of the equity volatility in cell G10. Run a static optimization using Risk Simulator.

If the model has a solution, the absolute error value in cell G29 will revert to zero (Figure 92.2). From here, the probability of default (measured in percent) and the distance to default (measured in standard deviations) are computed in cells G39 and G41. Then the relevant credit spread required can be determined using the *Credit Analysis – Credit Premium* model or some other credit spread tables (such as using the *Internal Credit Risk Rating* model).

The results indicate that the company has a probability of default at 0.56% with 2.54 standard deviations to default, indicating good creditworthiness (Figure 92.2).

A simpler approach is to use the Modeling Toolkit functions instead of manually running the optimization. These functions have internal intelligent optimization routines embedded in them. For instance, the following two functions perform multiple internal optimization routines of simultaneous stochastic equations to obtain their respective results, which are then used as an input into the MTProbabilityDefaultMertonII function to compute the probability of default:

MTProbabilityDefaultMertonImputedAssetValue
MTProbabilityDefaultMertonImputedAssetVolatility

See the model for more specific details.

Illustrative Example: Structural Probability
of Default Models on Private Firms

Several other structural models exist for computing the probability of default of a firm. Specific models are used depending on the need and availability of data. In the previous example, the firm is a publicly traded firm, with stock prices and equity volatility that can be readily obtained from the market. In the present example, we assume that the firm is privately held, meaning that there would be no market equity data available. This example essentially computes the probability of default or the point of default for the company when its liabilities exceed its assets, given the asset's growth rates and volatility over time (Figure 92.3). Before using this model, first review the preceding example using the *Probability of Default – External Options Model*. Similar methodological parallels exist between these two models, and this example builds on the knowledge and expertise of the previous example.

In Figure 92.3, the example firm with an asset value of $12M and a debt book value of $10M with significant growth rates of its internal assets and low volatility returns a 1.15% probability of default. Instead of relying on the valuation of the firm, external market benchmarks can be used, if such data are available. In Figure 92.4, we see that additional input assumptions are required, such as the market fluctuation (market returns and volatility) and relationship (correlation between the market benchmark and the company's assets). The model used is the *Probability of Default – Merton Market Options Model* accessible from **Modeling Toolkit | Prob of Default | Merton Market Options Model (Industry Comparable)**.

Figure 92.1: Default probability model setup

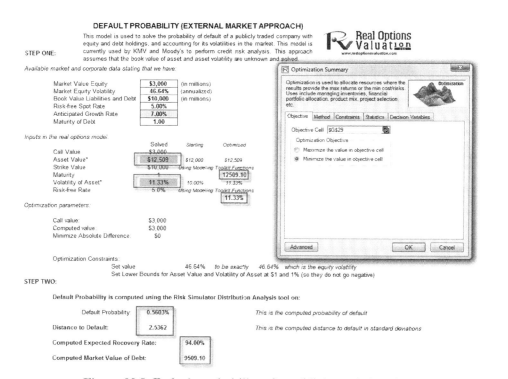

Figure 92.2: Default probability of a publicly traded entity

CREDIT RISK DEFAULT PROBABILITY (OPTIONS APPROACH)

VALUING DEFAULT PROBABILITY AND DISTANCE TO DEFAULT BASED ON OPTIONS MODELING OF INTERNAL DEBT

Input Assumptions

Asset Book Value	$12.0000
Debt Book Value	$10.0000
Maturity	1.0000
Risk-free Rate	5.00%
Volatility of Asset	10.00%

Probability of Default	1.1507%
Distance to Default	2.2732

Function: MTProbabilityDefaultMertonII
Function: MTProbabilityDefaultMertonDefaultDistance

Figure 92.3: Default probability of a privately held entity

MERTON MODEL OF DEBT DEFAULT PROBABILITY
VALUING THE PROBABILITY OF DEFAULT BASED ON MARKET RELATIONSHIPS

Input Assumptions

Asset Value	$100.0000
Debt Value	$50.0000
Time to Maturity	1.00
Risk-free Rate	5.00%
Volatility of Asset	20.00%
Market Volatility	10.00%
Market Return	8.00%
Correlation	0.00

Probability of Default	0.0150%

Function: MTProbabilityDefaultMertonI

Figure 92.4: Default probability of a privately held entity calibrated to market fluctuations

Empirical Models of Probability of Default

As mentioned, empirical models of probability of default are used to compute an individual's default probability, applicable within the retail banking arena, where empirical or actual historical or comparable data exist on past credit defaults. The dataset in Figure 92.5 represents a sample of several thousand previous loans, credit, or debt issues. The data show whether each loan had defaulted or not (0 for no default, and 1 for default) as well as the specifics of each loan applicant's age, education level (1 to 3 indicating high school, university, or graduate professional education), years with current employer, and so forth. The idea is to model these empirical data to see which variables affect the default behavior of individuals, using Risk Simulator's *Maximum Likelihood Model*. The resulting model will help the bank or credit issuer compute the expected probability of default of an individual credit holder having specific characteristics.

Illustrative Example on Applying Empirical Models of Probability of Default

The example file is *Probability of Default – Empirical* and can be accessed through **Modeling Toolkit | Prob of Default | Empirical (Individuals)**. To run the analysis, select the data on the left or any other dataset (include the headers) and make sure that the data have the same length for all variables, without any missing or invalid data. Then, using Risk Simulator, click on **Risk Simulator | Forecasting | Maximum Likelihood Models**. A sample set of results is provided in the *MLE* worksheet, complete with detailed instructions on how to compute the expected probability of default of an individual.

The Maximum Likelihood Estimates (MLE) approach on a binary multivariate logistic analysis is used to model dependent variables to determine the expected probability of success of belonging to a certain group. For instance, given a set of independent variables (e.g., age, income, education level of credit card or mortgage loan holders), we can model the probability of default using MLE. A typical regression model is invalid because the errors are heteroskedastic and non-normal, and the resulting estimated probability estimates will sometimes be above 1 or below 0. MLE analysis handles these problems using an iterative optimization routine. The computed results show the coefficients of the estimated MLE intercept and slopes.[*]

The coefficients estimated are actually the logarithmic odds ratios, and cannot be interpreted directly as probabilities. A quick but simple computation is first required. The approach is straightforward. To estimate the probability of success of belonging to a certain group (e.g., predicting if a debt holder will default given the amount of debt he holds), simply compute the estimated Y value using the MLE coefficients. Figure 92.6 illustrates an individual with 8 years at a current employer and current address, a low 3% debt to income ratio, and $2,000 in credit card debt has a log odds ratio of -3.1549. The inverse antilog of the odds ratio is obtained by computing:

$$\frac{\exp(estimated\ Y)}{1 + \exp(estimated\ Y)} = \frac{\exp(-3.1549)}{1 + \exp(-3.1549)} = 0.0409$$

---

[*] For instance, the coefficients are estimates of the true population b values in the following equation: $Y = b_0 + \beta_1 X_1 + \beta_2 X_2 + ... + \beta_n X_n$. The standard error measures how accurate the predicted coefficients are, and the Z-statistics are the ratios of each predicted coefficient to its standard error. The Z-statistic is used in hypothesis testing, where we set the null hypothesis (H_o) such that the real mean of the coefficient is equal to zero, and the alternate hypothesis (H_a) such that the real mean of the coefficient is not equal to zero. The Z-test is very important as it calculates if each of the coefficients is statistically significant in the presence of the other regressors. This means that the Z-test statistically verifies whether a regressor or independent variable should remain in the model or it should be dropped. That is, the smaller the p-value, the more significant the coefficient. The usual significant levels for the p-value are 0.01, 0.05, and 0.10, corresponding to the 99%, 95%, and 99% confidence levels.

So, such a person has a 4.09% chance of defaulting on the new debt. Using this probability of default, you can then use the *Credit Analysis – Credit Premium* model to determine the additional credit spread to charge this person given this default level and the customized cash flows anticipated from this debt holder.

PROBABILITY OF DEFAULT (EMPIRICAL USING MAXIMUM LIKELIHOOD)

Defaulted	Age	Education Level	Years with Current Employer	Years at Current Address	Household Income (Thousands $)	Debt to Income Ratio (%)	Credit Card Debt (Thousands $)	Other Debt (Thousands $)
1	41	3	17	12	176	9.3	11.36	5.01
0	27	1	10	6	31	17.3	1.36	4
0	40	1	15	14	55	5.5	0.86	2.17
0	41	1	15	14	120	2.9	2.66	0.82
1	24	2	2	0	28	17.3	1.79	3.06
0	41	2	5	5	25	10.2	0.39	2.16
0	39	1	20	9	67	30.6	3.83	16.67
0	43	1	12	11	38	3.6	0.13	1.24
1	24	1	3	4	19	24.4	1.36	3.28
0	36	1	0	13	25	19.7	2.78	2.15
0	27	1	0	1	16	1.7	0.18	0.09
0	25	1	4	0	23	5.2	0.25	0.94
0	52	1	24	14	64	10	3.93	2.47
0	37	1	6	9	29	16.3	1.72	3.01
0	48	1	22	15	100	9.1	3.7	5.4
1	36	2	9	6	49	8.6	0.82	3.4
1	36	2	13	6	41	16.4	2.92	3.81
0	43	1	23	19	72	7.6	1.18	4.29
0	39	1	6	9	61	5.7	0.56	2.91
0	41	3	0	21	26	1.7	0.1	0.34
0	39	1	22	3	52	3.2	1.15	0.51
0	47	1	17	21	43	5.6	0.59	1.82

Figure 92.5: Empirical analysis of probability of default

MLE Results

Log Likelihood Value   -200.51

Variable	Coefficients	Standard Error	Z-Statistic	p-Value		Sample Inputs
Intercept	-1.7003	0.7512	-2.2634	0.0236		
Age	0.0279	0.0205	1.3588	0.1742		
Education Level	0.0728	0.1447	0.5028	0.6151		
Years with Current Emplk	-0.2528	0.0391	-6.4644	0.0000		8.000
Years at Current Address	-0.0952	0.0271	-3.5064	0.0005		8.000
Household Income (Thou	0.0009	0.0125	0.0754	0.9399		
Debt to Income Ratio (%,	0.0750	0.0396	1.8934	0.0583		3.000
Credit Card Debt (Thous	0.5521	0.1324	4.1697	0.0000		2.000
Other Debt (Thousands $	0.0461	0.1005	0.4592	0.6461		

Log Odds Ratio	-3.1549
Default Probability	4.09%

Figure 92.6: MLE results

Loss Given Default and Expected Losses

As shown previously, probability of default is a key parameter for computing credit risk of a portfolio. In fact, the Basel II/III Accord requires that the probability of default as well as other key parameters, such as the loss given default (LGD) and exposure at default (EAD), be reported as well. The reason is that a bank's expected loss is equivalent to:

Expected Losses = (Probability of Default) × (Probability of Default) × (Exposure at Default)

or simply $EL = PD \times LGD \times EAD$.

PD and LGD are both percentages, whereas EAD is a value. As we have shown how to compute PD earlier, we will now revert to some estimations of LGD. There are several methods used to estimate LGD. The first is through a simple empirical approach where we set LGD = 1 – Recovery Rate. That is, whatever is not recovered at default is the loss at default, computed as the charge-off (net of recovery) divided by the outstanding balance:

LGD = 1 – Recovery Rate

or

$$LGD = \frac{\text{Charge Offs (Net of Recovery)}}{\text{Outstanding Balance at Default}}$$

Therefore, if market data or historical information are available, LGD can be segmented by various market conditions, types of obligor, and other pertinent segmentations. LGD can then be readily read off a chart.

A second approach to estimate LGD is more attractive in that if the bank has available information, it can attempt to run some econometric models to create the best-fitting model under an ordinary least squares approach. By using this approach, a single model can be determined and calibrated, and this same model can be applied under various conditions, with no data mining required. However, in most econometric models, a normal transformation will have to be performed first. Supposing the bank has some historical LGD data (Figure 92.7), the best-fitting distribution can be found using Risk Simulator (select the historical data, click on **Risk Simulator | Analytical Tools | Distributional Fitting (Single Variable)** to perform the fitting routine). The result is a beta distribution for the thousands of LGD values.

Past LGD	Normalized
49.69%	28.54%
25.76%	18.27%
14.61%	11.84%
26.91%	18.83%
18.47%	14.33%
21.29%	15.95%
26.00%	18.39%
11.84%	9.76%
51.85%	29.41%
19.35%	14.84%
24.74%	17.76%
15.68%	12.57%
14.35%	11.66%
21.36%	15.98%
35.31%	22.65%
50.71%	28.95%
28.58%	19.63%
5.96%	3.77%
3.84%	0.38%
21.70%	16.17%
71.28%	37.64%
23.49%	17.12%
20.25%	15.36%
44.01%	26.26%
31.27%	20.87%
40.86%	24.98%
26.54%	18.65%
25.29%	18.04%
28.51%	19.60%
55.40%	30.84%
31.57%	21.00%
16.30%	12.98%
24.37%	17.57%
8.46%	6.70%
77.08%	40.52%

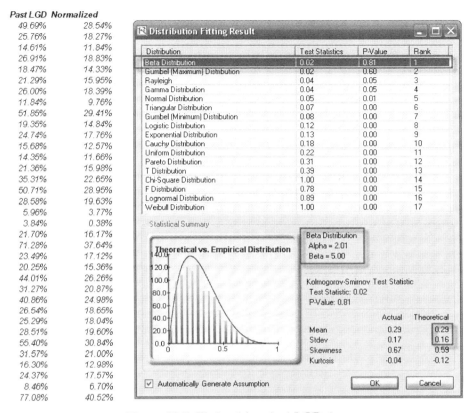

Figure 92.7: Fitting historical LGD data

Then, using the *Distribution Analysis* tool in Risk Simulator, obtain the theoretical mean and standard deviation of the fitted distribution (Figure 92.8). Then transform the LGD variable using the *MTNormalTransform* function in the Modeling Toolkit software. For instance, the value 49.69% will be transformed and normalized to 28.54%. Using this newly transformed dataset, you can run some nonlinear econometric models to determine LGD.

For instance, a partial list of independent variables that might be significant for a bank, in terms of determining and forecast the LGD value, might include:

- Debt to capital ratio
- Profit margin
- Revenue
- Current assets to current liabilities
- Risk rating at default and one year before default
- Industry
- Authorized balance at default
- Collateral value
- Facility type
- Tightness of covenant
- Seniority of debt
- Operating income to sales ratio (and other efficiency ratios)
- Total asset, total net worth, total liabilities

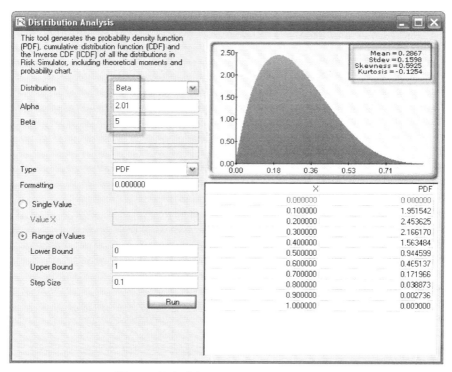

Figure 92.8: Distributional analysis tool

Economic Capital and Value at Risk

Economic capital is critical to a bank as it links a bank's earnings and returns to risks that are specific to business line or business opportunity. In addition, these economic capital measurements can be aggregated into a portfolio of holdings. Value at Risk (VaR) is used in trying to understand how the entire organization is affected by the various risks of each holding as aggregated into a portfolio, after accounting for cross-correlations among various holdings. VaR measures the maximum possible loss given some predefined probability level (e.g., 99.90%) over some holding period or time horizon (e.g., 10 days). Senior management at the bank usually selects the probability or confidence interval, which is typically a decision made by senior management at the bank, and reflects the board's risk appetite. Stated another way, we can define the probability level as the bank's desired probability of surviving per year. In addition, the holding period is usually chosen such that it coincides with the time period it takes to liquidate a loss position.

VaR can be computed several ways. Two main families of approaches exist: structural closed-form models and Monte Carlo risk simulation approaches. We showcase both methods in this chapter, starting with the structural models.

The second and much more powerful approach is Monte Carlo risk simulation. Instead of simply correlating individual business lines or assets, entire probability distributions can be correlated using mathematical copulas and simulation algorithms, by using Risk Simulator. In addition, tens to hundreds of thousands of scenarios can be generated using simulation, providing a very powerful stress-testing mechanism for valuing VaR. Distributional fitting methods are applied to reduce the thousands of data points into their appropriate probability distributions, allowing their modeling to be handled with greater ease.

Illustrative Example: Structural VaR Models

This first VaR example model used is *Value at Risk – Static Covariance Method*, accessible through **Modeling Toolkit | Value at Risk | Static Covariance Method**. This model is used to compute the portfolio's VaR at a given percentile for a specific holding period, after accounting for the cross-correlation effects between the assets (Figure 92.9). The daily volatility is the annualized volatility divided by the square root of trading days per year. Typically, positive correlations tend to carry a higher VaR compared to zero correlation asset mixes, whereas negative correlations reduce the total risk of the portfolio through the diversification effect (Figures 92.9 and 92.10). The approach used is a portfolio VaR with correlated inputs, where the portfolio has multiple asset holdings with different amounts and volatilities. Each asset is also correlated to each other. The covariance or correlation structural model is used to compute the VaR given a holding period or horizon and percentile value (typically 10 days at 99% confidence). Of course, the example illustrates only a few assets or business lines or credit lines for simplicity's sake. Nonetheless, using the VaR function (*MTVaRCorrelationMethod*) in the Modeling Toolkit, many more lines, assets, or businesses can be modeled.

VALUE AT RISK (VARIANCE-COVARIANCE METHOD)

Asset Allocation	Amount	Daily Volatility
Asset A	$1,000,000.00	1.20%
Asset B	$2,000,000.00	2.00%
Asset C	$3,000,000.00	1.89%
Asset D	$4,000,000.00	3.25%
Asset E	$5,000,000.00	4.20%

Correlation Matrix	Asset A	Asset B	Asset C	Asset D	Asset E
Asset A	1.0000	0.1000	0.1000	0.1000	0.1000
Asset B	0.1000	1.0000	0.1000	0.1000	0.1000
Asset C	0.1000	0.1000	1.0000	0.1000	0.1000
Asset D	0.1000	0.1000	0.1000	1.0000	0.1000
Asset E	0.1000	0.1000	0.1000	0.1000	1.0000

Horizon (Days)	10
Percentile	99.00%

Value at Risk (Daily)	$655,915.30
Value at Risk (Horizon)	$2,074,186.30

Daily Value at Risk (Positive Correlations)	$2,074,186.30
Daily Value at Risk (Zero Correlations)	$1,889,345.26
Daily Value at Risk (Negative Correlations)	$1,684,340.28

Figure 92.9: Computing Value at Risk using the structural covariance method

Correlation Matrix	Asset A	Asset B	Asset C	Asset D	Asset E
Asset A	1.0000	0.1000	0.1000	0.1000	0.1000
Asset B	0.1000	1.0000	0.1000	0.1000	0.1000
Asset C	0.1000	0.1000	1.0000	0.1000	0.1000
Asset D	0.1000	0.1000	0.1000	1.0000	0.1000
Asset E	0.1000	0.1000	0.1000	0.1000	1.0000

Correlation Matrix	Asset A	Asset B	Asset C	Asset D	Asset E
Asset A	1.0000	0.0000	0.0000	0.0000	0.0000
Asset B	0.0000	1.0000	0.0000	0.0000	0.0000
Asset C	0.0000	0.0000	1.0000	0.0000	0.0000
Asset D	0.0000	0.0000	0.0000	1.0000	0.0000
Asset E	0.0000	0.0000	0.0000	0.0000	1.0000

Correlation Matrix	Asset A	Asset B	Asset C	Asset D	Asset E
Asset A	1.0000	-0.1000	-0.1000	-0.1000	-0.1000
Asset B	-0.1000	1.0000	-0.1000	-0.1000	-0.1000
Asset C	-0.1000	-0.1000	1.0000	-0.1000	-0.1000
Asset D	-0.1000	-0.1000	-0.1000	1.0000	-0.1000
Asset E	-0.1000	-0.1000	-0.1000	-0.1000	1.0000

Figure 92.10: Different correlation levels

Illustrative Example: VaR Models Using Monte Carlo Risk Simulation

The model used is *Value at Risk – Portfolio Operational and Credit Risk VaR Capital Adequacy* and is accessible through **Modeling Toolkit | Value at Risk | Portfolio Operational and Credit Risk VaR Capital Adequacy**. This model shows how operational risk and credit risk parameters are fitted to statistical distributions and their resulting distributions are modeled in a portfolio of liabilities to determine the VaR (99.50th percentile certainty) for the capital requirement under Basel II/III requirements. It is assumed that the historical data of the operational risk impacts (*Historical Data* worksheet) are obtained through econometric modeling of the Key Risk Indicators.

The *Distributional Fitting Report* worksheet is a result of running a distributional fitting routine in Risk Simulator to obtain the appropriate distribution for the operational risk parameter. Using the resulting distributional parameter, we model each liability's capital requirements within an entire portfolio. Correlations can also be inputted if required, between pairs of liabilities or business units. The resulting Monte Carlo simulation results show the VaR capital requirements.

Note that an appropriate empirically based historical VaR cannot be obtained if distributional fitting and risk-based simulations were not first run. The VaR will be obtained only by running simulations. To perform distributional fitting, follow these steps:

1. In the *Historical Data* worksheet (Figure 92.11), select the data area (cells **C5:L104**) and click on **Risk Simulator | Analytical Tools | Distributional Fitting (Single Variable)**.

2. Browse through the fitted distributions and select the best-fitting distribution (in this case, the exponential distribution in Figure 92.12) and click **OK**.

Basel II - Credit Risk and Capital Requirement (Portfolio-Based)

This model applies the Basel II requirements on capital adequacy and modeling the operational risk of probability of default on 100 loans as well as the loss given default. These values are fitted based on the bank's historical loss data (Historical Data and Distributional Fitting Report sheets) using Risk Simulator. Then, the relevant historical simulation assumptions are set in this model (Credit Risk sheet) and a Monte Carlo risk-based simulation was run in Risk Simulator to determine the expected capital required and 99.50% Value at Risk (VaR). A simulation has to be run in order to determine the VaR.

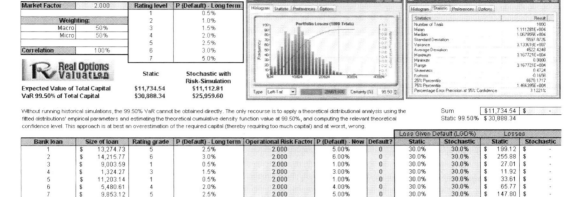

Market Factor	2.000

Weighting:	
Macro	50%
Micro	50%

Correlation	100%

Rating level	P (Default) - Long term
1	0.5%
2	1.0%
3	1.5%
4	2.0%
5	2.5%
6	3.0%
7	5.0%

	Static	Stochastic with Risk-Simulation
Expected Value of Total Capital	$11,734.54	$11,112.81
VaR 99.50% of Total Capital	$30,888.34	$25,959.60

Without running historical simulations, the 99.50% VaR cannot be obtained directly. The only recourse is to apply a theoretical distributional analysis using the fitted distributions' empirical parameters and estimating the theoretical cumulative density function value at 99.50%, and computing the relevant theoretical confidence level. This approach is at best an overestimation of the required capital (thereby requiring too much capital) and at worst, wrong.

Sum	$11,734.54	$ -
Static 99.50%	$30,888.34	

Bank loan	Size of loan	Rating grade	P (Default) - Long term	Operational Risk Factor	P (Default) - Now	Default?	Loss Given Default (LGD%) Static	Loss Given Default (LGD%) Stochastic	Losses Static	Losses Stochastic
1	$ 13,274.73	5	2.5%	2.000	5.00%	0	30.0%	30.0%	$ 199.12	$ -
2	$ 14,215.77	6	3.0%	2.000	6.00%	0	30.0%	30.0%	$ 255.88	$ -
3	$ 9,003.59	1	0.5%	2.000	1.00%	0	30.0%	30.0%	$ 27.01	$ -
4	$ 1,324.27	3	1.5%	2.000	3.00%	0	30.0%	30.0%	$ 11.92	$ -
5	$ 11,203.14	1	0.5%	2.000	1.00%	0	30.0%	30.0%	$ 33.61	$ -
6	$ 5,480.61	4	2.0%	2.000	4.00%	0	30.0%	30.0%	$ 65.77	$ -
7	$ 9,853.12	5	2.5%	2.000	5.00%	0	30.0%	30.0%	$ 147.80	$ -
8	$ 12,356.22	3	1.5%	2.000	3.00%	0	30.0%	30.0%	$ 111.21	$ -
9	$ 8,255.80	4	2.0%	2.000	4.00%	0	30.0%	30.0%	$ 99.07	$ -
10	$ 1,662.99	2	1.0%	2.000	2.00%	0	30.0%	30.0%	$ 9.98	$ -
11	$ 7,175.82	3	1.5%	2.000	3.00%	0	30.0%	30.0%	$ 64.58	$ -

Figure 92.11: Sample historical bank loans

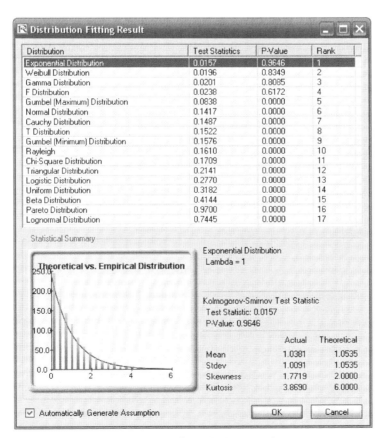

Distribution	Test Statistics	P-Value	Rank
Exponential Distribution	0.0157	0.9646	1
Weibull Distribution	0.0196	0.8349	2
Gamma Distribution	0.0201	0.8085	3
F Distribution	0.0238	0.6172	4
Gumbel (Maximum) Distribution	0.0838	0.0000	5
Normal Distribution	0.1417	0.0000	6
Cauchy Distribution	0.1487	0.0000	7
T Distribution	0.1522	0.0000	8
Gumbel (Minimum) Distribution	0.1576	0.0000	9
Rayleigh	0.1610	0.0000	10
Chi-Square Distribution	0.1709	0.0000	11
Triangular Distribution	0.2141	0.0000	12
Logistic Distribution	0.2770	0.0000	13
Uniform Distribution	0.3182	0.0000	14
Beta Distribution	0.4144	0.0000	15
Pareto Distribution	0.9700	0.0000	16
Lognormal Distribution	0.7445	0.0000	17

Statistical Summary

Theoretical vs. Empirical Distribution

Exponential Distribution
Lambda = 1

Kolmogorov-Smirnov Test Statistic
Test Statistic: 0.0157
P-Value: 0.9646

	Actual	Theoretical
Mean	1.0381	1.0535
Stdev	1.0091	1.0535
Skewness	1.7719	2.0000
Kurtosis	3.8690	6.0000

Figure 92.12: Data fitting results

3. You may now set the assumptions on the *Operational Risk Factors* with the exponential distribution (fitted results show *Lambda* = 1) in the *Credit Risk* worksheet. Note that the assumptions have already been set for you in advance. You may set the assumption by going to cell **F27** and clicking on **Risk Simulator | Set Input Assumption**, selecting **Exponential** distribution and entering **1** for the *Lambda* value and clicking **OK**. Continue this process for the remaining cells in column F, or simply perform a **Risk Simulator Copy** and **Risk Simulator Paste** on the remaining cells.

    a. Note that since the cells in column F have assumptions set, you will first have to clear them if you wish to reset and copy/paste parameters. You can do so by first selecting cells **F28:F126** and clicking on the **Remove Parameter** icon or select **Risk Simulator | Remove Parameter**.

    b. Then select cell **F27**, click on the **Risk Simulator Copy** icon or select **Risk Simulator | Copy Parameter**, and then select cells **F28:F126** and click on the **Risk Simulator Paste** icon or select **Risk Simulator | Paste Parameter**.

4. Next you can get assumptions can be set such as the probability of default using the *Bernoulli Distribution* (column H) and *Loss Given Default* (column J). Repeat the procedure in Step 3 if you wish to reset the assumptions.

5. Run the simulation by clicking on the **RUN** icon or clicking on **Risk Simulator | Run Simulation**.

6. Obtain the Value at Risk by going to the forecast chart once the simulation is done running and selecting **Left-Tail** and typing in **99.50**. Hit **TAB** on the keyboard to enter the confidence value and obtain the VaR of $25,959 (Figure 92.13).

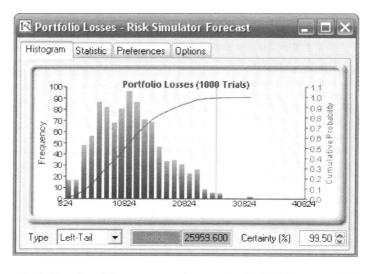

Figure 92.13: Simulated forecast results and the 99.50% Value at Risk value

222

Figure 92.13: Simulated forecast results and the 99.50% Value at Risk value
(continued)

Another example on VaR computation is shown next, where the model *Value at Risk – Right Tail Capital Requirements* is used, available through **Modeling Toolkit | Value at Risk | Right Tail Capital Requirements**.

This model shows the capital requirements per Basel II/III requirements (99.95th percentile capital adequacy based on a specific holding period's VaR). Without running risk-based historical and Monte Carlo simulation using Risk Simulator, the required capital is $37.01M (Figure 92.14) as compared to only $14.00M that is required using a correlated simulation (Figure 92.15). This is due to the cross-correlations between assets and business lines, and can only be modeled only using Risk Simulator. This lower VaR is preferred as banks can be required to hold less required capital and can reinvest the remaining capital in various profitable ventures, thereby generating higher profits.

TAIL VALUE AT RISK MODEL (BASEL II REQUIREMENT)

Line of Business	Mean Required Capital	99.95th Percentile	Capital Required	Allocation Weights	Minimum Allowed	Maximum Allowed			Correlation Matrix									
									1	2	3	4	5	6	7	8	9	10
Business 1	$10.50	$36.52	$26.01	10.00%	5.00%	15.00%	3.48	1										
Business 2	$11.12	$47.52	$36.39	10.00%	5.00%	15.00%	4.27	2	-0.20									
Business 3	$11.77	$48.99	$37.22	10.00%	5.00%	15.00%	4.16	3	-0.13	0.35								
Business 4	$10.77	$37.34	$26.56	10.00%	5.00%	15.00%	3.47	4	-0.05	0.01	0.00							
Business 5	$13.49	$49.52	$36.03	10.00%	5.00%	15.00%	3.67	5	0.23	0.50	0.15	0.00						
Business 6	$14.24	$55.59	$41.35	10.00%	5.00%	15.00%	3.91	6	0.00	0.00	-0.15	0.00	0.03					
Business 7	$15.60	$60.24	$44.64	10.00%	5.00%	15.00%	3.86	7	0.25	0.00	-0.26	0.01	0.10	-0.10				
Business 8	$14.95	$64.69	$49.74	10.00%	5.00%	15.00%	4.33	8	0.36	-0.25	-0.60	-0.30	0.00	0.00	-0.15			
Business 9	$14.15	$61.02	$46.87	10.00%	5.00%	15.00%	4.31	9	-0.01	-0.20	0.16	0.04	-0.01	0.01	0.00	0.00		
Business 10	$10.08	$35.37	$25.29	10.00%	5.00%	15.00%	3.51											
Portfolio Total	$12.67	$49.68	$37.01	100.00%														
Total Capital Required			$14.00															

Figure 92.14: Right-tail VaR model

To run the model, follow these steps:

1. Click on **Risk Simulator | Run Simulation.** If you had other models open, make sure you first click on **Risk Simulator | Change Profile**, and select the *Tail VaR* profile before starting.

2. When the simulation is complete, select **Left-Tail** in the forecast chart and enter in **99.95** in the *Certainty* box and hit **TAB** on the keyboard to obtain the value of $14.00M Value at Risk for this correlated simulation.

3. Note that the assumptions have already been set for you in advance in the model in cells **C6:C15**. However, you may set them again by going to cell **C6** and clicking on **Risk Simulator | Set Input Assumption**, selecting your distribution of choice or using the default *Normal Distribution* or performing a distributional fitting on historical data, then clicking **OK**. Continue this process for the remaining cells in column C. You may also decide to first *Remove Parameters* of these cells in column C and setting your own distributions. Further, correlations can be set manually when assumptions are set (Figure 92.16) or by going to **Risk Simulator | Edit Correlations** (Figure 92.17) after all the assumptions are set.

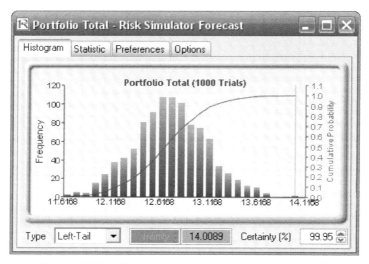

Figure 92.15: Simulated results of the portfolio VaR

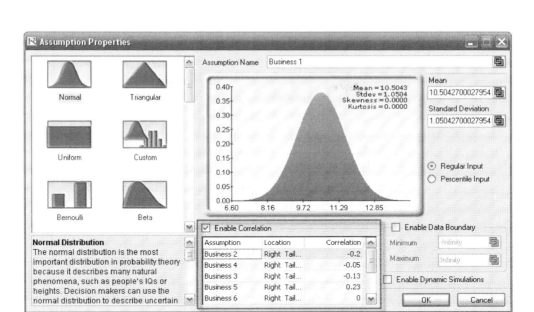

Figure 92.16: Setting correlations one at a time

Correlation Editor

Variables	Business 1	Business 2	Business 4	Business 3
Business 1	1.0000	-0.2000	-0.0500	-0.1300
Business 2	-0.2000	1.0000	0.0100	0.3500
Business 4	-0.0500	0.0100	1.0000	0.0000
Business 3	-0.1300	0.3500	0.0000	1.0000
Business 5	0.2300	0.5000	0.0000	0.1500
Business 6	0.0000	0.0000	-0.1500	-0.1500
Business 7	0.2500	0.0000	0.0100	-0.2600
Business 8	0.3600	-0.2500	-0.3000	-0.6000
Business 9	-0.0700	-0.2000	0.0400	0.1600

Figure 92.17: Setting correlations using the correlation matrix routine

If risk simulation was not run, the VaR or economic capital required would have been $37M, as opposed to only $14M. All cross-correlations between business lines have been modeled, as are stress and scenario tests, and thousands and thousands of possible iterations are run. Individual risks are now aggregated into a cumulative portfolio level VaR.

Efficient Portfolio Allocation and Economic Capital VaR

As a side note, by performing portfolio optimization, a portfolio's VaR actually can be reduced. We start by first introducing the concept of stochastic portfolio optimization through an illustrative hands-on example. Then, using this portfolio optimization technique, we apply it to four business lines or assets to compute the VaR or an un-optimized versus an optimized portfolio of assets, and see the difference in computed VaR. You will note that at the end, the optimized portfolio bears less risk and has a lower required economic capital.

Illustrative Example: Stochastic Portfolio Optimization

The optimization model used to illustrate the concepts of stochastic portfolio optimization is *Optimization – Stochastic Portfolio Allocation* and can be accessed via **Modeling Toolkit | Optimization | Stochastic Portfolio Allocation**. This model shows four asset classes with different risk and return characteristics. The idea here is to find the best portfolio allocation such that the portfolio's bang for the buck, or returns to risk ratio, is maximized. That is, in order to allocate 100% of an individual's investment among several different asset classes (e.g., different types of mutual funds or investment styles: growth, value, aggressive growth, income, global, index, contrarian, momentum, etc.), an optimization is used. This model is different from others in that there exist several simulation assumptions (risk and return values for each asset), as seen in Figure 92.18.

In other words, a simulation is first run, then optimization is executed, and the entire process is repeated multiple times to obtain distributions of each decision variable. The entire analysis can be automated using Stochastic Optimization.

In order to run an optimization, several key specifications on the model have to be identified first:

Objective: Maximize Return to Risk Ratio (C12)

Decision Variables: Allocation Weights (E6:E9)

Restrictions on Decision Variables: Minimum and Maximum Required (F6:G9)

Constraints: Portfolio Total Allocation Weights 100% (E11 is set to 100%)

Simulation Assumptions: Return and Risk Values (C6:D9)

The model shows the various asset classes. Each asset class has its own set of annualized returns and annualized volatilities. These return and risk measures are annualized values such that they can be compared consistently across different asset classes. Returns are computed using the geometric average of the relative returns, while the risks are computed using the logarithmic relative stock returns approach.

Column E, Allocation Weights, holds the decision variables, which are the variables that need to be tweaked and tested such that the total weight is constrained at 100% (cell E11). Typically, to start the optimization, we will set these cells to a uniform value, where in this case, cells E6 to E9 are set at 25% each. In addition, each decision variable may have specific restrictions in its allowed range. In this example, the lower and upper allocations allowed are 10% and 40%, as seen in columns F and G. This setting means that each asset class can have its own allocation boundaries.

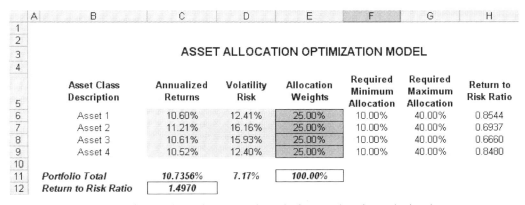

Figure 92.18: Asset allocation model ready for stochastic optimization

Column H shows the return to risk ratio, which is simply the return percentage divided by the risk percentage, where the higher this value, the higher the bang for the buck. The remaining sections of the model show the individual asset class rankings by returns, risk, return to risk ratio, and allocation. In other words, these rankings show at a glance which asset class has the lowest risk, or the highest return, and so forth.

Running an Optimization

To run this model, simply click on **Risk Simulator | Optimization | Run Optimization**. Alternatively, and for practice, you can set up the model using the following approach:

1. Start a new profile (**Risk Simulator | New Profile**).

2. For stochastic optimization, set distributional assumptions on the risk and returns for each asset class. That is, select cell **C6** and set an assumption (**Risk Simulator | Set Input Assumption**) and make your own assumption as required. Repeat for cells **C7** to **D9**.

3. Select cell **E6**, and define the decision variable (**Risk Simulator | Optimization | Decision Variables** or click on the **Define Decision** icon) and make it a **Continuous Variable** and then link the decision variable's name and minimum/maximum required to the relevant cells (**B6, F6, G6**).

4. Then use the **Risk Simulator Copy** on cell **E6**, select cells **E7 to E9**, and use **Risk Simulator's Paste** (**Risk Simulator | Copy Parameter** and **Risk Simulator | Paste Parameter** or use the Risk Simulator copy and paste icons). Make sure you do not use Excel's regular copy and paste functions.

5. Next, set up the optimization's constraints by selecting **Risk Simulator | Optimization | Constraints**, selecting **ADD**, and selecting the cell **E11**, and making it equal **100%** (total allocation, and do not forget the % sign).

6. Select cell **C12**, the objective to be maximized, and make it the objective: **Risk Simulator | Optimization | Set Objective** or click on the **O** icon.

7. Run the simulation by going to **Risk Simulator | Optimization | Run Optimization**. Review the different tabs to make sure that all the required inputs in steps 2 and 3 are correct. Select **Stochastic Optimization** and let it run for 500 trials repeated 20 times (Figure 92.19 illustrates these setup steps).

You may also try other optimization routines where:

Static Optimization is an optimization that is run on a static model, where no simulations are run. This optimization type is applicable when the model is assumed to be known and no uncertainties exist. Also, a static optimization can be run first to determine the optimal portfolio and its corresponding optimal allocation of decision variables before more advanced optimization procedures are applied. For instance, before running a stochastic optimization problem, a static optimization is run first to determine if there exist solutions to the optimization problem before a more protracted analysis is performed.

Dynamic Optimization is applied when Monte Carlo simulation is used together with optimization. Another name for such a procedure is Simulation-Optimization. In other words, a simulation is run for N trials, and then an optimization process is run for M iterations until the optimal results are obtained or an infeasible set is found. That is, using Risk Simulator's *Optimization* module, you can choose which forecast and assumption statistics to use and replace in the model after the simulation is run. Then, these forecast statistics can be applied in the optimization process. This approach is useful when you have a large model with many interacting assumptions and forecasts, and when some of the forecast statistics are required in the optimization.

Stochastic Optimization is similar to the dynamic optimization procedure except that the entire dynamic optimization process is repeated T times. The results will be a forecast chart of each decision variable with T values. In other words, a simulation is run and the forecast or assumption statistics are used in the optimization model to find the optimal allocation of decision variables. Then another simulation is run, generating different forecast statistics, and these new updated values are then optimized, and so forth. Hence, each of the final decision variables will have its own forecast chart, indicating the range of the optimal decision variables. For instance, instead of obtaining single-point estimates in the dynamic optimization procedure, you can now obtain a distribution of the decision variables, and, hence, a range of optimal values for each decision variable, also known as a stochastic optimization.

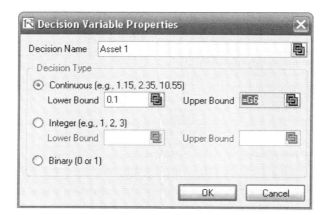

Figure 92.19: Setting up the stochastic optimization problem

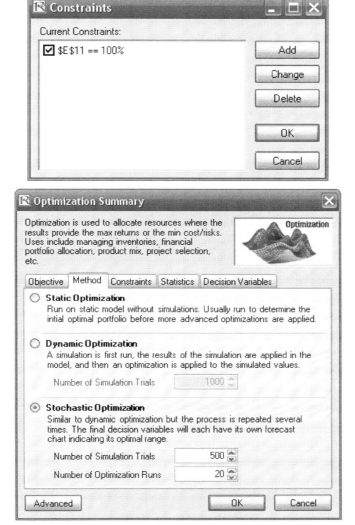

Figure 92.19: Setting up the stochastic optimization problem *(continued)*

Viewing and Interpreting Forecast Results

Stochastic optimization is performed when a simulation is first run and then the optimization is run. Then the whole analysis is repeated multiple times. The result is a distribution of each decision variable, rather than a single-point estimate (Figure 92.20). This means that instead of saying you should invest 30.57% in Asset 1, the optimal decision is to invest between 30.10% and 30.99% as long as the total portfolio sums to 100%. This way the optimization results provide management or decision makers a range of flexibility in the optimal decisions. Refer to Chapter 11 of *Modeling Risk: Applying Monte Carlo Simulation, Real Options Analysis, Forecasting, and Optimization* by Dr. Johnathan Mun for more detailed explanations about this model, the different optimization techniques, and an interpretation of the results. Chapter 11's appendix also details how the risk and return values are computed.

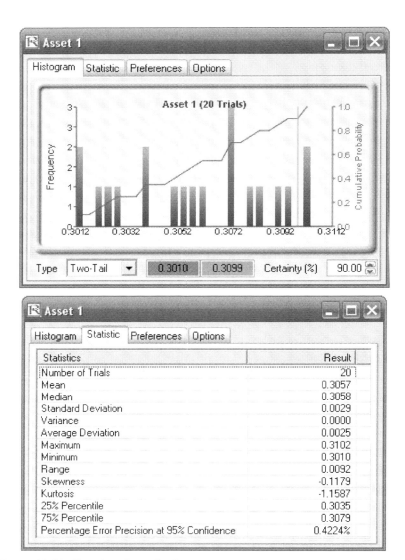

Figure 92.20: Simulated results from the stochastic optimization approach

Illustrative Example: Portfolio Optimization and Portfolio VaR

Now that we understand the concepts of optimized portfolios, let us see what the effects are on computed economic capital through the use of a correlated portfolio VaR. This model uses Monte Carlo simulation and optimization routines in Risk Simulator to minimize the Value at Risk of a portfolio of assets (Figure 92.21). The file used is *Value at Risk – Optimized and Simulated Portfolio VaR,* which is accessible via **Modeling Toolkit | Value at Risk | Optimized and Simulated Portfolio VaR**. In this example, we intentionally used only four asset classes to illustrate the effects of an optimized portfolio. In real life, we can extend this to cover a multitude of asset classes and business lines. Here we illustrate the use of a left-tail VaR, as opposed to a right-tail VaR, but the concepts are similar.

First, simulation is used to determine the 90% left-tail VaR. The 90% left-tail probability means that there is a 10% chance that losses will exceed this VaR for a specified holding period. With an equal allocation of 25% across the four asset classes, the VaR is determined using simulation (Figure 92.21). The annualized returns are uncertain and hence simulated. The VaR is then read off the forecast chart. Then optimization is run to find the best portfolio subject to the 100% allocation across the four projects that will maximize the portfolio's bang for the buck (returns to risk ratio). The resulting optimized portfolio is then simulated once again, and the new VaR is obtained (Figure 92.22). The VaR of this optimized portfolio is a lot less than the not-optimized portfolio.

VALUE AT RISK WITH ASSET ALLOCATION OPTIMIZATION MODEL

Asset Class Description	Annualized Returns	Volatility Risk	Allocation Weights	Required Minimum Allocation	Required Maximum Allocation
S&P 500	7.10%	9.80%	10.00%	10.00%	40.00%
Small Cap	9.51%	14.35%	27.30%	10.00%	40.00%
High Yield	15.90%	22.50%	22.70%	10.00%	40.00%
Govt Bonds	4.50%	7.25%	40.00%	10.00%	40.00%
		Total Weight:	100.00%		

Correlation Matrix	S&P 500	Small Cap	High Yield	Govt Bonds
S&P 500	1.0000	0.7400	0.6500	0.5500
Small Cap	0.7400	1.0000	0.4200	0.3100
High Yield	0.6500	0.4200	1.0000	0.2300
Govt Bonds	0.5500	0.3100	0.2300	1.0000

Covariance Matrix	S&P 500	Small Cap	High Yield	Govt Bonds
S&P 500	0.0096	0.0104	0.0143	0.0039
Small Cap	0.0104	0.0206	0.0136	0.0032
High Yield	0.0143	0.0136	0.0506	0.0038
Govt Bonds	0.0039	0.0032	0.0038	0.0053

Starting Value	$1,000,000.00
Term (Years)	5.00

Annualized Return	8.72%	Profit/Loss	$87,151.94
Portfolio Risk	9.84%	Return to Risk Ratio	88.59%
Ending Value	$1,087,151.94		

Specifications of the optimization model:

Objective:	*Maximize Return to Risk Ratio (E28)*
Decision Variables:	*Allocation Weights (E6:E9)*
Restrictions on Decision Variables:	*Minimum and Maximum Required (F6:G9)*
Constraints:	*Portfolio Total Allocation Weights 100% (E10 is set to 100%)*

Figure 92.21: Computing Value at Risk (VaR) with simulation

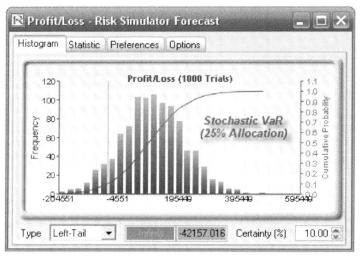

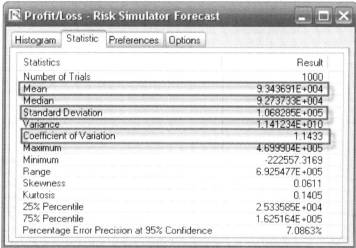

Figure 92.22: Non-optimized Value at Risk

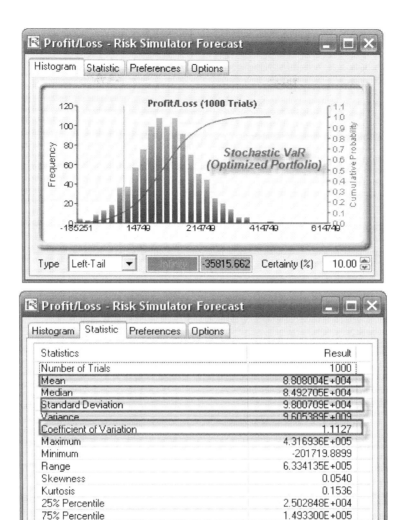

Figure 92.23: Optimal portfolio's Value at Risk through optimization and simulation

Hurdle Rates and Required Rate of Return

Another related item in the discussion of risk in the context of Basel II/III Accords is the issue of hurdle rates, or the required rate of return on investment that is sufficient to justify the amount of risk undertaken in the portfolio. There is a nice theoretical connection between uncertainty and volatility whereby the discount rate of a specific risk portfolio can be obtained. In a financial model, the old axiom of *high risk, high return* is seen through the use of a discount rate. That is, the higher the risk of a project, the higher the discount rate should be to risk-adjust this riskier project so that all projects are comparable.

There are two methods for computing the hurdle rate. The first is an internal model, where the VaR of the portfolio is computed first. This economic capital is then compared to the market risk premium. That is, we have

$$HurdleRate = \frac{MarketReturn - RiskfreeReturn}{RiskCapital}$$

That is, assuming that a similar set of comparable investments are obtained in the market, based on tradable assets, the market return is obtained. Using the bank's internal cash flow models, all future cash flows can be discounted at the risk-free rate in order to determine the risk-free return. Finally, the difference is then divided into the VaR risk capital to determine the required hurdle rate. This concept is very similar to the capital asset pricing model (CAPM), which often is used to compute the appropriate discount rate for a discounted cash flow model (weighted average cost of capital, hurdle rates, multiple asset pricing models, and arbitrage pricing models are the other alternatives but are based on similar principles). The second approach is the use of the CAPM to determine the hurdle rate.

93. Operational Risk – Queuing Models at Bank Branches

File Name: Operational – Queuing Models at Bank Branches

Location: Modeling Toolkit | Operational | Queuing Models at Bank Branches

Brief Description: Illustrates how to set up a queuing model, run a Monte Carlo simulation on a queuing model, and interpret the results of a queuing model

Requirements: Modeling Toolkit, Risk Simulator

Modeling Toolkit Functions Used: MTQueuingSCProbNoCustomer, MTQueuingSCAveCustomersWaiting, MTQueuingSCAveCustomersinSystem, MTQueuingSCAveTimeWaiting, MTQueuingSCAveTimeinSystem, MTQueuingSCProbHaveToWait, MTQueuingSCAProbNoCustomer, MTQueuingSCAAveCustomersWaiting, MTQueuingSCAAveCustomersinSystem, MTQueuingSCAAveTimeWaiting, MTQueuingSCAAveTimeinSystem, MTQueuingSCAProbHaveToWait, MTQueuingMCProbNoCustomer, MTQueuingMCAveCustomersWaiting, MTQueuingMCAveCustomersinSystem, MTQueuingMCAveTimeWaiting, MTQueuingMCAveTimeinSystem, MTQueuingMCProbHaveToWait, MTQueuingMGKProbBusy, MTQueuingMGKAveCustomersinSystem

Model Background

Think of how queuing models work; consider a customer service call center, a bank teller's waiting line, or the waiting line at an ATM machine. The queue is the line of people waiting to get served. Typically, the arrival rates of patrons follow a Poisson distribution on a per-period basis, per hour or per day, and so on. The number of checkout counters open is the number of channels in a queuing model. The rate at which servers are able to serve patrons typically follows an exponential distribution. The questions that a queuing model answers are how many servers or channels there should be if we do not want patrons to wait more than X minutes, or, if we have Y servers, what the probability is that a patron arriving will have to wait and what the average wait time is. These types of models are extremely powerful when coupled with simulation, where the arrival rates and service times are variable and simulated. Imagine applications from staffing call centers, customer service lines, and checkout counters to how many hospital beds should exist in a hospital per type of diagnostic-related group and the like.

These models are based on operations research queuing models. The single-channel queuing model and the multiple-channel queuing model assume a Poisson distribution of arrival rates and exponential distribution of service times, with the only difference between them being the number of channels. Both the *MG1 Single Arbitrary* model and *MGK Blocked Queuing* model assume the same Poisson distribution on arrival rates but do not rely on the exponential distribution for service times. The two main differences between these two general-distribution (G) models are that the MGK uses multiple channels as compared to the single-channel MG1, as well as the fact that the MG1 model assumes the possibility of waiting in line while the MGK model assumes customers will be turned away if the channels are loaded when they arrive.

Running a Monte Carlo Simulation

In all of these models, the results are closed form. Hence, only the input assumptions (arrival rates and service rates) are uncertain and should be simulated. The forecast results should be any of the outputs of interest. See Figures 93.1 and 93.2.

MG1 Single Channel Arbitrary Queuing Model

This model assumes a Poisson arrival rate with unknown distribution of service times

Mean Arrival Rate Per Period (λ)	0.35
Mean Service Rate Per Channel Per Period (μ)	0.5
Standard Deviation of Service Rate (σ)	1.2
Cost of waiting	$7,000.00
Adding the single channel	$5,000.00
Total cost per time period	$17,674.67
Probability that no customers are in the system, Po	**30.00%**
Average number of customers in the waiting line, Lq	**1.1107**
Average number of customers in the system, L	**1.8107**
Average time a customer spends in the waiting line, Wq	**3.1733**
Average time a customer spends in the system, W	**5.1733**
Probability an arriving customer has to wait, Pw	**70.00%**

Figure 93.1: Single channel queuing model

Multiple Channel Queuing Model

This model assumes a Poisson arrival rate with Exponential distribution of service times

Number of Channels (k)	2
Mean Arrival Rate Per Period (λ)	0.75
Mean Service Rate Per Channel Per Period (μ)	1

Cost of waiting	$7,000.00
Adding the single channel	$5,000.00
Total cost per time period	16109.09091

Probability that no customers are in the system, Po	**45.45%**
Average number of customers in the waiting line, Lq	**0.1227**
Average number of customers in the system, L	**0.8727**
Average time a customer spends in the waiting line, Wq	**0.1636**
Average time a customer spends in the system, W	**1.1636**
Probability an arriving customer has to wait, Pw	**20.45%**

Figure 93.2: Multiple channel queuing model

94. Optimization – Continuous Portfolio Allocation

File Name: Optimization – Continuous Portfolio Allocation

Location: Modeling Toolkit | Optimization | Continuous Portfolio Allocation

Brief Description: Illustrates how to run an optimization on continuous decision variables, and viewing and interpreting optimization results

Requirements: Modeling Toolkit, Risk Simulator

This model shows 10 asset classes with different risk and return characteristics. The idea here is to find the best portfolio allocation such that the portfolio's bang for the buck or returns to risk ratio is maximized; that is, to allocate 100% of an individual's investment portfolio among several different asset classes (e.g., different types of mutual funds or investment styles: growth, value, aggressive growth, income, global, index, contrarian, momentum, etc.). In order to run an optimization, several key specifications on the model have to first be identified:

Objective: Maximize Return to Risk Ratio (C18)

Decision Variables: Allocation Weights (E6:E15)

Restrictions on Decision Variables: Minimum and Maximum Required (F6:G15)

Constraints: Portfolio Total Allocation Weights 100% (E17 is set to 100%)

The model shows the 10 asset classes. Each asset class has its own set of annualized returns and risks, measured by annualized volatilities (Figure 94.1). These return and risk measures are annualized values such that they can be consistently compared across different asset classes. Returns are computed using the geometric average of the relative returns, while the risks are computed using the annualized standard deviation of the logarithmic relative historical stock returns approach.

Column E, Allocation Weights, holds the decision variables, which are the variables that need to be tweaked and tested such that the total weight is constrained at 100% (cell E17). Typically, to start the optimization, we will set these cells to a uniform value; in this case, cells E6 to E15 are set at 10% each. In addition, each decision variable may have specific restrictions in its allowed range. In this example, the lower and upper allocations allowed are 5% and 35%, as seen in columns F and G. This setting means that each asset class may have its own allocation boundaries (Figure 94.1).

Next, column H shows the return to risk ratio for each asset class, which is simply the return percentage divided by the risk percentage, where the higher this value, the higher the bang for the buck. The remaining sections of the model show the individual asset class rankings by returns, risk, return to risk ratio, and allocation. In other words, these rankings show at a glance which asset class has the lowest risk or the highest return, and so forth.

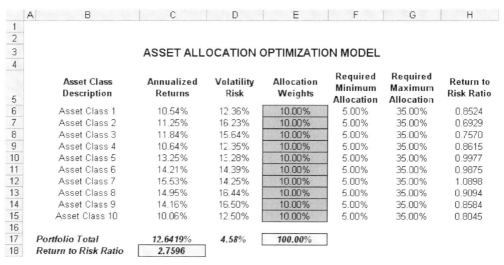

	Asset Class Description	Annualized Returns	Volatility Risk	Allocation Weights	Required Minimum Allocation	Required Maximum Allocation	Return to Risk Ratio
			ASSET ALLOCATION OPTIMIZATION MODEL				
6	Asset Class 1	10.54%	12.36%	10.00%	5.00%	35.00%	0.8524
7	Asset Class 2	11.25%	16.23%	10.00%	5.00%	35.00%	0.6929
8	Asset Class 3	11.84%	15.64%	10.00%	5.00%	35.00%	0.7570
9	Asset Class 4	10.64%	12.35%	10.00%	5.00%	35.00%	0.8615
10	Asset Class 5	13.25%	13.28%	10.00%	5.00%	35.00%	0.9977
11	Asset Class 6	14.21%	14.39%	10.00%	5.00%	35.00%	0.9875
12	Asset Class 7	15.53%	14.25%	10.00%	5.00%	35.00%	1.0898
13	Asset Class 8	14.95%	16.44%	10.00%	5.00%	35.00%	0.9094
14	Asset Class 9	14.16%	16.50%	10.00%	5.00%	35.00%	0.8584
15	Asset Class 10	10.06%	12.50%	10.00%	5.00%	35.00%	0.8045
17	Portfolio Total	12.6419%	4.58%	100.00%			
18	Return to Risk Ratio	2.7596					

Figure 94.1: Asset allocation optimization model

Running an Optimization

To run this model, simply click on **Risk Simulator | Optimization | Run Optimization**. Alternatively, for practice, you can try to set up the model again by doing the following (the steps are illustrated in Figure 94.2):

1. Start a new profile (**Risk Simulator | New Profile**) and give it a name.

2. Select cell **E6**, and define the decision variable (**Risk Simulator | Optimization | Set Decision,** or click on the **Set Decision D** icon) and make it a *Continuous Variable* and then link the decision variable's name and minimum/maximum required to the relevant cells (**B6, F6, G6**).

3. Then use the **Risk Simulator Copy** on cell **E6**, select cells **E7** to **E15**, and use **Risk Simulator's Paste** (**Risk Simulator | Copy Parameter** and **Risk Simulator | Paste Parameter** or use the copy and paste icons). To rerun the optimization, type in **10%** for all decision variables. Make sure you do not use Excel's regular copy and paste functions.

4. Next, set up the optimization's constraints by selecting **Risk Simulator | Optimization | Constraints**, selecting **ADD**, and selecting cell **E17**, and making it (==) equal **100%** (for total allocation, and remember to insert the % sign).

5. Select cell **C18** as the objective to be maximized (**Risk Simulator | Optimization | Set Objective**).

6. Select **Risk Simulator | Optimization | Run Optimization**. Review the different tabs to make sure that all the required inputs in steps 2–4 are correct.

7. You may now select the optimization method of choice and click **OK** to run the optimization:

    a. **Static Optimization** is an optimization that is run on a static model, where no simulations are run. This optimization type is applicable when the model is assumed to be known and no uncertainties exist. Also, a static optimization can be run first to determine the optimal portfolio and its corresponding optimal allocation of decision variables before applying more advanced optimization procedures. For instance, before running a stochastic optimization problem, first run a static optimization to determine if there exist solutions to the optimization problem before performing a more protracted analysis.

b. **Dynamic Optimization** is applied when Monte Carlo simulation is used together with optimization. Another name for such a procedure is Simulation-Optimization. In other words, a simulation is run for N trials, and then an optimization process is run for M iterations until the optimal results are obtained or an infeasible set is found. That is, using Risk Simulator's *Optimization* module, you can choose which forecast and assumption statistics to use and replace in the model after the simulation is run. Then, you can apply these forecast statistics in the optimization process. This approach is useful when you have a large model with many interacting assumptions and forecasts, and when some of the forecast statistics are required in the optimization.

c. **Stochastic Optimization** is similar to the dynamic optimization procedure except that the entire dynamic optimization process is repeated T times. The results will be a forecast chart of each decision variable with T values. In other words, a simulation is run and the forecast or assumption statistics are used in the optimization model to find the optimal allocation of decision variables. Then another simulation is run, generating different forecast statistics, and these new updated values are optimized, and so forth. Hence, each of the final decision variables will have its own forecast chart, indicating the range of the optimal decision variables. For instance, instead of obtaining single-point estimates in the dynamic optimization procedure, you can now obtain a distribution of the decision variables, and, hence, a range of optimal values for each decision variable, also known as a stochastic optimization.

Note: If you are to run either a dynamic or stochastic optimization routine, make sure that you first define the assumptions in the model. That is, make sure that some of the cells in C6:D15 are assumptions. The model setup is illustrated in Figure 94.2.

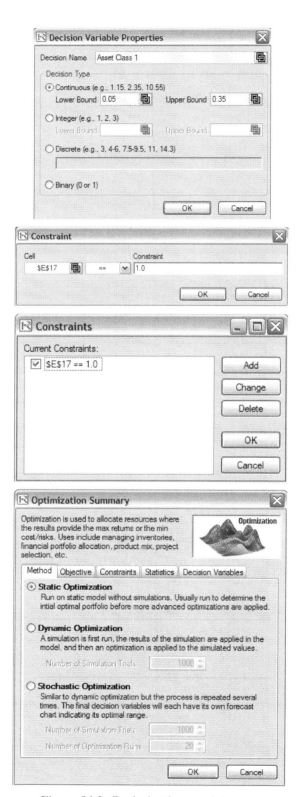

Figure 94.2: Optimization model setup

Briefly, the optimization results show the percentage allocation for each asset class (or projects or business lines, etc.) that would maximize the portfolio's bang for buck, that is, the allocation that would provide the highest returns subject to the least amount of risk. In other words, for the same amount of risk, what is the highest amount of returns that can be generated, or for the same amount of returns, what is the least amount of risk that can be obtained? See Figure 94.3. This is the concept of the Markowitz efficient portfolio analysis. For a comparable example, see Chapter 100 on the military portfolio model where we also generate the entire efficient frontier model.

ASSET ALLOCATION OPTIMIZATION MODEL

Asset Class Description	Annualized Returns	Volatility Risk	Allocation Weights	Required Minimum Allocation	Required Maximum Allocation	Return to Risk Ratio	Returns Ranking (Hi-Lo)	Risk Ranking (Lo-Hi)	Return to Risk Ranking (Hi-Lo)	Allocation Ranking (Hi-Lo)
Asset Class 1	10.54%	12.36%	11.09%	5.00%	35.00%	0.8524	9	2	7	4
Asset Class 2	11.25%	16.23%	6.87%	5.00%	35.00%	0.6929	7	8	10	10
Asset Class 3	11.84%	15.64%	7.78%	5.00%	35.00%	0.7570	6	7	9	9
Asset Class 4	10.64%	12.35%	11.22%	5.00%	35.00%	0.8615	8	1	5	3
Asset Class 5	13.25%	13.28%	12.08%	5.00%	35.00%	0.9977	5	4	2	2
Asset Class 6	14.21%	14.39%	11.04%	5.00%	35.00%	0.9875	3	6	3	5
Asset Class 7	15.53%	14.25%	12.30%	5.00%	35.00%	1.0898	1	5	1	1
Asset Class 8	14.95%	16.44%	8.90%	5.00%	35.00%	0.9094	2	9	4	7
Asset Class 9	14.16%	16.50%	8.37%	5.00%	35.00%	0.8584	4	10	6	8
Asset Class 10	10.06%	12.50%	10.35%	5.00%	35.00%	0.8045	10	3	8	6
Portfolio Total	12.6920%	4.52%	100.00%							
Return to Risk Ratio	2.8091									

Figure 94.3: Optimization results

95. Optimization – Discrete Project Selection

File Name: Optimization – Discrete Project Selection

Location: Modeling Toolkit | Optimization | Discrete Project Selection

Brief Description: Illustrates how to run an optimization on discrete integer decision variables in project selection in order to choose the best projects in a portfolio given a large variety of project options, subject to risk, return, budget, and other constraints

Requirements: Modeling Toolkit, Risk Simulator

This model shows 12 different projects with different risk and return characteristics. The idea here is to find the best portfolio allocation such that the portfolio's total strategic returns are maximized. That is, the model is used to find the best project mix in the portfolio that maximizes the total returns after considering the risks and returns of each project, subject to the constraints of number of projects and the budget. Figure 95.1 illustrates the model.

Objective: Maximize Total Portfolio Returns (C17) or Sharpe Ratio returns to risk ratio (C19)

Decision Variables: Allocation or Go/No-Go Decision (I4:I15)

Restrictions on Decision Variables: Binary decision variables (0 or 1)

Constraints: Total Cost (D17) is less than $5000 and less than or equal to 6 projects selected (I17)

Credit Line	ENPV	Cost	Risk $	Risk %	Return to Risk Ratio	Profitability Index	Selection
Project 1	$458.00	$1,732.44	$54.96	12.00%	8.33	1.26	1.0000
Project 2	$1,954.00	$859.00	$1,914.92	98.00%	1.02	3.27	1.0000
Project 3	$1,599.00	$1,845.00	$1,551.03	97.00%	1.03	1.87	1.0000
Project 4	$2,251.00	$1,645.00	$1,012.95	45.00%	2.22	2.37	1.0000
Project 5	$849.00	$458.00	$925.41	109.00%	0.92	2.85	1.0000
Project 6	$758.00	$52.00	$560.92	74.00%	1.35	15.58	1.0000
Project 7	$2,845.00	$758.00	$5,633.10	198.00%	0.51	4.75	1.0000
Project 8	$1,235.00	$115.00	$926.25	75.00%	1.33	11.74	1.0000
Project 9	$1,945.00	$125.00	$2,100.60	108.00%	0.93	16.56	1.0000
Project 10	$2,250.00	$458.00	$1,912.50	85.00%	1.18	5.91	1.0000
Project 11	$549.00	$45.00	$263.52	48.00%	2.08	13.20	1.0000
Project 12	$525.00	$105.00	$309.75	59.00%	1.69	6.00	1.0000
Total	$17,218.00	$8,197.44	$7,007	40.70%			12
Goal:	MAX	< =$5000					<=6
Sharpe Ratio	2.4573						

ENPV is the expected NPV of each credit line or project, while Cost can be the total cost of administration as well as required capital holdings to cover the credit line, and Risk is the Coefficient of Variation of the credit line's ENPV.

Figure 95.1: Discrete project selection model

Running an Optimization

To run this preset model, simply run the optimization (**Risk Simulator | Optimization | Run Optimization**) or for practice, set up the model yourself:

1. Start a new profile (**Risk Simulator | New Profile**) and give it a name.

2. In this example, all the allocations are required to be binary (0 or 1) values, so first select cell **I4** and make this a decision variable in the *Integer Optimization* worksheet, and select cell **I4** and define it as a decision variable (**Risk Simulator | Optimization | Decision Variables** or click on the **Define Decision** icon) and make it a **Binary Variable.** This setting automatically sets the minimum to 0 and maximum to 1 and can only take on a value of 0 or 1. Then use the **Risk Simulator Copy** on cell **I4**, select cells **I5** to **I15**, and use **Risk Simulator's Paste** (**Risk Simulator | Copy Parameter** and **Risk Simulator | Paste Parameter** or use the Risk Simulator copy and paste icons, NOT the Excel copy/paste).

3. Next, set up the optimization's constraints by selecting **Risk Simulator | Optimization | Constraints** and selecting **ADD**. Then link to cell **D17**, and make it **<= 5000**, and select **ADD** one more time and click on the **link** icon and point to cell **I17** and set it to **<=6**.

4. Select cell **C19**, the objective to be maximized, and select **Risk Simulator | Optimization | Set Objective** and then select **Risk Simulator | Optimization | Run Optimization**. Review the different tabs to make sure that all the required inputs in steps 2 and 3 above are correct.

5. You may now select the optimization method of choice and click **OK** to run the optimization.

Note: Remember that if you are to run either a dynamic or stochastic optimization routine, make sure that you first have assumptions defined in the model. That is, make sure that some of the cells in C4:C15 are assumptions. The suggestion for this model is to run a Discrete Optimization.

Viewing and Interpreting Forecast Results

In addition, you can create a Markowitz Efficient Frontier by running the optimization, then resetting the *budget* and *number of projects* constraints to a higher level, and rerunning the optimization. You can do this several times to obtain the Risk-Return efficient frontier. For a more detailed example, see Chapter 100 on the military portfolio and efficient frontier models.

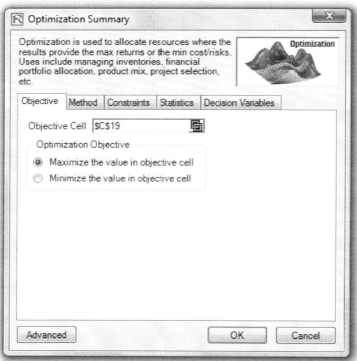

Figure 95.2: Setting up the optimization process

96. Optimization – Inventory Optimization

File Name: Optimization – Inventory Optimization

Location: Modeling Toolkit | Optimization | Inventory Optimization

Brief Description: Illustrates how to run an optimization on manufacturing inventory to maximize profits and minimize costs subject to manufacturing capacity constraints

Requirements: Modeling Toolkit, Risk Simulator

This model is used to find the optimal allocation of parts in a manufacturer's portfolio of inventory. In the model, eight different parts are shown, with their respective prices per unit (Figure 96.1). The demand for these parts is divided into four phases or cycles. For example, in the automotive aftermarket, certain parts are required more or less at certain times in the car's lifecycle (e.g., fewer parts may be needed during the first 3 years of a car's life than perhaps in years 4 to6, or years 7 to10, versus over 10 years) or parts of a machine, or the inventory in a retail shop during the four seasons in a year, and so forth. The demand levels in these cycles for each part is simulated (assumptions have already been preset in the model) and can be based on expert opinions, expectations, forecasts, or historical data (e.g., using distributional fitting methods in Risk Simulator).

In this model, if the manufacturer makes a higher quantity of a product than it can sell, there will be an added holding cost per unit (storage cost, opportunity cost, cost of money, etc.). Thus, it is less profitable to make too many units, but too few units mean lost sales. In other words, if the manufacturer makes too much, it loses money because it could have made some more of something else, but if it makes too little of a product, it should have made more to sell more of the product and make a profit. So an optimal inventory and manufacturing quantity is required. This model is used to find the best allocation of parts to manufacture given the uncertainty in demand and, at the same time, to maximize profits while minimizing cost.

However, the manufacturer has constraints. It cannot manufacture too many units of a single part due to resource, budget, and manufacturing constraints (size of factory, cycle time, manufacturing time, cost considerations, etc.). For example, say the firm cannot produce more than 100,000 units per part, and during each manufacturing or seasonal cycle, it cannot produce more than 250,000 units, and the total parts produced is set at no more than 800,000 units. In short, the problem can be summarized as:

Objective: Maximize total net revenues

Problem: Find the best allocation of parts to maximize net revenues (surplus and shortages are expensive)

Constraints: Each part cannot exceed 100,000 units
Each cycle cannot exceed 250,000 units
Each part in each cycle is between 15,000 and 35,000 units
Total parts cannot exceed 800,000 units

Assumptions: Surplus units has a holding inventory cost of $1

One very simple allocation is to produce an equal amount (e.g., 25,000 units per part, per cycle, thereby hitting all the constraints) as illustrated in Figure 96.1. The total net revenue from such a simple allocation is found to be $105,082,000.

Inventory Optimization

Units in '000s

Part	Part A512	Part V542	Part X221	Part AV12	Part CF88	Part X52	Part X72	Part FM2	TOTAL
Price	$154	$135	$188	$250	$54	$79	$155	$230	
Cycle 1 Demand	32.1200	18.1869	24.9693	17.1145	20.9422	21.8852	22.8831	15.9424	
Cycle 2 Demand	33.6296	29.1802	17.0791	20.0976	25.0521	19.9820	22.1348	22.8378	
Cycle 3 Demand	25.0197	33.0849	17.0325	24.0091	23.9793	28.8729	15.0658	19.0125	
Cycle 4 Demand	21.0919	15.0099	17.0732	31.2030	20.1536	21.9011	30.9182	21.0207	
Manufactured C1	25.000	25.000	25.000	25.000	25.000	25.000	25.000	25.000	200.00
Manufactured C2	25.000	25.000	25.000	25.000	25.000	25.000	25.000	25.000	200.00
Manufactured C3	25.000	25.000	25.000	25.000	25.000	25.000	25.000	25.000	200.00
Manufactured C4	25.000	25.000	25.000	25.000	25.000	25.000	25.000	25.000	200.00
Total Units	100.00	100.00	100.00	100.00	100.00	100.00	100.00	100.00	**800.000**
Surplus/Shortage	-11.86	4.54	23.85	7.58	9.87	7.36	9.00	21.19	
Gross Revenues	$14,798	$11,232	$14,317	$21,555	$4,864	$7,013	$13,188	$18,127	
Added Expenses	$12	$0	$0	$0	$0	$0	$0	$0	
Net Revenues	$14,786	$11,232	$14,317	$21,555	$4,864	$7,013	$13,188	$18,127	**$105,082**

Assumed Holding Cost (Per Unit) $1

Objective: Maximize total net revenues

Problem: Find the best allocation of parts to maximize net revenues
                Surplus and shortages are expensive

Constraints: Each part cannot exceed 100,000 units
                Each cycle cannot exceed 250,000 units
                Total parts cannot exceed 800,000 units

Assumptions: Surplus units has a holding inventory cost of $1

Figure 96.1: Inventory model before optimization

Optimization Procedure (Predefined)

In contrast, an optimization can be set up to solve this problem. The optimization has already been set up in the model and is ready to run. To run it:

1. Go to the *Optimization Model* worksheet and click on **Risk Simulator | Change Profile** and select the *Inventory Optimization* profile.

2. Click on the **Run Optimization** icon or click on **Risk Simulator | Optimization | Run Optimization** and click **OK**.

3. Click **Replace** when optimization is completed. The results show the optimal allocation of manufactured parts that maximizes the total net profit, increasing

it from \$105.082 million to \$110.116 million (Figure 96.2). Clearly optimization has created value.

4. Using these optimal allocations, run a simulation (the assumptions and forecasts have been predefined in the model) by clicking on the **RUN** icon or select **Risk Simulator | Run Simulation**.

5. On the Net Revenues forecast chart, select **Two-Tail** and type in **90** in the *Certainty* box and hit **TAB** on the keyboard to obtain the 90% confidence interval (between \$105 million and \$110 million). View the **Statistics** tab to obtain the mean expected value of \$108 million for the net revenues.

6. Select **Right-Tail** and type in **105082** in the *Value* box, to find the probability that this optimal allocation's portfolio of manufactured products (Figure 96.2) will exceed the simple equal allocation's net revenues seen in Figure 96.1. The results indicate that there is a 95.40% probability that by using this optimal portfolio, the manufacturer will make more net profits than going with a simple equal allocation (Figure 96.3).

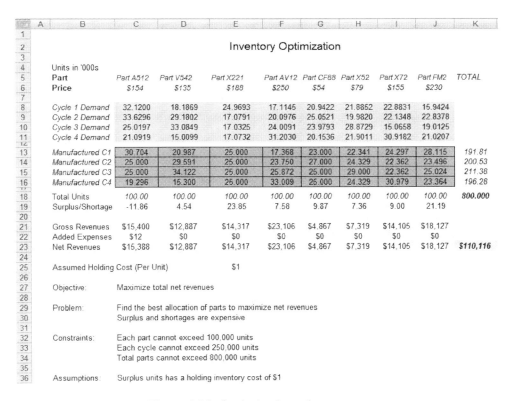

Figure 96.2: Optimized results

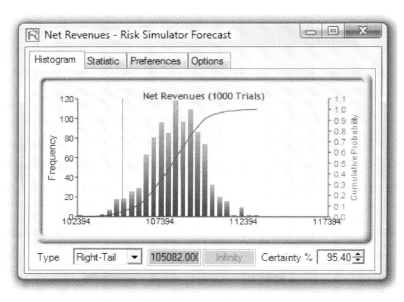

Figure 96.3: Optimized net revenues

Optimization Procedure (Manual)

To set up the model again from scratch, follow the instructions below:

1. Go to the *Optimization Model* worksheet and click on **Risk Simulator | New Profile** and give the profile a new name. You may have to reset the decision variables to some starting value (i.e., make the cells **C13:J16** all **25** as a starting point) so that you can immediately see when the optimization generates new values.

2. Click on cell **K23** and make it the objective to maximize (**Risk Simulator | Optimization | Set Objective**, and select **Maximize**).

3. Click on cell **C13** and make it a decision variable (**Risk Simulator | Optimization | Set Decision)**, and select **Continuous** for getting a continuous variable (we need this because the model's values are in thousands of units and thousands of dollars) and set the bounds to be between **15** and **35** (you can set your own bounds but these are typically constraints set by the manufacturer) to signify that the manufacturer can make only between 15,000 and 35,000 units of this part per cycle due to resource and budget or machine constraints.

4. Set the constraints by clicking on **Risk Simulator | Optimization | Constraints**, and select **ADD** for adding a new constraint. Add the three additional constraints in the model, namely, cells **K13** to **K16 <= 250** for each cell, **C18** to **J18 <= 100** for each cell, and **K18 <=800**. Do this one constraint at a time (Figure 96.4). Put your own constraints as required.

5. Click on the **Run Optimization** icon or click on **Risk Simulator | Optimization | Run Optimization**. Look through the tabs to make sure everything is set up correctly. Click on the **Method** tab and select **Static Optimization** and click **OK** to run the optimization.

6.   Click **Replace** when optimization is completed. The results illustrate that the optimal allocation of manufactured parts that maximizes net profit, increases it from $105.082 million to $110.116 million. Clearly optimization has created value.

7.   Using these optimal allocations, run a simulation (the assumptions and forecasts have been predefined in the model) by clicking on the **RUN** icon or select **Risk Simulator | Run Simulation**.

8.   On the Net Revenues forecast chart, select **Two-Tail** and type in **90** in the *Certainty* box and hit **TAB** on the keyboard to obtain the 90% confidence interval (between $105 million and $110 million). View the **Statistics** tab to obtain the mean expected value of $108 million for the net revenues.

9.   Select **Right-Tail** and type in **105082** in the *Value* box, to find the probability that this optimal allocation's portfolio of manufactured products will exceed the simple equal allocation's net revenues seen previously.

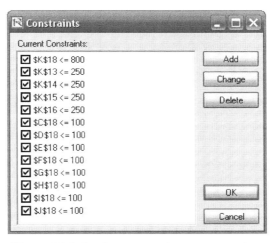

Figure 96.4: Setting constraints one at a time

97. Optimization – Investment Portfolio Allocation

File Name: Optimization – Investment Portfolio Allocation

Location: Modeling Toolkit | Optimization | Investment Portfolio Allocation

Brief Description: Illustrates how to run an optimization on investment decision variables in project allocation and new product mix

Requirements: Modeling Toolkit, Risk Simulator

This model looks at a set of new product lines that a company is thinking of investing in and the respective decisions on amounts to be invested to maximize profits (Figure 97.1). Each proposed new product line has its own estimated operating net returns and allowed investment range (lower and upper bounds). The idea is to maximize the total expected returns on the portfolio of investments subject to some budget constraint.

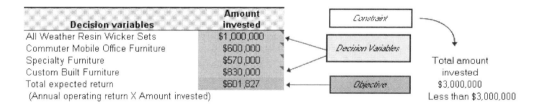

Strategic Investment Allocation

Proposed New Product Lines	Annual operating return	Lower bound	Upper bound
All Weather Resin Wicker Sets	19.40%	$1,000,000	$1,250,000
Commuter Mobile Office Furniture	19.27%	$600,000	$1,000,000
Specialty Furniture	19.95%	$570,000	$1,100,000
Custom Built Furniture	21.51%	$400,000	$900,000

Decision variables	Amount invested
All Weather Resin Wicker Sets	$1,000,000
Commuter Mobile Office Furniture	$600,000
Specialty Furniture	$570,000
Custom Built Furniture	$830,000
Total expected return	$601,827
(Annual operating return X Amount invested)	

Constraint

Decision Variables

Objective

Total amount invested
$3,000,000
Less than $3,000,000

Figure 97.1: Investment allocation model

98. Optimization – Investment Capital Allocation I (Basic Model)

File Name: Optimization – Capital Investments (Part A)

Location: Modeling Toolkit | Optimization | Investment Capital Allocation – Part I

Brief Description: Finds the optimal levels of capital investments in a strategic plan based on different risk and return characteristics of each type of product lines (the first of a two-part model)

Requirements: Modeling Toolkit, Risk Simulator

Companies restructure their product mix to boost sales and profits, increase shareholder value, or survive when the corporate structure becomes impaired. In successful restructurings, management not only actualizes lucrative new projects, but also abandons existing projects when they no longer yield sufficient returns, thereby channeling resources to more value-creating uses. At one level, restructuring can be viewed as changes in financing structures and management. At another level, it may be operational—in response to production overhauls, market trends, technology, and industry or macroeconomic disturbances.

For banks called on to finance corporate restructurings, things are a bit different. For example, most loans provide a fixed return over fixed periods that are dependent on interest rates and the borrower's ability to pay. A good loan will be repaid on time and in full. Hopefully, the bank's cost of funds will be low, with the deal providing attractive risk-adjusted returns. If the borrower's business excels, the bank will not participate in upside corporate values (except for a vicarious pleasure in the firm's success). However, if a borrower ends up financially distressed, lenders share much and perhaps most of the pain.

Two disparate goals—controlling default (credit) risk, the bank's objective, and value maximization, a traditional corporate aspiration—are often at odds, particularly if borrowers want the money to finance excessively aggressive projects. In the vast majority of traditional credit analyses, where the spotlight focuses on deterministically drawn projections, hidden risks are often exceedingly difficult to uncover. Devoid of viable projections, bankers will time and again fail to bridge gaps between their agendas and client aspirations. This chapter and the next offer ways for bankers to advance both their analytics and their communication skills; senior bank officials and clients alike, to "get the deal done" and ensure risk/reward agendas, are set in equilibrium. Undeniably, the direct way to achieve results is to take a stochastic view of strategic plans rather than rely inappropriately on deterministic base case/conservative scenarios.

ABC Bank is asked to approve a $3,410,000 loan facility for the hypothetical firm RI Furniture Manufacturing LTD. Management wants to restructure four of its operating subsidiaries. In support of the facility, the firm supplied the bank with deterministic base-case and conservative consolidating and consolidated projections—income statement, balance sheet, and cash flows. On the basis of deterministic consolidating projections, bankers developed the stochastic spreadsheet depicted in Figure 98.1. This spreadsheet includes maximum/minimum investments ranges supporting restructuring in each of the four product lines, and Risk Simulator is applied to run an optimization on the optimal amounts to invest in each product line. The annual operating returns are also set as assumptions in a stochastic optimization run. To run the Optimization in the preset model, click on **Risk Simulator | Optimization | Run Optimization** or click on the **Run Optimization** icon and select **Stochastic Optimization.** Figure 98.2 illustrates the results without (before) and with (after) optimization. Notice that the expected returns has increased through an optimal allocation of the investments in the four business units.

Figure 98.3 shows the results of two simulation runs (simulation is run on the original before-optimization allocation and is then rerun after the optimization). As expected, the mean or expected returns is higher with the optimization, but because we only set the total returns as the objective, risks also went up (as measured by standard deviation) by virtue of higher returns necessitating higher risks. However, at closer inspection, the coefficient of variation, which is computed by the standard deviation divided by the mean (risk to return ratio), actually stayed relatively constant (the small variations are due to random effects of simulation, which will dissipate with higher simulation trials).

Typically, at this point, as a prudent next step, the banker will have to discuss this first optimization run with the firm's management on three levels: the maximum expected return, the optimal investments/loan facility allocation, and the risk of expected returns. If the risk level is unacceptable, the standard deviation must be reduced to preserve credit grade integrity. In the next chapter, we take this simple model and add more levels of complexity by adding in an efficient frontier model and credit risk contribution effects on the portfolio.

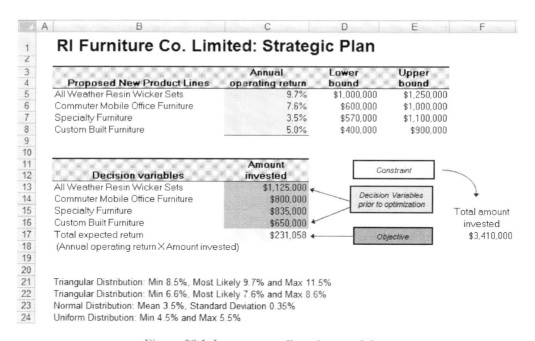

Figure 98.1: Investment allocation model

BEFORE OPTIMIZATION:

Decision variables	Amount invested
All Weather Resin Wicker Sets	$1,125,000
Commuter Mobile Office Furniture	$800,000
Specialty Furniture	$835,000
Custom Built Furniture	$650,000
Total expected return	$231,058
(Annual operating return X Amount invested)	

Total amount invested
$3,410,000

AFTER OPTIMIZATION:

Decision variables	Amount invested
All Weather Resin Wicker Sets	$1,250,000
Commuter Mobile Office Furniture	$1,000,000
Specialty Furniture	$570,000
Custom Built Furniture	$590,000
Total expected return	$246,072
(Annual operating return X Amount invested)	

Total amount invested
$3,410,000

Figure 98.2: Results from before and after an optimization run

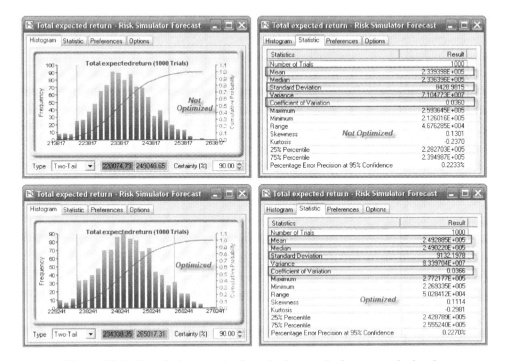

Figure 98.3: Simulation results from before and after an optimization

99. Optimization – Investment Capital Allocation II (Advanced Model)

File Name: Optimization – Capital Investments (Part B)

Location: Modeling Toolkit | Optimization | Investment Capital Allocation – Part II

Brief Description: Finds the optimal levels of capital investments in a strategic plan based on different risk and return characteristics of each type of product line as applied in an efficient frontier, and the contribution to the entire portfolio's credit risk is determined

Requirements: Modeling Toolkit, Risk Simulator

This model, Part B of the Capital Investments example, is the second of two parts, continued from the previous chapter. To get started, please first review Part A of the model before attempting to run this follow-up model. This follow-up model looks at a twist at the optimization procedures performed in Part A by now incorporating risk and the return to risk ratio (Sharpe Ratio, a Nobel Prize winning concept). As can be seen in Figure 99.1, the model is the same as Figure 98.1, with the exception of the inclusion of Column F, which is a measure of risk. This risk measure can be a probability of failure or volatility computation. Typically, for a project, the higher the expected value, the higher the risk. Therefore, with the inclusion of this risk value, we can now compute not only the expected returns for the portfolio, but also the expected risk for the entire portfolio, weighted to the various investment levels.

Simply maximizing returns in the portfolio (Opt Run 1 in Figure 99.1, based on the previous chapter's model) will, by definition, create a potentially higher risk portfolio (high risk equals high return). Instead, we may also want to maximize the Sharpe Ratio (portfolio returns to risk ratio), which will in turn provide the maximum levels of return subject to the least risk, or for the same risk, provide the highest returns, yielding an optimal point on the Markowitz Efficient Frontier for this portfolio (Opt Run 2 in Figure 99.1). As can be seen in the optimization results table, Opt Run 1 provides the highest returns ($246,072) as opposed to the original value of $231,058. Nonetheless, Opt Run 2, where we maximize the Sharpe Ratio instead, provides a slightly lower return ($238,816) but the total risk for the entire portfolio is reduced to 4.055% instead of 4.270%. A simulation is run on the original investment allocation, Opt Run 1, and Opt Run 2 and the results are shown in Figure 99.2. Here, we clearly see that the slightly lower returns provide a reduced level of risk, which is good for the bank.

To run this predefined optimization model, simple click on **Risk Simulator | Optimization | Run Optimization** and click **OK**. To change the objective from *Maximizing Returns to Risk*, to *Maximizing Returns*, simply click on the **Objective O** icon in the Risk Simulator toolbar or click on **Risk Simulator | Optimization | Set Objective** and link it to either cell **C20** for Sharpe Ratio, or **C17**, for Returns, and then run the optimization.

In addition, the total investment budget allowed can be changed to analyze what happens to the returns and risk of the portfolio. For instance, Figure 99.3 illustrates the results from such an analysis, and the resulting expected risk and return values. In order to better understand each point's risk structure, an optimization is carried out and a simulation is run. Further down, two sample extreme cases where $2.91M versus $3.61M are invested. From the results, one can see that the higher the risk (higher range of outcomes), the higher the returns (expected values are higher and the probability of beating the original expected value is also higher). Such analyses will provide the bank the ability to better analyze the risk and return characteristics.

Many additional analyses can be applied in this model. For instance, we can apply the Probability of Default computations of implied Asset Value and Implied Volatility to obtain the Cumulative Default Probability so that the bank can understand the risk of this deal and decide (based on the portfolio of deals) what the threshold of lending should be. For instance, if the bank does not want anything above a 3.5% probability of default for a 5-year cumulative loan, then $3.41M is the appropriate loan value threshold. In addition, Value at Risk for a portfolio of loans can also be determined for before and after this new loan, enabling the bank to decide if absorbing this new loan is possible, and the effects on the entire portfolio's VaR valuation and capital adequacy. Figure 99.4 shows some existing loans (grouped by tranches and types), and the new loan request. It is up to management to decide if the additional hit to capital requirements is reasonable. For details on credit risk analysis and Value at Risk models, please refer to the relevant chapters in this book.

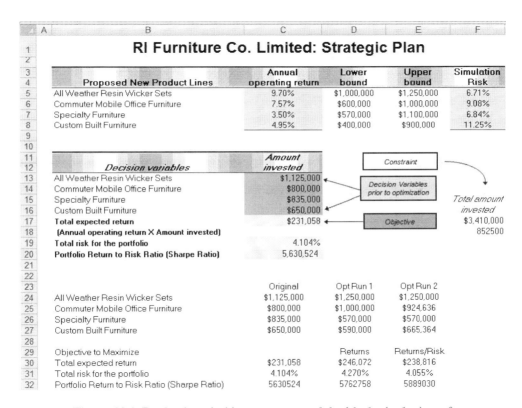

Figure 99.1: Revised capital investment model with the inclusion of stochastic risk elements

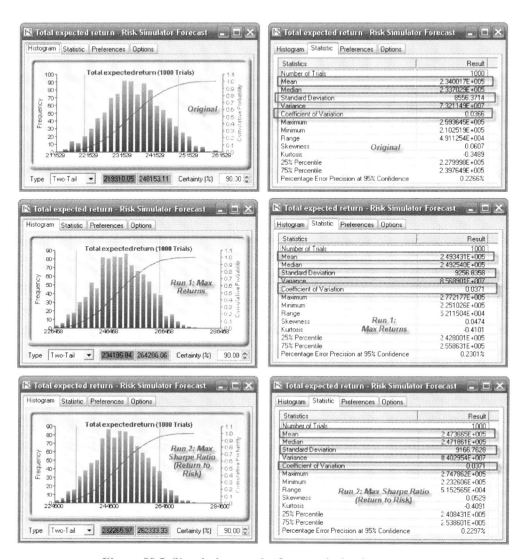

Figure 99.2: Simulation results from optimization runs

Maximizing Returns with different budget constraints:

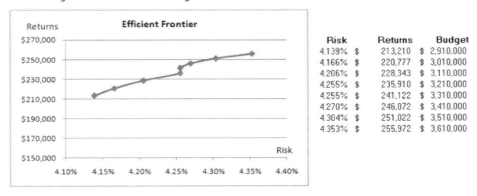

Risk		Returns		Budget
4.139%	$	213,210	$	2,910,000
4.166%	$	220,777	$	3,010,000
4.206%	$	228,343	$	3,110,000
4.255%	$	235,910	$	3,210,000
4.255%	$	241,122	$	3,310,000
4.270%	$	246,072	$	3,410,000
4.304%	$	251,022	$	3,510,000
4.353%	$	255,972	$	3,610,000

Figure 99.3: Efficient frontier results

Probability of Default Analysis to Determine Lending Threshold

Total Investment/Loan Required ($000)	$3,410	$2,910	$3,610
Other Liabilities and Debt ($000)	$3,512	$3,512	$3,512
Total Equity Value ($000)	$1,200	$1,200	$1,200
Equity Volatility	20.00%	20.00%	20.00%
Maturity of New Debt	5	5	5
Riskfree Rate	5.00%	5.00%	5.00%
Implied Asset Value	**$6,583.56**	**$6,196.20**	**$6,738.31**
Implied Asset Volatility	**4.75%**	**4.82%**	**4.73%**
Probability of Default	**3.3649%**	**2.6577%**	**3.6890%**

Value at Risk Contribution Analysis to the Bank's Portfolio of Holdings

	Daily Volatilities	Amounts
Existing Loan (Tranche 1)	0.1254%	$5,410,000
Existing Loan (Tranche 2)	0.3255%	$4,450,000
Existing Loan (Tranche 3)	0.1444%	$3,410,000
Existing Loan (Tranche 4)	0.1854%	$3,410,000
Existing Loan (Tranche 5)	0.2654%	$3,410,000
New Loan Addition	0.2163%	$3,410,000

Correlation Matrix	Existing Loan (Tranche 1)	Existing Loan (Tranche 2)	Existing Loan (Tranche 3)	Existing Loan (Tranche 4)	Existing Loan (Tranche 5)	New Loan Addition
Existing Loan (Tranche 1)	1.0000	0.2500	-0.1540	0.0250	0.0140	0.0200
Existing Loan (Tranche 2)	0.0000	1.0000	-0.1335	0.0020	0.1500	-0.1200
Existing Loan (Tranche 3)	0.0000	0.0000	1.0000	0.0255	0.0480	-0.1700
Existing Loan (Tranche 4)	0.0000	0.0000	0.0000	1.0000	0.0560	-0.2600
Existing Loan (Tranche 5)	0.0000	0.0000	0.0000	0.0000	1.0000	0.2500
New Loan Addition	0.0000	0.0000	0.0000	0.0000	0.0000	1.0000

Holding Days	365
Percentile	99.95%
Value at Risk of Portfolio Before New Loan	**$1,318,330**
Value at Risk of Portfolio After New Loan	**$1,378,376**

Figure 99.4: Probability of default and contributions to portfolio Value at Risk

100. Optimization – Military Portfolio and Efficient Frontier

File Name: Optimization – Military Portfolio and Efficient Frontier

Location: Modeling Toolkit | Optimization | Military Portfolio and Efficient Frontier

Brief Description: Illustrates how to run an optimization on discrete binary integer decision variables in project selection and mix; view and interpret optimization results; create additional qualitative constraints to the optimization model; and generate an investment Efficient Frontier by applying optimization on changing constraints

Requirements: Modeling Toolkit, Risk Simulator

This model shows 20 different projects with different risk-return characteristics as well as several qualitative measures such as strategic score, military readiness score, tactical score, comprehensive score, and so forth (see Figure 100.1). These scores are obtained through subject matter experts, for instance, decision makers, leaders, and managers of organizations, where their expert opinions are gathered through the double-blind Delphi Method. After being scrubbed (e.g., extreme values are eliminated, large data variations are analyzed, multiple iterations of the Delphi Method are performed, etc.), their respective scores can be entered into a Distributional Fitting routine to find the best-fitting distribution, or used to develop a Custom Distribution for each project.

The central idea of this model is to find the best portfolio allocation such that the portfolio's total comprehensive strategic score and profits are maximized. That is, it is used to find the best project mix in the portfolio that maximizes the total *Profit*Score* measure, where profit points to the portfolio level net returns after considering the risks and costs of each project, while the Score measures the total comprehensive score of the portfolio, all the while being subject to the constraints on number of projects, budget constraint, full-time equivalence resource (FTE) restrictions, and strategic ranking constraints.

Objective: Maximize Total Portfolio Returns times the Portfolio Comprehensive Score (C28)

Decision Variables: Allocation or Go/No-Go Decision (J5:J24)

Restrictions on Decision Variables: Binary decision variables (0 or 1)

Constraints: Total Cost (E26) is less than or equal to $3800 (in $thousands or $millions) Less than or equal to 10 projects selected (J26) in the entire portfolio Full-time Equivalence resources have to be less than or equal to 80 (M26) Total Strategic Ranking for entire portfolio must be less than or equal to 100 (F26)

Military Portfolio Optimization

Project Name	ENPV	NPV	Cost	Strategy Ranking	Return to Rank Ratio	Profitability Index	Selection	Military Score	Tactical Score	FTE Resources	Comprehensive Score
Project 1	$458.00	$150.76	$1,732.44	1.20	381.67	1.09	1	8.10	2.31	1.20	1.98
Project 2	$1,954.00	$245.00	$859.00	9.80	199.39	1.29	1	1.27	4.83	2.50	1.76
Project 3	$1,599.00	$458.00	$1,845.00	9.70	164.85	1.25	1	9.88	4.75	3.60	2.77
Project 4	$2,251.00	$529.00	$1,645.00	4.50	500.22	1.32	1	8.83	1.61	4.50	2.07
Project 5	$849.00	$564.00	$458.00	10.90	77.89	2.23	1	5.02	6.25	5.50	2.94
Project 6	$758.00	$135.00	$52.00	7.40	102.43	3.60	1	3.64	5.79	9.20	3.26
Project 7	$2,845.00	$311.00	$758.00	19.80	143.69	1.41	1	5.27	6.47	12.50	4.04
Project 8	$1,235.00	$754.00	$115.00	7.50	164.67	7.56	1	9.80	7.16	5.30	3.63
Project 9	$1,945.00	$198.00	$125.00	10.80	180.09	2.58	1	5.68	2.39	6.30	2.16
Project 10	$2,250.00	$785.00	$458.00	8.50	264.71	2.71	1	8.29	4.41	4.50	2.67
Project 11	$549.00	$35.00	$45.00	4.80	114.38	1.78	1	7.52	4.65	4.90	2.75
Project 12	$525.00	$75.00	$105.00	5.90	88.98	1.71	1	5.54	5.09	5.20	2.69
Project 13	$516.00	$451.00	$48.00	2.80	184.29	10.40	1	2.51	2.17	4.60	1.66
Project 14	$459.00	$458.00	$351.00	9.40	53.09	2.30	1	9.41	9.49	9.90	4.85
Project 15	$859.00	$125.00	$421.00	6.50	132.15	1.30	1	6.91	9.62	7.20	4.25
Project 16	$684.00	$458.00	$124.00	3.90	226.67	4.69	1	7.06	9.98	7.50	4.46
Project 17	$956.00	$124.00	$521.00	15.40	62.08	1.24	1	1.25	2.50	8.60	2.07
Project 18	$854.00	$164.00	$512.00	21.00	40.67	1.32	1	3.09	2.90	4.30	1.70
Project 19	$195.00	$45.00	$5.00	1.20	162.50	10.00	1	5.25	1.22	4.10	1.86
Project 20	$210.00	$85.00	$21.00	1.00	210.00	5.05	1	2.01	4.06	5.20	2.50
Total	$22,191.00		$10,200.44	162.00			20	116.32	97.65	116.60	56.08
Profit/Rank	$136.98										
Profit*Score	$1,244,365.33	Maximize	<=$3800	<=100			x<=10			<=80	

	Budget	Comprehensive Score	Tactical Score	Military Score	Allowed Projects	ROI-RANK Objective
	$3,800.00	33.15	62.64	58.58	10	$470,235.60
	$4,800.00	36.33	68.85	66.86	11	$521,645.92
	$5,800.00	38.40	70.46	75.69	12	$623,557.79
	$6,800.00	39.94	72.14	82.31	13	$659,947.99
	$7,800.00	39.76	70.05	86.54	14	$676,279.81

Figure 100.1: The project selection optimization model

Running an Optimization

To run this preset model, simply open the profile (**Risk Simulator | Change Profile**) and select *Military Portfolio and Efficient Frontier*. Then, run the optimization (**Risk Simulator | Optimization | Run Optimization**) or for practice, set up the model yourself:

1. Start a new profile (**Risk Simulator | New Profile**) and give it a name.

2. In this example, all the allocations are required to be binary (0 or 1) values, so, first select cell **J5** and make this a decision variable in the *Integer Optimization* worksheet. Select cell **J5** and define it as a decision variable (**Risk Simulator | Optimization | Set Decision** or click on the **Set Decision** icon) and make it a **Binary Variable**. This setting automatically sets the minimum to 0 and maximum to 1 and can only take on a value of 0 or 1. Then use the **Risk Simulator Copy** on cell **J5**, select cells **J6** to **J24**, and use **Risk Simulator's Paste** (**Risk Simulator | Copy Parameter** and **Risk Simulator | Paste Parameter** or use the Risk Simulator copy and paste icons, NOT the Excel copy/paste).

3. Next, set up the optimization's constraints by selecting **Risk Simulator | Optimization | Constraints**, and selecting **ADD**. Then link to cell **E26**, and make it **<= 3800**, select **ADD** one more time and click on the **link** icon and point to cell **J26** and set it to **<=10**. Continue with adding the other constraints (cell **M26 <= 80** and **F26 <= 100**).

4. Select cell **C28**, the objective to be maximized, **Risk Simulator | Optimization | Set Objective,** and then select **Risk Simulator | Optimization | Run Optimization**. Review the different tabs to make sure that all the required inputs in steps 2 and 3 above are correct.

5. You may now select the optimization method of choice and click **OK** to run the optimization. The model setup is illustrated in Figure 100.2.

Note: If you are to run either a dynamic or stochastic optimization routine, make sure that first you have assumptions defined in the model; that is, that some of the cells in **C5:C24** and **E5:F24** are assumptions. The suggestion for this model is to run a Discrete Optimization.

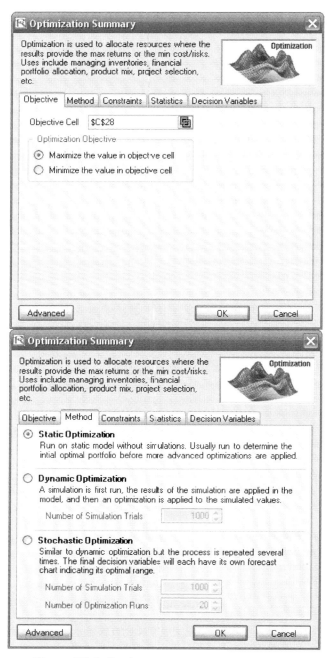

Figure 100.2: Setting up an optimization model

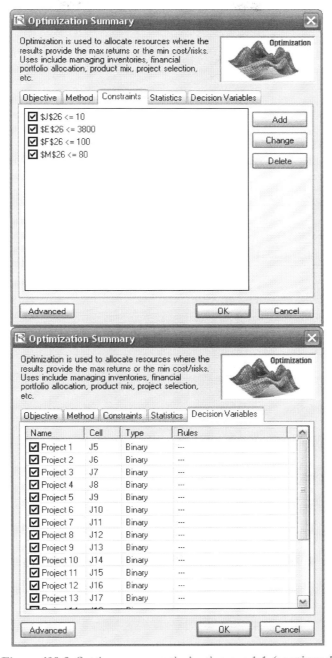

Figure 100.2: Setting up an optimization model *(continued)*

Portfolio Efficient Frontier

Clearly, running the optimization procedure will yield an optimal portfolio of projects where the constraints are satisfied. This represents a single optimal portfolio point on the efficient frontier, for example, Portfolio B on the chart in Figure 100.3. Then, by subsequently changing some of the constraints, for instance, by increasing the budget and allowed projects, we can rerun the optimization to produce another optimal portfolio given these new constraints. Therefore, a series of optimal portfolio allocations can be determined and graphed. This graphical representation of all optimal portfolios is called the Portfolio Efficient Frontier. At this juncture, each point represents a portfolio allocation, for instance, Portfolio B might represent projects 1, 2, 5, 6, 7, 8, 10, 15, and so forth, while Portfolio C might represent projects 2, 6, 7, 9, 12, 15, and so forth, each resulting in different tactical, military, or comprehensive scores and portfolio returns. It is up to the decision maker to decide which portfolio represents the best decision and if sufficient resources exist to execute these projects.

Typically, in an Efficient Frontier analysis, you would select projects where the marginal increase in benefits is positive and the slope is steep. In the next example, you would select Portfolio D rather than Portfolio E as the marginal increase is negative on the y-axis (e.g., Tactical Score). That is, spending too much money may actually reduce the overall tactical score, and hence this portfolio should not be selected. Also, in comparing Portfolios A and B, you would be more inclined to choose B as the slope is steep and the same increase in budget requirements (x-axis) would return a much higher percentage Tactical Score (y-axis). The decision to choose between Portfolios C and D would depend on available resources and the decision maker deciding if the added benefits warrant and justify the added budget and costs.

Budget	Comprehensive Score	Tactical Score	Military Score	Allowed Projects	ROI-RANK Objective
$3,800	33.15	62.64	58.58	10	$470,236
$4,800	36.33	68.85	66.86	11	$521,646
$5,800	38.40	70.46	75.69	12	$623,558
$6,800	39.94	72.14	82.31	13	$659,948
$7,800	39.76	70.05	86.54	14	$676,280

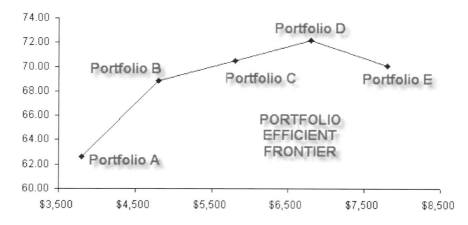

Figure 100.3: Efficient frontier

To further enhance the analysis, you can obtain the optimal portfolio allocations for C and D and then run a simulation on each optimal portfolio to decide what the probability that D will exceed C in value is, and whether this probability of occurrence justifies the added costs.

101. Optimization – Optimal Pricing with Elasticity

File Name: Optimization – Optimal Pricing with Elasticity

Location: Modeling Toolkit | Optimization | Optimal Pricing with Elasticity

Brief Description: Illustrates price optimization that maximizes total revenues based on price elasticity of demand

Requirements: Modeling Toolkit, Risk Simulator

This model is used to find the optimal pricing levels that will maximize revenues through the use of historical elasticity levels. The price elasticity of demand is a basic concept in microeconomics, which can be briefly described as the percentage change of quantity divided by the percentage change in prices. For example, if, in response to a 10% fall in the price of a good, the quantity demanded increases by 20%, the price elasticity of demand would be 20% / (−10 %) = −2. In general, a fall in the price of a good is expected to increase the quantity demanded, so the price elasticity of demand is negative but in some literature, the negative sign is omitted for simplicity (denoting only the absolute value of the elasticity). We can use this in several ways, including the point elasticity by taking the first derivative of the inverse of the demand function and multiplying it by the ratio of price to quantity at a particular point on the demand curve:

$$\varepsilon_d = \frac{\delta Q}{\delta P} \cdot \frac{P}{Q}$$

where ε is the price elasticity of demand, P is price, and Q is quantity demanded.

Instead of using instantaneous point elasticities, this example uses the discrete version, where we define elasticity as:

$$\varepsilon_d = \frac{\%\Delta Q}{\%\Delta P} = \frac{\dfrac{Q_2 - Q_1}{Q_2 + Q_1}}{2} \div \frac{\dfrac{P_2 - P_1}{P_2 + P_1}}{2} = \frac{Q_2 - Q_1}{Q_2 + Q_1} \cdot \frac{P_2 + P_1}{P_2 - P_1}$$

To further simplify things, we assume that in a category of hotel rooms, cruise ship tickets, airline tickets, or any other products with various categories (e.g., standard room, executive room, suite, etc.), there is an average price and average quantity of units sold per period. Therefore, we can further simplify the equation to:

$$\varepsilon_d = \frac{Q_2 - Q_1}{\overline{Q}} \div \frac{P_2 - P_1}{\overline{P}} = \frac{\overline{P}}{\overline{Q}} \cdot \frac{Q_2 - Q_1}{P_2 - P_1}$$

where we now use the average price and average quantity demanded values, $\overline{P}, \overline{Q}$.

If we have in each category the average price and average quantity sold, as in the model, we can compute the expected quantity sold given a new price if we have the historical elasticity of demand values. See Figure 101.1.

Type	Average Price Sold	Average Quantity Sold	Average Total Revenue
Single	$750	200	$150,000.00
Double	$812	180	$146,160.00
Deluxe	$865	150	$129,750.00
Executive	$1,085	100	$108,500.00
Premium Suite	$1,195	75	$89,625.00
Presidential	$1,458	50	$72,900.00

Figure 101.1: Sample historical pricing

In other words, if we take:

$$Q_1 - \varepsilon_d (P_2 - P_1) \frac{\overline{Q}}{\overline{P}} = Q_2$$

we would get:

$$Q_1 - \left[\frac{\overline{P}}{\overline{Q}} \cdot \frac{Q_2 - Q_1}{P_2 - P_1} \right] (P_2 - P_1) \frac{\overline{Q}}{\overline{P}} = Q_2$$

To illustrate, suppose the price elasticity of demand for a single room during high season at a specific hotel property is 3.15 (we use the absolute value), where the average price last season was $750 and the average quantity of rooms sold was 200 units. What would happen if prices were to change from $750 (P1) to $800 (P2)? That is, what would happen to the quantity sold from 200 units (Q1)? See Figure 101 2. Please note that ε is a negative value but we simplify as a positive value here to be consistent with economic literature.

Historical Analysis

Type	Average Price Sold	Average Quantity Sold	Average Total Revenue	Price Elasticity of Demand	Allocated New Price	Projected Quantity Sold
Single	$750	200	$150,000.00	3.15	$800.00	158
Double	$812	180	$146,160.00	2.85	$800.00	188
Deluxe	$865	150	$129,750.00	2.55	$1,000.00	90
Executive	$1,085	100	$108,500.00	2.35	$1,000.00	118
Premium Suite	$1,195	75	$89,625.00	1.65	$1,000.00	95
Presidential	$1,458	50	$72,900.00	1.45	$1,000.00	73

Figure 101.2: Elasticity simulation

Using the last equation, we compute the newly predicted quantity demanded at $800 per night to be:

$$Q_2 = Q_1 - \varepsilon_d (P_2 - P_1)\frac{\overline{Q}}{\overline{P}} = 200 - 3.15(800 - 750)\frac{200}{750} = 158$$

The higher the price, the lower the quantity demanded, and vice versa. Indeed, the entire demand curve can be reconstructed by applying different price levels. For instance, the demand curve for the Single room is reconstructed in Figure 101.3.

Note: See the *Simulation – Demand Curve and Elasticity Estimation* model for examples on how to obtain elasticity measures.

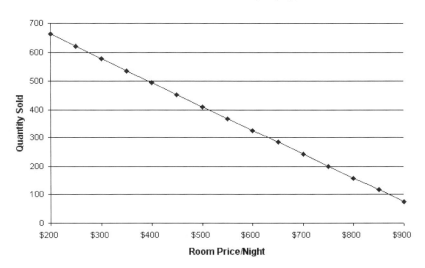

Figure 101.3: Reconstructed demand curve for a single room

Optimization Procedures

Using the principles of price elasticity of demand, we can now figure out the optimal pricing structure of these hotel rooms by setting:

Objective: Maximize Total Revenues

Constraints: Number of rooms available per type

Decision Variables: Price to charge for each type of room

This model already has the optimization set up. To run it directly, do the following:

1. Go to the *Model* worksheet and click on **Risk Simulator | Change Profile** and choose the *Optimal Pricing with Elasticity* profile.

2. Click on the **Run Optimization** icon or click on **Risk Simulator | Optimization | Run Optimization.**

3. Select the **Method** tab and select either **Static Optimization** if you wish to view the resulting optimal prices or **Stochastic Optimization** to run simulation with optimization multiple times, to obtain a range of optimal prices.

The results from a stochastic optimization routine are seen in the *Report* worksheet. In addition, several forecast charts will be visible once the stochastic optimization routine completes. For instance, looking at the Executive suites, select **Two-Tail**, type **90** in the Certainty box, and hit **TAB** on the keyboard to obtain the 90% confidence level (e.g., the optimal price to charge for the season is between $991 and $993 per night). See Figure 101.4.

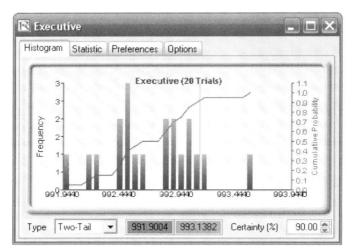

Figure 101.4: Distribution of stochastic optimization decision variable

To reset the model manually, do the following:

1.   Go to the *Model* worksheet and click on **Risk Simulator | New Profile** and give the new profile a name.

2.   *Reset* the values on prices. That is, enter **800** for cells **H7, H8** and **1000** for cells **H9** to **H12.** We do this so that we determine the initial starting prices that are easy to remember, versus the optimized price levels later on.

3.   Set the objective. Select cell **J15** and click on the **O** (set objective) icon or click **Risk Simulator | Optimization | Set Objective**.

4.   Set the decision variables. Select cell **H7** and click on the **D** (set decision variable) icon or click **Risk Simulator | Optimization | Set Decision**. Select **Continuous** and give it the relevant lower and upper bounds (see columns M and N) or click on the **link** icon and link the lower and upper bounds (cells **M7** and **N7**).

5.   Set the constraints. Click on the **C** icon or **Risk Simulator | Optimization | Constraints** and add the capacity constraints on the maximum number of available rooms (e.g., click **ADD** and link cell **I7** and make it **<= 250** and so forth).

6.   Click on the **Run Optimization** icon or click on **Risk Simulator | Optimization | Run Optimization.**

7.   Select the **Method** tab and select either **Static Optimization** if you wish to view the resulting optimal prices, or **Stochastic Optimization** to run simulation with optimization multiple times, to obtain a range of optimal prices. But remember that to run a stochastic optimization procedure, you need to have assumptions set up. Select cell **G7** and click on **Risk Simulator | Set Input Assumption** and set an assumption of your choice or choose Normal distribution and use the default values. Repeat for cells **G8** to **G12,** one at a time, then you can run a stochastic optimization.

102. Optimization – Optimization of a Harvest Model

File Name: Optimization – Optimization of a Harvest Model

Location: Modeling Toolkit | Optimization | Optimization of a Harvest Model

Brief Description: Illustrates how to find the optimal harvest rate for a population that maximizes return

Requirements: Modeling Toolkit, Risk Simulator

This is a population dynamics and harvest model, where, given an initial population and the growth rate of the population, we can determine the optimal harvest rate that maximizes the return on investment, given a specific cost of capital and carrying capacity of the population. For instance, this can be a model on a herd of cattle or a forest of trees, where there is a carrying or maximum capacity of the population. The population dynamics can be summarized as:

$Percentage\ Growth_t = Growth\ Rate\ (1 - Population_{t-1} \div Carrying\ Capacity)$

$Births_t = Percentage\ Growth_t\ Population_{t-1}$

$Continuing\ Population_t = Population_{t-1} - Harvest_t$

$Population_t = Births_t + Continuing\ Population_t$

A sample set of inputs is provided, as are the model computations, and the time-series chart shows the population dynamics and interactions. Typically, if there is no excess harvesting, the continuing graph should stabilize over time as shown in Figures 102.1 and 102.2.

Growth Rate	60.00%		
Maximum Capacity	1000	Ending Population	689
Annual Harvest	100.00	Total Harvested	5,000
Starting Value	300	Total Harvested PV Sales	$17,726.14
Harvest Sales Price	$10	Salvage Value	$8,086.05
PV Salvage Price Each	$12	Total Value of Property	$25,812.18
Cost of Capital	5.00%		
Minimum Harvest	50		
Maximum Harvest	200		

Figure 102.1: Harvest model

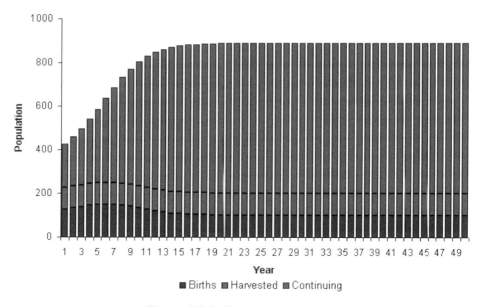

Figure 102.2: Harvest model chart

Procedure

The model has been preset with optimization parameters and simulation assumptions. To run this model, simply:

1. Go to the *Model* worksheet and click on **Risk Simulator | Change Profile** and select the *Population and Harvest Model* profile.

2. Click on the **Run Optimization** icon or **Risk Simulator | Optimization | Run Optimization**, and click **Replace** when the optimization routine is complete.

You will see the optimal annual harvest is 125.80 thousand, providing the highest total value of the property (Figure 102.3). In fact, after the optimization is run, run a simulation on the optimized annual harvest. You can then see that there is a 53% certainty that this optimized harvest level will result in values greater than those expected without optimization (Figure 102.4).

Growth Rate	60.00%
Maximum Capacity	1000
Annual Harvest	125.80
Starting Value	300
Harvest Sales Price	$10
PV Salvage Price Each	$12
Cost of Capital	5.00%
Minimum Harvest	50
Maximum Harvest	200

Ending Population	574
Total Harvested	6,290
Total Harvested PV Sales	$22,299.63
Salvage Value	$6,733.98
Total Value of Property	$29,033.61

Figure 102.3: Optimized results

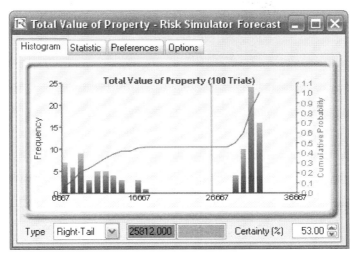

Figure 102.4: Total property value forecast chart

To replicate the model and create it from scratch, follow the instructions:

1. Go to the *Model* worksheet and click on **Risk Simulator | New Profile** and give the profile a name.

2. Set the objective. Select cell **H10** (Total Value of Property) and click on the **O** icon or **Risk Simulator | Optimization | Set Objective** (Figure 102.5).

3. Set the decision variable. Select cell **D7** (Annual Harvest) and click on the **D** icon or **Risk Simulator | Optimization | Set Decision**. Select **Continuous** and click on the **link** icon and link the lower bounds and upper bounds to **D12** and **D13** (Figure 102.6). Continuous decision variables can be chosen as the number of trees modeled is in thousands of units.

4. Reset the decision variable. Change the value in cell **D7** to some starting value, for example, **100**.

5. Prepare to run the optimization. Click on the **Run Optimization** icon or **Risk Simulator | Optimization | Run Optimization** (Figure 102.7).

6. Run the optimization. Click on the **Method** tab and select **Static Optimization** and click **OK**. Click **Replace** when the optimization routine is complete. You will see the optimal annual harvest is 125.80, providing the highest total value of the property.

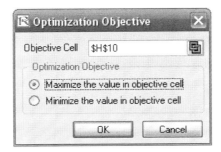

Figure 102.5: Setting optimization objective

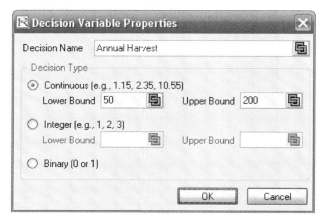

Figure 102.6: Continuous decision variables

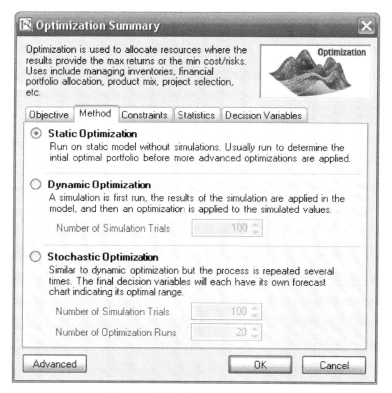

Figure 102.7: Optimization run

103. Optimization – Optimizing Ordinary Least Squares

File Name: Optimization – Optimizing Ordinary Least Squares

Location: Modeling Toolkit | Optimization | Optimizing Ordinary Least Squares

Brief Description: Illustrates how to solve a simple bivariate regression model with the ordinary least squares approach, using Risk Simulator's optimization and its *Regression Analysis* tool

Requirements: Modeling Toolkit, Risk Simulator

It is assumed that the user is sufficiently knowledgeable about the fundamentals of regression analysis. The general bivariate linear regression equation takes the form of $Y = \beta_0 + \beta_1 X + \varepsilon$ where β_0 is the intercept, β_1 is the slope, and ε is the error term. It is bivariate as there are only two variables, a Y or dependent variable, and an X or independent variable, where X is also known as the *regressor* (sometimes a bivariate regression is also known as a univariate regression as there is only a single independent variable X). The dependent variable is so named because it depends on the independent variable; for example, sales revenue depends on the amount of marketing costs expended on a product's advertising and promotion, making the dependent variable sales and the independent variable marketing costs. An example of a bivariate regression is seen as simply inserting the best-fitting line through a set of data points in a two-dimensional plane as seen in the graphs shown next.

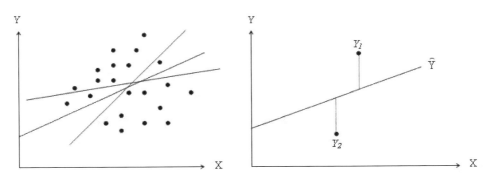

In other cases, a multivariate regression can be performed, where there are multiple or k number of independent X variables or regressors, where the general regression equation will now take the form:

$$Y = \beta_0 + \beta_1 X_1 + \beta_2 X_2 + \beta_3 X_3 ... + \beta_k X_k + \varepsilon$$

However, fitting a line through a set of data points in a scatter plot, as shown in the graphs, may result in numerous possible lines. The best-fitting line is defined as the single unique line that minimizes the total vertical errors. That is, the sum of the absolute distances between the actual data points and the estimated line. To find the best-fitting unique line that minimizes the errors, a more sophisticated approach is applied, using regression analysis. Regression analysis, therefore, finds the unique best-fitting line by requiring that the total errors be minimized, or by calculating:

$$Min \sum_{i=1}^{n} (Y_i - \hat{Y_i})^2 \quad \text{where } \hat{Y_i} \text{ is the predicted value and } Y_i \text{ is the actual value.}$$

Only one unique line minimizes this sum of squared errors. The errors (vertical distances between the actual data and the predicted line) are squared to prevent the negative errors from canceling out the positive errors. Solving this minimization problem with respect to the slope and intercept requires calculating first derivatives and setting them equal to zero:

$$\frac{d}{d\beta_0}\sum_{i=1}^{n}(Y_i - \hat{Y}_i)^2 = 0 \ \text{ and } \ \frac{d}{d\beta_1}\sum_{i=1}^{n}(Y_i - \hat{Y}_i)^2 = 0$$

which yields the bivariate regression's least squares equations:

$$\beta_1 = \frac{\sum_{i=1}^{n}(X_i - \overline{X})(Y_i - \overline{Y})}{\sum_{i=1}^{n}(X_i - \overline{X})^2} = \frac{\sum_{i=1}^{n}X_iY_i - \dfrac{\sum_{i=1}^{n}X_i\sum_{i=1}^{n}Y_i}{n}}{\sum_{i=1}^{n}X_i^2 - \dfrac{\left(\sum_{i=1}^{n}X_i\right)^2}{n}}$$

$$\beta_0 = \overline{Y} - \beta_1\overline{X}$$

Model Background

In the model, we have a set of Y and X values, and we need to find the slope and intercept coefficients that minimize the sum of squared errors of the residuals, which will hence yield the ordinary least squares (OLS) unique line and regression equation. We start off with some initial inputs (say, 3000 for both the intercept and slope, where we will then attempt to find the correct answer, but we need to insert some values here as placeholders for now). Then we compute the predicted values using the initial slope and intercept, and then the residual error between the predicted and actual Y values (Figure 103.1). These residuals are then squared and summed to obtain the *Sum of Squared Residuals*. In order to get the unique line that minimizes the sum of the squared residual errors, we employ an optimization process, then compare the results to manually computed values, and then reconfirm the results using Risk Simulator's *Multiple Regression* module.

Y	X	Slope	Intercept	Predicted	Residual	Squared Resid
1000	3	1000.00	1000.00	4000.00	3000.00	9000000.00
3333	3	1000.00	1000.00	4000.00	667.00	444889.00
2222	3	1000.00	1000.00	4000.00	1778.00	3161284.00
1111	2	1000.00	1000.00	3000.00	1889.00	3568321.00
5555	3	1000.00	1000.00	4000.00	-1555.00	2418025.00
2222	2	1000.00	1000.00	3000.00	778.00	605284.00
2222	3	1000.00	1000.00	4000.00	1778.00	3161284.00
5555	3	1000.00	1000.00	4000.00	-1555.00	2418025.00
4444	7	1000.00	1000.00	8000.00	3556.00	12645136.00
3333	6	1000.00	1000.00	7000.00	3667.00	13446889.00
2222	7	1000.00	1000.00	8000.00	5778.00	33385284.00
1111	8	1000.00	1000.00	9000.00	7889.00	62236321.00
5555	7	1000.00	1000.00	8000.00	2445.00	5978025.00
2222	6	1000.00	1000.00	7000.00	4778.00	22829284.00
2222	7	1000.00	1000.00	8000.00	5778.00	33385284.00
5555	6	1000.00	1000.00	7000.00	1445.00	2088025.00
4444	5	1000.00	1000.00	6000.00	1556.00	2421136.00
1111	6	1000.00	1000.00	7000.00	5889.00	34680321.00
2222	4	1000.00	1000.00	5000.00	2778.00	7717284.00
3333	5	1000.00	1000.00	6000.00	2667.00	7112889.00
2222	4	1000.00	1000.00	5000.00	2778.00	7717284.00
1111	4	1000.00	1000.00	5000.00	3889.00	15124321.00

Optimization Parameters

Intercept	1000.00
Slope	1000.00
Sum of Squared Residuals	285544595.00

Figure 103.1: Optimizing ordinary least squares approach

Procedure

1. Click on **Risk Simulator | Change Profile** and select *OLS Optimization* to open the preset profile.

2. Go to the *Model* worksheet and click on **Risk Simulator | Optimization | Run Optimization** and click **OK**. To obtain a much higher level of precision, rerun the optimization a second time to make sure the solution converges. This is important as sometimes the starting points (the placeholder values of 3000) chosen are important and may require a second or third optimization run to converge to a solution.

If you wish to recreate the optimization, you can attempt to do so by following the instructions next. The optimization setup is also illustrated in Figure 103.2.

1. Start a new profile (**Risk Simulator | New Profile**) and give it a name. Change the cells **F37** and **F38** back to some starting point, such as 3000 and 3000. This way, when the results are obtained, you see the new values.

2. Select cell **F39** and make it the **Objective** to minimize (this is the total sums of squares of the errors) by clicking on **Risk Simulator | Optimization | Set Objective**; then make sure **F39** is selected and click **Minimize**.

3. Set the decision variables as the intercept and slope (cells **F37** and **F38**, one at a time) by first selecting cell **F37** and clicking on **Risk Simulator | Optimization | Set Decision** or click on the **D** icon. Put in some large lower and upper bounds such as **–100000** and **100000**. Repeat for cell **F38**.

4. Click on **Risk Simulator | Optimization | Run Optimization** or click on the **Run Optimization** icon. Make sure to select **Static Optimization** and click **RUN**.

The optimized results are shown in Figure 103.3.

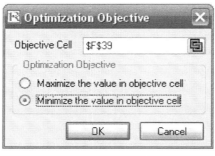

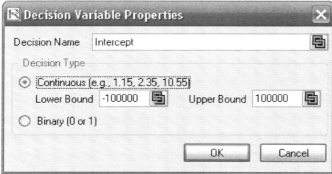

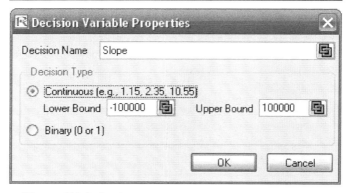

Figure 103.2: Setting up the least squares optimization

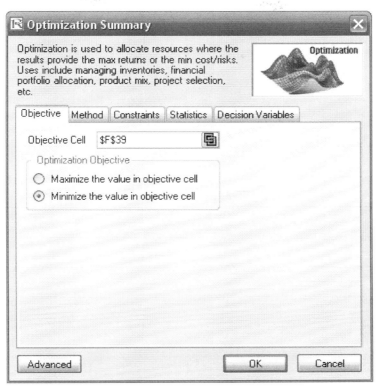

Figure 103.2: Setting up the least squares optimization *(continued)*

Optimization Parameters	
Intercept	2489.16
Slope	91.98
Sum of Squared Residuals	52991202.91

Figure 103.3: Optimized OLS results

The intercept is 2489.16 and the slope is 91.98, which means that the predicted regression equation is $Y = 2489.16 + 91.89X$. We can also recover these values if we computed these coefficients manually. The region B44 to G66 shows the manual computations and the results are shown in cells C71 and C72, which are identical to those computed using the optimization procedure (Figure 103.4).

Mean Y	2923.955	
Mean X	4.727	
B1	*91.98*	*Slope*
B0	*2489.16*	*Intercept*

Figure 103.4: Manual computations

The third and perhaps easiest alternative is to use Risk Simulator's *Multiple Regression* module. Perform the regression using these steps:

1. Select the **Y** and **X** values (including the header). That is, select the area **B12:C34**.

2. Click on **Risk Simulator | Forecasting | Multiple Regression Analysis.**

3. Make sure **Y** is selected as the dependent variable and click **OK.**

The results are generated as the *Report* worksheet in this file. Clearly, the regression report is a much more comprehensive than what we have done, complete with analytics and statistical results. The regression results using Risk Simulator shows the same values as we have computed using the two methods shown in Figure 103.5. Spend some time reading through the regression report.

Regression Results

	Intercept	X
Coefficients	2489.1583	91.9761
Standard Error	968.8464	191.3492
t-Statistic	2.5692	0.4807
p-Value	0.0183	**0.6360**
Lower 5%	468.1802	-307.1714
Upper 95%	4510.1364	491.1236

Figure 103.5: Risk Simulator results

Using Risk Simulator is a lot simpler and provides more comprehensive results than the alternative methods. In fact, the t-test shows that X is statistically not significant and hence is a worthless predictor of Y. This is a fact that we cannot determine using the first two methods. Indeed, when you have multiple independent X variables in a multivariate regression, you cannot compute the results manually using the second method. The only recourse and best alternative is to use this regression module.

104. Optimization – Stochastic Portfolio Allocation

File Name: Optimization – Stochastic Portfolio Allocation

Location: Modeling Toolkit | Optimization | Stochastic Portfolio Allocation

Brief Description: Illustrates how to run a stochastic optimization on continuous decision variables with simulation and interpret optimization results

Requirements: Modeling Toolkit, Risk Simulator

This model shows four asset classes with different risk and return characteristics. The idea here is to find the best portfolio allocation such that the portfolio's bang for the buck or returns to risk ratio is maximized. That is, the goal is to allocate 100% of an individual's investment among several different asset classes (e.g., different types of mutual funds or investment styles: growth, value, aggressive growth, income, global, index, contrarian, momentum, etc.). This model is different from others in that there exist several simulation assumptions (risk and return values for each asset), as seen in Figure 104.1.

A simulation is run, then optimization is executed, and the entire process is repeated multiple times to obtain distributions of each decision variable. The entire analysis can be automated using Stochastic Optimization.

In order to run an optimization, several key specifications on the model have to be identified first:

Objective: Maximize Return to Risk Ratio (C12)

Decision Variables: Allocation Weights (E6:E9)

Restrictions on Decision Variables: Minimum and Maximum Required (F6:G9)

Constraints: Portfolio Total Allocation Weights 100% (E11 is set to 100%)

Simulation Assumptions: Return and Risk Values (C6:D9)

The model shows the various asset classes. Each asset class has its own set of annualized returns and annualized volatilities. These return and risk measures are annualized values such that they can be consistently compared across different asset classes. Returns are computed using the geometric average of the relative returns, while the risks are computed using the logarithmic relative stock returns approach.

Column E, Allocation Weights, holds the decision variables, which are the variables that need to be tweaked and tested such that the total weight is constrained at 100% (cell E11). Typically, to start the optimization, we will set these cells to a uniform value. In this case, cells E6 to E9 are set at 25% each. In addition, each decision variable may have specific restrictions in its allowed range. In this example, the lower and upper allocations allowed are 10% and 40%, as seen in columns F and G. This setting means that each asset class may have its own allocation boundaries.

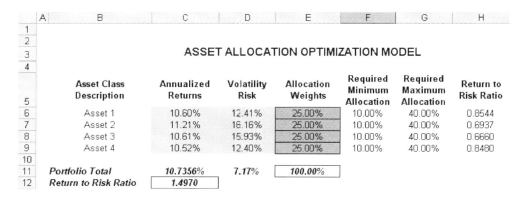

Figure 104.1: Asset allocation model ready for stochastic optimization

Next, column H shows the return to risk ratio, which is simply the return percentage divided by the risk percentage for each asset, where the higher this value, the higher the bang for the buck. The remaining parts of the model show the individual asset class rankings by returns, risk, return to risk ratio, and allocation. In other words, these rankings show at a glance which asset class has the lowest risk, or the highest return, and so forth.

Running an Optimization

To run this model, simply click on **Risk Simulator | Optimization | Run Optimization**. Alternatively, and for practice, you can set up the model using the following steps.

1. Start a new profile (**Risk Simulator | New Profile**).

2. For stochastic optimization, set distributional assumptions on the risk and returns for each asset class. That is, select cell **C6** and set an assumption (**Risk Simulator | Set Input Assumption**) and make your own assumption as required. Repeat for cells **C7** to **D9**.

3. Select cell **E6**, and define the decision variable (**Risk Simulator | Optimization | Set Decision** or click on the **Set Decision D** icon) and make it a **Continuous Variable,** and then link the decision variable's name and minimum/maximum required to the relevant cells (**B6, F6, G6**).

4. Then use the **Risk Simulator copy** on cell **E6**, select cells **E7** to **E9**, and use **Risk Simulator's paste** (**Risk Simulator | Copy Parameter**) and **Risk Simulator | Paste Parameter** or use the copy and paste icons). Remember not to use Excel's regular copy and paste functions.

5. Next, set up the optimization's constraints by selecting **Risk Simulator | Optimization | Constraints**, selecting **ADD**, and selecting the cell **E11**, and making it equal **100%** (total allocation, and do not forget the % sign).

6. Select cell **C12**, the objective to be maximized and make it the objective: **Risk Simulator | Optimization | Set Objective** or click on the **O** icon.

7. Run the optimization by going to **Risk Simulator | Optimization | Run Optimization**. Review the different tabs to make sure that all the required inputs in steps 2 and 3 are correct. Select **Stochastic Optimization** and let it run for 500 trials repeated 20 times (Figure 104.2 illustrates these setup steps).

Decision Variable Properties

Decision Name   Asset 1

Decision Type

○ Continuous (e.g., 1.15, 2.35, 10.55)

   Lower Bound 0.1   Upper Bound =GG

○ Integer (e.g., 1, 2, 3)

   Lower Bound   Upper Bound

○ Binary (0 or 1)

[OK] [Cancel]

Constraints

Current Constraints:

☑ $E$11 == 100%

[Add]
[Change]
[Delete]
[OK]
[Cancel]

Optimization Summary

Optimization is used to allocate resources where the results provide the max returns or the min cost/risks. Uses include managing inventories, financial portfolio allocation, product mix, project selection, etc.

Optimization

| Objective | Method | Constraints | Statistics | Decision Variables |

○ **Static Optimization**
   Run on static model without simulations. Usually run to determine the initial optimal portfolio before more advanced optimizations are applied.

○ **Dynamic Optimization**
   A simulation is first run, the results of the simulation are applied in the model, and then an optimization is applied to the simulated values.

   Number of Simulation Trials   1000

◉ **Stochastic Optimization**
   Similar to dynamic optimization but the process is repeated several times. The final decision variables will each have its own forecast chart indicating its optimal range.

   Number of Simulation Trials   500
   Number of Optimization Runs   20

[Advanced]   [OK]   [Cancel]

Figure 104.2: Setting up the stochastic optimization problem

Viewing and Interpreting Forecast Results

Stochastic optimization is performed when a simulation is first run and then the optimization is run. Then the whole analysis is repeated multiple times. The result is a distribution of each decision variable rather than a single-point estimate (Figure 104.3). This means that instead of saying you should invest 30.57% in Asset 1, the optimal decision is to invest between 30.10% and 30.99% as long as the total portfolio sums to 100%. This way, the results provide management or decision makers a range of flexibility in the optimal decisions.

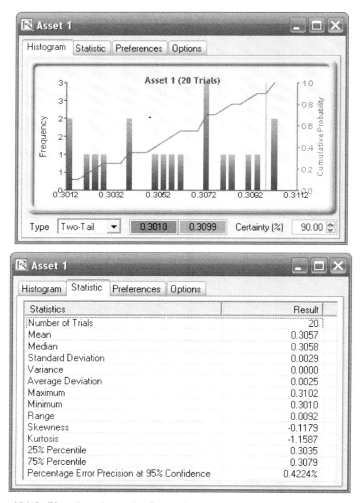

Figure 104.3: Simulated results from the stochastic optimization approach

105. Options Analysis – Binary Digital Instruments

File Name: Options Analysis – Binary Digital Instruments

Location: Modeling Toolkit | Options Analysis | Binary Digital Instruments

Brief Description: Values various types of binary digital instruments

Requirements: Modeling Toolkit

Modeling Toolkit Functions Used:

MTBinaryDownAndInCashAtExpirationOrNothing,
MTBinaryUpAndInCashAtExpirationOrNothing,
MTBinaryDownAndInAssetAtExpirationOrNothing,
MTBinaryUpAndInAssetAtExpirationOrNothing,
MTBinaryDownAndOutCashAtExpirationOrNothing,
MTBinaryUpAndOutCashAtExpirationOrNothing,
MTBinaryDownAndOutAssetAtExpirationOrNothing,
MTBinaryUpAndOutAssetAtExpirationOrNothing,
MTBinaryDownAndInCashAtHitOrNothing,
MTBinaryUpAndInCashAtHitOrNothing,
MTBinaryDownAndInAssetAtHitOrNothing,
MTBinaryUpAndInAssetAtHitOrNothing

Binary exotic instruments (also known as *Digital*, *Accrual* or *Fairway* instruments) become valuable only if a barrier (upper or lower) is breached (or not), and the payout could be in the form of some prespecified cash amount or the underlying asset itself. The cash or asset exchanges hands either at the point when the barrier is breached or at the end of the instrument's maturity (at expiration), assuming that the barrier is breached at some point prior to maturity.

For instance, in *Down and In Cash at Expiration* instruments, the instruments pay the specified cash amount at expiration if and only if the asset value breaches the lower barrier (asset value goes below the lower barrier), providing the holder of the instrument a safety net or a cash insurance in case the underlying asset does not perform well. *Up and In* instruments are such that the cash or asset is provided if the underlying asset goes above the upper barrier threshold. For *Up and Out* or *Down and Out* instruments, the asset or cash is paid as long as the barrier is not breached. In *At Expiration* instruments, cash and assets are paid at maturity, whereas *At Hit* instruments are payable at the point when the barrier is breached. Figure 105.1 shows a sample set of inputs in a binary digital instrument.

BINARY DIGITAL INSTRUMENTS

Input Assumptions

Asset Value or Stock Price	$10.00
Strike Price	$10.00
Upper Barrier Price	$8.00
Lower Barrier Price	$12.00
Cash Value	$10.00
Time to Maturity	1.00
Risk-free Rate	3.00%
Dividend Rate	0.00%
Annualized Volatility	25.00%
Delta T	0.00

Down and In Cash at Expiration	$14.83
Up and In Cash at Expiration	$4.50
Down and In Asset at Expiration	$18.80
Up and In Asset at Expiration	$5.50
Down and Out Cash at Expiration	$0.00
Up and Out Cash at Expiration	$5.20
Down and Out Asset at Expiration	$0.00
Up and Out Asset at Expiration	$4.50

Down and In Cash at Hit or Nothing	$15.66
Up and In Cash at Hit or Nothing	$4.58
Down and In Asset at Hit or Nothing	$15.66
Up and In Asset at Hit or Nothing	$4.58

Figure 105.1: Binary digital options

106. Options Analysis – Inverse Floater Bond

File Name: Options Analysis – Inverse Floater Bond Lattice

Location: Modeling Toolkit | Options Analysis | Inverse Floater Bond Lattice

Brief Description: Computes various inverse floater bond instruments using interest rate lattices

Requirements: Modeling Toolkit

Modeling Toolkit Functions Used: MTBDTInterestRateLattice, MTBDTFloatingCouponPriceLattice, MTBDTNoncallableDebtPriceLattice, MTBDTFloatingCouponPriceValue, MTBDTNoncallableDebtPriceValue

A floating coupon bond is a bond or other type of debt whose coupon rate has a direct or inverse relationship to short-term interest rates, and can be constructed using modified interest rate–based binomial lattices. With an inverse floater, as interest rates rise, the coupon rate falls. When short-term interest rates fall, an inverse floater holder benefits in two ways: The bond appreciates in price and the yield increases. The opposite is true for a direct floater bond. Alternatively, coupons could be allowed to float based on some external benchmark.

The only way such inverse floaters can be valued is through the use of modified binomial lattices, where the short rate or spot interest rate can be simulated using a discrete step approach in a lattice. Please note that a regular binomial or trinomial lattice used to model stock prices and options cannot be used. These stock price lattices assume a Brownian motion process versus the modified lattices used shown in this chapter (based on the Black-Derman-Toy methodology) that are calibrated to the term structure of interest rates with localized and changing volatilities over time.

At each step in the lattice, the yield curve or term structure of interest rates is mirrored, through a series of interest rates and instantaneous volatilities changing over time. The inverse rate, or the amount of coupon rate decrease per percent increase in interest rate, is an input used to compute this inverse floater. The result is the value of the inverse floater hedge. It is also assumed that this bond is callable, and the callable price and time step are also required inputs.

For instance, Figure 106.1 shows the input parameters required for solving this model (e.g., face value of the bond or principal of the debt, maturity, total steps in the lattice, current spot risk-free interest rate, the current coupon rate, market price of the bond, and if the bond is callable at certain steps and at a certain predetermined callable price). Further, the period-specific coupon payments, risk-free or external interest rate, and the interest rate volatilities can be entered as inputs. These three variables are entered as a time series (creating different interest yield curves with specific shapes and localized volatilities) in rows 13 to 15 of the model.

The first step is to create the short rate lattice, that is, the fluctuations of the interest rates based on the term structure of interest rates and localized volatilities entered in rows 14 and 15. In order to make sure that the interest rate lattice is built correctly, simply set all the volatilities to zero and use some simple interest rates such as those seen in Figure 106.3. Here we see that step 1's lattice rate of 3% is the sum of step 0 and step 1's spot rates (1% and 2%), and step 2's lattice rate of 5% is the same as the sum of step 1 and step 2's rates (2% and 3%), and so forth. This indicates that the interest rate lattice is calibrated correctly for interest rates.

Finally, we can check that the interest rate lattice is calibrated correctly for the localized volatility by putting in nonzero annualized volatilities and making the number of years match the number of lattice steps (this means each step taken on the lattice is one year). Figure 106.4 shows this calibration (cell C5 = C6 = 12, row 15 are all nonzero volatilities, and the volatility checks on row 19 are simply the natural logarithmic ratios of the upper and lower values on the lattice divided by two). As an example, the formula in cell D19 is LN(D21/D22)/2, which yields 2%, the input local volatility for that step. The remaining columns in row 19 match the input volatilities, indicating that the interest rate lattice is calibrated correctly for the yield curve and its corresponding volatilities.

To create this interest rate lattice, use the *MTBDTInterestRateLattice* function and link the inputs to the relevant locations in the spreadsheet. Figure 106.5 shows the function used and the input links for cell C21, the first input in the interest rate lattice. Once this function is completed, copy this cell **C21** and select the 13 × 13 matrix (we need a 13 ×13 matrix because we have a 12-step lattice starting at time 0, yielding a total of 13 steps) and paste the values in this area (**C21:O33**). Then, make sure the entire area is selected and click on **F2** and then hold down the **Shift + Control** keys and hit **Enter**. This will update the matrix to the results seen in Figure 106.1.

Replicate the steps above for the second matrix using the *MTBDTFloatingCouponPriceLattice* function, which computes the price of a bond with floating and changing coupon payments. Finally, generate the third lattice using the *MTBDTNoncallableDebtPriceLattice* for a noncallable straight bond value without any floating or changing coupons. The prices of these bonds are read directly off the lattices at step 0. For example, $108.79 and $97.59 for the two bonds respectively. The difference in price ($11.19 in cell K5) comes from the hedging effects of the floating coupons.

In addition, instead of having to build complete lattices, you can use the *MTBDTFloatingCouponPriceValue* and *MTBDTNoncallableDebtPriceValue* functions to obtain the values of the bonds (see cells F35 and F51), and the difference is the value of the floating coupon hedge. These "value" functions come in really handy as the results can be obtained immediately without having to recreate cumbersome lattice models.

INVERSE FLOATER WITH YIELD CURVE AND VOLATILITY TERM STRUCTURE

Real Options Valuation

Face Value	$100.00	Market Price of Debt	$102.00	Delta T 0.4167
Maturity	5	Callable Price	$100.00	Value of Hedge 11.1989
Total Steps	12	Callable Step	5	
Current Rate (Yield)	1.50%			
Initial Coupon Rate	3.50%			

Stepped Up Coupon Payments	$1.50	$2.00	$2.00	$2.00	$2.00	$3.00	$3.00	$3.00	$3.00	$3.00	$4.00	$4.00
Periodic Interest Rates (Yields)	6.00%	6.00%	5.50%	5.50%	5.25%	5.25%	5.00%	5.00%	4.50%	4.50%	4.00%	4.00%	4.00%
Interest Volatilities	0.00%	25.00%	25.00%	25.00%	25.00%	25.00%	25.00%	25.00%	25.00%	25.00%	25.00%	25.00%	25.00%

Short Rate Lattice

Steps	0	1	2	3	4	5	6	7	8	9	10	11	12
0	6.00%	5.62%	5.49%	7.40%	6.32%	8.53%	6.35%	10.03%	1.11%	11.03%	0.01%	8.95%	13.22%
1		5.38%	4.45%	6.01%	5.13%	7.00%	5.16%	8.14%	0.90%	8.95%	0.01%	7.27%	10.73%
2			3.62%	4.88%	4.17%	5.89%	4.19%	6.61%	0.73%	7.27%	0.01%	5.90%	8.71%
3				3.96%	3.38%	4.62%	3.40%	5.37%	0.59%	5.90%	0.01%	4.79%	7.08%
4					2.75%	3.75%	2.76%	4.36%	0.48%	4.79%	0.01%	3.89%	5.75%
5						3.04%	2.24%	3.54%	0.39%	3.89%	0.00%	3.16%	4.66%
6							1.82%	2.87%	0.32%	3.16%	0.00%	2.58%	3.79%
7								2.33%	0.26%	2.56%	0.00%	2.08%	3.08%
8									0.21%	2.08%	0.00%	1.69%	2.50%
9										1.69%	0.00%	1.37%	2.03%
10											0.00%	1.11%	1.65%
11												0.91%	1.34%
12													1.09%

Floater Price Lattice — Using Modeling Toolkit Function: 108.7943

Steps	0	1	2	3	4	5	6	7	8	9	10	11	12
0	108.7943	108.0641	107.1943	105.8311	105.4349	104.6346	104.0503	102.5540	102.9305	99.3574	100.3244	95.5588	94.6976
1		112.0328	109.9811	109.5144	108.8586	107.8621	106.8785	105.1301	104.9311	101.4562	101.7327	97.1018	95.6836
2			114.1615	112.6057	111.7256	110.5604	109.2349	107.2719	105.5853	103.1942	102.8917	98.3733	95.4918
3				115.1840	114.1127	112.8040	111.1887	109.0447	107.9507	104.6281	103.8432	99.4181	97.1530
4					116.0908	114.6612	112.8024	110.5067	108.0723	105.8075	104.6226	100.2748	97.6932
5						116.1930	114.1308	111.7090	108.9921	106.7752	105.2600	100.9758	98.1340
6							115.2217	112.6953	110.7451	107.5677	105.7806	101.5486	98.4933
7								113.5029	111.3608	108.2157	106.2053	102.0162	98.7861
8									111.8630	108.7448	106.5515	102.3974	99.0244
9										109.1763	106.8335	102.7080	99.2184
10											107.0630	102.9609	99.3761
11												103.1667	99.5044
12													99.6086

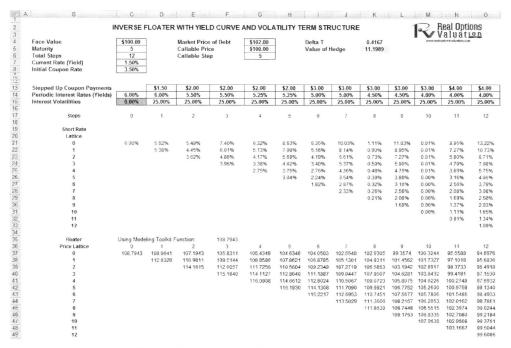

Figure 106.1: Inverse floater bond lattice I

Price Lattice

	0	1	2	3	4	5	6	7	8	9	10	11	12
0	97.5954	96.7341	96.1846	95.1933	95.0709	94.5850	95.1972	95.0106	96.5852	94.5019	96.7383	94.4701	96.0604
1		100.3979	99.8968	98.6233	98.2804	97.6305	97.8968	97.4921	98.5459	96.5525	98.1511	96.0180	97.0607
2			102.5487	101.5050	100.9701	100.1784	100.1474	99.5562	100.1683	98.2694	99.3139	97.2936	97.8805
3				103.9095	103.2107	102.2981	102.0143	101.2654	101.5062	99.6779	100.2685	98.3419	98.5512
4					105.0683	104.0535	103.5568	102.6754	102.6062	100.8368	101.0505	99.2014	99.0991
5						105.5019	104.8270	103.8352	103.5085	101.7878	101.6901	99.9048	99.5463
6							105.8703	104.7868	104.2471	102.5667	102.2125	100.4797	99.9108
7								105.5661	104.8509	103.2036	102.6387	100.9489	100.2078
8									105.3439	103.7237	102.9861	101.3314	100.4485
9										104.1479	103.2691	101.5431	100.5462
10											103.4994	101.8959	100.8063
11												102.1035	100.9364
12													101.0421

Figure 106.2: Inverse floater bond lattice II

Stepped Up Coupon Payments	$1.50	$2.00	$2.00	$2.00	$2.00	$3.00	$3.00	$3.00	$3.00	$3.00	$4.00	$4.00
Periodic Interest Rates (Yields)	1.00%	2.00%	3.00%	4.00%	5.00%	6.00%	7.00%	8.00%	9.00%	10.00%	11.00%	12.00%	13.00%
Interest Volatilities	0.00%	0.00%	0.00%	0.00%	0.00%	0.00%	0.00%	0.00%	0.00%	0.00%	0.00%	0.00%	0.00%

Short Rate Lattice

Steps	0	1	2	3	4	5	6	7	8	9	10	11	12
0	1.00%	3.00%	5.00%	7.00%	9.00%	11.00%	13.00%	15.00%	17.00%	19.00%	21.00%	23.00%	25.00%
1		3.00%	5.00%	7.00%	9.00%	11.00%	13.00%	15.00%	17.00%	19.00%	21.00%	23.00%	25.00%
2			5.00%	7.00%	9.00%	11.00%	13.00%	15.00%	17.00%	19.00%	21.00%	23.00%	25.00%
3				7.00%	9.00%	11.00%	13.00%	15.00%	17.00%	19.00%	21.00%	23.00%	25.00%
4					9.00%	11.00%	13.00%	15.00%	17.00%	19.00%	21.00%	23.00%	25.00%
5						11.00%	13.00%	15.00%	17.00%	19.00%	21.00%	23.00%	25.00%
6							13.00%	15.00%	17.00%	19.00%	21.00%	23.00%	25.00%
7								15.00%	17.00%	19.00%	21.00%	23.00%	25.00%
8									17.00%	19.00%	21.00%	23.00%	25.00%
9										19.00%	21.00%	23.00%	25.00%
10											21.00%	23.00%	25.00%
11												23.00%	25.00%
12													25.00%

Figure 106.3: Inverse floater bond lattice calibration of interest rates

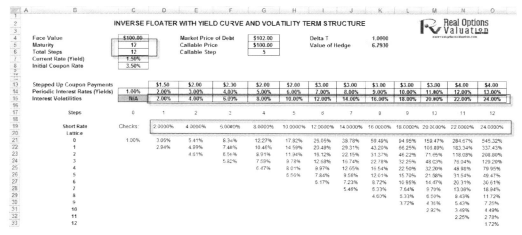

Figure 106.4: Inverse floater bond lattice calibration of volatilities

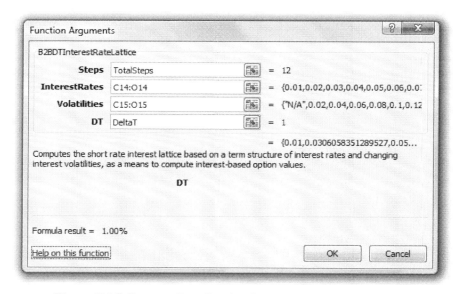

Figure 106.5: Interest Rate Lattice function in Modeling Toolkit

107. Options Analysis – Options Trading Strategies

File Name: Options Analysis – Options Strategies

Location: Modeling Toolkit | Options Analysis | Options Trading Strategies

Brief Description: Illustrates various options trading strategies such as covered calls, protective puts, bull and bear spreads, straddles, and strangles

Requirements: Modeling Toolkit

Modeling Toolkit Functions Used: MTOptionStrategyLongCoveredCall, MTOptionStrategyWriteCoveredCall, MTOptionStrategyLongProtectivePut, MTOptionStrategyWriteProtectivePut, MTOptionStrategyLongBullDebitSpread, MTOptionStrategyLongBearDebitSpread, MTOptionStrategyLongBullCreditSpread, MTOptionStrategyLongBearCreditSpread, MTOptionStrategyLongStraddle, MTOptionStrategyWriteStraddle, MTOptionStrategyLongStrangle, MTOptionStrategyWriteStrangle

We start by discussing a simple option example. Suppose ABC's stock is currently trading at $100, you can either purchase 1 share of ABC stock or purchase an options contract on ABC. Let's see what happens. If you purchase the stock at $100 and in 3 months the stock goes up to $110, you made $10 or 10%. And if it goes down to $90, you lost $10 or 10%. This is simple enough. Now, suppose you purchased a European call option with a strike price of $100 (at the money) for a 3-month expiration that cost $5. If the underlying stock price goes up to $110, you execute the call option, buy the stock at $100 contractually, and sell the stock in the market at $110; after the cost of the option, you net $110 – $100 – $5 = $5. The cost of the option was $5 and you made $5, so the return was 100%. If the stock goes down to $90, you let the option expire worthless and lose the $5 payment to buy the option, rather than lose $10 if you held the stock. In addition, if the stock goes to $0, you only lose $5 if you held the option versus losing $100 if you held the stock! This shows the limited downside of the option and unlimited upside leverage, the concept of hedging. The problem is, you can purchase many options through the leverage power of options. For instance, if you buy 20 options at $5 each, it costs you $100, the same as holding one stock. If the stock stays at $100 at maturity, you lose nothing on the stock, but you would lose 100% of your option premium. This is the concept of speculation!

Now, let's complicate things. We can represent the payoffs on call and put options graphically as seen in Figure 107.1. For instance, take the call option with a strike price of $10 purchased when the stock price was also $10. The premium paid to buy the option was $2. Therefore, if at maturity the stock price goes up to $15, the call option is executed (buy the stock at the contractual price of $10, turn around and sell the stock at the market price of $15, make $5 in gross profits, and deducting the cost of the option of $2 yields a net profit of $3). Following the same logic, the remaining payoff schedule can be determined as shown in Figure 107.1. Note that the break-even point is when the stock price is $12 (strike price plus the option premium). If the stock price falls to $10 or below, the net is –$2 (loss) because the option will never be exercised and the loss is the premium paid on the option. We can now chart the payoff schedules for buying (long) and selling (short) simple calls and puts. The "hockey stick" charts shown in Figure 107.1 are the various option payoff schedules.

Basic Options Positions

BASIC POSITIONS

Current Asset Price	$10.00										
Call Strike Price	$10.00		Put Strike Price			$10.00					
Call Option Premium	$2.00		Put Option Premium			$1.00					

Asset Price at Maturity	$5.00	$6.00	$7.00	$8.00	$9.00	$10.00	$11.00	$12.00	$13.00	$14.00	$15.00
Long Call	($2.00)	($2.00)	($2.00)	($2.00)	($2.00)	($2.00)	($1.00)	$0.00	$1.00	$2.00	$3.00
Short Call	$2.00	$2.00	$2.00	$2.00	$2.00	$2.00	$1.00	$0.00	($1.00)	($2.00)	($3.00)
Long Put	$4.00	$3.00	$2.00	$1.00	$0.00	($1.00)	($1.00)	($1.00)	($1.00)	($1.00)	($1.00)
Short Put	($4.00)	($3.00)	($2.00)	($1.00)	$0.00	$1.00	$1.00	$1.00	$1.00	$1.00	$1.00

Several key items:

• Limited downside and unlimited upside on long positions

• Limited upside and unlimited downside for short positions

• Symmetric around the x-axis creating a zero-sum game

• Breakeven profit ($0) is the strike price +/- option premium

Figure 107.1: Basic option payoff schedule

Next, we can use these simple calls and puts and put them in a portfolio or in various combinations to create options trading strategies. Options trading strategy refers to the use of multiple investment vehicles, including call options, put options, and the underlying stock. These vehicles can be purchased or sold at various strike prices to create strategies that will take advantage of certain market conditions. For instance, Figure 107.2 shows a Covered Call strategy, which comprises a long stock and short call combination. The position requires buying a stock and simultaneously selling a call option on that stock. The colored charts in the Excel model provide a better visual than those shown in this chapter. Please refer to the model for more details.

Just as in previous chapters, the functions used are matrices, where the first row is always the stock price at maturity, the second and third rows are the individual positions' net returns (e.g., in the case of the covered call, the second row represents the returns on the stock and the third row represents the short call position), and the fourth row is always the net total profit of the positions combined. As usual, apply the relevant Modeling Toolkit equations, copy and paste the cell's functions to a matrix comprising 4 rows by 18 columns, select the entire matrix area, hold down the **Shift + Control** keys and hit **Enter** to fill in the entire matrix. There are also two optional input parameters, the starting and ending points on the plot. These values refer to the starting and ending stock prices at maturity to analyze. If left empty, the software will automatically decide on these values.

The model also illustrates other options trading strategies. Figures 107.3 and 107.4 show the graphical representation of these positions, and the following lists these strategies and how they are obtained.

- A long covered call position is a combination of buying the stock (underlying asset) and selling a call of the same asset, typically at a different strike price than the starting stock price.

- A covered call is a combination of selling the stock (underlying asset) and buying a call of the same asset, typically at a different strike price than the starting stock price.

- A long protective put position is a combination of buying the stock (underlying asset) and buying a put of the same asset, typically at a different strike price than the starting stock price.

- Writing a protective put is a combination of selling the stock (underlying asset) and selling a put of the same asset, typically at a different strike price than the starting stock price.

- A long bull spread position is the same as writing a bearish spread, both of which are designed to be profitable if the underlying security rises in price. A bullish debit spread involves purchasing a call and selling a further out-of-the-money call. A bullish credit spread involves selling a put and buying a further out-of-the-money put.

- A long bearish spread takes advantage of a falling market and the strategy involves the simultaneous purchase and sale of options; both puts and calls can be used. Typically, a higher strike price option is purchased and a lower strike price option is sold. The options should have the same expiration date.

- A long bull spread position is the same as writing a bearish spread, both of which are designed to be profitable if the underlying security rises in price. A bullish debit spread involves purchasing a call and selling a further out-of-the-money call. A bullish credit spread involves selling a put and buying a further out-of-the money put.

- A long bearish spread takes advantage of a falling market and the strategy involves the simultaneous purchase and sale of options; both puts and calls can be used. Typically, a higher strike price is purchased and a lower strike price is sold. The options should have the same expiration date.

- A long straddle position requires the purchase of an equal number of puts and calls with identical strike price and expiration. A straddle provides the opportunity to profit from a prediction about the future volatility of the market. Long straddles are used to profit from high volatility but the direction of the move is unknown.

- Writing a straddle position requires the sale of an equal number of puts and calls with identical strike price and expiration. A straddle provides the opportunity to profit from a prediction about the future volatility of the market. Writing a straddles is used to profit from low volatility but the direction of the move is unknown.

- A long strangle requires the purchase of an out-of-the-money call and the purchase of an out-of-the-money put for a similar expiration (or within the same month), and profits from significant volatility of either directional move of the stock.

- Writing a strangle strategy requires the sale of an out-of-the-money call and the sale of an out-of-the-money put for a similar expiration (or within the same month), and profits from low volatility of either directional move of the stock.

LONG COVERED CALL

Asset Price	$8.00													
Call Strike Price	$10.00													
Option Premium	$3.00													

Asset Price at Maturity	$1.00	$2.00	$3.00	$4.00	$5.00	$6.00	$7.00	$8.00	$9.00	$10.00	$11.00	$12.00	$13.00	$14.00
Buy Stock	($7.00)	($6.00)	($5.00)	($4.00)	($3.00)	($2.00)	($1.00)	$0.00	$1.00	$2.00	$3.00	$4.00	$5.00	$6.00
Sell Call	$3.00	$3.00	$3.00	$3.00	$3.00	$3.00	$3.00	$3.00	$3.00	$3.00	$2.00	$1.00	$0.00	($1.00)
Total Profit	($4.00)	($3.00)	($2.00)	($1.00)	$0.00	$1.00	$2.00	$3.00	$4.00	$5.00	$5.00	$5.00	$5.00	$5.00

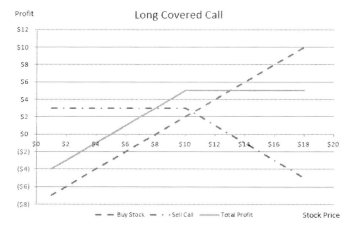

Figure 107.2: Covered call payoff schedule

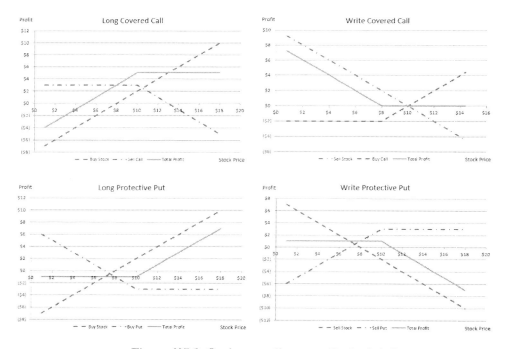

Figure 107.3: Options trading payoff schedule I

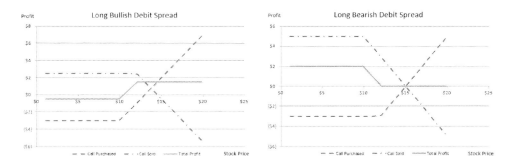

Figure 107.3: Options trading payoff schedule I *(continued)*

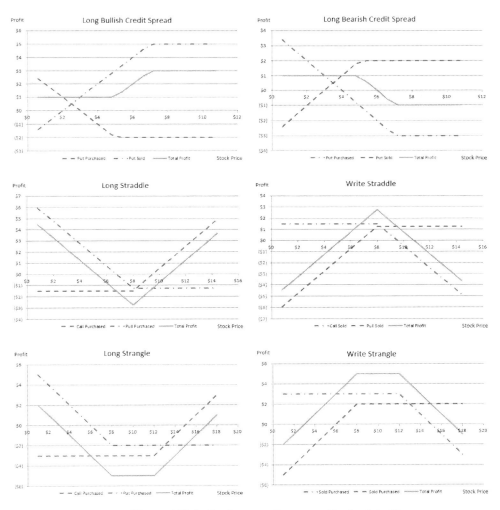

Figure 107.4: Options trading payoff schedule II

108. Options Analysis – Options-Adjusted Spreads Lattice

File Name: Options Analysis – Options Adjusted Spreads on Debt

Location: Modeling Toolkit | Options Analysis | Options Adjusted Spreads on Debt

Brief Description: Computes the option-adjusted spread, that is, the additional premium that should be charged on the option provision

Requirements: Modeling Toolkit

Modeling Toolkit Functions Used: MTBDTInterestRateLattice, MTBDTNoncallableDebtPriceLattice, MTBDTCallableDebtPriceLattice

Certain types of debt come with an option-embedded provision; for instance, a bond might be callable if the market price exceeds a certain value (when prevailing interest rates drop, making it more profitable for the issuing company to call the debt and reissue new ones at the lower rate) or have a prepayment allowance of mortgages or lines of credit and debt. Options-adjusted spreads, or OAS, value the spread between a straight bond and a bond with some embedded options, such as callability covenants, and are used to create modified binomial lattices to value such instruments, assuming changing interest rates and volatilities over time.

Figure 108.1 illustrates the *OAS Lattice* model with a set of sample inputs. The interest rates are assumed to be changing over time, with changing instantaneous volatilities, as in real life, where the yield curve or term structure of interest rates changes over time and has different volatilities at different ends of the curve. The entire yield curve may shift, twist, or bend, with higher maturity. See the *Yield Curve – Term Structure of Volatility* chapter for details on how to compute interest rate volatilities and the typical characteristics of volatility smiles and frowns.

Setting up this model is very similar to the one shown in Chapter 106 on the inverse floater bonds. Please review that chapter on how to create the lattice matrix as well as for information on calibrating the underlying interest rate lattice to make sure it models the term structure of interest rates and the corresponding localized volatilities of interest rates.

Note that one of the key inputs in the model is the call price of the bond and the time to call, translated into time steps. For instance, in a four-year debt modeled using an eight-step lattice, if the bond is callable starting in the third year, then the callable step is set as 6. Note that this model is the same as the last two chapters; the main difference being that this model allows you to generate your own modified binomial lattices to any number of steps. Be careful as the higher the number of steps, the longer it takes to generate and compute the lattices, depending on your computer's processor speed.

OPTIONS ADJUSTED SPREAD WITH YIELD CURVE AND VOLATILITY TERM STRUCTURE

Face Value	$100.00		Coupon Per Period	$2.50		Delta T	0.5000	
Maturity	4		Market Price of Debt	$100.00		Straight Spread	0.0000%	
Total Steps	8		Callable Price	$101.00		Callable Spread	0.0000%	
			Callable Step	6		Compute Spreads		

Modeling Toolkit Functions:
2.3387%
2.3896%

Interest Rates (Yields)	2.60%	2.60%	2.60%	2.60%	2.60%	2.60%	2.60%	2.60%	2.60%
Interest Volatilities	N/A	20.00%	20.00%	20.00%	20.00%	20.00%	20.00%	20.00%	20.00%

Steps	0	1	2	3	4	5	6	7	8

Short Rate Lattice

	0	1	2	3	4	5	6	7	8
0	2.60%	2.86%	3.14%	3.46%	3.80%	4.19%	4.61%	5.07%	5.58%
0		2.34%	2.57%	2.83%	3.11%	3.43%	3.77%	4.15%	4.57%
0			2.11%	2.32%	2.55%	2.81%	3.09%	3.40%	3.74%
0				1.90%	2.09%	2.30%	2.53%	2.79%	3.06%
0					1.71%	1.88%	2.07%	2.28%	2.51%
0						1.54%	1.69%	1.87%	2.05%
0							1.39%	1.53%	1.68%
0								1.25%	1.38%
8									1.13%

Straight Price Lattice — Using Function: 110.06

	0	1	2	3	4	5	6	7	8
0	110.06	107.95	106.01	104.26	102.73	101.45	100.48	99.87	99.68
1		110.04	108.00	106.13	104.43	102.95	101.72	100.78	100.19
2			109.65	107.68	105.85	104.19	102.74	101.53	100.60
3				108.97	107.02	105.22	103.59	102.15	100.94
4					107.99	106.07	104.29	102.66	101.22
5						106.77	104.86	103.08	101.45
6							105.34	103.43	101.64
7								103.71	101.80
8									101.92

Callable Debt Price Lattice — Using Function: 110.03

	0	1	2	3	4	5	6	7	8
0	110.03	108.25	106.63	105.15	103.77	102.32	100.48	99.87	99.68
1		109.68	107.99	106.48	105.21	104.20	103.50	100.78	100.19
2			108.97	107.29	105.80	104.52	103.50	103.50	100.60
3				107.95	106.28	104.79	103.50	103.50	100.94
4					106.68	105.01	103.50	103.50	103.50
5						105.19	103.50	103.50	103.50
6							103.50	103.50	103.50

Figure 108.1: Options-adjusted spreads lattice

109. Options Analysis – Options on Debt

File Name: Options Analysis – Options on Debt

Location: Modeling Toolkit | Options Analysis | Options on Debt

Brief Description: Computes options using the binomial lattice approach, assuming that the yield curve and term structure of interest rates change over time (both interest rates and volatility of interest rates are changing over time)

Requirements: Modeling Toolkit

Modeling Toolkit Functions Used: MTBDTInterestRateLattice, MTBDTZeroPriceLattice, MTBDTAmericanCallonDebtLattice, MTBDTAmericanPutonDebtLattice, MTBDTEuropeanCallonDebtLattice, MTBDTEuropeanPutonDebtLattice, MTBDTAmericanCallonDebtValue, MTBDTAmericanPutonDebtValue, MTBDTEuropeanCallonDebtValue, MTBDTEuropeanPutonDebtValue

This model is used to compute the American and European options on debt using a binomial lattice modified to account for changing volatilities and term structure of interest rates over the life of the option (Figure 109.1). It provides a sample template for building interest rate pricing lattices using the Modeling Toolkit functions and is set up to only compute up to 10 steps. Using this template, you can generate additional steps as required, as well as create customized lattices to value any types of embedded-option debt instruments. Also, you can use the Real Options SLS software to value many types of options and options-embedded instruments.

The modified lattices introduced in the preceding few chapters are specific to financial instruments that depend on interest rates, where the underlying asset's fundamental values are driven by interest rate fluctuations. Please see those chapters for instructions on setting up these lattice matrices and how to calibrate these matrices for the term structure of interest rates and their localized interest rate volatilities. The present model also shows how to compute the American and European call and put options on the bond. Note that entire lattices can be built using the "lattice" functions, or the value of the bond option can be computed simply by using the "value" functions in the model.

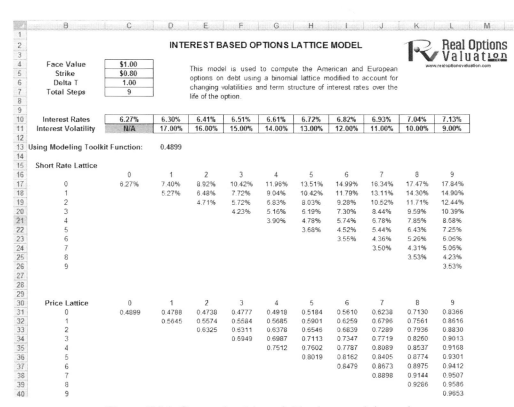

INTEREST BASED OPTIONS LATTICE MODEL

Real Options Valuation
www.realoptionsvaluation.com

Face Value	$1.00
Strike	$0.80
Delta T	1.00
Total Steps	9

This model is used to compute the American and European options on debt using a binomial lattice modified to account for changing volatilities and term structure of interest rates over the life of the option.

Interest Rates	6.27%	6.30%	6.41%	6.51%	6.61%	6.72%	6.82%	6.93%	7.04%	7.13%
Interest Volatility	N/A	17.00%	16.00%	15.00%	14.00%	13.00%	12.00%	11.00%	10.00%	9.00%

Using Modeling Toolkit Function: 0.4899

Short Rate Lattice

	0	1	2	3	4	5	6	7	8	9
0	6.27%	7.40%	8.92%	10.42%	11.96%	13.51%	14.99%	16.34%	17.47%	17.84%
1		5.27%	6.48%	7.72%	9.04%	10.42%	11.79%	13.11%	14.30%	14.90%
2			4.71%	5.72%	6.83%	8.03%	9.28%	10.52%	11.71%	12.44%
3				4.23%	5.16%	6.19%	7.30%	8.44%	9.59%	10.39%
4					3.90%	4.78%	5.74%	6.78%	7.85%	8.68%
5						3.68%	4.52%	5.44%	6.43%	7.25%
6							3.55%	4.36%	5.26%	6.06%
7								3.50%	4.31%	5.06%
8									3.53%	4.23%
9										3.53%

Price Lattice

	0	1	2	3	4	5	6	7	8	9
0	0.4899	0.4788	0.4738	0.4777	0.4918	0.5184	0.5610	0.6238	0.7130	0.8366
1		0.5645	0.5574	0.5584	0.5685	0.5901	0.6259	0.6796	0.7561	0.8616
2			0.6325	0.6311	0.6378	0.6546	0.6839	0.7289	0.7936	0.8830
3				0.6949	0.6987	0.7113	0.7347	0.7719	0.8260	0.9013
4					0.7512	0.7602	0.7787	0.8089	0.8537	0.9168
5						0.8019	0.8162	0.8405	0.8774	0.9301
6							0.8479	0.8673	0.8975	0.9412
7								0.8898	0.9144	0.9507
8									0.9286	0.9586
9										0.9653

Figure 109.1: Generating binomial lattices on debt options

110. Options Analysis –
Five Plain Vanilla Options

File Name: Options Analysis – Plain Vanilla Call Options (I-IV) and Plain Vanilla Put Options

Location: Modeling Toolkit | Options Analysis | Plain Vanilla Options (I-IV and Put Options)

Brief Description: Solves plain vanilla call and put option examples using the Real Options SLS software by applying advanced binomial lattices

Requirements: Real Options SLS, Modeling Toolkit

This chapter shows the five plain vanilla call and put options solved using Real Options SLS. These are plain vanillas as they are the simplest call and put options, without any exotic add-ons. A simple European call option is computed in this example using SLS. To follow along, start this example file by first starting the SLS software. Then click on the first icon, **Create a New Single Asset Model,** and when the single asset SLS opens, click on **File | Examples**. This is a list of the example files that come with the software for the single asset lattice solver. Start the Plain Vanilla Call Option I example. This example file will be loaded into the SLS software as seen in Figure 110.1. Alternatively, you can start the Modeling Toolkit software, click on **Modeling Toolkit** in Excel and select **Options Analysis,** and select the appropriate *Options Analysis* files. As this chapter uses the Real Options SLS software, it is recommended that readers unfamiliar with real options analysis or financial options analysis before proceeding with this chapter.

The starting PV Underlying Asset or starting stock price is $100, and the Implementation Cost or strike price is $100 with a 5-year maturity. The annualized risk-free rate of return is 5%, and the historical, comparable, or future expected annualized volatility is 10%. Click on **RUN** (or **ALT+R**) and a 100-step binomial lattice is computed. The results indicate a value of $23.3975 for both the European and American call options. Benchmark values using Black-Scholes and Closed-Form American approximation models as well as standard plain vanilla Binomial American and Binomial European Call and Put Options with 1,000-step binomial lattices are also computed. Notice that only the American and European Options are selected and the computed results are for these simple plain vanilla American and European call options.

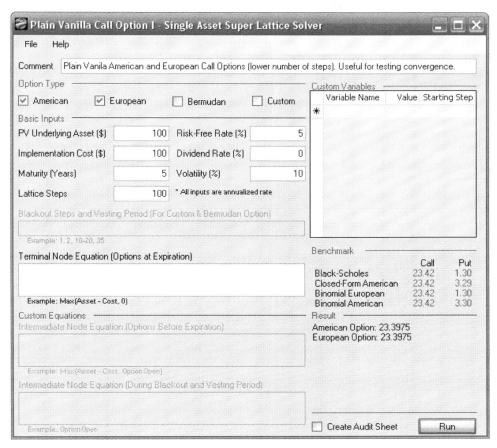

Figure 110.1: SLS Results of simple European and American call options

The benchmark results use both closed-form models (Black-Scholes and Closed-Form Approximation models) and 1,000-step binomial lattices on plain vanilla options. You can change the steps to **1000** in the basic inputs section (or open and use the *Plain Vanilla Call Option II* example model) to verify that the answers computed are equivalent to the benchmarks as seen in Figure 110.2. Notice that, of course, the values computed for the American and European options are identical to each other and identical to the benchmark values of $23.4187, as it is never optimal to exercise a standard plain vanilla call option early if there are no dividends. Be aware that the higher the lattice step, the longer it takes to compute the results. It is advisable to start with fewer lattice steps to make sure the analysis is robust and then progressively increase lattice steps to check for results convergence. See Chapter 6 of *Real Options Analysis,* Third Edition (Thomson–Shore, 2016) on convergence criteria on lattices regarding how many lattice steps are required for a robust option valuation. However, as a rule of thumb, the typical convergence occurs between 100 and 1,000 steps.

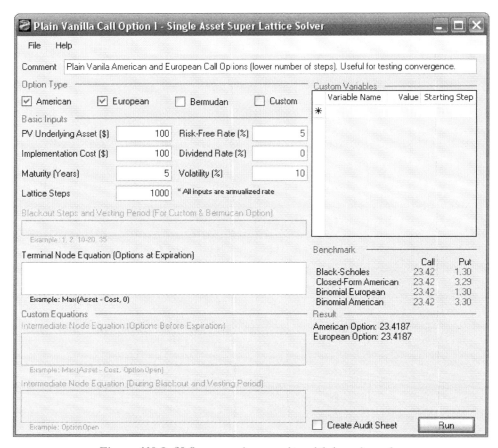

Figure 110.2: SLS comparing results with benchmarks

Alternatively, you can enter Terminal and Intermediate Node Equations for a call option to obtain the same results. Notice that using 100 steps and creating your own Terminal Node Equation of *Max(Asset-Cost,0)* and Intermediate Node Equation of *Max(Asset-Cost,OptionOpen)* will yield the same answer. When entering your own equations, make sure to first check **Custom Option**.

Figure 110.3 illustrates how the analysis is done. The example file used in this example is: *Plain Vanilla Call Option III*. Notice that the value $23.3975 in Figure 110.3 agrees with the value in Figure 110.1. The Terminal Node Equation is the computation that occurs at maturity, while the Intermediate Node Equation is the computation that occurs at all periods prior to maturity and is computed using backward induction. The term "OptionOpen" (one word, without spaces) represents "keeping the option open," and is often used in the Intermediate Node Equation when analytically representing the fact that the option is not executed but kept open for possible future execution. Therefore, in Figure 110.3, the Intermediate Node Equation *Max(Asset-Cost,OptionOpen)* represents the profit maximization decision of either executing the option or leaving it open for possible future execution. In contrast, the Terminal Node Equation of *Max(Asset-Cost,0)* represents the profit maximization decision at maturity of either executing the option if it is in the money, or allowing it to expire worthless if it is at the money or out of the money.

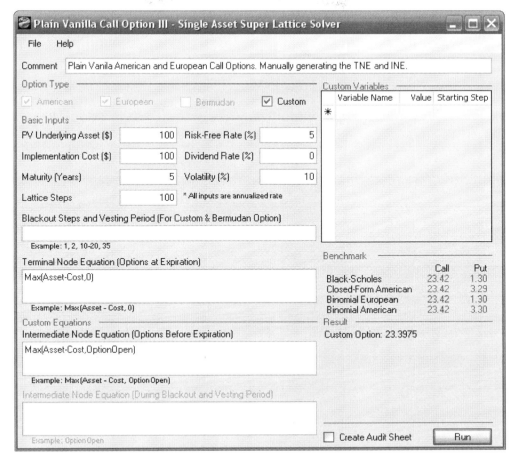

Figure 110.3: Custom equation inputs

In addition, you can create an *Audit* Worksheet in Excel to view a sample 10-step binomial lattice by checking the box *Generate Audit Worksheet*. For instance, loading the example file *Plain Vanilla Call Option I* and selecting the box creates a worksheet as seen in Figure 110.4. Two items on this audit worksheet are noteworthy:

- The audit worksheet generated will show the first 10 steps of the lattice, regardless of how many you enter. That is, if you enter **1000** steps, the first 10 steps will be generated. If a complete lattice is required, simply enter 10 steps in the SLS and the full 10-step lattice will be generated. The Intermediate Computations and Results are for the Super Lattice, based on the number of lattice steps entered and not based on the 10-step lattice generated. To obtain the Intermediate Computations for 10-step lattices, simply rerun the analysis inputting **10** as the lattice steps. This way, the audit worksheet generated will be for a 10-step lattice, and the results from SLS will now be comparable (Figure 110.5).

- The worksheet only provides values, as it is assumed that the user was the one who entered in the terminal and intermediate node equations, so there is no need to recreate these equations in Excel again. The user can always reload the SLS file and view the equations or print out the form if required (by clicking on **File | Print**).

The software also allows you to save or open analysis files. That is, all the inputs in the software will be saved and can be retrieved for future use. The results will not be saved because you may accidentally delete or change an input and the results would no longer be valid. In addition, rerunning the super lattice computations will take only a few seconds. It is always advisable for you to rerun the model when opening an old analysis file.

You may also enter in Blackout Steps, which are the steps on the super lattice that have different behaviors from the terminal or intermediate steps. For instance, you can enter **1000** as the lattice steps and enter **0-400** as the blackout steps, and some Blackout Equation (e.g., *OptionOpen*). This means that for the first 400 steps, the option holder can only keep the option open. Other examples include entering **1, 3, 5, 10** if these are the lattice steps where blackout periods occur. You will have to calculate the relevant steps within the lattice where the blackout exists. For instance, if the blackout exists in years 1 and 3 on a 10-year, 10-step lattice, then steps 1, 3 will be the blackout dates. This blackout step feature comes in handy when analyzing options with holding periods, vesting periods, or periods where the option cannot be executed. Employee stock options have blackout and vesting periods, and certain contractual real options have periods during which the option cannot be executed (e.g., cooling-off periods, or proof of concept periods).

If equations are entered into the Terminal Node Equation box and American, European, or Bermudan Options are chosen, the Terminal Node Equation entered will be the one used in the super lattice for the terminal nodes. However, for the intermediate nodes, the American option assumes the same Terminal Node Equation plus the ability to keep the option open; the European option assumes that the option can only be kept open and not executed; and the Bermudan option assumes that during the blackout lattice steps, the option will be kept open and cannot be executed. If you also enter the Intermediate Node Equation, first choose the Custom Option. Otherwise you cannot use the Intermediate Node Equation box. The Custom Option result uses all the equations you have entered in Terminal, Intermediate, and Intermediate with Blackout sections.

The Custom Variables list is where you can add, modify, or delete custom variables, the variables that are required beyond the basic inputs. For instance, when running an abandonment option, you need the salvage value. You can add this in the Custom Variables list and provide it a name (a variable name must be a single word), the appropriate value, and the starting step when this value becomes effective. That is, if you have multiple salvage values (i.e., if salvage values change over time), you can enter the same variable name (e.g., *salvage*) several times, but each time, its value changes and you can specify when the appropriate salvage value becomes effective. For instance, in a 10-year, 100-step super lattice problem where there are two salvage values—$100 occurring within the first 5 years and increases to $150 at the beginning of Year 6—you can enter two salvage variables with the same name, $100 with a starting step of 0 and $150 with a starting step of 51. Be careful here as Year 6 starts at step 51, not 61. That is, for a 10-year option with a 100-step lattice, we have: Steps 1–10 = Year 1; Steps 11–20 = Year 2; Steps 21–30 = Year 3; Steps 31–40 = Year 4; Steps 41–50 = Year 5; Steps 51–60 = Year 6; Steps 61–70 = Year 7; Steps 71–80 = Year 8; Steps 81–90 = Year 9; and Steps 91–100 = Year 10. Finally, incorporating **0** as a blackout step indicates that the option cannot be executed immediately.

Option Valuation Audit Sheet

Assumptions

PV Asset Value ($)	$100.00
Implementation Cost ($)	$100.00
Maturity (Years)	5.00
Risk-free Rate (%)	5.00%
Dividends (%)	0.00%
Volatility (%)	10.00%
Lattice Steps	100
Option Type	European

Terminal Equation	MAX(Asset-Cost, 0)
Intermediate Equation	@@
Intermediate Equation (Blackouts)	@@

Intermediate Computations

Stepping Time (dt)	0.0500
Up Step Size (up)	1.0226
Down Step Size (down)	0.9779
Risk-neutral Probability	0.5504

Results

Lattice Result	23.40

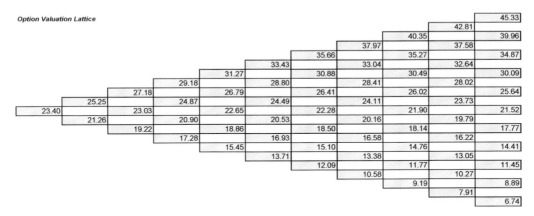

Figure 110.4: SLS-generated audit worksheet

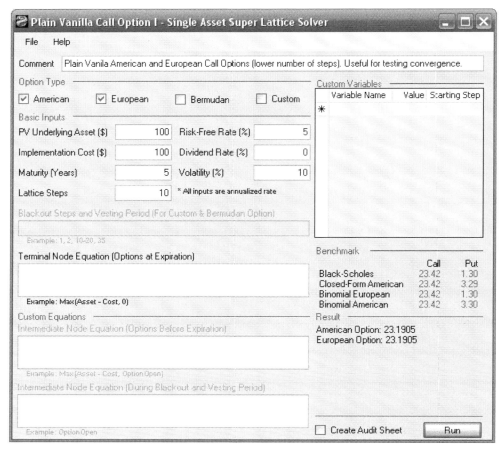

Figure 110.5: SLS results with a 10-step lattice

Finally, using the example file, *Plain Vanilla Option IV*, we see that when a dividend exists, the American option with its ability for early exercise is worth more than the Bermudan, which has early exercise but blackout periods when it cannot be exercised (e.g., Blackout Steps of 0–95 for a 100-step lattice on a 5-year maturity model means that for the first 4.75 years, the option cannot be executed), which in turn is worth more than the European option, which can be exercised only at expiration (Figure 110.6).

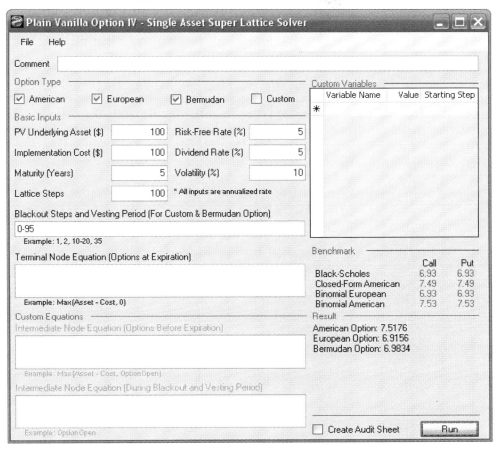

Figure 110.6: American, Bermudan, and European options

111. Personal Finance Models

File Names: Personal Finance (multiple models and examples in Modeling Toolkit)

Location: Modeling Toolkit | Personal Finance (multiple models)

Brief Description: Shows some of the personal finance models that exist in Modeling Toolkit (not all of the 30 models are shown)

Requirements: Modeling Toolkit and Risk Simulator

This chapter reviews several personal finance models, starting with a retirement savings growth model and modeling of sufficiency in retirement funds, to an analysis of whether you should buy or rent your home, saving and investing for your child's college, and accelerated amortization of home mortgages.

Retirement Savings Growth

If you participate in a 401(k) program or a similar retirement savings account, and your employer contributes or has some matching funds, how much money will you have saved by the time you intend to retire? Use this quick *401(k)* model (Figure 111.1) to determine the amount you will have at retirement. This model also shows you the difference between a taxable versus a nontaxable investment. Clearly, the model assumes that the economic and financial conditions remain stable over time, and for more detailed analysis, please see a certified financial analysts or financial planner. Nonetheless, this model helps you gauge how much you will have saved by retirement. If you wish to also include the payouts during retirement, please see the next section (*Retirement Funding with Inflation Adjustment* model) for more details. Finally, you can also model a stochastic or dynamic interest rate of return environment by setting Risk Simulator assumptions and running Monte Carlo simulations.

Retirement 401(k) Planner

Assumptions	
401(k) Contribution Each Paycheck ($)	$500.00
401(k) Employer Contribution Match Each Paycheck ($)	$0.00
Paychecks Per Year (12, 24, 26, or 52)	26
Expected Annual Rate of Return (%)	5.00%
Current Age	35
Anticipated Retirement Age	65
Current Value of 401(k) ($)	$100,000.00
Marginal Tax Rate (Federal and State %)	30.00%

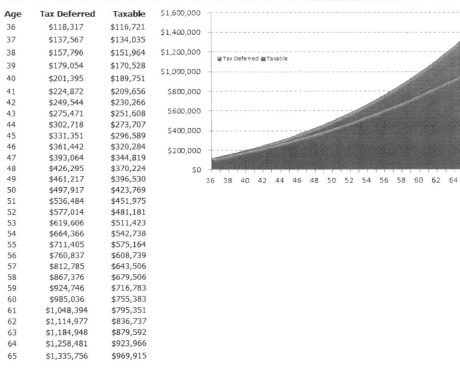

Age	Tax Deferred	Taxable
36	$118,317	$116,721
37	$137,567	$134,035
38	$157,796	$151,964
39	$179,054	$170,528
40	$201,395	$189,751
41	$224,872	$209,656
42	$249,544	$230,266
43	$275,471	$251,608
44	$302,718	$273,707
45	$331,351	$296,589
46	$361,442	$320,284
47	$393,064	$344,819
48	$426,295	$370,224
49	$461,217	$396,530
50	$497,917	$423,769
51	$536,484	$451,975
52	$577,014	$481,181
53	$619,606	$511,423
54	$664,366	$542,738
55	$711,405	$575,164
56	$760,837	$608,739
57	$812,785	$643,506
58	$867,376	$679,506
59	$924,746	$716,783
60	$985,036	$755,383
61	$1,048,394	$795,351
62	$1,114,977	$836,737
63	$1,184,948	$879,592
64	$1,258,481	$923,966
65	$1,335,756	$969,915

Figure 111.1: Retirement planning model

Retirement Funding with Inflation Adjustment

How soon do you need to start saving for your retirement? The short answer is that the sooner, the better! The earlier you start saving, the less monthly savings you will need to contribute towards your retirement fund. In this model (Figure 111.2), we look at your current salary and accounting for the inflation rate between now and the end of your natural life, and some investment returns on your savings, we can determine the minimum amount to save per year for retirement. The desired ending value of this retirement fund can also be set, using a value of $0 if you intend to exhaust the fund, or some positive value if you wish to provide a buffer amount in case inflation rises higher than expected, or to provide the family some lump sum amount to cover any unforeseen expenses. This model is built to intentionally not include any additional government sponsored programs (e.g., Social Security, Welfare) because different countries have different rules, regulations, and plans. Also, you can consider these plans as additional benefits above and beyond your retirement savings here. Note that the model screenshot intentionally has some hidden rows to conserve space.

Retirement Funding with Inflation Adjustment

Initial Savings Amount ($)	$100,000.00	Annual Salary ($)	$100,000.00
Annual Rate of Return (%)	8.00%	Replacement Ratio (%)	75%
Current Age	35.00		
Retirement Age	60.00	Inflation Rate (%)	3.00%
Average Terminal Age	90.00	Terminal Wealth Goal ($)	$0.00
Annual Contribution	$24,590.30	Terminal Wealth	$0

PAYOUT SCHEDULE

Age	Status	Starting Value	Contributions	Withdrawal	Wealth
35	Working	$100,000.00	$24,590.30	$0.00	$124,590.30
36	Working	$108,000.00	$51,147.83	$0.00	$159,147.83
37	Working	$116,640.00	$79,829.96	$0.00	$196,469.96
38	Working	$125,971.20	$110,806.66	$0.00	$236,777.86
39	Working	$136,048.90	$144,261.49	$0.00	$280,310.39
40	Working	$146,932.81	$180,392.72	$0.00	$327,325.52
56	Working	$503,383.37	$1,363,698.41	$0.00	$1,867,081.78
57	Working	$543,654.04	$1,497,384.58	$0.00	$2,041,038.62
58	Working	$587,146.36	$1,641,765.65	$0.00	$2,228,912.02
59	Working	$634,118.07	$1,797,697.21	$0.00	$2,431,815.28
60	Working	$684,847.52	$1,966,103.29	$0.00	$2,650,950.81
61	Retired	$0.00	$0.00	$161,744.35	$2,688,342.98
62	Retired	$0.00	$0.00	$166,596.68	$2,723,486.01
63	Retired	$0.00	$0.00	$171,594.58	$2,756,042.75
64	Retired	$0.00	$0.00	$176,742.41	$2,785,644.36
65	Retired	$0.00	$0.00	$182,044.69	$2,811,887.65
85	Retired	$0.00	$0.00	$328,792.95	$1,543,590.30
86	Retired	$0.00	$0.00	$338,656.74	$1,301,328.25
87	Retired	$0.00	$0.00	$348,816.44	$1,028,712.75
88	Retired	$0.00	$0.00	$359,280.94	$722,986.36
89	Retired	$0.00	$0.00	$370,059.36	$381,161.16
90	Retired	$0.00	$0.00	$381,161.14	$0.0

Figure 111.2: Retirement analysis

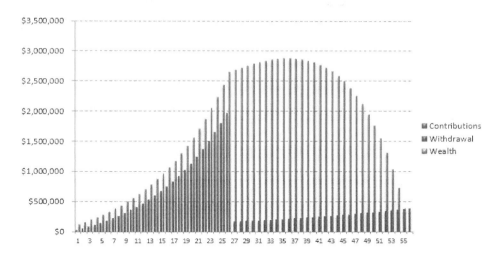

Figure 111.2: Retirement analysis *(continued)*

Is it better to buy your home or to rent? Well, it really depends on what type of house you are purchasing, the maintenance cost, rental price, down payment required for the house, the mortgage you will incur, whether you are retired empty nesters or just starting your career, and many other issues. This *Buy versus Rent* model (Figure 111.3) helps you make this determination quickly to see if it is indeed more financially profitable to buy versus rent your home. We will leave the other psychological factors up to you!

Buying versus Renting Your Home

After-tax Rate of Return on Investments (%)	8.00%
Marginal Tax Rate (%)	35.00%
Estimated Annual Appreciation of Home (%)	10.00%
Down Payment on Home ($)	$100,000
Estimated Closing Costs ($)	$10,000
Estimated Purchase Price of Home ($)	$500,000
Monthly Rent ($)	$1,500
Renter's Annual Insurance Premium ($)	$0
Annual Mortgage Interest Rate (%)	8.000%
Term of Mortgage (years)	30
Annual Property Taxes ($)	$5,000
Annual Homeowner's Insurance ($)	$1,500
Annual Home Maintenance ($)	$2,000

Total annual cost of renting	$18,000
Monthly mortgage payment	$2,935
Annual mortgage payment	$35,221
Opportunity cost of buying	$8,800
Total cost of buying	$52,521
Principal reduction in mortgage	$3,221
Tax savings of interest deductions	$11,200
Tax savings of property tax	$1,750
Total adjustments	$16,171
Annual after-tax cost of home ownership	$36,350
Estimated annual appreciation in value of home	$50,000
Net Annual Profit (Cost) of Home Ownership	**$13,650**

Figure 111.3: Buy versus rent

College Funding with Inflation Adjustment

How much money do you need to start saving for your child's college education? Well, as usual, the answer is always the sooner, the better! The earlier you start saving, the less monthly savings you will need to contribute towards that college fund. In this *College Funding* model (Figure 111.4), we look at what the current cost of attending college per year is, accounting for the inflation rate between now and the end of the college education, and some investment returns on your savings. You can also set the desired ending value of this college fund, using a value of $0 if you intend to only pay for the education, or some positive value if you wish to provide a cost buffer in case prices rise higher than expected, or to provide the fresh graduate some lump sum amount when s/he graduates (a nice car or apartment down payment, moving expenses, etc.).

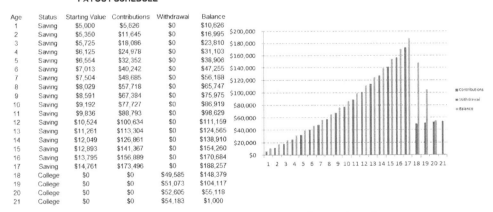

College Funding with Inflation Adjustment

Initial Amount Saved ($)	$5,000		Current Annual College Cost ($)	$30,000
Annual Investment Return (%)	7.00%		Inflation Rate (%)	3.00%
Current Age of Child	1.00		Target End Value of College Fund ($)	$1,000
Age Starting College	18.00			
Age Graduating College	21.00		Annual Investment Required	$5,626
			Monthly Investment Required	$469
			Ending Value of College Fund	$1,000

PAYOUT SCHEDULE

Age	Status	Starting Value	Contributions	Withdrawal	Balance
1	Saving	$5,000	$5,626	$0	$10,626
2	Saving	$5,350	$11,645	$0	$16,995
3	Saving	$5,725	$18,096	$0	$23,810
4	Saving	$6,125	$24,978	$0	$31,103
5	Saving	$6,554	$32,352	$0	$38,906
6	Saving	$7,013	$40,242	$0	$47,255
7	Saving	$7,504	$48,685	$0	$56,188
8	Saving	$8,029	$57,718	$0	$65,747
9	Saving	$8,591	$67,384	$0	$75,975
10	Saving	$9,192	$77,727	$0	$86,919
11	Saving	$9,836	$88,793	$0	$98,629
12	Saving	$10,524	$100,634	$0	$111,159
13	Saving	$11,261	$113,304	$0	$124,565
14	Saving	$12,049	$126,861	$0	$138,910
15	Saving	$12,893	$141,367	$0	$154,260
16	Saving	$13,795	$156,889	$0	$170,684
17	Saving	$14,761	$173,496	$0	$188,257
18	College	$0	$0	$49,585	$148,379
19	College	$0	$0	$51,073	$104,117
20	College	$0	$0	$52,605	$55,118
21	College	$0	$0	$54,183	$1,000

Figure 111.4: Saving for your child's college education

Mortgage Amortization and Accelerated Payoff

You frequently hear about biweekly mortgage payments, or friends say that you should put a little extra into your loan or mortgage to speed up the payoff on your home. This *Mortgage Accelerated Payoff* model (Figure 111.5) shows you how much time and how much interest you will be saving if you put some extra money into paying off the mortgage every month.

In an amortization schedule, you notice that the monthly payments are identical such that the remaining balance ends up as zero at the end of the mortgage life. Notice also that the principal paid per month increases and interest paid decreases over the life of the mortgage. This is because the monthly mortgage payment goes toward paying off the principal and interest on the remaining principal. Over time, as the principal of the mortgage is reduced, the interest on the remaining principal decreases. So, with the same monthly payment, a larger portion of the payment goes towards paying down the principal and less towards the interest.

Notice that by paying a little extra each month, you can drastically reduce the total interest you actually pay throughout the life of the mortgage and cut years from the life of the mortgage! Note that the model screenshot intentionally has some hidden rows to conserve space.

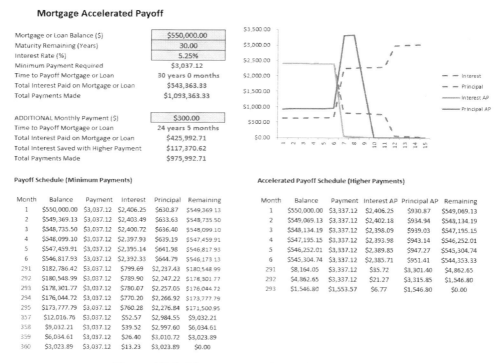

Figure 111.5: Mortgage accelerated payoff model

112. Probability of Default – Bond Yields and Spreads (Market Comparable Approach)

File Name: Probability of Default – Yields and Spreads

Location: Modeling Toolkit | Prob of Default | Bond Yields and Spreads (Market Comparable)

Brief Description: Generates the probability of default on a bond or debt by looking at market traded instruments' yields (bond)

Requirements: Modeling Toolkit

Modeling Toolkit Functions Used:
MTProbabilityDefaultCumulativeBondYieldApproach,
MTProbabilityDefaultHazardRate, MTProbabilityDefaultCumulativeSpreadApproach,
MTProbabilityDefaultAdjustedBondYield, MTProbabilityDefaultCorrelation,
MTProbabilityDefaultAverageDefaults, MTProbabilityDefaultPercentileDefaults

This chapter looks at the computation of probability of default on a bond or debt by looking at market traded instruments. Probability of default measures the degree of likelihood that the borrower of a loan or debt (an obligor) will be unable to make the necessary scheduled repayments on the debt, thereby defaulting on it. If the obligor is unable to pay, the debt is in default, and the lenders have legal avenues to attempt a recovery of the debt or at least partial repayment of the entire debt. The higher the default probability a lender estimates a borrower to have, the higher the interest rate the lender will charge the borrower as compensation for bearing the higher default risk. Probability of default models are categorized as structural or empirical.

Structural models compute probability of default based on market data (e.g., bond yields and spreads, equity prices, market and book values of asset and liabilities, as well as the volatility of these variables). In contrast, empirical models or credit scoring models are used to quantitatively determine the probability that a loan or loan holder will default, where the loan holder is an individual, by looking at historical portfolios of loans held, where individual characteristics are assessed (e.g., age, educational level, debt to income ratio, etc.).

The bond yield comparable approach is clearly a structural model. In these models, given the annualized spot risk-free yields over time, the corresponding corporate bond yields (both are zero coupon bonds), and the expected recovery rate upon default, we can compute the implied cumulative default probability, the default probability in a particular year, and the hazard rates for each year (Figure 112.1).

In addition, the cumulative default probability between two years can also be computed using the same bond yield approach. Sometimes, only the risky bond or debt's spread (the premium charged above the risk-free rate) is known. Using this credit spread, the cumulative probability of default can also be determined. To obtain the probability of default in a given year, compute two cumulative default probabilities and get the difference.

This model also exemplifies the use of the Credit Risk Plus method employed by Credit Suisse Financial Products and is used to compute the average number of credit defaults per period given the total number of credit exposures in the portfolio, the cumulative probability of default on average, and the percentile Value at Risk for the portfolio. The Credit Risk Plus method can also be used to compute the percentile given some estimated average number of defaults per period.

The downside to this method is the need for bond yield data that are comparable to the debt or bond to be analyzed. In contrast, the subsequent chapters look at other structural and empirical models that do not require a bond market.

Probability of Default Analysis

Maturity	Risk-Free Zero Yield	Corporate Bond Zero Yield	Cumulative Default Probability	Default Probability Specific Year	Hazard Rate Specific Year
1	5.00%	5.25%	0.3121%	0.3121%	1.1675%
2	5.00%	5.50%	1.2438%	0.9317%	1.7093%
3	5.00%	5.70%	2.5976%	1.3539%	2.0181%
4	5.00%	5.85%	4.1786%	1.5809%	2.0952%
5	5.00%	5.95%	5.7987%	1.6201%	1.9410%
6	5.00%	6.00%	7.2794%	1.4807%	2.0952%
7	5.00%	6.05%	8.8580%	1.5785%	2.0027%
8	5.00%	6.08%	10.3466%	1.4886%	1.9564%
9	5.00%	6.10%	11.7822%	1.4356%	2.0181%
10	5.00%	6.12%	13.2445%	1.4623%	

Assumed Recovery Rate: 20.00%

Modeling Toolkit Function Used: MTProbabilityDefaultCumulativeBondYieldApproach

Computing the Cumulative Default Probability between two time periods:

From Year	5
To Year	10
Cumulative Default Probability	**7.4458%**

Computing the Cumulative Probability between two time periods using Bond Spreads:

First Credit Spread above Risk-Free	0.9500%
First Credit Spread's Maturity	5
Second Credit Spread above Risk-Free	1.1200%
Second Credit Spread's Maturity	10
First Credit Spread's Cumulative Default Probability	**5.7987%**
Second Credit Spread's Cumulative Default Probability	**13.2445%**
Cumulative Default Probability between First and Second Maturity	**7.4458%**

Modeling Toolkit Function Used: MTProbabilityDefaultCumulativeSpreadApproach

Figure 112.1: Bond yield approach to probability of default

113. Probability of Default – Empirical Model

File Name: Probability of Default – Empirical

Location: Modeling Toolkit | Prob of Default | Empirical (Individuals)

Brief Description: Computes the probability of default on loans of individuals given some historical data on existing loans (age, educational levels, years at employment, etc.) and applies a maximum likelihood estimation approach

Requirements: Modeling Toolkit, Risk Simulator

Probability of default measures the degree of likelihood that the borrower of a loan or debt (also called an obligor) will be unable to make the necessary scheduled repayments on the debt, thereby defaulting on it. Should the obligor be unable to pay, the debt is in default, and the lenders of the debt have legal avenues to attempt a recovery of the debt, or at least partial repayment of the entire debt. The higher the default probability a lender estimates a borrower to have, the higher the interest rate the lender will charge the borrower as compensation for bearing the higher default risk.

Probability of default models are categorized as structural or empirical. Structural models are presented over the next few chapters, which look at a borrower's ability to pay based on market data such as equity prices, market and book values of asset and liabilities, as well as the volatility of these variables. Hence, they are used predominantly to estimate the probability of default of companies and countries. In contrast, empirical models or credit scoring models as presented here are used to quantitatively determine the probability that a loan or loan holder will default, where the loan holder is an individual, by looking at historical portfolios of loans held, where individual characteristics are assessed (e.g., age, educational level, debt to income ratio, and so forth). Other default models in the Modeling Toolkit handle corporations using market comparables and asset/liability valuations as seen in the next chapter.

The data here represents a sample of several hundred previous loans, credit, or debt issues. The data show whether each loan had defaulted or not, as well as the specifics of each loan applicant's age, education level (1–3 indicating high school, university, or graduate professional education), years with current employer, and so forth (Figure 113.1). The idea is to model these empirical data to see which variables affect the default behavior of individuals, using Risk Simulator's *Maximum Likelihood* models. The resulting model will help the bank or credit issuer compute the expected probability of default of an individual credit holder having specific characteristics.

To run the analysis, select the data (include the headers) and make sure that the data have the same length for all variables, without any missing or invalid data. Then, click on **Risk Simulator | Forecasting | Maximum Likelihood Models**. A sample set of results provided in the *MLE* worksheet in the model, complete with detailed instructions on how to compute the expected probability of default of an individual.

Maximum Likelihood Estimates (MLE) on a binary multivariate logistic analysis is used to model dependent variables to determine the expected probability of success of belonging to a certain group. For instance, given a set of independent variables (e.g., age, income, education level of credit card or mortgage loan holders), we can model the probability of default using MLE. A typical regression model is invalid because the errors are heteroskedastic and non-normal, and the resulting estimated probability estimates sometimes will be above 1 or below 0. MLE analysis handles these problems using an iterative optimization routine.

Use the MLE when the data are *ungrouped* (there is only one dependent variable, and its values are either 1 for success or 0 for failure). If the data are *grouped* into unique categories (for instance, the dependent variables are actually two variables, one for the *Total Events* T and another *Successful Events* S), and if, based on historical data for a given level of income, age, education level and so forth, data on how many loans had been issued (T) and of those, how many defaulted (S) are available, then use the *grouped* approach and apply the *Weighted Least Squares* and *Unweighted Least Squares* method instead.

The coefficients provide the estimated MLE intercept and slopes. For instance, the coefficients are estimates of the true population b values in the equation $Y = b_0 + b_1X_1 + MTX_2 + ... + b_nX_n$. The *standard error* measures how accurate the predicted coefficients are, and the Z-statistics are the ratios of each predicted coefficient to its standard error.

The Z-statistic is used in hypothesis testing, where we set the null hypothesis (H_o) such that the real mean of the coefficient is equal to zero, and the alternate hypothesis (H_a) such that the real mean of the coefficient is not equal to zero. The Z-test is very important as it calculates if each of the coefficients is statistically significant in the presence of the other regressors. This means that the Z-test statistically verifies whether a regressor or independent variable should remain in the model or should be dropped. That is, the smaller the p-value, the more significant the coefficient. The usual significant levels for the p-value are 0.01, 0.05, and 0.10, corresponding to the 99%, 95%, and 90% confidence levels.

The coefficients estimated are actually the logarithmic odds ratios and cannot be interpreted directly as probabilities. A quick computation is first required. The approach is simple. To estimate the probability of success of belonging to a certain group (e.g., predicting if a debt holder will default given the amount of debt held), simply compute the estimated Y value using the MLE coefficients. For instance, if the model is, say, $Y = -2.1 + 0.005$ (Debt in thousands), then someone with a \$100,000 debt has an estimated Y of $-2.1 + 0.005(100) = -1.6$. Then, calculate the inverse antilog of the odds ratio by computing:

$$\frac{\exp(\textit{estimated } Y)}{1 + \exp(\textit{estimated } Y)} = \frac{\exp(-1.6)}{1 + \exp(-1.6)} = 0.1679$$

Such a person has a 16.79% chance of defaulting on the new debt. Using this probability of default, you can then use the *Credit Analysis – Credit Premium* model to determine the additional credit spread to charge this person given this default level and the customized cash flows anticipated from this debt holder.

PROBABILITY OF DEFAULT (EMPIRICAL USING MAXIMUM LIKELIHOOD)

Defaulted	Age	Education Level	Years with Current Employer	Years at Current Address	Household Income (Thousands $)	Debt to Income Ratio (%)	Credit Card Debt (Thousands $)	Other Debt (Thousands $)
1	41	3	17	12	176	9.3	11.36	5.01
0	27	1	10	6	31	17.3	1.36	4
0	40	1	15	14	55	5.5	0.86	2.17
0	41	1	15	14	120	2.9	2.66	0.82
1	24	2	2	0	28	17.3	1.79	3.06
0	41	2	5	5	25	10.2	0.39	2.16
0	39	1	20	9	67	30.6	3.83	16.67
0	43	1	12	11	38	3.6	0.13	1.24
1	24	1	3	4	19	24.4	1.36	3.28
0	36	1	0	13	25	19.7	2.78	2.15
0	27	1	0	1	16	1.7	0.18	0.09
0	25	1	4	0	23	5.2	0.25	0.94
0	52	1	24	14	64	10	3.93	2.47
0	37	1	6	9	29	16.3	1.72	3.01
0	48	1	22	15	100	9.1	3.7	5.4
1	36	2	9	6	49	8.6	0.82	3.4
1	36	2	13	6	41	16.4	2.92	3.81
0	43	1	23	19	72	7.6	1.18	4.29
0	39	1	6	9	61	5.7	0.56	2.91
0	41	3	0	21	26	1.7	0.1	0.34
0	39	1	22	3	52	3.2	1.15	0.51
0	47	1	17	21	43	5.6	0.59	1.82

Figure 113.1: Empirical analysis of probability of default

114. Probability of Default – External Options Model (Public Company)

File Name: Probability of Default – External Options Model

Location: Modeling Toolkit | Prob of Default | External Options Model (Public Company)

Brief Description: Computes the probability of default and distance to default of a publicly traded company by decomposing the firm's book value and market value of liability, assets, and volatility using a simultaneous equations options model with optimization

Requirements: Modeling Toolkit, Risk Simulator

Modeling Toolkit Functions Used: MTMertonDefaultProbabilityII, MTMertonDefaultDistance, MTBlackScholesCall, MTProbabilityDefaultMertonImputedAssetValue, MTProbabilityDefaultMertonImputedAssetVolatility, MTProbabilityDefaultMertonRecoveryRate, MTProbabilityDefaultMertonMVDebt

Probability of default models is a category of models that assesses the likelihood of default by an obligor. These models differ from regular credit scoring models in several ways. First of all, credit scoring models usually are applied to smaller credits (individuals or small businesses) whereas default models are applied more to larger credits (corporation or countries). Credit scoring models are largely statistical, regressing instances of default against various risk indicators, such as an obligor's income, home renter or owner status, years at a job, educational level, debt to income ratio, and so forth. An example of such a model is seen in the previous chapter, *Probability of Default – Empirical Model*, where the maximum likelihood approach is used on an advanced econometric regression model. Default models, in contrast, directly model the default process and typically are calibrated to market variables, such as the obligor's stock price, asset value, debt book value, or credit spread on its bonds. Default models find many applications within financial institutions. They are used to support credit analysis and to find the probability that a firm will default, to value counterparty credit risk limits, or to apply financial engineering techniques in developing credit derivatives or other credit instruments.

This model is used to solve the probability of default of a publicly traded company with equity and debt holdings and accounting for its volatilities in the market (Figure 114.1). It is currently used by KMV and Moody's to perform credit risk analysis. This approach assumes that the book value of asset and asset volatility are unknown and solved in the model, and that the company is relatively stable and the growth rate of its assets are stable over time (e.g., not in start-up mode). The model uses several simultaneous equations in options valuation coupled with optimization to obtain the implied underlying asset's market value and volatility of the asset in order to compute the probability of default and distance to default for the firm.

It is assumed that at this point the reader is well versed in running simulations and optimizations in Risk Simulator. If not, it is suggested that the reader first spends some time on the *Simulation – Basic Simulation Model* as well as the *Continuous Portfolio Optimization* chapters before proceeding with the procedures discussed next.

To run this model, enter in the required inputs such as the market value of equity (obtained from market data on the firm's capitalization, i.e., stock price times number of stocks outstanding), market value of equity (computed in the *Volatility* or *LPVA* worksheets in the model), book value of debt and liabilities (the firm's book value of all debt and liabilities), the risk-free rate (the prevailing country's risk-free interest rate for the same maturity), the anticipated growth rate of the company (the expected annualized cumulative growth rate of the firm's assets, estimated using historical data over a long period of time, making this approach more applicable to mature companies rather than start-ups), and the debt maturity (the debt maturity to be analyzed, or enter **1** for the annual default probability). The comparable option parameters are shown in cells G18 to G23. All these comparable inputs are computed except for Asset Value (the market value of asset) and the Volatility of Asset. You will need to input some rough estimates as a starting point so that the analysis can be run. The rule of thumb is to set the volatility of the asset in G22 to be one-fifth to half of the volatility of equity computed in G10, and the market value of asset (G19) to be approximately the sum of the market value of equity and book value of liabilities and debt (G9 and G11).

Then you need to run an optimization in Risk Simulator in order to obtain the desired outputs. To do this, set *Asset Value* and *Volatility of Asset* as the decision variables (make them continuous variables with a lower limit of 1% for volatility and $1 for asset, as both these inputs can take on only positive values). Set cell **G29** as the objective to minimize as this is the absolute error value. Finally, the constraint is such that cell **H33**, the implied volatility in the default model, is set to exactly equal the numerical value of the equity volatility in cell G10. Run a static optimization using Risk Simulator.

If the model has a solution, the absolute error value in cell G29 will revert to zero (Figure 114.2). From here, the probability of default (measured in percent) and distance to default (measured in standard deviations) are computed in cells G39 and G41. Then the relevant credit spread required can be determined using the *Credit Analysis – Credit Premium* model or some other credit spread tables (such as using the *Internal Credit Risk Rating* model). The simpler alternative is to use Modeling Toolkit's prebuilt internally optimized functions (we embedded some artificial intelligence integrated with optimization of simultaneous stochastic equations to solve the problem) using

MTProbabilityDefaultMertonImputedAssetValue (cell I21) and

MTProbabilityDefaultMertonImputedAssetVolatility (cell I24)

for obtaining the probability of default (MTProbabilityDefaultMertonII in cell G39).

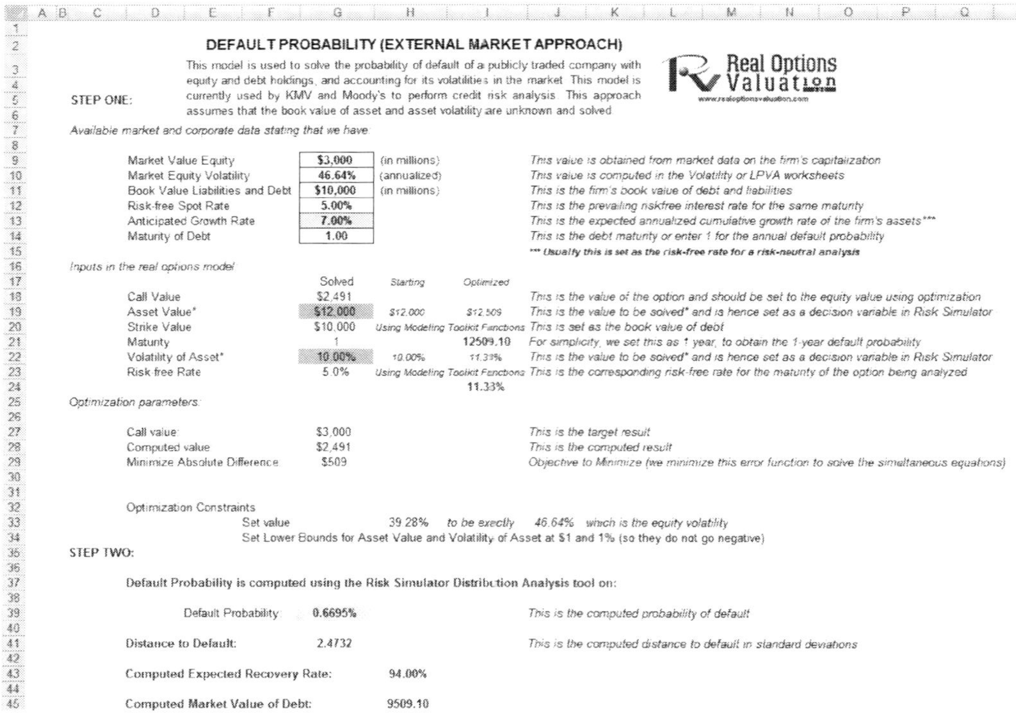

Figure 114.1: Default probability model

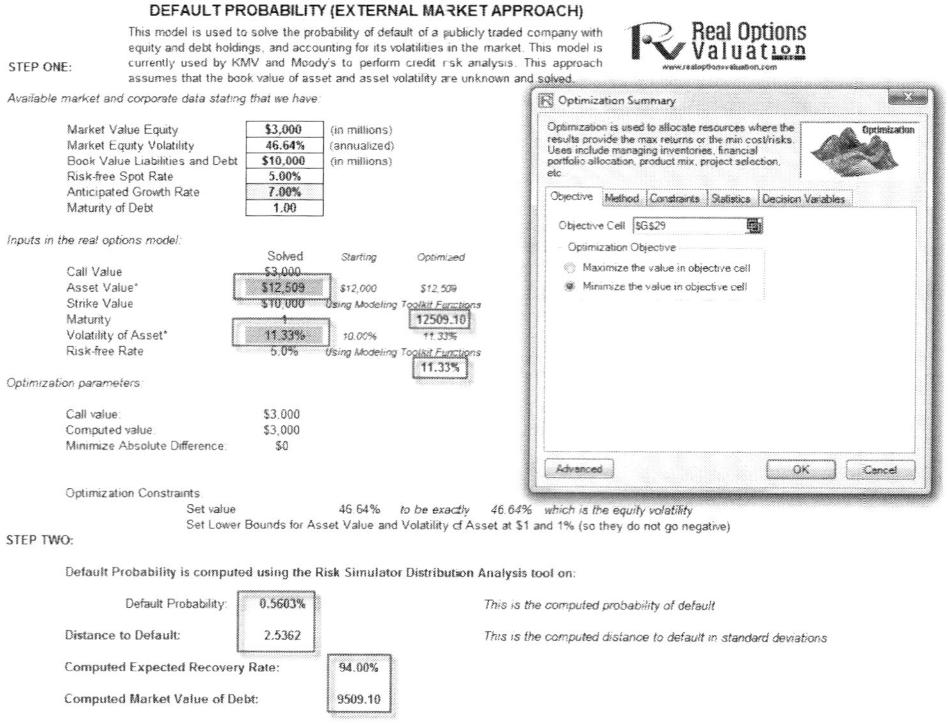

Figure 114.2: Default probability model setup

115. Probability of Default – Merton Internal Options Model (Private Company)

File Name: Probability of Default – Merton Internal Model

Location: Modeling Toolkit | Prob of Default | Merton Internal Model (Private Company)

Brief Description: Computes the probability of default and distance to default of a privately held company by decomposing the firm's book value of liability, assets, and volatility

Requirements: Modeling Toolkit, Risk Simulator

Modeling Toolkit Functions Used: MTMertonDefaultProbabilityII, MTMertonDefaultDistance

This model is a structural model that employs the options approach to computing the *probability of default* and *distance to default* of a company assuming that the book values of asset and debt are known, as are the asset volatilities and anticipated annual growth rates. If the book value of assets or volatility of assets is not known and the company is publicly traded, use the *External Options* model in the previous chapter instead. This model assumes these inputs are known or the company is privately held and not traded. It essentially computes the probability of default or the point of default for the company when its liabilities exceed its assets, given the asset's growth rates and volatility over time (Figure 115.1). It is recommended that the reader review the previous chapter's model on an external publicly traded company before using this model. Methodological parallels exist between these two models, with this chapter building on the knowledge and expertise of the last one.

CREDIT RISK DEFAULT PROBABILITY (OPTIONS APPROACH)

VALUING DEFAULT PROBABILITY AND DISTANCE TO DEFAULT BASED ON OPTIONS MODELING OF INTERNAL DEBT

Input Assumptions

Asset Book Value	$12.0000
Debt Book Value	$10.0000
Maturity	1.0000
Risk-free Rate	5.00%
Volatility of Asset	10.00%

Probability of Default	1.1507%
Distance to Default	2.2732

Function: MTProbabilityDefaultMertonII
Function: MTProbabilityDefaultMertonDefaultDistance

Figure 115.1: Credit default risk model with options modeling

116. Probability of Default – Merton Market Options Model (Industry Comparable)

File Name: Probability of Default – Merton Market Options Model

Location: Modeling Toolkit | Prob of Default | Merton Market Options Model (Industry Comparable)

Brief Description: Computes the probability of default and distance to default of a publicly or privately held company by decomposing the firm's book value of liability, assets, and volatility while benchmarking the company's returns to some external benchmark or index

Requirements: Modeling Toolkit, Risk Simulator

Modeling Toolkit Functions Used: MTMertonDefaultProbabilityI

This models the probability of default for both public and private companies using an index or set of comparables (the market), assuming that the company's asset and debt book values are known, as well as the asset's annualized volatility. Based on this volatility and the correlation of the company's assets to the market, we can determine the probability of default. This model is similar to the models in the last two chapters, which should be reviewed before attempting to run the model illustrated here, as the theoretical constructs of this model are derived from these last two structural models.

MERTON MODEL OF DEBT DEFAULT PROBABILITY
VALUING THE PROBABILITY OF DEFAULT BASED ON MARKET RELATIONSHIPS

Input Assumptions

Asset Value	$100.0000
Debt Value	$50.0000
Time to Maturity	1.00
Risk-free Rate	5.00%
Volatility of Asset	20.00%
Market Volatility	10.00%
Market Return	8.00%
Correlation	0.00

Probability of Default   0.0150%

Function: MTProbabilityDefaultMertonI

Figure 116.1: Merton market options model

117. Project Management – Cost Estimation Model

File Name: Project Management – Cost Estimation Model

Location: Modeling Toolkit | Project Management | Cost Estimation Model

Brief Description: Illustrates how to use Risk Simulator for running a Monte Carlo simulation on a multi-phased project to forecast costs and cost overruns, simulating discrete events (success/failure and go/no-go outcomes), linking these events, and linking the input parameters in a simulation assumption to calculated cells

Requirements: Modeling Toolkit, Risk Simulator

This is a cost estimation model used to forecast the potential cost and cost overruns of a multi-phased project, using simulation, where the later phases of the project will depend on the earlier phases. That is, you cannot proceed to the second phase unless the first phase is successful and so forth.

In this example, the model estimates the total cost of a project with five phases, where at each phase, there might be several subphases. For each phase or subphase, the minimum, maximum, and most likely estimates of costs are obtained and simulated (Figure 117.1). These cost estimates depend on the forecasts of weeks required in each phase and the cost per week. These costs are simulated through parameter linking to Triangular distributions. For instance, the cells in column G are distributional assumptions linked to columns H, I, and J. In addition, the estimates of minimum, likely, and maximum costs in these columns depend on the estimates of time to completion and cost per week in columns L to O. Cost overruns in each phase and their chances are also simulated in column P. A probability of success is estimated based on past experience and subject matter expert estimates, listed in column Q. Using these projections of project success/failure, Bernoulli distributions are set up in column R to simulate the discrete event of a success (1) or failure (0). We then link these events in column S where only if the previous period is successful will the current phase continue assuming that it too is successful. Otherwise, if the previous phase was a failure, all future phases are canceled and the project stops at that point. Finally, the values in column K are the expected values after accounting for the simulated results of time to completion, cost per week, overrun estimates, and success or failure of each phase.

B	C	D	E	F	G	H	I	J	K	L	M	N	O	P	Q	R	S
Work Breakout Structure					Cost					Time in Weeks				Overrun	Probability	Success/	Linked
					Assumption	Minimum	Likely	Maximum	Cost	Minimum	Likely	Maximum	Unit Cost	Assumption	of Success	Failure	Events
Phase 1 Conceptualization					$2,250	$1,500	$2,250	$4,500	*$2,295*	1	1.5	3	$1,500	2%	95%	1	1
Added time for remodeling product					$750	$150	$750	$1,500	*$750*	0.1	0.5	1	$1,500	0%	95%	1	1
Phase 2 Initiation					$7,500	$5,000	$7,500	$12,500	*$8,250*	2	3	5	$2,500	10%	93%	1	1
Reworking concept					$1,500	$750	$1,500	$3,000	*$1,500*	0.5	1	2	$1,500	0%	99%	1	1
Modification of existing concepts					$1,500	$750	$1,500	$2,250	*$1,500*	0.5	1	1.5	$1,500	0%	99%	1	1
Phase 3 Development					$21,000	$17,500	$21,000	$28,000	*$24,150*	5	6	8	$3,500	15%	97%	1	1
Additional R&D					$1,500	$1,000	$1,500	$2,000	*$1,530*	1	1.5	2	$1,000	2%	97%	1	1
Apply external IP					$5,000	$2,500	$5,000	$5,000	*$5,100*	0.5	1	1	$5,000	2%	98%	1	1
Phase 4 Manufacturing					$80,000	$50,000	$80,000	$100,000	*$96,000*	5	8	10	$10,000	20%	95%	1	1
Reprototyping					$12,000	$8,000	$12,000	$16,000	*$12,240*	1	1.5	2	$8,000	2%	98%	1	1
Recasting and rework					$12,000	$8,000	$12,000	$16,000	*$12,240*	1	1.5	2	$8,000	2%	98%	1	1
Phase 5 Market					$150,000	$120,000	$150,000	$240,000	*$765,000*	4	5	8	$30,000	10%	90%	1	1
Additional market research					$20,000	$10,000	$20,000	$30,000	*$22,000*	1	2	3	$10,000	10%	95%	1	1
Repositioning					$30,000	$20,000	$30,000	$50,000	*$33,000*	2	3	5	$10,000	10%	95%	1	1
Grand Total Cost									$385,555								

Figure 117.1: Cost estimation of a multi-phased project

Procedure

To run the model, simply:

1. Go to the *Model* worksheet and click on **Risk Simulator | Change Profile** and select the *Cost Estimation Model* profile.

2. Run the simulation by clicking on **Risk Simulator | Run Simulation**.

The forecast chart (Figure 117.2) results show a trimodal distribution (a distribution with three peaks) because of the discrete event simulation we ran (i.e., the success and failure probabilities). The right-tail probability past the single-point estimate is found to be 44.50%. This means that there is a 44.50% probability that the expected total cost of this project of $385,555 is not going to be enough (click on **Right-Tail** and enter **385555** then hit **TAB** on the keyboard). Therefore, to be 95% certain there are adequate funds to cover the cost of the project, you need $457,006 (click on **Left-Tail** and enter **95** in the Certainty box, then hit **TAB** on the keyboard).

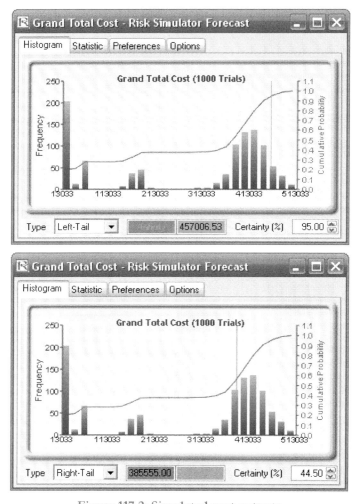

Figure 117.2: Simulated cost outputs

118. Project Management – Critical Path Analysis (CPM PERT GANTT)

File Name: Project Management – Critical Path Analysis (CPM PERT GANTT)

Location: Modeling Toolkit | Project Management | Critical Path Analysis (CPM PERT GANTT)

Brief Description: Illustrates how to use Risk Simulator for running simulations on time to completion of a project and critical path determination, creating GANTT charts and CPM/PERT models, simulating dates and binary variables, and linking input assumptions

Requirements: Modeling Toolkit, Risk Simulator

This model illustrates how a Project Management *Critical Path Analysis* and completion times can be modeled using Risk Simulator. The typical inputs of minimum, most likely, and maximum duration of each process or subproject can be modeled using the *triangular* distribution. This distribution typically is used in the *Critical Path Method* (CPM) and *Program Evaluation Review Technique* (PERT) in project management, together with the *beta* distribution. In other words, the assumptions in the model can also take the *beta* and *gamma* distributions rather than the *triangular* distribution. However, the *beta* and *gamma* distributions are more complex for project managers to use, hence the popularity of the *triangular* distribution.

In this two-part model, the first is a CPM critical path analysis to determine the critical path as well as the expected completion time of a project (Figure 118.1). The second part of the model is on the same project, but we are interested in the actual potential completion date with a GANTT chart analysis (Figure 118.2).

Critical Path Method and Time to Market Analysis

Task Number	Predecessor	Lead/Lag	Duration Optimistic	Duration Expected	Duration Pessimistic	Simulated Duration	Earliest Start Time	Earliest Finish Time	Last Start Time	Last Finish Time	Slack	On Critical Path 1=yes 0 = no
Start (S)						0.0	0.0	0.0	0.0	0.0		
Task 1	Start FS		10	15	20	15.0	0.0	15.0	3.0	18.0	3.0	0
Task 2	1 FS	-5	15	20	22	20.0	10.0	30.0	13.0	33.0	3.0	0
Task 3	2 FS		21	26	30	26.0	30.0	56.0	33.0	59.0	3.0	0
Task 4	2 SS	10	15	18	23	18.0	20.0	38.0	26.0	44.0	6.0	0
Task 5	4 FS		13	15	17	15.0	38.0	53.0	44.0	59.0	6.0	0
Task 6	3,5 FS		30	38	45	38.0	56.0	94.0	59.0	97.0	3.0	0
Task 7	6 FS	-5	20	25	30	25.0	89.0	114.0	92.0	117.0	3.0	0
Task 8	6 FS	5	10	15	20	15.0	99.0	114.0	102.0	117.0	3.0	0
Task 9	6 SS	20	11	18	22	18.0	76.0	94.0	99.0	117.0	23.0	0
Task 10	7,8,9 FS		23	30	45	30.0	114.0	144.0	117.0	147.0	3.0	0
Task 11	10 FS	5	22	28	39	28.0	149.0	177.0	152.0	180.0	3.0	0
Task 12	Start FS		120	140	180	140.0	0.0	140.0	0.0	140.0	0.0	1
Task 13	12 FS	-5	13	18	22	18.0	135.0	153.0	135.0	153.0	0.0	1
Task 14	13 SS	10	15	20	25	20.0	145.0	165.0	145.0	165.0	0.0	1
Task 15	14 FS		10	15	20	15.0	165.0	180.0	165.0	180.0	0.0	1
Task 16	11, 15 FS		30	33	44	33.0	180.0	213.0	180.0	213.0	0.0	1
Task 17	16 FS		5	8	11	8.0	213.0	221.0	213.0	221.0	0.0	1
Task 18	17 FS		10	15	25	15.0	221.0	236.0	223.0	238.0	2.0	0
Task 19	17 FS		13	17	19	17.0	221.0	238.0	221.0	238.0	0.0	1
Task 20	18, 19 FS		20	25	40	25.0	238.0	263.0	238.0	263.0	0.0	1
End (E)						0.0	263.0	263.0	263.0	263.0		

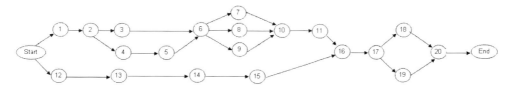

Figure 118.1: Critical path model and time to market analysis

	Start Date	Completed	Remaining	%Complete	Date Value
Start	1/1/2006	4.5	10.5	30.00%	38718
Task 1	1/16/2006	9.0	21.0	30.00%	38733
Task 2	2/5/2006	16.8	39.2	30.00%	38753
Task 3	3/3/2006	11.4	26.6	30.00%	38779
Task 4	3/21/2006	15.9	37.1	30.00%	38797
Task 5	4/5/2006	28.2	65.8	30.00%	38812
Task 6	5/13/2006	34.2	79.8	30.00%	38850
Task 7	6/7/2006	34.2	79.8	30.00%	38875
Task 8	6/22/2006	28.2	65.8	30.00%	38890
Task 9	7/10/2006	43.2	100.8	30.00%	38908
Task 10	8/9/2006	53.1	123.9	30.00%	38938
Task 11	9/6/2006	42.0	98.0	30.00%	38966
Task 12	1/24/2007	45.9	107.1	30.00%	39106
Task 13	2/11/2007	49.5	115.5	30.00%	39124
Task 14	3/3/2007	54.0	126.0	30.00%	39144
Task 15	3/18/2007	63.9	149.1	30.00%	39159
Task 16	4/20/2007	66.3	154.7	30.00%	39192
Task 17	4/28/2007	70.8	165.2	30.00%	39200
Task 18	5/13/2007	71.4	166.6	30.00%	39215
Task 19	5/30/2007	78.9	184.1	30.00%	39232
Task 20	6/24/2007	78.9	184.1	30.00%	39257

GANTT Chart

Figure 118.2: GANTT chart

Procedure

1. The cells in column G in the model already have simulation assumptions set. To view the assumptions, select cell **G5** and click on **Risk Simulator | Set Input Assumption.** You will see that a *triangular* distribution is set where the input parameters (minimum, most likely, and maximum) are linked to the corresponding cells in columns D to F (Figure 118.3). Note that when you click on the input parameters, you will see the links to D5, E5, and F5. Notice also that the input parameter boxes are now colored light green, indicating that the parameters are linked to a cell in the spreadsheet. If you entered or hard-coded a parameter, it would be white. You can link a parameter input to a cell in a worksheet by clicking on the **link** icon (beside the parameter input box) and clicking on the relevant cell in the worksheet.

2. For simplicity, other assumptions have already been preset for you, including the completion percentage in Column E of the second part of the model, where we use the *beta* distribution instead. Further, several forecasts have been set, including the Finish Time (L25), Ending Date (F63), and critical path binary values (N5:N24) for various tasks. All that needs to be done now is to run the simulation: **Risk Simulator | Run Simulation**.

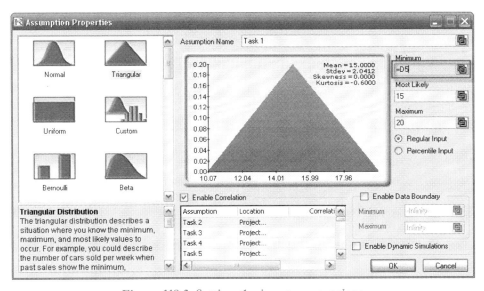

Figure 118.3: Setting the input assumptions

Results Interpretation

Several results are noteworthy:

- Looking at the Finish Time forecast chart after the simulation is completed, select **Left-Tail** and enter **95** in the *Certainty* box and hit **TAB** on the keyboard (Figure 118.4). This shows a value of 301.71, which means that there is a 95% chance that the project will complete in slightly under 302 days or that only a 5% chance exists where there will be an overrun of 301 days. Similarly, you can enter in **285** in the *Value* box and hit **TAB**. The forecast chart returns a value of 69.60%, indicating that there is only a 69.60% chance that the project can finish within 285 days, or a 30.40% chance the project will take longer than 285 days. Other values can be entered similarly.

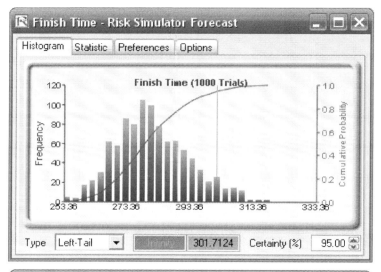

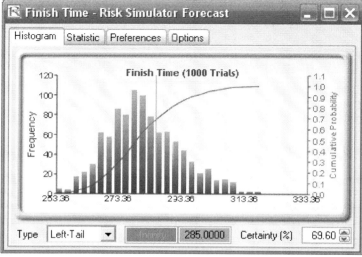

Figure 118.4: Forecast results

- Select one of the Tasks (e.g., **Task 10**). The forecast chart is bimodal, with two peaks, one at 0 and another at 1, indicating "NO" and "YES" on whether this particular task ends up being on the critical path (Figure 118.5). In this example, select the **Left-Tail** and type in **0.99** and hit **TAB** on the keyboard. Notice that the certainty value is 58.20%, indicating that this project has a 58.20% chance of not being on the critical path (the value 0) or 41.80% chance of being on the critical path (the value 1). This means that Task 10 is potentially very critical. In contrast, look at **Task 9**'s forecast chart. The **Left-Tail** certainty is 100% at the value **0.99**, indicating that 100% of the time, this project is not going to be on the critical path, and therefore has less worry for the project manager.

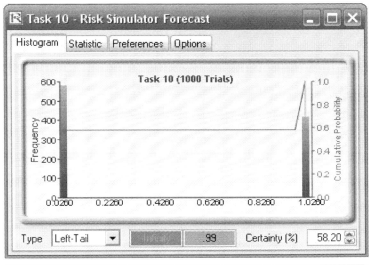

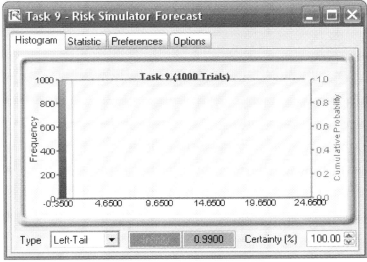

Figure 118.5: Task forecast

- Finally, the Ending Date forecast can be used to determine the potential ending date of the project. Looking at the forecast chart output, select the **Left-Tail**, enter **95,** and hit **TAB** (Figure 118.6). The corresponding 95th percentile returns a value of 39301. This is a text format for a specific date in Excel. To convert it into a date we understand, simply type this number in any empty cell and click on **Format | Cells** (or hit **Ctrl-1**) and select **Number | Date**, and the cell value changes to August 7, 2007. This means that there is a 95% chance that the project will be completed by August 7, 2007.

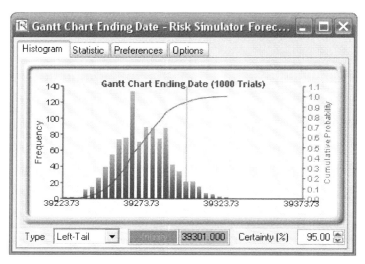

Figure 118.6: GANTT chart forecast end date

You can now experiment with other values and certainty levels as well as modify the model to suit your needs and project specifications. In addition, you can use the same methodology to simulate binary values (variables with 0/1 values) and dates.

119. Project Management – Project Timing

File Name: Project Management – Project Timing

Location: Modeling Toolkit | Project Management | Project Timing

Brief Description: Illustrates how to use Risk Simulator for simulating a project's completion date and how to revert the simulated results back to dates

Requirements: Modeling Toolkit, Risk Simulator

This project management model (Figure 119.1) is used to illustrate how the completion dates of a project can be simulated and the resulting values converted back into a regular date format. The model assumes that the tasks are all sequential. For nonsequential and path-independent projects, see the *Project Management – Critical Path Analysis (CPM PERT GANTT)* model instead.

Project Management and Timing

Contractual Start Date	30-Jan-06

	Start Date St	Duration in weeks				Finish Date	Probability	Start lag in weeks				Finish lag in weeks			
		Assumption	Min	ML	Max		y	Assumption	Min	ML	Max	Assumption	Min	ML	Max
CONCEPT PHASE (Task 01)															
Phase Completion	30-Jan-06	18.0	15	18	24	5-Jun-06	90%								
Rework risk	5-Jun-06	3.0	2	3	5	26-Jun-06	10%								
Total (c)						7-Jun-06									
INITIATION (Task 02)															
Phase Completion	30-Jan-06	5.0	3	5	9	6-Mar-06	85%								
Delay risk	6-Mar-06	5.0	3	5	7	10-Apr-06	15%								
Total (c)						11-Mar-06									
DEVELOPMENT (Task 03)															
Phase Completion	7-Jun-06	7.0	6	7	8	26-Jul-06	15%					2.5	1.1	2.5	3.1
MANUFACTURING (Task 04)															
Product A	13-Sep-06	5.0	3	5	7	18-Oct-06	85%	7.0	6	7	8				
Product B	18-Oct-06	4.0	3	4	5	15-Nov-06	10%								
Product C	15-Nov-06	5.0	3	5	9	20-Dec-06	5%								
Customized	20-Dec-06	9.0	4	9	11	13-Jan-16									
GO TO MARKET (Task 05)															
USA															
Product A	8-Nov-06	7.0	6	7	8	27-Dec-06	90%	3.0	1	3	4				
Product B	27-Dec-06	8.0	6	8	9	21-Feb-07									
Product C	21-Feb-07	7.0	6	7	9	11-Apr-07									
Europe															
Product A	8-Nov-06	8.0	7	8	9	3-Jan-07	10%	3.0	2	3	6				
Product B	3-Jan-07	6.0	5	6	10	14-Feb-07									
Product C	14-Feb-07	6.0	4	6	9	28-Mar-07									
Final Completion Date						9-Apr-07									

Figure 119.1: Project timing model

The input assumptions used for simulation are listed under the *Assumption* column, which are all set as *triangular* distributions (a typical distribution used in project management and related to the PERT distribution). These assumptions are then linked to the minimum (Min), most likely (ML), and maximum (Max) values of completion in weeks for each task and subtask. The final completion date is set as the output forecast. Because dates, when simulated, are presented in numerical values, using the forecast chart, you can determine the 90% certainty that the project will be completed by a certain time period, and so forth. In the example, the 90% Left-Tail confidence interval shows a value of 39210.046 as seen in Figure 119.2. Entering this value in any cell in Excel and then changing the properties of the cell to show dates rather than a numerical value (right-click on the cell, and select **Format Cells | Date**, and select the date format of your choice) will reveal that the 90th percentile date of completion is May 8, 2007.

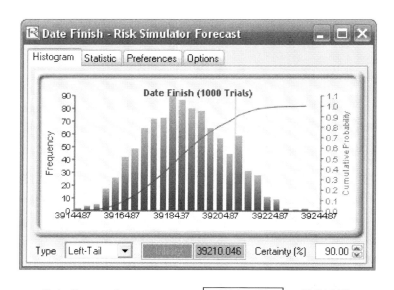

Date Conversion:

| 8-May-07 | 39,210.00 |
| 39,210.05 | 8-May-07 |

Figure 119.2: Probabilistic project completion dates

120. Real Estate – Commercial Real Estate ROI

File Name: Real Estate – Commercial ROI

Location: Modeling Toolkit | Industry Applications | Real Estate – Commercial ROI

Brief Description: Illustrates how to use Risk Simulator for simulating a financial ROI analysis for real estate projects and running scenario analysis on the optimal holding period of the asset that maximizes NPV

Requirements: Modeling Toolkit, Risk Simulator

This model is used to value the profit and loss from a real estate deal with industry standards, such as cap rates, vacancy and collection factors, and assumed growth rates and Consumer Price Index (CPI) adjusted pricings. The pro forma income statement and cash flow statement with the relevant salvage sale value of the property and amortization table of the mortgage are also included. The model uses function calls from the Modeling Toolkit and is simulated using Risk Simulator. See Figure 120.1.

Real Estate Valuation, Return on Investment and Financial Feasibility Studies

Global Assumptions	Expected	Min	Max			Expected	Min	Max
Annual Gross Rent (Year 1)	$2,000,000	$1,800,000	$2,200,000	Percent of Price in Improvements	85.00%	80.00%	88.00%
Vacancy and Collection Factor	7.00%	5.00%	10.00%	After Tax, Real Discount Rate	8.00%	7.75%	8.25%
Operating Expenses (Year 1)	$60,000	$50,000	$75,000	Cap Rate Assumed at Date of Sale	9.00%	8.75%	9.25%
Cap Rate at Purchase	9.00%	8.50%	12.00%	Transaction Costs % of Sales Price	9.00%	8.00%	10.00%
Loan to Value Ratio	75.00%	70.00%	80.00%	Loan Term (Years)	20		
Quoted Annual Interest Rate	6.00%	5.75%	6.25%	Holding Period	20		
CPI Annual Increase %	3.00%	2.50%	3.50%	Recovery Period for Depreciation	39		
Annual % Change in Rent	3.00%	2.75%	5.00%	Corporate Tax Rate	15.00%		
Annual % Change in Expenses	3.00%	2.50%	3.50%	Capital Gains Tax Rate	5.00%		

Property Valuation:	$20,000,000	Net Present Value	$7,285,096	Cap Rate = NOI / Sale Price
Loan Amount:	$15,000,000	Internal Rate of Return	9.51%	Market Value = NOI / (Cap Rate %)
Equity Required:	$5,000,000	Property Valuation + NPV	$27,285,096	
Mortgage Loan Payment:	8.72%			

Figure 120.1: Commercial real estate ROI analysis

Procedure

To run this model, simply click on **Risk Simulator | Run Simulation**. However, if you wish, you can create your own simulation model:

1. Start a new simulation profile and add various assumptions on cells **E5:E13** and **L5:L8**. You can make them all *triangular* distributions and link the input parameters to the relevant cells (e.g., for *Gross Rent the First Year*, link Min to F5, Likely to E5, and Max to G5). Define the assumption by first making sure there is a simulation profile (**Risk Simulator | New Profile**), then selecting the relevant cells and clicking on **Risk Simulator | Set Input Assumption**.

2. You can then select the predefined cell, click on **Risk Simulator | Copy Parameter**, hit the **Escape** key once (so that the values will not be copied; only the assumptions will be copied) and select the other cells to copy to (e.g., E6:E13 and later, L5:L8) and click on **Risk Simulator | Paste Parameter**.

3. Add **forecasts** to the key outputs such as *Net Present Value* (**Risk Simulator | Set Output Forecast**).

4. Run the simulation (**Risk Simulator | Run Simulation**) and interpret the results.

In addition, a tornado sensitivity analysis and a scenario analysis can be run on the model. The generated reports for both techniques are included in the model. To run these analyses, follow these instructions:

- **Tornado Analysis:** Select cell **I15** (*Net Present Value*) and start the tornado analysis (**Risk Simulator | Analytical Tools | Tornado Analysis**) and select the checkbox *Use Cell Addresses* and click **OK**. A report will be generated. Interpret the tornado results as usual.

- **Scenario Analysis:** Start the *Scenario Analysis* tool (**Risk Simulator | Analytical Tools | Sensitivity Analysis**) and enter the relevant inputs as seen in Figure 120.2.

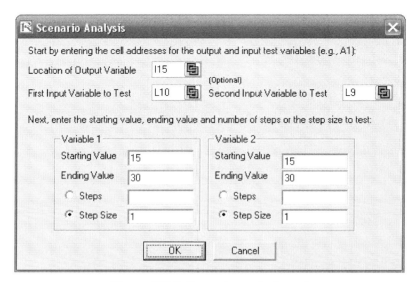

Figure 120.2: Scenario analysis tool

The scenario report worksheet will be generated, listing all the possible combinations of *Holding Periods* and *Mortgage Maturities* as well as the resulting NPV (Figure 120.3).

SCENARIO ANALYSIS TABLE

Output Variable:	$I$15	Initial Base Case Value:		7285096.36											
Column Variable:	$L$9	Min:	15.00	Max:	30.00	Steps:	—	Stepsize:	1.00	Initial Base Case Value:	20.00				
Row Variable:	$L$10	Min:	15.00	Max:	30.00	Steps:	—	Stepsize:	1.00	Initial Base Case Value:	20.00				

	15.00	16.00	17.00	18.00	19.00	20.00	21.00	22.00	23.00	24.00	25.00	26.00	27.00	28.00	29.00	30.00
15.00	6368723	6378891	6387783	6395612	6402548	6408724	6414251	6419217	6423697	6427752	6431434	6434787	6437847	6440647	6443215	6445575
16.00	6410437	6594333	6606592	6617385	6626947	6635462	6643081	6649928	6656104	6661694	6666770	6671392	6675611	6679472	6683012	6686265
17.00	6438608	6622505	6796885	6810912	6823338	6834404	6844305	6853203	6861229	6868494	6875091	6881097	6886580	6891597	6896198	6900425
18.00	6454730	6638626	6813007	6978347	6993861	7007678	7020041	7031151	7041172	7050243	7058479	7065979	7072825	7079089	7084834	7090112
19.00	6460158	6644055	6818435	6983775	7140528	7157284	7172276	7185749	7197901	7208902	7218889	7227984	7236286	7243883	7250849	7257250
20.00	6456129	6640025	6814406	6979746	7136499	7285096	7302875	7318851	7333262	7346306	7358150	7368934	7378779	7387788	7396049	7403639
21.00	6443763	6627660	6802040	6967380	7124134	7272731	7413584	7432194	7448981	7464176	7477972	7490535	7502003	7512496	7522119	7530961
22.00	6424081	6607978	6782358	6947698	7104452	7253049	7393902	7527400	7546671	7564115	7579954	7594375	7607541	7619588	7630635	7640785
23.00	6398007	6581904	6756284	6921624	7078377	7226975	7367827	7501326	7627841	7647624	7665586	7681942	7696872	7710535	7723063	7734574
24.00	6366379	6550275	6724656	6889996	7046749	7195346	7336199	7469697	7596213	7716099	7736260	7754617	7771375	7786709	7800771	7813691
25.00	6329955	6513851	6688232	6853572	7010325	7158922	7299775	7433273	7559789	7679675	7793269	7813689	7832331	7849389	7865031	7879403
26.00	6289421	6473318	6647698	6813038	6969791	7118389	7259241	7392740	7519255	7639142	7752736	7860357	7880932	7899760	7917025	7932888
27.00	6245398	6429295	6603675	6769015	6925768	7074366	7215218	7348716	7475232	7595118	7708712	7816334	7918287	7938925	7957851	7975239
28.00	6198444	6382341	6556721	6722061	6878814	7027412	7168264	7301762	7428278	7548164	7661758	7769380	7871333	7967908	7988527	8007472
29.00	6149063	6332960	6507340	6672680	6829433	6978031	7118883	7252381	7378897	7498783	7612377	7719999	7821952	7918527	3009998	8030526
30.00	6097708	6281604	6455985	6621325	6778078	6926676	7067528	7201026	7327542	7447428	7561022	7668644	7770597	7867172	⁷958643	8045272

Figure 120.3: Scenario analysis results table

121. Risk Analysis – Integrated Risk Management

File Name: Risk Analysis – Integrated Risk Analysis

Location: Modeling Toolkit | Risk Analysis | Integrated Risk Analysis

Brief Description: Integrates Monte Carlo simulation, forecasting, portfolio optimization, and real options analysis into a single unified model and shows how one plays off the other

Requirements: Modeling Toolkit, Risk Simulator

Before diving into the different risk analysis methods in the remaining chapters of the book, it is important to first understand *Integrated Risk Management* (IRM) and how these different techniques are related in a risk analysis and risk management context. This IRM framework comprises eight distinct phases of a successful and comprehensive risk analysis implementation, going from a qualitative management screening process to creating clear and concise reports for management. The process was developed by the author based on previous successful implementations of risk analysis, forecasting, real options, valuation, and optimization projects both in the consulting arena and in industry-specific problems. These phases can be performed either in isolation or together in sequence for a more robust integrated analysis. Figure 121.1 shows the Integrated Risk Management process up close. We can separate the process into the following eight simple steps:

1. Qualitative Management Screening

2. Forecast Predictive Modeling

3. Base Case Static Model

4. Monte Carlo Risk Simulation

5. Real Options Problem Framing

6. Real Options Valuation and Modeling

7. Portfolio and Resource Optimization

8. Reporting, Presentation, and Update Analysis

1. Qualitative Management Screening

Qualitative management screening is the first step in any Integrated Risk Management process. Management has to decide which projects, assets, initiatives, or strategies are viable for further analysis, in accordance with the firm's mission, vision, goal, or overall business strategy. The firm's mission, vision, goal, or overall business strategy may include market penetration strategies, and competitive advantage, technical, acquisition, growth, synergistic, or globalization issues. That is, the initial list of projects should be qualified in terms of meeting management's agenda. Often the most valuable insight is created as management frames the complete problem to be resolved. This is where the various risks to the firm are identified and fleshed out.

2. Forecast Predictive Modeling

The future is then forecasted using time-series analysis or multivariate regression analysis if historical or comparable data exist. Otherwise, other qualitative forecasting methods may be used (subjective guesses, growth rate assumptions, expert opinions, Delphi method, etc.). In a financial context, this is the step where future revenues, sale price, quantity sold, volume, production, and other key revenue and cost drivers are forecasted. See Chapter 9 of *Modeling Risk, Third Edition*, for details on forecasting and using the author's Risk Simulator software to run time-series, nonlinear extrapolation, stochastic process, ARIMA, multivariate regression forecasts, fuzzy logic, neural networks, econometric models, GARCH, and so on.

3. Base Case Static Model

For each project that passes the initial qualitative screens, a discounted cash flow model is created. This model serves as the base case analysis where a net present value is calculated for each project, using the forecasted values in the previous step. This step also applies if only a single project is under evaluation. This net present value is calculated using the traditional approach of modeling and forecasting revenues and costs, and discounting the net of these revenues and costs at an appropriate risk-adjusted rate. The return on investment and other profitability, cost-benefit, and productivity metrics are generated here.

4. Monte Carlo Risk Simulation

Because the static discounted cash flow produces only a single-point estimate result, there is oftentimes little confidence in its accuracy given that future events that affect forecast cash flows are highly uncertain. To better estimate the actual value of a particular project, Monte Carlo risk simulation should be employed next

Usually, a sensitivity analysis is first performed on the discounted cash flow model; that is, setting the net present value as the resulting variable, we can change each of its precedent variables and note the change in the resulting variable. Precedent variables include revenues, costs, tax rates, discount rates, capital expenditures, depreciation, and so forth, which ultimately flow through the model to affect the net present value figure. By tracing back all these precedent variables, we can change each one by a preset amount and see the effect on the resulting net present value. A graphical representation can then be created, which is oftentimes called a tornado chart because of its shape, where the most sensitive precedent variables are listed first, in descending order of magnitude. Armed with this information, the analyst can then decide which key variables are highly uncertain in the future and which are deterministic. The uncertain key variables that drive the net present value and, hence, the decision are called *critical success drivers*. These critical success drivers are prime candidates for Monte Carlo simulation. Because some of these critical success drivers may be correlated—for example, operating costs may increase in proportion to quantity sold of a particular product, or prices may be inversely correlated to quantity sold—a correlated Monte Carlo simulation may be required. Typically, these correlations can be obtained through historical data. Running correlated simulations provides a much closer approximation to the variables' real-life behaviors.

5. Real Options Problem Framing

After quantifying risks in the previous step, the question now is, what's next? The risk information obtained somehow needs to be converted into *actionable intelligence*. So what if risk has been quantified to be such and such using Monte Carlo simulation? What do we do about it? The answer is to use real options analysis to hedge these risks, to value these risks, and to position yourself to take advantage of the risks. The first step in real options is to generate a strategic map through the process of framing the problem. Based on the overall problem identification occurring during the initial qualitative management screening process, certain strategic optionalities would have become apparent for each particular project. The strategic optionalities may include, among other things, the option to expand, contract, abandon, switch, choose, and so forth. Based on the identification of strategic optionalities that exist for each project or at each stage of the project, the analyst can then choose from a list of options to analyze in more detail. Real options are added to the projects to hedge downside risks and to take advantage of upside swings.

6. Real Options Valuation and Modeling

Through the use of Monte Carlo risk simulation, the resulting stochastic discounted cash flow model will have a distribution of values. Thus, simulation models, analyzes, and quantifies the various risks and uncertainties of each project. The result is a distribution of the NPVs and the project's volatility. In real options, we assume that the underlying variable is the future profitability of the project, which is the future cash flow series. An implied volatility of the future free cash flow or underlying variable can be calculated through the results of a Monte Carlo simulation previously performed. Usually, the volatility is measured as the standard deviation of the logarithmic returns on the free cash flow stream (other approaches include running GARCH models and using simulated coefficients of variation as proxies). In addition, the present value of future cash flows for the base case discounted cash flow model is used as the initial underlying asset value in real options modeling. Using these inputs, real options analysis is performed to obtain the projects' strategic option values.

7. Portfolio and Resource Optimization

Portfolio optimization is an optional step in the analysis. If the analysis is done on multiple projects, management should view the results as a portfolio of rolled-up projects because the projects are, in most, cases correlated with one another, and viewing them individually will not present the true picture. As firms do not only have single projects, portfolio optimization is crucial. Given that certain projects are related to others, there are opportunities for hedging and diversifying risks through a portfolio. Because firms have limited budgets, as well as time and resource constraints, while at the same time have requirements for certain overall levels of returns, risk tolerances, and so forth, portfolio optimization takes into account all these to create an optimal portfolio mix. The analysis will provide the optimal allocation of investments across multiple projects.

8. Reporting, Presentation, and Update Analysis

The analysis is not complete until reports can be generated. Not only are results presented, but the process should also be shown. Clear, concise, and precise explanations transform a difficult black-box set of analytics into transparent steps. Management will never accept results coming from black boxes if it does not understand where the assumptions or data originate and what types of mathematical or financial massaging takes place.

Risk analysis assumes that the future is uncertain and that management has the right to make midcourse corrections when these uncertainties become resolved or risks become known; the analysis is usually done ahead of time and thus, ahead of such uncertainty and risks. Therefore, when these risks become known, the analysis should be revisited to incorporate the decisions made or to revise any input assumptions. Sometimes, for long-horizon projects, several iterations of the real options analysis should be performed, where future iterations are updated with the latest data and assumptions. Understanding the steps required to undertake an Integrated Risk Management analysis is important because it provides insight not only into the methodology itself but also into how it evolves from traditional analyses, showing where the traditional approach ends and where the advanced analytics start.

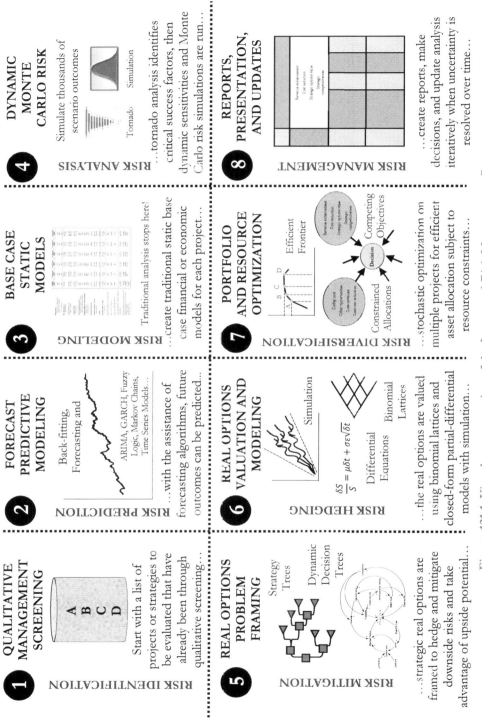

1 RISK IDENTIFICATION

QUALITATIVE MANAGEMENT SCREENING

A
B
C
D

Start with a list of projects or strategies to be evaluated that have already been through qualitative screening…

2 RISK PREDICTION

FORECAST PREDICTIVE MODELING

Back-fitting, Forecasting and

ARIMA, GARCH, Fuzzy Logic, Markov Chains, Time Series Models…

…with the assistance of forecasting algorithms, future outcomes can be predicted…

3 RISK MODELING

BASE CASE STATIC MODELS

Traditional analysis stops here!

…create traditional static base case financial or economic models for each project…

4 RISK ANALYSIS

DYNAMIC MONTE CARLO RISK

Simulate thousands of scenario outcomes

Tornado   Simulation

…tornado analysis identifies critical success factors, then dynamic sensitivities and Monte Carlo risk simulations are run…

5 RISK MITIGATION

REAL OPTIONS PROBLEM FRAMING

Strategy Trees

Dynamic Decision Trees

…strategic real options are framed to hedge and mitigate downside risks and take advantage of upside potential…

6 RISK HEDGING

REAL OPTIONS VALUATION AND MODELING

Simulation

$$\frac{\delta S}{S} = \mu \delta t + \sigma \epsilon \sqrt{\delta t}$$

Differential Equations   Binomial Lattices

…the real options are valued using binomial lattices and closed-form partial-differential models with simulation…

7 RISK DIVERSIFICATION

PORTFOLIO AND RESOURCE OPTIMIZATION

Efficient Frontier

Competing Objectives

Constrained Allocations

…stochastic optimization on multiple projects for efficient asset allocation subject to resource constraints…

8 RISK MANAGEMENT

REPORTS, PRESENTATION, AND UPDATES

…create reports, make decisions, and update analysis iteratively when uncertainty is resolved over time…

Figure 121.1: Visual representation of the Integrated Risk Management Process

Forecasting

In the *Forecasting* worksheet (Figure 121.2), first create a profile (**Risk Simulator | New Profile**) and give it a name, then select the area **G7:G26** of the data area and click on **Risk Simulator | Forecasting | Time-Series Analysis**. Suppose you know from experience that the seasonality of the revenue stream peaks every four years. Enter the **seasonality** of **4** and specify the number of **forecast periods** to **5**. The *Forecasting* tool automatically selects the best time-series model to forecast the results through backcast-fitting techniques and optimization, to find the best-fitting model and its associated parameters. The best-fitting time-series analysis model is chosen. Running this module on the historical data will generate a report with the five-year forecast revenues (*Forecast Report* worksheet) that are complete with Risk Simulator assumptions (cells D43:D47). These output forecasts then become the inputs into the *Valuation Model* worksheet (cells D19:H19).

Monte Carlo Simulation

The *Valuation Model* worksheet shows a simple discounted cash flow model (DCF) that calculates the relevant net present value (NPV) and internal rate of return (IRR) of a project or strategy. Notice that the output of the *Forecast Report* worksheet becomes an input into this *Valuation Model* worksheet. For instance, cells D19:H19 are linked from the first forecast worksheet. The model uses two discount rates for the two different sources of risk (market risk-adjusted discount rate of 12% for the risky cash flows, and a 5% cost of capital to account for the private risk of capital investment costs). Further, different discounting conventions are included (midyear, end-year, continuous, and discrete discounting), as well as a terminal value calculation assuming a constant growth model. Finally, the capital implementation costs are separated out of the model (row 46), but the regular costs of doing business (direct costs, cost of goods sold, operating expenses, etc.) are included in the computation of free cash flows. That is, this project has two phases. The first phase costs $5 and the second larger phase costs $2,000.

The statistic NPV shows a positive value of $123.26 while the IRR is 15.68%, both exceeding the zero-NPV and firm-specific hurdle rate of 12% required rate of return. Therefore, at first pass, the project seems to be profitable and justifiable. However, risk has not been considered. Without applying risk analysis, you cannot determine the chances this NPV and IRR are expected to occur. This is done by selecting the cells you wish to simulate (e.g., D20) and clicking on **Risk Simulator | Set Input Assumption** (Figure 121.3). For illustration purposes, select the *triangular* distribution and link to the input parameters to the appropriate cells. Continue the process to define input assumptions on all other relevant cells. Then select the output cells such as NPV, IRR, and so forth (cells **D14, D15, H14,** and **H15**) and set them as forecasts (i.e., select each cell one at a time and click on **Risk Simulator | Set Output Forecast** and enter the relevant variable names). Note that all assumptions and forecasts have already been set for you.

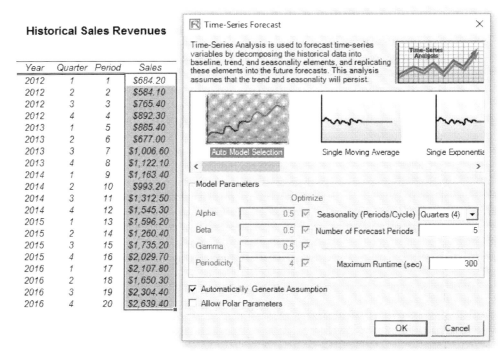

Figure 121.2: Stochastic time-series forecasting

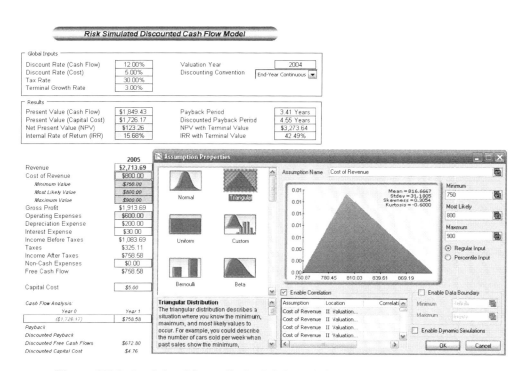

Figure 121.3: Applying Monte Carlo risk-based simulation on the model

Real Options Analysis

The next stop is real options analysis. In the previous simulation applications, risk was quantified and compared across multiple projects. The problem is, so what? That is, we have quantified the different levels of risks in different projects. Some are highly risky, some are somewhat risky, and some are not so risky. In addition, the relevant returns are also pretty variable as compared to the risk levels. Real options analysis takes this information to the next step. Looking at a specific project, real options identifies if there are ways to mitigate the downside risks while taking advantage of the upside uncertainty. In applying Risk Simulator, we have only quantified uncertainties, not risks! Downside uncertainty, if it is real and affects the firm, becomes risks, while upside uncertainty is a plus that firms should try to capitalize on.

At this point, we can either solve real options problems using Real Options SLS's multiple asset or *MSLS* module (install Real Options SLS and click on **Start | Real Options Valuation | Real Options SLS | Real Options SLS**) or apply its analytics directly in Excel by using the SLS Functions, which we will see later (Figures 121.5 and 121.6). The Real Options SLS is used to obtain a quick answer, but if a distribution of option values is required, then use the SLS Functions and link all the inputs into the function—we use the latter in this example. The real options analysis model's inputs are the outputs from the DCF model in the previous step. For instance, the free cash flows are computed previously in the DCF. The Expanded NPV value in cell C21 in the *Real Options* worksheet is obtained through the SLS Function call. Simulation was used to also obtain the volatility required in the real options analysis.

The Real Options SLS results (Figure 121.4) indicate an Expanded NPV of $388M, while the NPV was $123M. This means that there is an additional $265 expected value in creating a two-staged development of this project rather than jumping in first and taking all the risk. That is, NPV analysis assumed that you would definitely invest all $5M in year 1 and $2,000M in year 3 regardless of the outcome (see Figure 121.7). This view of NPV analysis is myopic. Real options analysis, however, assumes that if all goes well in Phase I ($5M), then you continue on to Phase II ($2,000M). Therefore, due to the volatility and uncertainty in the project (as obtained by Monte Carlo simulation), there is a chance that the $2,000M may not even be spent, as Phase II never materializes (due to a bad outcome in Phase I). In addition, there is a chance that valuation free cash flows exceeding $1,849M may occur. The expected value of all these happenstances yields an Expanded NPV of $388M (the average potential after a two-phased stage-gate development process is implemented). It is better to perform a stage-gate development process than to take all the risks immediately and invest everything. Figures 121.5 and 126.6 illustrate how the analysis can be performed in the Excel model by using function calls.

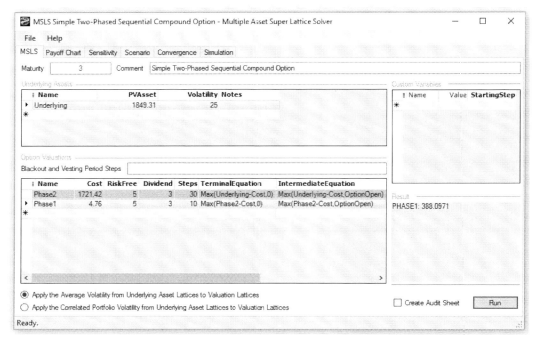

Figure 121.4: Applying real options on a two-phased project

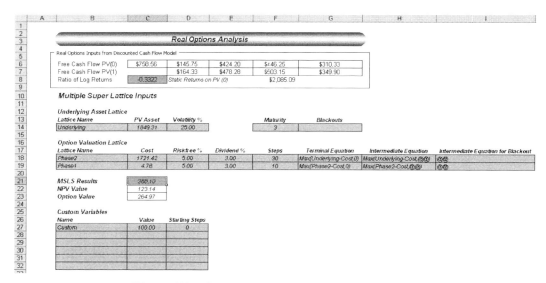

Figure 121.5: Linking real options in the spreadsheet

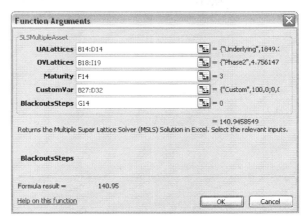

Figure 121.6: Real options function call in Excel

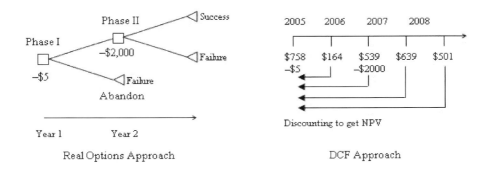

Figure 121.7: Graphical depiction of a two-phased sequential
compound option model

Notice that in the real options world, executing Phase II is an option, not a requirement or obligation, while in the DCF world all investments have been decreed in advance and thus will and must occur (Figure 121.7). Therefore, management has the legitimate flexibility and ability to abandon the project after Phase I and not continue on to Phase II if the outcome of the first phase is bad. Based on the volatility calculated in the real options model, there is a chance Phase II will never be executed, there is a chance that the cash flows could be higher and lower, and there is a chance that Phase II will be executed if the cash flows make it profitable. Therefore, the net expected value of the project after considering all these potential avenues is the option value calculated previously. In this example as well, we assumed a 3% annualized dividend yield, indicating that by stage-gating the development and taking our time, the firm loses about 3% of its *PV Asset* per year (lost revenues and opportunity costs as well as lower market share due to waiting and deferring action).

Note that as dividends increase, the option to wait and defer action goes down. In fact, the option value reverts to the NPV value when dividends exceed 32%. That is, the NPV or value of executing now is $123.26M (i.e., $1849.43M – $1721.41M – $4.76M). So, at any dividend yield exceeding 32%, the optimal decision is to execute immediately rather than to wait and phase the development.

Optimization

The next step is portfolio optimization, that is, how to efficiently and effectively allocate a limited budget (budget constraint and human resource constraints) across many possible projects while simultaneously accounting for their uncertainties, risks, and strategic flexibility, and all the while maximizing the portfolio's ENPV subject to the least amount of risk (Sharpe ratio). To this point we have shown how a single integrated model can be built utilizing simulation, forecasting, and real options. Figure 121.8 illustrates a summary of 12 projects (here we assume that you have re-created the simulation, forecasting, and real options models for each of the other 11 projects), complete with their expanded NPV, NPV, cost, risk, return to risk ratio, and profitability index. To simplify our analysis and to illustrate the power of optimization under uncertainty, the returns and risk values for projects B to L are simulated, instead of rebuilding this 11 other times.

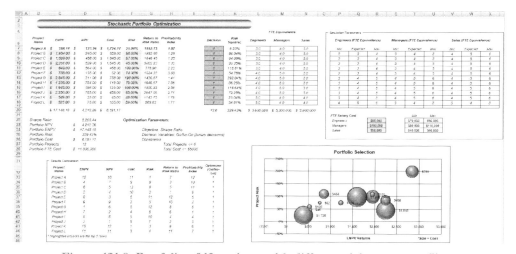

Figure 121.8: Portfolio of 12 projects with different risk-return profiles

Then the individual project's human resource requirements as measured by full-time equivalences (FTEs) are included. We simplify the problem by listing only the three major human resource requirements: engineers, managers, and salespeople. The FTE salary costs are simulated using Risk Simulator. Finally, decision variables (the *Decision Variables* in column J in the model) are constructed, with a binary variable of 1 or 0 for go and no-go decisions. The model also shows all 12 projects and their rankings sorted by returns, risk, cost, returns-to-risk ratio, and profitability ratio. Clearly, it is fairly difficult to determine simply by looking at this matrix which projects are the best to select in the portfolio.

The model also shows this matrix in graphical form, where the size of the balls is the cost of implementation, the x-axis shows the total returns including flexibility, and the y-axis lists the project risk as measured by volatility of the cash flows of each project. Again, it is fairly difficult to choose the right combinations of projects at this point. Optimization is required to assist in our decision making.

To set up the optimization process, first select each of the decision variables in column J and set the relevant decision variables by clicking on **Risk Simulator | Set Decision**. Alternatively, you can create one decision variable and copy/paste. The linear constraint is such that the total budget value for the portfolio has to be less than $5,000. Next, select *Portfolio Sharpe Ratio* (D22) as the objective to maximize.

The next section illustrates the results of the optimization under uncertainty and the results interpretation. Further, we can add additional constraints if required such as where the total FTE cannot exceed $9,500,000, and so forth. We can then change the constraint of number of projects allowed and we can marginally increase this constraint to see what additional returns and risks the portfolio will obtain. In each run, with a variable constraint inserted, an efficient frontier will be generated by connecting a sequence of optimal portfolios under different risk levels. That is, for a particular risk level, points on the frontier are the combinations of projects that maximize the returns of the portfolio subject to the lowest risk. Similarly, these are the points where, given a set of returns requirements, these combinations of projects provide the least amount of portfolio risk.

Optimization Parameters

For the first run, the following parameters were used:

Objective:	Maximize Portfolio Returns
Constraint:	Total Budget Allocation = $5,000
Constraint:	Total number of projects not to exceed 6 (we then change this from 5 to 9, to create an investment efficient frontier)

The results, including a portfolio efficient frontier (Figure 121.9) where, on the frontier, all the portfolio combinations of projects will yield the maximum returns (portfolio NPV) subject to the minimum portfolio risks, are shown in Figure 121.10. Clearly the first portfolio (with the 5-project constraint) is not a desirable outcome due to the low returns. So, the obvious candidates are the other portfolios. It is now up to management to determine what risk-return combination it wants; that is, depending on the risk appetite of the decision makers, the budget availability, and the capabilities of handling more projects, these five different portfolio combinations are the optimal portfolios of projects that maximize returns subject to the least risk, considering the uncertainties (simulation), strategic flexibility (real options), and uncertain future outcomes (forecasting). Of course, the results here are only for a specific set of input assumptions, constraints, and so forth. You may choose to change any of the input assumptions to obtain different variants of optimal portfolio allocations.

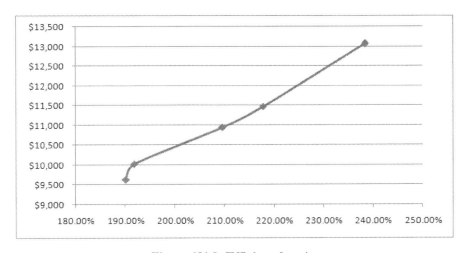

Figure 121.9: Efficient frontier

Investment Efficient Frontier

Total Projects Constraint	5	6	7	8	9
Budget Constraint	$ 5,000	$ 5,000	$ 5,000	$ 5,000	$ 5,500
Portfolio ENPV	$ 9,635	$10,023	$10,942	$ 11,467	$ 13,066
Portfolio Risk	190.11%	191.75%	209.58%	217.72%	238.35%
Portfolio Cost	$ 3,202	$ 4,928	$ 3,299	$ 3,404	$ 5,249
Project A	0	1	0	0	0
Project B	1	1	1	1	1
Project C	0	0	0	0	1
Project D	1	1	1	1	1
Project E	0	0	0	0	0
Project F	0	0	1	1	1
Project G	0	0	0	0	0
Project H	1	1	1	1	1
Project I	1	1	1	1	1
Project J	1	1	1	1	1
Project K	0	0	1	1	1
Project L	0	0	0	1	1

Figure 121.10: Project selection by multiple criteria

Many observations can be made from the summary of results. While all of the optimal portfolios are constrained at under a total cost budget and number of projects less than or equal to some value (in the efficient frontier, we change this constraint from 5 to 9 projects), all of these combinations of projects use the budget the most effectively as they generate the higher ENPV with the least amount of risk (Sharpe ratio is maximized) for the entire portfolio. However, the further on the right we go in the efficient frontier chart, the higher level of risk (wider range for ENPV and risk, higher volatility risk coefficient, requires more projects making it riskier, and higher total cost to implement) and the higher the returns. These values can be obtained from the forecast charts from Risk Simulator (not shown) by keeping the optimal project selections and running a simulation each time to view the ENPV and IRR forecast charts. It is at this point that the decision maker has to decide which risk-return profile to undertake.

All other combinations of projects in a portfolio are by definition suboptimal to these two, given the same constraints, and should not be entertained. Hence, from a possible portfolio combination of 12! or 479,000,000 possible outcomes, we have now isolated the decision down to these best portfolios. Finally, we can again employ a high-level portfolio real option on the decision. That is, because all portfolios require the implementation of projects B, D, H, I, J, do these first! Then leave the option open to execute the remaining projects (F, K, L) depending on which portfolios management decides to go with later. By doing so, we can buy additional time (portfolio level option to defer) before making the final determination, in case something happens during development, in which case the project can be terminated (option to abandon), the analysis can be rerun and different projects can be added, and new optimal portfolio can be obtained (option to switch).

122. Risk Analysis – Interest Rate Risk

File Name: Risk Analysis – Interest Rate Risk

Location: Modeling Toolkit | Risk Analysis | Interest Rate Risk

Brief Description: Applies duration and convexity measures to account for a bond's sensitivity and how interest rate shifts can affect the new bond price, and how this new bond price can be approximated using these sensitivity measures

Requirements: Modeling Toolkit, Risk Simulator

Modeling Toolkit Functions Used: MTBondPriceDiscrete, MTModifiedDuration, MTConvexityDiscrete

Banks selling fixed income products and vehicles need to understand interest rate risks. This model uses duration and convexity to show how fixed income products react under various market conditions. To compare the effects of interest rate and credit risks on fixed income investments, this model uses modified duration and convexity (discrete discounting) to analyze the effects of a change in interest rates on the value of a bond or debt. See Figure 122.1 for an example.

Duration and convexity are sensitivity measures that describe exposure to parallel shifts in the spot interest rate yield curve applicable to individual fixed income instruments or entire fixed income portfolios. These sensitivities cannot warn of exposure to more complex movements in the spot curve, including tilts and bends, only parallel shifts. The idea behind duration is simple. Suppose a portfolio has a duration measure of 2.5 years. This means that the portfolio's value will decline about 2.5% for each 1% increase in interest rates—or rise about 2.5% for each 1% decrease in interest rates. Typically, a bond's duration will be positive, but exotic instruments, such as mortgage-backed securities, may have negative durations or investment portfolios that short fixed income instruments or pay fixed for floating on an interest rate swap. Inverse floaters tend to have large positive durations. Their values change significantly for small changes in rates. Highly leveraged fixed income portfolios tend to have very large (positive or negative) durations.

In contrast, convexity summarizes the second most significant piece of information, the nonlinear curvature of the yield curve; duration measures the linear or first-approximation sensitivity. Duration and convexity traditionally have been used as tools for immunization or asset-liability management. To avoid exposure to parallel spot curve shifts, an organization (such as an insurance company or defined benefit pension plan) with significant fixed income exposures might perform duration matching by structuring its assets so that their duration matches the duration of its liabilities and the two offset each other. Even more effective (but less frequently practical) is duration-convexity matching, in which assets are structured so that durations and convexities match.

INTEREST RATE RISK

Face Value	$100.00
Coupon Rate	5.50%
Maturity	30.00
Current Interest Rate	5.50%
Interest Rate Shift	0.25%

Original Bond Price	$100.00	
Modified Duration	14.5337	
Convexity	321.0265	
	Duration and Convexity	**Using New Rates**
New Price After Shift	$96.47	$96.46
Price Change After Shift	-3.53%	-3.54%

Cash Flow	Interest Rates	Year	Shifted Interest Rates
$5.50	5.50%	1	5.75%
$5.50	5.50%	2	5.75%
$5.50	5.50%	3	5.75%
$5.50	5.50%	4	5.75%
$5.50	5.50%	5	5.75%
$5.50	5.50%	6	5.75%
$5.50	5.50%	7	5.75%
$5.50	5.50%	8	5.75%
$5.50	5.50%	9	5.75%
$5.50	5.50%	10	5.75%

Figure 122.1: Interest rate risk

123. Risk Analysis – Portfolio Risk and Return Profiles

File Name: Risk Analysis – Portfolio Risk and Return Profile

Location: Modeling Toolkit | Risk Analysis | Portfolio Risk and Return Profile

Brief Description: Computes the risk and return on a portfolio of multiple assets given each asset's own risk and return as well as its respective pairwise covariance

Requirements: Modeling Toolkit

Modeling Toolkit Functions Used: MTPortfolioReturns, MTPortfolioVariance, MTPortfolioRisk

As illustrated in Figure 123.1, this model computes the portfolio level of returns and risks given the percent allocated on various assets, the expected returns and risks on individual assets, and the variance-covariance matrix of the asset mix (you can use the *Variance-Covariance* tool in the Modeling Toolkit to compute this matrix if you have the raw stock returns data).

PORTFOLIO RISK-RETURN PROFILE USING VARIANCE-COVARIANCE MATRIX

Variance Covariance Matrix	S&P 500	High-Yield Bonds	Leveraged Loans	Corporate Bonds	7-10 Year Treasuries	3-5 Year Treasuries	International Equities
S&P 500	0.0001549	0.0000164	-0.0000001	0.0000299	0.0000374	0.0000189	0.0000970
High-Yield Bonds	0.0000164	1.0000000	0.0000012	0.0000147	0.0000179	0.0000106	0.0000145
Leveraged Loans	-0.0000001	0.0000012	1.0000000	0.0000008	0.0000009	0.0000008	0.0000003
Corporate Bonds	0.0000299	0.0000147	0.0000008	0.0000449	0.0000516	0.0000303	0.0000263
7-10 year Treasuries	0.0000374	0.0000179	0.0000009	0.0000516	0.0000686	0.0000408	0.0000345
3-5 year Treasuries	0.0000189	0.0000106	0.0000008	0.0000303	0.0000408	0.0000266	0.0000209
International Equities	0.0000970	0.0000145	0.0000003	0.0000263	0.0000345	0.0000209	0.0001721

	Asset Allocation	Returns			
S&P 500	14.29%	11.07%			
High-Yield Bonds	14.29%	11.52%			
Leveraged Loans	14.29%	7.61%			
Corporate Bonds	14.29%	7.56%	**Portfolio Expected Returns**	8.430%
7-10 year Treasuries	14.29%	7.09%	**Portfolio Variance**	4.084%
3-5 year Treasuries	14.29%	6.04%	**Portfolio Risk**	20.210%
International Equities	14.29%	8.11%			
TOTAL	100.00%	8.43%			

Figure 123.1: Portfolio risk-return profile

For instance, if raw data on various assets exist (Figure 123.2), simply select the data area and run the *Variance-Covariance* tool under the **Modeling Toolkit | Tools** menu item. The generated results are shown in the computed *Variance-Covariance* worksheet. This is a very handy tool indeed as the portfolio risk computations can sometimes be rather cumbersome. Consider that the portfolio risk (computed as volatility) is:

$$\sigma_P = \sqrt{\sum_{k=1}^{N} w_k^2 \sigma_k^2 + \sum_{i=1}^{m} \sum_{j=1}^{n} 2 w_i w_j \rho_{i,j} \sigma_i \sigma_j}$$

where the volatility of each asset k is squared and multiplied by its weight squared, summed, and added to the summation of all pairwise correlations among the assets (ρ), by their respective weights (w) and volatilities (σ). For the example model, this equation expands to 21 cross terms and 7 squared terms, creating a relatively complicated equation to compute manually. Using the single *MTPortfolioRisk* equation, the process is greatly simplified.

Dates	S&P 500	High-Yield Bonds	Leveraged Loans	Corporate Bonds	7-10 Year Treasuries	3-5 Year Treasuries	International Equities
1/3/1992	-1.011%	1.309%	-0.062%	0.098%	-0.096%	-0.169%	-2.226%
1/10/1992	0.906%	0.528%	0.111%	-0.836%	-1.349%	-0.662%	-0.378%
1/17/1992	-0.807%	0.640%	0.285%	-0.143%	-0.491%	-0.097%	0.543%
1/24/1992	-1.613%	0.651%	0.362%	0.014%	0.009%	0.013%	-0.310%
1/31/1992	0.565%	0.639%	0.131%	0.528%	0.667%	0.500%	0.690%
2/7/1992	0.338%	0.654%	0.125%	-0.759%	-1.074%	-0.829%	-2.883%
2/14/1992	-0.255%	0.526%	0.156%	-0.117%	-0.262%	-0.253%	-0.346%
2/21/1992	0.309%	0.403%	0.479%	0.995%	1.239%	0.841%	0.597%
2/28/1992	-2.001%	0.681%	0.240%	-0.573%	-1.143%	-0.864%	-2.727%
3/6/1992	0.346%	0.214%	0.140%	-0.774%	-1.160%	-0.848%	-1.689%
3/13/1992	1.333%	0.311%	0.073%	0.334%	0.549%	0.255%	0.123%
3/20/1992	-1.884%	0.323%	0.138%	0.641%	0.768%	0.665%	-0.649%
3/27/1992	-0.483%	0.203%	0.127%	1.020%	0.919%	0.960%	-2.460%
4/3/1992	0.682%	0.183%	0.218%	0.441%	0.498%	0.675%	0.543%
4/10/1992	2.906%	0.178%	0.126%	-0.253%	-0.384%	-0.321%	2.116%
4/17/1992	-1.687%	0.133%	0.003%	-0.305%	-0.184%	0.038%	-0.623%
4/24/1992	0.858%	0.178%	0.182%	0.299%	0.018%	0.226%	1.035%
5/1/1992	0.853%	0.329%	0.126%	0.668%	0.839%	0.503%	1.956%
5/8/1992	-1.433%	0.448%	0.265%	0.778%	0.835%	0.614%	-0.340%
5/15/1992	0.958%	0.291%	0.126%	-0.001%	-0.144%	-0.178%	1.349%
5/22/1992	0.321%	0.406%	0.126%	0.363%	0.354%	0.410%	0.897%
5/29/1992	-0.450%	0.297%	0.144%	0.215%	0.345%	0.276%	-0.813%
6/5/1992	-0.900%	0.312%	0.065%	0.307%	0.334%	0.403%	-1.176%
6/12/1992	-1.486%	0.343%	0.127%	0.356%	0.435%	0.335%	-2.126%
6/19/1992	-0.054%	0.234%	0.112%	0.504%	0.640%	0.528%	-0.391%

Figure 123.2: Raw stock returns data

124. Risk Hedging – Delta-Gamma Hedging

File Name: Risk Hedging – Delta Gamma Hedge

Location: Modeling Toolkit | Risk Hedging | Delta Gamma Hedge

Brief Description: Sets up a delta-gamma riskless and costless hedge in determining the number of call options to sell and buy, the number of common stocks to buy, and the borrowing amount required to set up a perfect arbitrage-free hedge

Requirements: Modeling Toolkit

Modeling Toolkit Functions Used: MTDeltaGammaHedgeCallSold, MTDeltaGammaHedgeSharesBought, MTDeltaGammaHedgeMoneyBorrowed

The delta-gamma hedge provides a hedge against larger changes in the asset value. This is done by buying some equity shares and a call option, which are funded by borrowing some amount of money and selling a call option at a different strike price. The net amount is a zero sum game, making this hedge completely effective in generating a zero delta and zero gamma for the portfolio, just as in a delta hedge, where the total portfolio's delta is zero (e.g., to offset a positive delta of some underlying assets, call options are sold to generate sufficient negative delta to completely offset the existing deltas to generate a zero delta portfolio). The problem with delta-neutral portfolios is that secondary changes (i.e., larger shocks) are not hedged. Delta-gamma hedged portfolios, on the contrary, hedge both delta and gamma risk, making them a lot more expensive to generate. The typical problem with such a hedging vehicle is that in larger quantities, buying and selling additional options or underlying assets may change the market value and prices of the same instruments used to perform the hedge. Therefore, typically, a dynamic hedge or continuously changing hedge portfolios might be required.

DELTA-GAMMA HEDGE

Asset	$100.00
Strike for Call Sold	$95.00
Strike for Call Bought	$100.00
Maturity for Call Sold	0.50
Maturity for Call Bought	0.75
Riskfree	8.00%
Volatility	20.00%
DividendRate	3.00%

Sell Calls	$9.7258
Shares to Buy	($6.9058)
Buy Calls	($9.1991)
Borrow This Amount	$6.3791
Delta-Gamma-Neutral Position Sum	$0.0000

Figure 124.1: Delta-gamma hedging

125. Risk Hedging – Delta Hedging

File Name: Risk Hedging – Delta Hedge

Location: Modeling Toolkit | Risk Hedging | Delta Hedge

Brief Description: Sets up a delta riskless and costless hedge in determining the number of call options to sell, the number of common stocks to buy, and the borrowing amount required to set up a costless hedge

Requirements: Modeling Toolkit

Modeling Toolkit Functions Used: MTDeltaHedgeCallSold, MTDeltaHedgeSharesBought, MTDeltaHedgeMoneyBorrowed

The delta hedge provides a hedge against small changes in the asset value by buying some equity shares of the asset and financing it through selling a call option and borrowing some money. The net should be a zero sum game to provide a hedge where the portfolio's delta is zero. For instance, an investor computes the portfolio delta of some underlying asset and offsets this delta through buying or selling some additional instruments such that the new instruments will offset the delta of the existing underlying assets. Typically, say an investor holds some stocks or commodity such as gold in the long position, creating a positive delta for the asset. To offset this, she sells some calls to generate negative delta, such that the amount of the call options sold on the gold is sufficient to offset the delta in the portfolio. See Figure 125.1 for an example.

DELTA HEDGE

Asset	$100.00
Strike	$95.00
Maturity	0.50
Riskfree	8.00%
Volatility	20.00%
DividendRate	3.00%

Sell 1 Call	$9.7258
Shares to Buy	($71.8275)
Borrow This Amount	$62.1018
Delta-Neutral Position Sum	$0.0000

Figure 125.1: Delta hedging

126. Risk Hedging – Effects of Fixed versus Floating Rates

File Name: Risk Hedging – Effects of Fixed versus Floating Rates

Location: Modeling Toolkit | Risk Hedging | Effects of Fixed versus Floating Rates

Brief Description: Sets up various levels of hedging to determine the impact on earnings per share

Requirements: Modeling Toolkit

This model illustrates the impact on financial earnings and earnings before interest and taxes (EBIT) of a hedged versus unhedged position. The hedge is done through interest rate swap payments. Various scenarios of swaps (different combinations of fixed rate versus floating rate debt) can be generated and tested in this model to determine the impact to earnings per share (EPS) and other financial metrics. See Figure 126.1. The foreign exchange cash flow hedge model shown in the next chapter goes into more detail on the hedging aspects of foreign exchange through the use of risk simulation.

This model looks at several scenarios of changes in interest rates (row 23 in the model), where a fixed rate versus a floating rate is applied (rows 26 and 27) based on the proportion of fixed to floating debt structure (rows 16 and 17). The fixed rate is fixed under all conditions whereas the floating rate is pegged to the LIBOR rate and some predetermined swap rate (where a floating is swapped with a fixed rate and vice versa) as well as the changes to the prevailing interest rate in the economy. For example, the floating rate will be equal to the fixed rate adjusted for the swap rate plus LIBOR and changes to the prevailing market rate (see row 27 of the model).

This model can then be simulated by adding assumptions to the LIBOR and change in the prevailing interest rates, to determine the probabilistic impacts to changes in the company's earnings based on a fixed versus floating rate regime.

IMPACTS OF FIXED VERSUS FLOATING RATE INTEREST PAYMENTS

Assumptions

EBIT	$3,000,000
Shares Outstanding	$500,000
Tax Rate	40.00%
Total Debt	$8,000,000
Fixed Interest Rate	7.00%
LIBOR	6.00%
10-Year Swap Rate	5.00%

		Scenarios		
	Current	1	2	3
Initial Debt Structure (before swap)				
% of Total Debt in Fixed-rate Debt	50.00%	50.00%	50.00%	50.00%
% of Total Debt in Floating-rate Debt	50.00%	50.00%	50.00%	50.00%
Desired Debt Structure (after swap)				
% of Total Debt in Fixed-rate Debt	50.00%	30.00%	100.00%	0.00%
% of Total Debt in Floating-rate Debt	50.00%	70.00%	0.00%	100.00%
Change in Interest Rates	0.00%	1.00%	0.50%	0.10%
Financials				
Fixed-rate Debt	7.00%	7.00%	7.00%	7.00%
Floating-rate Debt	8.00%	9.00%	8.50%	8.10%
EBIT	3,000,000	3,000,000	3,000,000	3,000,000
Interest Expense	(600,000)	(672,000)	(560,000)	(648,000)
Net Income before Taxes	2,400,000	2,328,000	2,440,000	2,352,000
Earnings	1,440,000	1,396,800	1,464,000	1,411,200
EPS	2.8800	2.7936	2.9280	2.8224
Change in Interest Expense		72,000	(40,000)	48,000
Change in Earnings		(43,200)	24,000	(28,800)

Figure 126.1: Impacts of an unhedged versus hedged position

127. Risk Hedging – Foreign Exchange Cash Flow Model

File Name: Risk Hedging – Foreign Exchange Cash Flow Model

Location: Modeling Toolkit | Risk Hedging | Foreign Exchange Cash Flow Model

Brief Description: Illustrates how to use Risk Simulator for simulating the foreign exchange rate to determine whether a hedged fixed exchange rate or floating unhedged rate is worth more

Requirements: Modeling Toolkit, Risk Simulator

This cash flow model is used to illustrate the effects of hedging foreign exchange rates. The tornado sensitivity analysis illustrates that foreign exchange rate, or forex, has the highest effects on the profitability of the project. Suppose that the project undertaken is in a foreign country (FC), the values obtained are denominated in FC currency, and the parent company is in the United States and requires that the net revenues be repatriated back to the United States. The questions we ask here are: What is the appropriate forex rate to hedge at, and what are the appropriate costs for that particular rate? Banks will be able to provide your firm with the appropriate pricing structure for various exchange forward rates, but by using the model here, you can determine the added value of the hedge and hence decide if the value added exceeds the cost to obtain the hedge. This model is preset for you to run a simulation on.

The *Forex Data* worksheet shows historical exchange rates between the FC and U.S. dollar. Using these values, we can create a *custom* distribution (we simply used the rounded values in our illustration), which is preset in this example model.

However, should you wish to replicate the model setup, you can follow these steps:

1. Start a new profile (**Risk Simulator | New Profile**) and give it an appropriate name.

2. Go to the *Forex Data* worksheet and select the data in cells **K6:K490** and click on **Edit | Copy** or **Ctrl + C**.

3. Select an empty cell (e.g., cell **K4**) and click on **Risk Simulator | Set Input Assumption** and select **Custom Distribution**.

4. Click on **Paste** to paste the data into the custom distribution, then **Update Chart** to view the results on the chart. Then, click **File | Save** and save the newly created distribution to your hard drive.

5. Go to the *Model* worksheet and select the **Forex** cell (**J9**). Click on **Risk Simulator | Set Input Assumption**, and choose **Custom**, then click on **Open** a distribution and select the previously saved custom distribution.

6. You may continue to set assumptions across the entire model, and set the **NPV** cell as a forecast (**Risk Simulator | Set Output Forecast**).

7. **RUN** the simulation with the custom distribution to denote an unhedged position. You can then rerun the simulation but this time, delete the custom distribution (use the **Delete Simulation Parameter** icon, not Excel's delete function or the keyboard's delete key) and enter in the relevant hedged exchange rate, indicating a fixed rate. You may create a report after each simulation to compare the results. A smarter approach is to duplicate the simulation profile and delete this input assumption on the duplicated profile. You can then switch between profiles to run the hedged and unhedged positions.

From the sample analysis, we obtain the following information:

	Mean ($'000)	Stdev ($'000)	% Confidence ($'000)	CV (%)
Unhedged	2292.82	157.94	2021 to 2550	6.89%
Hedged at 0.85	2408.81	132.63	2199 to 2618	5.51%
Hedged at 0.83	2352.13	129.51	2147 to 2556	5.51%
Hedged at 0.80	2267.12	124.83	2069 to 2463	5.51%

From this information, several things are evident:

- The higher the hedged exchange rate is, the more profitable the project (e.g., 0.85 USD/FC is worth more than 0.80 USD/FC).

- The relative risk ratio, computed as the coefficient of variation (CV, or the standard deviation divided by the mean) is the same regardless of the exchange rate, as long as it is hedged.

- The CV is lower for hedged positions than unhedged positions, indicating that the relative risk is reduced by hedging.

- It seems that the exchange rate hedge should be above 0.80, such that the hedged position is more profitable than the unhedged.

- In comparing a hedged versus an unhedged position, we can determine the amount of money the hedging is worth; for instance, going with a 0.85 USD/FC means that on average, the hedge is worth $115,990,000 (computed as $2,408.81 − $2,292.82 denominated in thousands). This means that as long as the cost of the hedge is less than this amount, it is a good idea to pursue the hedge. In fact, hedging at 0.83 USD/FC returns a lower expected value on the project, making this hedge level less optimal. Finally, the higher the hedge, the lower the risk to the project (as evident from the standard deviation), but again, a higher hedge costs more and the expected value of the project becomes lower. See Figures 127.1–127.4.

Cash Flow Model

Base Year	2006		Sum PV Net Benefits	FC 3,809.62						
Start Year	2006		Sum PV Investments	FC 1,389.08						
Discount Rate	15.00%		Net Present Value	FC 2,420.54						
Private-Risk Discount Rate	5.00%		Internal Rate of Return	54.64%						
Terminal Period Growth Rate	2.00%		Return on Investment	174.25%						
Tax Rate	40.00%		Profitability Index	2.74		Forex Rate (USD/FC)	0.85000			

	2006	2007	2008	2009	2010	2011	2012	2013	2014	2015
Prod A Price	FC 10.00	FC 10.50	FC 11.00	FC 11.50	FC 12.00	FC 12.00	FC 12.00	FC 12.00	FC 12.00	FC 12.00
Prod B Price	FC 12.25	FC 12.50	FC 12.75	FC 13.00	FC 13.25	FC 13.25	FC 13.25	FC 13.25	FC 13.25	FC 13.25
Prod C Price	FC 15.15	FC 15.30	FC 15.45	FC 15.60	FC 15.75	FC 15.75	FC 15.75	FC 15.75	FC 15.75	FC 15.75
Prod A Quantity	50	50	50	50	50	50	50	50	50	50
Prod B Quantity	35	35	35	35	35	35	35	35	35	35
Prod C Quantity	20	20	20	20	20	20	20	20	20	20
Total Revenues (Local Currency)	FC 1,231.75	FC 1,268.50	FC 1,305.25	FC 1,342.00	FC 1,378.75	FC 1,378.75	FC 1,378.75	FC 1,378.75	FC 1,378.75	FC 1,378.75
Direct Cost of Goods Sold	FC 184.76	FC 190.28	FC 195.79	FC 201.30	FC 206.81	FC 206.81	FC 206.81	FC 206.81	FC 206.81	FC 206.81
Gross Profit	FC 1,046.99	FC 1,078.23	FC 1,109.46	FC 1,140.70	FC 1,171.94	FC 1,171.94	FC 1,171.94	FC 1,171.94	FC 1,171.94	FC 1,171.94
Operating Expenses	FC 157.50	FC 157.50	FC 157.50	FC 157.50	FC 157.50	FC 157.50	FC 157.50	FC 157.50	FC 157.50	FC 157.50
Sales, General and Admin. Costs	FC 15.75	FC 15.75	FC 15.75	FC 15.75	FC 15.75	FC 15.75	FC 15.75	FC 15.75	FC 15.75	FC 15.75
Operating Income (EBITDA)	FC 873.74	FC 904.98	FC 936.21	FC 967.45	FC 998.69	FC 998.69	FC 998.69	FC 998.69	FC 998.69	FC 998.69
Depreciation	FC 10.00	FC 10.00	FC 10.00	FC 10.00	FC 10.00	FC 10.00	FC 10.00	FC 10.00	FC 10.00	FC 10.00
Amortization	FC 3.00	FC 3.00	FC 3.00	FC 3.00	FC 3.00	FC 3.00	FC 3.00	FC 3.00	FC 3.00	FC 3.00
EBIT	FC 860.74	FC 891.98	FC 923.21	FC 954.45	FC 985.69	FC 985.69	FC 985.69	FC 985.69	FC 985.69	FC 985.69
Interest	FC 2.00	FC 2.00	FC 2.00	FC 2.00	FC 2.00	FC 3.00	FC 4.00	FC 5.00	FC 6.00	FC 7.00
EBT	FC 858.74	FC 889.98	FC 921.21	FC 952.45	FC 983.69	FC 982.69	FC 981.69	FC 980.69	FC 979.69	FC 978.69
Taxes	FC 343.50	FC 355.99	FC 368.49	FC 380.98	FC 393.48	FC 393.08	FC 392.68	FC 392.28	FC 391.88	FC 391.48
Net Income	FC 515.24	FC 533.99	FC 552.73	FC 571.47	FC 590.21	FC 589.61	FC 589.01	FC 588.41	FC 587.81	FC 587.21
Depreciation/Amort	FC 13.00	FC 13.00	FC 13.00	FC 13.00	FC 13.00	FC 13.00	FC 13.00	FC 13.00	FC 13.00	FC 13.00
Net Working Capital	FC 0.00	FC 0.00	FC 0.00	FC 0.00	FC 0.00	FC 0.00	FC 0.00	FC 0.00	FC 0.00	FC 0.00
Capital Expenditures	FC 0.00	FC 0.00	FC 0.00	FC 0.00	FC 0.00	FC 0.00	FC 0.00	FC 0.00	FC 0.00	FC 0.00
Free Cash Flow	FC 528.24	FC 546.99	FC 565.73	FC 584.47	FC 603.21	FC 602.61	FC 602.01	FC 601.41	FC 600.81	FC 4,709.36
Investments	FC 500.00		FC 1,500.00							
Net Free Cash Flow	-FC 1,105.97	FC 546.99	FC 565.73	FC 584.47	FC 603.21	FC 602.61	FC 602.01	FC 601.41	FC 600.81	FC 4,709.36

Figure 127.1: Hedging cash flow models

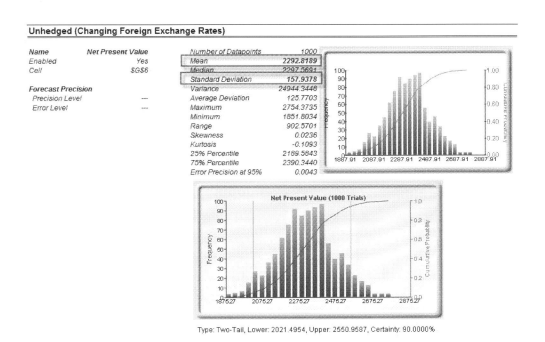

Unhedged (Changing Foreign Exchange Rates)

Name	Net Present Value		Number of Datapoints	1000
Enabled	Yes		Mean	2292.8189
Cell	$G$6		Median	2297.5691
			Standard Deviation	157.9378
Forecast Precision			Variance	24944.3446
Precision Level	---		Average Deviation	125.7703
Error Level	---		Maximum	2754.3735
			Minimum	1851.8034
			Range	902.5701
			Skewness	0.0236
			Kurtosis	-0.1093
			25% Percentile	2189.5843
			75% Percentile	2390.3440
			Error Precision at 95%	0.0043

Type: Two-Tail, Lower: 2021.4954, Upper: 2550.9587, Certainty: 90.0000%

Figure 127.2: Unhedged cash flow models

Hedged at 0.85

Name	Net Present Value
Enabled	Yes
Cell	$G$6
Forecast Precision	
Precision Level	---
Error Level	---

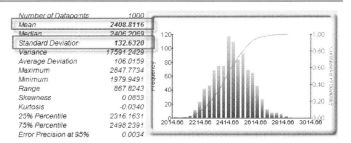

Number of Datapoints	1000
Mean	2408.8116
Median	2406.2069
Standard Deviation	132.6320
Variance	17591.2429
Average Deviation	106.0159
Maximum	2847.7734
Minimum	1979.9491
Range	867.8243
Skewness	0.0853
Kurtosis	-0.0340
25% Percentile	2316.1631
75% Percentile	2498.2391
Error Precision at 95%	0.0034

Type: Two-Tail, Lower: 2198.9784, Upper: 2617.5565, Certainty: 90.0000%

Figure 127.3: Hedged at 0.85 USD/FC

Hedged at 0.83

Name	Net Present Value
Enabled	Yes
Cell	$G$6
Forecast Precision	
Precision Level	---
Error Level	---

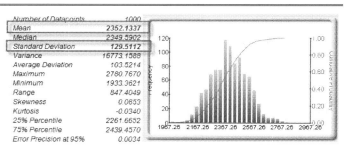

Number of Datapoints	1000
Mean	2352.1337
Median	2349.5902
Standard Deviation	129.5112
Variance	16773.1588
Average Deviation	103.5214
Maximum	2780.7670
Minimum	1933.3621
Range	847.4049
Skewness	0.0853
Kurtosis	-0.0340
25% Percentile	2261.6652
75% Percentile	2439.4570
Error Precision at 95%	0.0034

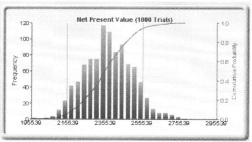

Type: Two-Tail, Lower: 2147.2378, Upper: 2555.9669, Certainty: 90.0000%

Figure 127.4: Hedged at 0.83 USD/FC

128. Risk Hedging – Hedging Foreign Exchange Exposure

File Name: Risk Hedging – Hedging Forex Exposures

Location: Modeling Toolkit | Risk Hedging | Foreign Exchange Exposure Hedging

Brief Description: Illustrates how to use Risk Simulator for simulating foreign exchange rates to determine the value of a hedged currency option position

Requirements: Modeling Toolkit, Risk Simulator

This model is used to simulate possible foreign exchange spot and future prices and the effects on the cash flow statement of a company under a freely floating exchange rate versus using currency options to hedge the foreign exchange exposure. See Figure 128.1.

Hedging Foreign Exchange Exposure with Currency Options

Months	Jan	Feb	Mar	April	May	June	July
FX Spot Rate (HKD/USD)	7.80	7.40	7.60	7.30	7.10	7.20	7.40
FX Strike Rate (HKD/USD)	7.80	7.80	7.80	7.80	7.80	7.80	7.80
Maturity (Years)	0.5833	0.5000	0.4167	0.3333	0.2500	0.1667	0.0833
Risk Free Rate US	6.08%	6.08%	6.08%	6.08%	6.08%	6.08%	6.08%
Risk Free Rate HK	5.06%	5.06%	5.06%	5.06%	5.06%	5.06%	5.06%
Volatility	15.00%	15.00%	15.00%	15.00%	15.00%	15.00%	15.00%
Quantity of Options Hedge Position	10,000,000	10,000,000	10,000,000	10,000,000	10,000,000	10,000,000	10,000,000
Currency Put Option Value (HKD/USD)	0.3229	0.5191	0.3795	0.5533	0.7012	0.6034	0.4102
Market Value of Hedge	3,229,135	5,191,009	3,794,813	5,532,845	7,012,229	6,034,435	4,102,320
Intrinsic Value	0	4,000,000	2,000,000	5,000,000	7,000,000	6,000,000	4,000,000
Time Value	3,229,135	1,191,009	1,794,813	532,845	12,229	34,435	102,320

FINANCIAL STATEMENTS IMPACTS - MARK TO MARKET

Balance Sheet (in 000's)	Jan	Feb	Mar	April	May	June	July
Option Contract	3,229,135	5,191,009	3,794,813	5,532,845	7,012,229	6,034,435	4,102,320
Other Comp Income (SE)		4,000,000	2,000,000	5,000,000	7,000,000	6,000,000	4,000,000

Income Statement (in 000's)							
Hedge Effectiveness gain or loss per period		(2,038,126)	603,805	(1,261,969)	(520,615)	22,206	67,884
Hedge Effectiveness sum of all periods							(3,126,816)
Market Cost of Hedge (Current Period)							3,229,135
Income from Option Exercise							4,000,000
Net Valuation of Hedging							770,865
Income from Hedging							74,770,865
Income from No Hedge							74,000,000
Loss Distribution from Hedging							3,229,135
Loss Distribution from No Hedge							4,000,000

Figure 128.1: Hedging currency exposures with currency options

Figure 128.2 shows the effects of the Value at Risk (VaR) of a hedged versus unhedged position. Clearly the right-tailed VaR of the loss distribution is higher without the currency options hedge. Figure 128.3 shows that there is a lower risk, lower risk to returns ratio, higher returns, and less swing in the outcomes of a currency-hedged position than an exposed position. Finally, Figure 128.4 shows the hedging effectiveness, that is, how often the hedge is in the money and become usable.

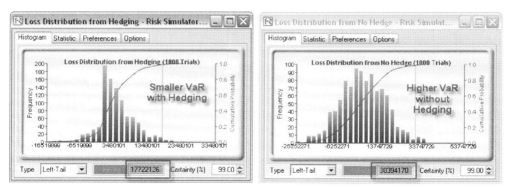

Figure 128.2: Values at Risk (VaR) of hedged versus unhedged positions

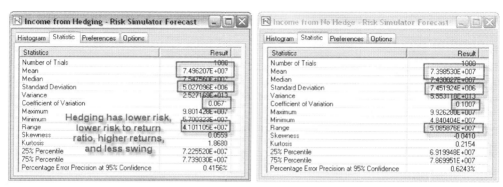

Figure 128.3: Forecast statistics of the loss distribution

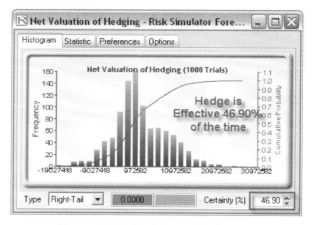

Figure 128.4: Hedging effectiveness

129. Sensitivity – Greeks

File Name: Sensitivity – Greeks

Location: Modeling Toolkit | Sensitivity | Greeks

Brief Description: Computes an option's instantaneous sensitivity parameters or Greeks

Requirements: Modeling Toolkit, Risk Simulator

Modeling Toolkit Functions Used: MTCallDelta, MTCallGamma, MTCallTheta, MTCallRho, MTCallVega, MTPutDelta, MTPutGamma, MTPutTheta, MTPutRho, MTPutVega

This model illustrates the option's *Greeks* to determine the instantaneous sensitivities to each of the inputs (Figure 129.1). Be careful as these values are based on partial differential equations for instantaneous changes and may not represent the changes of, say, some percentage differential. To determine the sensitivities of each input by varying one input at a time, use Risk Simulator's *Tornado* tool or see the *Sensitivity –Tornado and Sensitivity Nonlinear* model instead. Greeks are sometimes useful for setting up delta and delta-gamma hedges, to completely reduce the risk in a portfolio of options and underlying assets.

SENSITIVITY ANALYSIS - OPTION GREEKS

Input Assumptions

Asset Price	$20.00
Strike Price	$21.00
Maturity	10
Riskfree Rate	4.00%
Volatility	25.00%
Dividend Rate	2.00%

Call	Call	Put
Delta (Sensitivity to Stock Price)	0.5905	-0.2282
Gamma (Second Order Sensitivity to Delta)	0.0174	0.0174
Theta (Sensitivity to Maturity)	-0.2172	0.0183
Rho (Sensitivity to Risk-free Rate)	59.0054	-81.7618
Vega (Sensitivity to Volatility)	17.3929	17.3929

Figure 129.1: Option's Greeks

Using the corollary outputs generated by options theory, we can obtain the Greeks—namely, Delta, Gamma, Rho, Theta, Vega, and Xi—as a form of sensitivity analysis. By definition, sensitivity analysis, or stress testing, looks at the outcome of the change in the option price given a change in one unit of the underlying variables. In our case, these sensitivities reflect the instantaneous changes of the value of the option given a unit change in a particular variable, ceteris paribus. In other words, we can form a sensitivity table by simply looking at the corresponding values in Delta, Gamma, Rho, Theta, Vega, and Xi. Delta provides the change in value of the option given a unit change in the present value of the underlying asset's cash flow series. Gamma provides the rate of change in delta given a unit change in the underlying asset's cash flow series. Rho provides us with the change in the value of the option given that we change the interest rate one unit; Theta looks at the change per unit of time; Vega looks at the change per unit of volatility; and Xi looks at the change per unit of cost. In other words, one can provide a fairly comprehensive view of the way the value of the option changes given changes in these variables, thereby providing a test of the sensitivity of the option's value. A worst-case, nominal case, and best-case scenario can then be constructed. The sensitivity table not only provides a good test of the robustness of our results but also provides great insight into the value drivers in the firm, that is, which variables have the most impact on the firm's bottom line.

The following provides the derivations of these sensitivity measures for a European option without dividend payments. In actual options analysis, it might be easier to compute the sensitivities based on a percentage change to each input rather than instantaneous changes. Nonetheless, these Greeks are useful when modeling simultaneous hedging strategies (e.g., gamma and delta-gamma hedges as described previously in this book).

Call Delta

Starting from $C = S_t N(d_1) - Xe^{-rT} N(d_2)$, where

$$d_1 = \frac{\ln\left(\frac{S_t}{X}\right) + \left(r + \frac{1}{2}\sigma^2\right)(T)}{\sigma\sqrt{T}}$$ and $d_2 = d_1 - \sigma\sqrt{T}$, we can get the call Delta, defined as the change in call value for a change in the underlying asset value, that is, the partial derivative $\frac{\partial C_t}{\partial S_t}$

at an instantaneous time t. Differentiating, we obtain:

$$Delta = \Delta = \frac{\partial C_t}{\partial S_t} = N(d_1) + S_t \frac{\partial N(d_1)}{\partial S_t} - Xe^{-rT} \frac{\partial N(d_2)}{\partial S_t}$$

$$\frac{\partial C_t}{\partial S_t} = N(d_1) + S_t \frac{e^{-\frac{1}{2}d_1^2}}{\sqrt{2\pi}} \frac{\partial d_1}{\partial S_t} - Xe^{-rT} \frac{e^{-\frac{1}{2}d_2^2}}{\sqrt{2\pi}} \frac{\partial d_2}{\partial S_t}$$

$$\frac{\partial C_t}{\partial S_t} = N(d_1) + S_t \frac{e^{-\frac{1}{2}d_1^2}}{\sqrt{2\pi}} \frac{1/S_t}{\sigma\sqrt{T}} - Xe^{-rT} \frac{e^{-\frac{1}{2}(d_1 - \sigma\sqrt{T})^2}}{\sqrt{2\pi}} \frac{1/S_t}{\sigma\sqrt{T}}$$

$$\frac{\partial C_t}{\partial S_t} = N(d_1) + \frac{e^{-\frac{1}{2}d_1^2}}{\sigma\sqrt{2\pi T}}\left[1 - Xe^{-rT} \frac{e^{-\frac{1}{2}\sigma^2 T + d_1\sigma\sqrt{T}}}{S_t}\right]$$

$$\frac{\partial C_t}{\partial S_t} = N(d_1) + \frac{e^{-\frac{1}{2}d_1^2}}{\sigma\sqrt{2\pi T}}\left[1 - \frac{Xe^{-rT}}{S_t} e^{-\frac{1}{2}\sigma^2 T} e^{\ln(S_t/X)+(r+\sigma^2/2)T}\right]$$

$$\frac{\partial C_t}{\partial S_t} = N(d_1) + \frac{e^{-\frac{1}{2}d_1^2}}{\sigma\sqrt{2\pi T}}\left[1 - \frac{Xe^{-rT}}{S_t} e^{-\frac{1}{2}\sigma^2 T} \frac{S_t}{X} e^{rT} e^{\frac{1}{2}\sigma^2 T}\right]$$

$$Delta = \Delta = \frac{\partial C_t}{\partial S_t} = N(d_1)$$

Call Gamma

$$Gamma = \Gamma = \frac{\partial \Delta}{\partial S_t}$$

$$\frac{\partial \Delta}{\partial S_t} = \frac{1}{\sqrt{2\pi}} e^{-\frac{1}{2}d_1^2} \frac{\partial d_1}{\partial S_t}$$

$$\frac{\partial \Delta}{\partial S_t} = \frac{1}{\sqrt{2\pi}} e^{-\frac{1}{2}d_1^2} \frac{1}{S_t \sigma \sqrt{T}}$$

$$Gamma = \Gamma = \frac{\partial \Delta}{\partial S_t} = \frac{e^{\frac{-d_1^2}{2}}}{S_t \sigma \sqrt{2\pi T}}$$

Call Rho

$$Rho = P = \frac{\partial C_t}{\partial r} = S_t \frac{\partial N(d_1)}{\partial r} + XTe^{-rT} N(d_2) - Xe^{-rT} \frac{\partial N(d_2)}{\partial r}$$

$$\frac{\partial C_t}{\partial r} = S_t \frac{e^{-\frac{1}{2}d_1^2}}{\sqrt{2\pi}} \frac{\partial d_1}{\partial r} + XTe^{-rT} N(d_2) - Xe^{-rT} \frac{e^{-\frac{1}{2}d_2^2}}{\sqrt{2\pi}} \frac{\partial d_2}{\partial r}$$

$$\frac{\partial C_t}{\partial r} = \frac{e^{-\frac{1}{2}d_1^2}}{\sqrt{2\pi}} \left[S_t \frac{\partial d_1}{\partial r} - Xe^{-rT} e^{\frac{1}{2}\left(d_1^2 - d_2^2\right)} \frac{\partial d_1}{\partial r} \right] + XTe^{-rT} N(d_2)$$

$$\frac{\partial C_t}{\partial r} = \frac{e^{-\frac{1}{2}d_1^2}}{\sqrt{2\pi}} \frac{\partial d_1}{\partial r} \left[S_t - Xe^{-rT} e^{-\frac{1}{2}\sigma^2 T} e^{\ln(S/X) + (r + \sigma^2/2)T} \right] + XTe^{-rT} N(d_2)$$

$$\frac{\partial C_t}{\partial r} = \frac{e^{-\frac{1}{2}d_1^2}}{\sqrt{2\pi}} \frac{\partial d_1}{\partial r} \left[S_t - \frac{XS_t}{X} \right] + XTe^{-rT} N(d_2)$$

$$Rho = P = \frac{\partial C_t}{\partial r} = XTe^{-rT} N(d_2)$$

Call Theta

$$Theta = \Theta = \frac{\partial C_t}{\partial T} = S_t \frac{\partial N(d_1)}{\partial T} - X \frac{\partial}{\partial T} \left[e^{-rT} N(d_2) \right]$$

$$\frac{\partial C_t}{\partial T} = S_t \frac{1}{\sqrt{2\pi}} e^{-\frac{1}{2}d_1^2} \frac{\partial d_1}{\partial t} - rXe^{-rT} N(d_2) - Xe^{-rT} \frac{1}{\sqrt{2\pi}} e^{-\frac{1}{2}d_2^2} \frac{\partial d_2}{\partial t}$$

as $\dfrac{\partial d_1}{\partial t} = \dfrac{\ln \frac{S_t}{X}}{2\sigma T^{3/2}} + \dfrac{1}{2\sigma\sqrt{T}}\left[r + \dfrac{\sigma^2}{2} \right]$ we have $\dfrac{\partial d_2}{\partial t} = \dfrac{\partial d_1}{\partial t} + \dfrac{\sigma}{2\sqrt{T}}$ and

$$\frac{\partial C_t}{\partial T} = S_t \frac{1}{\sqrt{2\pi}} e^{-\frac{1}{2}d_1^2} \frac{\partial d_1}{\partial t} - rXe^{-rT} N(d_2) - Xe^{-rT} \frac{1}{\sqrt{2\pi}} e^{-\frac{1}{2}d_2^2} \left[\frac{\partial d_1}{\partial t} + \frac{\sigma}{2\sqrt{T}} \right]$$

$$\frac{\partial C_t}{\partial T} = \frac{e^{-\frac{1}{2}d_1^2}}{\sqrt{2\pi}}\left[S_t\frac{\partial d_1}{\partial t} - Xe^{-rT}e^{-\frac{1}{2}\left(d_1^2-d_2^2\right)}\left(\frac{\partial d_1}{\partial t} + \frac{\sigma}{2\sqrt{T}}\right)\right] - rXe^{-rT}N(d_2)$$

$$\frac{\partial C_t}{\partial T} = \frac{e^{-\frac{1}{2}d_1^2}}{\sqrt{2\pi}}\left[S_t\frac{\partial d_1}{\partial t} - Xe^{-rT}e^{-\frac{1}{2}\left(\sigma^2 T\right)}e^{d_1\sigma\sqrt{T}}\left(\frac{\partial d_1}{\partial t} + \frac{\sigma}{2\sqrt{T}}\right)\right] - rXe^{-rT}N(d_2)$$

$$\frac{\partial C_t}{\partial T} = \frac{e^{-\frac{1}{2}d_1^2}}{\sqrt{2\pi}}\left[S_t\frac{\partial d_1}{\partial t} - Xe^{-rT-\frac{1}{2}\left(\sigma^2 T\right)+\ln(S/X)+(r+\sigma^2/2)T}\left(\frac{\partial d_1}{\partial t} + \frac{\sigma}{2\sqrt{T}}\right)\right] - rXe^{-rT}N(d_2)$$

$$\frac{\partial C_t}{\partial T} = \frac{e^{-\frac{1}{2}d_1^2}}{\sqrt{2\pi}}\left[S_t\frac{\partial d_1}{\partial t} - S_t\frac{\partial d_1}{\partial t} - \frac{S_t\sigma}{2\sqrt{T}}\right] - rXe^{-rT}N(d_2)$$

$$Theta = \Theta = \frac{\partial C_t}{\partial T} = \frac{-S\sigma e^{-\frac{d_1^2}{2}}}{2\sqrt{2\pi T}} - rXe^{-rT}N(d_2)$$

Call Vega

$$Vega = V = \frac{\partial C_t}{\partial \sigma} = \frac{\partial}{\partial \sigma}\left[S_t N(d_1) - Xe^{-rT}N(d_2)\right]$$

$$\frac{\partial C_t}{\partial \sigma} = \frac{S_t}{\sqrt{2\pi}}e^{-\frac{1}{2}d_1^2}\frac{\partial d_1}{\partial \sigma} - Xe^{-rT}e^{-\frac{1}{2}d_2^2}\frac{\partial d_2}{\partial \sigma}$$

$$\frac{\partial C_t}{\partial \sigma} = \frac{1}{\sqrt{2\pi}}e^{-\frac{1}{2}d_1^2}\left[S_t\frac{\partial d_1}{\partial \sigma} - Xe^{-rT}e^{-\left(d_1^2-d_2^2\right)}\frac{\partial d_2}{\partial \sigma}\right]$$

$$\frac{\partial C_t}{\partial \sigma} = \frac{1}{\sqrt{2\pi}}e^{-\frac{1}{2}d_1^2}\left[S_t\frac{\partial d_1}{\partial \sigma} - Xe^{-rT}e^{-\frac{1}{2}\sigma^2 T + d_1\sigma\sqrt{T}}\frac{\partial d_2}{\partial \sigma}\right]$$

$$\frac{\partial C_t}{\partial \sigma} = \frac{1}{\sqrt{2\pi}}e^{-\frac{1}{2}d_1^2}\left[S_t\frac{\partial d_1}{\partial \sigma} - Xe^{-rT}e^{-\frac{1}{2}\sigma^2 T}e^{\ln(S/X)+(r+\sigma^2/2)T}\frac{\partial d_2}{\partial \sigma}\right]$$

$$\frac{\partial C_t}{\partial \sigma} = \frac{1}{\sqrt{2\pi}}e^{-\frac{1}{2}d_1^2}\left[S_t\frac{\partial d_1}{\partial \sigma} - S_t\frac{\partial d_2}{\partial \sigma}\right]$$

$$\frac{\partial C_t}{\partial \sigma} = \frac{1}{\sqrt{2\pi}}e^{-\frac{1}{2}d_1^2}S_t\left[\frac{\partial d_1}{\partial \sigma} - \frac{\partial d_1}{\partial \sigma} + \sqrt{T}\right]$$

$$Vega = V = \frac{\partial C_t}{\partial \sigma} = \frac{S_t\sqrt{T}e^{-\frac{d_1^2}{2}}}{\sqrt{2\pi}}$$

Call Xi

$$Xi = \Xi = \frac{\partial C_t}{\partial X_t} = -N(d_2) + S_t \frac{\partial N(d_1)}{\partial X_t} - Xe^{-rT}\frac{\partial N(d_2)}{\partial X_t}$$

$$\frac{\partial C_t}{\partial X_t} = -N(d_2) + S_t \frac{e^{-\frac{1}{2}d_1^2}}{\sqrt{2\pi}}\frac{\partial d_1}{\partial X_t} - Xe^{-rT}\frac{e^{-\frac{1}{2}d_2^2}}{\sqrt{2\pi}}\frac{\partial d_2}{\partial X_t}$$

$$\frac{\partial C_t}{\partial X_t} = -N(d_2) + S_t \frac{e^{-\frac{1}{2}d_1^2}}{\sqrt{2\pi}}\frac{1/S_t}{\sigma\sqrt{T}} - Xe^{-rT}\frac{e^{-\frac{1}{2}(d_1-\sigma\sqrt{T})_2^2}}{\sqrt{2\pi}}\frac{1/S_t}{\sigma\sqrt{T}}$$

$$\frac{\partial C_t}{\partial X_t} = -N(d_2) + \frac{e^{-\frac{1}{2}d_1^2}}{\sigma\sqrt{2\pi T}}\left[1 - Xe^{-rT}\frac{e^{-\frac{1}{2}\sigma^2 T + d_1\sigma\sqrt{T}}}{S_t}\right]$$

$$\frac{\partial C_t}{\partial X_t} = -N(d_2) + \frac{e^{-\frac{1}{2}d_1^2}}{\sigma\sqrt{2\pi T}}\left[1 - \frac{Xe^{-rT}}{S_t}e^{-\frac{1}{2}\sigma^2 T}e^{\ln(S_t/X)+(r+\sigma^2/2)T}\right]$$

$$\frac{\partial C_t}{\partial X_t} = -N(d_2) + \frac{e^{-\frac{1}{2}d_1^2}}{\sigma\sqrt{2\pi T}}\left[1 - \frac{Xe^{-rT}}{S_t}e^{-\frac{1}{2}\sigma^2 T}\frac{S_t}{X}e^{rT}e^{\frac{1}{2}\sigma^2 T}\right]$$

$$Xi = \Xi = \frac{\partial C_t}{\partial X_t} = -N(d_2)$$

130. Sensitivity – Tornado and Linear Sensitivity Charts

File Name: Sensitivity – Tornado and Sensitivity Linear

Location: Modeling Toolkit | Sensitivity | Tornado and Sensitivity Linear

Brief Description: Illustrates how to use Risk Simulator for running a pre-simulation sensitivity analysis (tornado and spider charts) and running a post-simulation sensitivity analysis (sensitivity charts)

Requirements: Modeling Toolkit, Risk Simulator

This example illustrates a simple discounted cash flow model and shows how sensitivity analysis can be performed prior to running a simulation and after a simulation is run. Tornado and spider charts are static sensitivity analysis tools useful for determining which variables impact the key results the most. That is, each precedent variable is perturbed a set amount and the key result is analyzed to determine which input variables are the critical success factors with the most impact. In contrast, sensitivity charts are dynamic, in that all precedent variables are perturbed together in a simultaneous fashion (the effects of autocorrelations, cross-correlations, and interactions are all captured in the resulting sensitivity chart). Therefore, a tornado static analysis is run before a simulation while a sensitivity analysis is run after a simulation.

The precedents in a model are used in creating the tornado chart. Precedents are all the input variables that affect the outcome of the model. For instance, if a model consists of A = B + C, and where C = D + E, then B, D, and E are the precedents for A (C is not a precedent as it is only an intermediate calculated value). The testing range of each precedent variable can be set when running a tornado analysis and is used to estimate the target result. If the precedent variables are simple inputs, then the testing range will be a simple perturbation based on the range chosen (e.g., the default is ±10%). Each precedent variable can be perturbed at different percentages if required. A wider range is important as it is better able to test extreme values rather than smaller perturbations around the expected values. In certain circumstances, extreme values may have a larger, smaller, or unbalanced impact (e.g., nonlinearities may occur where increasing or decreasing economies of scale and scope creep in for larger or smaller values of a variable) and only a wider range will capture this nonlinear impact.

Creating a Tornado and Sensitivity Chart

To run this model, simply:

1. Go to the *DCF Model* worksheet and select the NPV result (cell **G6**) as seen in Figure 130.1.

2. Select **Risk Simulator | Analytical Tools | Tornado Analysis** (or click on the **Tornado Chart** icon).

3. Check that the software's intelligent naming is correct or, better still, click on **Use Cell Address** to use the cell address as the name for each precedent variable and click **OK** (Figure 130.2).

Discounted Cash Flow Model

Base Year	2016		Sum PV Net Benefits	$1,896.63
Market Risk-Adjusted Discount Rate	15.00%		Sum PV Investments	$1,800.00
Private-Risk Discount Rate	5.00%		Net Present Value	$96.63
Annualized Sales Growth Rate	2.00%		Internal Rate of Return	18.80%
Price Erosion Rate	5.00%		Return on Investment	5.37%
Effective Tax Rate	40.00%			

	2016	2017	2018	2019	2020
Prod A Avg Price	$10.00	$9.50	$9.03	$8.57	$8.15
Prod B Avg Price	$12.25	$11.64	$11.06	$10.50	$9.98
Prod C Avg Price	$15.15	$14.39	$13.67	$12.99	$12.34
Prod A Quantity	50.00	51.00	52.02	53.06	54.12
Prod B Quantity	35.00	35.70	36.41	37.14	37.89
Prod C Quantity	20.00	20.40	20.81	21.22	21.65
Total Revenues	$1,231.75	$1,193.57	$1,156.57	$1,120.71	$1,085.97
Cost of Goods Sold	$184.76	$179.03	$173.48	$168.11	$162.90
Gross Profit	$1,046.99	$1,014.53	$983.08	$952.60	$923.07
Operating Expenses	$157.50	$160.65	$163.86	$167.14	$170.48
SG&A Costs	$15.75	$16.07	$16.39	$16.71	$17.05
Operating Income (EBITDA)	$873.74	$837.82	$802.83	$768.75	$735.54
Depreciation	$10.00	$10.00	$10.00	$10.00	$10.00
Amortization	$3.00	$3.00	$3.00	$3.00	$3.00
EBIT	$860.74	$824.82	$789.83	$755.75	$722.54
Interest Payments	$2.00	$2.00	$2.00	$2.00	$2.00
EBT	$858.74	$822.82	$787.83	$753.75	$720.54
Taxes	$343.50	$329.13	$315.13	$301.50	$288.22
Net Income	$515.24	$493.69	$472.70	$452.25	$432.33
Depreciation	$13.00	$13.00	$13.00	$13.00	$13.00
Change in Net Working Capital	$0.00	$0.00	$0.00	$0.00	$0.00
Capital Expenditures	$0.00	$0.00	$0.00	$0.00	$0.00
Free Cash Flow	$528.24	$506.69	$485.70	$465.25	$445.33
Investments	$1,800.00				

Figure 130.1: Discounted cash flow model

Interpreting the Results

The report generated illustrates the sensitivity table (starting base value of the key variable as well as the perturbed values and the precedents). The precedent with the highest impact (range of output) is listed first. The tornado chart illustrates this analysis graphically (Figure 130.3). The spider chart performs the same analysis but also accounts for nonlinear effects. That is, if the input variables have a nonlinear effect on the output variable, the lines on the spider chart will be curved. Rerun the analysis on the *Black-Scholes* model sheet in the tornado and sensitivity charts (nonlinear) example file.

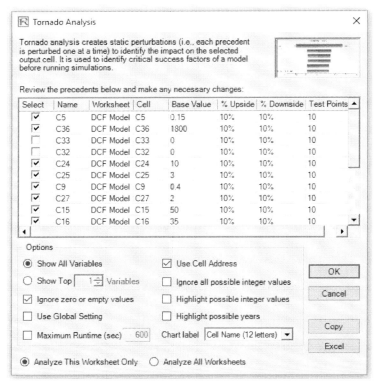

Figure 130.2: Setting up a tornado analysis

Tornado and Spider Charts

Statistical Summary

One of the powerful simulation tools is the tornado chart—it captures the static impacts of each variable on the outcome of the model. That is, the tool automatically perturbs each precedent variable in the model a user-specified preset amount, captures the fluctuation on the model's forecast or final result, and lists the resulting perturbations ranked from the most significant to the least. Precedents are all the input and intermediate variables that affect the outcome of the model. For instance, if the model consists of $A = B + C$, where $C = D + E$, then B, D, and E are the precedents for A (C is not a precedent as it is only an intermediate calculated value). The range and number of values perturbed is user-specified and can be set to test extreme values rather than smaller perturbations around the expected values. In certain circumstances, extreme values may have a larger, smaller, or unbalanced impact (e.g., nonlinearities may occur where increasing or decreasing economies of scale and scope creep occurs for larger or smaller values of a variable) and only a wider range will capture this nonlinear impact.

A tornado chart lists all the inputs that drive the model, starting from the input variable that has the most effect on the results. The chart is obtained by perturbing each precedent input at some consistent range (e.g., ±10% from the base case) one at a time, and comparing their results to the base case. A spider chart looks like a spider with a central body and its many legs protruding. The positively sloped lines indicate a positive relationship, while a negatively sloped line indicates a negative relationship. Further, spider charts can be used to visualize linear and nonlinear relationships. The tornado and spider charts help identify the critical success factors of an output cell in order to identify the inputs to simulate. The identified critical variables that are uncertain are the ones that should be simulated. Do not waste time simulating variables that are neither uncertain nor have little impact on the results.

Result

	Base Value: 96.6261638553219			Input Changes		
Precedent Cell	Output Downside	Output Upside	Effective Range	Input Downside	Input Upside	Base Case Value
Investment	$276.63	($83.37)	360.00	$1,620.00	$1,980.00	$1,800.00
Tax Rate	$219.73	($26.47)	246.20	36.00%	44.00%	40.00%
A Price	$3.43	$189.83	186.40	$9.00	$11.00	$10.00
B Price	$16.71	$176.55	159.84	$11.03	$13.48	$12.25
A Quantity	$23.18	$170.07	146.90	45.00	55.00	50.00
B Quantity	$30.53	$162.72	132.19	31.50	38.50	35.00
C Price	$40.15	$153.11	112.96	$13.64	$16.67	$15.15
C Quantity	$48.05	$145.20	97.16	18.00	22.00	20.00
Discount Rate	$138.24	$57.03	81.21	13.50%	16.50%	15.00%
Price Erosion	$116.80	$76.64	40.16	4.50%	5.50%	5.00%
Sales Growth	$90.59	$102.69	12.10	1.80%	2.20%	2.00%
Depreciation	$95.08	$98.17	3.08	$9.00	$11.00	$10.00
Interest	$97.09	$96.16	0.93	$1.80	$2.20	$2.00
Amortization	$96.16	$97.09	0.93	$2.70	$3.30	$3.00
CapEx	$96.63	$96.63	0.00	$0.00	$0.00	$0.00
Working Capital	$96.63	$96.63	0.00	$0.00	$0.00	$0.00

Figure 130.3: Tornado analysis result

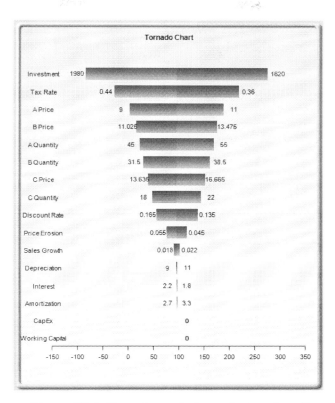

Figure 130.3: Tornado analysis result *(continued)*

The sensitivity table in Figure 130.3 shows the starting NPV base value of $96.63 and how each input is changed (e.g., Investment is changed from $1,800 to $1,980 on the upside with a +10% swing, and from $1,800 to $1,620 on the downside with a –10% swing). The resulting upside and downside values on NPV are –$83.37 and $276.63, with a total change of $360, making it the variable with the highest impact on NPV. The precedent variables are ranked from the highest impact to the lowest impact.

The spider chart illustrates these effects graphically. The y-axis is the NPV target value while the x-axis depicts the percentage change on each of the precedent values (the central point is the base case value at $96.63 at 0% change from the base value of each precedent). Positively sloped lines indicate a positive relationship or effect while negatively sloped lines indicate a negative relationship (e.g., investment is negatively sloped, which means that the higher the investment level, the lower the NPV). The absolute value of the slope indicates the magnitude of the effect computed as the percentage change in the result given a percentage change in the precedent (a steep line indicates a higher impact on the NPV y-axis given a change in the precedent x-axis).

The tornado chart illustrates the results in another graphical manner, where the highest impacting precedent is listed first. The x-axis is the NPV value with the center of the chart being the base case condition. Green (lighter) bars in the chart indicate a positive effect while red (darker) bars indicates a negative effect. Therefore, for investments, the red (darker) bar on the right side indicate a negative effect of investment on higher NPV—in other words, capital investment and NPV are negatively correlated. The opposite is true for price and quantity of products A to C (their green or lighter bars are on the right side of the chart).

Although the tornado chart is easier to read, the spider chart is important to determine if there are any nonlinearities in the model. Such nonlinearities are harder to identify in a tornado chart and may be important information in the model or provide decision makers important insight into the model's dynamics. For instance, in the Black-Scholes model (see the next chapter on nonlinear sensitivity analysis), the fact that stock price and strike price are nonlinearly related to the option value is important to know. This characteristic implies that option value will not increase or decrease proportionally to the changes in stock or strike price, and that there might be some interactions between these two prices as well as other variables. As another example, an engineering model depicting nonlinearities might indicate that a particular part or component, when subjected to a high enough force or tension, will break. Clearly, it is important to understand such nonlinearities.

Remember that tornado analysis is a static sensitivity analysis applied on each input variable in the model—that is, each variable is perturbed individually and the resulting effects are tabulated. This makes tornado analysis a key component to execute before running a simulation. One of the very first steps in risk analysis is where the most important impact drivers in the model are captured and identified. The next step is to identify which of these important impact drivers are uncertain. These uncertain impact drivers are the critical success drivers of a project, where the results of the model depend on these critical success drivers. These variables are the ones that should be simulated. Do not waste time simulating variables that are neither uncertain nor have little impact on the results. Tornado charts assist in identifying these critical success drivers quickly and easily. According to this example, it might be that price and quantity should be simulated, assuming if the required investment and effective tax rate are both known in advance and unchanging.

Creating a Sensitivity Chart

To run this model, simply:

1. Create a new simulation profile called (**Risk Simulator | New Profile**).

2. Set the relevant assumptions and forecasts on the *DCF Model* worksheet.

3. Run the simulation (**Risk Simulator | Run Simulation**).

4. Select **Risk Simulator | Analytical Tools | Sensitivity Analysis.**

Interpreting the Results

Notice that if correlations are turned off, the results of the sensitivity chart are similar to the tornado chart. Now, reset the simulation, and turn on correlations (select **Risk Simulator | Reset Simulation** then select **Risk Simulator | Edit Profile** and check **Apply Correlations**, and then **Risk Simulator | Run Simulation**), and repeat the steps above for creating a sensitivity chart. Notice that when correlations are applied, the resulting analysis may be different due to the interactions among variables. Of course, you will need to set the relevant correlations among the assumptions.

Sometimes the chart axis variable names can be too long (Figure 130.4). If that happens, simply rerun the tornado but truncate or rename some of the long variable names to something more concise. Then the charts will be more visually appealing.

The results of the sensitivity analysis comprise a report and two key charts. The first is a nonlinear rank correlation chart that ranks from highest to lowest the assumption-forecast correlation pairs. These correlations are nonlinear and nonparametric, making them free of any distributional requirements (i.e., an assumption with a Weibull distribution can be compared to another with a Beta distribution). The results from this chart are fairly similar to that of the tornado analysis seen previously (of course, without the capital investment value, which we decided was a known value and hence was not simulated), with one special exception. Tax rate was relegated to a much lower position in the sensitivity analysis chart as compared to the tornado chart. This is because by itself, tax rate will have a significant impact but once the other variables are interacting in the model, it appears that tax rate has less of a dominant effect (this is because tax rate has a smaller distribution as historical tax rates tend not to fluctuate too much, and also because tax rate is a straight percentage value of the income before taxes, where other precedent variables have a larger effect on NPV). This example proves that performing sensitivity analysis after a simulation run is important to ascertain if there are any interactions in the model and if the effects of certain variables still hold. The second chart illustrates the percent variation explained; that is, of the fluctuations in the forecast, how much of the variation can be explained by each of the assumptions after accounting for all the interactions among variables? Notice that the sum of all variations explained is usually close to 100% (sometimes other elements impact the model but they cannot be captured here directly), and if correlations exist, the sum may sometimes exceed 100% (due to the interaction effects that are cumulative).

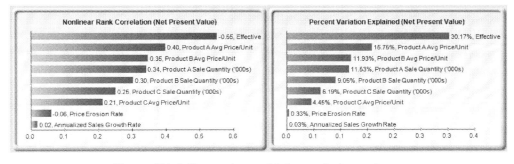

Figure 130.4: Dynamic sensitivity analysis results

131. Sensitivity – Tornado and Nonlinear Sensitivity Charts

File Name: Sensitivity – Tornado and Sensitivity Nonlinear

Location: Modeling Toolkit | Sensitivity | Tornado and Sensitivity Nonlinear

Brief Description: Illustrates how to use Risk Simulator for running a pre-simulation sensitivity analysis (tornado and spider charts) and running a post-simulation sensitivity analysis (sensitivity charts)

Requirements: Modeling Toolkit, Risk Simulator

This example illustrates a simple option valuation model and shows how sensitivity analysis can be performed prior to running a simulation and after a simulation is run. Tornado and spider charts are static sensitivity analysis tools useful for determining which variables impact the key results the most. That is, each precedent variable is perturbed a set percentage amount, and the key result is analyzed to determine which input variables are the critical success factors with the most impact. In contrast, sensitivity charts are dynamic, in that all precedent variables are perturbed together in a simultaneous fashion. The effects of autocorrelations, cross-correlations, and interactions are all captured in the resulting sensitivity chart. Therefore, a tornado analysis is done before a simulation whereas a sensitivity analysis is done after a simulation. Please review the previous chapter for more theoretical details on tornado and sensitivity analysis before proceeding.

Creating a Tornado and Spider Chart

To run this model, simply:

1. Go to the *Black-Scholes Model* worksheet and select the Black-Scholes result (cell **E13**).

2. Select **Risk Simulator | Analytical Tools | Tornado Analysis** (or click on the **Tornado Chart** icon).

3. Check that the software's intelligent naming is correct for the precedent values.

4. Change the upper and lower test values from *10%* to ***80%*** on all variables and click **OK** (Figure 131.1).

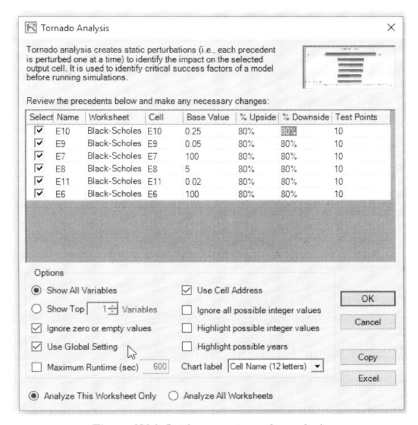

Figure 131.1: Setting up a tornado analysis

Interpreting the Results

The report generated (Figure 131.2) illustrates the sensitivity table (starting base value of the key variable as well as the perturbed values and the precedents). The precedent with the highest impact (range of output) is listed first. The tornado chart illustrates this analysis graphically. The spider chart performs the same analysis but also accounts for nonlinear effects. That is, if the input variables have a nonlinear effect on the output variable, the lines on the spider chart will be curved. Notice that the stock price and strike price have the highest effects (positive and negative effects, respectively) and the inputs are nonlinear. Positively sloped lines indicate positive relationships, while negatively sloped lines indicate negative relationships. The steeper the slope of the line, the higher the impact on the bottom line value.

In this special case where the option pricing model is nonlinear, you will see that the tornado chart is not symmetrical and the spider chart has a few lines that are curved. These are key characteristics of nonlinear models. This means that an X percentage change in one variable will not always mean a Y percentage change in the forecast result. To understand the variables in a model, it is important to identify nonlinearities.

Tornado and Spider Charts

Statistical Summary

One of the powerful simulation tools is the tornado chart—it captures the static impacts of each variable on the outcome of the model. That is, the tool automatically perturbs each precedent variable in the model a user-specified preset amount, captures the fluctuation on the model's forecast or final result, and lists the resulting perturbations ranked from the most significant to the least. Precedents are all the input and intermediate variables that affect the outcome of the model. For instance, if the model consists of $A = B + C$, where $C = D + E$, then B, D, and E are the precedents for A (C is not a precedent as it is only an intermediate calculated value). The range and number of values perturbed is user-specified and can be set to test extreme values rather than smaller perturbations around the expected values. In certain circumstances, extreme values may have a larger, smaller, or unbalanced impact (e.g., nonlinearities may occur where increasing or decreasing economies of scale and scope creep occurs for larger or smaller values of a variable) and only a wider range will capture this nonlinear impact.

A tornado chart lists all the inputs that drive the model, starting from the input variable that has the most effect on the results. The chart is obtained by perturbing each precedent input at some consistent range (e.g., ±10% from the base case) one at a time, and comparing their results to the base case. A spider chart looks like a spider with a central body and its many legs protruding. The positively sloped line indicates a positive relationship, while a negatively sloped line indicates a negative relationship. Further, spider charts can be used to visualize linear and nonlinear relationships. The tornado and spider charts help identify the critical success factors of an output cell in order to identify the inputs to simulate. The identified critical variables that are uncertain are the ones that should be simulated. Do not waste time simulating variables that are neither uncertain nor have little impact on the results.

Result

	Base Value: 25.4786764688884			Input Changes		
Precedent Cell	Output Downside	Output Upside	Effective Range	Input Downside	Input Upside	Base Case Value
Stock Price	0.028731	87.66505	87.64	$20.00	$180.00	$100.00
Strike Price	74.91229	7.619643	67.29	$20.00	$180.00	$100.00
Annualized Volatility	12.99407	39.05116	26.06	5.00%	45.00%	25.00%
Maturity in Years	11.12376	32.71824	21.59	1.00	9.00	5.00
Risk-free Rate	18.19017	33.43947	15.25	1.00%	9.00%	5.00%
Dividend Yield	30.99746	20.72544	10.27	0.40%	3.60%	2.00%

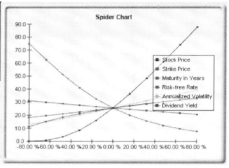

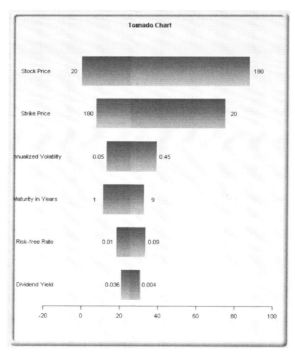

Figure 131.2: Nonlinear and asymmetrical tornado chart

Creating a Sensitivity Chart

To run this model, simply:

1. Create a new simulation profile (**Risk Simulator | New Profile**).

2. Set some assumptions on the inputs (with correlations) and set the output forecast.

3. Run the simulation (**Risk Simulator | Run Simulation**).

4. Select **Risk Simulator | Analytical Tools | Sensitivity Analysis**.

Interpreting the Results

Notice that if correlations are turned off, the results of the sensitivity chart are similar to those of the tornado chart. Now reset the simulation, and turn on correlations (select **Risk Simulator | Reset Simulation**, then select **Risk Simulator | Edit Profile** and check **Apply Correlations**, then **Risk Simulator | Run Simulation**) and repeat the steps for creating a sensitivity chart (Figure 131.3). Notice that when correlations are applied, the resulting analysis may be slightly different due to the interactions among variables (Figure 131.4). Notice that when correlations are turned on, the *Stock Price* position is reduced to a less prominent effect as it is correlated to *Dividend Yield*, a less dominant variable. Note that in the sensitivity chart, *Volatility* has a larger effect once the interactions among variables have all been accounted for. Volatility in real life is a key indicator of option value, and the analysis here proves this fact.

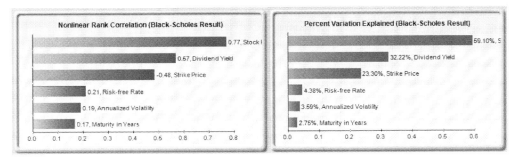

Figure 131.3: Dynamic sensitivity analysis charts

Sensitivity Analysis with No Correlations

Statistical Summary

Sensitivity charts are dynamic perturbations created after the simulation run. Sensitivity charts are dynamic perturbations in the sense that multiple assumptions are perturbed simultaneously and their interactions are captured in the fluctuations of the results. In contrast, Tornado charts are static perturbations, meaning that each precedent or assumption variable is perturbed a preset amount and the fluctuations in the results are tabulated. Tornado charts therefore identify which variables drive the results the most and hence are suitable for determining which variables to simulate (that is, they are used before a simulation), whereas sensitivity charts identify the impact to the results when multiple interacting variables are simulated together in the model (that is, they are used after a simulation).

The Nonlinear Rank Correlation charts indicate the rank correlations between each assumption and the target forecast, and are depicted from the highest absolute value to the lowest absolute value. Positive correlations are shown in green while negative correlations are shown in red. Rank correlation is used instead of a regular correlation coefficient as it captures nonlinear effects between variables. In contrast, the Percent Variation Explained computes how much of the variation in the forecast variable can be explained by the variations in each of the assumptions by itself in a dynamic simulated environment. These charts show the sensitivity of the target forecast to the simulated assumptions.

Figure 131.4: Dynamic sensitivity charts

132. Simulation – Basic Simulation Model

File Name: Simulation – Basic Simulation Model

Location: Modeling Toolkit | Risk Simulator | Basic Simulation Model

Brief Description: Illustrates how to use Risk Simulator for running a Monte Carlo simulation, viewing and interpreting forecast results, setting seed values, setting run preferences, extracting simulation data, and creating new and switching among simulation profiles

Requirements: Modeling Toolkit, Risk Simulator

The model in the *Static and Dynamic Model* worksheet illustrates a very simple model with two input assumptions (revenue and cost) and an output forecast (income). In Figure 132.1, the model on the left is a static model with single-point estimates; the model on the right is a dynamic model on which Monte Carlo assumptions and forecasts can be created. After running the simulation, the results can be extracted and further analyzed. In this model we can also learn to set different simulation preferences, run a simulation with error and precision controls, and set seed values. This should be the first model you run to get started with Monte Carlo simulation.

Figure 132.1 shows this basic model, which is a very simplistic model of revenue minus cost to equal income. On the static model, the input and output values are unchanging or static. This means that if revenue is $2 and cost is $1, then the income must be $2 – $1, or $1. We replicate the same model on the right and call it a dynamic model, where we will run a simulation.

	A	B	C	D	E	F	G	H	I	J
1										
2										
3										
4										
5										
6			STATIC MODEL			DYNAMIC MODEL				
7										
8			Revenue	$ 2.00		Revenue	$ 2.00	<<---This is an Input Assumption		
9			Cost	$ 1.00		Cost	$ 1.00	<<---This is an Input Assumption		
10			Income	$ 1.00		Income	$ 1.00	<<---This is an Output Forecast		
11										
12										

Figure 132.1: The world's simplest model

Running a Monte Carlo Simulation

To run this model, simply:

1. Select **Risk Simulator | New Simulation Profile** (or click on the **New Profile** icon in Figure 132.2) and provide it with a name.
2. Select cell **G8** and click on **Risk Simulator | Set Input Assumption** (or click on the **Set Input Assumption** icon shown in Figure 132.2).

3. Select **Triangular Distribution** and set the **Min = 1.50, Most Likely = 2.00,** and **Max = 2.25** and hit **OK** (Figure 132.3).

4. Select cell **G9** and set another input assumption. This time use **Uniform Distribution** with **Min = 0.85** and **Max = 1.25**.

5. Select cell **G10** and set that cell as the output forecast by clicking on **Risk Simulator | Set Output Forecast**.

6. Select **Risk Simulator | Run Simulation** (or click on the **RUN** icon in Figure 132.2) to start the simulation.

Figure 132.2: Risk Simulator toolbar

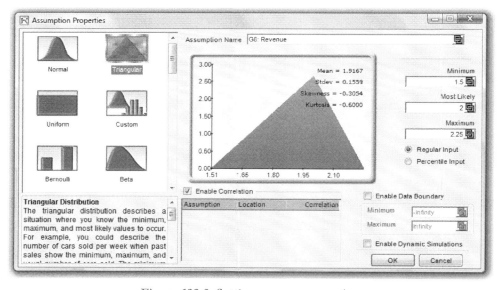

Figure 132.3: Setting up an assumption

Viewing and Interpreting Forecast Results

The forecast chart is shown when the simulation is running. Once simulation is completed, the forecast chart can be used (Figure 132.4). The forecast chart has several tabs, including *Histogram, Statistics, Preferences*, and *Options* tabs. Of particular interest are the first two tabs. For instance, the *Histogram* shows the output forecast's probability distribution in the form of a histogram, where the specific values can be determined using the certainty boxes. For example, select **Two-Tail**, enter **90** in the certainty box, and hit **TAB** on the keyboard. The 90% confidence interval is shown (0.5273 and 1.1739), meaning that there is a 5% chance that the income will fall below $0.5273 and another 5% chance that it will be above $1.1739. Alternatively, you can select **Left-Tail** and enter **1.0** on the input box, hit **TAB**, and see that the left-tail certainty is 74.30%, indicating that there is a 74.30% chance that the income will fall below $1.0 (alternatively, there is a 25.70% chance that income will exceed $1.0).

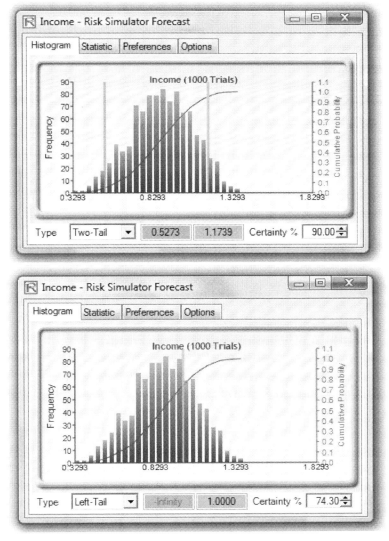

Figure 132.4: Forecast charts

The *Statistics* tab (Figure 132.5) illustrates the statistical results of the forecast variable. Note that your results will not be exactly the same as those illustrated here because a simulation (random number generation) was run. By definition, the results will not be exactly the same every time. However, if a seed value is set (see next section), the results will be identical in every single run. Setting a seed value is important especially when you wish to obtain the same values in each simulation run (e.g., you need the live model to return the same results as a printed report during a presentation).

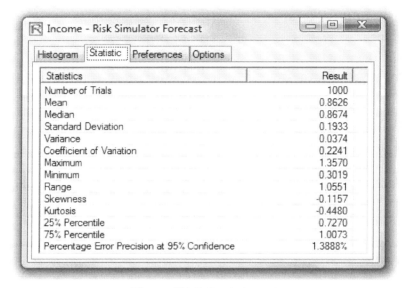

Figure 132.5: Statistics tab

Setting a Seed Value

1. Reset the simulation by selecting **Risk Simulator | Reset Simulation**.

2. Select **Risk Simulator | Edit Simulation Profile**.

3. Select the check box for random number sequence.

4. Enter in a seed value (e.g., 999) and hit **OK** (Figure 132.6).

5. Run the simulation and note the results, then rerun the simulation a few times and verify that the results are the same as those obtained earlier.

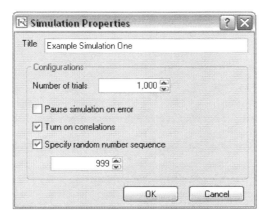

Figure 132.6: Setting a random number sequence seed

Note that the random number sequence or seed number has to be a positive integer value. Running the same model with the same assumptions and forecasts with the identical seed value and same number of trials will always yield the same results. The number of simulation trials to run can be set in the same run properties box.

Setting Run Preferences

The run preferences dialog box allows you to specify the number of trials to run in a particular simulation. In addition, the simulation can be paused if a computational error in Excel is encountered (e.g., #NUM or #ERROR). Correlations can also be specified between pairs of input assumptions (Figure 132.3), and if *Turn on Correlations* is selected, these specified correlations will be imputed in the simulation.

Extracting Simulation Data

The simulation's assumptions and forecast data are stored in memory until the simulation is reset or when Excel is closed. If required, these raw data can be extracted into a separate Excel spreadsheet. To extract the data, simply:

1. Run the simulation.

2. After the simulation is completed, select **Risk Simulator | Analytical Tools | Extract Data**.

3. Choose the relevant assumptions or forecasts to extract and click **OK** (Figure 132.7).

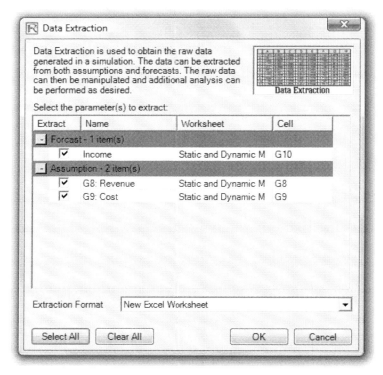

Figure 132.7: Data extraction

Creating New and Switching Among Simulation Profiles

The same model can have multiple simulation profiles in Risk Simulator. That is, different users of the same model can create their own simulation assumptions, forecasts, run preferences, and so forth. All these preferences are stored in separate simulation profiles, and each profile can be run independently. This powerful feature allows multiple users to run the same model their own way or allows the same user to run the model under different simulation conditions, thereby allowing for scenario analysis on Monte Carlo simulation. To create different profiles and switch among different profiles, simply:

1. Create several new profiles by clicking on **Risk Simulator | New Simulation Profile**.

2. Add the relevant assumptions and forecasts, or change the run preferences as desired in each simulation profile.

3. Switch among different profiles by clicking on **Risk Simulator | Change Active Simulation** (Figure 132.8).

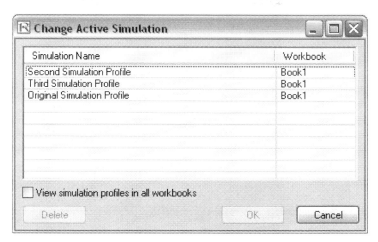

Figure 132.8: Switching among profiles

133. Simulation – Best Surgical Team

File Name: Simulation – Best Surgical Team

Location: Modeling Toolkit | Risk Simulator | Best Surgical Team

Brief Description: Illustrates how to use Risk Simulator for simulating the chances of a successful surgery and understanding the distribution of successes, using the *Distribution Analysis* tool to compute the CDF and ICDF of the population distribution, and using Bootstrap Simulation to obtain the statistical confidence of success rates

Requirements: Modeling Toolkit, Risk Simulator

In this model, we analyze six hospitals and look at their respective successes and failures when it comes to a specific type of surgical procedure. This historical information is tabulated in the *Model* worksheet and is summarized in Figure 133.1.

Hospital Name	Total Operations	Number of Successes	Number of Failures	Sample Success Rate	True Success Rate	True Success Rate
Boston	1254	1024	230	81.66%	81.66%	81.66%
Conrad	1264	954	310	75.47%	75.47%	75.47%
Detroit	1648	895	753	54.31%	54.31%	54.31%
Johns Hopkins	954	901	53	94.44%	94.44%	94.44%
Mayo	1994	1895	99	95.04%	95.04%	95.04%
Mass General	2561	2441	120	95.31%	95.31%	95.31%

Figure 133.1: Historical surgical success rates

For instance, Boston General Hospital had 1,254 surgical cases of a specific nature within the past five years, and out of those cases, 1,024 were considered successful while 230 cases were not successful (based on predefined requirements for failures and successes). Therefore, the sample success rate is 81.66%. The problem is, this is only a small sample and is not indicative of the entire population (i.e., all possible outcomes). In this example, we simply assume that history repeats itself. Because there are dozens of surgeons performing the same surgery and the tenure of a surgeon extends multiple years, we assume this is adequate, and that any small changes in staffing do not necessarily create a significant change in the success rates. Otherwise, more data should be collected and multivariate regressions and other econometric modeling should be performed to determine if the composition of surgeons and other medical practitioners will contribute in a statistically significant way to the rates of success, and we use simulation as well as distributional and probabilistic models to predict the successful outcomes. In addition, jump-diffusion or new medical technology advances might also contribute to a higher success rate. The advent of these technologies and their corresponding contributions to success rates can be modeled using the custom distribution through solicitation from subject matter experts in the area. Nonetheless, for this example, we look at using historical data to forecast the potential current success rate and to determine the entire population's distribution of success rates.

Monte Carlo Simulation

Success rates are distributed following a Beta distribution, where the *alpha* parameter is the number of successes in a sample, and the *beta* parameter is the number of failures. For instance, the Boston hospital's distribution of success rates is a Beta (1024, 230). Using Risk Simulator's set input assumption (Figure 133.2), you can see that the theoretical mean is 0.8166, equivalent to the sample success rate of 81.66% computed previously.

Just knowing the sample mean is insufficient. By using simulation, we can now reconstitute the entire population based on the sample success rate. For instance, running a simulation on the model yields the forecast results shown in Figures 133.3 and 133.4 for the Boston hospital.

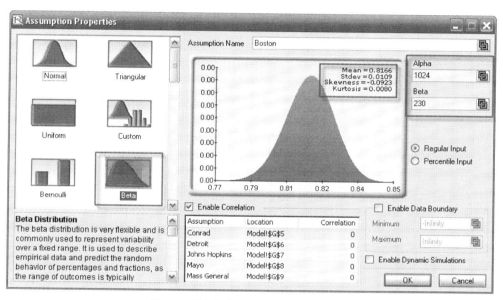

Figure 133.2: Set input assumption

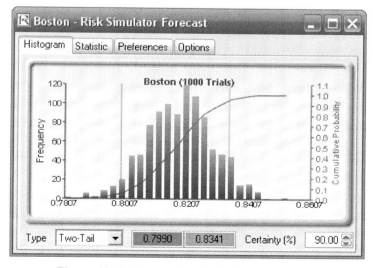

Figure 133.3: Boston hospital's forecast output

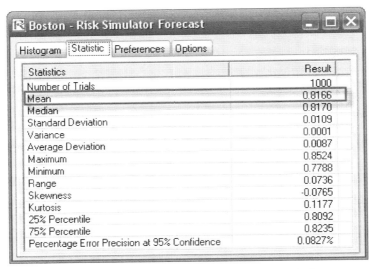

Figure 133.4: Boston hospital's forecast statistics

After running 1,000 trials, the expected value is 81.66%. In addition, we now have a slew of statistics associated with the success rate at Boston. The theoretical success rate is between 77.88% and 85.24%, and is fairly symmetrical with a skew close to zero (Figure 133.4). Further, the 90% confidence puts the success rate at between 79.90% and 83.41% (Figure 133.3). You can now perform a comparison among all the hospitals surveyed and see which hospital is the safest place to get the procedure done.

Procedures for Running Monte Carlo Simulation

This model already has assumptions and forecasts predefined for you. To run the predefined model, simply:

1. Go to the *Model* worksheet and click on **Risk Simulator | Change Profile** and select the *Best Surgical Team* profile.

2. Click on the **RUN** icon or select **Risk Simulator | Run Simulation.**

3. Select the forecast chart of your choice (e.g., Boston) and use the **Two-Tail** analysis. Type **90** in the *Certainty* box and hit **TAB** on the keyboard.

4. You can enter in other certainty values and hit **TAB** to obtain other confidence results. Also, click on the **Statistics** tab to view the distributional statistics.

To recreate the model's assumptions and forecasts, simply:

1. Go to the *Model* worksheet and click on **Risk Simulator | New Profile** and give it a new profile name of your choice.

2. Select cell **G4** and click on **Risk Simulator | Set Input Assumption**. Select the **BETA** distribution and enter in the relevant parameters (e.g., type in **1024** for Alpha and **230** for Beta) and click **OK**. Repeat for the other cells in **G5** to **G9**.

3. Select **H4** and click on **Risk Simulator | Set Output Forecast** and give it a relevant name (e.g., Boston), and repeat by setting the rest of the cells in **H5** to **H9** as forecast cells.

4. Click on the **RUN** icon or select **Risk Simulator | Run Simulation.**

5. Select the forecast chart of your choice (e.g., Boston) and use the **Two-Tail** analysis. Type **90** in the *Certainty* box and hit **TAB** on the keyboard.

6. You can enter in other certainty values and hit **TAB** to obtain other confidence results. Also, click on the **Statistics** tab to view the distributional statistics.

Distribution Analysis

In addition, because we are now able to reconstitute the entire distribution, we can use the information to compute and see the various confidence levels and their corresponding success rates by using the *Distribution Analysis* tool. For instance, selecting the Beta distribution and entering the relevant input parameters and choosing the cumulative distribution function (CDF), we can now see that, say, 81.5% success rate has a CDF of about 43.6% (Figure 133.5). This means that you have a 43.6% chance that the success rate is less than or equal to 81.5%, or that you have a 56.4% chance that your success rate will be at least 81.5%, and so forth. These values are theoretical values. An alternative approach is to use the forecast chart and compute the left-tail probability (CDF). Here we see the empirical results show that the probability of getting less than 81.5% success rate is 43.9% (Figure 133.6), close enough to the theoretical. Clearly the theoretical results are more reliable and accurate. Nonetheless, the empirical results approach the theoretical when enough trials are run in the simulation.

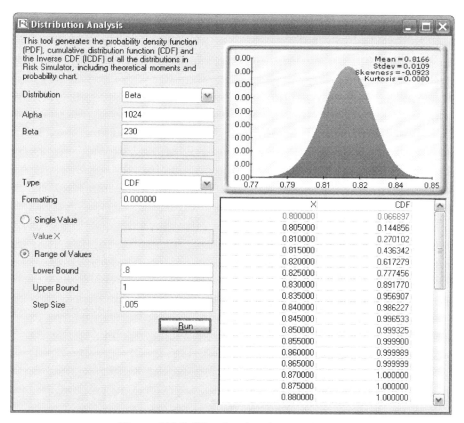

Figure 133.5: Distributional analysis tool

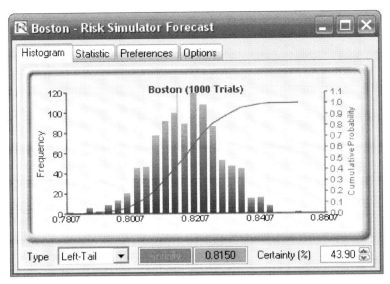

Figure 133.6: Empirical results

Conversely, you can compute the Inverse CDF or ICDF of the distribution. For instance, the 10% CDF shows an ICDF value of 80.24%, which means that you have a 10% chance of getting a success rate below or equal to 80.24% or that, from a more positive point of view, you have a 90% chance that the success rate is at least 80.24% (Figure 133.7).

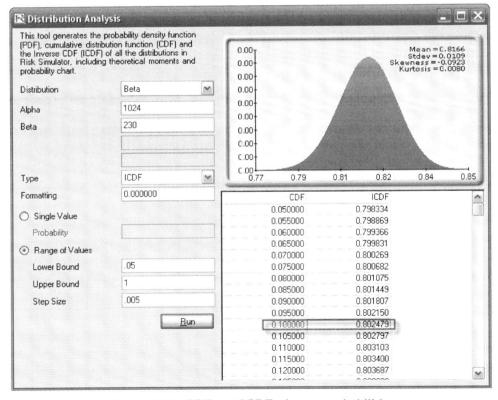

Figure 133.7: CDF and ICDF of exact probabilities

Procedures for Running a Distribution Analysis

1. Start the *Distribution Analysis* tool (click on **Risk Simulator | Tools | Distribution Analysis**).

2. Select the Beta distribution and enter **1024** for Alpha and **230** for Beta parameters, and select **CDF** as the analysis type. Then, select **Range of Values** and enter **0.8** and **1** as the lower and upper bounds, with a step of **0.005** and click **RUN**.

3. Now change the analysis type to **ICDF** and the bounds to between **0.05** and **1** with a step size of **0.005** and click **RUN**.

Bootstrap Simulation

A *Bootstrap* simulation can also be run on the resulting forecast. For instance, after running a simulation on the model, a bootstrap is run on the Boston hospital on its mean, maximum, and minimum values (Figure 133.8).

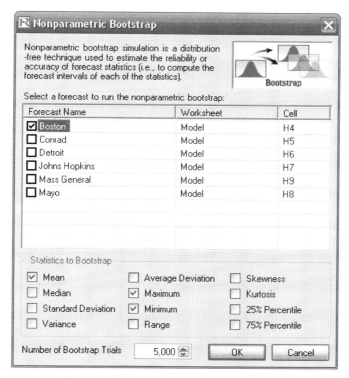

Figure 133.8: Bootstrap simulation tool

The results indicate that there is a 90% statistical confidence that the average success rate of the true population is between 81.6% and 81.7%, with the lowest or minimum success rate you can be assured of, at a 90% confidence, of between 77.8% and 78.5%. This means that 90 out of a 100 times a surgery is performed, or 90% confidence, the lowest and most conservative success rate is between 77.8% and 78.5%. For an additional exercise, change the confidence levels to 95% and 99% and analyze the results. Repeat for all other hospitals.

Procedures for Bootstrap Simulation

To run a bootstrap simulation, follow the steps below:

1. Run a simulation based on the steps outlined above. You cannot run a bootstrap unless you first run a simulation.

2. Click on **Risk Simulator | Analytical Tools | Nonparametric Bootstrap** and select the hospital of your choice (e.g., Boston), and then select the statistics of your choice (e.g., mean, maximum, minimum), enter **5000** as the number of bootstrap trials, and click **OK**.

3. Select **Two-Tail** on the statistics forecast chart of your choice (e.g., Mean), type in **90** in the *Certainty* box, and hit **TAB** on the keyboard to obtain the 90% statistical confidence interval of that statistic. Repeat on other statistics or use different tails and confidence levels (Figures 133.9 and 133.10).

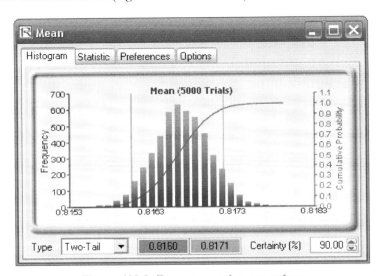

Figure 133.9: Bootstrapped mean values

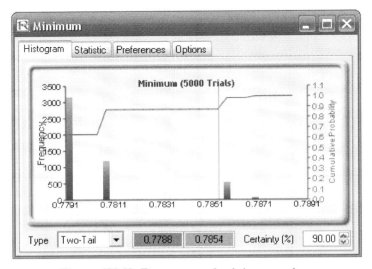

Figure 133.10: Bootstrapped minimum values

134. Simulation – Correlated Simulation

File Name: Simulation – Correlated Simulation

Location: Modeling Toolkit | Risk Simulator | Correlated Simulation

Brief Description: Illustrates how to use Risk Simulator for running a simulation with correlated variables, as well as extracting data and determining the final correlations

Requirements: Modeling Toolkit, Risk Simulator

This model illustrates how to set up basic correlated variables in a Monte Carlo simulation, extract the data, and confirm that the resulting correlations closely match the input correlations in the model.

Correlated Model

Simply open the existing profile, run the simulation, extract the data, and compute a correlation matrix. The results for 5,000 trials are provided in this example. Note that the input pairwise correlations were all 0.50, and the resulting correlations computed from the data are very close to the required input correlations. Figure 134.1 illustrates the sample correlated model. Figure 134.2 shows the simulated results that have been extracted. A correlation analysis was run on the results using Excel, and the results indicate that the empirical simulated data match the correlations required and entered in the model. Therefore, this model is used to illustrate how correlations can be inputted in a simulation model. The next chapter shows the effects of correlations on a model, specifically on the risk and return profile of the model.

For the sake of completion, Figure 134.3 shows how pairwise correlations can be set in Risk Simulator. Simply select any of the cells with predefined assumption and click on **Risk Simulator | Set Assumption** and in the set assumption dialog box, enter in the correlations (see the highlighted section in Figure 134.3). Be aware that entering correlations this way requires manual pairwise inputs. That is, suppose there are three assumptions in the model, A, B, and C. There will be three pairs of correlations: AB, AC, and BC. In order to insert these three pairwise correlations, you will have to select variable A and manually type in the correlations for AB and AC (note that inserting a correlation between A and B within the A variable will automatically update variable B to show this same correlation back to variable A), and then select variable B to correlate it to variable C.

Alternatively, Figure 134.4 shows how all pairwise correlations can be entered in a matrix. This matrix is available after assumptions have been first set, and then going to **Risk Simulator | Edit Correlations**. You can also select a predefined correlation matrix in Excel and click on the **Paste** button in the edit correlations dialog to update the matrix.

Pairwise correlations of 0.50 on all variables:

A	100.00	D	100.00
B	100.00	E	100.00
C	100.00	F	100.00

To replicate the dataset, simply set all variables to Normal (100, 10) and correlated at 0.5 to each other, and run 5,000 trials with a seed value of 123456.

Figure 134.1: Example correlated simulation model

A	B	C	D	E	F
93.75	86.07	77.84	86.76	96.26	89.35
91.36	93.30	95.84	102.04	86.40	91.38
102.29	90.24	102.00	108.01	104.83	103.31
104.64	90.19	97.91	89.48	99.95	105.91
86.79	89.54	80.49	70.12	89.42	87.11
97.32	100.99	110.57	92.41	107.92	91.80
105.90	102.93	101.27	105.66	95.94	106.76
84.60	77.91	84.40	75.55	88.60	85.29
79.74	85.90	87.52	86.16	81.27	93.13
106.69	93.61	98.69	91.62	93.50	97.38
97.70	91.11	100.40	116.27	99.43	100.63
98.40	98.83	93.95	99.96	90.52	90.85
92.06	78.97	101.03	98.26	82.84	94.65

Correlation Matrix

	A	B	C	D	E	F
A	1					
B	0.49	1				
C	0.52	0.49	1			
D	0.51	0.51	0.50	1		
E	0.52	0.51	0.51	0.51	1	
F	0.50	0.48	0.50	0.49	0.50	1

Average Correlation: 0.50

Figure 134.2: Computed empirical correlations

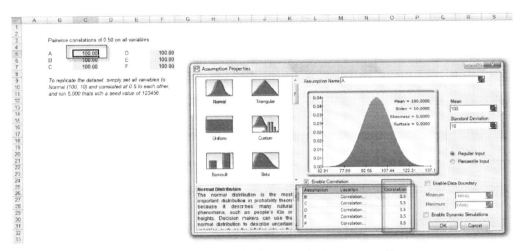

Figure 134.3: Setting pairwise correlations manually

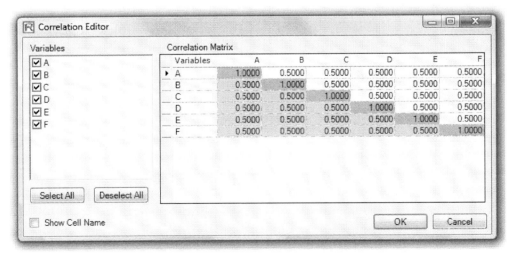

Figure 134.4: Setting pairwise correlations using a matrix

135. Simulation – Correlation Effects on Risk

File Name: Simulation – Correlation Effects Model

Location: Modeling Toolkit | Risk Simulator | Correlation Effects Model

Brief Description: Illustrates how to use Risk Simulator for creating correlated simulations and comparing the results between correlated and uncorrelated models, as well as extracting and manually computing (verifying) the assumptions' correlations

Requirements: Modeling Toolkit, Risk Simulator

This model illustrates the effects of correlated simulation compared to uncorrelated simulation, that is, when a pair of simulated assumptions is not correlated, positively correlated, and negatively correlated. Sometimes the results can be very different. In addition, the raw data of the simulated assumptions are extracted after the simulation, and manual computations of their pairwise correlations are performed. The results indicate that the correlations hold after the simulation.

Running a Monte Carlo Simulation

To run this model, simply:

1. Click on *Correlation* model and replicate the assumptions and forecasts.

2. Run the simulation by clicking on the **RUN** icon or **Risk Simulator | Run Simulation**.

Viewing and Interpreting Forecast Results

The resulting simulation statistics indicate that the negatively correlated variables provide a tighter or smaller standard deviation or overall risk level on the model. See Figure 135.1.

This relationship exists because negative correlations provide a diversification effect on the variables and hence tend to make the standard deviation slightly smaller. Thus, we need to make sure to input correlations when there indeed are correlations between variables. Otherwise this interacting effect will not be accounted for in the simulation.

The positive correlation model has a larger standard deviation, as a positive correlation tends to make both variables travel in the same direction, which make the extreme ends wider and hence increases the overall risk. Therefore, the model without any correlations will have a standard deviation between the positive and negative correlation models.

Notice that the expected value or mean does not change much. In fact, if sufficient simulation trials are run, the theoretical and empirical values of the mean remain the same. The first moment (central tendency) does not change with correlations. Only the second moment (spread) will change.

Note that this characteristic exists only in simple models with a positive relationship. That is, a *Price* × *Quantity* model is considered a "positive" relationship model (as is a *Price* + *Quantity* model), where a negative correlation decreases the range and a positive correlation increases the range. The opposite is true for negative relationship models. For instance, *Price ÷ Quantity* or *Price* – *Quantity* would be a negative relationship model, and a positive correlation will reduce the range of the forecast variable, whereas a negative correlation will increase the range. Finally, for more complex models (e.g., larger models with multiple variables interacting with positive and negative relationships and sometimes with positive and negative correlations), the results are hard to predict and cannot be determined theoretically. Only by running a simulation would the true results of the range and outcomes be determined. In such a scenario, tornado analysis and sensitivity analysis would be more appropriate.

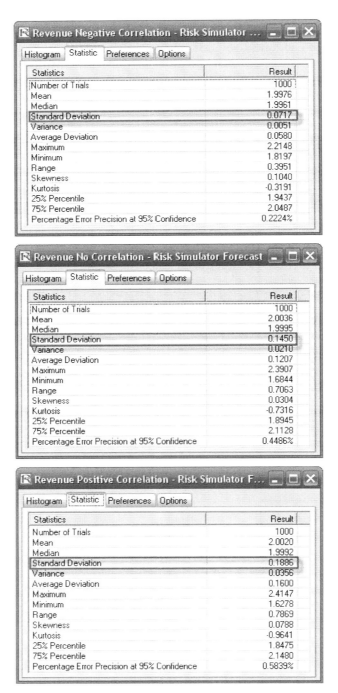

Figure 135.1: Effects on forecast statistics when variables are correlated

136. Simulation – Custom Simulation Equations

Brief Description: This chapter provides some examples of how Risk Simulator and Modeling Toolkit functions can be used inside Excel to create your own custom simulation assumptions

Requirements: Modeling Toolkit, Risk Simulator

This chapter reviews the use of Risk Simulator functions and Modeling Toolkit functions in Excel to set up and run Monte Carlo simulations. Specifically, these two sets of functions perform different tasks.

The Risk Simulator functions are used to manually set assumptions in your model (Figures 136.1 and 136.2) in lieu of using the *Set Input Assumption* icon. In contrast, the Modeling Toolkit functions can be used to customize a cell with any combinations of distributions, linking the assumption's inputs to other cells which are also assumptions, and these can be used in conjunction with Risk Simulator (Figures 136.3, 136.4, and 136.5).

Risk Simulator Functions

Typically, to set up and run a simulation, you would first create a *New Profile* in Risk Simulator, and then enter your preferences at the relevant cells, *Set Input Assumptions* and *Output Forecasts*, prior to running a simulation. However, there is an alternative, that is, using *RS Functions* to set these assumptions. Figure 136.1 shows an example where cell A2 is first selected as the "control cell" and the RSAssumption function is called (click on the **Insert Function** or **FX** icon in Excel, select **All Categories,** and scroll down to the *RSAssumption* functions). The figure shows the *RSAssumptionBeta* function, where cell A1 is linked as the assumption cell, the cell's default *Value* is set to 3 (this is a placeholder value, where instead of leaving the cell empty, it will show this value before a simulation is run), and a *Variable Name* can be set (this will become the Risk Simulator assumption name), as well as the relevant parameters (e.g., *Alpha* and *Beta*). Clicking on **OK** will set the Risk Simulator assumption in cell A1.

To make sure the assumption was set up correctly, you can select cell **A1** and click on the **Set Input Assumption** icon (Figure 136.2). You can see that the relevant distribution was set, with the parameters and assumption name. At this point, a regular simulation using Risk Simulator can be run. If you also wish to obtain forecast charts, do not forget to first set output forecasts in your model prior to running the simulation.

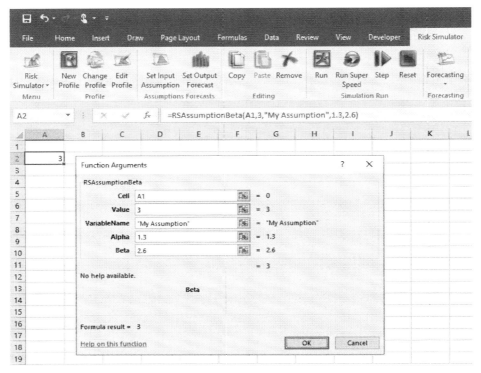

Figure 136.1: Using RS Functions to manually set assumptions

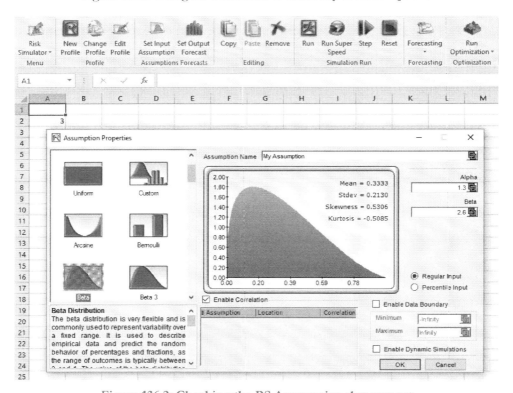

Figure 136.2: Checking the RS Assumption that was set

Modeling Toolkit Simulation Functions

There are over three dozen *MTSimulate* functions in Modeling Toolkit. Each function will simulate a specific probability distribution. For instance, Figure 136.3 shows the *MTSimulateGamma* function where a gamma distribution with Alpha = 2.3 and Beta = 4.2 is set in cell A1. The *Random* input in the function is a standard uniform distribution between 0 and 1. You can use Excel's *RAND()* function (Figure 136.3) and you will need to manually hit **F9** on the keyboard to manually simulate the *RAND()* function and, hence, generate the beta distribution. The problem with this approach is you will need to run each simulation trial manually, or write complex VBA codes to run multiple trials. The benefit is that you can control the function in VBA to incorporate any external databases or external data sources to be used in your model.

In contrast, Figure 136.4 shows a better and simpler approach that is the most commonly used method, where the *MTSimulate* function can be used in conjunction with Risk Simulator assumptions. Specifically, instead of using *MTSimulateGamma(2.3, 4.2, RAND())*, we now first set a new Risk Simulator *Profile* and then a new Risk Simulator *Assumption* in cell B1 with a *Uniform* distribution with Min = 0 and Max = 1. You can further add a seed value to the Risk Simulator profile such that the results will be replicated each time the simulation is rerun. By embedding Risk Simulator assumptions and seed values, we can now automate the model (i.e., thousands of simulation trials can be run at once by clicking on the Risk Simulator **Run** icon) and the results will be replicated each time.

You can also embed additional MT simulation functions within a function, link the function to other cells, and make the input assumptions of a function to be the output of another function, and so forth. As an example, Figure 136.5 shows how you can use the following simple function to simulate a normal distribution with a mean of 10 and a standard deviation of 2 in a specific Excel cell B4:

=MTSimulateNormal(10,2,RAND()).

Similarly, instead of setting the input parameters (mean and standard deviation) as static inputs, you can set them as dynamic outputs of another simulation (cell B7):

=MTSimulateNormal(MTSimulateGamma(1.2,1.5,RAND()),MTSimulateTriangular(0.5,0.8,1.2,RAND()),RAND()).

Of course, you can also link the three RAND() functions to three separate cells in Excel with Risk Simulator assumptions set (i.e., Uniform (0,1) in cells B9 to B11) and add a seed value to the Risk Simulator settings such that the results will be replicated each time.

Finally, cell B7 can be set as a forecast using Risk Simulator such that when the simulation is run, you will obtain the Risk Simulator forecast chart (see Figure 136.5).

Risk Simulator Results Function

Figure 136.6 shows a final function in Risk Simulator, called *RSForecastStatistic*. To make this function work, you need to first set a simulation profile, input assumption, and output forecasts, and then run a simulation. Once the simulation is done, set up the *RSForecastStatistic* as illustrated in Figure 136.6. It will call the simulation results and put them into Excel cells. Every time a simulation is run, these cells will update accordingly. Be aware that you might get an error message if there are no output forecasts set or no simulations have yet been run.

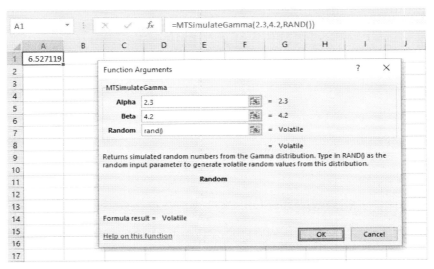

Figure 136.3: Using Modeling Toolkit MT Functions to set simulation assumptions

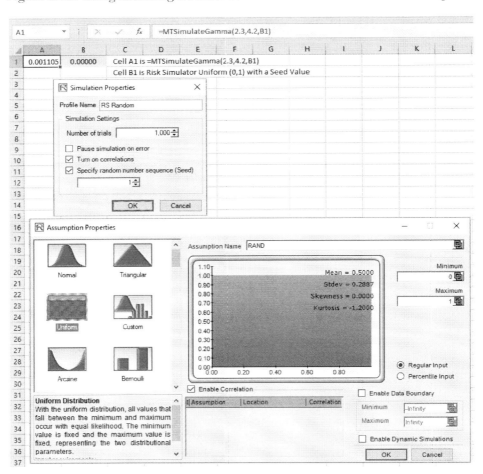

Figure 136.4: Mixing RS and MT capabilities to customize simulations

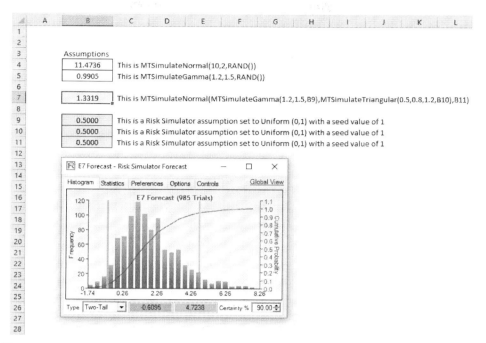

Figure 136.5: Embedded MT simulation with Risk Simulator charting and seed value

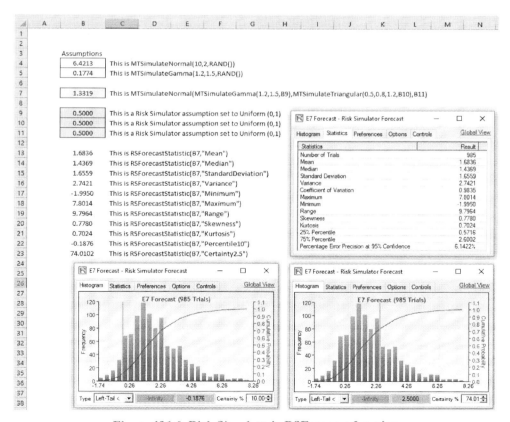

Figure 136.6: Risk Simulator's RSForecast function

137. Simulation – Data Fitting

File Name: Simulation – Data Fitting

Location: Modeling Toolkit | Risk Simulator | Data Fitting

Brief Description: Illustrates how to use Risk Simulator for fitting a single variable to existing data, fitting multiple variables to existing data, and simulating, extracting data, and refitting to distributions

Requirements: Modeling Toolkit, Risk Simulator

This example illustrates how existing sample data can be used to find the statistically best-fitting distribution. By doing so, we also confirm the simulation results through the distributional fitting routine; that is, we simulate a particular distribution, extract its raw data, and refit the simulated data back to all distributions.

Running a Single-Fit

To run this model, simply:

1. Go to the *Raw Data* worksheet in the model and select cells **C2:C201**.

2. Click on **Risk Simulator | Analytical Tools | Distributional Fitting (Single Variable)**.

3. Make sure **Fit Continuous Distributions** is selected and all distributions are checked, then click **OK** (Figure 137.1).

4. The resulting fit of all distributions is shown. Select the best fit (ranked first), view the statistics, and click **OK** (Figure 137.2).

5. A report will be generated indicating all the relevant statistics as well as the data used for fitting (for future reference).

Note that if a profile exists and if the *Automatically Generate Assumption* choice is selected (Figure 137.2), the report will contain an assumption that is the best fit. Otherwise, only the type of distribution and its relevant input assumptions are provided. You can repeat this exercise on the remaining data points provided.

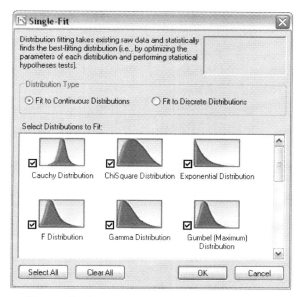

Figure 137.1: Fitting to multiple distributions

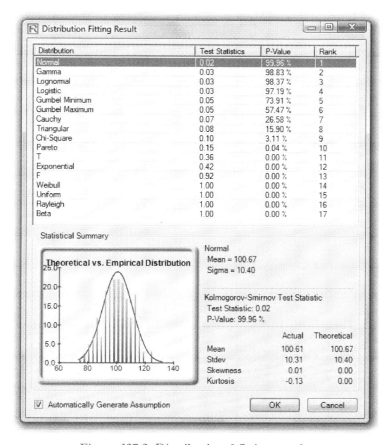

Figure 137.2: Distributional fitting results

You can replicate the fitting routine on multiple variables simultaneously (variables must be arranged in contiguous columns) instead of one at a time. Select the area **C2:E201** and run the multiple variable fitting routine by selecting **Risk Simulator | Analytical Tools | Distributional Fitting (Multi-Variable)**.

However, there are several key points to remember. First, more data implies a better statistical fit. Do not fit to very few data points and expect a good fit. Second, only positive discrete data (integers) can be fitted to discrete distributions. When negative values or continuous data exist, you should always fit to continuous distributions (or first transpose them to the positive region). Third, certain distributions are related to other distributions through their statistical properties. For example, a t-distribution becomes a normal distribution when degrees of freedom is high; a Poisson distribution can be used to approximate a binomial; or a normal can be used to approximate a Poisson, hypergeometric, and binomial. In addition, the beta and gamma distributions are highly flexible. For instance, in the beta distribution, if the two inputs parameters, *alpha* and *beta*, are equal, then the distribution is symmetrical. If either parameter is 1 while the other parameter is greater than 1, the distribution is triangular or J-shaped. If alpha is less than beta, the distribution is said to be positively skewed (most of the values are near the minimum value). If alpha is greater than beta, the distribution is negatively skewed (most of the values are near the maximum value). There are many other such relationships. Just because the fit is not exactly to the distribution expected does not mean the data are bad or the routine is incorrect. It simply means that another distribution is better suited for the data.

When performing a *Multiple Variable Fitting*, make sure to select the right distribution type for the variables (e.g., continuous for the first two and discrete for the third distribution in our model). Further, do not select the variable name when fitting; instead, enter the variable name in the fitting dialog box. Also, if you have an existing simulation profile (**Risk Simulator | New Simulation Profile**), you can select the *Automatically Generate Assumptions* option such that the report will have assumptions set up for you.

Further, these assumptions will also include correlations. Then the question is what correlation coefficient is significant for this dataset (i.e., is a correlation of 0.0151 significant or merely a residual effect of randomness and should not be incorporated? What about 0.016 or 0.15, etc.?). Risk Simulator automatically computes the statistical significance cutoff level (in this case, any correlations above the absolute value of 0.0910 are statistically significant). If you select this option, the software will ignore all correlations below this significance level. See Figure 137.3.

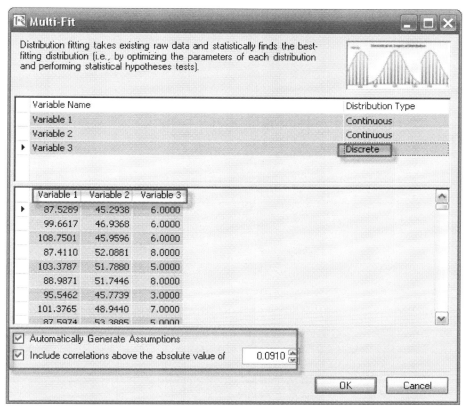

Figure 137.3: Multiple variables simultaneous fitting

138. Simulation – Debt Repayment and Amortization

File Name: Simulation – Debt Repayment and Amortization

Location: Modeling Toolkit | Risk Simulator | Debt Repayment and Amortization

Brief Description: Illustrates how to use Risk Simulator for simulating interest rates in a mortgage and amortization schedule to determine the potential savings on interest payments if additional payments are made each period and when the interest rates can become variable and unknown over time

Requirements: Modeling Toolkit, Risk Simulator

This is an amortization model examining a debt repayment schedule. In this example, we look at a 30-year mortgage with a portion of that period on a fixed interest rate and a subsequent period of variable rates with minimum and maximum caps. This model illustrates how the mortgage or debt is amortized and paid off over time, resulting in a final value of zero at the end of the debt's maturity. Further, this model allows for some additional periodic (monthly, quarterly, semiannually, annually) payment, which will reduce the total amount of payments, reduce the total interest paid, and reduce the length of time it takes to pay off the loan. Notice that initially the principal paid off is low, but it increases over time. Because of this, the initial interest portion of the loan is high but decreases over time as the principal is paid off.

The required input parameters of the model are highlighted in boxes, and an assumption on the uncertain interest rate is set in cell D8, with a corresponding forecast cell at I12. By entering additional payments per period, you can significantly reduce the term of the mortgage (i.e., pay it off faster), and at a much lower total payment (you end up saving a lot on interest payments). A second forecast cell is set on J12 to find out the number of years it takes to pay off the loan if additional periodic payments are made.

Procedure

You can either change the assumptions or keep the existing assumptions and run the simulation:

1. Click on **Risk Simulator | Change Profile** and select the *Debt Repayment and Amortization* profile and click **OK**.

2. Run the simulation by clicking on **Risk Simulator | Run Simulation**.

Interpretation

The resulting forecast charts (Figure 138.1) on the example inputs indicate that the least amount of money that can be saved by paying an additional $500 per month can potentially save the mortgage holder $136,985 (minimum), and at most $200,406 (maximum) given the assumed uncertainty fluctuations of interest rates during the variable rate period. The 90% confidence level can also be obtained, meaning that 90% of the time, the total interest saved is between $145,749 and $191,192.

In addition, the *Payoff Year with Extra Payment* forecast chart (Figure 138.1) shows that given the expected fluctuations of interest rates and the additional payments made per period, there is a 90% chance that the mortgage will be paid off between 20.9 and 21.8 years, with an average of 21.37 years (mean value). The quickest payoff is 20.67 years (minimum). If interest rates are on the high end, the payoff may take up to 22 years (maximum).

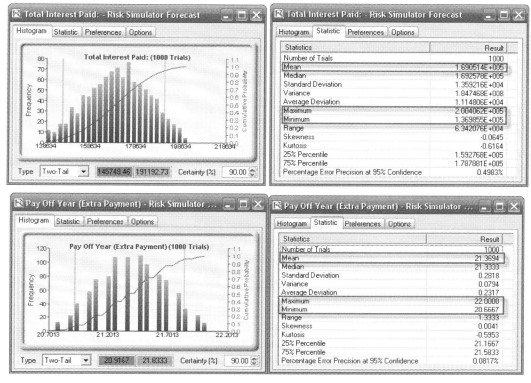

Figure 138.1: Interest paid and payoff year on long-term debt

139. Simulation – Demand Curve and Elasticity Estimation

File Name: Simulation – Demand Curve and Elasticity Estimation

Location: Modeling Toolkit | Risk Simulator | Demand Curve and Elasticity Estimation

Brief Description: Illustrates how to use Risk Simulator for determining the price elasticity of demand for a historical set of price and quantity sold data for linear and nonlinear functions

Requirements: Modeling Toolkit, Risk Simulator

This model illustrates how the price elasticity of demand can be computed from historical sale price and quantity sold. The resulting elasticity measure is then used in the *Optimization – Optimal Pricing with Elasticity* model to determine the optimal prices to charge for a product in order to maximize total revenues.

This model is used to find the optimal pricing levels that will maximize revenues through the use of historical elasticity levels. The price elasticity of demand is a basic concept in microeconomics, which can be briefly described as the percentage change of quantity divided by the percentage change in prices. For example, if, in response to a 10% fall in the price of a good, the quantity demanded increases by 20%, the price elasticity of demand would be 20% / (−10%) = −2. In general, a fall in the price of a good is expected to increase the quantity demanded, so the price elasticity of demand is negative. In some literature, the negative sign is omitted for simplicity (denoting only the absolute value of the elasticity).

We can model this elasticity in several ways, including the point elasticity by taking the first derivative of the inverse of the demand function and multiplying it by the ratio of price to quantity at a particular point on the demand curve:

$$\varepsilon_d = \frac{\delta Q}{\delta P} \cdot \frac{P}{Q}$$

where ε is the price elasticity of demand, P is price, and Q is quantity demanded.

Instead of using instantaneous point elasticities, this example uses the discrete version, where we define elasticity as:

$$\varepsilon_d = \frac{\%\Delta Q}{\%\Delta P} = \frac{Q_2 - Q_1}{\frac{Q_2 + Q_1}{2}} \div \frac{P_2 - P_1}{\frac{P_2 + P_1}{2}} = \frac{Q_2 - Q_1}{Q_2 + Q_1} \cdot \frac{P_2 + P_1}{P_2 - P_1}$$

To further simplify things, we assume that in a group of hotel rooms, cruise ship tickets, airline tickets, or any other products with various categories (e.g., standard room, executive room, suite, etc.), there is an average price and average quantity of units sold per period. Therefore, we can further simplify the equation to:

$$\varepsilon_d = \frac{Q_2 - Q_1}{\overline{Q}} \div \frac{P_2 - P_1}{\overline{P}} = \frac{\overline{P}}{\overline{Q}} \cdot \frac{Q_2 - Q_1}{P_2 - P_1}$$

where we now use the average price and average quantity demanded values $\overline{P}, \overline{Q}$.

If we have in each category the average price and average quantity sold such as in the model, we can compute the expected quantity sold given a new price if we have the historical elasticity of demand values.

The example model in Figure 139.1 shows how a nonlinear price-quantity relationship yields a static and unchanging elasticity, whereas a linear price-quantity relationship typically yields changing elasticities over the entire price range. Nonlinear extrapolation and linear regression are run to determine the linearity and nonlinearity of the prices. For the nonlinear relationship, a loglinear regression can be run to determine the single elasticity value (Figure 139.2). Elasticities of a linear relationship have to be determined at every price level using the aforementioned equations.

Nonlinear Demand Curve (A)

Original Data		Modified Data		Confirmation Computation	
Price	Quantity	LN(Q)	LN(P)	(Quantity)	Elasticity
$30	111.11	4.7105	3.4012	111.11	-2.0
$35	81.63	4.4022	3.5553	81.63	-2.0
$40	62.50	4.1352	3.6889	62.50	-2.0
$45	49.38	3.8996	3.8067	49.38	-2.0
$50	40.00	3.6889	3.9120	40.00	-2.0
$55	33.06	3.4983	4.0073	33.06	-2.0
$60	27.78	3.3242	4.0943	27.78	-2.0
$65	23.67	3.1642	4.1744	23.67	-2.0
$70	20.41	3.0159	4.2485	20.41	-2.0
$75	17.78	2.8779	4.3175	17.78	-2.0
$80	15.63	2.7489	4.3820	15.63	-2.0
$85	13.84	2.6276	4.4427	13.84	-2.0
$90	12.35	2.5133	4.4998	12.35	-2.0
$95	11.08	2.4052	4.5539	11.08	-2.0
$100	10.00	2.3026	4.6052	10.00	-2.0
$105	9.07	2.2050	4.6540	9.07	-2.0
$110	8.26	2.1120	4.7005	8.26	-2.0
$115	7.56	2.0231	4.7449	7.56	-2.0
$120	6.94	1.9379	4.7875	6.94	-2.0
$125	6.40	1.8563	4.8283	6.40	-2.0
$130	5.92	1.7779	4.8675	5.92	-2.0
$135	5.49	1.7024	4.9053	5.49	-2.0
$140	5.10	1.6296	4.9416	5.10	-2.0
$145	4.76	1.5595	4.9767	4.76	-2.0
$150	4.44	1.4917	5.0106	4.44	N/A

For nonlinear or power demand curves, the price elasticity of demand is unchanging regardless of the price level. In this case, the elasticity is found to be -2.0.

Linear Demand Curve (B)

Original Data		Confirmation Computation	
Price	Quantity	(Quantity)	Elasticity
$30	97.00	97.00	-0.03
$35	96.50	96.50	-0.04
$40	96.00	96.00	-0.04
$45	95.50	95.50	-0.05
$50	95.00	95.00	-0.06
$55	94.50	94.50	-0.06
$60	94.00	94.00	-0.07
$65	93.50	93.50	-0.07
$70	93.00	93.00	-0.08
$75	92.50	92.50	-0.08
$80	92.00	92.00	-0.09
$85	91.50	91.50	-0.10
$90	91.00	91.00	-0.10
$95	90.50	90.50	-0.11
$100	90.00	90.00	-0.11
$105	89.50	89.50	-0.12
$110	89.00	89.00	-0.13
$115	88.50	88.50	-0.13
$120	88.00	88.00	-0.14
$125	87.50	87.50	-0.15
$130	87.00	87.00	-0.15
$135	86.50	86.50	-0.16
$140	86.00	86.00	-0.17
$145	85.50	85.50	-0.17
$150	85.00	85.00	N/A

For linear demand curves, the price elasticity of demand is constantly changing depending on the price level.

Figure 139.1: Nonlinear demand curve with static elasticity versus linear demand curve with changing elasticity

Regression Analysis Report

Regression Statistics

R-Squared (Coefficient of Determination)	1.0000
Adjusted R-Squared	1.0000
Multiple R (Multiple Correlation Coefficient)	1.0000
Standard Error of the Estimates (SEy)	0.0000
Number of Observations	25

Regression Results

	Intercept	LNP
Coefficients	11.5129	-2.0000
Standard Error	0.0000	0.0000
t-Statistic	60157349.4365	-46275857.0777
p-Value	0.0000	0.0000
Lower 5%	11.5129	-2.0000
Upper 95%	11.5129	-2.0000

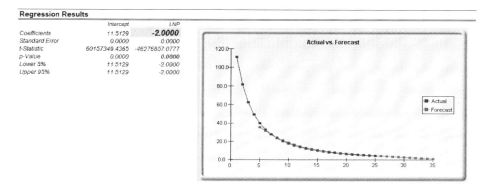

Figure 139.2: Nonlinear demand curve's elasticity estimated using a nonlinear regression

140. Simulation – Discounted Cash Flow, Return on Investment, and Volatility Estimates

File Name: Simulation – DCF, ROI and Volatility

Location: Modeling Toolkit | Risk Simulator | DCF, ROI and Volatility

Brief Description: Illustrates how to use Risk Simulator for running a Monte Carlo simulation in a financial return on investment (ROI) analysis, incorporating various correlations among variables (time-series and cross-sectional relationships), and calculating forward-looking volatility based on the PV Asset approach

Requirements: Modeling Toolkit, Risk Simulator

This is a generic discounted cash flow (DCF) model showing the net present value (NPV), internal rate of return (IRR), and return on investment (ROI) calculations. This model can be adapted to any industry and is used to illustrate how a Monte Carlo simulation can be applied to actual investment decisions and capital budgeting. In addition, the project's or asset's volatility is also computed in this example model. Volatility is a measure of risk and is a key input in financial option and real options analysis.

Procedure

To run this model, simply click on **Risk Simulator | Run Simulation**. However, if you wish you can create your own simulation model:

1. Start a new simulation profile and add various assumptions on the price and quantity inputs.

2. Remember to add correlations between the different years of price and quantity (autocorrelation).

3. Continue to add correlations between price and quantity (cross-correlations).

4. Add forecasts to the key outputs (*NPV* and *Intermediate X Variable* to obtain the project's volatility).

Results Interpretation

If you run the existing simulation profile, you will obtain two forecast charts, the *NPV* and *Intermediate X* forecasts.

1. From the NPV forecast chart (Figure 140.1), select **Two-Tail** and enter in **95** in the *Certainty* box and hit **TAB** on the keyboard. The results show that the 95% confidence interval for the NPV falls between $2429 and $3485. If you click on the **Statistics** tab, the expected value or mean shows the value $2941. Alternatively, select **Left-Tail** and enter in **5** in the *Certainty* box and hit **TAB**. The results indicate that the 5% worst-case scenario will still yield a positive NPV of $2488, indicating that this is a good project. You can now compare this with other projects to decide which project should be chosen. Finally, because probabilities of left and right tails in the same forecast distribution are complementary, if you select **Right-Tail** and enter **2.5** in the *Certainty* box and hit **TAB**, the result is $3485, identical to the 95% confidence level's right-tail value (95% confidence interval means there is a 2.5% probability in each tail).

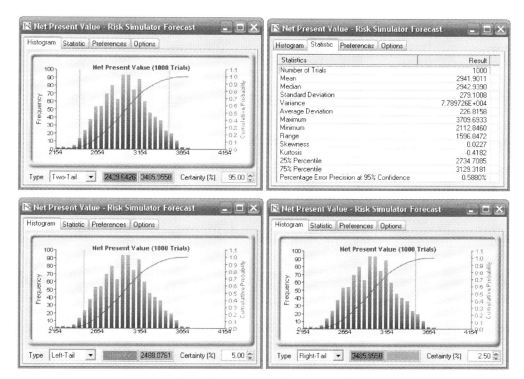

Figure 140.1: NPV forecast results

2. The *Intermediate X Variable* is used to compute the project's volatility. To obtain a volatility measure, first modify the model as appropriate and then click on **Set Static CF** in the model (near cell B46) to generate a static cash flow. Then **RUN** the simulation and view the *Intermediate Variable X*'s forecast chart (Figure 140.2). Go to the **Statistics** tab and obtain the *standard deviation*, and annualize it by multiplying the value with the square root of the number of periods per year In this case, the annualized volatility is 6.45% as the periodicity of the cash flows in the model is annual, otherwise multiply the standard deviation by the square root of 4 if quarterly data is used, or the square root of 12 if monthly data is used, and so forth.

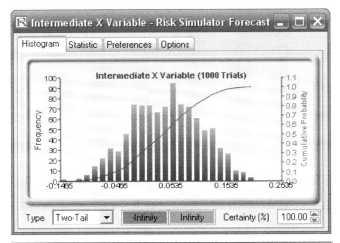

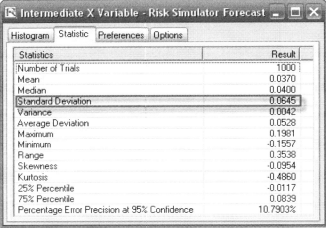

Figure 140.2: Forecast results of the *X* variable

141. Simulation – Infectious Diseases

File Name: Simulation – Infectious Diseases

Location: Modeling Toolkit | Risk Simulator | Infectious Diseases

Brief Description: Illustrates how to build an epidemic diseases model and use Risk Simulator for running a Monte Carlo simulation on the epidemic model to determine survival probabilities

Requirements: Modeling Toolkit, Risk Simulator

Remember the science fiction movies where some terrorist cell sets off a chemical or biological weapon in a major cosmopolitan area and the heroes in the movie will be in a high-tech situation room with the president and high-ranking military officials looking at a large screen indicating the possible scenarios with the number of people perishing within a day, within two days, and so forth?

Well, the model in this chapter briefly illustrates how an epidemic can spread within a population and how the input assumptions that are uncertain (as in any rampant disease) can be simulated (Figures 141.1 and 141.2). By simulating these assumptions, we can obtain the number of people who might perish if this disease becomes an epidemic. The input parameters include the total population size in the infected area, the probability of contact with an infected person, the initial number of infected individuals, and the potential healing rate. The total numbers of people who might be susceptible, the infected individuals, and those removed from the infected list (cured) are shown over several time periods. The output forecast of interest is the total number of people who perished in this epidemic.

Infectious Diseases Epidemic Model

Population	1000	
Contact Probability	0.30%	3
Initial Infected Size	3	
Healing Rate	20.00%	200

Period	Susceptible	Infected	Removals	Newly Infected	New Removals	Perished
0	997.0	3.0	0.0	8.9	0.6	8.3
1	988.1	11.3	0.6	33.1	2.3	30.8
2	954.9	42.2	2.9	113.7	8.4	105.3
3	841.2	147.4	11.3	301.1	29.5	271.6
4	540.2	419.0	40.8	386.8	83.8	303.0
5	153.4	722.0	124.6	135.8	144.4	0.0
6	17.5	713.5	269.0	15.5	142.7	0.0
7	2.1	586.2	411.7	1.7	117.2	0.0
8	0.4	470.7	529.0	0.3	94.1	0.0
9	0.1	376.8	623.1	0.1	75.4	0.0
10	0.0	301.5	698.5	0.0	60.3	0.0
11	0.0	241.2	758.8	0.0	48.2	0.0
12	0.0	193.0	807.0	0.0	38.6	0.0
13	0.0	154.4	845.6	0.0	30.9	0.0
14	0.0	123.5	876.5	0.0	24.7	0.0
15	0.0	98.8	901.2	0.0	19.8	0.0
16	0.0	79.1	920.9	0.0	15.8	0.0
17	0.0	63.2	936.8	0.0	12.6	0.0
18	0.0	50.6	949.4	0.0	10.1	0.0
19	0.0	40.5	959.5	0.0	8.1	0.0
20	0.0	32.4	967.6	0.0	6.5	0.0

Total Perished   719.0

Figure 141.1: Simulating an infectious diseases epidemic model

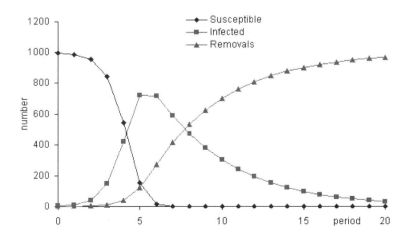

Figure 141.2: Epidemic interactive model

142. Simulation – Recruitment Budget (Negative Binomial and Multidimensional Simulation)

File Name: Simulation – Recruitment Budget (Negative Binomial and Multidimensional Simulation)

Location: Modeling Toolkit | Risk Simulator | Recruitment Budget (Negative Binomial and Multidimensional Simulation)

Brief Description: Illustrates how to use Risk Simulator in applying the Negative Binomial distribution to compute the required budget to obtain the desired outcomes given probabilities of failure, using the *Distribution Analysis* tool to determine the theoretical probabilities of success, and applying a Multidimensional Simulation approach where the inputs into a simulation are uncertain

Requirements: Modeling Toolkit, Risk Simulator

Negative Binomial Simulation

The negative binomial distribution is useful for modeling the distribution of the number of additional trials required on top of the number of successful occurrences required (R). For instance, in order to close a total of 10 sales opportunities, how many extra sales calls would you need to make above 10 calls given some probability of success in each call? The x-axis shows the number of additional calls required or the number of failed calls. The number of trials is not fixed, the trials continue until the Rth success, and the probability of success is the same from trial to trial. Probability of success (P) and number of successes required (R) are the distributional parameters. Such a model can be applied in a multitude of situations, such as the cost of cold sales calls, the budget required to train military recruits, and so forth.

The simple example shown illustrates how a negative binomial distribution works. Suppose that a salesperson is tasked with making cold calls and a resulting sale is considered a success while no sale means a failure. Suppose that historically the proportion of sales to all calls is 30%. We can model this using the negative binomial distribution by setting the *Successes Required* (R) to equal 2 and the *Probability of Success* (P) as 0.3.

For instance, as illustrated in Figure 142.1, say the sales person makes two calls. The success rate is 30% per call, and the success or failure of one call versus another are statistically independent of one another. There can be four possible outcomes (SS, SF, FS, FF, where S stands for success, and F for failure). The probability of SS is 0.3 ×0.3 or 9%; SF and FS is 0.3 × 0.7 or 21% each; and FF is 0.7 × 0.7 or 49%. The total probability is 100%. Therefore, there is a 9% chance that two calls are sufficient and no additional calls are required to get the two successes required. In other words, X = 0 has a probability of 9% if we define X as the additional calls required beyond the two calls.

Extending this to three calls, we have many possible outcomes, but the key outcomes we care about are two successful calls, which we can define as the following combinations: SSS, SSF, SFS, and FSS, and their respective probabilities are computed (e.g., FSS is computed by 0.7 × 0.3 × 0.3 = 6.30%). Now, the combinatorial sequence SSS and SSF do not require a third call because the first two calls have already been successful. Further, SFF, FSF, FFS, and FFF all fail the required two-call success as they only have either zero or one successful call. So, the sum total probability of the situations requiring a third call to make exactly two calls successful out of three is 12.60%.

	2 Call Example	
	Success	Failure
Call 1	30%	70%
Call 2	30%	70%

Success + Success	**9%**
Success + Failure	21%
Failure + Success	21%
Failure + Failure	49%
Sum	100%
Both Successful (R = 2)	**9%**

	3 Call Example	
	Success	Failure
Call 1	30%	70%
Call 2	30%	70%
Call 3	30%	70%

Success + Success + Success	2.70%	*Not require 3rd call*
Success + Success + Failure	6.30%	*Not require 3rd call*
Success + Failure + Success	**6.30%**	***Requires 3rd call***
Failure + Success + Success	**6.30%**	***Requires 3rd call***
Success + Failure + Failure	14.70%	*Fails 2-call required*
Failure + Success + Failure	14.70%	*Fails 2-call required*
Failure + Failure + Success	14.70%	*Fails 2-call required*
Failure + Failure + Failure	34.30%	*Fails 2-call required*
Sum	100.00%	
Sum (Requires 3rd call)	**12.60%**	

Figure 142.1: Sample negative binomial distribution

Clearly, doing this exercise for a large combinatorial problem with many required successes is difficult and intractable. However, we can obtain the same results using Risk Simulator. For instance, creating a new profile and setting an input assumption and choosing the negative binomial distribution with $R = 2$ and $P = 0.3$ provides the chart in Figure 142.2. Notice that the probability of $X = 0$ is exactly what we had computed, 9%, and $X = 1$ yields 12.60%.

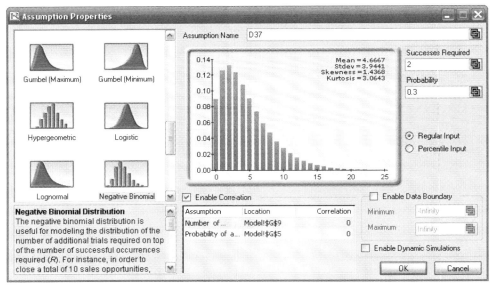

Figure 142.2: Negative binomial distribution

It is easier if you use Risk Simulator's *Distribution Analysis* tool (Figure 142.3) to obtain the same results with a table of numerical values. If you choose the *PDF* type, you obtain the exact probabilities. That is, there is a 12.6% probability you will need to make three calls (or one additional call on top of the required two calls), or 13.23% with four calls, and so forth.

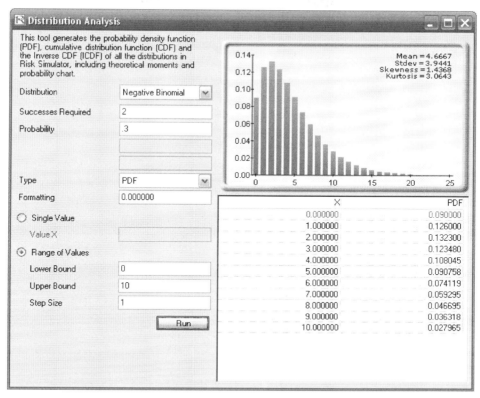

Figure 142.3: Negative binomial distribution's theoretical PDF properties

If you select *CDF* (Figure 142.4), the cumulative probabilities will be computed. For instance, the *CDF* value when *X* = *1* is 9% + 12.6% or 21.6%, which means that 21.6% of the time, making three calls (or *X* = *1* extra call beyond the required two) is sufficient to get two successful calls to be, say, 80% sure, you should be prepared to make up to seven additional calls, or nine calls total, but you can stop once two successes have been achieved.

Procedure for Computing Probabilities in a Negative Binomial Distribution

1. Start the *Distribution Analysis* tool (click on **Risk Simulator | Tools | Distribution Analysis**).

2. Select **Negative Binomial** from the Distribution drop list, and enter **2** for successes required and **0.3** for the probability of success, then select **Range of Values** and enter **0** and **10** for the *Lower* and *Upper Bounds*, with **1** as the *Step Size* and click **RUN**.

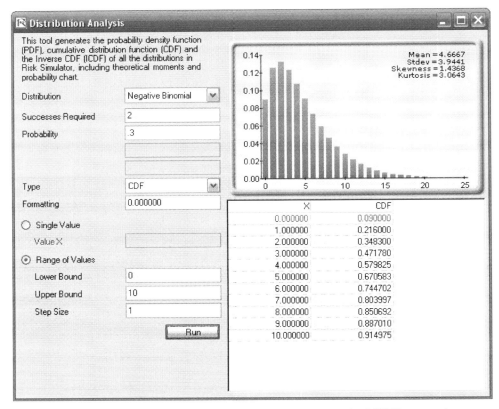

Figure 142.4: Negative binomial distribution's theoretical CDF properties

Multidimensional Simulation

The *Model* worksheet shows a simple recruitment budget example, where the task is to determine the total cost required to obtain the required number of qualified and trained recruits, when, in fact, only a small percentage of recruits will successfully complete the training course. The required weeks of training and cost per week are also used as inputs. The question is, how much money (budget) is required to train these recruits given these uncertainties? In Figure 142.5, G9 is a Risk Simulator assumption with a Negative Binomial distribution with $R = 10$ (linked to cell G4) and $P = 0.25$ (linked to cell G5). Cell G12 is the model's forecast. You can now run a simulation and obtain the distribution forecast of the required budget.

In contrast, if the 25% rate is an unknown and uncertain input, you can set it as an assumption, and make the value in cell G9 a link to the 25% cell, and check the box *Enable Dynamic Simulation*. This means that the value 25% is an assumption and changes with each trial, and the number of recruits failing is also an assumption but is linked to this changing 25% value. This is termed a multidimensional simulation model (Figure 142.6).

	A	B	C	D	E	F	G
1							
2				**Recruitment Budget**			
3							
4		New recruits required at the end of the training					10
5		Probability of a recruit being successful					25%
6		Cost of training a recruit per week					$500
7		Number of weeks of training					10
8							
9		Number of recruits failing					0
10		Cost of successful recruits					$50,000
11		Cost of failing recruits					$0
12		Total cost required for training					$50,000

Figure 142.5: Recruitment model

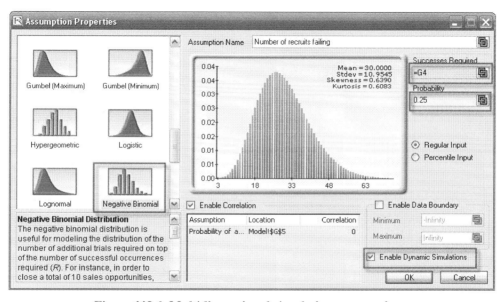

Figure 142.6: Multidimensional simulation assumptions

The results show that on a 90% confidence, the required budget should be between $115,000 and $315,000 (Figure 142.7), with an expected value of $200,875 (Figure 142.8).

Procedure for Running a Multidimensional Simulation

The model is also preset with assumptions and forecasts. To run this model:

1. Go to the *Model* worksheet and click on **Risk Simulator | Change Profile** and select the *Recruitment Budget* profile.

2. Click on the **RUN** icon or **Risk Simulator | Run Simulation.**

3. On the forecast chart, select **Two-Tail**, enter in **90** in the *Certainty* box and hit **TAB** on the keyboard.

To recreate the assumptions and forecasts:

1. Go to the *Model* worksheet and click on **Risk Simulator | New Profile** and give the profile a name.

2. Select cell **G5** and click on **Risk Simulator | Set Input Assumption.** Choose a **Uniform** distribution and enter in **0.2** and **0.3** as min and max values. (You may enter your own values if required, as long as they are positive and maximum exceeds minimum).

3. Select cell **G9** and click on **Risk Simulator | Set Input Assumption.** Choose a **Negative Binomial** distribution, click on the **Link** icon for *Successes Required* and link it to cell **G4**. Repeat for the *Probability* input by linking to cell **G5**.

4. Click on the checkbox **Enable Dynamic Simulation** and click **OK**.

5. Select cell **G12** and click on **Risk Simulator | Set Output Forecast** and click **OK**.

6. Click on the **RUN** icon or **Risk Simulator | Run Simulation.**

7. On the forecast chart, select **Two-Tail**, enter in **90** in the *Certainty* box and hit **TAB** on the keyboard.

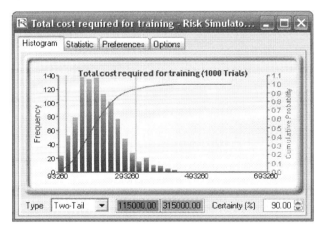

Figure 142.7: Statistical confidence levels

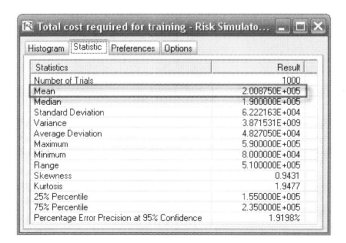

Figure 142.8: Simulated statistics

143. Simulation – Retirement Funding with VBA Macros

File Name: Simulation – Retirement Funding with VBA Macros

Location: Modeling Toolkit | Risk Simulator | Retirement Funding with VBA Macros

Brief Description: Illustrates how to use Risk Simulator for running Monte Carlo simulation and capturing the output results, and for running VBA macros in your models together with Monte Carlo simulation

Requirements: Modeling Toolkit, Risk Simulator

This model illustrates a simplified retirement amortization computation allowing for inflation adjustments. That is, given how much you currently have and the expected rate of return on your investment vehicles, the expected inflation rates, your current salary, and the expected amount you wish to have starting at retirement, this model computes how much annual investment is required to sufficiently fund your retirement (Figure 143.1).

RETIREMENT FUNDING (INFLATION ADJUSTED)

Input Data

Initial Savings Amount	$100,000.00		Annual Salary	$100,000.00
Annual Required Rate of Return	8.00%		Replacement Ratio at Retirement	70%
Current Age	32.00		*(The percentage of your current income required at retirement)*	
Retirement Age	55.00		Inflation Rate	2%
Average Terminal Age	90.00		Terminal Wealth	$0
			Terminal Wealth Goal	$0.00
			Annual Contribution	$17,454.71

PAYOUT SCHEDULE

Age	Status	Starting Value	Contributions	Withdrawal	Wealth
32	Working	$100,000.00	$17,454.71	$0.00	$117,454.71
33	Working	$108,000.00	$36,305.79	$0.00	$144,305.79
34	Working	$116,640.00	$56,664.96	$0.00	$173,304.96
35	Working	$125,971.20	$78,652.86	$0.00	$204,624.06
36	Working	$136,048.90	$102,399.79	$0.00	$238,448.69
37	Working	$146,932.81	$128,046.48	$0.00	$274,979.29
38	Working	$158,687.43	$155,744.90	$0.00	$314,432.34
39	Working	$171,382.43	$185,659.20	$0.00	$357,041.63
40	Working	$185,093.02	$217,966.64	$0.00	$403,059.66
41	Working	$199,900.46	$252,858.68	$0.00	$452,759.14
42	Working	$215,892.50	$290,542.08	$0.00	$506,434.58
43	Working	$233,163.90	$331,240.15	$0.00	$564,404.05
44	Working	$251,817.01	$375,194.07	$0.00	$627,011.08
45	Working	$271,962.37	$422,664.30	$0.00	$694,626.67
46	Working	$293,719.36	$473,932.15	$0.00	$767,651.51
47	Working	$317,216.91	$529,301.42	$0.00	$846,518.34
48	Working	$342,594.26	$589,100.24	$0.00	$931,694.51
49	Working	$370,001.81	$653,682.97	$0.00	$1,023,684.77
50	Working	$399,601.95	$723,432.31	$0.00	$1,123,034.26
51	Working	$431,570.11	$798,761.60	$0.00	$1,230,331.71
52	Working	$466,095.71	$880,117.23	$0.00	$1,346,212.95
53	Working	$503,383.37	$967,981.32	$0.00	$1,471,364.69
54	Working	$543,654.04	$1,062,874.53	$0.00	$1,606,528.57
55	Working	$587,146.36	$1,165,359.20	$0.00	$1,752,505.56
56	Retired	$0.00	$0.00	$112,590.61	$1,771,108.15
57	Retired	$0.00	$0.00	$114,842.42	$1,788,766.99
58	Retired	$0.00	$0.00	$117,139.27	$1,805,357.94
59	Retired	$0.00	$0.00	$119,482.05	$1,820,745.95
60	Retired	$0.00	$0.00	$121,871.69	$1,834,784.20

Figure 143.1: Retirement funding model (inflation adjusted)

The required inputs and computed outputs are summarized below:

Required Inputs
- Initial Savings Amount: How much you have currently
- Annual Required Rate of Return: The expected annualized rate of return on the investment vehicle
- Current Age: Your current age right now, corresponding to the initial savings
- Retirement Age: Your proposed age at retirement
- Average Terminal Age: The expected age at death (life expectancy)
- Annual Salary: Your current salary level
- Replacement Ratio: Percentage of your current salary required at retirement
- Inflation Rate: Annualized inflation rate expected
- Terminal Wealth Goal: Typically, $0 (complete amortization)

Computed Results
- Terminal Wealth: How much you have left at terminal age
- Annual Contribution: Required annual contribution to have sufficient funds for retirement

Monte Carlo Simulation

As returns on investment and inflation rates are both uncertain and vary, these two variables are defined as input assumptions. The output forecast is the required annual contribution. This model already has a simulation profile, assumptions, forecasts, and VBA macros created.

To run this model, simply:

1. Go to the *Payments Per Period* worksheet

2. Select **Risk Simulator | New Profile** and define assumptions on Rate of Return (**E6**) and Inflation (**I8**) and then click on the **RUN** icon or **Risk Simulator | Run Simulation**

Model Analysis

You can recreate the model's simulation and VBA analysis by repeating the following steps:

1. Click on **Alt-F11** to get to the Excel VBA environment (Figure 143.2).

2. Double click on **Sheet 1** and you will see the VBA macro code used to compute the Annual Contribution. Notice that the codes are listed under the *Private Sub* called *Worksheet Change*. This setup means that every time a value changes in the worksheet (i.e., when a simulation trial occurs), the macro will be executed and the value of the annual contribution will be computed accordingly in each simulation trial.

3. Exit the VBA environment and go back to the *Payments Per Period* worksheet.

4. Create a New Simulation Profile and give it an appropriate name.

5. Define Assumptions on the *Interest Annual Required Rate of Return* and *Inflation Rate*.

6. Define Forecast on *Annual Contribution*.

7. Run the simulation.

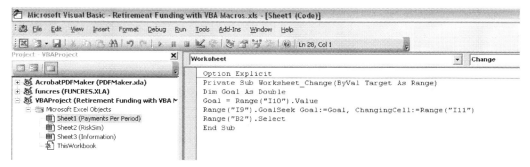

Figure 143.2: Visual Basic for Applications (VBA) code with simulation

144. Simulation – Roulette Wheel

File Name: Simulation – Roulette Wheel

Location: Modeling Toolkit | Risk Simulator | Roulette Wheel

Brief Description: Illustrates how to use Risk Simulator for running Monte Carlo simulation on a roulette wheel

Requirements: Modeling Toolkit, Risk Simulator

This is a fun model to illustrate how Visual Basic for Applications can be used in conjunction with Risk Simulator to generate random simulations of a roulette wheel and the subsequent payoffs.

To run the model, go to the *Roulette* worksheet and click on **Reset** to get started. You can then click on the **Step Simulation** icon (the icon that looks like a play button between the *Run* and *Reset* icons). You can do this one click at a time or just run the entire simulation to see what the payoff looks like.

A roulette wheel has 38 slots or possible outcomes, and the first 36 slots represent the 36 numbers, and each number is assigned either a red or black color (Figure 144.1). Values 37 and 38 are the 0 or 00 outcomes, where for the former, it is a value you can bet on but the latter means house wins. Further, in a real roulette game, you can bet on even or odd values; the first second; or third set of 12 numbers; and so forth. However, for simplicity, we only allow the possibilities of betting on a number and color.

To run more trials, simply change the number of bets (cell **M3**) and edit the simulation profile to change the number of trials to equal this new number of bets (**Risk Simulator | Edit Profile**).

	Number	Color
1	1	Red
2	2	Black
3	3	Red
4	4	Black
5	5	Red
6	6	Black
7	7	Red
8	8	Black
9	9	Red
10	10	Black
11	11	Black
12	12	Red
13	13	Black
14	14	Red
15	15	Black
16	16	Red
17	17	Black
18	18	Red
19	19	Red
20	20	Black
21	21	Red
22	22	Black
23	23	Red
24	24	Black
25	25	Red
26	26	Black
27	27	Red
28	28	Black
29	29	Black
30	30	Red
31	31	Black
32	32	Red
33	33	Black
34	34	Red
35	35	Black
36	36	Red
37	0	Green
38	00	Green

Figure 144.1: Roulette wheel equivalent

145. Simulation – Time Value of Money

File Name: Simulation – Time Value of Money

Location: Modeling Toolkit | Risk Simulator | Time Value of Money

Brief Description: Illustrates how to solve time value of money problems, and how to add simulation to time value of money problems to account for uncertainties

Requirements: Modeling Toolkit, Risk Simulator

Time value of money (TVM) is one of the most fundamental yet important concepts in the world of finance and decision analysis. It provides a robust framework to value and decide the best course of action among multiple projects, based on an equal footing. For instance, one project might have a 10-year life providing high cash flow returns in the future but also costs more while another costs less and returns slightly lower cash flows. By applying TVM methods, the net present value (NPV) of a project can be easily determined, and the correct and optimal course of action can be taken. The examples in the file start off easy with the basics of future value and present value, then on to annuities with equal payments per period. Then we have different period analysis (monthly versus annual payments), NPV, internal rate of return, and return on investment analysis. A TVM amortization table example is also presented.

Clearly these are simple, getting-started examples. Also, see the *Simulation –Discounted Cash Flow, Return on Investment, and Volatility Estimates* chapter for an example of a more protracted NPV analysis with various end-of-period, beginning-of-period, discrete discounting, and continuous discounting approaches. Some quick manual computations are shown here. The examples in the *Models* worksheet use Excel functions as well as manual computations.

Figure 145.1 illustrates the basic theoretical concepts of the time value of money. The Excel worksheet model provides more step-by-step examples of these applications.

Future Value

As an example, if you saved $100 today in a savings account yielding 5% a year, how much will you have at the end of 3 years?

Year 0	Year 1	Year2	Year 3
PV = 100	$FV_1 = 100(1+0.05)$ $= 105$ $FV_1 = PV(1+i)^1$	$FV_2 = 100(1+0.05)(1+0.05)$ $= PV(1+0.05)^2$ $= 110.25$ $FV_2 = PV(1+i)^2$	$FV_3 = 100(1+0.05)(1+0.05)\ (1+0.05)$ $= PV(1+0.05)^3$ $= 115.76$ $FV_3 = PV(1+i)^3$

$$FV_3 = FV_2(1+i)^1 = FV_1(1+i)^1(1+i)^1 = PV_0(1+i)^1(1+i)^1(1+i)^1 = PV_0(1+i)^3$$

This conforms to the equation: $FV_n = PV_0(1+i)^n = PV_0[FVIF_{i,n}]$

Present Value

Similarly, we can compute the PV manually as well as by using Excel's *PV* function:

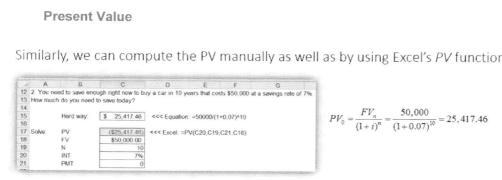

$$PV_0 = \frac{FV_n}{(1+i)^n} = \frac{50,000}{(1+0.07)^{10}} = 25,417.46$$

Ordinary Annuities

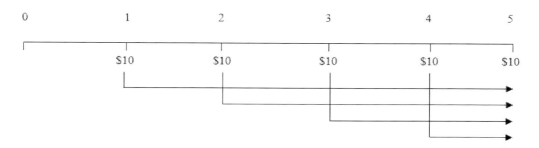

$$FVA_n = PMT_1(1+i)^4 + PMT_2(1+i)^3 + PMT_3(1+i)^2 + PMT_4(1+i)^1 + PMT_5(1+i)^0$$

Since this is an annuity, $PMT_1 = PMT_2 = PMT_3 = PMT_4 = PMT_5$

$$FVA_n = PMT\left[(1+i)^4 + (1+i)^3 + (1+i)^2 + (1+i)^1 + (1+i)^0\right]$$

$$FVA_n = PMT\left[\sum_{i=1}^{n}(1+i)^{n-t}\right] = PMT\left[\frac{(1+i)^n}{i} - \frac{1}{i}\right]$$

Figure 145.1: The underlying theory of time value of money

146. Six Sigma – Obtaining Statistical Probabilities, Basic Hypothesis Tests, Confidence Intervals, and Bootstrapping Statistics

File Names: Six Sigma – Hypothesis Testing and Bootstrap Simulation; Six Sigma – Probabilities and Hypothesis Tests (CDF, PDF, ICDF)

Location: Modeling Toolkit | Six Sigma | Hypothesis Testing and Bootstrap Simulation, and Probabilities and Hypothesis Tests (CDF, PDF, ICDF)

Brief Description: Illustrates how to use Risk Simulator's *Distributional Analysis* tool and Modeling Toolkit's probability functions to obtain exact probabilities of events, and confidence intervals and hypothesis testing for quality control, as well as using Risk Simulator for running hypothesis tests after a simulation run, generating a hypothesis test with raw data, understanding the concept of random seeds, and running a nonparametric bootstrap simulation to obtain the confidence intervals of the statistics

Requirements: Modeling Toolkit, Risk Simulator

Computing Theoretical Probabilities of Events for Sig Sigma Quality Control

In this chapter, we use Risk Simulator's *Distribution Analysis* tool and Modeling Toolkit's functions to obtain exact probabilities of the occurrence of events for quality control purposes. These will be illustrated through some simple discrete distributions. The chapter also provides some continuous distributions for the purposes of theoretical hypotheses tests. Then hypothesis testing on empirically simulated data is presented, where we use theoretical distributions to simulate empirical data and run hypotheses tests. The next chapter goes into more detail on using the Modeling Toolkit's modules on one-sample and two-sample hypothesis tests using t-tests and Z-tests for values and proportions, analysis of variance (ANOVA) techniques, and some powerful nonparametric tests for small sample sizes. This chapter is a precursor and provides the prerequisite knowledge to the materials presented in the next chapter.

Binomial Distribution

The binomial distribution describes the number of times a particular event occurs in a fixed number of trials, such as the number of heads in 10 flips of a coin or the number of defective items out of 50 items chosen. For each trial, only two outcomes are possible that are mutually exclusive. The trials are independent, where what happens in the first trial does not affect the next trial. The probability of an event occurring remains the same from trial to trial. Probability of success (p) and the number of total trials (n) are the distributional parameters. The number of successful trials is denoted x (the x-axis of the probability distribution graph). The input requirements in the distribution include Probability of success > 0 and < 1 (for example, $p \geq 0.0001$ and $p \leq 0.9999$) and Number of Trials ≥ 1 and integers and ≤ 1000.

Example: If the probability of obtaining a part that is defective is 50%, what is the probability that in selecting four parts at random, there will be no defective part, or one defective part, or two defective parts, and so forth? Recreate the probability mass function or probability density function (PDF), where we define P(x=0) as the probability (P) of the number of successes of an event (x), and the mathematical combination (C):

Probability of no defects P(x=0): 6.25% using MTDistributionPDFBinomial(4,0.5,0) or computed: $C_0^4(.5)^0(.5)^{4-0} = \dfrac{4!}{0!(4-0)!}(.5)^0(.5)^{4-0} = \dfrac{1}{16} = 6.25\%$

Probability of one defect P(x=1): 25.00% using MTDistributionPDFBinomial(4,0.5,1) or computed: $C_1^4(.5)^1(.5)^{4-1} = \dfrac{4!}{1!(4-1)!}(.5)^1(.5)^3 = \dfrac{4}{16} = 25\%$

Probability of two defects P(x=2): 37.50% using MTDistributionPDFBinomial(4,0.5,2) or computed: $C_2^4(.5)^2(.5)^{4-2} = \dfrac{4!}{2!(4-2)!}(.5)^2(.5)^2 = \dfrac{6}{16} = 37.50\%$

Probability of three defects P(x=3): 25.00% using MTDistributionPDFBinomial(4,0.5,3) or computed: $C_3^4(.5)^3(.5)^{4-3} = \dfrac{4!}{3!(4-3)!}(.5)^3(.5)^1 = \dfrac{4}{16} = 25\%$

Probability of four defects P(x=4): 6.25% using MTDistributionPDFBinomial(4,0.5,4) or computed: $C_4^4(.5)^4(.5)^{4-4} = \dfrac{4!}{4!(4-4)!}(.5)^4(.5)^0 = \dfrac{1}{16} = 6.25\%$

Total probabilities: 100.00%

In addition, you can sum up the probabilities to obtain the cumulative distribution function (CDF):

Probability of no defects P(x=0): 6.25%
   using MTDistributionCDFBinomial(4,0.5,0) or computed as P(x=0)

Probability of up to one defect P(x<=1): 31.25%
   using MTDistributionCDFBinomial(4,0.5,1) or computed as P(x=0) + P(x=1)

Probability of up to two defects P(x<=2): 68.75%
   using MTDistributionCDFBinomial(4,0.5,2) or computed as P(x=0) + P(x=1) + P(x=2)

Probability of up to three defects P(x<=3): 93.75%
   using MTDistributionCDFBinomial(4,0.5,3) or computed as P(x=0) + P(x=1) + P(x=2) + P(x=3)

Probability of up to four defects P(x<=4): 100.00%
   using MTDistributionCDFBinomial(4,0.5,4) or computed as P(x=0) + P(x=1) + P(x=2) + P(x=3) + P(x=4)

The same analysis can be performed using the *Distribution Analysis* tool in Risk Simulator. For instance, you can start the tool by clicking on **Risk Simulator | Analytical Tools | Distributional Analysis**, selecting **Binomial**, entering in **4** for **Trials, 0.5** for **Probability**, and then selecting PDF as the type of analysis, and a range of between 0 and 4 with a step of **1**. The resulting table and PDF distribution is exactly as computed using the Modeling Toolkit functions as seen in Figure 146.1.

The four distributional moments can also be determined using the tool as well as using the MT functions:

Mean or Average	2.00	using MTDistributionBinomialMean(4,0.5)
Standard Deviation	1.00	using MTDistributionBinomialStdev(4,0.5)
Skewness Coefficient	0.00	using MTDistributionBinomialSkew(4,0.5)
Kurtosis (Excess)	–0.50	using MTDistributionBinomialKurtosis(4,0.5)

In addition, typically, for discrete distributions, the exact probabilities are called probability mass functions (PMFs); they are called probability density functions (PDFs) for continuous distributions. However, in this book, we use both terms interchangeably. Also, this chapter highlights only some of the examples illustrated in the model. To view more detailed examples, please see the Excel model in the Modeling Toolkit.

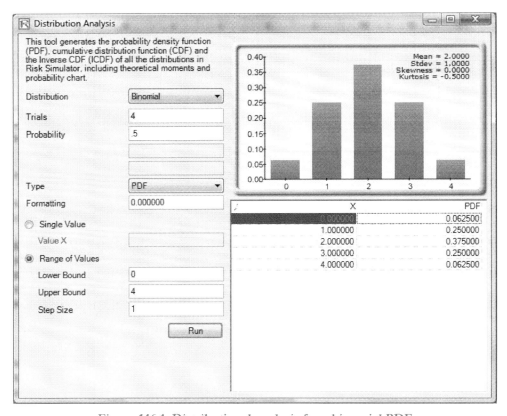

Figure 146.1: Distributional analysis for a binomial PDF

Poisson Distribution

The Poisson distribution describes the number of times an event occurs in a given space or time interval, such as the number of telephone calls per minute or the number of errors per page in a document. The number of possible occurrences in any interval is unlimited; the occurrences are independent. The number of occurrences in one interval does not affect the number of occurrences in other intervals, and the average number of occurrences must remain the same from interval to interval. Rate or Lambda is the only distributional parameter. The input requirements for the distribution are Rate > 0 and ≤ 1000.

Example: A tire service center has the capacity of servicing six customers in an hour. From prior experience, on average three show up an hour. The owner is afraid that there might insufficient manpower to handle an overcrowding of more than six customers. What is the probability that there will be exactly six customers? What about six or more customers?

Using the *Distribution Analysis* tool, we see that the PDF of exactly six customers is 5.04% (Figure 146.2) and the probability of six or more is the same as 1 – the CDF probability of five or less, which is 1 – 91.61% or 8.39% (Figure 146.3).

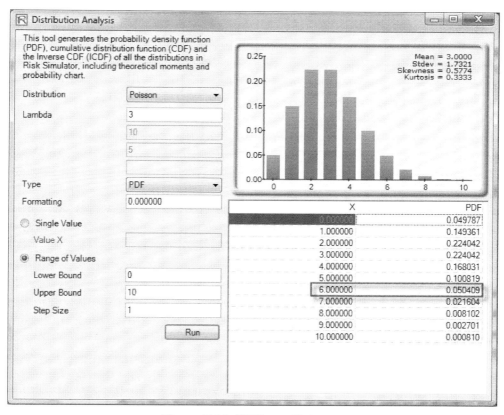

Figure 146.2: PDF on a Poisson

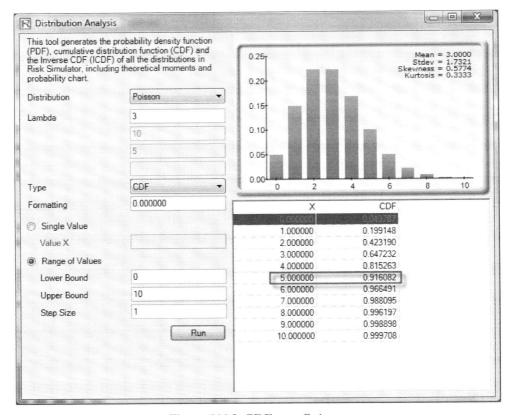

Figure 146.3: CDF on a Poisson

C. Normal Distribution

The normal distribution is the most important distribution in probability theory because it describes many natural phenomena, such as people's IQs or heights. Decision makers can use the normal distribution to describe uncertain variables such as the inflation rate or the future price of gasoline. Some value of the uncertain variable is the most likely (the mean of the distribution), the uncertain variable could as likely be above the mean as it could be below the mean (symmetrical about the mean), and the uncertain variable is more likely to be in the vicinity of the mean than farther away. Mean (μ) and standard deviation (σ) are the distributional parameters. The input requirements are that Mean can take on any value and Standard Deviation > 0 and can be any positive value.

Example: You observe that in the past, on average, your manufactured batteries last for 15 months with a standard deviation of 1.5 months. Assume that the battery life is normally distributed. If a battery is randomly selected, find the probability that it has a life of less than 16.5 months or over 16.5 months.

Using the tool, we obtain CDF of X = 16.5 months as 84.13%, which means that there is 84.13% chance that the manufactured batteries last up to 16.5 months and $1 - 0.8413$ or 15.87% chance the batteries will last over 16.5 months (Figure 146.4). The same value of 84.13% can be obtained using the function MTDistributionCDFNormal(15,1.5,16.5) to obtain 84.13% (Figure 146.5).

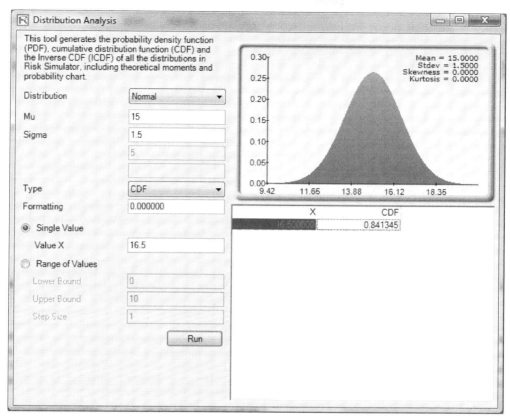

Figure 146.4: CDF of a normal distribution

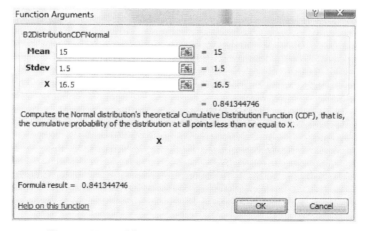

Figure 146.5: CDF of normal using function calls

Example: Alternatively, if you wish to provide a 12-month warranty on your batteries, that is, if the battery dies before 12 months, you will give a full refund. What are the chances that you may have to provide this refund?

Using the tool, we find that the CDF for $X = 12$ is 2.28% chance that a refund will have to be issued (Figure 146.6).

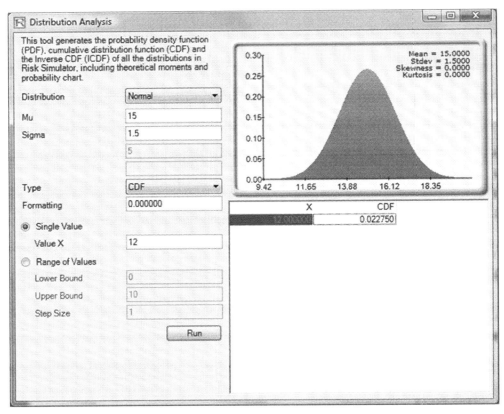

Figure 146.6: Probability of a guarantee refund

So far, we have been computing the probabilities of events occurring using the PDF and CDF functions and tools. We can also reverse the analysis and obtain the X values given some probability, using the inverse cumulative distribution function (ICDF), as seen next.

Example: If the probability calculated in the preceding example is too high, hence, too costly for you and you wish to minimize the cost and probability of having to refund your customers down to a 1% probability, what would be a suitable warranty date (in months)?

The answer is that to provide anything less than an 11.51-month guarantee will most likely result in less than or equal to a 1% chance of a return. To obtain the results here, we use the ICDF analysis in the *Distribution Analysis* tool (Figure 146.7). Alternatively, we can use the Modeling Toolkit function MTDistributionICDFNormal(15,1.5,0.01) to obtain 11.510478 (Figure 146.8).

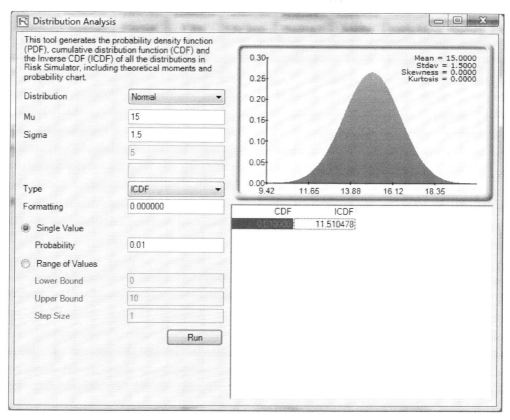

Figure 146.7: Obtaining the inverse cumulative distribution function (ICDF)

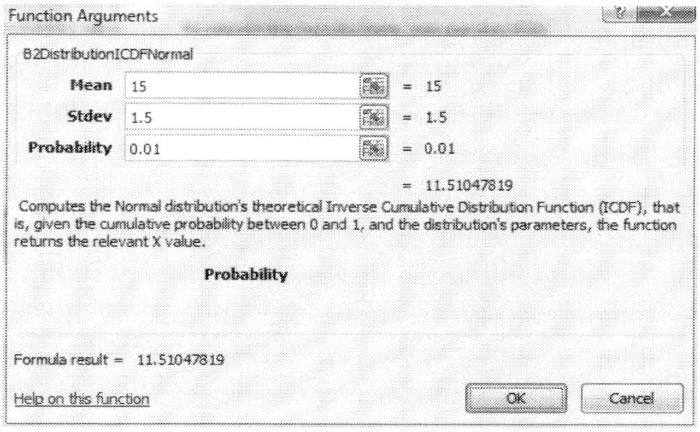

Figure 146.8: Function call for ICDF

Hypothesis Tests in a Theoretical Situation

This section illustrates how to continue using the *Distribution Analysis* tool to simplify theoretical hypothesis tests.

Example: Sometimes we need to obtain certain X values given a certainty and probability level for the purposes of hypothesis testing. This is where the ICDF comes in handy. For instance, suppose a lightbulb manufacturer needs to test if its bulbs can last on average 1,000 burning hours. If the plant manager randomly samples 100 lightbulbs and finds that the sample average is 980 hours with a standard deviation of 80 hours, at a 5% significance level (two-tails), do the lightbulbs last an average of 1,000 hours?

There are several methods to solve this problem, including the use of confidence intervals, Z-scores, and p-values. For example, we are testing the null hypothesis H_o: Population Mean = 1,000 and the alternate hypothesis H_a: Population Mean is NOT 1,000. Using the Z-score approach, we first obtain the Z-score equivalent to a two-tail alpha of 5% (which means one tail is 2.5%, and using the *Distribution Analysis* tool we get the Z = 1.96 at a CDF of 97.50%, equivalent to a one tail p-value of 2.5%). Using the *Distribution Analysis* tool, set the distribution to Normal with a mean of zero and standard deviation of 1 (this is the standard normal Z distribution). Then, compute the ICDF for 0.975 or 97.5% CDF, which provides an X value of 1.9599 or 1.96 (Figure 146.9).

Using the confidence interval formula, we get:

$$\mu \pm Z\left(\frac{s}{\sqrt{n}}\right)$$

$$1000 \pm 1.96\left(\frac{80}{\sqrt{100}}\right)$$

$$1000 \pm 15.68$$

This means that the statistical confidence interval is between 984.32 and 1015.68. As the sample mean of 980 falls outside this confidence interval, we reject the null hypothesis and conclude that the true population mean is different from 1,000 hours.

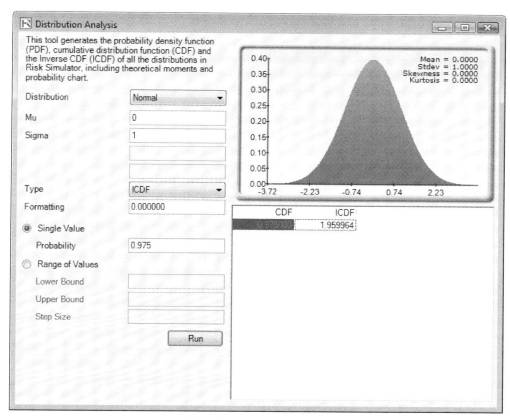

Figure 146.9: Standard normal Z-score

A much quicker and simpler approach is to use the *Distribution Analysis* tool directly. Seeing that we are performing a statistical sample, we first need to correct for small sampling size bias by correcting the standard deviation to get:

$$\frac{s}{\sqrt{n}} = \frac{80}{\sqrt{100}} = 8$$

Then, we can find the CDF relating to the sample mean of 980. We see that the CDF p-value is 0.0062, less than the alpha of 0.025 one tail (or 0.50 two tail), which means we reject the null hypothesis and conclude that the population mean is statistically significantly different from the 1,000 hours tested (Figure 146.10).

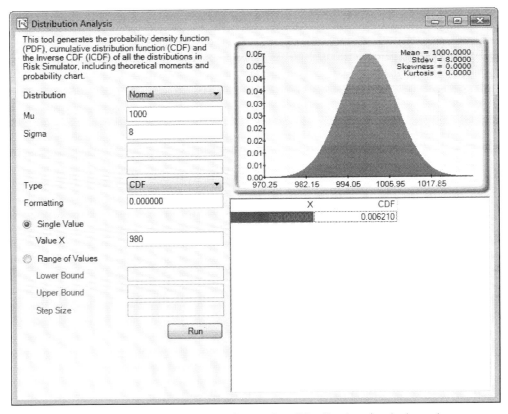

Figure 146.10: Obtaining p-values using Distribution Analysis tool

Yet another alternative is to use the ICDF method for the mean and sampling adjusted standard deviation and compute the X values corresponding to the 2.5% and 97.5% levels. The results indicate that the 95% two-tail confidence interval is between 984.32 and 1,015.68 as computed previously. Hence, 980 falls outside this range; this means that the sample value of 980 is statistically far away from the hypothesized population of 1,000 (i.e., the unknown true population based on a statistical sampling test can be determined to be not equal to 1,000). See Figure 146.11.

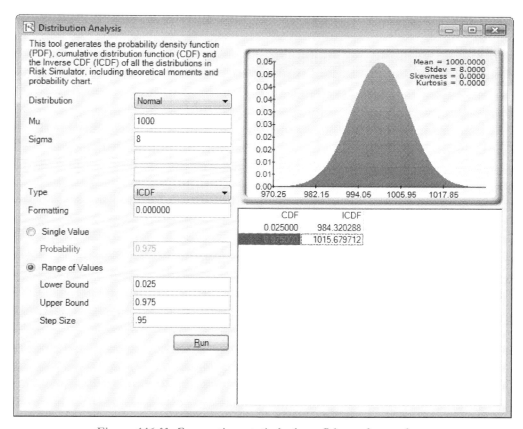

Figure 146.11: Computing statistical confidence intervals

Note that we adjust the sampling standard deviation only because the population is large and we sample a small size. However, if the population standard deviation is known, we do not divide it by the square root of N (sample size).

Example: In another example, suppose it takes on average 20 minutes with a standard deviation of 12 minutes to complete a certain manufacturing task. Based on a sample of 36 workers, what is the probably that you will find someone completing the task taking between 18 and 24 minutes?

Again, we adjust the sampling standard deviation to be 12 divided by the square root of 36 or equivalent to 2. The CDFs for 18 and 24 are 15.86% and 97.72%, respectively, yielding the difference of 81.86%, which is the probability of finding someone taking between 18 and 24 minutes to complete the task. See Figure 146.12.

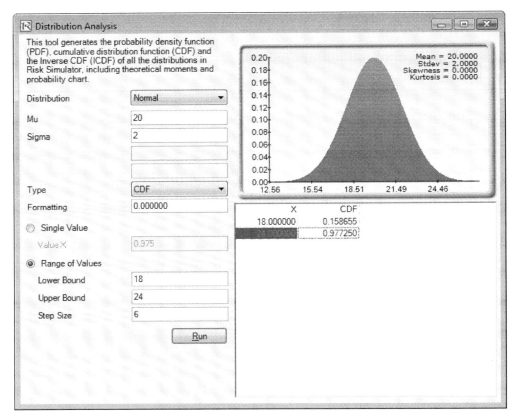

Figure 146.12: Sampling confidence interval

Example: Sometimes, when the sample size is small, we need to revert to using the Student's T distribution. For instance, suppose a plant manager studies the life of a particular battery and samples 10 units. The sample mean is 5 hours with a sample standard deviation of 1 hour. What is the 95% confidence interval for the battery life?

Using the T distribution, we set the degrees of freedom as $n-1$ or 9, with a mean location of 0 for a standard T distribution. The ICDF for 0.975 or 97.5% (5% two tail means 2.5% on one tail, creating a complement of 97.5%) is equivalent to 2.262 (Figure 146.13). So, the 95% statistical confidence interval is:

$$\bar{x} \pm t\frac{s}{\sqrt{n}}$$

$$5 \pm 2.262 \frac{1}{\sqrt{10}}$$

$$5 \pm 0.71$$

Therefore, the confidence interval is between 4.29 and 5.71.

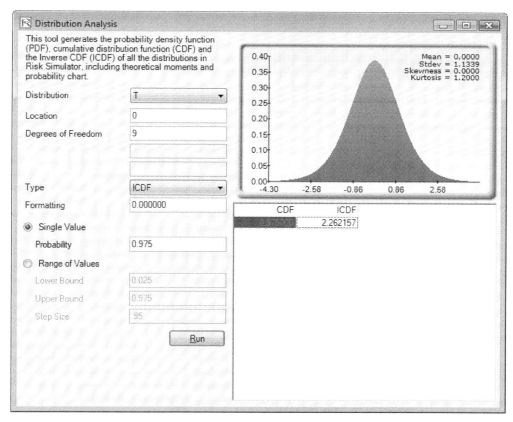

Figure 146.13: Standard T distribution

Hypothesis Tests in an Empirical Simulation

This next example shows how two different forecasts or sets of data can be tested against one another to determine if they have the same means and variances. That is, if the first distribution has a mean of 100, how far away does the mean of the second distribution have to be such that they are considered statistically different? The example illustrates two models (A and B) with the same calculations (see *Simulation Model* worksheet) where the income is revenue minus cost. Both sets of models have the same inputs and the same distributional assumptions on the inputs, and the simulation is run on the random seed of 123456.

Two major items are noteworthy. The first is that the means and variances (as well as standard deviations) are slightly different. These differences raise the question as to whether the means and variances of these two distributions are identical. A hypothesis test can be applied to answer this first question. A nonparametric bootstrap simulation can also be applied to test the other statistics to see if they are statistically valid. The second item of interest is that the results from A and B are different although the input assumptions are identical and an overall random seed has been applied (Figure 146.14). The different results occur because with a random seed applied, each distribution is allowed to vary independently as long as it is not correlated to another variable. This is a key and useful fact in Monte Carlo simulation.

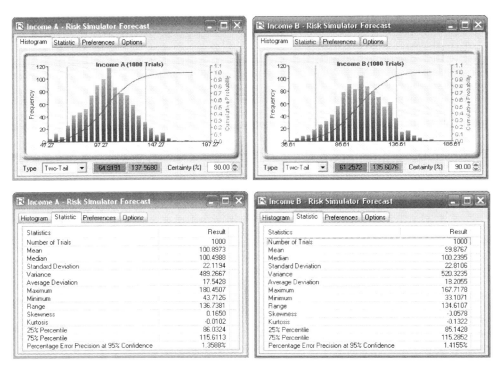

Figure 146.14: Simulation results

Running a Hypothesis Test

To run this model, simply:

1. Open the existing simulation profile by selecting **Risk Simulator | Change Simulation Profile**. Choose the *Hypothesis Testing* profile.

2. Select **Risk Simulator | Run Simulation** or click on the **RUN** icon.

3. After the simulation run is complete, select **Risk Simulator | Analytical Tools | Hypothesis Test**.

4. Make sure both forecasts are selected and click **OK**.

The report and results are provided in Figure 146.15. The results indicate that the p-value for the t-test is higher than 0.05, indicating that both means are statistically identical and that any variations are due to random white noise. Further, the p-value is also high for the F-test, indicating that both variances are also statistically identical to one another.

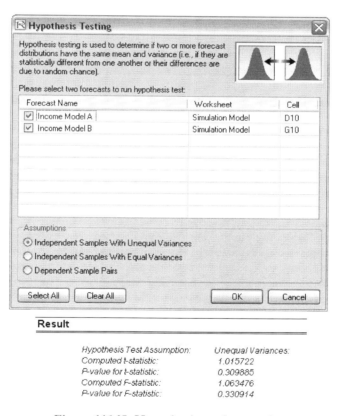

Figure 146.15: Hypothesis testing results

The preceding hypothesis test is a theoretical test and is thus more accurate than empirical tests (e.g., bootstrap simulation). However, these tests do not exist for other statistics; hence, an empirical approach is required, namely, nonparametric bootstrap simulation. To run the bootstrap simulation, simply reset and rerun the simulation; then, once the simulation is complete, click on **Risk Simulator | Analytical Tools | Nonparametric Bootstrap**. Choose one of the forecasts (only one forecast can be chosen at a time when running bootstrap simulation), select the statistics of interest, and click **OK** (Figure 146.16).

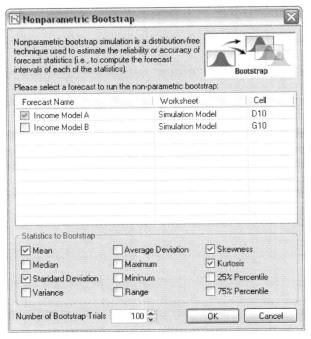

Figure 146.16: Nonparametric bootstrap simulation

The resulting forecast charts are empirical distributions of the statistics. By typing in **90** on the certainty box and hitting **TAB** on the keyboard, the 90% confidence is displayed for each statistic. For instance, the skewness interval is between 0.0452 and 0.2877, indicating that the value zero is outside this interval; that is, at the 90% two-tail confidence (or significance of 0.10 two-tailed), model A has a statistically significant positive skew. Clearly, the higher the number of bootstrap trials, the more accurate the results (recommended trials are between 1,000 and 10,000). Think of bootstrap simulation in this way: Imagine you have 100 people with the same exact model running the simulation without any seed values. At the end of the simulations, each person will have a set of means, standard deviations, skewness, and kurtosis. Clearly, some people will have exactly the same results while others are going to be slightly off, by virtue of random simulation. The question is, how close or variable is the mean or any of these statistics? In order to answer that question, you collect all 100 means and show the distribution and figure out the 90% confidence level (Figure 146.17). This is what bootstrap does. It creates alternate realities of hundreds or thousands of runs of the same model, to see how accurate and what the spread of the statistic is. This also allows us to perform hypothesis tests to see if the statistic of interest is statistically significant or not.

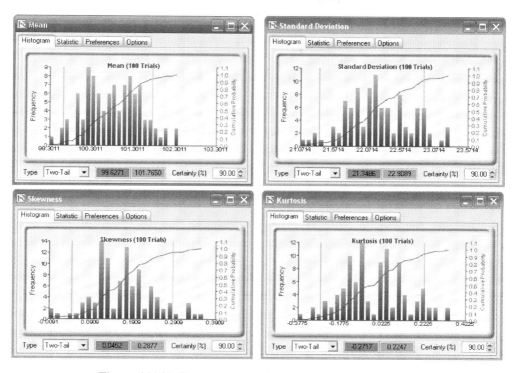

Figure 146.17: Bootstrap simulation's forecast results

147. Six Sigma – One- and Two-Sample Hypothesis Tests Using T-Tests, Z-Tests, F-Tests, ANOVA, and Nonparametric Tests (Friedman, Kruskal-Wallis, Lilliefors, and Runs Test)

File Name: Six Sigma – Hypothesis Testing (Advanced Techniques)

Location: Modeling Toolkit | Six Sigma | Hypothesis Testing (Advanced Techniques)

Brief Description: Illustrates how to use Modeling Toolkit's Statistical Tools to run single, two-variable, and multivariate hypothesis tests using parametric and nonparametric techniques

Requirements: Modeling Toolkit, Risk Simulator

This chapter is a follow-up to the preceding chapter on hypothesis testing. As a primer to the more advanced applications described here, please first review the materials in that chapter. Here we continue the quest of quality control and sampling to test one, two, and multiple different variables to see if they are statistically significantly similar or different from each other or from some hypothesized value. The methodologies introduced in this chapter are more advanced than those presented in the last chapter, but build on similar concepts. All the statistical tests shown in this chapter are available in the *Statistical Tools* section of Modeling Toolkit.

A hypothesis test is a statistical test of the characteristics of a population by testing a small sample collected. In most cases, the population to be studied might be too large, difficult, or expensive to be completely sampled (e.g., all 100 million registered voters in the United States in a particular election). Hence, a smaller sample (e.g., a random sample of 1,100 voters from 20 cities) is collected, and the sample statistics are tabulated. Then, using hypothesis tests, the characteristics of the entire population can be inferred from this small sample. Modeling Toolkit allows the user to test one-variable, two-variable, and multiple-variable hypotheses tests using t-tests, Z-tests, analysis of variance (ANOVA), and advanced nonparametric techniques.

To perform a hypothesis test, first set up the null hypothesis (H_o) and the alternate hypothesis (H_a). Here are some quick rules:

- Always set up the alternate hypothesis first, then the null hypothesis.

- The alternate hypothesis always has these signs: $>$ or $<$ or $\neq$.

- The null hypothesis always has these signs: $\geq$ or $\leq$ or $=$.

- If the alternate hypothesis is $\neq$, then it's a 2-tailed test; if $<$, then it is a left- (one-) tailed test; if $>$, then it is a right- (one-) tailed test

If the p-value is less than the significance level (the significance level α is selected by the user and is usually 0.10, 0.05, or 0.01) tested, reject the null hypothesis and accept the alternate hypothesis.

Two-Tailed Hypothesis Test

A two-tailed hypothesis tests the null hypothesis of whether the population mean, median, or other statistic of the sample dataset is statistically identical to the hypothesized mean, median, or the specified statistic. The alternative hypothesis is that the real population mean, median, or other statistic is statistically different from the hypothesized mean, median, or the specified statistic when tested using the sample dataset. If the calculated p-value is less than or equal to the alpha significance value, then reject the null hypothesis and accept the alternate hypothesis. Otherwise, if the p-value is higher than the alpha significance value, do not reject the null hypothesis.

Right-Tailed Hypothesis Test

A right-tailed hypothesis tests the null hypothesis such that the population mean, median, or other statistic of the sample dataset is statistically less than or equal to the hypothesized mean, median, or the specified statistic. The alternative hypothesis is that the real population mean, median, or other statistic is statistically greater than the hypothesized mean, median, or specified statistic when tested using the sample dataset. If the calculated p-value is less than or equal to the alpha significance value, then reject the null hypothesis and accept the alternate hypothesis. Otherwise, if the p-value is higher than the alpha significance value, do not reject the null hypothesis.

Left-Tailed Hypothesis Test

A left-tailed hypothesis tests the null hypothesis such that the population mean, median, or other statistic of the sample dataset is statistically greater than or equal to the hypothesized mean, median, or specified statistic. The alternative hypothesis is that the real population mean, median, or other statistic is statistically less than the hypothesized mean, median, or specified statistic when tested using the sample dataset. If the calculated p-value is less than or equal to the alpha significance value, then reject the null hypothesis and accept the alternate hypothesis. Otherwise, if the p-value is higher than the alpha significance value, do not reject the null hypothesis.

Example: A lightbulb manufacturing company wants to test the hypothesis that its bulbs can last on average at least 1,000 burning hours. Hence, the company randomly selects 20 sample bulbs. The 20 bulbs' burning hours are 1100, 1095, 997, 1010, 1001, 1000, 995, 995, 1005, 1070, 998, 950, 1020, 1035, 1050, 999, 1021, 998, 1010, and 1002. At a 5% significance level, what is the conclusion?

Figure 147.1 illustrates the sample data of 20 lightbulbs randomly selected and tested using the One-Variable T-Test. Figure 147.2 illustrates the results obtained. The hypothesis tested is, of course, a one-tail right-tail test. As the sample size is less than 30, we use a one-variable t-test. Figure 147.1 also illustrates the data setup and requirements to run a one-variable t-test.

Clearly, the null hypothesis tested is such that the population average life of the lightbulbs is $\leq 1,000$ hours, while the alternate hypothesis is such that the population life of the lightbulbs $> 1,000$ hours. The calculated p-value for the right tail is 0.0220, which is less than the 5% significance (α) level. Hence we reject the null hypothesis and conclude that the population average of the life of the lightbulbs exceeds 1,000 hours.

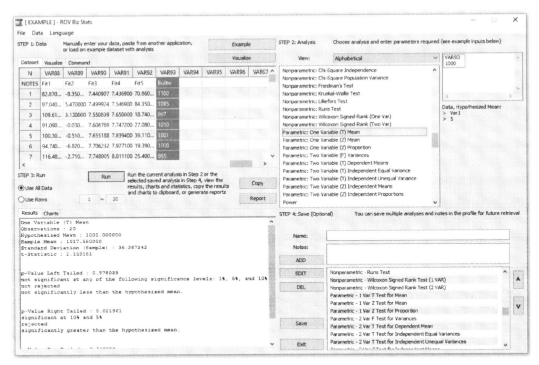

Figure 147.1: One-variable t-test

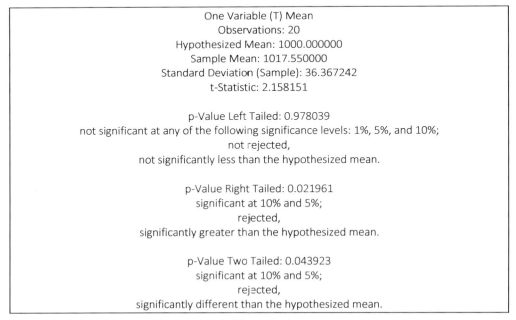

Figure 147.2: Hypothesis test results

One-Variable Testing for Means (T-Test)

This one-variable t-test of means is appropriate when the population standard deviation is not known but the sampling distribution is assumed to be approximately normal. The t-test is used when the sample size is less than 30. This t-test can be applied to three types of hypothesis tests: a two-tailed test, a right-tailed test, and a left-tailed test, to examine based on the sample dataset if the population mean is equal to, less than, or greater than some hypothesized mean.

If the calculated p-value is less than or equal to the significance level in the test, then reject the null hypothesis and conclude that the true population mean is not equal to (two-tail test), less than (left-tail test), or greater than (right-tail test) the hypothesized mean based on the sample tested. Otherwise, the true population mean is statistically similar to the hypothesized mean.

Data Requirements

For the **One-Variable T-Tests**, create data tables such as the one in Figure 147.3, and select the data area *one variable* at a time. Repeat this process for other variables. To extend the dataset, just add more observations (rows) or more variables (columns), as illustrated in Figures 147.3 and 147.4.

[C:\Users\jcmun\Desktop\AAM2E Models.bizstats] - ROV Biz Stats

File   Data   Language   Help

STEP 1. Data   Manually enter your data, paste from another application, or load an example dataset with analysis   [Example]   [Visualize]

N	VAR1	VAR2	VAR3	VAR4	VAR5	VAR6	VAR7	VAR8	VAR9	VAR10	VAR11	VAR12
NOTES	One	Two	Three	Four	Five	Six	Seven	Eight	Nine	Ten		
1	10.00	26.00	55.00	88.00	99.00	10.00	23.00	10.00	10.00	10.00		
2	13.00	28.00	57.00	89.00	104.00	13.00	13.00	43.00	13.00	13.00		
3	14.00	29.00	66.00	90.00	110.00	14.00	14.00	14.00	3.00	14.00		
4	15.00	30.00	78.00	93.00	111.00	15.00	15.00	15.00	15.00	43.00		
5	18.00	33.00	79.00	99.00	145.00	18.00	18.00	18.00	32.00	18.00		
6	6.00	37.00	88.00	99.00	155.00	19.00	19.00	19.00	24.00	32.00		
7	87.00	39.00	89.00	104.00	169.00	19.00	19.00	19.00	55.00	19.00		
8	21.00	44.00	90.00	110.00	188.00	21.00	23.00	21.00	3.00	21.00		
9	23.00	44.00	93.00	111.00	190.00	22.00	24.00	22.00	3.00	22.00		
10	34.00	46.00	99.00	145.00	200.00	21.00	54.00	21.00	22.00	21.00		
11	26.00	48.00	99.00	221.00	202.00	26.00	26.00	26.00	23.00	26.00		
12	28.00	55.00	104.00	169.00	212.00	28.00	28.00	28.00	28.00	34.00		
13	29.00	57.00	110.00	188.00	345.00	29.00	29.00	29.00	56.00	29.00		
14	30.00	66.00	147.00	190.00	280.00	30.00	30.00	30.00	30.00	30.00		
15	33.00	78.00	145.00	200.00	56.00	34.00	33.00	33.00	33.00	33.00		
16	23.00	79.00	155.00	202.00	300.00	37.00	23.00	32.00	37.00	11.00		
17	39.00	88.00	169.00	212.00	300.00	39.00	32.00	39.00	75.00	39.00		
18	44.00	89.00	199.00	222.00	400.00	44.00	44.00	44.00	44.00	33.00		
19	44.00	90.00	190.00	280.00	401.00	44.00	44.00	44.00	44.00	44.00		
20	46.00	93.00	200.00	300.00	555.00	46.00	23.00	46.00	46.00	4.00		
21	48.00	99.00	202.00	300.00	565.00	48.00	48.00	48.00	48.00	23.00		
22	55.00	99.00	212.00	300.00	577.00	55.00	55.00	55.00	55.00	55.00		
23	57.00	104.00	222.00	400.00	587.00	57.00	13.00	57.00	57.00	57.00		
24	66.00	110.00	299.00	401.00	599.00	66.00	66.00	66.00	66.00	66.00		

Figure 147.3: Data requirements for a one-variable t-test

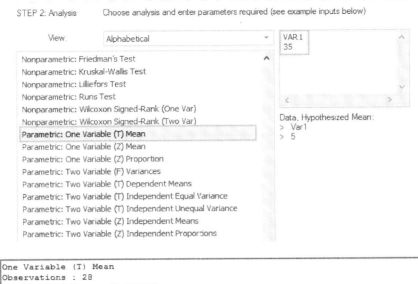

STEP 2: Analysis   Choose analysis and enter parameters required (see example inputs below)

View: Alphabetical   VAR1
                                                          35

Nonparametric: Friedman's Test
Nonparametric: Kruskal-Wallis Test
Nonparametric: Lilliefors Test
Nonparametric: Runs Test
Nonparametric: Wilcoxon Signed-Rank (One Var)   Data, Hypothesized Mean:
Nonparametric: Wilcoxon Signed-Rank (Two Var)   > Var1
Parametric: One Variable (T) Mean   > 5
Parametric: One Variable (Z) Mean
Parametric: One Variable (Z) Proportion
Parametric: Two Variable (F) Variances
Parametric: Two Variable (T) Dependent Means
Parametric: Two Variable (T) Independent Equal Variance
Parametric: Two Variable (T) Independent Unequal Variance
Parametric: Two Variable (Z) Independent Means
Parametric: Two Variable (Z) Independent Proportions

```
One Variable (T) Mean
Observations : 28
Hypothesized Mean : 35.000000
Sample Mean : 36.964286
Standard Deviation (Sample) : 19.891338
t-Statistic : 0.522540


p-Value Left Tailed : 0.697222
not significant at any of the following significance levels: 1%, 5%, and 10%
not rejected
not significantly less than the hypothesized mean.


p-Value Right Tailed : 0.302778
not significant at any of the following significance levels: 1%, 5%, and 10%
not rejected
not significantly greater than the hypothesized mean.


p-Value Two Tailed : 0.605556
not significant at any of the following significance levels: 1%, 5%, and 10%
not rejected
not significantly different than the hypothesized mean.
```

Figure 147.4: Running a one-variable t-test

One-Variable Testing for Means (Z-Test)

The one-variable Z-test is appropriate when the population standard deviation is known, and the sampling distribution is assumed to be approximately normal. This applies when the number of data points exceeds 30. This Z-test can be applied to three types of hypothesis tests: a two-tailed test, a right-tailed test, and a left-tailed test, to examine based on the sample dataset if the population mean is equal to, less than, or greater than some hypothesized mean.

If the calculated p-value is less than or equal to the significance level in the test, then reject the null hypothesis and conclude that the true population mean is not equal to (two-tail test), less than (left-tail test), or greater than (right-tail test) the hypothesized mean based on the sample tested. Otherwise, the true population mean is statistically similar to the hypothesized mean.

Data Requirements

For the **One-Variable Z-Test**, create data tables such as the one in Figure 147.5, and select the data area *one variable* at a time. Repeat this process for other variables. To extend the dataset, just add more observations (rows) or more variables (columns) but make sure that you have at least 30 data points to run a Z-test (Figures 147.5 and 147.6).

[C:\Users\jcmun\Desktop\AAM2E Models.bizstats] – ROV Biz Stats

File   Data   Language   Help

STEP 1: Data   Manually enter your data, paste from another application, or load an example dataset with analysis

Example   Visualize

N	VAR4	VAR5	VAR6	VAR7	VAR8	VAR9	VAR10	VAR11	VAR12	VAR13	VAR14	VAR15
NOTES	Four	Five	Six	Seven	Eight	Nine	Ten	Eleven	Twelve	Thirteen	Fourteen	Fifteen
1	88.00	99.00	10.00	23.00	10.00	10.00	10.00	10.00	10.00	99.00	0.0360	0.0340
2	89.00	104.00	13.00	13.00	43.00	13.00	13.00	17.00	14.00	36.00	0.0990	0.0360
3	90.00	110.00	14.00	14.00	14.00	3.00	14.00	14.00	14.00	74.00	0.0360	0.0380
4	93.00	111.00	15.00	15.00	15.00	15.00	43.00	12.00	15.00	30.00	0.0740	0.0330
5	99.00	145.00	18.00	18.00	18.00	32.00	18.00	18.00	18.00	54.00	0.0300	0.0340
6	99.00	155.00	19.00	19.00	19.00	24.00	32.00	19.00	32.00	17.00	0.0540	0.0310
7	104.00	169.00	19.00	19.00	19.00	55.00	19.00	19.00	19.00	21.00	0.0170	0.0390
8	110.00	188.00	21.00	23.00	21.00	3.00	21.00	21.00	21.00	89.00	0.0320	0.0300
9	111.00	190.00	22.00	24.00	22.00	3.00	22.00	22.00	22.00	77.00	0.0890	0.0290
10	145.00	200.00	21.00	54.00	21.00	22.00	21.00	21.00	21.00	86.00	0.0770	0.0280
11	221.00	202.00	26.00	26.00	26.00	23.00	26.00	26.00	26.00	33.00	0.0860	0.0270
12	169.00	212.00	28.00	28.00	28.00	28.00	34.00	28.00	28.00	11.00	0.0330	0.0290
13	188.00	345.00	29.00	29.00	29.00	56.00	29.00	29.00	29.00	74.00	0.0900	0.0300
14	190.00	280.00	30.00	30.00	30.00	30.00	30.00	30.00	30.00	7.00	0.0740	0.0310
15	200.00	56.00	34.00	33.00	33.00	33.00	33.00	33.00	22.00	54.00	0.0070	0.0330
16	202.00	300.00	37.00	23.00	32.00	37.00	11.00	44.00	53.00	98.00	0.0540	0.0290
17	212.00	300.00	39.00	32.00	39.00	75.00	39.00	39.00	39.00	50.00	0.0980	0.0280
18	222.00	400.00	44.00	44.00	44.00	44.00	33.00	44.00	44.00	86.00	0.0500	0.0270
19	280.00	401.00	44.00	44.00	44.00	44.00	44.00	44.00	44.00	90.00	0.0860	0.0430
20	300.00	555.00	46.00	23.00	46.00	46.00	4.00	46.00	46.00	65.00	0.0900	0.0450
21	300.00	565.00	48.00	48.00	48.00	48.00	23.00	21.00	48.00	20.00	0.0650	0.0410
22	300.00	577.00	55.00	55.00	55.00	55.00	55.00	55.00	55.00	17.00	0.0200	0.0440
23	400.00	587.00	57.00	13.00	57.00	57.00	57.00	57.00	57.00	45.00	0.0170	0.0410

Figure 147.5: Data requirements for a one-variable Z-test

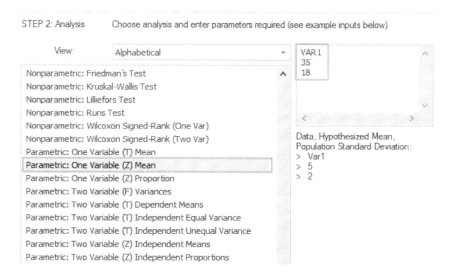

STEP 2: Analysis   Choose analysis and enter parameters required (see example inputs below)

View: Alphabetical

VAR1
35
18

Nonparametric: Friedman's Test
Nonparametric: Kruskal-Wallis Test
Nonparametric: Lilliefors Test
Nonparametric: Runs Test
Nonparametric: Wilcoxon Signed-Rank (One Var)
Nonparametric: Wilcoxon Signed-Rank (Two Var)
Parametric: One Variable (T) Mean
Parametric: One Variable (Z) Mean
Parametric: One Variable (Z) Proportion
Parametric: Two Variable (F) Variances
Parametric: Two Variable (T) Dependent Means
Parametric: Two Variable (T) Independent Equal Variance
Parametric: Two Variable (T) Independent Unequal Variance
Parametric: Two Variable (Z) Independent Means
Parametric: Two Variable (Z) Independent Proportions

Data, Hypothesized Mean,
Population Standard Deviation:
> Var1
> 5
> 2

Figure 147.6: Running a one-variable Z-test

```
One Variable (Z) Mean
Observations : 28
Hypothesized Mean : 35.000000
Sample Mean : 36.964286
Standard Deviation (Sample) : 19.891338
Z-Statistic : 0.577446


p-Value Left Tailed : 0.718181
not significant at any of the following significance levels: 1%, 5%, and 10%
not rejected
not significantly less than the hypothesized mean.


p-Value Right Tailed : 0.281819
not significant at any of the following significance levels: 1%, 5%, and 10%
not rejected
not significantly greater than the hypothesized mean.


p-Value Two Tailed : 0.563638
not significant at any of the following significance levels: 1%, 5%, and 10%
not rejected
not significantly different than the hypothesized mean.
```

Figure 147.6: Running a one-variable Z-test *(continued)*

One-Variable Testing for Proportions (Z-Test)

The one-variable Z-test for proportions is appropriate when the sampling distribution is assumed to be approximately normal. This applies when the number of data points exceeds 30, and when the number of data points, N, multiplied by the hypothesized population proportion mean, P, is greater than or equal to five, $NP \geq 5$. The data used in the analysis have to be proportions and be between 0 and 1. This Z-test can be applied to three types of hypothesis tests: a two-tailed test, a right-tailed test, and a left-tailed test, to examine based on the sample dataset if the population mean is equal to, less than, or greater than the hypothesized mean.

If the calculated p-value is less than or equal to the significance level in the test, then reject the null hypothesis and conclude that the true population mean is not equal to (two-tail test), less than (left-tail test), or greater than (right-tail test) the hypothesized mean based on the sample tested. Otherwise, the true population mean is statistically similar to some hypothesized mean.

For data requirements, see One Variable Testing for Means (Z-Test). However, make sure that the data are proportions between 0 and 1 (not including 1).

Two Variables with Dependent Means (T-Test)

The two-variable dependent t-test is appropriate when the population standard deviation is not known but the sampling distribution is assumed to be approximately normal. The t-test is used when the sample size is less than 30. In addition, this test is specifically formulated for testing the same or similar samples before and after an event (e.g., measurements taken before a medical treatment are compared against those measurements taken after the treatment to see if there is a difference). This t-test can be applied to three types of hypothesis tests: a two-tailed test, a right-tailed test, and a left-tailed test.

Suppose that a new heart medication was administered to 100 patients ($N = 100$) and the heart rates before and after the medication was administered were measured. The Two Dependent Variables t-Test can be applied to test if the new medication is effective by testing to see if there is a statistically different "before and after" averages. The Dependent Variables test is used here because there is only a single sample collected (the heartbeats of the same patients were measured before and after administration of the new drug).

The two-tailed null hypothesis tests that the true population's mean of the difference between the two variables is zero, versus the alternate hypothesis that the difference is statistically different from zero. The right-tail null hypothesis test is such that the differences in the population means (first mean less second mean) is statistically less than or equal to zero (which is identical to saying that the mean of the first sample is less than or equal to the mean of the second sample). The alternative hypothesis is that the mean difference of the real populations is statistically greater than zero when tested using the sample dataset (which is identical to saying that the mean of the first sample is greater than the mean of the second sample). The left-tail null hypothesis test is such that the differences in the population means (first mean less second mean) is statistically greater than or equal to zero (which is the same as saying that the mean of the first sample is greater than or equal to the mean of the second sample). The alternative hypothesis is that the mean difference of the real population is statistically less than zero when tested using the sample dataset (which is identical to saying that the mean of the first sample is less than the mean of the second sample).

If the calculated p-value is less than or equal to the significance level in the test, reject the null hypothesis and conclude that the true population difference of the population means is not equal to (two-tail test), less than (left-tail test), or greater than (right-tail test) zero based on the sample tested. Otherwise, the true population and hypothesized means are statistically similar.

Data Requirements

For the **Two-Variable T-Tests**, create data tables such as the one shown in Figure 147.7, and select the data area *two variables* at a time. Repeat this process for other pairs of variables. To extend the existing dataset, just add more observations (rows) or more variables (columns). See Figures 147.7 and 147.8.

[C:\Users\jcmun\Desktop\AAM2E Models.bizstats] - ROV Biz Stats

File Data Language Help

STEP 1. Data   Manually enter your data, paste from another application, or load an example dataset with analysis   [Example]   [Visualize]

N	VAR1	VAR2	VAR3	VAR4	VAR5	VAR6	VAR7	VAR8	VAR9	VAR10	VAR11	VAR12
NOTES	One	Two	Three	Four	Five	Six	Seven	Eight	Nine	Ten		
1	10.00	26.00	55.00	88.00	99.00	10.00	23.00	10.00	10.00	10.00		
2	13.00	28.00	57.00	89.00	104.00	13.00	13.00	43.00	13.00	13.00		
3	14.00	29.00	66.00	90.00	110.00	14.00	14.00	14.00	3.00	14.00		
4	15.00	30.00	78.00	93.00	111.00	15.00	15.00	15.00	15.00	43.00		
5	18.00	33.00	79.00	99.00	145.00	18.00	18.00	18.00	32.00	18.00		
6	6.00	37.00	88.00	99.00	155.00	19.00	19.00	19.00	24.00	32.00		
7	87.00	39.00	89.00	104.00	169.00	19.00	19.00	19.00	55.00	19.00		
8	21.00	44.00	90.00	110.00	138.00	21.00	23.00	21.00	3.00	21.00		
9	23.00	44.00	93.00	111.00	190.00	22.00	24.00	22.00	3.00	22.00		
10	34.00	46.00	99.00	145.00	200.00	21.00	54.00	21.00	22.00	21.00		
11	26.00	48.00	99.00	221.00	202.00	26.00	26.00	26.00	23.00	26.00		
12	28.00	55.00	104.00	169.00	212.00	28.00	28.00	28.00	28.00	34.00		
13	29.00	57.00	110.00	188.00	345.00	29.00	29.00	29.00	56.00	29.00		
14	30.00	66.00	147.00	190.00	280.00	30.00	30.00	30.00	30.00	30.00		
15	33.00	78.00	145.00	200.00	56.00	34.00	33.00	33.00	33.00	33.00		
16	23.00	79.00	155.00	202.00	300.00	37.00	23.00	32.00	37.00	11.00		
17	39.00	88.00	169.00	212.00	300.00	39.00	32.00	39.00	75.00	39.00		
18	44.00	89.00	199.00	222.00	400.00	44.00	44.00	44.00	44.00	33.00		
19	44.00	90.00	190.00	280.00	401.00	44.00	44.00	44.00	44.00	44.00		
20	46.00	93.00	200.00	300.00	555.00	46.00	23.00	46.00	46.00	4.00		
21	48.00	99.00	202.00	300.00	565.00	48.00	48.00	48.00	48.00	23.00		
22	55.00	99.00	212.00	300.00	577.00	55.00	55.00	55.00	55.00	55.00		
23	57.00	104.00	222.00	400.00	587.00	57.00	13.00	57.00	57.00	57.00		
24	66.00	110.00	300.00	401.00	500.00	66.00	66.00	66.00	66.00	66.00		

Figure 147.7: Data requirements for a two-variable dependent means t-test

Figure 147.8: Running a two-variable dependent means t-test

Two Variables That Are Independent with Equal Variances (T-Test)

The two-variable t-test with equal variances is appropriate when the population standard deviation is not known but the sampling distribution is assumed to be approximately normal. The t-test is used when the sample size is less than 30. In addition, the two independent samples are assumed to have similar variances.

For illustration, suppose that a new engine design is tested against an existing engine design to see if there is a statistically significant different between the two. The t-Test on Two (Independent) Variables with Equal Variances can be applied. This test is used here because there are two distinctly different samples collected here (new engine and existing engine) but the variances of both samples are assumed to be similar (the means may or may not be similar but the fluctuations around the mean are assumed to be similar).

This t-test can be applied to three types of hypothesis tests: a two-tailed test, a right-tailed test, and a left-tailed test. A two-tailed hypothesis tests the null hypothesis H_0 such that the mean difference of the population between the two variables is statistically identical to the hypothesized mean differences (HMD). If HMD is set to zero, this is the same as saying that the first mean equals the second mean. The alternative hypothesis is that the difference between the real population means is statistically different from the hypothesized mean differences when tested using the sample dataset. If HMD is set to zero, this is the same as saying that the first mean does not equal the second mean in the alternate hypothesis.

A right-tailed hypothesis tests the null hypothesis H_0 such that the population mean difference between the two variables is statistically less than or equal to the hypothesized mean differences. If HMD is set to zero, this is the same as saying that the first mean is less than or equals the second mean. The alternative hypothesis is that the real difference between population means is statistically greater than the hypothesized mean differences when tested using the sample dataset. If HMD is set to zero, this is the same as saying that the first mean is greater than the second mean.

A left-tailed hypothesis tests the null hypothesis H_0 such that the differences between the population means of the two variables is statistically greater than or equal to the hypothesized mean differences. If HMD is set to zero, this is the same as saying that the first mean is greater than or equals the second mean. The alternative hypothesis is that the real difference between population means is statistically less than the hypothesized mean difference when tested using the sample dataset. If HMD is set to zero, this is the same as saying that the first mean is less than the second mean.

If the calculated p-value is less than or equal to the significance level in the test, reject the null hypothesis and conclude that the true population difference of the population means is not equal to (two-tail test), less than (left-tail test), or greater than (right-tail test) HMD based on the sample tested. Otherwise, the true difference of the population means is statistically similar to the HMD.

For data requirements, see Two Variables with Dependent Means (T-Test).

Two Variables That Are Independent with Unequal Variances (T-Test)

The two-variable t-test with unequal variances (the population variance of sample 1 is expected to be different from the population variance of sample 2) is appropriate when the population standard deviation is not known but the sampling distribution is assumed to be approximately normal. The t-test is used when the sample size is less than 30. In addition, the two independent samples are assumed to have similar variances.

To illustrate, suppose that a new customer relationship management (CRM) process is being evaluated for its effectiveness. The customer satisfaction ranking between two hotels (one with and the other without CRM implemented) are collected. The t-Test on Two (Independent) Variables with Unequal Variances can be applied. This test is used here because there are two distinctly different samples collected (customer survey results of two different hotels) and the variances of both samples are assumed to be dissimilar (due to the difference in geographical location plus the different demographics and psychographics of customers at both properties).

This t-test can be applied to three types of hypothesis tests: a two-tailed test, a right-tailed test, and a left-tailed test. A two-tailed hypothesis tests the null hypothesis H_0 such that the population mean differences between the two variables is statistically identical to the hypothesized mean differences. If HMD is set to zero, this is the same as saying that the first mean equals the second mean. The alternative hypothesis is that the real difference between the population means is statistically different from the hypothesized mean differences when tested using the sample dataset. If HMD is set to zero, this is the same as saying that the first mean does not equal the second mean.

A right-tailed hypothesis tests the null hypothesis H_0 such that the difference between the means of the populations of the two variables is statistically less than or equal to the hypothesized mean differences. If HMD is set to zero, this is the same as saying that the first mean is less than or equals the second mean. The alternative hypothesis is that the mean of the differences of the real populations is statistically greater than the hypothesized mean difference when tested using the sample dataset. If HMD is set to zero, this is the same as saying that the first mean is greater than the second mean.

A left-tailed hypothesis tests the null hypothesis H_0 such that the difference between the population means of the two variables is statistically greater than or equal to the hypothesized mean differences. If HMD is set to zero, this is the same as saying that the first mean is greater than or equals the second mean. The alternative hypothesis is that the real difference between population means is statistically less than the hypothesized mean difference when tested using the sample dataset. If HMD is set to zero, this is the same as saying that the first mean is less than the second mean.

If the calculated p-value is less than or equal to the significance level in the test, reject the null hypothesis and conclude that the true population difference of the population means is not equal to (two-tail test), less than (left-tail test), or greater than (right-tail test) the hypothesized mean based on the sample tested. Otherwise, the true difference of the population means is statistically similar to the hypothesized mean.

For data requirements, see Two Variables with Dependent Means (T-Test).

Two Variables That Are Independent Testing for Means (Z-Test)

The two-variable Z-test is appropriate when the population standard deviations are known for the two samples, and the sampling distribution of each variable is assumed to be approximately normal. This applies when the number of data points of each variable exceeds 30.

To illustrate, suppose that a market research was conducted on two different markets and the sample collected is large (N must exceed 30 for both variables). The researcher is interested in testing whether there is a statistically significant difference between the two markets. Further suppose that such a market survey has been performed many times in the past and the population standard deviations are known. A Two Independent Variables Z-Test can be applied because the sample size exceeds 30 on each market, and the population standard deviations are known.

This Z-test can be applied to three types of hypothesis tests: a two-tailed test, a right-tailed test, and a left-tailed test. A two-tailed hypothesis tests the null hypothesis H_0 such that the difference between the two population means is statistically identical to the hypothesized mean. The alternative hypothesis is that the real difference between the two population means is statistically different from the hypothesized mean when tested using the sample dataset.

A right-tailed hypothesis tests the null hypothesis H_0 such that the difference between the two population means is statistically less than or equal to the hypothesized mean. The alternative hypothesis is that the real difference between the two population means is statistically greater than the hypothesized mean when tested using the sample dataset.

A left-tailed hypothesis tests the null hypothesis H_0 such that the difference between the two population means is statistically greater than or equal to the hypothesized mean. The alternative hypothesis is that the real difference between the two population means is statistically less than the hypothesized mean when tested using the sample dataset.

Data Requirements

For the **Two Independent Variables Z-Test**, create data tables such as the one in Figure 147.9, and select the data area *two variables* at a time. To extend the dataset, just add more observations (rows) or more variables (columns) but make sure that you have at least 30 data points in each variable to run a Z-test. See Figure 147.10.

[C:\Users\jcmun\Desktop\AAM2E Models.bizstats] – ROV Biz Stats

File   Data   Language   Help

STEP 1: Data   Manually enter your data, paste from another application, or load an example dataset with analysis   Example   Visualize

N	VAR4	VAR5	VAR6	VAR7	VAR8	VAR9	VAR10	VAR11	VAR12	VAR13	VAR14	VAR15
NOTES	Four	Five	Six	Seven	Eight	Nine	Ten	Eleven	Twelve	Thirteen	Fourteen	Fifteen
1	88.00	99.00	10.00	23.00	10.00	10.00	10.00	10.00	10.00	99.00	0.0360	0.0340
2	89.00	104.00	13.00	13.00	43.00	13.00	13.00	17.00	14.00	36.00	0.0990	0.0360
3	90.00	110.00	14.00	14.00	14.00	3.00	14.00	14.00	14.00	74.00	0.0360	0.0380
4	93.00	111.00	15.00	15.00	15.00	15.00	43.00	12.00	15.00	30.00	0.0740	0.0330
5	99.00	145.00	18.00	18.00	18.00	32.00	18.00	18.00	18.00	54.00	0.0300	0.0340
6	99.00	155.00	19.00	19.00	19.00	24.00	32.00	19.00	32.00	17.00	0.0540	0.0310
7	104.00	169.00	19.00	19.00	19.00	55.00	19.00	19.00	19.00	21.00	0.0170	0.0390
8	110.00	188.00	21.00	23.00	21.00	3.00	21.00	21.00	21.00	89.00	0.0320	0.0300
9	111.00	190.00	22.00	24.00	22.00	3.00	22.00	22.00	22.00	77.00	0.0890	0.0290
10	145.00	200.00	21.00	54.00	21.00	22.00	21.00	21.00	21.00	86.00	0.0770	0.0280
11	221.00	202.00	26.00	26.00	26.00	23.00	26.00	26.00	26.00	33.00	0.0860	0.0270
12	169.00	212.00	28.00	28.00	28.00	28.00	34.00	28.00	28.00	11.00	0.0330	0.0290
13	188.00	345.00	29.00	29.00	29.00	56.00	29.00	29.00	29.00	74.00	0.0900	0.0300
14	190.00	280.00	30.00	30.00	30.00	30.00	30.00	30.00	30.00	7.00	0.0740	0.0310
15	200.00	56.00	34.00	33.00	33.00	33.00	33.00	33.00	22.00	54.00	0.0070	0.0330
16	202.00	300.00	37.00	23.00	32.00	37.00	11.00	44.00	53.00	98.00	0.0540	0.0290
17	212.00	300.00	39.00	32.00	39.00	75.00	39.00	39.00	39.00	50.00	0.0980	0.0280
18	222.00	400.00	44.00	44.00	44.00	44.00	33.00	44.00	44.00	86.00	0.0500	0.0270
19	280.00	401.00	44.00	44.00	44.00	44.00	44.00	44.00	44.00	90.00	0.0860	0.0430
20	300.00	555.00	46.00	23.00	46.00	46.00	4.00	46.00	46.00	65.00	0.0900	0.0450
21	300.00	565.00	48.00	48.00	48.00	48.00	23.00	21.00	48.00	20.00	0.0650	0.0410
22	300.00	577.00	55.00	55.00	55.00	55.00	55.00	55.00	55.00	17.00	0.0200	0.0440
23	400.00	587.00	57.00	13.00	57.00	57.00	57.00	57.00	57.00	45.00	0.0170	0.0410

Figure 147.9: Data requirements for a two-variable independent Z-test

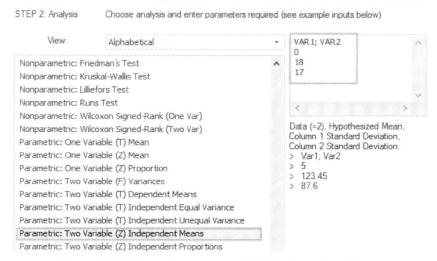

STEP 2: Analysis   Choose analysis and enter parameters required (see example inputs below)

View: Alphabetical

VAR1; VAR2
0
18
17

Nonparametric: Friedman's Test
Nonparametric: Kruskal-Wallis Test
Nonparametric: Lilliefors Test
Nonparametric: Runs Test
Nonparametric: Wilcoxon Signed-Rank (One Var)
Nonparametric: Wilcoxon Signed-Rank (Two Var)
Parametric: One Variable (T) Mean
Parametric: One Variable (Z) Mean
Parametric: One Variable (Z) Proportion
Parametric: Two Variable (F) Variances
Parametric: Two Variable (T) Dependent Means
Parametric: Two Variable (T) Independent Equal Variance
Parametric: Two Variable (T) Independent Unequal Variance
Parametric: Two Variable (Z) Independent Means
Parametric: Two Variable (Z) Independent Proportions

Data (=2), Hypothesized Mean, Column 1 Standard Deviation, Column 2 Standard Deviation:
> Var1; Var2
> 5
> 123.45
> 87.6

Figure 147.10: Running a two-variable independent Z-test

```
Two Variable (Z) Independent Means
Column 1 Observations : 28
Column 1 Sample Mean : 36.964286
Column 1 Sample Standard Deviation : 19.891338
Column 2 Observations : 28
Column 2 Sample Mean : 68.678571
Column 2 Sample Standard Deviation : 29.694810
Z-Statistic : -6.778034
Hypothesized Mean : 0.000000

p-Value Left Tailed : 0.000000
significant at 1%, 5% and 10%
rejected
significantly less than the hypothesized mean.

p-Value Right Tailed : 1.000000
not significant at any of the following significance levels: 1%, 5%, and 10%
not rejected
not significantly greater than the hypothesized mean.

p-Value Two Tailed : 0.000000
significant at 1%, 5% and 10%
rejected
significantly different than the hypothesized mean.
```

Figure 147.10: Running a two-variable independent Z-test *(continued)*

Two Variables That Are Independent Testing for Proportions (Z-Test)

The two-variable Z-test on proportions is appropriate when the sampling distribution is assumed to be approximately normal. This applies when the number of data points of both samples exceeds 30. Further, the data should all be proportions and be between 0 and 1.

To illustrate, suppose that brand research was conducted on two different headache pills and the sample collected is large (N must exceed 30 for both variables). The researcher is interested in testing whether there is a statistically significant difference between the proportion of headache sufferers of both samples using the different headache medication. A Two Independent Variables Z-Test for Proportions can be applied because the sample size exceeds 30 on each market, and the data collected are proportions.

This Z-test can be applied to three types of hypothesis tests: a two-tailed test, a right-tailed test, and a left-tailed test. A two-tailed hypothesis tests the null hypothesis H_0 such that the difference in the population proportion is statistically identical to the hypothesized difference (if the hypothesized difference is set to zero, the null hypothesis tests if the population proportions of the two samples are identical). The alternative hypothesis is that the real difference in population proportions is statistically different from the hypothesized difference when tested using the sample dataset.

A right-tailed hypothesis tests the null hypothesis H_0 such that the difference in the population proportion is statistically less than or equal to the hypothesized difference. If the hypothesized difference is set to zero, the null hypothesis tests if the population proportion of Sample 1 is equal or less than the population proportion of Sample 2. The alternative hypothesis is that the real difference in population proportions is statistically greater than the hypothesized difference when tested using the sample dataset.

A left-tailed hypothesis tests the null hypothesis H_0 such that the difference in the population proportion is statistically greater than or equal to the hypothesized difference. If the hypothesized difference is set to zero, the null hypothesis tests if the population proportion of Sample 1 is equal or greater than the population proportion of Sample 2. The alternative hypothesis is that the real difference in population proportions is statistically less than the hypothesized difference when tested using the sample dataset.

Data Requirements

For the **Two Independent Variables Z-Test for Proportions**, create data tables such as the one in Figure 147.11, and select the data area *two variables* at a time. To extend the dataset, just add more observations (rows) or more variables (columns) but make sure that the data are proportions between 0 and 1 (not inclusive of 1). Finally, make sure that you have at least 30 data points to run a Z-test (see Figures 147.11 and 147.12).

[C:\Users\jcmun\Desktop\AAM2E Models.bizstats] - ROV Biz Stats

File   Data   Language   Help

STEP 1: Data   Manually enter your data, paste from another application, or load an example dataset with analysis   [Example]   [Visualize]

N	VAR4	VAR5	VAR6	VAR7	VAR8	VAR9	VAR10	VAR11	VAR12	VAR13	VAR14	VAR15
NOTES	Four	Five	Six	Seven	Eight	Nine	Ten	Eleven	Twelve	Thirteen	Fourteen	Fifteen
1	88.00	99.00	10.00	23.00	10.00	10.00	10.00	10.00	10.00	99.00	0.0360	0.0340
2	89.00	104.00	13.00	13.00	43.00	13.00	13.00	17.00	14.00	36.00	0.0990	0.0360
3	90.00	110.00	14.00	14.00	14.00	3.00	14.00	14.00	14.00	74.00	0.0360	0.0380
4	93.00	111.00	15.00	15.00	15.00	15.00	43.00	12.00	15.00	30.00	0.0740	0.0330
5	99.00	145.00	18.00	18.00	18.00	32.00	18.00	18.00	18.00	54.00	0.0300	0.0340
6	99.00	155.00	19.00	19.00	19.00	24.00	32.00	19.00	32.00	17.00	0.0540	0.0310
7	104.00	169.00	19.00	19.00	19.00	55.00	19.00	19.00	19.00	21.00	0.0170	0.0390
8	110.00	188.00	21.00	23.00	21.00	3.00	21.00	21.00	21.00	89.00	0.0320	0.0300
9	111.00	190.00	22.00	24.00	22.00	3.00	22.00	22.00	22.00	77.00	0.0890	0.0290
10	145.00	200.00	21.00	54.00	21.00	22.00	21.00	21.00	21.00	86.00	0.0770	0.0280
11	221.00	202.00	26.00	26.00	26.00	23.00	26.00	26.00	26.00	33.00	0.0860	0.0270
12	169.00	212.00	28.00	28.00	28.00	28.00	34.00	28.00	28.00	11.00	0.0330	0.0290
13	188.00	345.00	29.00	29.00	29.00	56.00	29.00	29.00	29.00	74.00	0.0900	0.0300
14	190.00	280.00	30.00	30.00	30.00	30.00	30.00	30.00	30.00	7.00	0.0740	0.0310
15	200.00	56.00	34.00	33.00	33.00	33.00	33.00	33.00	22.00	54.00	0.0070	0.0330
16	202.00	300.00	37.00	23.00	32.00	37.00	11.00	44.00	53.00	98.00	0.0540	0.0290
17	212.00	300.00	39.00	32.00	39.00	75.00	39.00	39.00	39.00	50.00	0.0980	0.0280
18	222.00	400.00	44.00	44.00	44.00	44.00	33.00	44.00	44.00	86.00	0.0500	0.0270
19	280.00	401.00	44.00	44.00	44.00	44.00	44.00	44.00	44.00	90.00	0.0860	0.0430
20	300.00	555.00	46.00	23.00	46.00	46.00	4.00	46.00	46.00	65.00	0.0900	0.0450
21	300.00	565.00	48.00	48.00	48.00	48.00	23.00	21.00	48.00	20.00	0.0650	0.0410
22	300.00	577.00	55.00	55.00	55.00	55.00	55.00	55.00	55.00	17.00	0.0200	0.0440
23	400.00	587.00	57.00	13.00	57.00	57.00	57.00	57.00	57.00	45.00	0.0170	0.0410

Figure 147.11: Data requirements for a two-variable Z-test for proportions

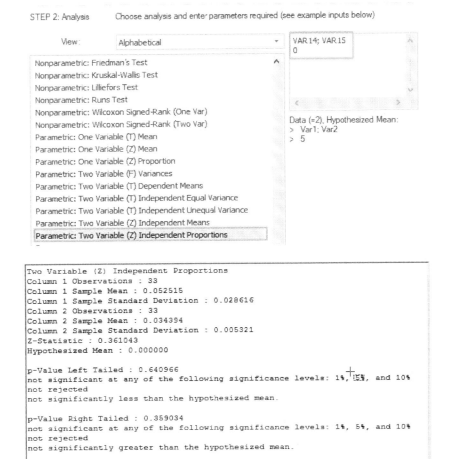

Figure 147.12: Running a two-variable Z-test for proportions

Two Variables That Are Independent Testing for Variances (F-Test)

The two-variable F-test analyzes the variances from two samples. The population variance of sample 1 is tested with the population variance of sample 2 to see if they are equal. This test is appropriate when the population standard deviation is not known and the sampling distribution is assumed to be approximately normal.

The measurement of variation is a key issue in Six Sigma and quality control applications. In this illustration, suppose that the variation or variance around the units produced in a manufacturing process is compared to another process to determine which process is more variable and, hence, less predictable in quality.

This F-test typically can be applied to a single hypothesis test: a two-tailed test. A two-tailed hypothesis tests the null hypothesis H_o such that the population variance of the two variables is statistically identical. The alternative hypothesis is that the population variances are statistically different from one another when tested using the sample dataset.

If the calculated p-value is less than or equal to the significance level in the test, reject the null hypothesis and conclude that the true population variances of the two variables are not statistically equal to one another. Otherwise, the true population variances are statistically similar to each other.

For data requirements, see Two Variables That Are Independent Testing for Proportions (Z-Test).

The Basics of Nonparametric Methodologies

Nonparametric techniques make no assumptions about the specific shape or distribution from which the sample is drawn. This is different from the other hypotheses tests, such as ANOVA or t-Tests (parametric tests) where the sample is assumed to be drawn from a population that is normally or approximately normally distributed. If normality is assumed, the power of the test is higher due to this normality restriction. However, if flexibility on distributional requirements is needed, nonparametric techniques are superior. In general, nonparametric methodologies provide these advantages over other parametric tests:

- Normality or approximate normality does not have to be assumed.
- Fewer assumptions about the population are required, that is, nonparametric tests do not require that the population assume any specific distribution.
- Smaller sample sizes can be analyzed.
- Samples with nominal and ordinal scales of measurement can be tested.
- Sample variances do not have to be equal, which is required in parametric tests.

However, two caveats are worthy of mention:

- Compared to parametric tests, nonparametric tests use data less efficiently.
- The power of nonparametric tests is lower than that of parametric tests.

Therefore, if all the required assumptions are satisfied, it is better to use parametric tests. However, in reality, it may be difficult to justify these distributional assumptions, or small sample sizes may exist, requiring the need for nonparametric tests. Thus, nonparametric tests should be used when the data are nominal or ordinal, or when the data are interval or ratio but the normality assumption is not met.

The following lists each of the nonparametric tests available for use in the software.

Chi-Square Goodness of Fit Test

The Chi-Square test for goodness of fit is used to examine if a sample dataset could have been drawn from a population having a specified probability distribution. The probability distribution tested here is the normal distribution. The null hypothesis tested is such that the sample is randomly drawn from the normal distribution, versus the alternate hypothesis that the sample is not from a normal distribution. If the calculated p-value is less than or equal to the alpha significance value, reject the null hypothesis and accept the alternate hypothesis. Otherwise, if the p-value is higher than the alpha significance value, do not reject the null hypothesis. For testing other distributions, use Risk Simulator's distributional fitting tool instead.

Data Requirements

For the **Chi-Square Goodness of Fit Test**, create data tables such as the one shown in Figure 147.13, and select the data area. To extend the dataset, just add more observations (rows) as seen in Figures 147.13 and 147.14.

Chi-Square Goodness of Fit

Category	Upper Limit	Frequency
700-800	800	36
800-900	900	96
900-1000	1000	78
1000-1100	1100	48
1100-1200	1200	25
1200-1300	1300	10
1300-1400	1400	3
1400-1500	1500	4

STEP 1: Data   Manually enter your data, paste from another application, or load an example dataset with analysis   Example   Visualize

N	VAR39	VAR40	VAR41	VAR42	VAR43	VAR=4	VAR45	VAR46	VAR47	VAR48	VAR49	VAR50	VAR51	VAR!
NOTES	Upper Limit	Frequency												
1	800.00	36.00												
2	900.00	96.00												
3	1000.00	78.00												
4	1100.00	48.00												
5	1200.00	25.00												
6	1300.00	10.00												
7	1400.00	3.00												
8	1500.00	4.00												
9														

Figure 147.13: Data requirements for the chi-square goodness-of-fit test

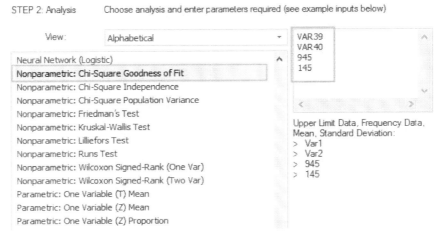

STEP 2: Analysis   Choose analysis and enter parameters required (see example inputs below)

View: Alphabetical

VAR39
VAR40
945
145

Neural Network (Logistic)
Nonparametric: Chi-Square Goodness of Fit
Nonparametric: Chi-Square Independence
Nonparametric: Chi-Square Population Variance
Nonparametric: Friedman's Test
Nonparametric: Kruskal-Wallis Test
Nonparametric: Lilliefors Test
Nonparametric: Runs Test
Nonparametric: Wilcoxon Signed-Rank (One Var)
Nonparametric: Wilcoxon Signed-Rank (Two Var)
Parametric: One Variable (T) Mean
Parametric: One Variable (Z) Mean
Parametric: One Variable (Z) Proportion

Upper Limit Data, Frequency Data, Mean, Standard Deviation:
> Var1
> Var2
> 945
> 145

Figure 147.14: Running a chi-square goodnes of fit test

```
Chi Square Goodness of Fit
Mean : 945.000000
Standard Deviation : 145.000000
Chi-Square Stat : 23.711983
Chi-Square Critical 1% : 11.344867
Chi-Square Critical 5% : 7.814728
Chi-Square Critical 10% : 6.251389
Calculated p-Value : 0.000029

Expected Frequencies
          47.596576
          65.848236
          80.886575
          62.905832
          30.966488
          11.796293
           2.153126
           0.255217
```

Figure 147.14: Running a chi-square goodnes of fit test *(continued)*

Chi-Square Test of Independence

The Chi-Square test for independence examines two variables to see if there is some statistical relationship between them. This test is not used to find the exact nature of the relationship between the two variables but simply to test if the variables could be independent of each other. The null hypothesis tested is such that the variables are independent of each other, versus the alternate hypothesis that the variables are not independent of each other. The Chi-Square test looks at a table of observed frequencies and a table of expected frequencies. The amount of disparity between these two tables is calculated and compared with the Chi-Square test statistic. The observed frequencies reflect the cross-classification for members of a single sample, and the table of expected frequencies is constructed under the assumption that the null hypothesis is true.

Data Requirements

For the **Chi-Square Test of Independence**, create data tables such as the one in Figure 147.15, and select the data area (blue area) two variables at a time. To extend the dataset, just add more observations (rows) as seen in Figure 147.15.

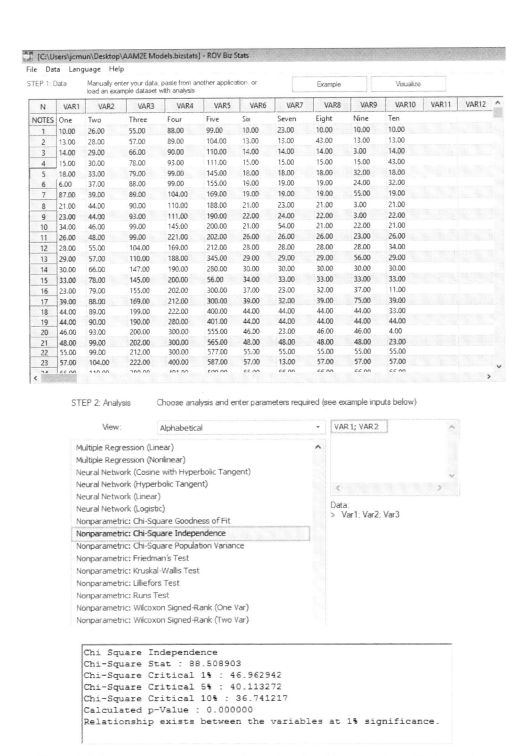

Figure 147.15: Data requirements and running the chi-square test of independence

Chi-Square Population Variance Test

The Chi-Square test for population variance is used for hypothesis testing and confidence interval estimation for a population variance. The population variance of a sample is typically unknown; hence, the need for quantifying this confidence interval. The population is assumed to be normally distributed. See the Excel model for details of this test.

Friedman's Test

The Friedman test is a form of nonparametric test that makes no assumptions about the specific shape of the population from which the sample is drawn, allowing for smaller sample datasets to be analyzed. This method is the extension of the Wilcoxon Signed Rank test for paired samples. The corresponding parametric test is the Randomized Block Multiple Treatment ANOVA, but unlike the ANOVA, the Friedman test does not require that the dataset be randomly sampled from normally distributed populations with equal variances. See later sections of this chapter for details of these tests.

The Friedman test uses a two-tailed hypothesis test where the null hypothesis is such that the population *medians* of each treatment are statistically identical to the rest of the group. That is, there is no effect on the treatment among the different groups. The alternative hypothesis is such that the real population *medians* are statistically different from one another when tested using the sample dataset. That is, the medians are statistically different, which means that there is a statistically significant effect among the different treatment groups. If the calculated p-value is less than or equal to the alpha significance value, then reject the null hypothesis and accept the alternate hypothesis. Otherwise, if the p-value is higher than the alpha significance value, do not reject the null hypothesis.

Data Requirements

For the **Friedman's Test**, create data tables such as the one shown in Figure 147.16, and select the data area. If selecting the headers, remember to select "Treat first row as headers." To extend the dataset, just add more observations (rows). See Figure 147.16.

STEP 1: Data		Manually enter your data, paste from another application, or load an example dataset with analysis				Example		Visualize		

N	VAR35	VAR36	VAR37	VAR38	VAR39	VAR40	VAR41	VAR42	VAR43	VAR44	^
NOTES	TREATMENT AAA	TREATMENT BBB	TREATMENT CCC	TREATMENT DDD							
1	90.00	87.00	93.00	85.00							
2	86.00	79.00	87.00	83.00							
3	76.00	77.00	91.00	85.00							
4	75.00	78.00	92.00	83.00							
5	79.00	79.00	89.00	82.00							
6	68.00	75.00	88.00	83.00							
7	69.00	74.00	87.00	84.00							
8	68.00	76.00	82.00	81.00							
9	59.00	72.00	91.00	81.00							
10	62.00	71.00	90.00	80.00							
11											

Figure 147.16: Data requirements and running the Friedman test for randomized block design

STEP 2: Analysis   Choose analysis and enter parameters required (see example inputs below)

View: Alphabetical

VAR35;VAR36;VAR37;VAR38

Lag
Lead
Linear Interpolation
LN
Log
Logistic S Curve
Markov Chain
Markov Chain Transition Risk Matrix
Max
Median
Min
Mode
Multiple Regression (Linear)
Multiple Regression (Nonlinear)
Neural Network (Cosine with Hyperbolic Tangent)
Neural Network (Hyperbolic Tangent)
Neural Network (Linear)
Neural Network (Logistic)
Nonparametric: Chi-Square Goodness of Fit
Nonparametric: Chi-Square Independence
Nonparametric: Chi-Square Population Variance
Nonparametric: Friedman's Test
Nonparametric: Kruskal-Wallis Test
Nonparametric: Lilliefors Test
Nonparametric: Runs Test
Nonparametric: Wilcoxon Signed-Rank (One Var)
Nonparametric: Wilcoxon Signed-Rank (Two Var)

Data:
> Var1; Var2; Var3

```
Friedman's Test
Friedman Statistic : 22.890000
p-Value : 0.000043
Chi-Square Critical 1% : 11.344867
Chi-Square Critical 5% : 7.814728
Chi-Square Critical 10% : 6.251389
The population medians are statistically not equal at 1%, 5%, or 10% significance.
Rank Sum :   14.500000  18.500000  40.000000  27.000000
```

Figure 147.16: Data requirements and running the Friedman test for randomized block design *(continued)*

Kruskal-Wallis Test

The Kruskal-Wallis test is a form of nonparametric test that makes no assumptions about the specific shape of the population from which the sample is drawn, allowing for smaller sample datasets to be analyzed. This method is the extension of the Wilcoxon Signed Rank test for paired samples that compares the statistical properties of more than two independent samples. The corresponding parametric test is the One-Way ANOVA, but unlike the ANOVA, the Kruskal-Wallis test does not require that the dataset be randomly sampled from normally distributed populations with equal variances. The Kruskal-Wallis test is a two-tailed hypothesis test where the null hypothesis is such that the population medians of each treatment are statistically identical to the rest of the group. That is, there are no different effects among the different treatment groups. The alternative hypothesis is such that the real population medians are statistically different from one another when tested using the sample dataset. That is, the medians are statistically different, which means that there is a statistically significant effect among the different treatment groups. If the calculated p-value is less than or equal to the alpha significance value, reject the null hypothesis and accept the alternate hypothesis. Otherwise, if the p-value is higher than the alpha significance value, do not reject the null hypothesis.

The benefit of the Kruskal-Wallis Test is that it can be applied to ordinal, interval, and ratio data; ANOVA, however, is applicable only for interval and ratio data. Also, the Kruskal-Wallis test can be run with fewer data points.

To illustrate, suppose that three different drug indications ($T = 3$) were developed and tested on 100 patients each ($N = 100$). The Kruskal-Wallis Test can be applied to test if these three drugs are all equally effective statistically. If the calculated p-value is less than or equal to the significance level used in the test, reject the null hypothesis and conclude that there is a significant difference among the different treatments. Otherwise, the treatments are all equally effective.

Data Requirements

For the **Kruskal-Wallis Test**, create data tables such as the one in Figure 115.17, and select the data area. To extend the dataset, just add more observations (rows) or more treatment variables to compare (columns). If selecting the variable names, remember to select "Treat first row as headers."

STEP 1. Data	Manually enter your data, paste from another application, or load an example dataset with analysis			Example			Visualize			
N	VAR35	VAR36	VAR37	VAR38	VAR39	VAR40	VAR41	VAR42	VAR43	VAR44
NOTES	TREATMENT AAA	TREATMENT BBB	TREATMENT CCC	TREATMENT DDD						
1	90.00	87.00	93.00	85.00						
2	86.00	79.00	87.00	83.00						
3	76.00	77.00	91.00	85.00						
4	75.00	78.00	92.00	83.00						
5	79.00	79.00	89.00	82.00						
6	68.00	75.00	88.00	83.00						
7	69.00	74.00	87.00	84.00						
8	68.00	76.00	82.00	81.00						
9	59.00	72.00	91.00	81.00						
10	62.00	71.00	90.00	80.00						
11										

Figure 147.17: Data requirements and running the Kruskal-Wallis test for a nonparametric one-way ANOVA equivalence

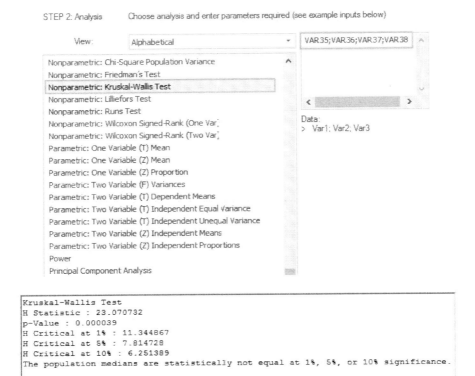

Figure 147.17: Data requirements and running the Kruskal-Wallis test for a nonparametric one-way ANOVA equivalence *(continued)*

Lilliefors Test

The Lilliefors test is a form of nonparametric test that makes no assumptions about the specific shape of the population from which the sample is drawn, allowing for smaller sample datasets to be analyzed. This test evaluates the null hypothesis of whether the data sample was drawn from a normally distributed population versus an alternate hypothesis that the data sample is not normally distributed. If the calculated p-value is less than or equal to the alpha significance value, reject the null hypothesis and accept the alternate hypothesis. Otherwise, if the p-value is higher than the alpha significance value, do not reject the null hypothesis. This test relies on two cumulative frequencies: one derived from the sample dataset, the second derived from a theoretical distribution based on the mean and standard deviation of the sample data. An alternative to this test is the Chi-Square test for normality, which requires more data points to run than the Lilliefors test.

Data Requirements

For the **Lilliefors Test for Normality**, create data tables such as the one shown in Figure 147.18, and select the data area *one variable* at a time. To extend the dataset, just add more observations (rows).

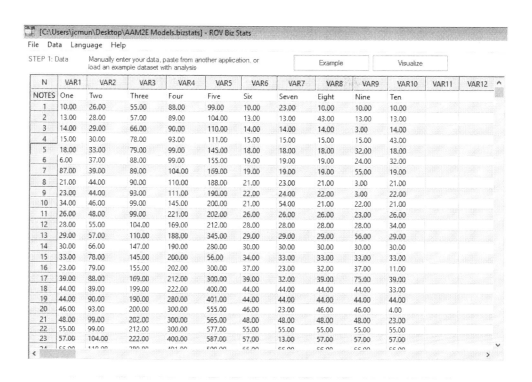

File   Data   Language   Help

STEP 1: Data   Manually enter your data, paste from another application, or load an example dataset with analysis

Example   Visualize

N	VAR1	VAR2	VAR3	VAR4	VAR5	VAR6	VAR7	VAR8	VAR9	VAR10	VAR11	VAR12
NOTES	One	Two	Three	Four	Five	Six	Seven	Eight	Nine	Ten		
1	10.00	26.00	55.00	88.00	99.00	10.00	23.00	10.00	10.00	10.00		
2	13.00	28.00	57.00	89.00	104.00	13.00	13.00	43.00	13.00	13.00		
3	14.00	29.00	66.00	90.00	110.00	14.00	14.00	14.00	3.00	14.00		
4	15.00	30.00	78.00	93.00	111.00	15.00	15.00	15.00	15.00	43.00		
5	18.00	33.00	79.00	99.00	145.00	18.00	18.00	18.00	32.00	18.00		
6	6.00	37.00	88.00	99.00	155.00	19.00	19.00	19.00	24.00	32.00		
7	87.00	39.00	89.00	104.00	169.00	19.00	19.00	19.00	55.00	19.00		
8	21.00	44.00	90.00	110.00	188.00	21.00	23.00	21.00	3.00	21.00		
9	23.00	44.00	93.00	111.00	190.00	22.00	24.00	22.00	3.00	22.00		
10	34.00	46.00	99.00	145.00	200.00	21.00	54.00	21.00	22.00	21.00		
11	26.00	48.00	99.00	221.00	202.00	26.00	26.00	26.00	23.00	26.00		
12	28.00	55.00	104.00	169.00	212.00	28.00	28.00	28.00	28.00	34.00		
13	29.00	57.00	110.00	188.00	345.00	29.00	29.00	29.00	56.00	29.00		
14	30.00	66.00	147.00	190.00	280.00	30.00	30.00	30.00	30.00	30.00		
15	33.00	78.00	145.00	200.00	56.00	34.00	33.00	33.00	33.00	33.00		
16	23.00	79.00	155.00	202.00	300.00	37.00	23.00	32.00	37.00	11.00		
17	39.00	88.00	169.00	212.00	300.00	39.00	32.00	39.00	75.00	39.00		
18	44.00	89.00	199.00	222.00	400.00	44.00	44.00	44.00	44.00	33.00		
19	44.00	90.00	190.00	280.00	401.00	44.00	44.00	44.00	44.00	44.00		
20	46.00	93.00	200.00	300.00	555.00	46.00	23.00	46.00	46.00	4.00		
21	48.00	99.00	202.00	300.00	565.00	48.00	48.00	48.00	48.00	23.00		
22	55.00	99.00	212.00	300.00	577.00	55.00	55.00	55.00	55.00	55.00		
23	57.00	104.00	222.00	400.00	587.00	57.00	13.00	57.00	57.00	57.00		
24	55.00	110.00	200.00	401.00	500.00	55.00	55.00	55.00	55.00	55.00		

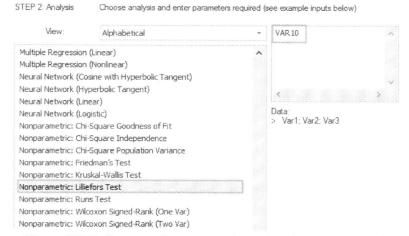

STEP 2: Analysis   Choose analysis and enter parameters required (see example inputs below)

View: Alphabetical   ▾   VAR 10

Multiple Regression (Linear)
Multiple Regression (Nonlinear)
Neural Network (Cosine with Hyperbolic Tangent)
Neural Network (Hyperbolic Tangent)
Neural Network (Linear)
Neural Network (Logistic)
Nonparametric: Chi-Square Goodness of Fit
Nonparametric: Chi-Square Independence
Nonparametric: Chi-Square Population Variance
Nonparametric: Friedman's Test
Nonparametric: Kruskal-Wallis Test
Nonparametric: Lilliefors Test
Nonparametric: Runs Test
Nonparametric: Wilcoxon Signed-Rank (One Var)
Nonparametric: Wilcoxon Signed-Rank (Two Var)

Data:
> Var1; Var2; Var3

Figure 147.18: Data requirements and running the nonparametric Lilliefors test for normality

```
Lilliefors Test
Average : 32.964286
Stdev : 17.639354
D Statistic : 0.119446
D Critical at 1% : 0.158000
D Critical at 5% : 0.173000
D Critical at 10% : 0.200000
The sequence is normally distributed at 1% significance.

           Data    Relative Frequency        Observed        Expected
       4.000000              0.035714        0.035714        0.050292
      10.000000              0.035714        0.071429        0.096479
      11.000000              0.035714        0.107143        0.106532
      13.000000              0.035714        0.142857        0.128858
      14.000000              0.035714        0.178571        0.141162
      18.000000              0.035714        0.214286        0.198122
      19.000000              0.035714        0.250000        0.214281
      21.000000              0.071429        0.321429        0.248800
      22.000000              0.035714        0.357143        0.267109
      23.000000              0.035714        0.392857        0.286074
      26.000000              0.035714        0.428571        0.346490
      29.000000              0.035714        0.464286        0.411090
      30.000000              0.035714        0.500000        0.433272
      32.000000              0.035714        0.535714        0.478202
```

Figure 147.18: Data requirements and running the nonparametric
Lilliefors test for normality *(continued)*

Runs Test

The Runs test is a form of nonparametric test that makes no assumptions about the specific shape of the population from which the sample is drawn, allowing for smaller sample datasets to be analyzed. This test evaluates the randomness of a series of observations by analyzing the number of runs it contains. A run is a consecutive appearance of one or more observations that are similar. The null hypothesis tested is whether the data sequence is random versus the alternate hypothesis that the data sequence is not random. If the calculated p-value is less than or equal to the alpha significance value, reject the null hypothesis and accept the alternate hypothesis. Otherwise, if the p-value is higher than the alpha significance value, do not reject the null hypothesis.

Data Requirements

For the **Runs Test for Randomness**, create data tables such as the one shown in Figure 147.19, and select the data area *multiple variables* at a time. To extend the dataset, just add more observations (rows) and variables (columns).

File   Data   Language   Help

STEP 1: Data   Manually enter your data, paste from another application, or load an example dataset with analysis

| Example | Visualize |

N	VAR1	VAR2	VAR3	VAR4	VAR5	VAR6	VAR7	VAR8	VAR9	VAR10	VAR11	VAR12
NOTES	One	Two	Three	Four	Five	Six	Seven	Eight	Nine	Ten		
1	10.00	26.00	55.00	88.00	99.00	10.00	23.00	10.00	10.00	10.00		
2	13.00	28.00	57.00	89.00	104.00	13.00	13.00	43.00	13.00	13.00		
3	14.00	29.00	66.00	90.00	110.00	14.00	14.00	14.00	3.00	14.00		
4	15.00	30.00	78.00	93.00	111.00	15.00	15.00	15.00	15.00	43.00		
5	18.00	33.00	79.00	99.00	145.00	18.00	18.00	18.00	32.00	18.00		
6	6.00	37.00	88.00	99.00	155.00	19.00	19.00	19.00	24.00	32.00		
7	87.00	39.00	89.00	104.00	169.00	19.00	19.00	19.00	55.00	19.00		
8	21.00	44.00	90.00	110.00	188.00	21.00	23.00	21.00	3.00	21.00		
9	23.00	44.00	93.00	111.00	190.00	22.00	24.00	22.00	3.00	22.00		
10	34.00	46.00	99.00	145.00	200.00	21.00	54.00	21.00	22.00	21.00		
11	26.00	48.00	99.00	221.00	202.00	26.00	26.00	26.00	23.00	26.00		
12	28.00	55.00	104.00	169.00	212.00	28.00	28.00	28.00	28.00	34.00		
13	29.00	57.00	110.00	188.00	345.00	29.00	29.00	29.00	56.00	29.00		
14	30.00	66.00	147.00	190.00	280.00	30.00	30.00	30.00	30.00	30.00		
15	33.00	78.00	145.00	200.00	56.00	34.00	33.00	33.00	33.00	33.00		
16	23.00	79.00	155.00	202.00	300.00	37.00	23.00	32.00	37.00	11.00		
17	39.00	88.00	169.00	212.00	300.00	39.00	32.00	39.00	75.00	39.00		
18	44.00	89.00	199.00	222.00	400.00	44.00	44.00	44.00	44.00	33.00		
19	44.00	90.00	190.00	280.00	401.00	44.00	44.00	44.00	44.00	44.00		
20	46.00	93.00	200.00	300.00	555.00	46.00	23.00	46.00	46.00	4.00		
21	48.00	99.00	202.00	300.00	565.00	48.00	48.00	48.00	48.00	23.00		
22	55.00	99.00	212.00	300.00	577.00	55.00	55.00	55.00	55.00	55.00		
23	57.00	104.00	222.00	400.00	587.00	57.00	13.00	57.00	57.00	57.00		
24	55.00	110.00	200.00	401.00	500.00	55.00	55.00	55.00	55.00	55.00		

Figure 147.19: Data requirements for the nonparametric Runs test for randomness

Wilcoxon Signed-Rank Test (One Variable)

The single variable Wilcoxon Signed Rank test is a form of nonparametric test that makes no assumptions about the specific shape of the population from which the sample is drawn, allowing for smaller sample datasets to be analyzed. This method looks at whether a sample dataset could have been randomly drawn from a particular population whose median is being hypothesized. The corresponding parametric test is the one-sample t-test, which should be used if the underlying population is assumed to be normal, providing a higher statistical power on the test. The Wilcoxon Signed Rank test can be applied to three types of hypothesis tests: a two-tailed test, a right-tailed test, and a left-tailed test. If the calculated Wilcoxon statistic is outside the critical limits for the specific significance level in the test, reject the null hypothesis and conclude that the true population median is not equal to (two-tail test), less than (left-tail test), or greater than (right-tail test) the hypothesized median based on the sample tested. Otherwise, the true population median is statistically similar to the hypothesized median.

For data requirements, see One-Variable Testing for Means (T-Test).

Wilcoxon Signed-Rank Test (Two Variables)

The Wilcoxon Signed Rank test for paired variables is a form of nonparametric test that makes no assumptions about the specific shape of the population from which the sample is drawn, allowing for smaller sample datasets to be analyzed. This method looks at whether the median of the differences between the two paired variables is equal. This test is specifically formulated for testing the same or similar samples before and after an event (e.g., measurements taken before a medical treatment are compared against those measurements taken after the treatment to see if there is a difference). The corresponding parametric test is the two-sample t-test with dependent means, which should be used if the underlying population is assumed to be normal, providing a higher statistical power on the test. The Wilcoxon Signed Rank test can be applied to three types of hypothesis tests: a two-tailed test, a right-tailed test, and a left-tailed test.

To illustrate, suppose that a new engine design is tested against an existing engine design to see if there is a statistically significant difference between the two. The Paired Variable Wilcoxon Signed-Rank Test can be applied. If the calculated Wilcoxon statistic is outside the critical limits for the specific significance level in the test, reject the null hypothesis and conclude that the difference between the true population medians is not equal to (two-tail test), less than (left-tail test), or greater than (right-tail test) the hypothesized median difference based on the sample tested. Otherwise, the true population median is statistically similar to the hypothesized median.

For data requirements, see Two Dependent Variables Testing for Means (Z-Test).

Single-Factor Multiple Treatments ANOVA

The One-Way ANOVA for Single Factor with Multiple Treatments is an extension of the two-variable t-test, looking at multiple variables simultaneously. The ANOVA is appropriate when the sampling distribution is assumed to be approximately normal. ANOVA can be applied only to the two-tailed hypothesis test. A two-tailed hypothesis tests the null hypothesis such that the population means of each treatment are statistically identical to the rest of the group, which means that there is no effect among the different treatment groups. The alternative hypothesis is such that the real population means are statistically different from one another when tested using the sample dataset.

To illustrate, suppose that three different drug indications ($T = 3$) were developed and tested on 100 patients each ($N = 100$). The One-Way ANOVA can be applied to test if these three drugs are all equally effective statistically. If the calculated p-value is less than or equal to the significance level used in the test, reject the null hypothesis and conclude that there is a significant difference among the different treatments. Otherwise, the treatments are all equally effective.

Data Requirements

For the *One-Way ANOVA* module, create tables such as the one in Figure 147.20, and select the data area. You can extend the data by adding rows of observations and columns of treatments.

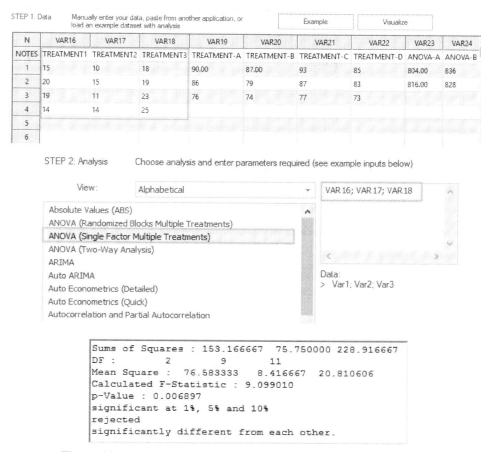

Figure 147.20: Data requirements and running a one-way ANOVA

Randomized Block Multiple Treatments ANOVA

The One-Way Randomized Block ANOVA is appropriate when the sampling distribution is assumed to be approximately normal and when there exists a Block variable for which ANOVA will Control (block the effects of this variable by controlling it in the experiment). ANOVA can be applied only to the two-tailed hypothesis test. This analysis can test for the effects of the treatments as well as the effectiveness of the control or block variable. If the calculated p-value for the treatment is less than or equal to the significance level used in the test, reject the null hypothesis and conclude that there is a significant difference among the different treatments. If the calculated p-value for the block variable is less than or equal to the significance level used in the test, reject the null hypothesis and conclude that there is a significant difference among the different block variables.

To illustrate, suppose that three different headlamp designs ($B = 3$) were developed and tested on four groups of volunteer drivers grouped by their age ($T = 4$). The One-Way Randomized Block ANOVA can be applied to test if these three headlamps are all equally effective statistically when tested using the volunteers' driving test grades. Otherwise, the treatments are all equally effective. This test can determine if the difference occur because of the treatment (that the type of headlamp will determine differences in driving test scores) or from the Block or controlled variable (that age may yield different driving abilities).

Data Requirements

For the *Randomized Block ANOVA* module, create tables such as the one in Figure 147.21, and select the data area. You can extend the data by adding rows of blocks and columns of treatments.

Randomized Block Design ANOVA

Blocks	Treatment 1	Treatment 2	Treatment 3	Treatment 4
1	90	87	93	85
2	86	79	87	83
3	76	74	77	73

STEP 1: Data — Manually enter your data, paste from another application, or load an example dataset with analysis [Example] [Visualize]

N	VAR19	VAR20	VAR21	VAR22	VAR23	VAR24	VAR25	VAR26	VAR27	VAR28
NOTES	TREATMENT-A	TREATMENT-B	TREATMENT-C	TREATMENT-D	ANOVA-A	ANOVA-B	ANOVA-C	ANOVA-D	ANOVA-E	ANOVA-F
1	90.00	87.00	93	85	804.00	836	804	819	844	807
2	86	79	87	83	816.00	828	808	813	836	819
3	76	74	77	73						
4										
5										
6										
7										

STEP 2: Analysis — Choose analysis and enter parameters required (see example inputs below)

View: [Alphabetical ▼]   [VAR19;VAR20;VAR21;VAR22]

Absolute Values (ABS)
ANOVA (Randomized Blocks Multiple Treatments)
ANOVA (Single Factor Multiple Treatments)
ANOVA (Two-Way Analysis)
ARIMA
Auto ARIMA
Auto Econometrics (Detailed)
Auto Econometrics (Quick)
Autocorrelation and Partial Autocorrelation

Data:
> Var1; Var2; Var3

```
Sums of Squares :   69.666667 -26851.416667 27254.750000 473.000000
DF :        3        6        2        11
Mean Square :   23.222222 -4475.236111 13627.375000  43.000000
Calculated F-Statistic :   -0.005189  -3.045063
p-Value :    0.999426   0.122225
not significant at any of the following significance levels: 1%, 5%, and 10%
not rejected
not significantly different from each other.
not significant at any of the following significance levels: 1%, 5%, and 10%
not rejected
not significantly affected by the Control or Block variable.
```

Figure 147.21: Data requirements and running a randomized block ANOVA

Two-Way ANOVA

The Two-Way ANOVA is an extension of the Single Factor and Randomized Block ANOVA by simultaneously examining the effects of two factors on the dependent variable, along with the effects of interactions between the different levels of these two factors. Unlike the randomized block design, this model examines the interactions between different levels of the factors, or independent variables. In a two-factor experiment, interaction exists when the effect of a level for one factor depends on which level of the other factor is present.

There are three sets of null and alternate hypotheses to be tested in the two-way analysis of variance.

The first test is on the first independent variable, where the null hypothesis is that no level of the first factor has an effect on the dependent variable. The alternate hypothesis is that there is at least one level of the first factor having an effect on the dependent variable. If the calculated p-value is less than or equal to the alpha significance value, reject the null hypothesis and accept the alternate hypothesis. Otherwise, if the p-value is higher than the alpha significance value, do not reject the null hypothesis.

The second test is on the second independent variable, where the null hypothesis is that no level of the second factor has an effect on the dependent variable. The alternate hypothesis is that there is at least one level of the second factor having an effect on the dependent variable. If the calculated p-value is less than or equal to the alpha significance value, reject the null hypothesis and accept the alternate hypothesis. Otherwise, if the p-value is higher than the alpha significance value, do not reject the null hypothesis.

The third test is on the interaction of both the first and second independent variables, where the null hypothesis is that there are no interacting effects between levels of the first and second factors. The alternate hypothesis is that there is at least one combination of levels of the first and second factors having an effect on the dependent variable. If the calculated p-value is less than or equal to the alpha significance value, reject the null hypothesis and accept the alternate hypothesis. Otherwise, if the p-value is higher than the alpha significance value, do not reject the null hypothesis.

Data Requirements

For the *Two-Way ANOVA* module, create tables such as the one in Figure 147.22, and select the data area. You can extend the data by adding rows of factors and columns of treatments. Note that the number of replications in the table is 2 (i.e., two rows of observations per Factor A type). Of course, you can increase the number of replications as required. The number of replications has to be consistent if you wish to extend the dataset.

Two-Way ANOVA

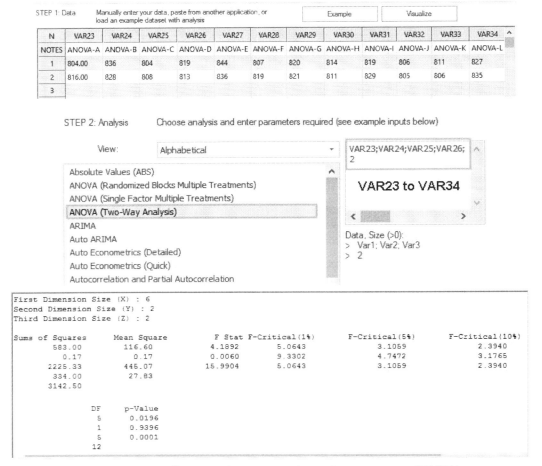

		Factor B		
		j =1	*j* =2	*j* =3
Factor A	*i* = 1	804 816	836 828	804 808
	i = 2	819 813	844 836	807 819
	i = 3	820 821	814 811	819 829
	i = 4	806 805	811 806	827 835

*For the Two-Way ANOVA, create tables such as the one above, and select the data area in blue (804 to 835). You can extend the data by adding rows of factors and columns of treatments. Note that the number of replications in the table above is 2 (i.e., two rows of observations per Factor A type. The number of replications has to be consistent if you wish to extend the data set.

STEP 1: Data   Manually enter your data, paste from another application, or load an example dataset with analysis   [Example]   [Visualize]

N	VAR23	VAR24	VAR25	VAR26	VAR27	VAR28	VAR29	VAR30	VAR31	VAR32	VAR33	VAR34
NOTES	ANOVA-A	ANOVA-B	ANOVA-C	ANOVA-D	ANOVA-E	ANOVA-F	ANOVA-G	ANOVA-H	ANOVA-I	ANOVA-J	ANOVA-K	ANOVA-L
1	804.00	836	804	819	844	807	820	814	819	806	811	827
2	816.00	828	808	813	836	819	821	811	829	805	806	835
3												

STEP 2: Analysis   Choose analysis and enter parameters required (see example inputs below)

View: [Alphabetical ▾]

VAR23;VAR24;VAR25;VAR26;
2

Absolute Values (ABS)
ANOVA (Randomized Blocks Multiple Treatments)
ANOVA (Single Factor Multiple Treatments)
ANOVA (Two-Way Analysis)
ARIMA
Auto ARIMA
Auto Econometrics (Detailed)
Auto Econometrics (Quick)
Autocorrelation and Partial Autocorrelation

VAR23 to VAR34

Data, Size (>0):
> Var1; Var2; Var3
> 2

```
First Dimension Size (X) : 6
Second Dimension Size (Y) : 2
Third Dimension Size (Z) : 2

Sums of Squares     Mean Square      F Stat F-Critical(1%)    F-Critical(5%)    F-Critical(10%)
      583.00          116.60         4.1892      5.0643           3.1059            2.3940
        0.17            0.17         0.0060      9.3302           4.7472            3.1765
     2225.33          445.07        15.9904      5.0643           3.1059            2.3940
      334.00           27.83
     3142.50

                DF      p-Value
                 5       0.0196
                 1       0.9396
                 5       0.0001
                12
```

Figure 147.22: Data requirements and running a two-way ANOVA

148. Six Sigma – Sample Size Determination and Design of Experiments

File Names: Six Sigma – Sample Size Correlation; Six Sigma – Sample Size DPU; Six Sigma – Sample Size Mean; Six Sigma – Sample Size Proportion; Six Sigma – Sample Size Sigma, Six Sigma – Delta Precision; Six Sigma – Design of Experiments and Combinatorics

Location: Modeling Toolkit | Six Sigma

Brief Description: Illustrate how to obtain the required sample size in performing hypotheses testing from means to standard deviations and proportions

Requirements: Modeling Toolkit, Risk Simulator

Modeling Toolkit Functions Used: MTSixSigmaSampleSize, MTSixSigmaSampleSizeProportion, MTSixSigmaSampleSizeZeroCorrelTest, MTSixSigmaSampleSizeDPU, MTSixSigmaSampleSizeStdev, MTSixSigmaDeltaPrecision

In performing quality controls and hypothesis testing, the size of the samples collected is of paramount importance. Theoretically, it would be impossible or too expensive and impractical to collect information and data on the entire population to be tested (e.g., all outputs from a large manufacturing facility). Therefore, statistical sampling is required. The question is: What size sample is sufficient? The size of a statistical sample is the number of repeated measurements that are collected. It is typically denoted n, a positive integer. Sample size determination is critical in Six Sigma and quality analysis as different sample sizes lead to different accuracies and precision of measurement. This can be seen in such statistical rules as the Law of Large Numbers and the Central Limit Theorem. With all else being equal, a larger sample size n leads to increased precision in estimates of various properties of the population. The question that always arises is: How many sample data points are required? The answer is: it depends. It depends on the error tolerances and precision required in the analysis. This model is used to compute the minimum required sample size given the required error, precision, and variance levels.

There are five different sample size determination models in the Modeling Toolkit. The first model (*Six Sigma – Sample Size Mean*) computes the minimum required sample size for a hypothesis test (one- or two-tailed test), where the required errors and precisions are stated, as is the sample standard deviation (Figure 148.1). Alpha Error is the Type I error, also known as the significance level in a hypothesis test. It measures the probability of not having the true population mean included in the confidence interval of the sample. That is, it computes the probability of rejecting a true hypothesis. *1 – Alpha* is, of course, the confidence interval, or the probability that the true population mean resides in the sample confidence interval. Beta Error is the Type II error, or the probability of accepting a false hypothesis or of not being able to detect the mean's changes. *1 – Beta* is the power of the test. Delta Precision is the accuracy or precision with which the standard deviation may be estimated. For instance, a 0.10% Delta with 5% Alpha for two tails means that the estimated mean is plus or minus 0.10%, at a 90% (*1 – 2 ×Alpha*) confidence level. Finally, the Sigma Sample is the sample standard deviation of the dataset.

SAMPLE SIZE REQUIREMENTS (MEAN)

Input Assumptions

Alpha Error	10.00%
Beta Error	5.00%
Delta Precision	3.00%
Sigma Sample	0.15
One or Two-Tail Test	2

Required Sample Size   273

Figure 148.1: Sample size determination model for the mean

The remaining models are very similar in that they determine the appropriate sample size to test the standard deviation or sigma levels given some Alpha and Beta levels (*Six Sigma – Sample Size Sigma*), testing proportions (*Six Sigma – Sample Size Proportion*), or defect per unit (*Six Sigma – Sample Size DPU*). In addition, the *Six Sigma – Sample Size Correlation* model is used to determine the minimum required sample size to perform a hypothesis test on correlations. Finally, the *Six Sigma – Delta Precision* model works backwards in that given some Alpha and Beta errors and a given sample size, the Delta precision level is computed instead.

Design of Experiments (DOE) and Combinatorics

Another issue related to sampling and testing or experimentation is that of generating the relevant combinations and permutations of experimental samples to test. Let us say you have five different projects and need to decide all the combinations of projects that can occur. For instance, the value 00000 means no projects are chosen; or 10000, where project 1 is chosen and no others; or 010000 where project 2 is chosen and no others; and so forth. This result can also include multiple projects such as 10101 where projects 1, 3, and 5 are chosen. Clearly, if the portfolio has more projects, the combinations can become rather intractable. This is where combinatorial math comes in. We use Excel to determine the combinatorials.

Procedure

1.   Start Excel's Analysis Toolpak (**Tools | Add-Ins | Analysis Toolpak**).

2.   Go to the *Combinatorics* model and view the examples.

The example shown illustrates how to convert a five-project or five-asset portfolio into all the possible combinations by using the *DEC2BIN* function in Excel. The *DEC2BIN* function stands for decimal to binary function. Specifically, it takes the value of a decimal or number and converts it into the relevant binary structure of 0s and 1s.

For instance, if there are five projects in a portfolio, then there are 32 combinations or 2^5 combinations. As binary coding starts from 0, we can number these outcomes from 0, 1, 2, all the way to 31 (providing 32 possible outcomes). We then convert these to a five-digit binary sequence using the function *DEC2BIN(0,5),* which yields 00000. As another example, *DEC2BIN(10,5)* yields 01010, and so forth. By creating this combinatorial matrix, we see all the possible combinations for five projects. We can then pick out the ones required. For example, say we need to select two out of five projects, and need all the possible combinations. We know that there are 10 combinations, and by using the example model, we can determine exactly what they are. Figure 148.2 shows an example.

Using this approach, we can add in Risk Simulator to randomly select the projects and cycle through all possible combinations of projects that can be executed in time. As an example, say you have five projects in a portfolio and you would like to randomly choose three projects to execute in a sequence of three years. In each year you cannot execute more than three projects, and no project can repeat itself. In addition, you wish to run all possible combinations of possibilities. Such an example is also included in the model and is self-explanatory.

Design of Experiments and Combinatorics

Combinatorial Matrix for 5 Projects		Decomposed					Total	Feasible	Feasible	Feasible
Value	Combinations	1	2	3	4	5		5 Choose 4	5 Choose 3	5 Choose 2
0	00000	0	0	0	0	0	0	0	0	0
1	00001	0	0	0	0	1	1	0	0	0
2	00010	0	0	0	1	0	1	0	0	0
3	00011	0	0	0	1	1	2	0	0	1
4	00100	0	0	1	0	0	1	0	0	0
5	00101	0	0	1	0	1	2	0	0	1
6	00110	0	0	1	1	0	2	0	0	1
7	00111	0	0	1	1	1	3	0	1	0
8	01000	0	1	0	0	0	1	0	0	0
9	01001	0	1	0	0	1	2	0	0	1
10	01010	0	1	0	1	0	2	0	0	1
11	01011	0	1	0	1	1	3	0	1	0
12	01100	0	1	1	0	0	2	0	0	1
13	01101	0	1	1	0	1	3	0	1	0
14	01110	0	1	1	1	0	3	0	1	0
15	01111	0	1	1	1	1	4	1	0	0
16	10000	1	0	0	0	0	1	0	0	0
17	10001	1	0	0	0	1	2	0	0	1
18	10010	1	0	0	1	0	2	0	0	1
19	10011	1	0	0	1	1	3	0	1	0
20	10100	1	0	1	0	0	2	0	0	1
21	10101	1	0	1	0	1	3	0	1	0
22	10110	1	0	1	1	0	3	0	1	0
23	10111	1	0	1	1	1	4	1	0	0
24	11000	1	1	0	0	0	2	0	0	1
25	11001	1	1	0	0	1	3	0	1	0
26	11010	1	1	0	1	0	3	0	1	0
27	11011	1	1	0	1	1	4	1	0	0
28	11100	1	1	1	0	0	3	0	1	0
29	11101	1	1	1	0	1	4	1	0	0
30	11110	1	1	1	1	0	4	1	0	0
31	11111	1	1	1	1	1	5	0	0	0
							SUM	5	10	10

Figure 148.2: Combinatorics results

149. Six Sigma – Statistical and Unit Capability Measures, Specification Levels, and Control Charts

File Names: Six Sigma – Statistical Capability; Six Sigma – Unit Capability; Six Sigma – Control Charts

Location: Modeling Toolkit | Six Sigma

Brief Description: Illustrate how to obtain the various capability measures such as the capability index (Cpk and Cp), yields, defects per million opportunities (DPMO), and others

Requirements: Modeling Toolkit, Risk Simulator

Modeling Toolkit Functions Used: MTSixSigmaStatCP, MTSixSigmaStatCPK, MTSixSigmaStatDPU, MTSixSigmaStatDPMO, MTSixSigmaStatProcessSigma, MTSixSigmaUnitDPU, MTSixSigmaUnitDPMO, MTSixSigmaUnitYield, MTSixSigmaUnitCPK, MTSixSigmaUnitProcessSigma

Capability Measures (Cp and Cpk) and
Specification Levels (USL and LSL)

Capability measures in Six Sigma are the central analytics in quality control. Defective Proportion Units (DPUs) are the number of defects observed with respect to the total opportunities or outcomes, and can be measured with respect to a million opportunities (defective parts per million, DPPM, or also known as the defects per million opportunities, DPMO). The Process Capability Index or Cpk takes into account the off-centered distribution and analyzes it as a centered process producing a similar level of defects (defined as the ratio between permissible deviation, measured from the mean value to the nearest specific limit of acceptability, and the actual one-sided 3-sigma spread of the process). Simplistically, it measures how many times you can fit three standard deviations of the process between the mean of the process and the nearest specification limit. Assuming that the process is stable and predictable, if you can do this once, Cpk is 1, and your process probably needs attention. If you can do it 1.5 times, your process is excellent, and you are on the path to being able to discontinue final inspection. If you can do it twice, you have an outstanding process. If Cpk is negative, the process mean is outside the specification limits. Cpk of at least 1.33 is desired. Finally, the sigma of the process is determined. Typically, this process sigma value can be used to compare before and after effects of some quality improvement program, or to see if the process is up to par in terms of a target sigma level.

This statistical capability model uses as inputs the statistical properties of the process, including the observed mean and standard deviation (sigma), as well as predefined lower and upper specification limits (LSLs and USLs). In contrast, the *Unit Capability* model computes some of the same capability measures but uses the actual number of defects and population size. In addition, the Cp index is computed, which relates to the potential of the process to meet specification, regardless of where the process distribution falls. The process may not be performing within specifications, but the index tells you how the process will perform if you can shift the distribution mean to the desired target (without changing the distribution). If we have a Cp of 2.0, it has the potential to be a Six Sigma process. In contrast, Cpk actually compares the distribution of the data to the specification limits to determine its actual performance. If we have a Cpk of 2.0, you have a Six Sigma process. As discussed, a Cpk of at least 1.33 is desired, and 1.5 is excellent. See Figure 149.1.

STATISTICAL CAPABILITY

Input Assumptions

Mean	2.2500
Sigma	0.0500
USL	2.8000
LSL	2.2000

Process Capability C_P	2.0000
Process Capability $C_{PK} P_{PK}$	0.3333
Defective Proportion Units (DPU)	0.1587
Defective Per Million Opportunities (DPMO)	158655.260
Output Yield (%)	84.1345%
Process Sigma	2.5000

Figure 149.1: Six Sigma capability modeling

Quality Control Charts

Sometimes the specification limits are not set; instead, statistical control limits are computed based on the actual data collected (e.g., the number of defects in a manufacturing line). For instance, in Figure 149.2, we see 20 sample experiments or samples taken at various times of a manufacturing process. The number of samples taken varied over time, and the number of defective parts were also gathered. The upper control limit (UCL) and lower control limit (LCL) are computed, as are the central line (CL) and other sigma levels. The resulting chart is called a control chart, and if the process if out of control, the actual defect line will be outside of the UCL and LCL lines. Typically, when the LCL is a negative value, we set the floor as zero, as illustrated in Figure 149.2.

Subgroup	Defective Units	Sample Size	Defect Proportion	LCL	CL	UCL
1	5	25	20.00%	0.00%	24.76%	53.71%
2	3	23	13.04%	0.00%	24.76%	53.71%
3	4	19	21.05%	0.00%	24.76%	53.71%
4	2	18	11.11%	0.00%	24.76%	53.71%
5	6	19	31.58%	0.00%	24.76%	53.71%
6	12	20	60.00%	0.00%	24.76%	53.71%
7	5	17	29.41%	0.00%	24.76%	53.71%
8	6	25	24.00%	0.00%	24.76%	53.71%
9	4	26	15.38%	0.00%	24.76%	53.71%
10	3	24	12.50%	0.00%	24.76%	53.71%
11	5	21	23.81%	0.00%	24.76%	53.71%
12	4	26	15.38%	0.00%	24.76%	53.71%
13	5	25	20.00%	0.00%	24.76%	53.71%
14	1	19	5.26%	0.00%	24.76%	53.71%
15	11	20	55.00%	0.00%	24.76%	53.71%
16	5	19	26.32%	0.00%	24.76%	53.71%
17	6	18	33.33%	0.00%	24.76%	53.71%
18	6	18	33.33%	0.00%	24.76%	53.71%
19	4	16	25.00%	0.00%	24.76%	53.71%
20	5	14	35.71%	0.00%	24.76%	53.71%

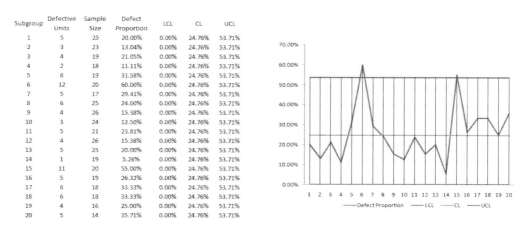

Figure 149.2: Example quality control p-chart

In the interpretation of a control chart, by adding in the $+/-1$ and 2 sigma lines, we can divide the control charts into several areas or zones, as illustrated in Figure 149.3. The following are rules of thumb that typically apply to control charts to determine if the process is out of control:

- If one point is beyond Area A
- If two out of three consecutive points are in Area A or beyond
- If four out of five consecutive points are in Area B or beyond
- If eight consecutive points are in Area C or beyond

Additionally, a potential structural shift can be detected if any one of the following occurs:

- At least 10 out of 11 sequential points are on one side of the CL
- At least 12 out of 14 sequential points are on one side of the CL
- At least 14 out of 17 sequential points are on one side of the CL
- At least 16 out of 20 sequential points are on one side of the CL

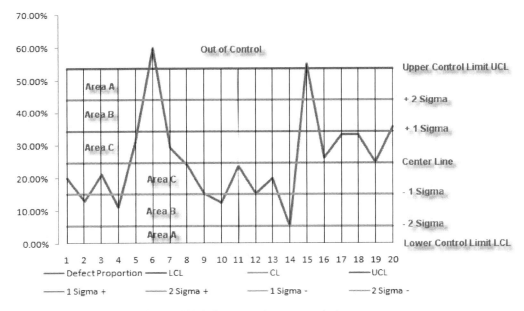

Figure 149.3: Interpreting control charts

The Modeling Toolkit presents several control chart types, and each type is used under different circumstances:

- $\overline{X}$ chart: used when the variable has raw data values and there are multiple measurements in a sample experiment, and multiple experiments are run, and the average of the collected data is of interest.

- $\overline{R}$ chart: used when the variable has raw data values and there are multiple measurements in a sample experiment, and multiple experiments are run, and the range of the collected data is of interest.

- *XmR* chart: used when the variable has raw data values and is a single measurement taken in each sample experiment, and multiple experiments are run, and the actual value of the collected data is of interest.

- *P*-chart: used when the variable of interest is an attribute (e.g., defective or non-defective) and the data collected are in proportions of defects (or number of defects in a specific sample) and there are multiple measurements in a sample experiment, and multiple experiments are run, and the average proportion of defects of the collected data is of interest, also, the number of samples collected in each experiment differs.

- *NP*-chart: used when the variable of interest is an attribute (e.g., defective or non-defective) and the data collected are in proportions of defects (or number of defects in a specific sample) and there are multiple measurements in a sample experiment, and multiple experiments are run, and the average proportion of defects of the collected data is of interest, also, the number of samples collected in each experiment is constant for all experiments.

- *C*-chart: used when the variable of interest is an attribute (e.g., defective or non-defective) and the data collected are in total number of defects (actual count in units) and there are multiple measurements in a sample experiment, and multiple experiments are run, and the average number of defects of the collected data is of interest, also, the number of samples collected in each experiment the same.

- *U*-chart: used when the variable of interest is an attribute (e.g., defective or non-defective) and the data collected are in total number of defects (actual count in units) and there are multiple measurements in a sample experiment, and multiple experiments are run, and the average number of defects of the collected data is of interest, also, the number of samples collected in each experiment differs.

150. Valuation – Buy versus Lease

File Name: Valuation – Buy versus Lease

Location: Modeling Toolkit | Valuation | Buy versus Lease

Brief Description: Illustrates how to compute the net advantage to leasing by comparing the cash flow differential between purchasing an asset or equipment versus leasing it

Requirements: Modeling Toolkit, Risk Simulator

Leasing versus buying decisions have plagued decision makers ever since a choice was made available. A lease is simply a contractual agreement between a lessee and lessor. This agreement specifies that the lessee has the right to use the asset in return for a periodic payment to the lessor who owns the asset. Typically, the lessor is the equipment or asset manufacturer or a third-party leasing company that purchases the asset from the manufacturer in order to provide a lease to the user. Leases usually are divided into two categories: operating and financial. An operating lease is a lease for a certain period of time that is typically less than the economic life of the asset, which means that the lease is not fully amortized (the total of lease payments received does not cover the cost of the asset). In addition, the lessor or owner of the asset has to cover the maintenance of the asset throughout the life of the lease, and the lease can be terminated early (with an option to abandon) whereby the lessor has the ability to sell the asset at some residual value to recoup the value of the initial asset cost. A financial lease, in contrast, is usually fully amortized and the lease cannot be canceled. In addition, no maintenance is provided for the lessee. In order to entice the lessee into a financial lease, several provisions can be included in the lease. In a sale and leaseback provision, the lessee owns the asset but sells it to the lessor and receives some cash payment upfront, and leases the asset back from the lessor for periodic lease payments. In leveraged leases, a third-party finances the lessor and obtains periodic payments from the lessor, and part of the payments go toward paying off the third-party financing the deal. Other types of leases exist, and exotic instruments and options can be embedded into the contract. For financial reporting purposes, certain leases are classified as capital leases, which will appear on the balance sheet (the present value of future lease payments appear as a liability, with a counterbalance on the asset side for the same amount) whereas operating leases do not appear on the balance sheet and are captured only in the income statement. Therefore, sometimes debt displacement is a hidden cost of leases and should be considered as part of the overall optimal capital allocation in a company.

Figure 150.1 illustrates how to compute a purchase versus a lease, specifically looking at the net advantage to leasing. In the first scenario, the asset or equipment is purchased, with the cost of the machine if purchased immediately, and the potential operating savings of having the machine. The corporate tax rate and before-tax discount rate are the required inputs. Using these values, the after-tax operating savings are computed, over the life of the lease, and the tax shield or tax savings from depreciation by owning the equipment (assuming a simple straight-line depreciation, or you may insert your own accelerated depreciation schedule if required), and the net cash flow for purchasing the equipment is computed.

In the lease scenario, the lease payments are listed and the benefits of tax savings from the lease are also included. The after-tax operating savings are added to this tax savings to obtain the net cash flow to leasing. To compute the net advantage to leasing (NAL), the net of the cash flows between the lease and purchase scenarios are computed and discounted back to time zero using an after-tax discount rate. If the NAL is positive, leasing is the better decision. Conversely, if the NAL is negative, purchasing the equipment is the better decision.

In addition, sometimes leases are based on a fluctuation of interest rates that can be uncertain, or the cost of funds can be fluctuating. These inputs can be subjected to simulation, and the resulting NAL is set as the forecast. The probability that NAL is positive can be determined. Hence, this is the same probability that the lease will be more advantageous than the purchase scenario.

	A	B	C	D	E	F	G	H	I	J
2						BUY VERSUS LEASE				
3										
4				Corporate Tax		34.00%		Discount Rate		12.0000%
5				Economic Life		5		(Before tax)		
6										
7		Buy Scenario		Years		0	1	2	3	4	5
8										
9		Cost of Machine			($10,000)					
10		Operating Savings				$4,500	$4,500	$4,500	$4,500	$4,500
11		Savings 1				$1,000	$1,000	$1,000	$1,000	$1,000
12		Savings 2				$1,500	$1,500	$1,500	$1,500	$1,500
13		Savings 3				$2,000	$2,000	$2,000	$2,000	$2,000
14		After Tax Operating Savings				$2,970	$2,970	$2,970	$2,970	$2,970
15		Depreciation Tax Benefit				$680	$680	$680	$680	$680
16		Net Cash Flow for Purchase				$3,650	$3,650	$3,650	$3,650	$3,650
17										
18		Lease Scenario								
19										
20		Lease Payments				($2,500)	($2,500)	($2,500)	($2,500)	($2,500)
21		Tax Benefits from Lease Payment				$850	$850	$850	$850	$850
22		After Tax Operating Savings				$2,970	$2,970	$2,970	$2,970	$2,970
23		Net Cash Flow for Leasing				$1,320	$1,320	$1,320	$1,320	$1,320
24										
25		Net Cash Flow Lease Minus Buy			$10,000	($2,330)	($2,330)	($2,330)	($2,330)	($2,330)
26		PV Net Cash Flow (After Tax)			$10,000	($2,159)	($2,001)	($1,854)	($1,718)	($1,592)
27		Net Advantage to Leasing			$677.34	Leasing is the better alternative				

Figure 150.1: Buy versus lease scenario cash flows

151. Valuation – Classified Loan Borrowing Base

File Name: Valuation – Classified Loan Borrowing Base

Location: Modeling Toolkit | Valuation | Classified Loan Borrowing Base

Brief Description: Illustrates how to value and classify a loan based on accounts receivable valuation

Requirements: Modeling Toolkit, Risk Simulator

Modeling Toolkit Functions Used: MTCreditAcceptanceCost, MTCreditRejectionCost

Special Credits: This model was contributed by Prof. Morton Glantz. He is a financial consultant, educator, and advisor to corporate financial executives, government ministers, privatization managers, investment and commercial bankers, public accounting firms, members of merger and acquisition teams, strategic planning executives, management consultants, attorneys, and representatives of foreign governments and international banks. As a senior officer of JP Morgan Chase, he specialized in credit analysis and credit risk management, risk grading systems, valuation models and professional training. Morton is on the finance faculty at the Fordham Graduate School of Business. He has appeared in the Harvard University International Directory of Business and Management Scholars and Research and earned Fordham University Deans Award for Faculty Excellence on three occasions, a school record. His areas of expertise include Advanced Forecasting Methods, Advanced Credit Risk Analysis, Credit Portfolio Risk Management, Essentials of Corporate Finance, Corporate Valuation Modeling and Analysis, Credit Risk Analysis and Modeling, Project Finance, and Corporate Failure. He has authored a number of books including: *Credit Derivatives: Techniques to Manage Credit Risk for Financial Professionals,* (with Erik Banks and Paul Siegel), McGraw Hill 2006; *Optimal Trading Strategies,* AMACOM 2003 (co-author: Dr. Robert Kissell); *Managing Bank Risk: An Introduction to Broad-Base Credit Engineering,* Academic Press/Elsevier 2002 (RISKBOOK.COM Award: Best Finance Books of 2003); *Scientific Financial Management,* AMACOM 2000; *Loan Risk Management,* McGraw Hill (1995); and *The Banker's Handbook on Credit Risk,* with Dr. Johnathan Mun, Academic Press (2008).

The key characteristic of a borrowing base workout loan is the fact that the amount a borrower may borrow at any one time is restricted by both the total exposure allowed under the applicable workout agreement and by the borrowing base. Borrowing base loans are not limited to workout loans. This is in contrast to the traditional loans where, as long as the borrower complies with loan covenants, he or she may draw down the entire loan facility. The borrowing base in an asset-based loan may consist of accounts receivable, inventory, equipment, and even real estate. Collateral quality and these collaterals can be converted into cash influences amount (the level of cash advance) approved. This models the creditworthiness of a borrower given that the loan is backed by accounts receivables of the debt holder's firm. In this model, we can determine the probability that the loan will be paid back and determine if the loan should be issued or not. See Figure 151.1.

Borrowing Base Analysis
Accounts Receivable Financing

Accounts Receivable Analysis		
Accounts receivable balance last report	12,003,020	
Plus new accounts receivable	3,400,345	
Plus (minus) adjustments	(100,340)	
Less deposits to cash collateral account	(567,666)	
Less collections not deposited to cash collateral account	(900,900)	
Total value of outstanding accounts receivable	13,834,459	
Less accounts over 90 days per aging 7/31/95	(350,000)	
Less other ineligible accounts	(650,500)	
Net eligible accounts receivable for this period		12,833,959
Inventory Analysis		
Inventory balance last report	9,500,000	
Plus inventory incoming	1,250,060	
Less inventory outgoing	(1,550,000)	
Plus (minus) adjustments	(35,500)	
Less other ineligible inventory	(76,550)	
Net eligible inventory for this period		9,088,010
Loan Request		
Loan Value Of The Accounts Receivable and Inventory Collateral		
Allowable advances against eligible receivables	70.0%	
Allowable advances against eligible receivables	50.0%	
Accounts receivable eligible against loan (borrowing base)	8,983,771	
Inventory eligible against loan (borrowing base)	4,544,005	
Collateral loan value for this period		13,527,776
Loan Balance Last Report	11,500,000	
Less deposits in cash collateral account to be applied to loan	(2,555,550)	
Less loan payments	(1,500,000)	
Present loan balance		7,444,450
Excess (Deficit) collateral loan value over loan balance		6,083,326
Borrowers request for additional advances		5,000,000
Surplus (shortfall)		1,083,326
Advances to be approved		5,000,000

Figure 151.1: Borrowing base accounts receivable model

This model is similar to accept-reject decisions in capital budgeting whereby the specific application introduced here is in the area of "problem loans" where the loan workout exercise is to control the distressed-borrower approval based on orders sold on credit, such as accounts receivable. The model reveals the relationship between marginal returns and marginal costs of approving an order and granting credit terms. For example, if acceptance costs are below rejection costs on an incremental order, the opportunity cost of rejecting the credit is too much; thus the credit would be accepted. The model is a powerful tool in problem loan turnarounds. For example, the banker would allow the distressed borrower to approve a weak credit order, if the incremental cost of production was very low because even if the receivable went bad, the borrower would not lose much if the incremental cost of manufacturing a widget was $1.00 while the widget was sold for $100.00.

The model can be made stochastic because there are assumption variables, forecast variables, and possibly constraints. The Acceptance/Rejection Costs part of the model serves as a framework for evaluating decisions on changing credit policies (Figure 151.2).

ACCEPTANCE VS. REJECTION COSTS MODEL

Inputs

Acceptance Costs

Clerical Costs Associated With Opening Account	$30
Credit Investigation Cost	$40
Collection Costs	$130
Dollars Tied Up In Receivables (Sale Price)	$100,000
Probability of Non Payment	4.00%
Incremental Cost of Production and Selling	$60,000
Average Time in Days between Sale and Payment	45
Cost of Funds	15.00%

Rejection Costs

Marginal Profit From Sale	$40,000
Probability of Payment	96.00%

Outputs

Acceptance Cost $4,449

Rejection Cost $38,400

Accept/Reject Credit: ACCEPT CREDIT

Probability B/E   0.380

Figure 151.2: Acceptance and rejection costs of new credit

152. Valuation – Break-Even Inventory: Seasonal Lending Trial Balance Analysis

File Name: Valuation – Break Even Inventory: Seasonal Lending Trial Balance Analysis

Location: Modeling Toolkit | Valuation | Valuation – Break Even Inventory Seasonal Lending Trial Balance Analysis

Brief Description: Illustrates how to value the creditworthiness of a line of credit or debt based on the company's loan inventory

Requirements: Modeling Toolkit, Risk Simulator

Special Credits: This model was contributed by Prof. Morton Glantz.

Trial balances take snapshots of general ledger accounts for assets, liabilities, and owner's equity during any point in the season. Lenders, to detect liquidity problems that compromise repayment, use the break-even inventory method, derived from a trial balance. Liquidity problems stem from inventory devaluations (write-downs). And trouble can surface quickly—two or three months down the season—often on the heels of disappointing bookings. At this point, inventory value usually falls below recorded book value (Figure 152.1).

Trial balances are associated with the periodic inventory method, where inventory is counted and valued at the lower of cost or market periodically, as opposed to the perpetual inventory system, where inventory is counted and valued frequently. Because ending inventory determines cost of goods sold and ultimately profits, bankers should know inventory value throughout the season. Examples of perpetual inventory include items scanned into the computer a shopper sees at cash registers and high-ticket items painstakingly monitored. Of the two methods, periodic inventory is more uncertain, rendering seasonal analysis indefinable at best if not impossible unless break-even techniques are employed effectively.

Though accountants have not appraised inventory value, assuming periodic inventory, management certainly has. Thus, lenders derive break-even inventory by first asking management for estimated lower of cost or market inventory values. They then figure spreads between the two, breakeven and estimated. For example, In Figure 152.1, if inventory required to break even is $7,500 while management estimated inventory is $6,000, net loss for the period is $1,500. Interim losses caused by large inventory write-downs reduce chances of a short-term loan cleanup. The logic is that write-downs follow production problems, poor strategic planning, stockpiling, canceled orders, overly optimistic sales projections, and flawed cash budgets.

Break Even Inventory Analysis

			Beg Inv.	Purchases	Overhead	Labor	Depr.	less X
Sales	28,000							
Cost of Goods Sold	25,500	CGS =	25,500	8,000 12,000	5,000	6,000	2,000	less X
Gross Profit	2,500							less X
Selling Expenses	1,500							
Administration Exp	500	BE =	X=	7,500				
Other Expenses	500		Act Inv	6,000				
Profit	0		Loss	(1,500)				

Proof

Sales	28,000		
Cost of Goods Sold	27,000		Substitute 6,000 (Actual Inventory) in the formula and
Gross Profit	1,000	GPM= 3.57%	solve for the real (not Break Even)
Selling Expenses	1,500		CGS
Administration Exp	500		
Other Expenses	500		
Profit	(1,500)		

Figure 152.1: Inventory valuation model

153. Valuation – Firm in Financial Distress

File Name: Valuation – Firm in Financial Distress

Location: Modeling Toolkit | Valuation | Firm in Financial Distress

Brief Description: Illustrates how to value the continued operations of a firm under distress, as well as to ascertain its creditworthiness

Requirements: Modeling Toolkit, Risk Simulator

Special Credits: This model was contributed by Prof. Morton Glantz.

In this model, the publicly available McKinsey discounted cash flow (DCF) model is employed to value the probability that the equity value of a company falls below zero. (This is set as an output forecast variable in a simulation.) A sample snapshot of the model is shown in Figure 153.1.

When equity values fall below zero, the firm has an excess of economic liabilities above and beyond its economic assets. (The assets are underwater.) Using this approach, bankers, under the Basel II/III requirements, can internally access the expected default frequency (EDF) or obligor risk, using their own assumptions and projections of the company's financial health. Finally, positive economic equity implies a call option whereby the shareholders can purchase the assets from creditors by paying off all the loans and continue business well past the residual period. A negative economic equity implies a put option whereby shareholders put or sell the assets to the creditors and can walk away from the bankrupt business exactly as if they purchased an out-of-the-money option and walked away losing only their initial investment.

Value of Operations: DCF approach

Year	Free Cash Flow	Discount Factor	PV of FCF
2002	74,330	0.931	69,264
2003	55,889	0.867	48,453
2004	64,761	0.807	52,276
2005	74,460	0.752	55,964
2006	85,053	0.700	59,520
2007	72,733	0.636	46,272
2008	70,872	0.578	40,983
2009	74,416	0.526	39,126
2010	78,136	0.478	37,347
2011	82,043	0.435	35,650
2012	86,145	0.395	34,029
2013	90,453	0.359	32,483
2014	94,975	0.326	31,006
2015	99,724	0.297	29,597
2016	104,710	0.270	28,251
Cont. Value	1,409,561	0.270	380,308
Operating Value			1,020,536

Continuing value % Operating value	37.3%

Mid-Year Adjustment Factor	1.036
Operating Value (Adjusted)	**1,057,622**

Value of Operations: Economic Profit

Year	Economic Profit	Discount Factor	PV of EP
2002	31,880	0.931	29,684
2003	39,186	0.867	33,972
2004	45,180	0.807	36,454
2005	53,538	0.752	40,239
2006	62,475	0.700	43,720
2007	43,287	0.636	27,539
2008	46,426	0.578	26,851
2009	49,172	0.526	25,854
2010	52,056	0.478	24,881
2011	55,083	0.435	23,935
2012	58,263	0.395	23,015
2013	61,601	0.359	22,122
2014	65,106	0.326	21,255
2015	68,786	0.297	20,415
2016	72,650	0.270	19,602
Cont. Value	829,805	0.270	223,886
Present Value of Economic Profit			643,923
Invested Capital (incl. goodwill)			376,613

Operating Value	1,020,536

Mid-Year Adjustment Factor	1.036
Operating Value (Adjusted)	**1,057,622**

Value of Equity

Operating Value	1,057,622
Excess Mkt Securities	0
Financial Investments	99,257
Excess Pension Assets	0
Enterprise Value	1,156,878
Debt	(980,000)
Capitalized Operating Leases	(33,400)
Retirement Related Liability	(2,351)
Preferred Stock	0
Minority Interest	0
Restructuring Provision	0
Stock options	0
Equity Value	141,127
No. shares (thousands)	30,001
Value per Share	4.70
12 month -High	34.81
12 month -Low	18.93
Value Difference - High	-86.5%
Value Difference - Low	-75.1%
Debt/Equity	720%
Debt/Assets	88%

Comparison of key ratios

	Averages			
From:	1999	2002	2007	2012
To:	2001	2006	2011	2016
Revenue growth (CAG)	-0.8%	5.0%	5.0%	5.0%
Adjusted EBITA growth (CAG)	#DIV/0!	9.5%	0.6%	5.0%
NOPLAT growth (CAG)	#DIV/0!	11.3%	2.0%	5.0%
Invested capital growth (CAG)	-6.2%	0.9%	3.7%	4.2%
Adj. EBIT/Revenues	6.5%	14.0%	13.0%	13.0%
Revenues/Invested Capital (pre-Goodwill)	2.3	2.8	3.0	3.0
ROIC (after tax, pre-Goodwill)	18.2%	26.8%	27.2%	27.2%
ROIC (after tax, including Goodwill)	13.3%	19.8%	21.6%	22.7%
Average Economic Profit	2,636	46,572	43,205	65,281
Cash Tax Rate	33.6%	32.7%	30.0%	30.0%
WACC	7.4%	7.4%	10.0%	10.0%

Evaluation of entry and exit multiples

	2001	2011
Operating Value	1,057,622	1,409,561
Excess Mkt Securities	0	
Financial Investments	99,257	
Enterprise Value	1,156,878	1,409,561
Revenue	678,023	1,409,561
Adjusted EBITA	88,427	183,243
NOPLAT	53,370	128,270
Enterprise / Revenue	1.7	1.0
Enterprise / Adjusted EBITA	13.1	7.7
Enterprise / NOPLAT	21.7	11.0

Figure 153.1: Firm in financial distress

154. Valuation – Banking and Pricing Loan Fees Model

File Name: Banking – Stochastic Loan Pricing Model

Location: Modeling Toolkit | Banking | Stochastic Loan Pricing Model

Brief Description: Illustrates how to price a bank loan based on commercial lending practices

Requirements: Modeling Toolkit, Risk Simulator

Special Credits: This model was contributed by Prof. Morton Glantz.

Stochastic models (Figure 154.1) produce an entire range of results and confidence levels feasible for the pricing run. Monte Carlo simulation fosters a more realistic (pricing) environment, and, as a result, involves elements of uncertainty too complex to be solved with deterministic pricing models.

PRICING MODEL

Facility Information
Borrower Picnic Furniture Manufacturing Co
Lenders: Second City Bank
Amount: $1,000,000 Five Year Unsecured Facility
Purpose:Expansion
Bank ROA Guideline: 1.16%

Facility Information

Enter Unsecured Line of Credit (Assumed To Be Fully Utilized)	1,000,000	
Enter 12 Month Average Balances (Assume Balances Not Free)	50,000	
Enter Base Rate (Prime or LIBOR) Rate	10.5%	
Enter Spread Over Base	1.75%	
Enter % Facility Fees (Not Connected To Balances!)	2.00%	
Enter Funding Costs	8.43%	
Enter Servicing: Enter % or complete Schedule Two	3.23%	
Enter Loan loss expense (Applied To Income Statement)	1.50%	Function of *Expected* Risk
Enter % Equity Reserve Requirement (Function of Unexpected Risk)	9.00%	Function of *Unexpected* Risk
Enter Taxes	35%	

Deposit Information

12 month average balances	50,000
Enter Activity costs as a percent of balances	**4.09%**
Enter Balance Requirement	**8.75%**

Net Borrowed Funds	950,000
Interest rate: Prime + 1.5%	12.21%
Fees in lieu of balances	7,673

Schedule One Types of Facility Fees
Agent Fees
Management Fees
Compensation Balances - See Schedule Two
Fees In Lieu of Balances - See Sehedule Two

Schedule Two - Servicing Costs (See Definations
Do Not Complete Schedule If % Was Entered

Direct Variable	0
Allocated Variable	0
Direct fixed	0
Allocated fixed	0

Figure 154.1: Pricing of loan fees

155. Valuation – Simulation and Valuation

File Names: Valuation – Valuation Model; Valuation – Financial Statements; Valuation – Financial Ratios Analysis

Location: Modeling Toolkit | Valuation | Valuation Model, Financial Statements, Financial Ratios Analysis

Brief Description: Illustrates the use of Monte Carlo simulation methods on standard discounted cash flow models

Requirements: Modeling Toolkit, Risk Simulator

These valuation models are based on standard discounted cash flow and financial statement approaches, useful for generating standard financial statements and computing financial ratios, and have been modified to account for the earnings per share of a company under uncertainty.

In this example model, we run a Monte Carlo simulation on the forecast projections of a company's profitability, as modeled in an income statement and earnings per share valuation. Figure 155.1 shows a simple screenshot of the *Valuation* model, where the boxed cells are the input assumptions in the valuation of the firm. The model then takes these input assumptions as starting points and forecasts the income statement, balance sheet, cash flow statement, and some financial ratios. Using these financial statements, the valuation of the firm is obtained (Figure 155.2). The valuation flows through these financial statements in order to obtain the net operating profit after taxes (NOPAT). From this NOPAT value, adjustments on tax-related items and noncash expenses are added back to determine the free cash flows available to the firm.

Then, the company's net present value is computed as the sum of the present value of future cash flows. This is the firm's present value of operations (PVO). We then add PVO to the value of continuation (value of the firm to perpetuity) assuming some growth rate and weighted average cost of capital. The total value is called the enterprise value, which is the valuation of the firm.

To get a more detailed look at the three key financial statements, refer to the **Modeling Toolkit | Valuation | Financial Statements** model. These models also provide a list of typical financial ratios. Please refer to Appendix B for details and definitions of these ratios (see the functions list with a *MTRatios* prefix).

Assumptions

Base Year (Valuation Year)	2008					
Start of Forecast Year	2008					
Years to Forecast	5					

Discounting | Discrete End-of-Year Discounting ▼ |

	0	1	2	3	4	5
Forecast Year						
Year	2008	2009	2010	2011	2012	2013
Weighted Average Cost of Capital	15.00%	15.00%	15.00%	15.00%	15.00%	15.00%

Currency Units (e.g., in $000's)	1000	
Equity Starting Value	129567	
Marginal Tax Rate	35%	
Return on Invested Capital	10%	
Assumed Terminal WACC	10.00%	
Assumed Terminal Growth Rate	5.00%	
Current Stock Price	10.00	

This is the Corporate Valuation Model used for developing financial statements as well as for enterprise valuation, and computing the total enterprise value, earnings per share, economic profit, and other financial metrics. The inputs are the boxed cells. You can extend the model to additional years by first entering the Years to Forecast (cell E7) and typing in the various required values in these future years (the boxes will automatically appear).

Revenues	678023	711924	747520	784896	824141	865348
Revenue: % Growth		5.00%	5.00%	5.00%	5.00%	5.00%
Other Operating Revenues	14554	17465	20958	25149	30179	36215
Other Operating Revenues: % Growth		20.00%	20.00%	20.00%	20.00%	20.00%
Cost of Goods Sold	180054	194458	210015	226816	244961	264558
Cost of Goods Sold: % Growth		8.00%	8.00%	8.00%	8.00%	8.00%
Selling, Gen & Admin Expenses	385447	393156	401019	409039	417220	425565
Selling, Gen & Admin Expenses: % Growth		2.00%	2.00%	2.00%	2.00%	2.00%
Non-Operating Income	7345	8080	8887	9776	10754	11829
Non-Operating Income: % Growth		10.00%	10.00%	10.00%	10.00%	10.00%
Interest Expense	23190	24350	25567	26845	28188	29597
Interest Expense: % Growth		5.00%	5.00%	5.00%	5.00%	5.00%
Cash	12826	14109	15519	17071	18779	20656
Cash: % Growth		10.00%	10.00%	10.00%	10.00%	10.00%
Accounts Receivable	24611	27072	29779	32757	36033	39636
Accounts Receivable: % Growth		10.00%	10.00%	10.00%	10.00%	10.00%
Inventories	16080	17688	19457	21402	23543	25897
Inventories: % Growth		10.00%	10.00%	10.00%	10.00%	10.00%
Other Current Assets	5692	6546	7528	8657	9955	11449
Other Current Assets: % Growth		15.00%	15.00%	15.00%	15.00%	15.00%
Wages and Accounts Payable	28738	30175	31684	33268	34931	36678
Wages and Accounts Payable: % Growth		5.00%	5.00%	5.00%	5.00%	5.00%
Other Current Liabilities	50915	56007	61607	67768	74545	81999
Other Current Liabilities: % Growth		10.00%	10.00%	10.00%	10.00%	10.00%

Figure 155.1: Simulation and valuation on income statements and earnings per share

DCF Valuation

Free Cash Flow	14854	64498	68498	79699	91261	103502
Discount Factor	1.0000	0.8696	0.7561	0.6575	0.5718	0.4972
Present Value of Operations	**278774**					
Computed Terminal NOPAT	114450					
Continuing Value	1201729					
Present Value of Continuing Value	**60086**					
Total Enterprise Value	**338860**					
Projected EPS	1.32	1.83	2.12	2.46	2.85	3.29
Projected Stock Price	10.00	13.81	16.03	18.61	21.58	24.87

Note that this model uses a growth rate approach where starting values are entered and the subsequent annualized growth rates of the variables are entered and the model computes the future values of these variables. You can override any of the assumption cells above by simply typing over the values (changing growth rates over time or using actual values rather than growth rates). In addition, some sample input assumptions have been set up (cells in green) and an example simulation was run. The following illustrates the same results from the simulation, indicating that there is a 12.90% chance that the stock price at the end of 5 years will fall below $23 per share, and the total enterprise value at the worst case scenario (5th percentile) Value at Risk is $309,892,000. You may override these input assumptions as required to create your own valuation model.

Figure 155.2: Valuation results

156. Value at Risk – Optimized and Simulated Portfolio VaR

File Name: Value at Risk – Optimized and Simulated Portfolio VaR

Location: Modeling Toolkit | Value at Risk | Optimized and Simulated Portfolio VaR

Brief Description: Computes the Value at Risk (VaR) of a portfolio of assets and uses Monte Carlo simulation to perform historical simulation to determine the tail-end confidence interval for determining VaR

Requirements: Modeling Toolkit, Risk Simulator

This model uses Monte Carlo simulation and optimization routines in Risk Simulator to minimize the Value at Risk (VaR) of a portfolio of assets (Figure 156.1).

VALUE AT RISK WITH ASSET ALLOCATION OPTIMIZATION MODEL

Asset Class Description	Annualized Returns	Volatility Risk	Allocation Weights	Required Minimum Allocation	Required Maximum Allocation
S&P 500	7.10%	9.80%	10.00%	10.00%	40.00%
Small Cap	9.51%	14.35%	27.30%	10.00%	40.00%
High Yield	15.90%	22.50%	22.70%	10.00%	40.00%
Govt Bonds	4.50%	7.25%	40.00%	10.00%	40.00%
		Total Weight:	100.00%		

Correlation Matrix	S&P 500	Small Cap	High Yield	Govt Bonds
S&P 500	1.0000	0.7400	0.6500	0.5500
Small Cap	0.7400	1.0000	0.4200	0.3100
High Yield	0.6500	0.4200	1.0000	0.2300
Govt Bonds	0.5500	0.3100	0.2300	1.0000

Covariance Matrix	S&P 500	Small Cap	High Yield	Govt Bonds
S&P 500	0.0096	0.0104	0.0143	0.0039
Small Cap	0.0104	0.0206	0.0136	0.0032
High Yield	0.0143	0.0136	0.0506	0.0038
Govt Bonds	0.0039	0.0032	0.0038	0.0053

Starting Value	$1,000,000.00
Term (Years)	5.00

Annualized Return	8.72%	Profit/Loss	$87,151.94
Portfolio Risk	9.84%	Return to Risk Ratio	88.59%
Ending Value	$1,087,151.94		

Specifications of the optimization model:

Objective:	*Maximize Return to Risk Ratio (E28)*
Decision Variables:	*Allocation Weights (E6:E9)*
Restrictions on Decision Variables:	*Minimum and Maximum Required (F6:G9)*
Constraints:	*Portfolio Total Allocation Weights 100% (E10 is set to 100%)*

Figure 156.1: Computing Value at Risk (VaR) with simulation

First, simulation is used to determine the 90% left-tail VaR. This means that there is a 10% chance that losses will exceed this VaR for a specified holding period. With an equal allocation of 25% across the four asset classes, the VaR is determined using simulation (Figure 156.2). The annualized returns are uncertain and hence simulated. The VaR is then read off the forecast chart. Then optimization is run to find the best portfolio subject to the 100% total allocation across the four projects that will maximize the portfolio's bang for the buck (returns to risk ratio). The resulting optimized portfolio is then simulated once again, and the new VaR is obtained (Figure 156.3). The VaR of this optimized portfolio is a lot less than the non-optimized portfolio.

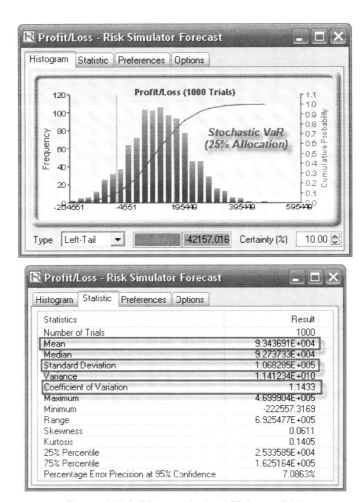

Figure 156.2: Non-optimized Value at Risk

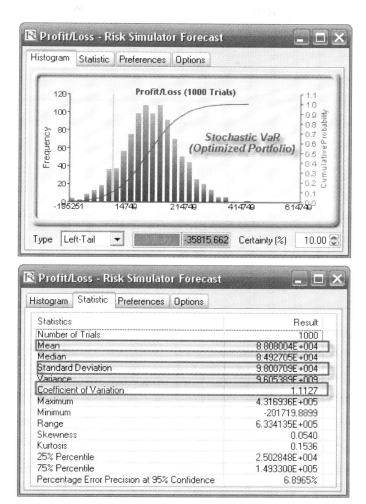

Figure 156.3: Optimal portfolio's Value at Risk through optimization and simulation

157. Value at Risk – Options Delta Portfolio VaR

File Name: Value at Risk – Options Delta Portfolio VaR

Location: Modeling Toolkit | Value at Risk | Options Delta Portfolio VaR

Brief Description: Computes the Value at Risk (VaR) of a portfolio of options and uses closed-form structural models to determine the VaR, after accounting for the cross-correlations among the various options

Requirements: Modeling Toolkit, Risk Simulator

Modeling Toolkit Functions Used: MTVaROptions, MTCallDelta

There are two examples in this *Value at Risk* (VaR) model . The first example illustrates how to compute the portfolio Value at Risk of a group of options, given the options' deltas (Figure 157.1). The option delta is the instantaneous sensitivity of the option's value to the stock price (see the *Sensitivity – Greeks* chapter for more details on computing an option's delta sensitivity measure). Given the underlying stock price of the option, the quantity of options held in the portfolio, each option's delta levels, and the daily volatility, we can compute the portfolio's VaR measure. In addition, given a specific holding period (typically between 1 and 10 days) or risk horizon days and the percentile required (typically between 90% and 99.95%), we can compute the portfolio's VaR for that holding period and percentile. If the option's delta is not available, use the *MTCallDelta* function instead, or see the *Given Option Inputs* worksheet.

VALUE AT RISK (DELTA OPTIONS PORTFOLIO)

Asset Allocation	Stock Price	Quantity Held	Delta	Daily Volatility
Asset A	$120.00	10000	0.1000	2.00%
Asset B	$30.00	200000	0.1000	1.00%
Asset C	$75.00	5000	0.2000	3.00%
Asset D	$48.00	10000	0.2500	4.00%
Asset E	$98.00	12500	0.2900	5.00%

Correlation Matrix	Asset A	Asset B	Asset C	Asset D	Asset E
Asset A	1.0000	0.1000	0.1000	0.1000	0.1000
Asset B	0.1000	1.0000	0.1000	0.1000	0.1000
Asset C	0.1000	0.1000	1.0000	0.1000	0.1000
Asset D	0.1000	0.1000	0.1000	1.0000	0.1000
Asset E	0.1000	0.1000	0.1000	0.1000	1.0000

Horizon Days for VaR	5
VaR Percentile	95.00%

Portfolio Value at Risk $78,638.72

Figure 157.1: Delta options VaR with known options delta values

The second example (Figure 157.2) illustrates how to compute the portfolio VaR of a group of options, given the option inputs (stock price, strike price, risk-free rate, maturity, annualized volatilities, and dividend rate). The option delta is then computed using the *MTCallDelta* function. The delta measure is the instantaneous sensitivity of the option's value to the stock price. Given the underlying stock price of the option, the quantity of options held in the portfolio, each option's delta levels, and the daily volatility, we can compute the portfolio's VaR measure. In addition, given a specific holding period (typically between 1 and

10 days) or risk horizon days and the percentile required (typically between 90% and 99.95%), we can compute the portfolio's VaR for that holding period and percentile. Finally, the daily volatility is computed by dividing the annualized volatility by the square root of trading days per year.

VALUE AT RISK (DELTA OPTIONS PORTFOLIO)

Asset Allocation	Stock Price	Strike Price	Maturity in Years	Annualized Risk-Free Rate	Annualized Volatility	Annualized Dividend Rate	Quantity	Delta	Daily Volatility
Asset A	$120.00	$100.00	1.00	5.00%	31.62%	0.00%	1250	0.8140	2.00%
Asset B	$30.00	$30.00	1.00	5.00%	15.81%	0.00%	30000	0.6537	1.00%
Asset C	$50.00	$50.00	2.00	5.00%	25.00%	0.00%	5000	0.6771	1.58%
Asset D	$75.00	$70.00	3.00	5.00%	23.60%	0.10%	7500	0.7659	1.49%
Asset E	$36.00	$31.00	5.00	5.00%	18.90%	0.20%	10000	0.8627	1.20%

Correlation Matrix	Asset A	Asset B	Asset C	Asset D	Asset E
Asset A	1.0000	0.1000	0.1000	0.1000	0.1000
Asset B	0.1000	1.0000	0.1000	0.1000	0.1000
Asset C	0.1000	0.1000	1.0000	0.1000	0.1000
Asset D	0.1000	0.1000	0.1000	1.0000	0.1000
Asset E	0.1000	0.1000	0.1000	0.1000	1.0000

Horizon Days for VaR	5
VaR Percentile	95.00%
Trading Days Per Year	250

Portfolio Value at Risk	$43,093.78

Figure 157.2: Delta options VaR with options input parameters

158. Value at Risk – Portfolio Operational and Credit Risk VaR Capital Adequacy

File Name: Value at Risk – Portfolio Operational and Capital Adequacy

Location: Modeling Toolkit | Value at Risk | Portfolio Operational and Capital Adequacy

Brief Description: Illustrates how to use Risk Simulator for distributional fitting, to find the best-fitting distributions for credit risk and operational risk parameters, and how to run Monte Carlo simulation on these credit and operational risk variables to determine the total capital required under a 99.50% Value at Risk

Requirements: Modeling Toolkit, Risk Simulator

This model shows how operational risk and credit risk parameters are fitted to statistical distributions and their resulting distributions are modeled in a portfolio of liabilities to determine the Value at Risk (VaR) 99.50th percentile certainty for the capital requirement under Basel II/III requirements. It is assumed that the historical data of the operational risk impacts (*Historical Data* worksheet) are obtained through econometric modeling of the *Key Risk Indicators*.

The *Distributional Fitting Report* worksheet is a result of running a distributional fitting routine in Risk Simulator to obtain the appropriate distribution for the operational risk parameter. Using the resulting distributional parameter, we model each liability's capital requirements within an entire portfolio. Correlations can also be inputted if required, between pairs of liabilities or business units. The resulting Monte Carlo simulation results show the VaR capital requirements.

Note that an appropriate empirically based historical VaR cannot be obtained if distributional fitting and risk-based simulations were not first run. Only by running simulations will the VaR be obtained.

Procedure

To perform distributional fitting, follow the steps below:

1. In the *Historical Data* worksheet (Figure 158.1), select the data area (cells **C5:L104**) and click on **Risk Simulator | Analytical Tools | Distributional Fitting (Single Variable)**.

2. Browse through the fitted distributions and select the best-fitting distribution (in this case, the exponential distribution in Figure 158.2) and click **OK**.

Basel II - Credit Risk and Capital Requirement (Portfolio-Based)

This model applies the Basel II requirements on capital adequacy and modeling the operational risk of probability of default on 100 loans as well as the loss given default. These values are fitted based on the bank's historical loss data (Historical Data and Distributional Fitting Report sheets) using Risk Simulator. Then, the relevant historical simulation assumptions are set in this model (Credit Risk sheet) and a Monte Carlo risk-based simulation was run in Risk Simulator to determine the expected capital required and 99.50% Value at Risk (VaR). A simulation has to be run in order to determine the VaR.

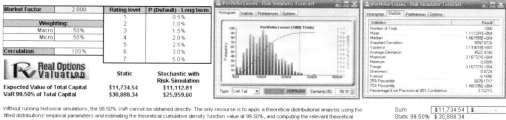

Market Factor	2.000

Weighting:	
Macro	50%
Micro	50%

Correlation	100%

Rating level	P (Default) - Long term
1	0.5%
2	1.0%
3	1.5%
4	2.0%
5	2.5%
6	3.0%
7	5.0%

	Static	Stochastic with Risk-Simulation
Expected Value of Total Capital	$11,734.54	$11,112.81
VaR 99.50% of Total Capital	$30,888.34	$25,959.60

Without running historical simulations, the 99.50% VaR cannot be obtained directly. The only recourse is to apply a theoretical distributional analysis using the fitted distributions' empirical parameters and estimating the theoretical cumulative density function value at 99.50%, and computing the relevant theoretical confidence level. This approach is at best an overestimation of the required capital (thereby requiring too much capital) and at worst, wrong.

Sum	$11,734.54	$ -
Static 99.50%	$30,888.34	

Bank loan	Size of loan	Rating grade	P (Default) - Long term	Operational Risk Factor	P (Default) - Now	Default?	Loss Given Default (LGD%) Static	Loss Given Default (LGD%) Stochastic	Losses Static	Losses Stochastic
1	$ 13,274.73	5	2.5%	2.000	5.00%	0	30.0%	30.0%	$ 199.12	$ -
2	$ 14,215.77	6	3.0%	2.000	6.00%	0	30.0%	30.0%	$ 255.88	$ -
3	$ 9,003.59	1	0.5%	2.000	1.00%	0	30.0%	30.0%	$ 27.01	$ -
4	$ 1,324.27	3	1.5%	2.000	3.00%	0	30.0%	30.0%	$ 11.92	$ -
5	$ 11,203.14	1	0.5%	2.000	1.00%	0	30.0%	30.0%	$ 33.61	$ -
6	$ 5,480.61	4	2.0%	2.000	4.00%	0	30.0%	30.0%	$ 65.77	$ -
7	$ 9,853.12	5	2.5%	2.000	5.00%	0	30.0%	30.0%	$ 147.80	$ -
8	$ 12,356.22	3	1.5%	2.000	3.00%	0	30.0%	30.0%	$ 111.21	$ -
9	$ 8,255.80	4	2.0%	2.000	4.00%	0	30.0%	30.0%	$ 99.07	$ -
10	$ 1,662.99	2	1.0%	2.000	2.00%	0	30.0%	30.0%	$ 9.98	$ -
11	$ 7,175.82	3	1.5%	2.000	3.00%	0	30.0%	30.0%	$ 64.58	$ -

Figure 158.1: Sample historical bank loans

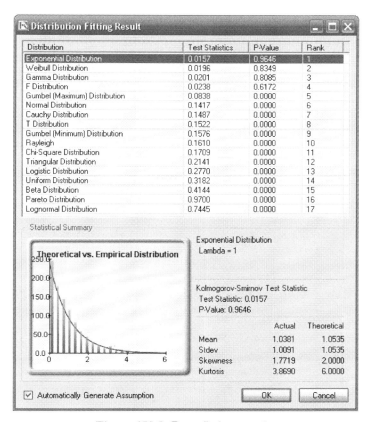

Figure 158.2: Data fitting results

To run a simulation in the portfolio model:

1. You may now set the assumptions on the *Operational Risk Factors* with the exponential distribution (fitted results show *Lambda* = 1) in the *Credit Risk* worksheet. Note that the assumptions have been set for you in advance. You may set it by going to cell **F27** and clicking on **Risk Simulator | Set Input Assumption**, selecting **Exponential** distribution and entering **1** for the *Lambda* value and clicking **OK**. Continue this process for the remaining cells in column F or simply perform a **Risk Simulator Copy** and **Risk Simulator Paste** on the remaining cells:

   a. Note that since the cells in column F have assumptions set, you will first have to clear them if you wish to reset and copy/paste parameters. You can do so by first selecting cells **F28:F126** and clicking on the **Remove Parameter** icon or select **Risk Simulator | Remove Parameter**.

   b. Then select cell **F27**, click on the **Risk Simulator Copy** icon or select **Risk Simulator | Copy Parameter**, and then select cells **F28:F126** and click on the **Risk Simulator Paste** icon or select **Risk Simulator | Paste Parameter**.

2. Next, additional assumptions can be set such as the probability of default using the Bernoulli distribution (column H) and *Loss Given Default* (column J). Repeat the procedure in Step 3 if you wish to reset the assumptions.

3. Run the simulation by clicking on the **RUN** icon or clicking on **Risk Simulator | Run Simulation**.

4. Obtain the Value at Risk by going to the forecast chart once the simulation is done running and selecting **Left-Tail** and typing in **99.50**. Hit **TAB** on the keyboard to enter the confidence value and obtain the VaR of $25,959 (Figure 158.3).

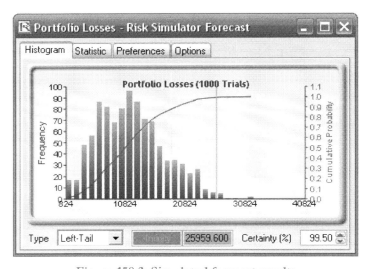

Figure 158.3: Simulated forecast results

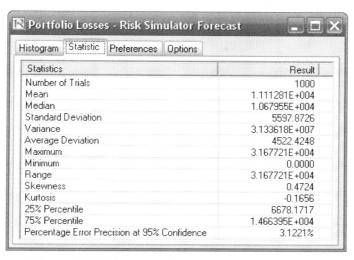

Statistics	Result
Number of Trials	1000
Mean	1.111281E+004
Median	1.067955E+004
Standard Deviation	5597.8726
Variance	3.133618E+007
Average Deviation	4522.4248
Maximum	3.167721E+004
Minimum	0.0000
Range	3.167721E+004
Skewness	0.4724
Kurtosis	-0.1656
25% Percentile	6678.1717
75% Percentile	1.466395E+004
Percentage Error Precision at 95% Confidence	3.1221%

Figure 158.3: Simulated forecast results *(continued)*

159. Value at Risk – Right-Tail Capital Requirements

File Name: Value at Risk – Right Tail Capital Requirements

Location: Modeling Toolkit | Value at Risk | Right Tail Capital Requirements

Brief Description: Illustrates how to use Risk Simulator for running a risk-based correlated Monte Carlo simulation to obtain the right-tailed Value at Risk for Basel II/III requirements

Requirements: Modeling Toolkit, Risk Simulator

This model shows the capital requirements per Basel II/III requirements (99.95th percentile capital adequacy based on a specific holding period's Value at Risk). Without running risk-based historical and Monte Carlo simulation using Risk Simulator, the required capital is $37.01M (Figure 159.1) as compared to only $14.00M required using a correlated simulation (Figure 159.2). This is due to the cross-correlations between assets and business lines, and can only be modeled using Risk Simulator. This lower VaR is preferred as banks can now be required to hold less required capital and can reinvest the remaining capital in various profitable ventures, thereby generating higher profits.

TAIL VALUE AT RISK MODEL (BASEL II REQUIREMENT)

Line of Business	Mean Required Capital	99.95th Percentile	Capital Required	Allocation Weights	Minimum Allowed	Maximum Allowed	
Business 1	$10.50	$36.52	$26.01	10.00%	5.00%	15.00%	3.48
Business 2	$11.12	$47.52	$36.39	10.00%	5.00%	15.00%	4.27
Business 3	$11.77	$48.99	$37.22	10.00%	5.00%	15.00%	4.16
Business 4	$10.77	$37.34	$26.56	10.00%	5.00%	15.00%	3.47
Business 5	$13.49	$49.52	$36.03	10.00%	5.00%	15.00%	3.67
Business 6	$14.24	$55.59	$41.35	10.00%	5.00%	15.00%	3.91
Business 7	$15.60	$60.24	$44.64	10.00%	5.00%	15.00%	3.86
Business 8	$14.95	$64.69	$49.74	10.00%	5.00%	15.00%	4.33
Business 9	$14.15	$61.02	$46.87	10.00%	5.00%	15.00%	4.31
Business 10	$10.08	$35.37	$25.29	10.00%	5.00%	15.00%	3.51
Portfolio Total	$12.67	$49.68	$37.01	100.00%			
Total Capital Required			$14.00				

Correlation Matrix

	1	2	3	4	5	6	7	8	9	10
1										
2	-0.20	0.35								
3	-0.13	0.01	0.00							
4	-0.05	0.01	0.00							
5	0.23	0.50	0.15	0.00						
6	0.00	0.00	-0.15	0.00	0.03					
7	0.25	0.00	-0.26	0.01	0.10	-0.10				
8	0.36	-0.25	-0.60	-0.30	0.00	0.00	-0.15			
9	-0.01	-0.20	0.16	0.04	-0.01	0.01	0.00	0.00		

Figure 159.1: Right-tail VaR model

Procedure

1. To run the model, click on **Risk Simulator | Run Simulation** (if you had other models open, make sure you first click on **Risk Simulator | Change Profile**, and select the *Tail VaR* profile before starting).

2. When simulation is complete, select **Left-Tail** in the forecast chart and enter in **99.95** in the *Certainty* box and hit **TAB** on the keyboard to obtain the value of $14.00M Value at Risk for this correlated simulation.

3. Note that the assumptions have been set for you in advance in the model in cells C6:C15. However, you may set it again by going to cell **C6** and clicking on **Risk Simulator | Set Input Assumption**, selecting your distribution of choice or use the default *Normal Distribution* (as a quick example) or perform a distributional fitting on historical data and click **OK**. Continue this process for the remaining cells in column C. You may also decide to first *Remove Parameters* of these cells in column C and set your own distributions. Further, correlations can be set manually when assumptions are set (Figure 159.3) or by going to **Risk Simulator | Edit Correlations** (Figure 159.4) after all the assumptions are set.

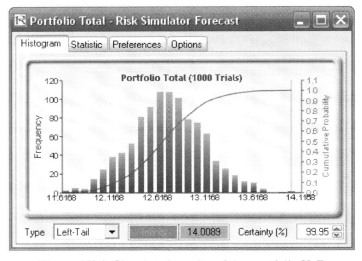

Figure 159.2: Simulated results of the portfolio VaR

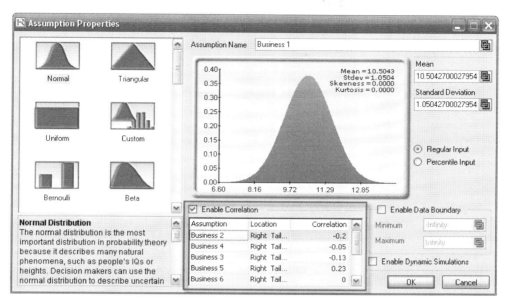

Figure 159.3: Setting correlations one at a time

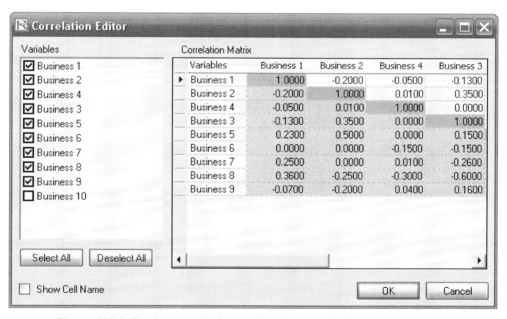

Figure 159.4: Setting correlations using the correlation matrix routine

160. Value at Risk – Static Covariance Method

File Name: Value at Risk – Static Covariance Method

Location: Modeling Toolkit | Value at Risk | Static Covariance Method

Brief Description: Computes a static Value at Risk (VaR) using a correlation and covariance method, to obtain the portfolio's VaR after accounting for the individual component's returns, volatility, cross-correlations, holding period, and VaR percentile

Requirements: Modeling Toolkit, Risk Simulator

Modeling Toolkit Function Used: MTVaRCorrelationMethod

This model is used to compute the portfolio's Value at Risk (VaR) at a given percentile for a specific holding period, after accounting for the cross-correlation effects between the assets (Figure 160.1). The daily volatility is the annualized volatility divided by the square root of trading days per year. Typically, positive correlations tend to carry a higher VaR compared to zero correlation asset mixes, whereas negative correlations reduce the total risk of the portfolio through the diversification effect (Figure 160.2). The approach used is a portfolio VaR with correlated inputs, where the portfolio has multiple asset holdings with different amounts and volatilities. Each asset is also correlated to each other. The covariance or correlation structural model is used to compute the VaR given a holding period or horizon and percentile value (typically 10 days at 99% confidence).

VALUE AT RISK (VARIANCE-COVARIANCE METHOD)

Asset Allocation	Amount	Daily Volatility
Asset A	$1,000,000.00	1.20%
Asset B	$2,000,000.00	2.00%
Asset C	$3,000,000.00	1.89%
Asset D	$4,000,000.00	3.25%
Asset E	$5,000,000.00	4.20%

Correlation Matrix	Asset A	Asset B	Asset C	Asset D	Asset E
Asset A	1.0000	0.1000	0.1000	0.1000	0.1000
Asset B	0.1000	1.0000	0.1000	0.1000	0.1000
Asset C	0.1000	0.1000	1.0000	0.1000	0.1000
Asset D	0.1000	0.1000	0.1000	1.0000	0.1000
Asset E	0.1000	0.1000	0.1000	0.1000	1.0000

Horizon (Days)	10
Percentile	99.00%

Value at Risk (Daily)	$655,915.30
Value at Risk (Horizon)	$2,074,186.30

Daily Value at Risk (Positive Correlations)	$2,074,186.30
Daily Value at Risk (Zero Correlations)	$1,389,345.26
Daily Value at Risk (Negative Correlations)	$1,684,340.28

Figure 160.1: Computing Value at Risk using the covariance method

Correlation Matrix	Asset A	Asset B	Asset C	Asset D	Asset E
Asset A	1.0000	0.1000	0.1000	0.1000	0.1000
Asset B	0.1000	1.0000	0.1000	0.1000	0.1000
Asset C	0.1000	0.1000	1.0000	0.1000	0.1000
Asset D	0.1000	0.1000	0.1000	1.0000	0.1000
Asset E	0.1000	0.1000	0.1000	0.1000	1.0000

Correlation Matrix	Asset A	Asset B	Asset C	Asset D	Asset E
Asset A	1.0000	0.0000	0.0000	0.0000	0.0000
Asset B	0.0000	1.0000	0.0000	0.0000	0.0000
Asset C	0.0000	0.0000	1.0000	0.0000	0.0000
Asset D	0.0000	0.0000	0.0000	1.0000	0.0000
Asset E	0.0000	0.0000	0.0000	0.0000	1.0000

Correlation Matrix	Asset A	Asset B	Asset C	Asset D	Asset E
Asset A	1.0000	-0.1000	-0.1000	-0.1000	-0.1000
Asset B	-0.1000	1.0000	-0.1000	-0.1000	-0.1000
Asset C	-0.1000	-0.1000	1.0000	-0.1000	-0.1000
Asset D	-0.1000	-0.1000	-0.1000	1.0000	-0.1000
Asset E	-0.1000	-0.1000	-0.1000	-0.1000	1.0000

Figure 160.2: Value at Risk results with different correlation levels

161. Volatility – Implied Volatility

File Name: Volatility – Implied Volatility

Location: Modeling Toolkit | Volatility | Implied Volatility

Brief Description: Computes the implied volatilities using an internal optimization routine, given the fair market values of a call or put option as well as all their required inputs

Requirements: Modeling Toolkit, Risk Simulator

Modeling Toolkit Functions Used: MTImpliedVolatilityCall, MTImpliedVolatilityPut

This implied volatility computation is based on an internal iterative optimization, which means it will work under typical conditions (without extreme volatility values, i.e., too small or too large). It is always good modeling technique to recheck the imputed volatility using an options model to make sure the answer coincides before adding more sophistication to the model. That is, given all the inputs in an option analysis as well as the option value, the volatility can be imputed. See Figure 161.1.

IMPLIED VOLATILITY FUNCTION

Asset	$100.00
Strike	$95.00
Maturity	0.50
Riskfree	8.00%
Volatility	25.00%
DividendRate	3.00%

Call Option	$10.9126
Put Option	$3.6764

Implied Volatility Calculation	
Call Option	25.00%
Put Option	25.00%

Figure 161.1: Getting the implied volatility from options

162. Volatility – Volatility Computations

File Name: Volatility – Volatility Computations

Location: Modeling Toolkit | Volatility, and Applying Log Cash Flow Returns, Log Asset Returns, Probability to Volatility, EWMA, and GARCH Models

Brief Description: Uses Risk Simulator to apply Monte Carlo simulation to compute a project's volatility measure

Requirements: Modeling Toolkit, Risk Simulator

There are several ways to estimate the volatility used in the option models. The most common and valid approaches are:

Logarithmic Cash Flow Returns Approach or Logarithmic Stock Price Returns Approach: This method is used mainly for computing the volatility on liquid and tradable assets, such as stocks in financial options. However, sometimes it is used for other traded assets, such as the price of oil or electricity. The drawback is that discounted cash flow models with only a few cash flows generally will overstate the volatility, and this method cannot be used when negative cash flows occur. Thus, this volatility approach is applicable only for financial instruments and not for real options analysis. The benefits include its computational ease, transparency, and modeling flexibility. In addition, no simulation is required to obtain a volatility estimate. The approach is simply to take the annualized standard deviation of the logarithmic relative returns of the time-series data as the proxy for volatility. The Modeling Toolkit function **MTVolatility** is used to compute this volatility, where the time series of stock prices can be arranged in either chronological or reverse chronological order when using the function. See the *Log Cash Flow Returns* example model in the Volatility section of Modeling Toolkit for details.

Exponentially Weighted Moving Average (EWMA) Models: This approach is similar to the logarithmic cash flow returns approach. It uses the **MTVolatility** function to compute the annualized standard deviation of the natural logarithms of relative stock returns. The difference here is that the most recent value will have a higher weight than values farther in the past. A lambda, or weight variable, is required (typically, industry standards set this at 0.94). The most recent volatility is weighted at this lambda value, and the period before that is (1 – lambda), and so forth. See the *EWMA* example model in the Volatility section of Modeling Toolkit for details.

Logarithmic Present Value Returns Approach: This approach is used mainly when computing the volatility on assets with cash flows. A typical application is in real options. The drawback of this method is that simulation is required to obtain a single volatility, and it is not applicable for highly traded liquid assets, such as stock prices. The benefits include the ability to accommodate certain negative cash flows. Also, this approach applies more rigorous analysis than the logarithmic cash flow returns approach, providing a more accurate and conservative estimate of volatility when assets are analyzed. In addition, within, say, a cash flow model, you can set up multiple simulation assumptions (insert any types of risks and uncertainties, such as related assumptions, correlated distributions and nonrelated inputs, multiple stochastic processes, etc.) and allow the model to distill all the interacting risks and uncertainties in these simulations. You then obtain the single-value volatility, which represents the integrated risk of the project. See the *Log Asset Returns* example model in the Volatility section of Modeling Toolkit for details.

Management Assumptions and Guesses: This approach is used for both financial options and real options. The drawback is that the volatility estimates are very unreliable and are only subjective best guesses. The benefit of this approach is its simplicity—using this method, you can easily explain to management the concept of volatility, both in execution and interpretation. Most people understand what probability is but have a hard time understanding what volatility is. Using this approach, you can impute one from another. See the *Probability to Volatility* example model in the Volatility section of Modeling Toolkit for details.

Generalized Autoregressive Conditional Heteroskedasticity (GARCH) Models: These methods are used mainly for computing the volatility on liquid and tradable assets, such as stocks in financial options. However, sometimes they are used for other traded assets, such as the price of oil or electricity. The drawback is that these models require a lot of data and advanced econometric modeling expertise is required. In addition, these models are highly susceptible to user manipulation. The benefit is that rigorous statistical analysis is performed to find the best-fitting volatility curve, providing different volatility estimates over time. The *EWMA* model is a simple weighting model; the *GARCH* model is a more advanced analytical and econometric model that requires advanced algorithms, such as generalized method of moments, to obtain the volatility forecasts.

This chapter only provides a high-level review of all these methods as they pertain to hands-on applications. For detailed technical details on volatility estimates, including the theory and step-by-step interpretation of the method, please refer to Chapter 7 of Dr. Johnathan Mun's *Real Options Analysis*, Third Edition (Thomson–Shore, 2016).

Procedure

1. For the **Log Cash Flow** or **Log Returns Approach**, make sure that your data are all positive (this approach cannot apply negative values). The *Log Cash Flow Approach* worksheet illustrates an example computation of downloaded Microsoft stock prices (Figure 162.1). You can perform **Edit | Copy** and **Edit | Paste Special | Values Only** using your own stock closing prices to compute the volatility. The MTVolatility function is used to compute volatility. Enter in the positive integer for periodicity as appropriate (e.g., to annualize the volatility using monthly stock prices, enter in 12, or 52 for weekly stock prices, etc.), as seen in the example model.

Downloaded Weekly Historical Stock Prices of Microsoft | Volatility Computations

Date	Open	High	Low	Close	Volume	Adj Close*	LN Relative Returns	Moving Average Volatilities
27-Dec-04	27.01	27.10	26.68	26.72	52388840	26.64	-0.0108	17.87%
20-Dec-04	27.01	27.17	26.78	27.01	77413174	26.93	0.0019	17.84%
13-Dec-04	27.10	27.40	26.80	26.96	108628300	26.88	-0.0045	17.85%
6-Dec-04	27.10	27.44	26.91	27.08	83312720	27.00	-0.0055	18.00%
29-Nov-04	26.64	27.44	26.61	27.23	83103200	27.15	0.0235	18.13%
22-Nov-04	26.75	26.82	26.10	26.60	61834599	26.52	-0.0098	18.03%
15-Nov-04	27.34	27.50	26.84	26.86	75375960	26.78	-0.0011	18.10%
8-Nov-04	29.18	30.20	29.13	29.97	109385736	26.81	0.0223	18.20%
1-Nov-04	28.16	29.36	27.96	29.31	85044019	26.22	0.0468	18.28%
25-Oct-04	27.67	28.54	27.55	27.97	70791679	25.02	0.0084	17.71%
18-Oct-04	28.07	28.89	27.58	27.74	74671318	24.81	-0.0092	17.80%
11-Oct-04	28.20	28.27	27.80	27.99	48396360	25.04	0.0000	19.68%
4-Oct-04	28.44	28.59	27.97	27.99	52998320	25.04	-0.0091	19.69%
27-Sep-04	27.17	28.32	27.04	28.25	61783760	25.27	0.0346	19.68%
20-Sep-04	27.44	27.74	27.07	27.29	59162520	24.41	-0.0082	19.62%
13-Sep-04	27.53	27.57	26.74	27.51	51599880	24.61	0.0008	20.52%
7-Sep-04	27.29	27.51	27.14	27.49	51935175	24.59	0.0139	21.30%
30-Aug-04	27.30	27.68	26.85	27.11	45125980	24.25	-0.0127	21.25%
23-Aug-04	27.27	27.67	27.09	27.46	40526880	24.56	0.0123	22.29%
16-Aug-04	27.03	27.50	26.89	27.20	52571740	24.26	0.0066	22.29%
9-Aug-04	27.26	27.75	26.86	27.02	51244080	24.10	-0.0041	22.42%
2-Aug-04	28.27	28.55	27.06	27.14	56739100	24.20	-0.0488	22.42%
26-Jul-04	28.36	28.81	28.13	28.49	65555220	25.41	0.0163	21.97%
19-Jul-04	27.62	29.89	27.60	28.03	114579322	25.00	0.0198	22.11%
12-Jul-04	27.67	28.36	27.25	27.48	57970740	24.51	-0.0138	22.02%
6-Jul-04	28.32	28.33	27.55	27.86	61197249	24.85	-0.0250	22.04%
28-Jun-04	28.60	28.84	28.17	28.57	66214339	25.48	0.0000	22.07%
21-Jun-04	28.22	28.66	27.81	28.57	82202478	25.48	0.0079	22.30%
14-Jun-04	26.55	28.50	26.53	28.35	97727643	25.28	0.0574	22.48%
7-Jun-04	26.02	26.79	25.97	26.77	55540250	23.87	0.0311	22.71%
1-Jun-04	26.13	26.28	25.86	25.95	49284475	23.14	-0.0107	22.86%
24-May-04	26.05	26.35	25.60	26.23	51927460	23.39	0.0129	23.19%
17-May-04	25.47	26.27	25.42	25.89	56652040	23.09	0.0013	23.21%
10-May-04	25.63	26.19	25.43	25.86	58864200	23.06	0.0030	23.87%
3-May-04	26.19	26.60	25.75	25.78	60847680	22.99	-0.0134	24.07%
26-Apr-04	27.45	27.55	25.96	26.13	77381899	23.30	-0.0527	24.05%
19-Apr-04	25.08	27.72	25.06	27.54	102244677	24.56	0.0903	23.67%
12-Apr-04	25.48	25.77	25.10	25.16	56472679	22.44	-0.0124	21.92%
5-Apr-04	25.81	25.98	25.35	25.48	52838950	22.72	-0.0144	22.50%
29-Mar-04	25.25	25.90	24.85	25.85	69704180	23.05	0.0322	22.76%
22-Mar-04	24.48	25.51	24.01	25.03	92829802	22.32	0.0158	22.59%

One-Year Annualized Volatility Analysis

Average	21.89%
Median	22.30%

Figure 162.1 Historical stock prices and volatility estimates

2. For the **Log Present Value Approach**, negative cash flows are allowed. In fact, this approach is preferred to the *Log Cash Flow* approach when modeling volatilities in a real options world. First, set some assumptions in the model or use the preset assumptions as is. The *Intermediate X Variable* is used to compute the project's volatility (Figure 162.2). Run the simulation and view the Intermediate Variable X's forecast chart. Go to the **Statistics** tab and obtain the **Standard Deviation** (Figure 162.3). Annualize it by multiplying the value with the square root of the number of periods per year (in this case, the annualized volatility is 11.64% as the periodicity is annual, otherwise multiply the standard deviation by the square root of 4 if quarterly data is used, the square root of 12 if monthly data is used, etc.).

Log Present Value Approach

Input Parameters		Results	
Discount Rate (Cash Flow)	15.00%	Present Value (Cash Flow)	**$286.66**
Discount Rate (Impl. Cost)	5.00%	Present Value (Impl. Cost)	**$189.58**
Tax Rate	10.00%	Net Present Value	**$97.09**

	2002	2003	2004	2005	2006
Revenue	$100.00	$200.00	$300.00	$400.00	$500.00
Cost of Revenue	$40.00	$80.00	$120.00	$160.00	$200.00
Gross Profit	$60.00	$120.00	$180.00	$240.00	$300.00
Operating Expenses	$22.00	$44.00	$66.00	$88.00	$110.00
Depreciation Expense	$5.00	$10.00	$15.00	$20.00	$25.00
Interest Expense	$3.00	$6.00	$9.00	$12.00	$15.00
Income Before Taxes	$30.00	$60.00	$90.00	$120.00	$150.00
Taxes	$3.00	$6.00	$9.00	$12.00	$15.00
Income After Taxes	$27.00	$54.00	$81.00	$108.00	$135.00
Non-Cash Expenses	$12.00	$12.00	$12.00	$12.00	$12.00
Cash Flow	$39.00	$66.00	$93.00	$120.00	$147.00
Implementation Cost	$25.00	$25.00	$50.00	$50.00	$75.00

Volatility Estimates (Logarithmic PV Approach)

PV (0)	$39.00	$57.39	$70.32	$78.90	$84.05
PV (1)	N/A	$66.00	$80.87	$90.74	$96.65
Static PV (0)	$39.00	$63.65	$81.21	$93.10	$100.51
Variable X	-0.1216				
Volatility	Simulate to obtain volatility				

Figure 162.2: Using the PV Asset approach to model volatility

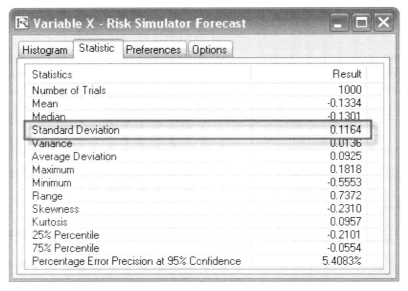

Figure 162.3: Volatility estimates using the PV Asset approach and simulation

3. The **Volatility to Probability** approach can provide rough estimates of volatility, or you can use it to explain to senior management the concept of volatility. To illustrate, say your model has an expected value of $100M, and the best-case scenario as modeled or expected or anticipated by subject matter experts or senior management is $150M with a 10% chance of exceeding this value. We compute the implied volatility as 39.02% (Figure 162.4).

Probability to Volatility (Best-Case Scenario)

Expected NPV of the Asset:	$100.00
Alternate Best-Case Scenario NPV:	$150.00
Percentile of Best-Case Scenario:	90.00%
Implied Volatility Estimate:	39.02%

Figure 162.4: Probability to volatility approximation approach

Clearly this is a rough estimate, but it is a good start if you do not wish to perform elaborate modeling and simulation to obtain a volatility measure. Further, this approach can be reversed. That is, instead of getting volatility from probability, you can get probability from volatility. This reversed method is very powerful in explaining to senior management the concept of volatility. To illustrate, we use the *Worst-Case Scenario* model next.

Suppose you run a simulation model and obtain an annualized volatility of 35% and need to explain what this means to management. Well, 35% volatility does not mean that there is a 35% chance of something happening, nor does it mean that the expected value can go up 35%, and so forth. Management has a hard time understanding volatility, whereas probability is a simpler concept. For instance, if you state that there is a 10% chance of something happening (such as a product being successful in the market), management understands this to mean that 1 out of 10 products will be a superstar. You can take advantage of this fact and impute the probability from the analytically computed volatility to explain the concept in a simplified manner. Using the *Probability to Volatility Worst-Case Scenario* model, assume that the worst-case is defined as the 10% left tail (you can change this if you wish), and that your analytical model provides a 35% volatility. Simply click on **Tools | Goal Seek** and set the cell **F24** (the volatility cell) to change to the value **35%** (your computed volatility) by *changing the alternate worst-case scenario* cell (**F21**). Clicking **OK** returns the value $55.15 in cell F21. This means that a 35% volatility can be described as a project with an expected NPV of $100M. It is risky enough that the worst-case scenario can occur less than 10% of the time, and if it does, it will reduce the project's NPV to $55.15M. In other words, there is a 1 in 10 chance the project will be below $55.15M or 9 out of 10 times it will make at least $55.15M (Figure 162.5).

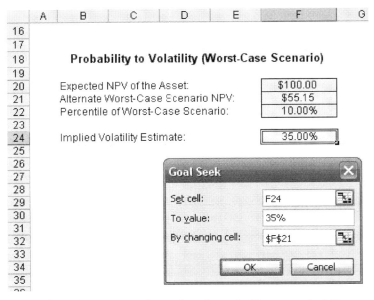

Figure 162.5: Sample computation using the volatility to probability approach

4. For the **EWMA** and **GARCH** approaches, time-specific multiple volatility forecasts are obtained. That is, a term structure of volatility can be determined using these approaches. GARCH models are used mainly in analyzing financial time-series data, in order to ascertain their conditional variances and volatilities. These volatilities are then used to value the options as usual, but the amount of historical data necessary for a good volatility estimate remains significant. Usually, several dozen—and even up to hundreds—of data points are required to obtain good GARCH estimates. GARCH is a term that incorporates a family of models that can take on a variety of forms, known as GARCH(p,q), where p and q are positive integers that define the resulting GARCH model and its forecasts. In most cases for financial instruments, a GARCH(1,1) is sufficient and is most generally used.

    For instance, a GARCH (1,1) model takes the form of

$$y_t = x_t \gamma + \varepsilon_t$$
$$\sigma_t^2 = \omega + \alpha \varepsilon_{t-1}^2 + \beta \sigma_{t-1}^2$$

where the first equation's dependent variable (y_t) is a function of exogenous variables (x_t) with an error term (ε_t). The second equation estimates the variance (squared volatility σ_t^2) at time t, which depends on a historical mean (ω), news about volatility from the previous period, measured as a lag of the squared residual from the mean equation (ε_{t-1}^2), and volatility from the previous period (σ_{t-1}^2). The exact modeling specification of a GARCH model is beyond the scope of this book. Suffice it to say that detailed knowledge of econometric modeling (model specification tests, structural breaks, and error estimation) is required to run a GARCH model, making it less accessible to the general analyst. The other problem with GARCH models is that the model usually does not provide a good statistical fit. That is, it is impossible to predict the stock market and, of course, equally if not harder to predict a stock's volatility over time. Figure 162.6 shows a GARCH (1,1) on a sample set of historical stock prices using the *MTGARCH* model.

	A	B		I	J
1				Computed Alpha	0.082019894
2	User Data			Couted Beta	0.914890346
3	Period	Inputs		Computed Omega	0.000000968
4	1	459.11			0.00%
5	2	460.71		Periods/Year	0.00%
6	3	460.34		252	17.80%
7	4	460.68			17.10%
8	5	460.83			16.44%
9	6	461.68			15.80%
10	7	461.66			15.22%
11	8	461.64			14.64%
12	9	465.97			14.09%
13	10	469.38			14.21%
14	11	470.05			14.08%
15	12	469.72			13.57%
16	13	466.95			13.08%
17	14	464.78			12.89%
18	15	465.81			12.61%
19	16	465.86			12.20%
20	17	467.44			11.78%

Figure 162.6: Sample GARCH (1,1) model

In order to create GARCH forecasts, start the Modeling Toolkit and open the **Volatility | GARCH** model. You will see a model that resembles Figure 162.7. Follow the next procedures to create the volatility estimates:

1. Enter the **Stock Prices** in chronological order (e.g., cells **I6:I17**).

2. Use the *MTGARCH* function call in Modeling Toolkit. For instance, cell K3 has the function call "MTGARCH($I$6:$I$17,$I$19,1,3)" where the stock price inputs are in cells I6:I17, the periodicity is 12 (i.e., there are 12 months in a year, to obtain the annualized volatility forecasts), and the predictive base is 1, and we forecast for a sample of 3 periods into the future. Because we will copy and paste the function down the column, make sure that absolute addressing is used, i.e., **$I$6** and not relative addressing I6.

3. Copy cell **K3** and paste the function on cells **K3:K20** (select cell **K3** and drag the fill handle to copy the function down the column). You do this because the first three values are the GARCH estimated parameters of Alpha, Beta, and Gamma, and at the bottom (e.g., cells K18:K20) are the forecast values.

4. With the entire column selected (cells **K3:K20** selected), hit **F2** on the keyboard, and then hold down **Shift+Ctrl** and hit **Enter**. This will update the entire matrix with GARCH forecasts.

Alternatively, and probably a simpler method, is to use Risk Simulator's *Forecast GARCH* module as seen in Figure 162.8, select the data location of raw stock prices, and enter in the required parameters (see below for a description of these parameters). The result is a GARCH volatility report seen in Figure 162.9.

Note that the GARCH function has several inputs as follow:

Stock Prices: This is the time series of stock prices in chronological order. Typically, dozens of data points are required for a decent volatility forecast.

Periodicity: This is a positive integer indicating the number of periods per year (e.g., 12 for monthly data, 252 for daily trading data, etc.), assuming you wish to annualize the volatility. For getting periodic volatility, enter 1.

Predictive Base: This is the number of periods (the time-series data) back to use as a base to forecast volatility. The higher this number, the longer the historical base is used to forecast future volatility.

Forecast Period: This is a positive integer indicating how many future periods beyond the historical stock prices you wish to forecast.

Variance Targeting: This variable is set as False by default (even if you do not enter anything here) but can be set as True. False means the omega variable is automatically optimized and computed. The suggestion is to leave this variable empty. If you wish to create mean-reverting volatility with variance targeting, set this variable as True.

P: This is the number of previous lags on the mean equation.

Q: This is the number of previous lags on the variance equation.

		GARCH (1,1)
	Alpha	0.1939450
	Beta	0.0000000
Periods (Months)	Stock Price	Omega	0.0013381
Jan	10.25	0.00%
Feb	13.25	0.00%
Mar	15.36	41.16%
Apr	15.95	25.86%
May	16.15	13.92%
Jun	15.45	12.81%
Jul	14.55	14.36%
Aug	15.50	15.63%
Sep	16.00	15.93%
Oct	16.20	13.57%
Nov	16.90	12.81%
Dec	17.50	14.22%
		13.74%
Periodicity	12	13.74%
		13.74%

Figure 162.7: Setting up a GARCH model

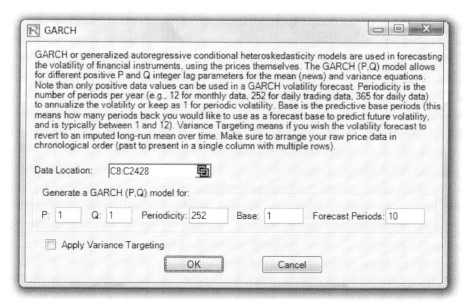

Figure 162.8: Running a GARCH model in Risk Simulator

GARCH: Generalized Autoregressive Conditional Heteroskedasticity (Volatility Forecast)

GARCH models are used mainly for computing the volatility on liquid and tradable assets such as stocks in financial options; this model is sometimes used for other traded assets such as price of oil and price of electricity. The drawback is that a lot of data is required, advanced econometric modeling expertise is required, and this approach is highly susceptible to user manipulation. The benefit is that rigorous statistical analysis is performed to find the best-fitting volatility curve, providing different volatility estimates over time. GARCH is a term that incorporates a family of models that can take on a variety of forms, known as GARCH (P,Q), where P and Q are positive integers that define the resulting GARCH model and its forecasts. In most cases for financial instruments, a GARCH (1,1) is sufficient and is most generally used.

GARCH Model (P, Q)		1,1	Periodicity (Periods/Year)	252
Optimized Alpha		0.0820	Predictive Base	1
Optimized Beta		0.9149	Forecast Periods	10
Optimized Omega		0.0000	Variance Targeting	FALSE

Period	Data	Volatility
0	459.11	
1	460.71	
2	460.34	17.80%
3	460.68	17.10%
4	460.83	16.44%
5	461.68	15.80%
6	461.66	15.22%
7	461.64	14.64%
8	465.97	14.09%
9	469.38	14.21%
10	470.05	14.08%
11	469.72	13.57%
12	466.95	13.08%
13	464.78	12.89%
14	465.81	12.61%
15	465.86	12.20%
16	467.44	11.78%
17	468.32	11.48%
18	470.39	11.12%
19	468.51	10.94%
20	470.42	10.73%
21	470.40	10.55%
22	472.78	10.21%
23	478.64	10.15%
24	481.14	11.32%
25	480.81	11.19%
26	481.19	10.82%
27	480.19	10.47%
28	481.46	10.18%

GARCH or generalized autoregressive conditional heteroskedasticity models are used in forecasting the volatility of financial instruments, using the prices themselves. The GARCH (P,Q) model allows for different positive P and Q integer lag parameters for the mean (news) and variance equations. Note than only positive data values can be used in a GARCH volatility forecast. Periodicity is the number of periods per year (e.g., 12 for monthly data, 252 for daily trading data, 365 for daily data) to annualize the volatility or keep as 1 for periodic volatility. Base is the predictive base periods (this means how many periods back you would like to use as a forecast base to predict future volatility, and is typically between 1 and 12). Variance Targeting means if you wish the volatility forecast to revert to an imputed long-run mean over time. Make sure to arrange

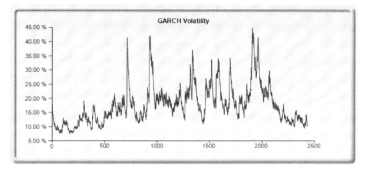

Figure 162.9: GARCH forecast results

163. Yield Curve – CIR Model

File Name: Yield Curve – CIR Model

Location: Modeling Toolkit | Yield Curve | CIR Model

Brief Description: Estimates and models the term structure of interest rates and yield curve approximation assuming the interest rates are mean-reverting

Requirements: Modeling Toolkit, Risk Simulator

Modeling Toolkit Function Used: MTCIRBondYield

The yield curve is the time-series relationship between interest rates and the time to maturity of some underlying debt. The more formal mathematical description of this relationship is called the term structure of interest rates. The yield curve can take on various shapes. In the normal yield curve, yields rise as maturity lengthens and the yield curve is positively sloped, reflecting investor expectations for the economy to grow in the future (and hence an expectation that inflation rates will rise in the future). An inverted yield curve occurs when long-term yields fall below short-term yields, and long-term investors will settle for lower yields now if they think the economy will slow or even decline in the future. This situation is indicative of a worsening economy in the future (and hence an expectation that inflation will remain low in the future). Another potential situation is a flat yield curve, signaling uncertainty in the economy. The yield curve also can be humped or show a smile or a frown. The yield curve over time can change in shape through a twist or bend, a parallel shift, or a movement on one end versus another.

As the yield curve is related to inflation rates, and central banks in most countries have the ability to control monetary policy to target inflation rates, inflation rates are mean-reverting in nature. This also implies that interest rates are mean-reverting as well as stochastically changing over time.

This chapter shows the *Cox-Ingersoll-Ross (CIR)* model, which is used to compute the term structure of interest rates and yield curve. The CIR model assumes a mean-reverting stochastic interest rate. The rate of reversion and long-run mean rates can be determined using Risk Simulator's *Statistical Analysis* tool. If the long-run rate is higher than the current short rate, the yield curve is upward sloping, and vice versa. Please see Figure 163.1.

CIR MODEL
YIELD CURVE CONSTRUCTION

Input Assumptions

Time to Maturity of the Bond or Debt (Years)	1.00
Riskfree Rate (Short Rate)	3.00%
Long-run Mean Rate	8.00%
Annualized Volatility of Interest Rate	6.00%
Market Price of Interest Rate Risk	0.00%
Rate of Mean Reversion	25.00%

Yield of Zero Coupon Bond   3.5744%

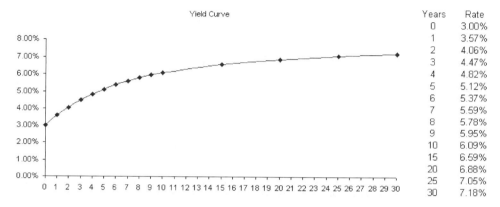

Yield Curve

Years	Rate
0	3.00%
1	3.57%
2	4.06%
3	4.47%
4	4.82%
5	5.12%
6	5.37%
7	5.59%
8	5.78%
9	5.95%
10	6.09%
15	6.59%
20	6.88%
25	7.05%
30	7.18%

Figure 163.1: CIR model on yield curve construction

164. Yield Curve – Curve Interpolation BIM Model

File Name: Yield Curve – Curve Interpolation BIM

Location: Modeling Toolkit | Yield Curve | Curve Interpolation BIM

Brief Description: Estimates and models the term structure of interest rates and yield curve approximation using a curve interpolation method

Requirements: Modeling Toolkit, Risk Simulator

Modeling Toolkit Function Used: MTYieldCurveBIM

A number of alternative methods exist for estimating the term structure of interest rates and the yield curve. Some are fully specified stochastic term structure models while others are simply interpolation models. The former include the *CIR* and *Vasicek* models (illustrated in other chapters in this book), while the latter are interpolation models such as the Bliss or Nelson approach. This chapter looks at the *Bliss Interpolation* model (BIM) (Figure 164.1) for generating the term structure of interest rates and yield curve estimation. Some econometric modeling techniques are required to calibrate the values of several input parameters in this model. The Bliss approach modifies the Nelson-Siegel method by adding an additional generalized parameter. Virtually any yield curve shape can be interpolated using these models, which are widely used at banks around the world.

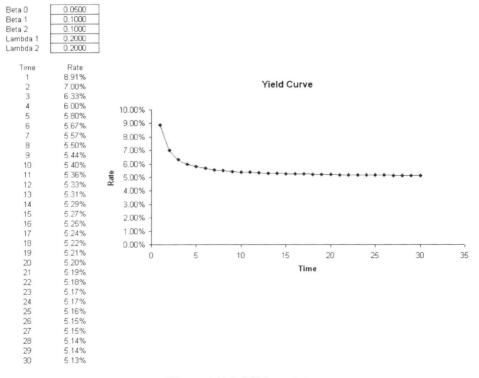

Figure 164.1: BIM model

165. Yield Curve – Curve Interpolation NS Model

File Name: Yield Curve – Curve Interpolation NS

Location: Modeling Toolkit | Yield Curve | Curve Interpolation NS

Brief Description: Estimates and models the term structure of interest rates and yield curve approximation using a curve interpolation method

Requirements: Modeling Toolkit, Risk Simulator

Modeling Toolkit Function Used: MTYieldCurveNS

This is the *Nelson-Siegel (NS) Interpolation* model for generating the term structure of interest rates and yield curve estimation. Some econometric modeling techniques are required to calibrate the values of several input parameters in this model. Just like the Bliss model in the previous chapter, the NS model (Figure 165.1) is purely an interpolation model, with four estimated parameters. If properly modeled, it can be made to fit almost any yield curve shape. Calibrating the inputs in the NS model requires facility with econometric modeling and error optimization techniques. Typically, if some interest rates exist, a better approach is to use the spline interpolation method (see Chapter 168 for details).

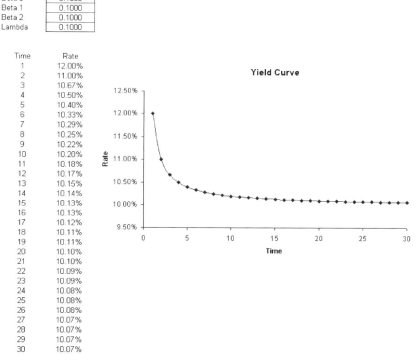

Figure 165.1: NS model

166. Yield Curve – Forward Rates from Spot Rates

File Name: Yield Curve – Forward Rates from Spot Rates

Location: Modeling Toolkit | Yield Curve | Forward Rates from Spot Rates

Brief Description: Determines the implied forward rate given two spot rates

Requirements: Modeling Toolkit, Risk Simulator

Modeling Toolkit Function Used: MTForwardRate

Given two spot rates (from Year 0 to some future time periods), you can determine the implied forward rate between these two time periods using this bootstrap model. For instance, if the spot rate from Year 0 to Year 1 is 8%, and the spot rate from Year 0 to Year 2 is 7% (both yields are known currently), the implied forward rate from Year 1 to Year 2 (that will occur based on current expectations) is 6%. See Figure 166.1.

FORWARD RATES
COMPUTING FORWARD RATES FROM SPOT RATES

Input Assumptions

Spot Rate 1	8.00%
Spot Rate 2	7.00%
Time of Spot Rate 1	1.00
Time of Spot Rate 2	2.00

Forward Rate　　　　　　　　　　6.00%

Figure 166.1: Forward rate extrapolation

167. Yield Curve – Term Structure of Volatility

File Name: Yield Curve – Term Structure of Volatility

Location: Modeling Toolkit | Yield Curve | Term Structure of Volatility

Brief Description: Illustrates the term structure of volatilities of interest rates

Requirements: Modeling Toolkit, Risk Simulator

Not only are interest rates themselves critical but their underlying volatility is also key. Interest rate volatilities change over time and, depending on the maturity, also are different during the same time period. Are shorter-term rates more volatile or long-term rates more volatile? It depends on the liquidity preference, trading market depth, economic outlook, and so forth. Using multiple years of historical data, spot interest rates are analyzed and their respective volatilities are tabulated in the model, and the results are shown in Figures 167.1 and 167.2.

Term Structure of Volatility

	3 Month	6 Month	1 Year	2 Year	3 Year	5 Year	7 Year	10 Year	20 Year
Average	8.65%	8.58%	9.29%	13.06%	13.39%	13.79%	13.62%	12.80%	12.12%

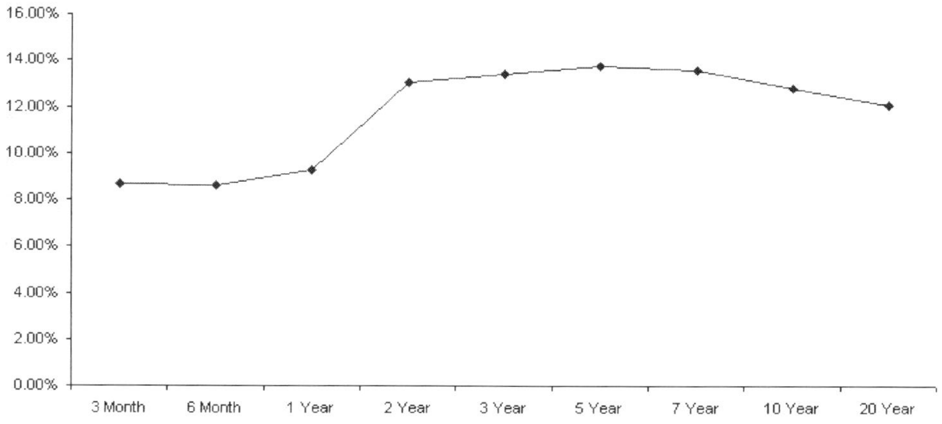

Figure 167.1: Term structure of average volatility

Notice that longer-term yields tend to have smaller volatilities than shorter-term, more liquid and highly traded instruments (Figure 167.2), such as one-year Treasury bills.

Note that in the *Bond Options* models, we use the BDT lattices to model the term structure of interest rates accounting for different spot rates and local volatilities over time. In contrast, this chapter uses actual empirically based models to determine the historical term structure of interest rates and their local volatilities.

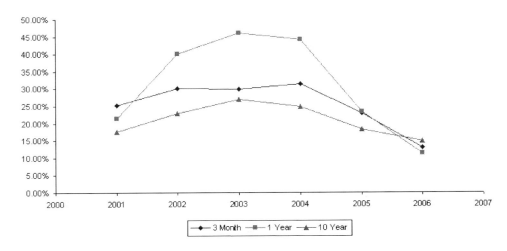

Figure 167.2: Term structure of volatility by maturity

168. Yield Curve – U.S. Treasury Risk-free Rates and Cubic Spline Curves

File Name: Yield Curve – U.S. Treasury Risk-free Rates and Yield Curve – Spline Interpolation and Extrapolation

Location: Modeling Toolkit | Yield Curve | U.S. Treasury Risk-free Rates and Modeling Toolkit | Yield Curve | Spline Interpolation and Extrapolation

Brief Description: Illustrates how to use Risk Simulator for applying distributional fitting and computing volatilities of risk-free rates (application of a Cubic Spline curve to interpolate and extrapolate missing risk-free rates also includes)

Requirements: Modeling Toolkit, Risk Simulator

This model shows the daily historical yield of the U.S. Treasury securities, from 1 month to 30 years, for the years 1990 to 2006. The volatilities of these time-series yields are also computed, and they are then put through a distributional fitting routine in Risk Simulator to determine if they can be fitted to a particular distribution and hence used in a model elsewhere.

There are several ways to compute the volatility of a time series of data, including:

- **Logarithmic Cash Flow or Stock Returns Approach:** This method is used mainly for computing the volatility on liquid and tradable assets, such as stocks in financial options; however, sometimes it is used for other traded assets, such as price of oil and electricity. The drawback is that discounted cash flow models with only a few cash flows generally will overstate the volatility, and this method cannot be used when negative cash flows occur. The benefits include its computational ease, transparency, and modeling flexibility of the method. In addition, no simulation is required to obtain a volatility estimate.

- **Logarithmic Present Value Returns Approach:** This approach is used mainly when computing the volatility on assets with cash flows. A typical application is in real options. The drawback of this method is that simulation is required to obtain a single volatility, and it is not applicable for highly traded liquid assets such as stock prices. The benefits include the ability to accommodate certain negative cash flows. Also this approach applies more rigorous analysis than the logarithmic cash flow returns approach, providing a more accurate and conservative estimate of volatility when assets are analyzed.

- **Management Assumptions and Guesses:** This approach is used for both financial options and real options. The drawback is that the volatility estimates are very unreliable and are only subjective best guesses. The benefit of this approach is its simplicity—using this method, you can easily explain to management the concept of volatility, both in execution and interpretation.

- **Generalized Autoregressive Conditional Heteroskedasticity (GARCH) Models:** These methods are used mainly for computing the volatility on liquid and tradable assets, such as stocks in financial options. However, sometimes they are used for other traded assets, such as the price of oil or electricity. The drawback is that these models require a lot of data and advanced econometric modeling expertise is required. In addition, these models are highly susceptible to user manipulation. The benefit is that rigorous statistical analysis is performed to find the best-fitting volatility curve, providing different volatility estimates over time.

This model applies the first method and only describes the approach on a very superficial level. For detailed technical details on volatility estimates, including the theory and step-by-step interpretation of the method, please refer to Chapter 7 of Dr. Johnathan Mun's *Real Options Analysis*, Third Edition (Thomson–Shore, 2016).

The *Risk-Free Rate Volatility* worksheet shows the computed annualized volatilities for each term structure, together with the average, median, minimum, and maximum values. These volatilities are also fitted to continuous distributions and the results are shown in the Fitting *Volatility* worksheet. Notice that longer-term yields tend to have smaller volatilities than shorter-term more liquid and highly traded instruments.

Procedure

The volatilities and their distributions have already been determined in this model. To review them, follow these instructions:

1. Select any of the worksheets (1990 to 2006) and look at the historical risk-free rates as well as how the volatilities are computed using the logarithmic returns approach.

2. Go to the *Fitting Volatility* worksheet and view the resulting fitted distributions, their p-values, theoretical versus empirical values, and cross-correlations (Figure 168.1).

3. Notice that in most cases, the p-values are pretty high. For example, the p-value for the 3-month volatilities for the past 17 years is 0.9853, or roughly, about 98.53% of the fluctuations in the actual data can be accounted for by the fitted lognormal distribution, which is indicative of an extremely good fit. We can use this information to model and simulate short-term volatilities very robustly. In addition, the cross-correlations indicate that yields of closely related terms are highly correlated, but the correlation decreases over time. For instance, the 3-month volatilities tend to be highly correlated to the 6-month volatilities but only have negligible correlations to longer term yields' (e.g., 10-year) volatilities. This is highly applicable for simulating and modeling options-embedded instruments, such as options-adjusted spreads, which require the term structure of interest rates and volatility structure.

Multiple Variable Distributional Fitting

Statistical Summary

Variable Name	3 Month		Variable Name	6 Month		Variable Name	1 Year	
Best-Fit Assumption	0.32		Best-Fit Assumption	0.30		Best-Fit Assumption	0.33	
Fitted Distribution	**Lognormal**		Fitted Distribution	**Triangular**		Fitted Distribution	**Gumbel (Maximum)**	
Mu	-1.36		Minimum	-0.05		Alpha	0.23	
Sigma	0.70		Most Likely	0.08		Beta	0.22	
			Maximum	0.84				
Kolmogorov-Smirnov Statistic	0.11		Kolmogorov-Smirnov Statistic	0.15		Kolmogorov-Smirnov Statistic	0.15	
P-Value for Test Statistic	**0.9853**		P-Value for Test Statistic	**0.8181**		P-Value for Test Statistic	**0.8180**	
	Actual	Theoretical		Actual	Theoretical		Actual	Theoretical
Mean	0.32	0.33	Mean	0.30	0.29	Mean	0.33	0.36
Standard Deviation	0.22	0.26	Standard Deviation	0.21	0.20	Standard Deviation	0.20	0.29
Skewness	1.28	2.87	Skewness	1.05	0.52	Skewness	0.46	1.14
Excess Kurtosis	1.51	17.51	Excess Kurtosis	0.98	-0.60	Excess Kurtosis	-0.48	2.40

Variable Name	2 Year	Variable Name	3 Year	Variable Name	5 Year
Best-Fit Assumption	0.34	Best-Fit Assumption	0.31	Best-Fit Assumption	0.26
Fitted Distribution	**Lognormal**	Fitted Distribution	**Lognormal**	Fitted Distribution	**Lognormal**
Mu	-1.21	Mu	-1.31	Mu	-1.51
Sigma	0.76	Sigma	0.66	Sigma	0.52

Figure 168.1: P-values and cross-correlations of fitting routines

Correlation Matrix

	3 Month	6 Month	1 Year	2 Year	3 Year	5 Year	7 Year	10 Year
3 Month	1							
6 Month	0.986068	1						
1 Year	0.907243	0.958162	1					
2 Year	0.578518	0.684161	0.8539608	1				
3 Year	0.449018	0.56911	0.7588623	0.981742	1			
5 Year	0.201037	0.337348	0.5485411	0.869494	0.944104	1		
7 Year	0.137761	0.273914	0.472691	0.789994	0.881749	0.983872	1	
10 Year	0.085105	0.217716	0.3945755	0.684885	0.788038	0.931852	0.9798362	1

Figure 168.1: P-values and cross-correlations of fitting routines *(continued)*

To replicate the distributional fitting routine, follow the instructions below. You can perform a single-variable fitting and replicate the steps for multiple variables or perform a multiple fitting routine once. To perform individual fits:

1. Start a new profile by clicking on **Risk Simulator | New Simulation Profile** and give it a name.

2. Go to the *Risk-Free Rate Volatility* worksheet and select a data column (e.g., select cells **K6:K22**).

3. Start the single-fitting procedure by clicking on **Risk Simulator | Analytical Tools | Distributional Fitting (Single-Variable)**.

4. Select **Fit to Continuous Distributions** and make sure all distributions are checked (by default) and click **OK**.

5. Review the results. Note that the best-fitting distribution is listed or ranked first, complete with its p-value. A high p-value is considered statistically to be a good fit. That is, the null hypothesis that the fitted distribution is the right distribution cannot be rejected; therefore, we can conclude that the distribution fitted is the best fit. Thus, the higher the p-value, the better the fit. Alternatively, you can roughly think of the p-value as the percentage fit, for example, the Gumbel Maximum Distribution fits the 10-year volatilities at about 95.77%. You also can review the theoretical and empirical statistics to see how closely the theoretical distribution matches the actual empirical data. If you click **OK**, a single-fit report will be generated together with the assumption. See Figure 168.2.

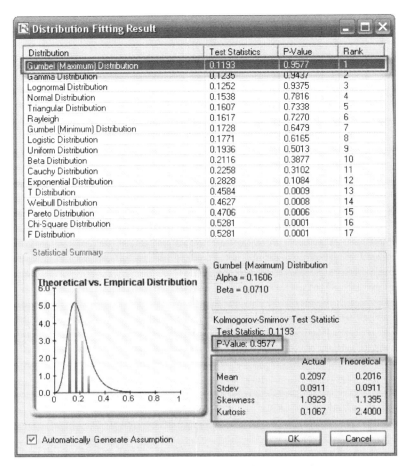

Figure 168.2: Distributional fitting results

Alternatively, you can perform a multiple-variable fitting routine to fit multiple variables at the same time. The problem here is that the data must be complete. In other words, there must be no gaps in the area selected. Looking at the *Risk-Free Rate Volatility* worksheet, there are gaps as in certain years, the 1-month Treasure Bill, 20-year Treasury Note, and 30-year Treasury Bond are not issued, hence the empty cells. You may have to perform a multi-variable fitting routine on the 3-month to 10-year volatilities and perform single-variable fits on the remaining 1-month, 20-year, and 30-year issues. To perform a multi-variable fit, follow these steps:

1. Make sure you have already created a simulation profile. Then, select the cells **D6:K22** and start the multi-fit routine: **Risk Simulator | Analytical Tools | Distributional Fitting (Multi-Variable)**.

2. You can rename each of the variables if desired, and make sure that the distribution types are all set to **Continuous**. Click **OK** when ready. A multiple distribution fitting report will then be generated (see the *Fitting Volatility* spreadsheet). See Figure 168.3.

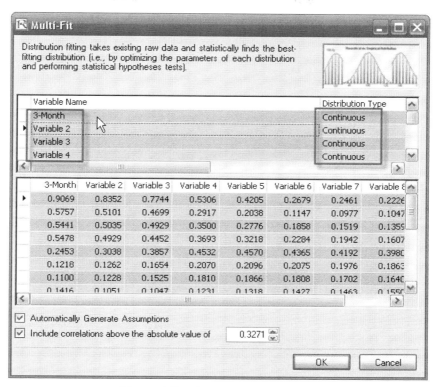

Figure 168.3: Multiple fitting result

Cubic Spline Curves

The cubic spline polynomial interpolation and extrapolation model is used to "fill in the gaps" of missing values in a time-series dataset. In this chapter, we illustrate the model application on spot yields and term structure of interest rates whereby the model can be used to both interpolate missing data points within a time series of interest rates (as well as other macroeconomic variables such as inflation rates and commodity prices or market returns) and also used to extrapolate outside of the given or known range, useful for forecasting purposes.

To illustrate, Figure 168.4 shows the published zero coupon government bonds (risk-free rates) issued by the U.S. Department of Treasury. The values provided are 1-month, 3-month, 6-month, 1–3 years, and then skips to years 5, 7, 10, 20 and 30. We can apply the cubic spline methodology to interpolate the missing values from 1 month to 30 years, and extrapolate beyond 30 years. Figure 168.5 shows the interest rates plotted as a yield curve, and Figure 168.6 shows how to run the cubic spline forecasts. You can use either Modeling Toolkit's *MTCubicSpline* function or **Risk Simulator | Forecasting | Cubic Spline**. The *Known X Values* input are the values on the x-axis (in the example, we are interpolating interest rates, a time series of values, making the x-axis time). The *Known Y Values* are the published interest rates. With this information, we can determine the required Y values (missing interest rates) by providing the required X values (the time periods where we want to predict the interest rates).

Daily Treasury Yield Curve Rates

✉ Get e-mail updates when this information changes.

Historical Data

XML This data is also available in XML format by clicking on the XML icon

September 2007

Date	1 mo	3 mo	6 mo	1 yr	2 yr	3 yr	5 yr	7 yr	10 yr	20 yr	30 yr
09/04/07	4.55	4.47	4.52	4.39	4.13	4.16	4.26	4.38	4.56	4.88	4.84
09/05/07	4.41	4.36	4.41	4.28	4.03	4.05	4.16	4.29	4.48	4.82	4.78
09/06/07	4.28	4.29	4.42	4.30	4.08	4.09	4.20	4.32	4.51	4.84	4.79
09/07/07	4.03	4.07	4.20	4.10	3.90	3.92	4.03	4.17	4.38	4.73	4.70
09/10/07	3.93	3.96	4.20	4.09	3.87	3.89	4.00	4.13	4.34	4.68	4.65
09/11/07	4.13	4.11	4.27	4.16	3.95	3.97	4.07	4.19	4.37	4.68	4.65
09/12/07	4.00	4.03	4.20	4.12	3.95	3.99	4.11	4.23	4.41	4.72	4.68
09/13/07	4.04	4.08	4.27	4.20	4.08	4.11	4.22	4.33	4.49	4.79	4.75
09/14/07	3.85	4.01	4.22	4.16	4.05	4.07	4.18	4.30	4.47	4.77	4.72
09/17/07	3.82	4.15	4.31	4.23	4.08	4.11	4.21	4.32	4.48	4.76	4.72
09/18/07	3.87	4.01	4.12	4.08	4.00	4.04	4.19	4.32	4.50	4.81	4.77

Daily Treasury
Yield Curve Rates

Daily Treasury Bill
Rates

Daily Treasury
Long-Term Rates

Daily Treasury Real
Yield Curve Rates

Daily Treasury Real
Long-Term Rates

Figure 168.4: Sample U.S. Treasury risk-free interest rates

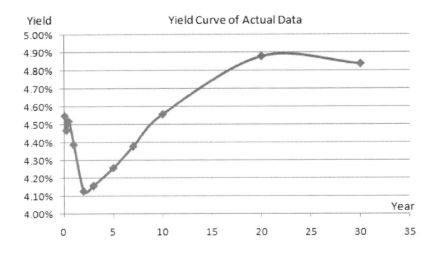

Figure 168.5: Yield curve of published rates

Function: B2CubicSpline (Known X, Known Y, Required X)

Years	Spot Yields
0.0833	4.55%
0.2500	4.47%
0.5000	4.52%
1.0000	4.39%
2.0000	4.13%
3.0000	4.16%
5.0000	4.26%
7.0000	4.38%
10.0000	4.56%
20.0000	4.88%
30.0000	4.84%

These are the yields that are known and are used as inputs in the Cublic Spline Interpolation and Extrapolation model

Figure 168.6: Modeling cubic spline

Figure 168.7 shows the results from a cubic spline forecast. The entire term structure of interest rates for every six months is obtained, from the period of 6 months to 50 years. The interest rates obtained up to year 30 are interpolated. Interest rates beyond year 30 are extrapolated from the original known dataset. Notice that the time-series chart shows a nonlinear polynomial function that is obtained using spline curve methodology.

Spline Interpolation and Extrapolation Results

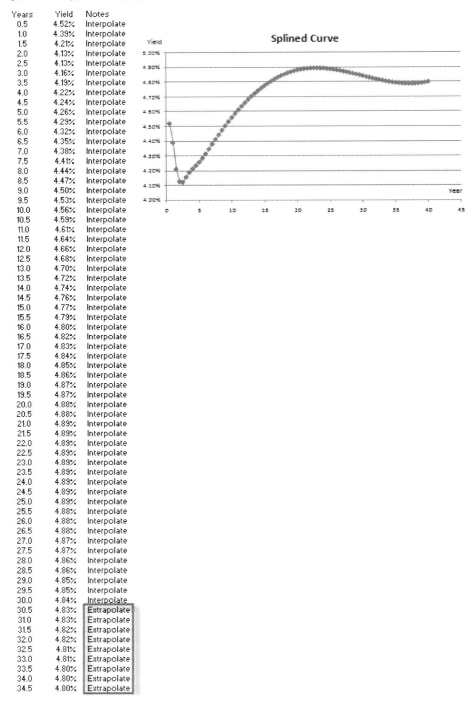

Years	Yield	Notes
0.5	4.52%	Interpolate
1.0	4.39%	Interpolate
1.5	4.21%	Interpolate
2.0	4.13%	Interpolate
2.5	4.13%	Interpolate
3.0	4.16%	Interpolate
3.5	4.19%	Interpolate
4.0	4.22%	Interpolate
4.5	4.24%	Interpolate
5.0	4.26%	Interpolate
5.5	4.29%	Interpolate
6.0	4.32%	Interpolate
6.5	4.35%	Interpolate
7.0	4.38%	Interpolate
7.5	4.41%	Interpolate
8.0	4.44%	Interpolate
8.5	4.47%	Interpolate
9.0	4.50%	Interpolate
9.5	4.53%	Interpolate
10.0	4.56%	Interpolate
10.5	4.59%	Interpolate
11.0	4.61%	Interpolate
11.5	4.64%	Interpolate
12.0	4.66%	Interpolate
12.5	4.68%	Interpolate
13.0	4.70%	Interpolate
13.5	4.72%	Interpolate
14.0	4.74%	Interpolate
14.5	4.76%	Interpolate
15.0	4.77%	Interpolate
15.5	4.79%	Interpolate
16.0	4.80%	Interpolate
16.5	4.82%	Interpolate
17.0	4.83%	Interpolate
17.5	4.84%	Interpolate
18.0	4.85%	Interpolate
18.5	4.86%	Interpolate
19.0	4.87%	Interpolate
19.5	4.87%	Interpolate
20.0	4.88%	Interpolate
20.5	4.88%	Interpolate
21.0	4.89%	Interpolate
21.5	4.89%	Interpolate
22.0	4.89%	Interpolate
22.5	4.89%	Interpolate
23.0	4.89%	Interpolate
23.5	4.89%	Interpolate
24.0	4.89%	Interpolate
24.5	4.89%	Interpolate
25.0	4.89%	Interpolate
25.5	4.88%	Interpolate
26.0	4.88%	Interpolate
26.5	4.88%	Interpolate
27.0	4.87%	Interpolate
27.5	4.87%	Interpolate
28.0	4.86%	Interpolate
28.5	4.86%	Interpolate
29.0	4.85%	Interpolate
29.5	4.85%	Interpolate
30.0	4.84%	Interpolate
30.5	4.83%	Extrapolate
31.0	4.83%	Extrapolate
31.5	4.82%	Extrapolate
32.0	4.82%	Extrapolate
32.5	4.81%	Extrapolate
33.0	4.81%	Extrapolate
33.5	4.80%	Extrapolate
34.0	4.80%	Extrapolate
34.5	4.80%	Extrapolate

Figure 168.7: Cubic spline results

169. Yield Curve – Vasicek Model

File Name: Yield Curve – Vasicek Model

Location: Modeling Toolkit | Yield Curve | Vasicek Model

Brief Description: Creates the term structure of interest rates and reconstructs the yield curve assuming the underlying interest rates are mean-reverting and stochastic

Requirements: Modeling Toolkit, Risk Simulator

Modeling Toolkit Function Used: MTVasicekBondYield

A Vasicek model is used to compute the term structure of interest rates and yield curve; it assumes a mean-reverting stochastic interest rate. The rate of reversion and long-run mean rates can be determined using Risk Simulator's *Statistical Analysis* tool. If the long-run rate is higher than the current short rate, the yield curve is upward sloping, and vice versa.

The yield curve is the time-series relationship between interest rates and the time to maturity of some underlying debt. The more formal mathematical description of this relationship is called the term structure of interest rates. The yield curve can take on various shapes. In the normal yield curve, yields rise as maturity lengthens and the yield curve is positively sloped, reflecting investor expectations for the economy to grow in the future (and hence an expectation that inflation rates will rise in the future). An inverted yield curve occurs when the long-term yields fall below short-term yields, and long-term investors settle for lower yields now if they think the economy will slow or even decline in the future, indicative of a worsening economic situation in the future (and hence an expectation that inflation will remain low in the future). Another potential situation is a flat yield curve, signaling uncertainty in the economy. The yield curve also can be humped or show a smile or a frown. The yield curve over time can change in shape through a twist or bend, a parallel shift, or a movement on one end versus another.

As the yield curve is related to inflation rates, and as central banks in most countries have the ability to control monetary policy to target inflation rates, inflation rates are mean-reverting in nature. This also implies that interest rates are mean-reverting as well as stochastically changing over time.

In a 1977 paper, a Czech mathematician, Oldrich Vasicek, proved that bond prices on a yield curve over time and various maturities are driven by the short end of the yield curve, or the short-term interest rates, using a risk-neutral martingale measure. In his work the mean-reverting Ornstein-Uhlenbeck process was assumed, hence the resulting Vasicek model requires that a mean-reverting interest rate process be modeled (rate of mean reversion and long-run mean rates are both inputs in the Vasicek model). See Figure 169.1.

VASICEK MODEL
YIELD CURVE CONSTRUCTION

Input Assumptions

Time to Maturity of the Bond or Debt (Years)	1.00
Riskfree Rate (Short Rate)	2.00%
Long-run Mean Rate	8.00%
Annualized Volatility of Interest Rate	2.00%
Market Price of Interest Rate Risk	0.00%
Rate of Mean Reversion	20.00%

Yield of Zero Coupon Bond   **2.5562%**

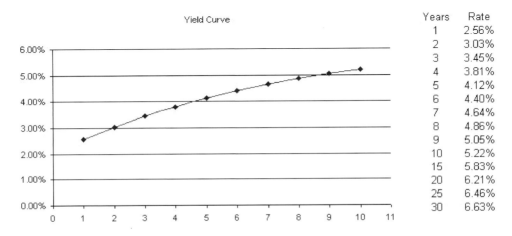

Years	Rate
1	2.56%
2	3.03%
3	3.45%
4	3.81%
5	4.12%
6	4.40%
7	4.64%
8	4.86%
9	5.05%
10	5.22%
15	5.83%
20	6.21%
25	6.46%
30	6.63%

Figure 169.1: Using the Vasicek model to generate a yield curve

PART II: REAL OPTIONS SLS APPLICATIONS

This section goes into more detail in terms of the applications and computations of real options problems using the *Real Options SLS* software. Each option is discussed in detail followed by simple case studies and solutions using the SLS software. Additional study questions and hands-on exercises are also included at the end of some of the case studies. For more details on Real Options Analysis and the applications of the SLS software, please refer to the book, *Real Options Analysis,* Third Edition (Thomson–Shore, 2016), also by the author, which provides more detailed and protracted discussions, including the analytics behind the computations Those discussions are focused on understanding how the real options analysis process works, whereas this section's short cases are focused on how the real options computations and software work. The *Real Options SLS* software comprises several modules listed below.

- The *Single Asset Super Lattice Solver (SLS)* module is used primarily for solving options with a single underlying asset using binomial lattices. Even highly complex options with a single underlying asset can be solved using the SLS included in this module.

- The *Multiple Asset/Phase Super Lattice Solver (MSLS)* module is used for solving options with multiple underlying assets and sequential compound options with multiple phases using binomial lattices. Highly complex options with multiple underlying assets and phases can be solved using the MSLS found in this module.

- The *Multinomial Lattice Solver (MNLS)* module uses multinomial lattices (trinomial, quadranomial, pentanomial) to solve specific options that cannot be solved using binomial lattices.

- The *Lattice Maker* is used to create lattices in Excel with visible and live equations, useful for running Monte Carlo simulations with the Risk Simulator software (an Excel add-in, risk-based simulation, forecasting, and optimization software also developed by ROV) or for linking to and from other spreadsheet models. The lattices generated also include decision lattices where the strategic decisions to execute certain options and the optimal timing to execute these options are shown.

- The *Advanced Exotic Financial Options Valuator* is a comprehensive calculator of more than 250 functions and models, from basic options to exotic options (e.g., from Black-Scholes to multinomial lattices to closed-form differential equations and analytical methods for valuing exotic options, as well as other options-related models such as bond options, volatility computations, delta-gamma hedging, etc.).

- The *SLS Excel Solution* implements the SLS and MSLS computations within the Excel environment, allowing users to access the SLS and MSLS functions directly in Excel. This feature facilitates model building, formula and value linking and embedding, and running simulations, and provides the user sample templates to create such models.

- The *SLS Functions* are additional real options and financial options models accessible directly through Excel. This module facilitates model building, linking and embedding, and running simulations.

- The *Strategy Tree* module is used to simplify the drawing and creation of strategy trees but is not used for the actual real options valuation modeling. This module helps you to create visually appealing representations of strategic real options during the options framing portion of your analysis.

170. Employee Stock Options – Simple American Call Option

File Name: Employee Stock Options – Simple American Call Option

Location: Modeling Toolkit | Real Options Models

Brief Description: Computes the American call option (the option is exercisable at any time up to and including maturity) using binomial lattices and closed-form solutions

Requirements: Modeling Toolkit, Real Options SLS

Figure 170.1 shows how an American Call Option can be computed using the Real Options SLS software. American options are, of course, exercisable at any time prior to and up to and including the maturity period.

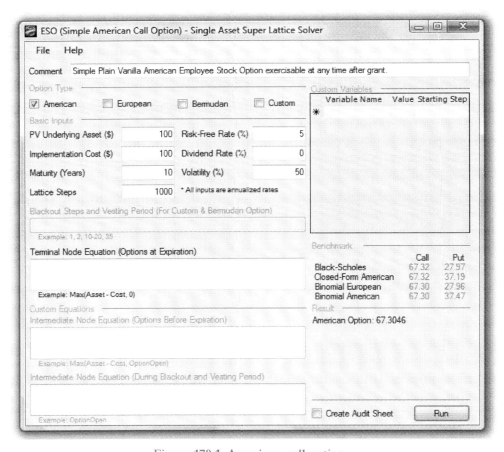

Figure 170.1: American call option

171. Employee Stock Options – Simple Bermudan Call Option with Vesting

File Name: Employee Stock Options – Simple Bermudan Call Option

Location: Modeling Toolkit | Real Options Models

Brief Description: Computes the Bermudan call option (the option is exercisable at any time up to and including maturity except during certain blackout periods) using binomial lattices and closed-form solutions

Requirements: Modeling Toolkit, Real Options SLS

Figure 171.1 illustrates the Real Options SLS model *Employee Stock Options – Simple Bermudan Call Option with Vesting* on how an employee stock option (ESO) with a vesting period and blackout dates can be modeled. Enter the blackout steps (0-39). Because the blackout dates input box has been used, you will need to enter the Terminal Node Equation (TE), Intermediate Node Equation (IE), and Intermediate Node Equation During Vesting and Blackout Periods (IEV). Enter *Max(Stock-Strike,0)* for the TE; *Max(Stock-Strike,0,OptionOpen)* for the IE; and *OptionOpen* for IEV (example file used: *ESO Vesting*). This means the option is executed or left to expire worthless at termination; execute early or keep the option open during the intermediate nodes; and keep the option open only and no executions are allowed during the intermediate steps when blackouts or vesting occurs. The result is $49.73 (Figure 171.1), which can be corroborated with the use of the ESO Valuation Toolkit (Figure 171.2).

ESO Valuation Toolkit is another software tool developed by the author at Real Options Valuation, Inc. (see www.realoptionsvaluation.com for more details), specifically designed to solve ESO problems following the 2004 FAS 123R. In fact, this software was used by the Financial Accounting Standards Board to model the valuation example in its final FAS 123R Statement in December 2004. Before starting with ESO valuations, it is suggested that you read *Valuing Employee Stock Options* (Wiley, 2004), another book by the author, as a primer.

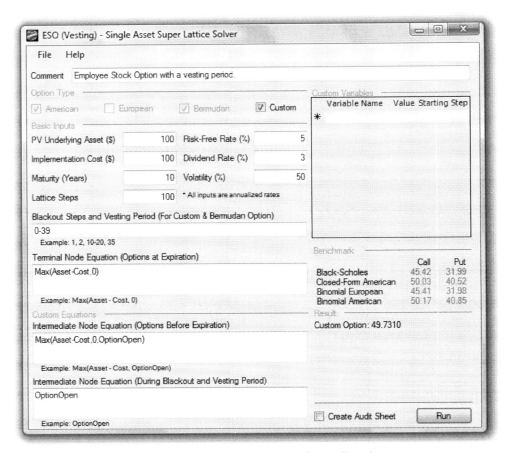

Figure 171.1: SLS results of a vesting call option

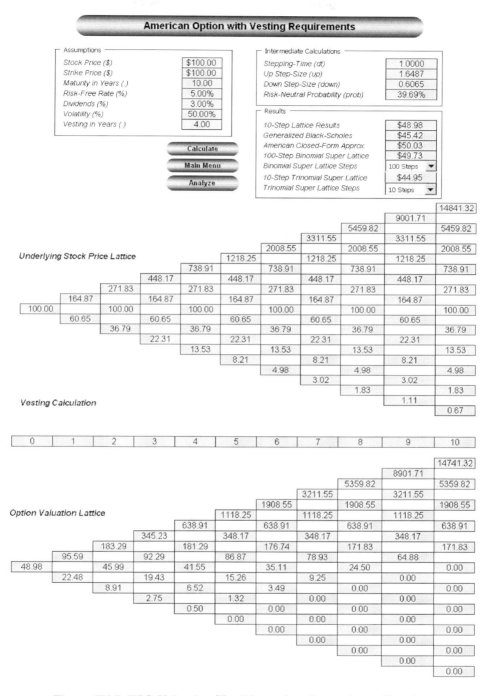

Figure 171.2: ESO Valuation Toolkit results of a vesting call option

172. Employee Stock Options – Simple European Call Option

File Name: Employee Stock Options – Simple European Call Option

Location: Modeling Toolkit | Real Options Models

Brief Description: Computes the European call option (the option is exercisable only at maturity) using binomial lattices and closed-form solutions

Requirements: Modeling Toolkit, Real Options SLS

The European call option can be exercised only at maturity. In most typical cases where the underlying asset of stock pays a dividend, an American call option is typically worth more than a Bermudan call option, which in turn is worth more than a European call option, due to each preceding option's ability to exercise early. Simple European options can be computed using closed-form models (e.g., Black-Scholes; Figure 172.1) as well as binomial lattices. The results are identical when sufficient lattice steps are applied. However, for more complex options models, only binomial lattices are appropriate or can be used to perform the valuation, as will be seen in later chapters.

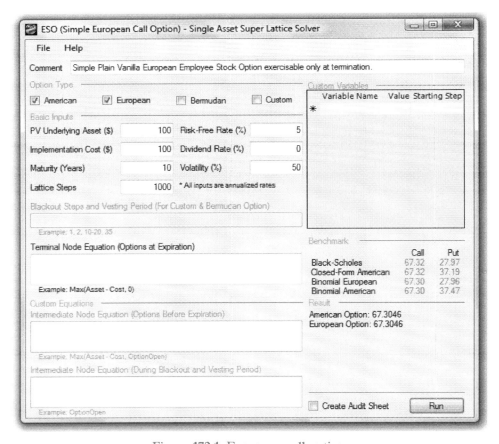

Figure 172.1: European call option

173. Employee Stock Options – Suboptimal Exercise

File Name: Employee Stock Options – Suboptimal Exercise

Location: Modeling Toolkit | Real Options

Brief Description: Values an employee stock option where suboptimal exercise behavior is considered and modeled

Requirements: Modeling Toolkit, Real Options SLS

This model shows how suboptimal exercise behavior multiples can be included in the analysis and how the custom variables list can be used as seen in Figure 173.1 (example file used: *ESO Suboptimal Behavior*). The terminal equation (TE) is the same as the previous example, but the intermediate equation (IE) assumes that the option will be suboptimally executed if the stock price in some future state exceeds the suboptimal exercise threshold times the strike price. Notice that the intermediate equation during vesting and blackout periods (IEV) is not used because we did not assume any vesting or blackout periods. Also, the *Suboptimal* exercise multiple variable is listed on the customs variable list with the relevant value of 1.85 and a starting step of 0. This means that 1.85 is applicable starting from step 0 in the lattice all the way through to step 100. The results again are verified through the ESO Toolkit (Figure 173.2).

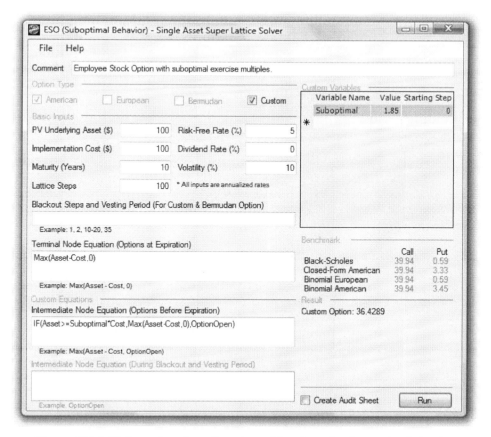

Figure 173.1: SLS results of a call option with suboptimal exercise behavior

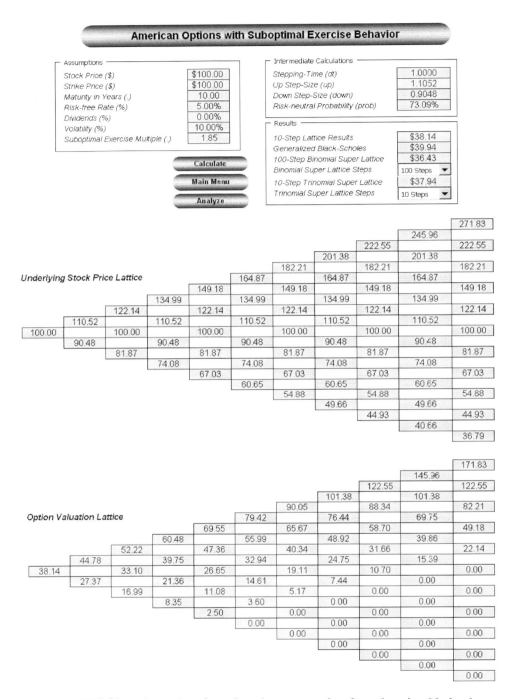

Figure 173.2: ESO Toolkit results of a call option accounting for suboptimal behavior

174. Employee Stock Options – Vesting, Blackout, Suboptimal, Forfeiture

File Name: Employee Stock Options – Vesting, Blackout, Suboptimal, Forfeiture

Location: Modeling Toolkit | Real Options

Brief Description: Computes an employee stock option after considering the real-life elements of vesting, blackout periods, suboptimal exercise behaviors, and forfeiture rates, which usually significantly lower the value of the option to be expensed and are solved only using a customized Real Options SLS approach (closed-form models are inadequate and inappropriate)

Requirements: Modeling Toolkit, Real Options SLS

This model incorporates the element of forfeiture into the model as seen in Figure 174.1 (example file used: *ESO Vesting, Blackout, Suboptimal, Forfeiture*). This means that if the option is vested and the prevailing stock price exceeds the suboptimal threshold above the strike price, the option will be executed summarily and suboptimally. If vested but not exceeding the threshold, the option will be executed only if the postvesting forfeiture occurs; otherwise the option is kept open. This means that the intermediate step is a probability-weighted average of these occurrences. Finally, when an employee forfeits the option during the vesting period, all options are forfeited, with a prevesting forfeiture rate. In this example, we assume identical pre- and postvesting forfeitures so that we can verify the results using the ESO Toolkit (Figure 174.2). In certain other cases, a different rate may be assumed. The next chapter applies these methodologies to solve actual business cases, where the process of options framing can be seen.

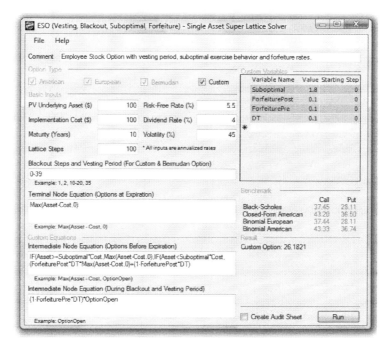

Figure 174.1: SLS results of a call option accounting for vesting, forfeiture, suboptimal behavior, and blackout periods

Customized American Option

Assumptions

Stock Price ($)	$100.00
Strike Price ($)	$100.00
Maturity in Years (.)	10.00
Risk-free Rate (%)	5.50%
Dividends (%)	4.00%
Volatility (%)	45.00%
Suboptimal Exercise Multiple (.)	1.80
Vesting in Years (.)	4.00
Forfeiture Rate (%)	10.00%

Results

Generalized Black-Scholes	$37.45
100-Step Super Lattice	$26.18
Super Lattice Steps	100 Steps

Calculate

Main Menu

Analyze

Additional Assumptions

Year	Volatility %		Year	Risk-free %
10.00	45.00%		10.00	5.50%
10.00	45.00%		10.00	5.50%
10.00	45.00%		10.00	5.50%
10.00	45.00%		10.00	5.50%
10.00	45.00%		10.00	5.50%
10.00	45.00%		10.00	5.50%
10.00	45.00%		10.00	5.50%
10.00	45.00%		10.00	5.50%
10.00	45.00%		10.00	5.50%
10.00	45.00%		10.00	5.50%

Please be aware that by applying multiple changing volatilities over time, a nonrecombining lattice is required, which increases the computation time significantly. In addition, only smaller lattice steps may be computed. When many volatilities over time and many lattice steps are required, use Monte Carlo simulation on the volatilities and run the Basic or Advanced Custom Option module instead.

Figure 174.2: ESO Toolkit results after accounting for vesting, forfeiture, suboptimal behavior, and blackout periods

175. Exotic Options – American and European Lower Barrier Options

File Names: Exotic Options – Barrier Option – Down and In Lower Barrier Call; Exotic Options – Barrier Option – Down and Out Lower Barrier Call

Location: Modeling Toolkit | Real Options

Brief Description: Computes upper barrier options, that is, options that either get kicked in the money or out of the money when they breach a lower barrier

Requirements: Modeling Toolkit, Real Options SLS

The *Lower Barrier Option* measures the strategic value of an option (this applies to both calls and puts) that comes either in the money or out of the money when the *Asset Value* hits an artificial *Lower Barrier* that is currently lower than the asset value. Therefore, a *Down and In* option (for both calls and puts) becomes live if the asset value hits the lower barrier. Conversely, a *Down and Out* option is live only when the lower barrier is not breached.

Examples of this option include contractual agreements whereby if the lower barrier is breached, some event or clause is triggered. The value of a barrier option is lower than standard options, as the barrier option will be valuable only within a smaller price range than the standard option. The holder of a barrier option loses some of the traditional option value, and therefore a barrier option should sell at a lower price than a standard option. An example would be a contractual agreement whereby the writer of the contract can get into or out of certain obligations if the asset or project value breaches a barrier.

Figure 175.1 shows a Lower Barrier Option for a Down and In Call. Notice that the value is only $7.3917, much lower than a regular American call option of $42.47. This is because the barrier is set low, at $90. This means that all of the upside potential that the regular call option can have will be reduced significantly, and the option can be exercised only if the asset value falls below this lower barrier of $90 (example file used: *Barrier Option – Down and In Lower Barrier Call*). To make such a Lower Barrier option *binding*, the *lower barrier level must be below the starting asset value but above the implementation cost*. If the barrier level is above the starting asset value, it becomes an upper barrier option. If the lower barrier is below the implementation cost, the option will be worthless under all conditions. When the lower barrier level is between the implementation cost and starting asset value, the option is potentially worth something. However, the value of the option is dependent on volatility. Using the same parameters as in Figure 175.1 and changing the volatility, the following examples illustrate what happens:

- At a volatility of 75%, the option value is $4.34.

- At a volatility of 25%, the option value is $3.14.

- At a volatility of 5%, the option value is $0.01.

The lower the volatility, the lower the probability that the asset value will fluctuate enough to breach the lower barrier such that the option will be executed. By balancing volatility with the threshold lower barrier, you can create optimal trigger values for barriers.

Figure 175.2 shows the Lower Barrier Option for Down and Out Call option. Here, if the asset value breaches this lower barrier, the option is worthless; it is valuable only when it does not breach this lower barrier. As call options have higher values when the asset value is high, and lower values when the asset value is low, this Lower Barrier Down and Out Call Option is worth almost the same as the regular American option. The higher the barrier, the lower the value of the lower barrier option will be (example file used here is the *Barrier Option – Down and Out Lower Barrier Call*). For instance,

- At a lower barrier of $90, the option value is $42.19

- At a lower barrier of $100, the option value is $41.58

Figures 175.1 and 175.2 illustrate American Barrier Options. To change these into European Barrier Options, set the Intermediate Node Equation to *OptionOpen*. In addition, for certain types of contractual options, vesting and blackout periods can be imposed. For solving such Bermudan Barrier Options, keep the same Intermediate Node Equation as the American Barrier Options but set the Intermediate Node Equation During Blackout and Vesting Periods to *OptionOpen* and insert the corresponding blackout and vesting period lattice steps. Finally, if the barrier is a changing target over time, put in several custom variables named *Barrier* with the different values and starting lattice steps.

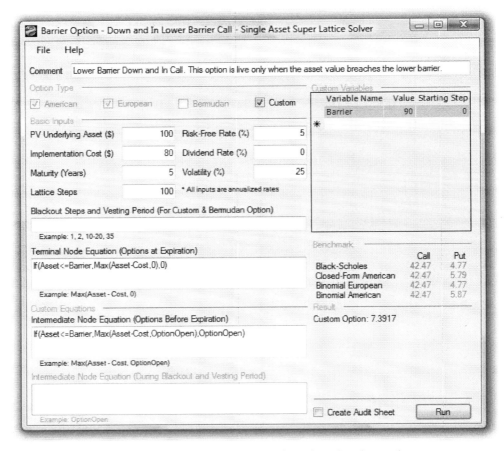

Figure 175.1: Down and in lower American barrier option

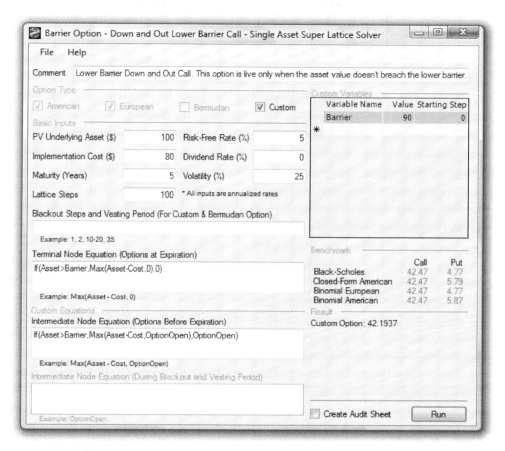

Figure 175.2: Down and out lower American barrier option

176. Exotic Options – American and European Upper Barrier Option

File Names: Exotic Options – Barrier Option – Up and In Upper Barrier Call; Real Options – Barrier Option – Up and Out Upper Barrier Call

Location: Modeling Toolkit | Real Options

Brief Description: Computes upper barrier options, that is, options that either get kicked in the money or out of the money when they breach an upper barrier

Requirements: Modeling Toolkit, Real Options SLS

The *Upper Barrier Option* measures the strategic value of an option (this applies to both calls and puts) that comes either in the money or out of the money when the *Asset Value* hits an artificial *Upper Barrier* that is currently higher than the asset value. Therefore, in an *Up and In* option (for both calls and puts), the option becomes live if the asset value hits the upper barrier. Conversely, for the *Up and Out* option, the option is live only when the upper barrier is not breached. This is very similar to the Lower Barrier Option but now the barrier is above the starting asset value, and for a binding barrier option, the implementation cost is typically lower than the upper barrier. That is, the *upper barrier is usually greater than implementation cost and the upper barrier is also greater than starting asset value.*

Examples of this option include contractual agreements whereby if the upper barrier is breached some event or clause is triggered. The values of barrier options typically are lower than standard options, as the barrier option will have value within a smaller price range than the standard option. The holder of a barrier option loses some of the traditional option value; therefore, a barrier option should sell at a lower price than a standard option. An example would be a contractual agreement whereby the writer of the contract can get into or out of certain obligations if the asset or project value breaches a barrier.

The Up and In Upper American Barrier Option has slightly lower value than a regular American call option, as seen in Figure 176.1, because some of the option value is lost when the asset is less than the barrier but greater than the implementation cost. Clearly, the *higher the upper barrier, the lower the up and in barrier option value* will be as more of the option value is lost due to the inability to execute when the asset value is below the barrier (example file used: *Barrier Option – Up and In Upper Barrier Call*). For instance:

- When the upper barrier is $110, the option value is $41.22.
- When the upper barrier is $120, the option value is $39.89.

In contrast, an Up and Out Upper American Barrier Option is worth a lot less because this barrier truncates the option's upside potential. Figure 176.2 shows the computation of such an option. Clearly, the *higher the upper barrier, the higher the option value* will be (example file used: *Barrier Option – Up and Out Upper Barrier Call*). For instance:

- When the upper barrier is $110, the option value is $23.69.
- When the upper barrier is $120, the option value is $29.59.

Finally, note the issues of nonbinding barrier options. Examples of **nonbinding options** are:

- Up and Out Upper Barrier Calls, where the option will be worthless when the Upper Barrier ≤ Implementation Cost

- Up and In Upper Barrier Calls, where the option value reverts to a simple call option when Upper Barrier ≤ Implementation Cost

Upper Barrier Options are contractual options; typical examples are:

- A manufacturer contractually agrees not to sell its products at prices higher than a prespecified upper barrier price level.

- A client agrees to pay the market price of a good or product until a certain amount and then the contract becomes void if it exceeds some price ceiling.

Figures 176.1 and 176.2 illustrate American Barrier Options. To change these into European Barrier Options, set the Intermediate Node Equation to *OptionOpen*. In addition, for certain types of contractual options, vesting and blackout periods can be imposed. For solving such Bermudan Barrier Options, keep the same Intermediate Node Equation as the American Barrier Options but set the Intermediate Node Equation During Blackout and Vesting Periods to *OptionOpen* and insert the corresponding blackout and vesting period lattice steps. Finally, if the barrier is a changing target over time, put in several custom variables named *Barrier* with the different values and starting lattice steps.

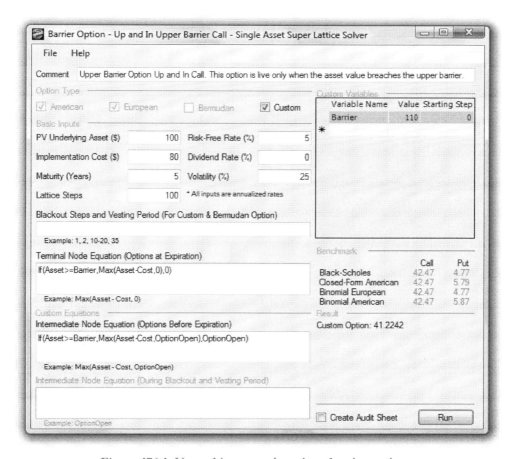

Figure 176.1: Up and in upper American barrier option

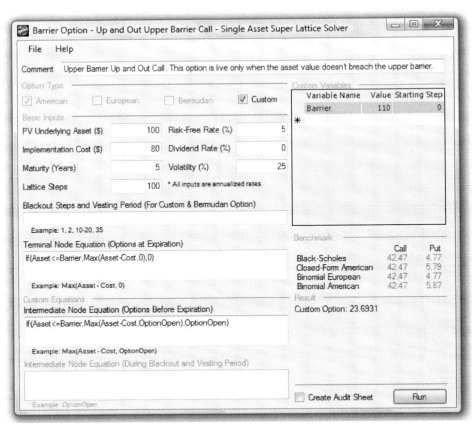

Figure 176.2: Up and out upper American barrier option

177. Exotic Options – American and European Double Barrier Options and Exotic Barriers

File Names: Exotic Options – Barrier Option – Up and In, Down and In Double Barrier Call; Exotic Options – Barrier Option – Up and Out, Down and Out Double Barrier Call

Location: Modeling Toolkit | Real Options Models

Brief Description: Computes American and European double barrier options where the option gets kicked in the money or out of the money if the underlying asset or stock breaches an upper or lower barrier

Requirements: Modeling Toolkit, Real Options SLS

The *Double Barrier Option* is solved using the binomial lattice. This model measures the strategic value of an option (this applies to both calls and puts) that comes either in the money or out of the money when the *Asset Value* hits either the artificial *Upper* or *Lower Barriers*. Therefore, an *Up and In* and *Down and In* option (for both calls and puts) indicates that the option becomes live if the asset value hits either the upper or lower barrier. Conversely, for the *Up and Out* and *Down and Out* option, the option is live only when neither the upper nor the lower barrier is breached. Examples of this option include contractual agreements whereby if the upper barrier is breached, some event or clause is triggered. The value of barrier options is lower than standard options, as the barrier option will have value within a smaller price range than the standard option. The holder of a barrier option loses some of the traditional option value; therefore, such options should be worth less than a standard option.

Figure 177.1 illustrates an American Up and In, Down and In Double Barrier Option, which is a combination of the Upper and Lower Barrier Options shown previously. Exactly the same logic applies to this Double Barrier Option.

Figure 177.1 illustrates the American Barrier Option solved using the SLS. To change these into a European Barrier Option, set the Intermediate Node Equation to *OptionOpen*. In addition, for certain types of contractual options, vesting and blackout periods can be imposed. For solving such Bermudan Barrier Options, keep the same Intermediate Node Equation as the American Barrier Options but set the Intermediate Node Equation During Blackout and Vesting Periods to *OptionOpen* and insert the corresponding blackout and vesting period lattice steps. Finally, if the barrier is a changing target over time, put in several custom variables named *Barrier* with the different values and starting lattice steps.

Exotic Barrier Options exist when other options are combined with barriers. For instance, an option to expand can be executed only if the PV Asset exceeds some threshold, or a contraction option to outsource manufacturing can only be executed when it falls below some break-even point. Again, such options can be easily modeled using the SLS.

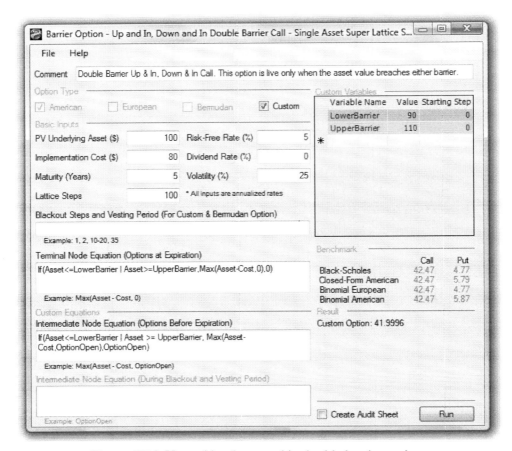

Figure 177.1: Up and in, down and in double barrier option

Exercise: Barrier Options

Barrier options are combinations of call and put options such that they become in the money or out of the money when the asset value breaches an artificial barrier. Standard single upper barrier options can be call up and in, call up and out, put up and in, and put up and out. Standard single lower barrier options can be call down and in, call down and out, put down and in, and put down and out. Double barrier options are combinations of standard single upper and lower barriers.

1. Assume that the PV Asset is $200, maturity is 5 years, risk-free rate is 5%, no dividends, and 25% volatility. For each of the barrier option types (upper, lower, and double barrier options), determine:

    a. What are some examples of nonbinding inputs? That is, show the combinations of cost and barrier levels that make the options nonbinding.

    b. How do you know the option is nonbinding?

    c. Show some binding inputs and explain the differences between binding results and nonbinding results.

2. Now run the double barrier option, change each input parameter, and explain the effects on the up and in and down and in call option, up and in and down and in put option, up and out and down and out call option, and up and out and down and out put option. Explain your observations when the barrier levels change or when volatility increases.

   a. Replicate the analysis using a standard lower barrier option.

   b. Replicate the analysis using a standard upper barrier option.

3. Suppose a chemical manufacturer executes sales contracts with a customer and agrees to charge the customer $8/pound of a particular reagent if the customer agrees to purchase 1 million pounds per year for the next 5 years. The market price of the reagent is currently $10/pound. Thus, the customer receives a $2 million discount per year. In addition, if the price is always set at $8/pound, the manufacturer might be losing out on being able to sell products at the higher market prices. Therefore, an agreement is struck whereby the contract holds as long as the market price is below $11/pound. If the prevailing price exceeds this threshold, the product will be sold at this market price. Assume a 25% annualized volatility and a 5% risk-free rate over the next 5 years.

   a. How much is such a price protection contact worth to the customer if this upper barrier does not exist?

   b. How much is such a price protection contact worth to the customer if this upper barrier is implemented?

   c. What happens when the upper threshold is increased?

   d. What happens when the price volatility of this compound is lower than 25%? Are the price differentials between the option with and without barrier constant for various volatility levels? In other words, is the barrier option a linear function of volatility?

178. Exotic Options – Basic American, European, and Bermudan Call Options

File Name: Basic American, European, versus Bermudan Call Options

Location: Modeling Toolkit | Real Options

Brief Description: Compares and values the three different types of option, American (exercisable at any time), Bermudan (exercisable at certain times), and European (exercisable only at expiration), where dividends exist and when dividends do not exist

Requirements: Modeling Toolkit, Real Options SLS

Figure 178.1 shows the computation of basic American, European, and Bermudan Options without dividends, while Figure 178.2 shows the computation of the same options but with a dividend yield. Of course, European Options can be executed only at termination and not before, while in American Options, early exercise is allowed, versus a Bermudan Option where early exercise is allowed except during blackout or vesting periods. Notice that the results for the three options without dividends are identical for simple call options, but they differ when dividends exist. When dividends are included, the simple call option values for American $\geq$ Bermudan $\geq$ European in most basic cases, as seen in Figure 178.2. Of course, these generalities can be applied only to plain vanilla call options and do not necessarily apply to other exotic options (e.g., Bermudan options with vesting and suboptimal exercise behavior multiples sometimes carry a higher value when blackouts and vesting occur than regular American options with the same suboptimal exercise parameters).

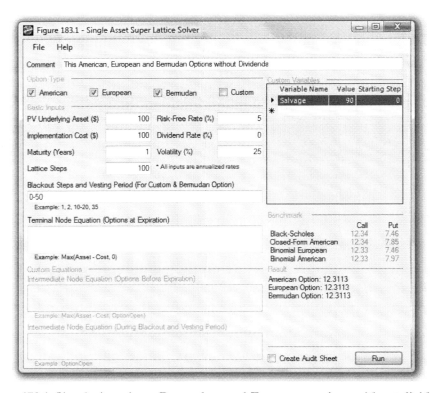

Figure 178.1: Simple American, Bermudan, and European options without dividends

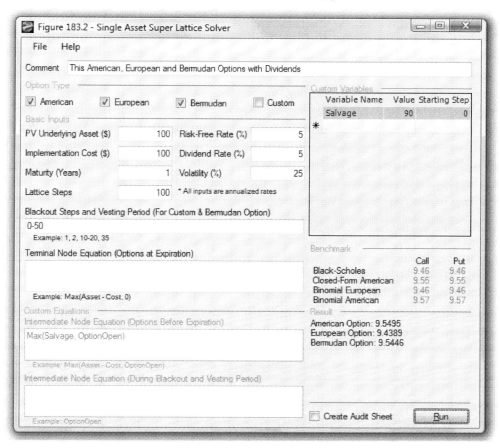

Figure 178.2: Simple American, Bermuda, and European options with dividends

179. Exotic Options – Basic American, European, and Bermudan Put Options

File Name: Basic American, European, versus Bermudan Put Options

Location: Modeling Toolkit | Real Options

Brief Description: Compares and values the three different types of option, American (exercisable at any time), Bermudan (exercisable at certain times), and European (exercisable only at expiration), where dividends exist and when dividends do not exist

Requirements: Modeling Toolkit, Real Options SLS

The *American and European Put Options* without dividends are calculated using the SLS in Figure 179.1. The sample results of this calculation indicate the strategic value of the project's NPV and provide an option to sell the project within the specified *Maturity* in years. There is a chance that the project value can significantly exceed the single-point estimate of *PV Asset Value* (measured by the present value of all uncertain future cash flows discounted at the risk-adjusted rate of return) or be significantly below it. Hence, the option to **defer** and **wait** until some of the uncertainty becomes resolved through the passage of time is worth more than executing immediately. The value of being able to wait before executing the option and selling the project at the *Implementation Cost* in present values is the value of the option. The NPV of executing immediately is simply the *Implementation Cost* less the *Asset Value* ($0). The option value of being able to wait and defer selling the asset only if the condition goes bad and becomes optimal is the difference between the calculated results (total strategic value) and the NPV or $24.42 for the American option and $20.68 for the European option. The American put option is worth more than the European put option even when no dividends exist, contrary to the call options seen previously. For simple call options, when no dividends exist, it is never optimal to exercise early. However, sometimes it may be optimal to exercise early for put options, regardless of whether dividend yields exist. In fact, a dividend yield will decrease the value of a call option but increase the value of a put option because when dividends are paid out, the value of the asset decreases. Thus, the call option will be worth less and the put option will be worth more. The higher the dividend yield, the earlier the call option should be exercised and the later the put option should be exercised.

The put option can be solved by setting the Terminal Node Equation as *Max(Cost–Asset,0)* as seen in Figure 179.1 (example file used: *Plain Vanilla Put Option*).

Puts have a similar result as calls in that when dividends are included, the basic put option values for American ≥ Bermudan ≥ European in most basic cases. You can confirm this by simply setting the Dividend Rate at **3%** and Blackout Steps at **0-80** and rerunning the *SLS* module.

Recall that a higher dividend means a higher put option value but a lower abandonment option value (see the next chapter on abandonment real options). Thus, a put option is not exactly identical to an abandonment option. A high dividend means the abandonment option's cost of waiting and holding on to the option is high (e.g., not selling a piece of land means having to pay the taxes, insurance, and maintenance on it, reducing the value of waiting before abandoning). However, for a put option, the asset price or value in the market decreases because of this dividend, making the put option (the ability to sell the asset at a predetermined contractual price) worth more. Dividends in the abandonment option affect the holding cost of the option, but dividends in the put option affect the underlying asset value. Therefore, care has to be taken to choose the relevant option model to use.

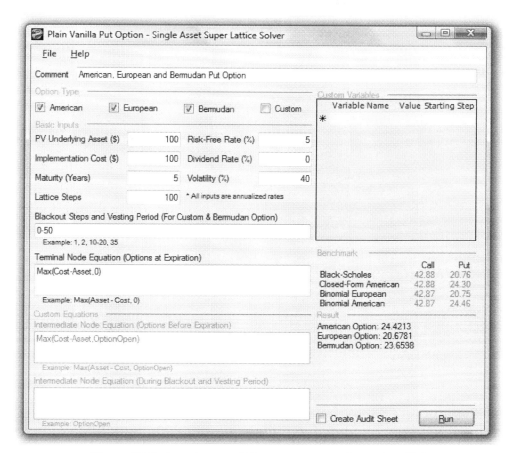

Figure 179.1: American and European put option using SLS

Exercise: American, Bermudan, and European Options

These exercises allow us to compare the results of a European option with American and Bermudan options. In addition, the Black-Scholes model is used to compare the results. The Black-Scholes equation is applicable for analyzing European-type options—that is, options that can be executed only at maturity and not before. The original Black-Scholes model cannot solve an option problem when there are dividend payments. However, extensions of the Black-Scholes model, termed the Generalized Black-Scholes model, can accommodate a continuous dividend payout for a European Option.

Perform the exercises that follow. Assume that a call option's asset value and strike price are both $100, subject to 25% volatility. The maturity on this option is 5 years, and the corresponding risk-free rate on a similar asset maturity is 5%. Finally, for the Bermudan option, assume a 4-year vesting period.

1. Using the Single Asset SLS software, calculate the American, European, and Bermudan call options using a 100-step lattice.

2. Compare your results using 5, 10, 50, 100, 300, 500, and 1,000 steps in the SLS software. Explain what happens when the number of steps gets higher.

3. Now assume that a continuous dividend payout yielding 3% exists. What happens to the value of the option?

4. Show that the value of an American call option is identical to the European call option when no dividends are paid. That is, it is never optimal to execute an American call option early when no dividend payouts exist. Now consider the Bermudan option. What generalities can you come up with?

5. Repeat exercise 4 on the put option. Here you will see a very different set of results. What generalities can you come up with?

6. Show that as a 3% dividend yield exists, the value of the American call option exceeds the value of a European option. Why is this so? How does the Bermudan option compare? What happens when the blackout steps are significant in the Bermudan option (e.g., increase the vesting period from 4 to 4.5 years and then to 5 years)? What happens when the blackout vesting period is identical to the maturity of the option? How do you model this in the software?

7. Repeat exercise 6 on the put option. Here you will see a very different set of results. What generalities can you come up with?

180. Real Options – American, European, Bermudan, and Customized Abandonment Option

File Names: Real Options – Abandonment American Option; Real Options – Abandonment Bermudan Option; Real Options – Abandonment Customized Option; Real Options – Abandonment European Option

Location: Modeling Toolkit | Real Options Models

Brief Description: Computes the abandonment option assuming American, Bermudan, and European flavors as well as customized inputs and parameters to mirror real-life situations using closed-form models and customized binomial lattices

Requirements: Modeling Toolkit, Real Options SLS

The *Abandonment Option* looks at the value of a project's or asset's flexibility in being abandoned over the life of the option. As an example, suppose that a firm owns a project or asset and that, based on traditional discounted cash flow (DCF) models, it estimates the present value of the asset (*PV Underlying Asset*) to be $120M. For the abandonment option this is the net present value of the project or asset. Monte Carlo simulation using the *Risk Simulator* software indicates that the *Volatility* of this asset value is significant, estimated at 25%. Under these conditions, there is a lot of uncertainty as to the success or failure of this project. The volatility calculated models the different sources of uncertainty and computes the risks in the DCF model including price uncertainty, probability of success, competition, cannibalization, and so forth. Thus, the value of the project might be significantly higher or lower than the expected value of $120M. Suppose an abandonment option is created whereby a counterparty is found and a contract is signed that lasts five years (*Maturity*) such that for some monetary consideration now, the firm has the ability to sell the asset or project to the counterparty at any time within these five years (indicative of an American option) for a specified *Salvage* of $90M. The counterparty agrees to this $30M discount and signs the contract.

What has just occurred is that the firm bought itself a $90M insurance policy. That is, if the asset or project value increases above its current value, the firm may decide to continue funding the project, or sell it off in the market at the prevailing fair market value. Alternatively, if the value of the asset or project falls below the $90M threshold, the firm has the right to execute the option and sell off the asset to the counterparty at $90M. In other words, a safety net of sorts has been erected to prevent the value of the asset from falling below this salvage level. Thus, how much is this safety net or insurance policy worth? You can create competitive advantage in negotiation if the counterparty does not have the answer and you do. Further assume that the five-year Treasury Note *Risk-Free Rate* (zero coupon) is 5% from the U.S. Department of Treasury (http://www.treasury.gov). The *American Abandonment Option* results in Figure 180.1 show a value of $125.48M, indicating that the option value is $5.48M as the present value of the asset is $120M. Hence, the **maximum** value you should be willing to pay for the contract on **average** is $5.48M. This resulting expected value weights the continuous probabilities that the asset value exceeds $90M versus when it does not (where the abandonment option is valuable). Also, it weights when the timing of executing the abandonment is optimal such that the expected value is $5.48M.

In addition, some experimentation can be conducted. Changing the salvage value to $30M (this means a $90M discount from the starting asset value) yields a result of $120M, or $0M for the option. This result means that the option or contract is worthless because the safety net is set so low that it will never be utilized. Conversely, setting the salvage level to three times the prevailing asset value, or $360M, would yield a result of $360M, and the options valuation

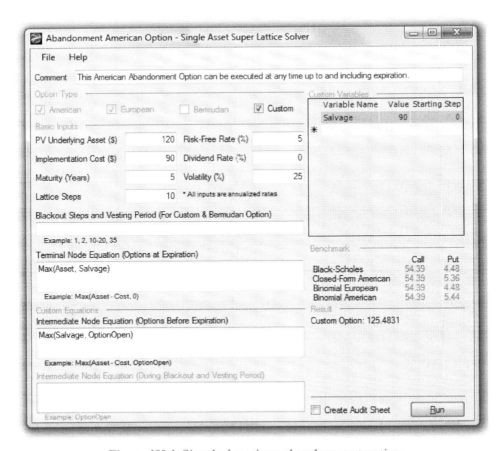

Figure 180.1: Simple American abandonment option

results indicate $360M, which means that there is no option value; there is no value in waiting and having this option, or simply, execute the option immediately and sell the asset if someone is willing to pay three times the value of the project right now. Thus, you can keep changing the salvage value until the option value disappears, indicating the ***optimal trigger value*** has been reached. For instance, if you enter $166.80 as the salvage value, the abandonment option analysis yields a result of $166.80, indicating that at this price and above, the optimal decision is to sell the asset immediately, given the assumed volatility and the other input parameters. At any lower salvage value, there is option value, and at any higher salvage value, there will be no option value. This break-even salvage point is the optimal trigger value. Once the market price of this asset exceeds this value, it is optimal to abandon. Finally, adding a *Dividend Rate*, the ***cost of waiting before abandoning the asset*** (e.g., the annualized taxes and maintenance fees that have to be paid if you keep the asset and not sell it off, measured as a percentage of the present value of the asset) will decrease the option value. Hence, the break-even trigger point, where the option becomes worthless, can be calculated by successively choosing higher dividend levels. This break-even point again illustrates the trigger value at which the option should be optimally executed immediately, but this time with respect to a dividend yield. That is, if the ***cost of carry*** or holding on to the option, or the option's ***leakage value*** is high (i.e., if the ***cost of waiting*** is too high), do not wait and execute the option immediately.

Other applications of the abandonment option include buy-back lease provisions in a contract (guaranteeing a specified asset value); asset preservation flexibility; insurance policies; walking away from a project and selling off its intellectual property; purchase price of an acquisition; and so forth. To illustrate, here are some additional examples of the abandonment option:

- An aircraft manufacturer sells its planes of a particular model in the *primary* market for, say, $30M each to various airline companies. Airlines are usually risk-averse and may find it hard to justify buying an additional plane with all the uncertainties in the economy, demand, price competition, and fuel costs. When uncertainties become resolved over time, actions, and events, airline carriers may have to reallocate and reroute their existing portfolio of planes globally, and an excess plane on the tarmac is very costly. The airline can sell the excess plane in the *secondary* market where smaller regional carriers buy used planes, but the price uncertainty is very high and is subject to significant volatility, of, say, 45%, and may fluctuate wildly between $10M and $25M for this class of aircraft. The aircraft manufacturer can reduce the airline's risk by providing a *buyback provision* or abandonment option, where at any time within the next five years, the manufacturer agrees to buy back the plane at a guaranteed residual salvage price of $20M, at the request of the airline. The corresponding risk-free rate for the next five years is 5%. **This reduces the downside risk of the airline, and hence reduces its risk, chopping off the left tail of the price fluctuation distribution, and shifting the expected value to the right. This abandonment option provides risk reduction and value enhancement to the airline.** *Applying the abandonment option in SLS using a 100-step binomial lattice, we find that this option is worth $3.52M. If the airline is the smarter counterparty and calculates this value and gets this buyback provision for free as part of the deal, the aircraft manufacturer has just left over 10% of its aircraft value on the negotiation table. Information and knowledge is highly valuable in this case.*

- A high-tech disk-drive manufacturer is thinking of acquiring a small start-up firm with a new microdrive technology (a super-fast and high-capacity pocket hard drive) that may revolutionize the industry. The start-up is for sale and its asking price is $50M based on an NPV fair market value analysis some third-party valuation consultants have performed. The manufacturer can either develop the technology itself or acquire this technology through the purchase of the firm. The question is, how much is this firm worth to the manufacturer, and is $50M a good price? Based on internal analysis by the manufacturer, the NPV of this microdrive is expected to be $45M, with a cash flow volatility of 40%, and it would take another three years before the microdrive technology is successful and goes to market. Assume that the three-year risk-free rate is 5%. In addition, it would cost the manufacturer $45M in present value to develop this drive internally. If using an NPV analysis, the manufacturer should build the drive itself. However, if you include an abandonment option analysis whereby if this specific microdrive does not work, the start-up still has an abundance of intellectual property (patents and proprietary technologies) as well as physical assets (buildings and manufacturing facilities) that can be sold in the market at up to $40M, *the abandonment option together with the NPV yields $51.83, making buying the start-up worth more than developing the technology internally, and making the purchase price of $50M worth it.* (See the section on Expansion Option for more examples on how this start-up's technology can be used as a platform to further develop newer technologies that can be worth a lot more than just the abandonment option.)

Real Options – Abandonment American Option

Figure 180.1 shows the results of a simple abandonment option with a 10-step lattice as discussed, while Figure 180.2 shows the audit sheet that is generated from this analysis.

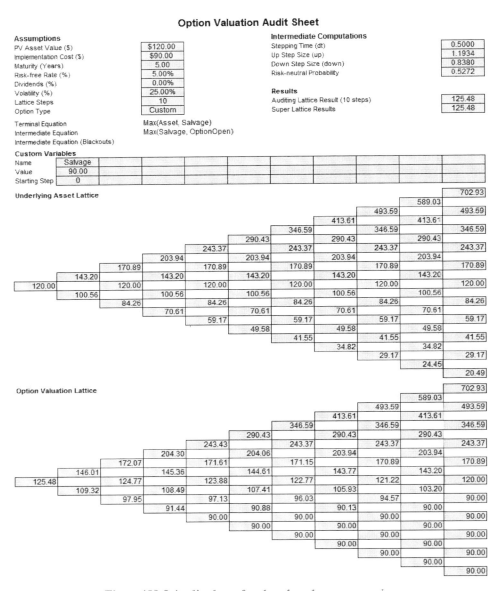

Option Valuation Audit Sheet

Assumptions

PV Asset Value ($)	$120.00
Implementation Cost ($)	$90.00
Maturity (Years)	5.00
Risk-free Rate (%)	5.00%
Dividends (%)	0.00%
Volatility (%)	25.00%
Lattice Steps	10
Option Type	Custom

Terminal Equation — Max(Asset, Salvage)
Intermediate Equation — Max(Salvage, OptionOpen)
Intermediate Equation (Blackouts)

Intermediate Computations

Stepping Time (dt)	0.5000
Up Step Size (up)	1.1934
Down Step Size (down)	0.8380
Risk-neutral Probability	0.5272

Results

Auditing Lattice Result (10 steps)	125.48
Super Lattice Results	125.48

Custom Variables

Name	Salvage
Value	90.00
Starting Step	0

Figure180.2 Audit sheet for the abandonment option

Figure 180.3 shows the same abandonment option but with a 100-step lattice. To follow along, open the example file by first starting the SLS software. Then click on **Single Asset Option Model** and then **File | Examples | Abandonment American Option**. Notice that the 10-step lattice yields $125.48 while the 100-step lattice yields $125.45, indicating that the lattice results have achieved convergence. The Terminal Node Equation is *Max(Asset,Salvage)*, which means the decision at maturity is to decide if the option should be executed, selling the asset and receiving the salvage value, or not to execute, holding on to the asset. The Intermediate Node Equation used is *Max(Salvage, OptionOpen)* indicating that before maturity, the decision is either to execute early in this American option to abandon and receive the salvage value, or to hold on to the asset and, hence, hold on to and keep the option open for potential future execution, denoted simply as *OptionOpen*.

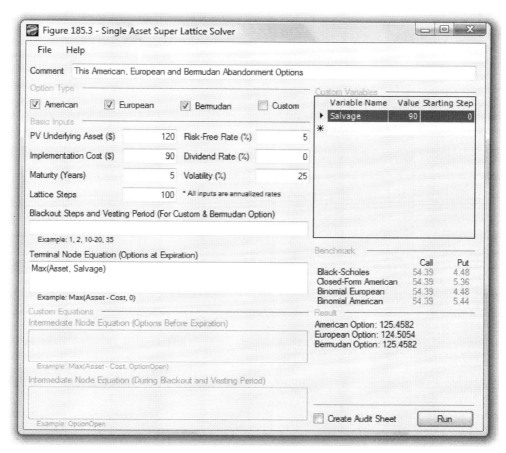

Figure 180.3: American, European, and Bermudan Abandonment
option with 100-step lattice

Real Options – Abandonment European Option

Figure 180.4 shows the European version of the abandonment option, where the Intermediate Node Equation is simply *OptionOpen*, as early execution is prohibited before maturity. Of course, being able to execute the option only at maturity is worth less ($124.5054 compared to $125.4582) than being able to exercise earlier. The example files used are *Abandonment American Option* and *Abandonment European Option*. For example, the airline manufacturer in the previous case example can agree to a buy-back provision that can be exercised at any time by the airline customer versus only at a specific date at the end of five years—the former American option will clearly be worth more than the latter European option.

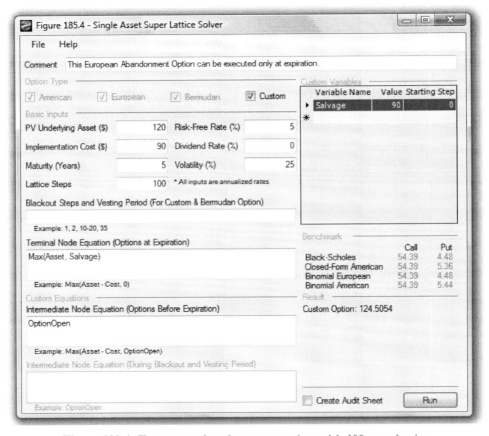

Figure 180.4: European abandonment option with 100-step lattice

Real Options – Abandonment Bermudan Option

Sometimes, a Bermudan option is appropriate, as when there might be a vesting period or blackout period when the option cannot be executed. For instance, if the contract stipulates that for the 5-year abandonment buyback contract, the airline customer cannot execute the abandonment option within the first 2.5 years. This is shown in Figure 180.5 using a Bermudan option with a 100-step lattice on 5 years, where the blackout steps are from **0-50**. This means that during the first 50 steps (as well as right now or step 0), the option cannot be executed. This is modeled by inserting **OptionOpen** into the Intermediate Node Equation During Blackout and Vesting Periods. This forces the option holder only to keep the option open during the vesting period, preventing execution during this blackout period.

Figure 180.5 shows that the American option is worth more than the Bermudan option, which is worth more than the European option, by virtue of the ability of each option type to execute early and the frequency of execution possibilities.

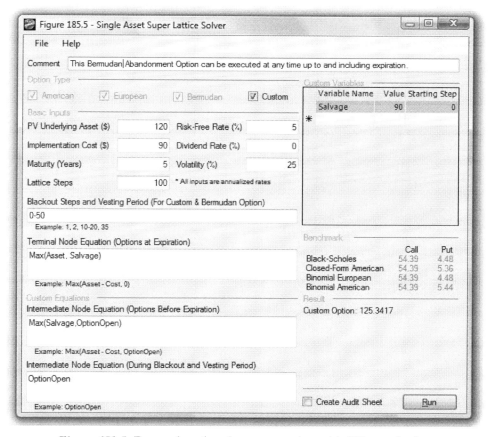

Figure 180.5: Bermudan abandonment option with 100-step lattice

Real Options – Abandonment Customized Option

Sometimes, the salvage value of the abandonment option may change over time. To illustrate, in the previous example of an acquisition of a start-up firm, the intellectual property will most probably increase over time because of continued research and development activities, thereby changing the salvage values over time. An example is seen in Figure 180.6, where there are five salvage values over the five-year abandonment option. This can be modeled by using the Custom Variables. Type in the input variables one at a time as seen in Figure 180.6's *Custom Variables* list. Notice that the same variable name (*Salvage*) is used but the values change over time, and the starting steps represent when these different values become effective. For instance, the salvage value $90 applies at step 0 until the next salvage value of $95 takes over at step 21. This means that for a five-year option with a 100-step lattice, the first year including the current period (steps 0 to 20) will have a salvage value of $90, which then increases to $95 in the second year (steps 21 to 40), and so forth. Notice that as the value of the firm's intellectual property increases over time, the option valuation results also increase, which makes logical sense. You can also model in blackout vesting periods for the first six months (steps **0-10** in the blackout area). The blackout period is very typical of contractual obligations of abandonment options where during specified periods, the option cannot be executed (a cooling-off period).

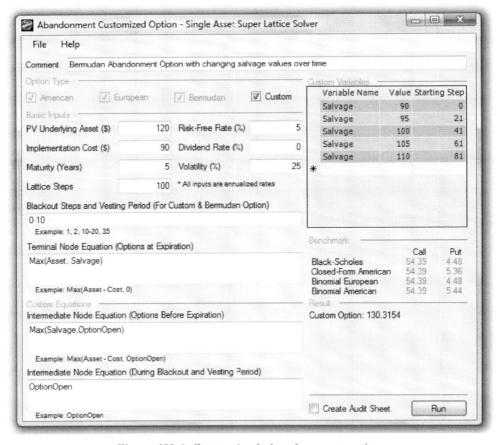

Figure 180.6: Customized abandonment option

Suppose a pharmaceutical company is developing a particular drug. However, due to the uncertain nature of the drug's development progress, market demand, success in human and animal testing, and Food and Drug Administration approval, management has decided that it will create a strategic abandonment option. That is, at any time period within the next five years of development, management can review the progress of the research and development effort and decide whether to terminate the drug development program. After five years, the firm would have either succeeded or completely failed in its drug development initiative, and there exists no option value after that time period. If the program is terminated, the firm can potentially sell off its intellectual property rights to the drug in question to another pharmaceutical firm with which it has a contractual agreement. This contract with the other firm is exercisable at any time within this time period, at the whim of the firm owning the patents.

Using a traditional DCF model, you find the present value of the expected future cash flows discounted at an appropriate market risk-adjusted discount rate to be $150 million. Using Monte Carlo simulation, you find the implied volatility of the logarithmic returns on future cash flows to be 30%. The risk-free rate on a riskless asset for the same time frame is 5%, and you understand from the intellectual property officer of the firm that the value of the drug's patent is $100 million contractually, if sold within the next five years. For simplicity, you assume that this $100 million salvage value is fixed for the next five years. You attempt to calculate how much this abandonment option is worth and how much this drug development effort on the whole is worth to the firm. By virtue of having this safety net of being able to abandon drug development, the value of the project is worth more than its net present value. You decide to use a closed-form approximation of an American put option because the option to abandon drug development can be exercised at any time up to and including the expiration date. You also decide to confirm the value of the closed-form analysis with a binomial lattice calculation. With these assumptions, do the following exercises, answering the questions posed:

1. Solve the abandonment option problem manually using a 10-step lattice and confirm the results by generating an audit sheet using the SLS software.

2. Select the right choice for each of the following:

    a. Increases in maturity (increase/decrease) an abandonment option value.

    b. Increases in volatility (increase/decrease) an abandonment option value.

    c. Increases in asset value (increase/decrease) an abandonment option value.

    d. Increases in risk-free rate (increase/decrease) an abandonment option value.

    e. Increases in dividend (increase/decrease) an abandonment option value.

    f. Increases in salvage value (increase/decrease) an abandonment option value.

3. Apply 100 steps using the software's binomial lattice.

    a. How different are the results as compared to the 5-step lattice?

    b. How close are the closed-form results compared to the 100-step lattice?

4. Apply a 3% continuous dividend yield to the 100-step lattice.

    a. What happens to the results?

    b. Does a dividend yield increase or decrease the value of an abandonment option? Why?

5. Assume that the salvage value increases at a 10% annual rate. Show how this can be modeled using the software's *Custom Variables List*.

6. Explain the differences in results when using the *Black-Scholes* and *American Put Option Approximation* in the benchmark section of the Single Asset SLS software.

181. Real Options – American, European, Bermudan, and Customized Contraction Option

File Names: Real Options – Contraction American and European Option; Real Options – Contraction Bermudan Option; Real Options – Contraction Customized Option

Location: Modeling Toolkit | Real Options Models

Brief Description: Computes the contraction option (American, Bermudan, and European) with customizable and changing input parameters using closed-form models and custom binomial lattices

Requirements: Modeling Toolkit, Real Options SLS

A *Contraction Option* evaluates the flexibility value of being able to reduce production output or to contract the scale and scope of a project when conditions are not as amenable, thereby reducing the value of the asset or project by a *Contraction Factor*, but at the same time creating some cost *Savings*. As an example, suppose you work for a large aeronautical manufacturing firm that is unsure of the technological efficacy and market demand for its new fleet of long-range supersonic jets. The firm decides to hedge itself through the use of strategic options, specifically an option to contract 10% of its manufacturing facilities at any time within the next five years (i.e., the *Contraction Factor* is 0.9).

Suppose that the firm has a current operating structure whose static valuation of future profitability using a DCF model (in other words, the present value of the expected future cash flows discounted at an appropriate market risk-adjusted discount rate) is found to be $1,000M (*PV Asset*). Using Monte Carlo simulation, you calculate the implied volatility of the logarithmic returns of the asset value of the projected future cash flows to be 30%. The risk-free rate on a riskless asset (five-year U.S. Treasury Note with zero coupons) is found to be yielding 5%.

Further, suppose the firm has the option to contract 10% of its current operations at any time over the next five years, thereby creating an additional $50 million in savings after this contraction. These terms are arranged through a legal contractual agreement with one of the firm's vendors, which had agreed to take up the firm's excess capacity and space. At the same time, the firm can scale back and lay off part of its existing workforce to obtain this level of savings (in present values).

The results indicate that the strategic value of the project is $1,001.71M (using a 10-step lattice as seen in Figure 181.1), which means that the NPV currently is $1,000M and the additional $1.71M comes from this contraction option. This result is obtained because contracting now yields 90% of $1,000M + $50M, or $950M, which is less than staying in business and not contracting and obtaining $1,000M. Therefore, the optimal decision is not to contract immediately but keep the ability to do so open for the future. Hence, in comparing this optimal decision of $1,000M to $1,001.71M of being able to contract, the option to contract is worth $1.71M. This should be the maximum amount the firm is willing to spend to obtain this option (contractual fees and payments to the vendor counterparty).

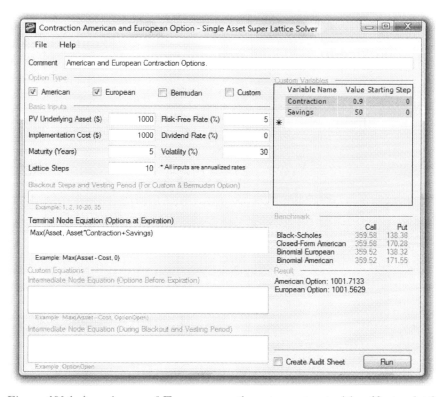

Figure 181.1: American and European options to contract with a 10-step lattice

In contrast, if *Savings* were $200M instead, then the strategic project value becomes $1,100M, which means that starting at $1,000M and contracting 10% to $900M and keeping the $200 in savings yields $1,100M in total value. Hence, the additional option value is $0M which means that it is optimal to execute the contraction option immediately as there is no option value and no value to wait to contract. The value of executing now is $1,100M as compared to the strategic project value of $1,100M; there is no additional option value, and the contraction should be executed immediately. That is, instead of asking the vendor to wait, the firm is better off executing the contraction option now and capturing the savings.

Other applications include shelving an R&D project by spending a little to keep it going but reserving the right to come back to it should conditions improve; the value of synergy in a merger and acquisition where some management personnel are let go to create the additional savings; reducing the scope and size of a production facility; reducing production rates; a joint venture or alliance, and so forth.

To illustrate, here are some additional examples of the contraction option:

- A large oil and gas company is embarking on a deep-sea drilling platform that will cost the company billions to implement. A DCF analysis is run and the NPV is found to be $500M over the next 10 years of economic life of the offshore rig. The 10-year risk-free rate is 5%, and the volatility of the project is found to be at an annualized 45% using historical oil prices as a proxy. If the expedition is highly successful (oil prices are high and production rates are soaring), then the company will continue its operations. However, if things are not looking too good (oil prices are low or moderate and production is only decent), it is very difficult for the company to abandon operations (why lose everything when net income is still positive although not as high as anticipated, not to mention the environmental and legal ramifications of simply abandoning an oil rig in the middle of the ocean). Hence, the oil company decides to hedge its downside risk through an American Contraction Option. The oil company was able to find a smaller oil and gas company (a former partner on other explorations) interested in a joint venture. The joint venture is structured such that the oil company pays this smaller counterparty a lump sum right now for a 10-year contract whereby at any time and at the oil company's request, the smaller counterparty will have to take over all operations of the offshore oil rig (i.e., taking over all operations and hence all relevant expenses) and keep 30% of the net revenues generated. The counterparty is in agreement because it does not have to spend the billions of dollars required to implement the rig in the first place, and it actually obtains some cash up front for this contract to assume the downside risk. The oil company is also in agreement because it reduces its own risks if oil prices are low and production is not up to par, and it ends up saving over $75M in present value of total overhead expenses, which it can reallocate and invest somewhere else. *In this example, the contraction option using a 100-step lattice is valued to be $14.24M using SLS. This means that the maximum amount the counterparty should be paid should not exceed this amount. Of course, the option analysis can be further complicated by analyzing the actual savings on a present value basis. For instance, if the option is exercised within the first five years, the savings is $75M but if exercised during the last five years then the savings is only $50M. The revised option value is now $10.57M.*

- A manufacturing firm is interested in outsourcing its manufacturing of children's toys to a small province in China. By doing so, it will produce overhead savings of over $20M in present value over the economic life of the toys. However, outsourcing this internationally will mean lower quality control, problems in delayed shipping, added importing costs, and assuming the added risks of unfamiliarity with the local business practices. In addition, the firm will consider outsourcing only if the quality of the workmanship in this firm is up to the stringent quality standards it requires. The NPV of this particular line of toys is $100M with a 25% volatility. The firm's executives decide to purchase a contraction option by locating a small manufacturing firm in China, spending some resources to try out a *small-scale proof of concept* (thereby reducing the uncertainties of quality, knowledge, import-export issues, health-related issues like checking for lead in the toys, etc.). If successful, the firm will agree to give this small Chinese manufacturer 20% of its net income as remuneration for its services, plus some start-up fees. The question is how much is this option to contract worth, that is, how much should the firm be willing to pay, on average, to cover the initial start-up fees plus the costs of this proof of concept stage? *A contraction option valuation result using SLS shows that the option is worth $1.59M, assuming a 5% risk-free rate for the one-year test period. As long as the total costs for a pilot test are less than $1.59M, it is optimal to obtain this option, especially if it means potentially being able to save more than $20M.*

Real Options – Contraction American and European Option

Figure 181.1 illustrates a simple 10-step Contraction Option while Figure 181.2 shows the same option using 100 lattice steps (example file: *Contraction American and European Option*).

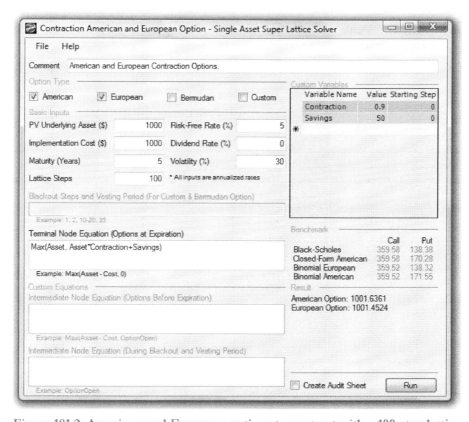

Figure 181.2: American and European options to contract with a 100-step lattice

Real Options – Contraction Bermudan Option

Figure 181.3 illustrates a five-year Bermudan Contraction Option with a four-year vesting period (blackout steps of 0 to 80 out of a five-year, 100-step lattice) where for the first four years, the option holder can only keep the option open and not execute it (example file used is *Contraction Bermudan Option*).

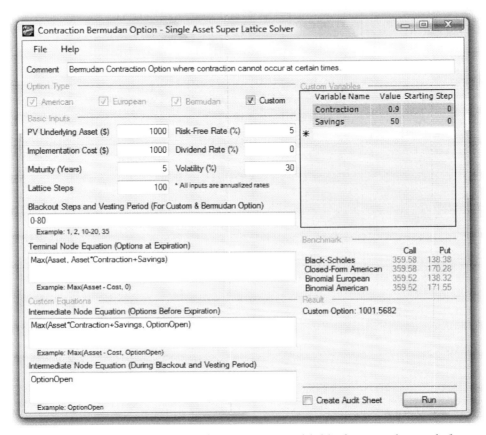

Figure 181.3: A Bermudan option to contract with blackout vesting periods

Real Options – Contraction Customized Option

Figure 181.4 shows a customized option where there is a blackout period and the savings from contracting change over time (example file used is *Contraction Customized Option*). These results are for the aeronautical manufacturing example presented at the beginning of the chapter.

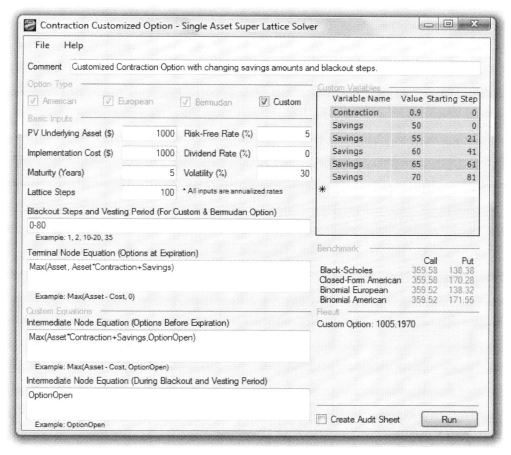

Figure 181.4: A customized option to contract with changing savings levels

Exercise: Option to Contract

You work for a large automobile spare parts manufacturing firm that is unsure of the technological efficacy and market demand of its products. The firm decides to hedge itself through the use of strategic options, specifically an option to contract 50% of its manufacturing facilities at any time within the next five years.

Suppose the firm has a current operating structure whose static valuation of future profitability using a DCF model (in other words, the present value of the expected future cash flows discounted at an appropriate market risk-adjusted discount rate) is found to be $1 billion. Using Monte Carlo simulation, you calculate the implied volatility of the logarithmic returns on the projected future cash flows to be 50%. The risk-free rate on a riskless asset for the next five years is found to be yielding 5%. Suppose the firm has the option to contract 50% of its current operations at any time over the next five years, thereby creating an additional $400 million in savings after this contraction. This is done through a legal contractual agreement with one of its vendors, which had agreed to take up the firm's excess capacity and space. Then, the firm can scale back its existing workforce to obtain this level of savings.

A *Closed-Form American Approximation Model* can be used, because the option to contract the firm's operations can be exercised at any time up to the expiration date and can be confirmed with a binomial lattice calculation. Do the following exercises, answering the questions that are posed:

1. Solve the contraction option problem manually using a 10-step lattice and confirm the results by generating an audit sheet using the software.

2. Modify the continuous dividend payout rate until the option breaks even. What observations can you make at this break-even point?

3. Use the *Closed-Form American Approximation Model* in the benchmark area of the software by using the corresponding put option. In order to do this appropriately, you will need to rerun the model with modified input parameters. What are these required input parameters?

4. How can you use the *American Abandonment Option* as a benchmark to estimate the contraction option? If it is used, are the resulting option values comparable?

5. Change the contraction factor to 0.7, and answer the questions in item 4. Why are the answers different? Suppose the initial estimate of $400 million in savings is applicable only if the contraction option is executed immediately. However, due to opportunity costs and time value of money, assume that the $400 million goes down by $10 million each year. What happens to the value of this option and how much is it worth now?

182. Real Options – American, European, Bermudan, and Customized Expansion Option

File Names: Real Options – Expansion American and European Option; Real Options – Expansion Bermudan Option; Real Options – Expansion Customized Option

Location: Modeling Toolkit | Real Options Models

Brief Description: Computes expansion options with multiple flavors (American, Bermudan, and European) with customizable and changing inputs using closed-form and customized binomial lattices

Requirements: Modeling Toolkit, Real Options SLS

The *Expansion Option* values the flexibility to expand from a current existing state to a larger or expanded state. Therefore, an existing state or condition must be present in order to use the expansion option. That is, there must be a base case on which to expand. If there is no base case state, then the simple *Execution Option* (calculated using the simple *Call Option*) is more appropriate, where the issue at hand is whether to execute a project immediately or to defer execution.

As an example, suppose a growth firm has a static valuation of future profitability using a DCF model (in other words, the present value of the expected future cash flows discounted at an appropriate market risk-adjusted discount rate) that is found to be $400 million (*PV Asset*). Using Monte Carlo simulation, you calculate the implied *Volatility* of the logarithmic returns on the assets based on the projected future cash flows to be 35%. The *Risk-Free Rate* on a riskless asset (five-year U.S. Treasury note with zero coupons) for the next five years is found to be 7%.

Further suppose that the firm has the option to expand and double its operations by acquiring its competitor for a sum of $250 million (*Implementation Cost*) at any time over the next five years (*Maturity*). What is the total value of this firm, assuming that you account for this expansion option? The results in Figure 182.1 indicate that the strategic project value is $638.73M (using a 10-step lattice), which means that the expansion option value is $88.73M. This result is obtained because the NPV of executing immediately is $400M × 2 – $250M, or $550M. Thus, $638.73 less $550M is $88.73M, the value of the ability to *defer* and to wait and see before executing the expansion option. The example file used is *Expansion American and European Option*.

Increase the dividend rate to, say, 2% and notice that both the American and European Expansion Options are now worth less, and that the American Expansion Option is worth more than the European Expansion Option by virtue of the American Option's ability to be executed early (Figure 182.2). The dividend rate is the cost of waiting to expand or to defer and not execute. That is, this rate is the opportunity cost of waiting on executing the option, and the cost of holding the option. If the dividend rate is high, then the ability to defer reduces and the option to wait decreases.

Increase the *Dividend Rate* to 4.9% and see that the binomial lattice's Custom Option result reverts to $550, (the static, expand-now scenario), indicating that the option is worthless (Figure 182.3). This result means if the cost of waiting as a proportion of the asset value (as measured by the dividend rate) is too high, then execute now and stop wasting time deferring the expansion decision! Of course, this decision can be reversed if the volatility is significant enough to compensate for the cost of waiting. That is, it might be worth something to wait and see if the uncertainty is too high even if the cost to wait is high.

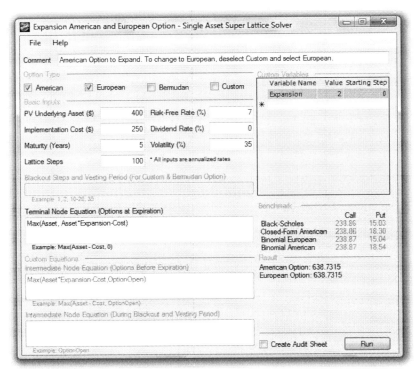

Figure 182.1: American and European options to expand with a 100-step lattice

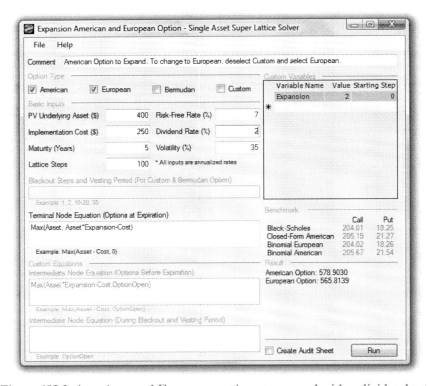

Figure 182.2: American and European options to expand with a dividend rate

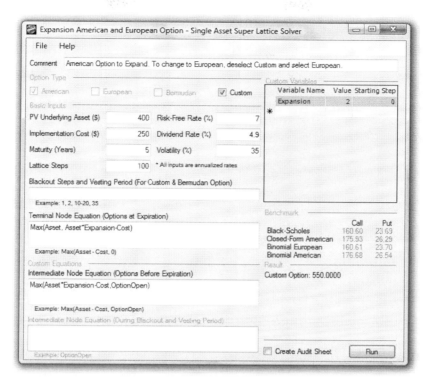

Figure 182.3: Dividend rate optimal trigger value

Other applications of this option abound! To illustrate, here are some additional examples of the contraction option:

- Suppose a pharmaceutical firm is thinking of developing a new type of insulin that can be inhaled and the drug will be absorbed directly into the blood stream. A novel and honorable idea. Imagine what this means to diabetics, who will no longer need painful and frequent injections. The problem is, this new type of insulin requires a brand-new development effort. If the uncertainties of the market, competition, drug development, and Food and Drug Administration approval are high, perhaps a base insulin drug that can be ingested is developed first. The ingestible version is a required precursor to the inhaled version. The pharmaceutical firm can decide either to take the risk and fast-track development into the inhaled version or to buy an option to defer, to first wait and see if the ingestible version works. If this precursor works, then the firm has the option to expand into the inhaled version. How much should the firm be willing to spend on performing additional tests on the precursor, and under what circumstances should the inhaled version be implemented directly? Suppose the intermediate precursor development work yields an NPV of $100M, but at any time within the next two years, an additional $50M can be invested into the precursor to develop it into the inhaled version, which will triple the NPV. However, after modeling the risk of technical success and uncertainties in the market (competitive threats, sales, and pricing structure), the annualized volatility of the cash flows using the logarithmic present value returns approach comes to 45%. Suppose the risk-free rate is 5% for the two-year period. *Using the SLS, the analysis results yields $254.95M, indicating that the option value to wait and defer is worth more than $4.95M after accounting for the $250M NPV if executing now. In playing with several scenarios, the break-even* *point is found when dividend yield is 1.34%. This means that if the cost of waiting (lost net revenues in sales by pursuing the smaller market rather than the larger market, and loss of market share by delaying) exceeds $1.34M per year, it is not optimal to wait, and the pharmaceutical firm should invest in the inhaled version immediately. The loss in returns generated each year does not sufficiently cover the risks incurred.*

- An oil and gas company is currently deciding on a deep-sea exploration and drilling project. The platform provides an expected NPV of $1,000M. This project is fraught with risks (price of oil and production rate are both uncertain) and the annualized volatility is computed to be 55%. The firm is thinking of purchasing an expansion option by spending an additional $10M to build a slightly larger platform that it does not currently need. If the price of oil is high, or when production rate is low, the firm can execute this expansion option and execute additional drilling to obtain more oil to sell at the higher price, which will cost another $50M, thereby increasing the NPV by 20%. The economic life of this platform is 10 years and the risk-free rate for the corresponding term is 5%. Is obtaining this slightly larger platform worth it? *Using the SLS, the option value is worth $27.12M when applying a 100-step lattice. Therefore, the option cost of $10M is worth it. However, this expansion option will not be worth it if annual dividends exceed 0.75% or $7.5M a year—this is the annual net revenues lost by waiting and not drilling as a percentage of the base case NPV.*

Figure 182.4 shows a Bermudan Expansion Option with certain vesting and blackout steps, while Figure 182.5 shows a Customized Expansion Option to account for the expansion factor changing over time. Of course, other flavors of customizing the expansion option exist, including changing the implementation cost to expand, and so forth.

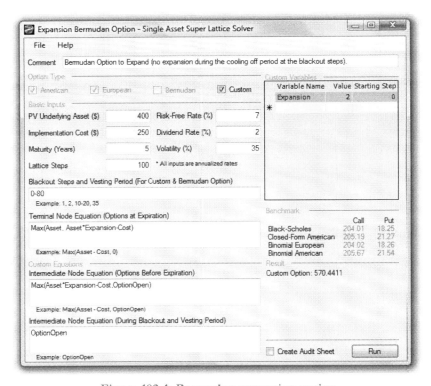

Figure 182.4: Bermudan expansion option

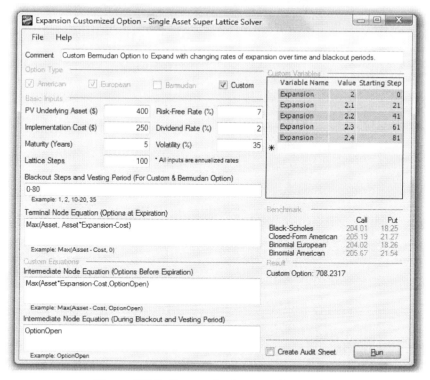

Figure 182.5: Customized expansion option

Exercise: Option to Expand

As another example, suppose a growth firm exists, and its static valuation of future profitability using a DCF model (in other words, the present value of the expected future cash flows discounted at an appropriate market risk-adjusted discount rate) is found to be $400 million. Using Monte Carlo simulation, you calculate the implied volatility of the logarithmic returns on the projected future cash flows to be 35%. The risk-free rate on a riskless asset for the next five years is found to be yielding 7%. Suppose that the firm has the option to expand and double its operations by acquiring its competitor for a sum of $250 million at any time over the next five years. What is the total value of this firm assuming you account for this expansion option?

You decide to use a closed-form approximation of an American call option as a benchmark because the option to expand the firm's operations can be exercised at any time up to the expiration date. You also decide to confirm the value of the closed-form analysis with a binomial lattice calculation. Do the following exercises, answering the questions that are posed:

1. Solve the expansion option problem manually using a 10-step lattice and confirm the results by generating an audit sheet using the software.

2. Rerun the expansion option problem using the software for 100 steps, 300 steps, and 1,000 steps. What are your observations?

3. Show how you would use the *Closed-Form American Approximation Model* to estimate and benchmark the results from an expansion option. How comparable are the results?

4. Show the different levels of expansion factors but still yielding the same expanded asset value of $800. Explain your observations of why, when the expansion value changes, the *Black-Scholes* and *Closed-Form American Approximation* models are insufficient to capture the fluctuation in value.

    a. Use an expansion factor of 2.00 and an asset value of $400.00 (yielding an expanded asset value of $800).

    b. Use an expansion factor of 1.25 and an asset value of $640.00 (yielding an expanded asset value of $800).

    c. Use an expansion factor of 1.50 and an asset value of $533.34 (yielding an expanded asset value of $800).

    d. Use an expansion factor of 1.75 and an asset value of $457.14 (yielding an expanded asset value of $800).

5. Add a dividend yield and see what happens. Explain your findings.

    a. What happens when the dividend yield equals or exceeds the risk-free rate?

    b. What happens to the accuracy of closed-form solutions such as the *Black-Scholes* and *Closed-Form American Approximation* models when used as benchmarks?

6. What happens to the decision to expand if a dividend yield exists? Now suppose that although the firm has an annualized volatility of 35%, the competitor has a volatility of 45%. This means that the expansion factor of this option changes over time, comparable to the volatilities. In addition, suppose the implementation cost is a constant 120% of the existing firm's asset value at any point in time. Show how this problem can be solved using the Multiple Asset SLS. Is there option value in such a situation?

183. Real Options – Contraction, Expansion, and Abandonment Option

File Names: Real Options – Expand Contract Abandon American and European Option; Real Options – Expand Contract Abandon Bermudan Option; Real Options – Expand Contract Abandon Customized Option I; Real Options – Expand Contract Abandon Customized Option II

Location: Modeling Toolkit | Real Options Models

Brief Description: Models a combination of mutually exclusive chooser options (contraction, expansion, and abandonment) with customizable inputs

Requirements: Modeling Toolkit, Real Options SLS

The *Contraction, Expansion, and Abandonment Option* applies when a firm has three ***competing and mutually exclusive*** options on a single project to choose from at different times up to the time of expiration. Be aware that this is a mutually exclusive set of options. That is, you cannot execute any combinations of expansion, contraction, or abandonment at the same time. Only one option can be executed at any time.

For mutually exclusive options, use a single model to compute the option value as seen in Figure 183.1 (*Expand Contract Abandon American and European Option*). However, if the options are not mutually exclusive, calculate them individually in different models and add up the values for the total value of the strategy.

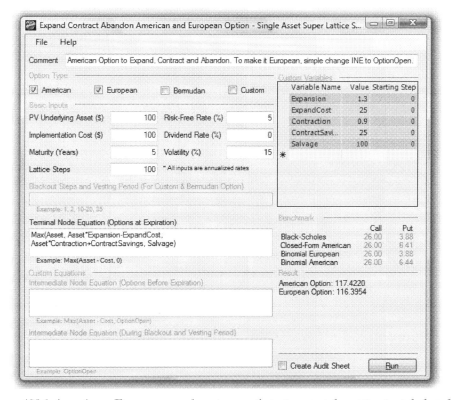

Figure 183.1: American, European, and custom options to expand, contract, and abandon

Figure 183.2 illustrates a Bermudan Option with the same parameters but with certain blackout periods (example file used: *Expand Contract Abandon Bermudan Option*), while Figure 183.3 (example file used: *Expand Contract Abandon Customized Option I*) illustrates a more complex Custom Option where during some earlier period of vesting, the option to expand does not exist yet (perhaps the technology being developed is not yet mature enough in the early stages to be expanded into some spin-off technology). In addition, during the post-vesting period but prior to maturity, the option to contract or abandon does not exist. Perhaps the technology is now being reviewed for spin-off opportunities, and so forth. Figure 183.4 uses the same example as in Figure 183.3, but now the input parameters (salvage value) are allowed to change over time, perhaps accounting for the increase in project, asset, or firm value if abandoned at different times (example file used: *Expand Contract Abandon Customized Option II*).

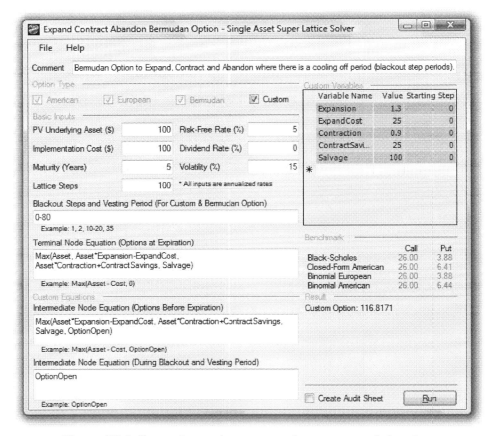

Figure 183.2: Bermudan option to expand, contract, and abandon

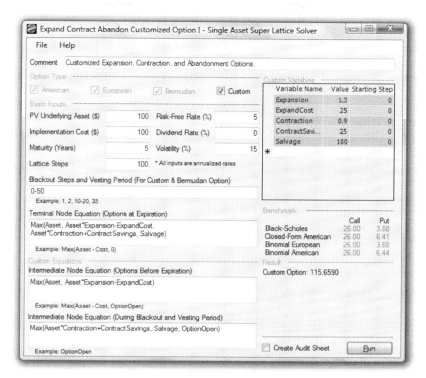

Figure 183.3: Custom options with mixed expand, contract, and abandon capabilities

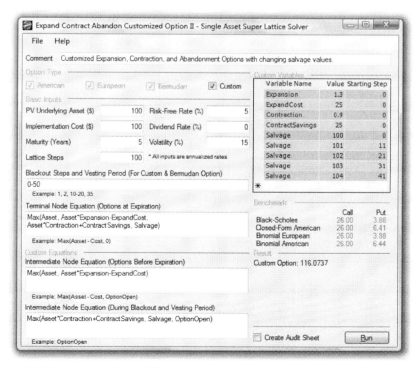

Figure 183.4: Custom options with mixed expand, contract, and abandon capabilities with changing input parameters

Exercise: Option to Choose – Contraction, Expansion, Abandonment (Dominant Option)

Suppose a large manufacturing firm decides to hedge itself through the use of strategic options. Specifically, it has the option to choose among three strategies: expanding its current manufacturing operations, contracting its manufacturing operations, or completely abandoning its business unit at any time within the next five years. Suppose the firm has a current operating structure whose static valuation of future profitability using a DCF model (in other words, the present value of the future cash flows discounted at an appropriate market risk-adjusted discount rate) is found to be $100 million.

Using Monte Carlo simulation, you calculate the implied volatility of the logarithmic returns on the projected future cash flows to be 15%. The risk-free rate on a riskless asset for the next five years is found to be yielding 5% annualized returns. Suppose the firm has the option to contract 10% of its current operations at any time over the next five years, thereby creating an additional $25 million in savings after this contraction. The expansion option will increase the firm's operations by 30%, with a $20 million implementation cost. Finally, by abandoning its operations, the firm can sell its intellectual property for $100 million. Do the following exercises, answering the questions posed:

1. Solve the chooser option problem manually using a 10-step lattice and confirm the results by generating an audit sheet using the SLS software.

2. Recalculate the option value in exercise 1 accounting only for an expansion option.

3. Recalculate the option value in exercise 1 accounting only for a contraction option.

4. Recalculate the option value in exercise 1 accounting only for an abandonment option.

5. Compare the results of the sum of these three individual options in exercises 2 to 4 with the results obtained in exercise 1 using the chooser option.

    a. Why are the results different?

    b. Which value is correct?

6. Prove that if there are many interacting options, if there is a single dominant strategy, then the value of the project's option value approaches this dominant strategy's value. That is, perform the following steps, then compare and explain the results.

    a. Reduce the expansion cost to $1.

    b. Increase the contraction savings to $100.

    c. Increase the salvage value to $150.

    d. What inferences can you make based on these results?

7. Solve this Contraction and Abandonment option: Asset value of $100, five-year economic life, 5% annualized risk-free rate of return, 25% annualized volatility, 25% contraction with a $25 savings, and a $70 abandonment salvage value.

8. Show and explain what happens when the salvage value of abandonment far exceeds any chances of a contraction. For example, set the salvage value at $200.

9. In contrast, set the salvage value back to $70, and increase the contraction savings to $100. What happens to the value of the project?

10. Solve just the contraction option in isolation. That is, set the contraction savings to $25 and explain what happens. Change the savings to $100 and explain the change in results. What can you infer from dominant option strategies? Solve just the abandonment option in isolation. That is, set the salvage value to $70, and explain what happens. Change the salvage value to $200, and explain the change in results. What can you infer from dominant option strategies?

184. Real Options – Dual-Asset Rainbow Option Using Pentanomial Lattices

File Name: Real Options – Dual-Asset Rainbow Option Pentanomial Lattice

Location: Modeling Toolkit | Real Options Models

Brief Description: Solves a rainbow option made up of two correlated underlying assets by applying a pentanomial lattice

Requirements: Modeling Toolkit, Real Options SLS

The *Dual Asset Rainbow Option* for both American and European options requires the *Pentanomial Lattice* approach. Rainbows on the horizon after a rainy day comprise various colors of the light spectrum, and although rainbow options are not as colorful as their physical counterparts, they get their name from the fact that they have two or more underlying assets rather than one. In contrast to standard options, the value of a rainbow option is determined by the behavior of two or more underlying elements and by the correlation between these underlying elements. That is, the value of a rainbow option is determined by the performance of two or more underlying asset elements. This particular model is appropriate when there are two underlying variables in the option (e.g., *Price of Asset* and *Quantity*) where each fluctuates at different rates of volatilities but at the same time might be correlated (Figure 184.1). These two variables are usually correlated in the real world, and the underlying asset value is the product of price and quantity. Due to the different volatilities, a pentanomial or five-branch lattice is used to capture all possible combinations of products (Figure 184.2). Be aware that certain combinations of inputs may yield an unsolvable lattice with negative implied probabilities. If that result occurs, a message will appear. Try a different combination of inputs as well as higher lattice steps to compensate.

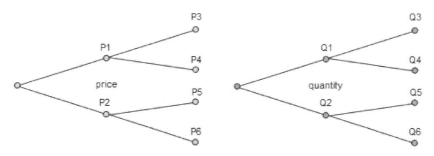

Figure 184.1: Two binomial lattices (asset prices and quantity)

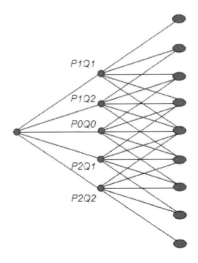

Figure 184.2: Pentanomial lattice (combining two binomial lattices)

Figure 184.3 shows an example *Dual Asset Rainbow Option* (example file used: *Dual-Asset Rainbow Option Pentanomial Lattice*). Notice that a high positive correlation will increase both call option and put option values, because if both underlying elements move in the same direction, there is a higher overall portfolio volatility. Price and quantity can fluctuate at high-high and low-low levels, generating a higher overall underlying asset value. In contrast, negative correlations will reduce the call and put option values for the opposite reason due to the portfolio diversification effects of negatively correlated variables. Of course, correlation here is bounded between −1 and +1 inclusive. If a real options problem has more than two underlying assets, use either the SLS or Risk Simulator to simulate the underlying asset's trajectories and capture their interacting effects in a DCF model. See the varied examples in SLS using pentanomial lattices to solve 3D dual-asset (e.g., spreads, exchange, dual strike, and portfolio) options.

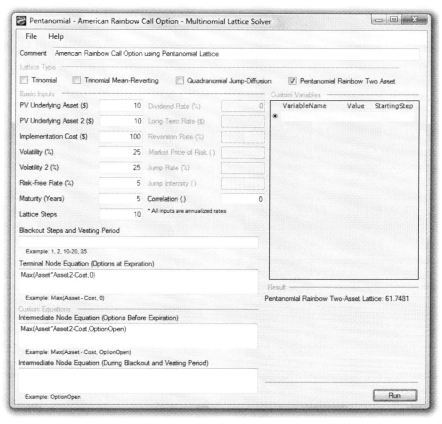

Figure 184.3: Pentanomial lattice solving a dual-asset rainbow option

185. Real Options – Exotic Chooser Options

File Name: Exotic Options – Exotic Chooser Option

Location: Modeling Toolkit | Real Options Models

Brief Description: Values a hybrid or chooser option

Requirements: Modeling Toolkit, Real Options SLS

A Chooser option is a single option that allows the holder to decide if the option becomes a call or a put at some future time, essentially creating two options in one where the cost of the single option is lower than purchasing two options.

Many types of user-defined and exotic options can be solved using the SLS software. For instance, Figure 185.1 shows a simple *Exotic Chooser Option*. In this simple analysis, the option holder has two options, a call and a put. Instead of having to purchase or obtain two separate options, one single option is obtained, which allows the option holder to choose whether the option will be a call or a put, thereby reducing the total cost of obtaining two separate options. For instance, with the same input parameters in Figure 185.1, the American Chooser Option is worth $6.7168, as compared to $4.87 for the call and $2.02 for the put ($6.89 total cost for two separate options).

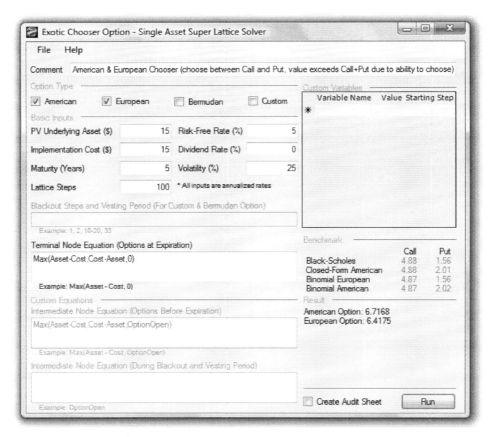

Figure 185.1: American and European exotic chooser option using SLS

186. Real Options – Exotic Complex Floating American and European Chooser

File Names: Exotic Complex Floating European Chooser; Exotic Complex Floating American Chooser

Location: Modeling Toolkit | Real Options Models

Brief Description: Values an exotic chooser option with changing parameters

Requirements: Modeling Toolkit, Real Options SLS

A Chooser option is a single option that allows the holder to decide if the option becomes a call or a put at some future time, with different parameters such as different strike levels, essentially creating two options in one where the cost of the single option is lower than purchasing two options.

A more complex Chooser Option can be constructed using the SLS software as seen in Figures 186.1 and 186.2. In these examples, the execution costs of the call versus put are set at different levels. An interesting example of a Complex Chooser Option is a firm developing a highly uncertain and risky new technology. The firm tries to hedge its downside as well as capitalize its upside by creating a Chooser Option. That is, the firm can decide to build the technology itself once the research and development phase is complete or it can sell the intellectual property of the technology, both at different costs. You can also use the SLS software to easily and quickly solve the situation where building and selling off the option each has a different volatility and time to choose.

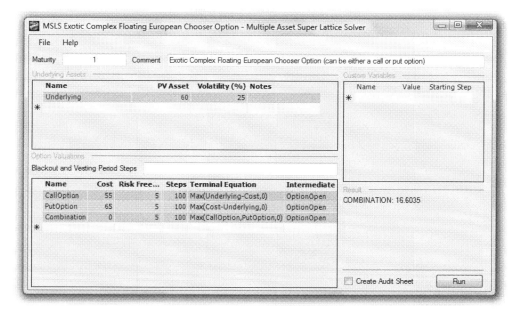

Figure 186.1: Complex European exotic chooser option using SLS

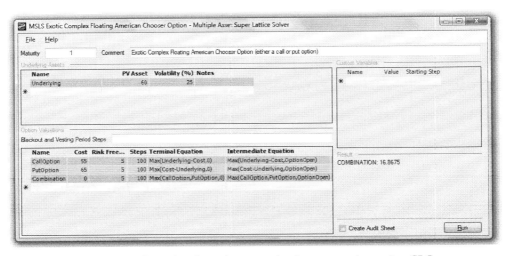

Figure 186.2: Complex American exotic chooser option using SLS

187. Real Options – Jump-Diffusion Option Using Quadranomial Lattices

File Name: Real Options – Jump-Diffusion Calls and Puts Using Quadranomial Lattices

Location: Modeling Toolkit | Real Options Models

Brief Description: Computes the options where the underlying asset follows a jump-diffusion process (e.g., oil and electricity prices), using quadranomial lattices

Requirements: Modeling Toolkit, Real Options SLS

The *Jump-Diffusion Calls and Puts model* for both American and European options applies the *Quadranomial Lattice* approach. This model is appropriate when the underlying variable in the option follows a jump-diffusion stochastic process. Figure 187.1 illustrates an underlying asset modeled using a jump-diffusion process. Jumps are commonplace in certain business variables such as the price of oil and price of gas where prices take sudden and unexpected jumps (e.g., during a war). The underlying variable's frequency of jump is denoted as its *Jump Rate*, and the magnitude of each jump is its *Jump Intensity*.

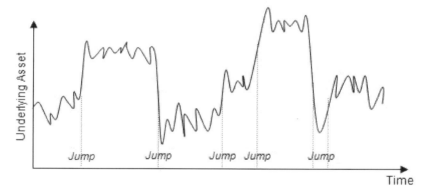

Figure 187.1: Jump-diffusion process

The binomial lattice is able to capture only a stochastic process without jumps (e.g., Brownian Motion and Random Walk processes). When there is a probability of jump (albeit a small probability that follows a Poisson distribution), additional branches are required. The quadranomial lattice (four branches on each node) is used to capture these jumps, as seen in Figure 187.2.

Be aware that due to the complexity of the models, some calculations with higher lattice steps may take slightly longer to compute. Furthermore, certain combinations of inputs may yield negative implied risk-neutral probabilities and result in a noncomputable lattice. In that case, make sure the inputs are correct (e.g., *Jump Intensity* has to exceed 1, where 1 implies no jumps; check for erroneous combinations of *Jump Rates*, *Jump Sizes*, and *Lattice Steps*). The probability of a jump can be computed as the product of the *Jump Rate* and time-step δt. Figure 187.3 illustrates a sample Quadranomial Jump-Diffusion Option analysis (example file used: *Jump Diffusion Calls and Puts Using Quadranomial Lattices*). Notice that the Jump-Diffusion call and put options are worth more than regular calls and puts. This is because with the positive jumps (10% probability per year with an average jump size of 1.50 times the previous values) of the underlying asset, the movements of the asset are more significant than without any jumps. This results in the call and put options being worth more, even with the same volatility (i.e., $34.69 compared to $31.99 and $15.54 compared to $13.14).

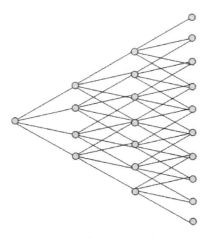

Figure 187.2: Quadranomial lattice

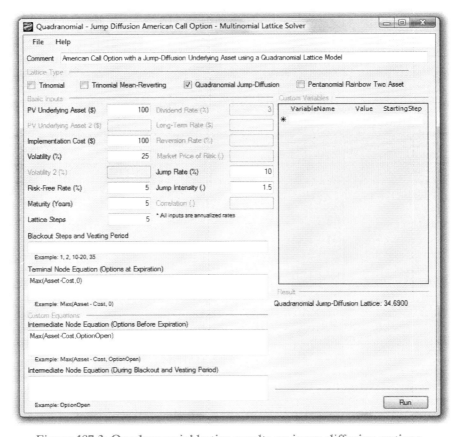

Figure 187.3: Quadranomial lattice results on jump-diffusion options

188. Real Options – Mean-Reverting Calls and Puts Using Trinomial Lattices

File Name: Real Options – Mean-Reverting Calls and Puts Using Trinomial Lattices

Location: Modeling Toolkit | Real Options Models

Brief Description: Computes the options where the underlying asset follows a mean-reverting process (e.g., interest rates), using trinomial lattices

Requirements: Modeling Toolkit, Real Options SLS

The *Mean-Reversion Option* in the SLS software calculates both the American and European options when the underlying asset value is mean reverting. A mean-reverting stochastic process reverts back to the long-term mean value (*Long-Term Rate Level*) at a particular speed of reversion (*Reversion Rate*). Examples of variables following a mean-reversion process include inflation rates, interest rates, gross domestic product growth rates, optimal production rates, price of natural gas, and so forth. Certain variables such as these succumb either to natural tendencies or economic/business conditions to revert to a long-term level when the actual values stray too far above or below this level. For instance, monetary and fiscal policy will prevent the economy from significant fluctuations, while policy goals tend to have a specific long-term target rate or level. Figure 188.1 illustrates a regular stochastic process (dotted line) versus a mean-reversion process (solid line). Clearly the mean-reverting process with its dampening effects will have a lower level of uncertainty than the regular process with the same volatility measure.

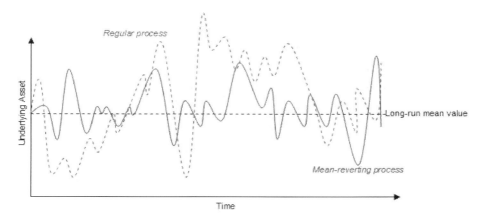

Figure 188.1: Mean reversion in action

Figure 188.2 shows the mean-reverting call option computed using the SLS *Multinomial Lattice* module. Using this module, we can compute additional call and put results from a regular option modeled using the Trinomial Lattice versus calls and puts assuming a mean-reverting (MR) tendency of the underlying asset using the Mean-Reverting Trinomial Lattice. Based on the results, several items are worthy of notice:

- The MR Calls ≤ regular Calls because of the dampening effect of the mean-reversion asset. The MR asset value will not increase as high as the regular asset value.

591

- Conversely, the MR Puts ≥ regular Puts because the asset value will not rise as high, indicating that there will be a higher chance that the asset value will hover around the PV Asset, and a higher probability it will be below the PV Asset, making the put option more valuable.

- With the dampening effect, the MR Call and MR Put ($18.62 and $18.76) are more symmetrical in value than with a regular call and put ($31.99 and $13.14).

- The regular American Calls = regular European Calls without dividends because without dividends, it is never optimal to execute early. However, because of the mean-reverting tendencies, being able to execute early is valuable, especially before the asset value decreases. So, we see that MR American Calls > MR European Calls but, of course, both are less than the regular Calls.

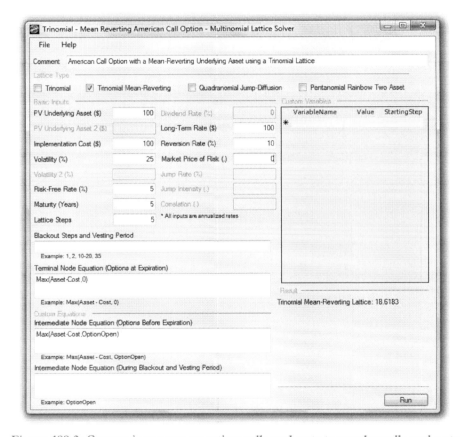

Figure 188.2: Comparing mean-reverting calls and puts to regular calls and puts

Other items of interest in mean-reverting options include:

- The higher (lower) the long-term rate level, the higher (lower) the call options.

- The higher (lower) the long-term rate level, the lower (higher) the put options.

Finally, be careful when modeling mean-reverting options. Higher lattice steps usually are required, and certain combinations of reversion rates, long-term rate level, and lattice steps may yield unsolvable trinomial lattices. When this occurs, the software will return error messages.

189. Real Options – Multiple Assets Competing Options

File Name: Real Options – Multiple Assets Competing Options (3D Binomial)

Location: Modeling Toolkit | Real Options Models

Brief Description: Computes a 3D binomial option where there are multiple underlying assets and the option holder has the ability to purchase the asset with the highest value

Requirements: Modeling Toolkit, Real Options SLS

This model illustrates the power of real options analysis and the ability for the Real Options SLS software to solve customizable options. This two-underlying-assets model is sometimes called a 3D binomial model, as there are multiple assets (Figure 189.1). The problem is solved using the multiple assets and multiple phased *MNLS* module in the SLS software. The critical pieces are the terminal and intermediate equations. In this example, we solve a call option on the maximum (i.e., given that there are multiple underlying assets, this option allows the holder to execute and purchase the asset that is the highest when executed). The option can be an American, Bermudan, or European option.

To create an American option, use:

Terminal equation: Max(FirstAsset-Cost,SecondAsset-Cost,0)

Intermediate equation: Max(FirstAsset-Cost,SecondAsset-Cost,OptionOpen)

To create a Bermudan option, simply add in the Blackout and Vesting Period Steps to cover the appropriate time periods in the lattice when the option cannot be executed. For instance, for a five-year project solved using a 100-step lattice, if the blackout or vesting period is the first three years (option cannot be executed in Years 0 to 3, including the current time zero), then set the blackout steps to be 0–60, and make sure you type in *OptionOpen* for the blackout equation. To create a European option, keep the same terminal equation but change the intermediate equation to *OptionOpen*.

Note that 3D options can also be solved using pentanomial lattices in SLS.

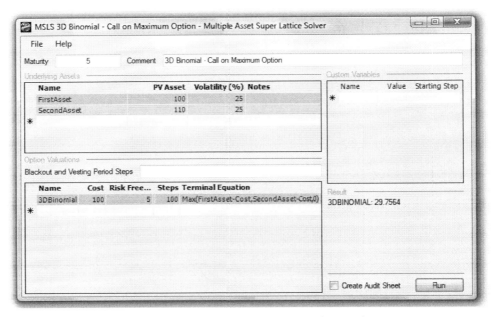

Figure 189.1: Multiple assets competing option

190. Real Options – Path-Dependent, Path-Independent, Mutually Exclusive, Nonmutually Exclusive, and Complex Combinatorial Nested Options

Sequential Compound Options are *path-dependent options*, where one phase depends on the success of another, in contrast to *path-independent options* such as those solved using SLS. These options can be *mutually exclusive* or *nonmutually exclusive*. In all these types of options, there might be multiple underlying assets (e.g., Japan has a different risk-return or profitability-volatility profile from the United Kingdom or Australia). You can build multiple underlying asset lattices this way using the SLS, and combine them in many various ways depending on the options. Some examples of path-dependent versus path-independent and mutually exclusive versus nonmutually exclusive options follow:

- **Path-Independent and Mutually Exclusive Options**: Use the SLS to solve these types of options by combining all the options into a single valuation lattice. Examples include the option to expand, contract, and expand. They are mutually exclusive if you cannot both expand into a different country while abandoning and selling the company. These are path independent if there are no restrictions on timing (i.e., you can expand, contract, and abandon at any time within the confines of the maturity period).

- **Path-Independent and Nonmutually Exclusive Options:** Use the SLS to solve these types of options by running each of the options that are nonmutually exclusive one at a time in SLS. Examples include the option to expand your business into Japan, the United Kingdom, and Australia. These are not mutually exclusive if you can choose to expand to any combinations of countries (e.g., Japan only, Japan and the United Kingdom, United Kingdom and Australia, etc.). They are path independent if there are no restrictions on timing (i.e., you can expand to any country at any time within the maturity of the option). Add the individual option values to obtain the total option value for expansion.

- **Path-Dependent and Mutually Exclusive Options:** Use the SLS software to solve these types of options by combining all the options into one valuation lattice. Examples include the option to expand into the three countries: Japan, the United Kingdom, and Australia. However, this time, the expansions are mutually exclusive and path dependent. That is, you can expand into only one country at a time, but at certain periods you can expand only into certain countries (e.g., Japan is optimal only in three years due to current economic conditions, export restrictions, etc., as compared to the United Kingdom expansion, which can be executed right now).

- **Path-Dependent and Nonmutually Exclusive Options:** Use the SLS software to solve these. These are typically simple Sequential Compound Options with multiple phases. If more than one nonmutually exclusive option exists, rerun the SLS for each option. Examples include the ability to enter Japan from Years 0–3, Australia in Years 3–6, and the United Kingdom at any time between Years 0–10. Each entry strategy is not mutually exclusive if you can enter more than one country. The strategies and are path dependent as they are time dependent.

- **Nested Combinatorial Options:** These are the most complicated options and can take a combination of any of the four types preceding types. In addition, the options are nested within one another in that the expansion into Japan must come only after Australia, and cannot be executed without heading to Australia first. In addition, Australia and the United Kingdom are okay, but you cannot expand to the United Kingdom and Japan (e.g., certain trade restrictions, antitrust issues, competitive considerations, strategic issues, restrictive agreements with alliances). For such options, draw all the scenarios on a strategy tree and use IF, AND, OR, and MAX statements in SLS to solve the option. That is, if you enter into United Kingdom, that is it, but *if* you enter into Australia, you can still enter into Japan *or* the United Kingdom but *not* Japan and the United Kingdom.

191. Real Options – Sequential Compound Options

File Names: Real Options – Simple Two-Phased Sequential Compound Option; Real Options – Multiple-Phased Sequential Compound Option; Real Options – Multiple-Phased Complex Sequential Compound Option

Location: Modeling Toolkit | Real Options Models

Brief Description: Computes sequential compound options with multiple-phased and complex interrelationships between phases and customizable and changing input parameters

Requirements: Modeling Toolkit, Real Options SLS

Sequential Compound Options are applicable for research and development investments or any other investments that have multiple stages. The Real Options SLS software is required for solving Sequential Compound Options. The easiest way to understand this option is to start with a two-phased example as seen in Figure 191.1. In a two-phased example, management has the ability to decide if Phase II (PII) should be implemented after obtaining the results from Phase I (PI). For example, a pilot project or market research in PI indicates that the market is not yet ready for the product, hence PII is not implemented. All that is lost is the PI sunk cost, not the entire investment cost of both PI and PII. The next section illustrates how the option is analyzed.

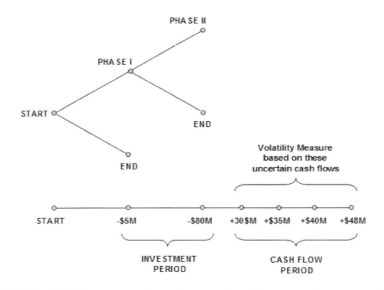

Figure 191.1: Graphical representation of a two-phased sequential compound option

Real Options – Simple Two-Phased Sequential Compound Option

Figure 191.1 is valuable in explaining and communicating to senior management the aspects of an American Sequential Compound Option and its inner workings. In the illustration, the Phase I investment of –$5M (in present value dollars) in Year 1 is followed by Phase II investment of –$80M (in present value dollars) in Year 2. It is hoped that positive net free cash flows (CF) will follow in Years 3 to 6, yielding a sum of *PV Asset* of $100M (CF discounted at, say, a 9.7% discount or hurdle rate), and the *Volatility* of these CFs is 30%. At a 5% risk-free rate, the strategic value is calculated at $27.67 as seen in Figure 191.2 using a 100-step lattice, which means that the strategic option value of being able to **defer** investments and to **wait and see** until more information becomes available and uncertainties become resolved is worth $12.67M because the NPV is worth $15M ($100M – $5M – $80M). In other words, the ***Expected Value of Perfect Information*** is worth $12.67M, which indicates that if market research can be used to obtain credible information to decide if this project is a good one, the maximum the firm should be willing to spend in Phase I is *on average no more than* $17.67M (i.e., $12.67M + $5M) if PI is part of the market research initiative, or simply $12.67M otherwise. If the cost to obtain the credible information exceeds this value, then it is optimal to take the risk and execute the entire project immediately at $85M. The example file used is *Simple Two-Phased Sequential Compound Option*.

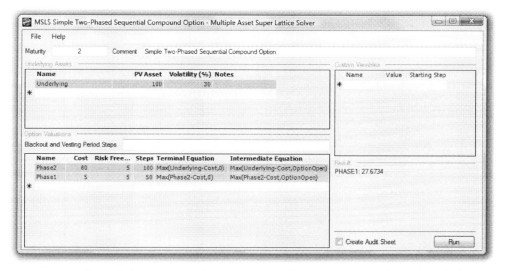

Figure 191.2: Solving a two-phased sequential compound option using SLS

In contrast, if the volatility decreases (uncertainty and risk are lower), the strategic option value decreases. In addition, when the cost of waiting (as described by the *Dividend Rate* as a percentage of the *Asset Value*) increases, it is better not to defer and wait that long. Therefore, the higher the dividend rate, the lower the strategic option value. For instance, at an 8% dividend rate and 15% volatility, the resulting value reverts to the NPV of $15M, which means that the option value is zero, and that it is better to execute immediately as the cost of waiting far outstrips the value of being able to wait given the level of volatility (uncertainty and risk). Finally, if risks and uncertainty increase significantly even with a high cost of waiting (e.g., 7% dividend rate at 30% volatility), it is still valuable to wait.

This model provides the decision maker with a view into the optimal balancing between *waiting for more information* (Expected Value of Perfect Information) and the *cost of waiting*. You can analyze this balance by creating strategic *options to defer* investments through development stages where at every stage the project is reevaluated as to whether it is beneficial to proceed to the next phase. Based on the input assumptions used in this model, the *Sequential Compound Option* results show the strategic value of the project, and the NPV is simply the *PV Asset* less the *Implementation Costs* of both phases. In other words, the strategic option value is the difference between the calculated strategic value minus the NPV. It is recommended that you vary the volatility and dividend inputs to determine their interactions—specifically, where the break-even points are for different combinations of volatilities and dividends. Using this information, you can make better *go* or *no-go decisions* based on the resulting option value (for instance, break-even volatility points can be traced back into the discounted cash flow model to estimate the probability of crossing over and this ability to wait becomes valuable).

Note that the investment costs of $80M and $5M are in present values for several reasons. The first is that only the PV Asset undergoes an underlying asset lattice evolution to future values; costs do not undergo such an evolution, and are hence in present values. Also, for example, in a five-year option, an implementation that can occur at any time within these five years will have very different actual implementation costs. To make these costs comparable, we use their present values. Thus, an $80M cost can occur at any time within some specified time period; the present value of the cost is still $80M regardless of when it hits. Finally, the risk-free rate discounts the expected value of keeping the option open, not the cost. So, there is no double-discounting and using the present value for these costs is correct.

Real Options – Multiple-Phased Sequential Compound Option

The Sequential Compound Option can similarly be extended to multiple phases with the use of the SLS software. A graphical representation of a multi-phased or stage-gate investment is seen in Figure 191.3. The example illustrates a ten-phase project, where, at every phase, management has the option and flexibility either to continue to the next phase if everything goes well, or to terminate the project otherwise. Based on the input assumptions, the results in the SLS indicate the calculated strategic value of the project, while the NPV of the project is simply the *PV Asset* less all *Implementation Costs* (in present values) if implementing all phases immediately. Therefore, with the strategic option value of being able to defer and wait before implementing future phases (due to the volatility, there is a possibility that the asset value will be significantly higher) the strategic value of the project is higher. Hence, the ability to wait before making the investment decisions in the future is the option value or the strategic value of the project less the NPV.

Figure 191.4 shows the results using the SLS software. Notice that due to the backward induction process used, the analytical convention is to start with the last phase and go all the way back to the first phase (example file used: *Multiple Phased Sequential Compound Option*). In NPV terms the project is worth –$500. However, the total strategic value of the stage-gate investment option is worth $41.78. This means that although the investment looks bad on an NPV basis, in reality, by hedging the risks and uncertainties through sequential investments, the option holder can pull out at any time and not have to keep investing unless things look promising. If after the first phase things look bad, the option holder can pull out and stop investing; the maximum loss will be $100 (Figure 191.4), not the entire $1,500 investment. If, however, things look promising, the option holder can continue to invest in stages. The expected value of the investments in present values after accounting for the probabilities that things will look bad (and hence stop investing) versus things looking great (and hence continuing to invest) is worth an average of $41.78M.

Notice that the option valuation result will always be greater than or equal to zero (e.g., try reducing the volatility to 5% and increasing the dividend yield to 8% for all phases). When the option value is very low or zero, this means that it is not optimal to defer investments. The stage-gate investment process is not optimal here. The cost of waiting is too high (high dividend) or the uncertainties in the cash flows are low (low volatility); hence, invest if the NPV is positive. In such a case, although you obtain a zero value for the option, the analytical interpretation is significant! A zero or very low value is indicative of an optimal decision not to wait.

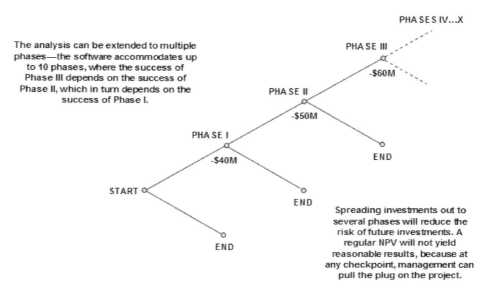

The analysis can be extended to multiple phases—the software accommodates up to 10 phases, where the success of Phase III depends on the success of Phase II, which in turn depends on the success of Phase I.

Spreading investments out to several phases will reduce the risk of future investments. A regular NPV will not yield reasonable results, because at any checkpoint, management can pull the plug on the project.

Figure 191.3: Graphical representation of a multi-phased sequential compound option

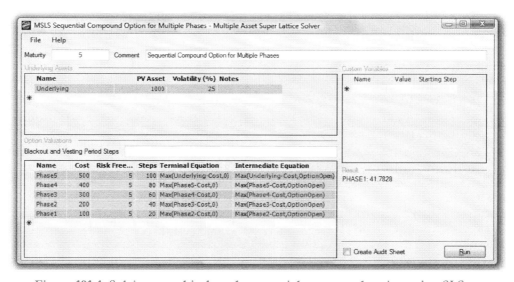

Figure 191.4: Solving a multi-phased sequential compound option using SLS

Real Options – Multiple-Phased Complex Sequential Compound Option

The Sequential Compound Option can be further complicated by adding customized options at each phase as illustrated in Figure 191.5. In the figure, at every phase, there may be different combinations of mutually exclusive options including the flexibility to stop investing, *abandon* and *salvage* the project in return for some value, *expand* the scope of the project into another project (e.g., spin off projects and expand into different geographical locations), *contract* the scope of the project resulting in some savings, or continue on to the next phase. The seemingly complicated option can be very solved easily using SLS as seen in Figure 191.6 (example file used: *Real Options – Multiple Phased Complex Sequential Compound Option*).

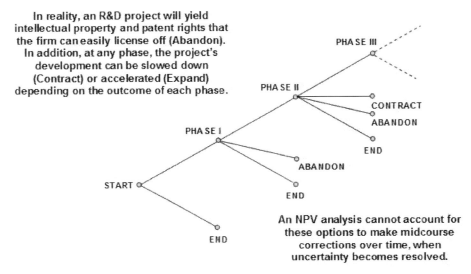

Figure 191.5: Graphical representation of a complex multi-phased sequential compound option

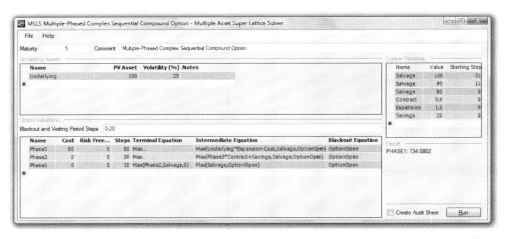

Figure 191.6: Solving a complex multi-phased sequential compound option using SLS

To illustrate, Figure 191.6's SLS path-dependent sequential option uses the following inputs:

Phase 3:   Terminal: Max(Underlying*Expansion-Cost,Underlying,Salvage)

Intermediate: Max(Underlying*Expansion-Cost,Salvage,OptionOpen)

Steps: 50

Phase 2:   Terminal: Max(Phase3,Phase3*Contract+Savings,Salvage,0)

Intermediate: Max(Phase3*Contract+Savings,Salvage,OptionOpen)

Steps: 30

Phase 1:   Terminal: Max(Phase2,Salvage,0)

Intermediate: Max(Salvage,OptionOpen)

Steps: 10

Exercise: Sequential Compound Option

A sequential compound option exists when a project has multiple phases and latter phases depend on the success of previous ones. Suppose a project has two phases, of which the first has a one-year expiration that costs $500 million. The second phase's expiration is three years and costs $700 million. Suppose that the implied volatility of the logarithmic returns on the projected future cash flows is calculated to be 20%. The risk-free rate on a riskless asset for the next three years is found to be yielding 7.7%. The static valuation of future profitability using a discounted cash flow model—in other words, the present value of the future cash flows discounted at an appropriate market risk-adjusted discount rate—is found to be $1,000 million. Do the following exercises, answering the questions posed:

1.   Solve the sequential compound option problem manually using a 10-step lattice and confirm the results by generating an audit sheet using the software.

2.   Change the sequence of the costs. That is, set the first phase's cost to $700 and the second phase's cost to $500 (both in present values). Compare your results. Explain what happens.

3.   Now suppose the total cost of $1,200 (in present values) is spread out equally over six phases in six years. How would the analysis results differ?

4.   Suppose that the project is divided into three phases with the following options in each phase as described. Solve the option using Multiple Asset SLS.

a.   Phase 3 occurs in three years, the implementation cost is $300, but the project can be abandoned and salvaged to receive $300 at any time within the first year, $350 within the second year, and $400 within the third year.

b.   Phase 2 occurs in two years, and the project can be spun off to a partner. In doing this, the partner keeps 15% of the NPV and saves the firm $200.

c.   Phase 1 occurs in one year, and the only thing that can be done is to invest the $300 implementation cost and continue to the next phase.

192. Real Options – Simultaneous Compound Options

File Names: Real Options – Simple Two-Phased Simultaneous Compound Option; Real Options – Multiple-Phased Simultaneous Compound Option

Location: Modeling Toolkit | Real Options Models

Brief Description: Computes simultaneous compound options with multiple options executed simultaneously with complex interrelationships between phases and customizable and changing input parameters

Requirements: Modeling Toolkit, Real Options SLS

The Simultaneous Compound Option evaluates a project's strategic value when the value of the project depends on the success of *two or more* investment initiatives executed *simultaneously in time*. The Sequential Compound Option evaluates these investments in stages, one after another over time, while the simultaneous option evaluates these options concurrently. Clearly, the sequential compound is worth more than the simultaneous compound option by virtue of staging the investments. Note that the simultaneous compound option acts like a regular execution call option. Hence, the *American Call Option* is a good benchmark for such an option.

Real Options – Two-Phased Simultaneous Compound Option

Figure 192.1 shows how a Simultaneous Compound Option can be solved using the SLS (example file used: *Simple Two-Phased Simultaneous Compound Option*). Like the sequential compound option analysis, the existence of an option value implies that the ability to defer and wait for additional information prior to executing is valuable due to the significant uncertainties and risks as measured by *Volatility*. However, when the cost of waiting as measured by the *Dividend Rate* is high, the option to wait and defer becomes less valuable, until the break-even point where the option value equals zero and the strategic project value equals the NPV of the project. This break-even point gives the decision maker valuable insights into the interactions between the levels of uncertainty inherent in the project and the cost of waiting to execute.

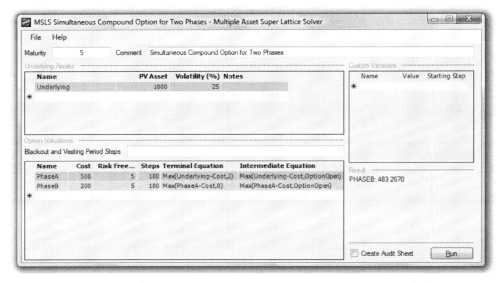

Figure 192.1: Solving a simultaneous compound option using SLS

Real Options – Multiple-Phased Simultaneous Compound Option

The same analysis can be extended to Multiple Investment Simultaneous Compound Options as seen in Figure 192.2 (example file used: *Multiple-Phased Simultaneous Compound Option*).

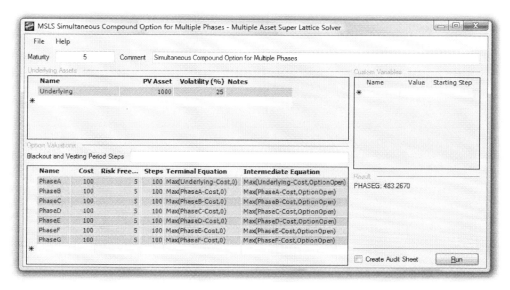

Figure 192.2: Solving a multiple investment simultaneous
compound option using SLS

Exercise: Simultaneous Compound Option

In a compound option analysis, the value of the option depends on the value of another option. For instance, a pharmaceutical company currently going through a particular Food and Drug Administration (FDA) drug approval process has to go through human trials. The success of the FDA approval depends heavily on the success of human testing, both occurring at the same time. Suppose that the former costs $900 million and the latter $500 million. Further suppose that both phases occur simultaneously and take five years to complete. Using Monte Carlo simulation, you calculate the implied volatility of the logarithmic returns on the projected future cash flows to be 25%. The risk-free rate on a riskless asset for the next five years is found to be yielding 7.7%. The drug development effort's static valuation of future profitability using a DCF model (in other words, the present value of the future cash flows discounted at an appropriate market risk-adjusted discount rate) is found to be $1 billion. Do the following exercises, answering the questions posed:

1. Solve the simultaneous compound option problem manually using a 10-step lattice and confirm the results by generating an Audit Sheet using the software.

2. Swap the implementation costs such that the first cost is $500 and the second cost is $900. Is the resulting option value similar or different? Why?

3. What happens when part of the cost of the first option is allocated to the second option? For example, make the first cost $450 and the second cost $950. Does the result change? Explain.

4. Show how a *Closed-Form American Approximation Model* can be used to benchmark the results from a simultaneous compound option.

5. Show how a *Sequential Compound Option* can also be used to calculate or at least approximate the simultaneous compound option result.

6. Assume that the total $1,400 implementation cost (in present values) is now distributed equally across seven simultaneous projects. Does the result change? Why or why not?

193. Real Options – Simple Calls and Puts Using Trinomial Lattices

File Name: Real Options – Simple Calls and Puts Using Trinomial Lattices

Location: Modeling Toolkit | Real Options Models

Brief Description: Solves simple call and put options using trinomial lattices and used to compare with the results from binomial lattices

Requirements: Modeling Toolkit, Real Options SLS

Building and solving trinomial lattices is similar to building and solving binomial lattices, complete with the up/down jumps and risk-neutral probabilities, but it is more complicated due to more branches stemming from each node. At the limit, both the binomial and trinomial lattices yield the same result, as seen in the following table. However, the lattice-building complexity is much higher for trinomial or multinomial lattices. The only reason to use a trinomial lattice is because the level of convergence to the correct option value is achieved more quickly than by using a binomial lattice. In the table below showing the convergence of trinomials and binomials, notice how the trinomial lattice yields the correct option value with fewer steps than it takes for a binomial lattice (1,000 as compared to 5,000). Because both yield identical results at the limit but trinomials are much more difficult to calculate and take a longer computation time, the binomial lattice is usually used instead. However, a trinomial is required when the underlying asset follows a *mean-reverting process*.

Steps	5	10	100	1,000	5,000
Binomial Lattice	$30.73	$29.22	$29.72	$29.77	$29.78
Trinomial Lattice	$29.22	$29.50	$29.75	$29.78	$29.78

Figure 193.1 shows another example. To run this model, use the SLS software and click on **Create a New Multinomial Option Model**. The computed American Call is $31.99 using a 5-step trinomial, and is identical to a 10-step binomial lattice seen in Figure 193.2. Therefore, due to the simpler computation and the speed of computation, the SLS software uses binomial lattices instead of trinomials or other multinomial lattices. As noted previously, the only time a trinomial lattice is truly useful is when the underlying asset of the option follows a mean-reversion tendency.

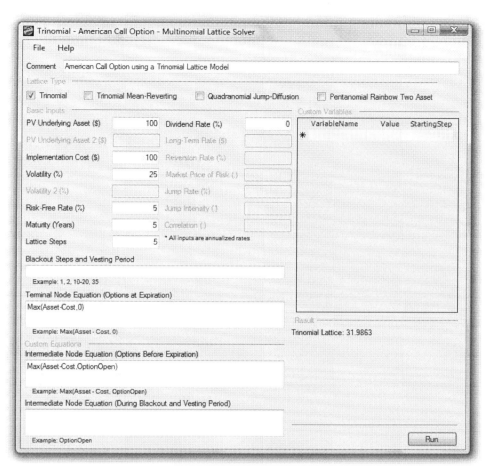

Figure 193.1: Simple trinomial lattice solution

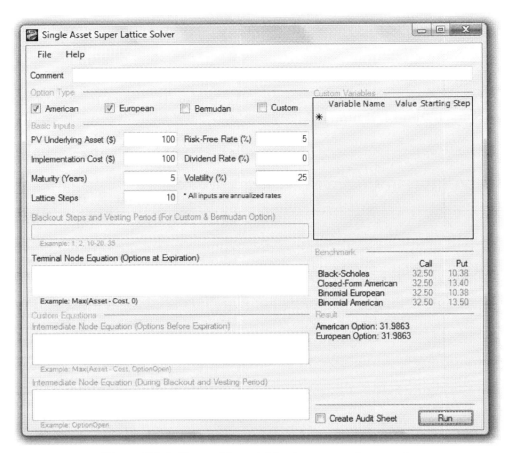

Figure 193.2: 10-step binomial lattice comparison result

PART III: REAL OPTIONS STRATEGIC CASE STUDIES – FRAMING THE OPTIONS

This part of the book presents several actual cases and real-life applications of real options, financial options, and employee stock options, with particular emphasis on framing the options or framing the problems. You can use the *ROV Strategy Trees* module available on the main *Real Options SLS* user interface to create visually appealing representations of strategic real options. This module is used to simplify the drawing and creation of strategy trees but is not used for the actual real options valuation modeling. Use the other *Real Options SLS* software modules such as Single Asset or Multiple Asset SLS for actual modeling purposes.

In the Integrated Risk Management process, after modeling the decision and quantifying risks using Monte Carlo simulation, the question that should be asked is, what's next? The risk information obtained somehow needs to be converted into actionable intelligence. So what if risk has been quantified to be such and such using Monte Carlo simulation? What do we do about it? The answer is to use real options analysis to hedge these risks, to value these risks, and to position yourself to take advantage of the risks. The first step in real options is to generate a strategy tree through the process of framing the problem. Based on the overall problem identification occurring during the initial qualitative management screening process, certain strategic optionalities would have become apparent for each particular project. The strategic optionalities may include, among other things, the option to expand, contract, abandon, switch, choose, and so forth. Based on the identification of strategic optionalities that exist for each project or at each stage of the project, the analyst can then choose from a list of options to analyze in more detail. Real options are added to the projects to hedge downside risks and to take advantage of upside swings.

One major misunderstanding that analysts tend to have about real options is that they can be solved using decision trees alone. Instead, decision trees are a great way of depicting strategic pathways that a firm can take, showing graphically a decision road map of management's strategic initiatives and opportunities over time. However, to solve a real options problem, it is better to combine decision tree analytics with real options analytics, rather than solely relying on decision trees. When used in framing real options, these trees should be more appropriately called strategy trees (used to define optimal strategic pathways).

In summary, decision tree analysis is incomplete as a stand-alone analysis in complex situations. Both the decision tree and real options methodologies discussed approach the same problem from different perspectives. However, a common ground could be reached. Taking the advantages of both approaches and melding them into an overall valuation strategy, decision trees should be used to frame the problem, real options analytics should be used to solve any existing strategic optionalities (either by pruning the decision tree into subtrees or solving the entire strategy tree at once), and the results should be presented back on a decision tree. These so-called option strategy trees are useful for determining the optimal decision paths the firm should take.

194. Real Options Strategic Cases – High-Tech Manufacturing: Build or Buy Decision with Real Options

File Names: Real Options Strategic Cases – High-Tech Manufacturing's Strategy A; Real Options Strategic Cases – High-Tech Manufacturing's Strategy B; Real Options Strategic Cases – High-Tech Manufacturing's Strategy C

Location: Modeling Toolkit | Real Options Models

Brief Description: Frames and solves a real options problem of choosing between build and buy strategies when the underlying project is filled with risk and uncertainty

Requirements: Modeling Toolkit, Real Options SLS

Microtech, Inc. is a billion-dollar high-tech manufacturing firm interested in developing a new state-of-the-art, high-capacity micro hard drive that fits into the palm of your hand. The problem is, the larger the capacity, the larger the magnetic disk has to be, and the faster it has to spin. Therefore, making small hard drives is difficult enough, let alone a high-capacity hard drive that is reliable and state-of-the-art. The risks the firm faces include market risks—will this product sell, will it sell enough, and at what price?—and private risks—will the technology work and can we develop it fast enough ahead of the competition?—both of which are significant enough to yield disasters in the project. In performing its due diligence, the vice president of the firm's advanced emerging technologies found a small start-up that is currently developing such a technology, and it is approximately three-quarters of the way there. This start-up will initiate a patent process in the next few weeks. Microtech would like to consider acquiring the start-up prior to initiation of the patent process. The start-up has shown interest in being acquired and based on preliminary discussions, requested $50M for the firm.

The question is, should Microtech acquire the firm and mitigate some development risk but still face the market risk and some residual development risk? After all, the start-up has the technology only partially completed. Then again, through the acquisition, Microtech can take a potential rival out of the picture and even mitigate the chances of its competitors acquiring this firm's technologies. How much is this firm really worth, compared to its asking price of $50M? What options exist to mitigate some of the market and development risks? Can Microtech take advantage of additional opportunities in the market through the acquisition?

The finance staff at Microtech with the assistance of several external consultants began to collect all the relevant data and created a DCF model. The best-guess present value of the benefits from the firm is $100M. This means that the NPV of buying the firm is $50M after accounting for the acquisition cost of $50M. In the DCF model, the probability of technical success is also modeled (using several binomial distributions and their relevant probabilities of success in several phases multiplied together) as well as the market positioning (triangular distributions were used to simulate the different market conditions in the future). Using *Risk Simulator* software, the Monte Carlo simulation's resulting annualized volatility is found to be 25%, a somewhat moderate level of risk. The finance staff also created another DCF with which to compare the result. This second DCF models the scenario of building the technology in-house. The total de*velopment cost in present value* will be $40M, a lot less than the acquisition cost of $50M. At first glance, Microtech might be better off building the technology in-house, providing an NPV of $60M. However, the volatility is found to be 30% as it is riskier to develop the technology from scratch than to buy a firm with the technology almost completed.

The question now becomes: What, if any, strategic real options exist for Microtech to consider? Is the NPV analysis sufficient to justify doing it itself? What about all the market and private risks in the project? If acquiring the firm, are there any options to protect Microtech from failure? If building the technology itself, are there any options to mitigate the development risks?

Microtech then proceeded to perform some ***real options framing exercises*** with its executives, facilitated by an external real options expert consultant. The questions raised included what risks exist and how can they be reduced. The real options consultant then put a real options framework around the discussions and came up with a preliminary ***strategy tree*** (Figure 194.1). For the first pass, four main options were conceived: mitigate the development risk of building themselves; mitigate the risk of the market; mitigate the risk of failure if acquiring the firm; and take advantage of the upside risks whenever possible. These options are compiled into path-dependent strategies in Figure 194.1.

Strategy A is to develop the technology in-house with the R&D risk mitigated through a stage-gate investment process, where the total $40M required investment is spread into four steps of $10M each (in present values). At any phase of the development, the fate of the next stage is determined (i.e., to decide if the R&D initiative should continue depending on the outcome of the current phase). The investment can be terminated at any time, and the maximum loss will be the total investment up to that point. That is, if R&D shows bad results after one year, the initiative is abandoned, the firm exits the project, and the maximum loss is $10M, not the entire $40M as defined in the DCF model. The questions are: How much is this strategic path worth? Is stage-gating the process worth it?

Strategy B is to develop the technology but hedge the market risk. That is, a preliminary Phase I market research is performed for $5M in the first year to obtain competitive intelligence on Microtech's competitors and to see if the market and complementary technologies exist such that the microdrive will indeed be successful. Then, depending on the results of this market research, Phase II's R&D initiative will or will not be executed. Because the market research takes an entire year to complete, further stage-gating the R&D initiative is not an option because it will significantly delay product launch. So Phase II is a full-scale R&D. In this strategic path, although the market risk is mitigated through market research, the development risk still exists. Hence, a contraction option is conceived. That is, Microtech finds another counterparty to assume the manufacturing risks by signing a two-year contract whereby at any time within the next two years, Microtech can have this counterparty firm take over the development of the increased rotational latency and seek times of the microdrives during the R&D process. The counterparty shares in 30% of the net profits without undertaking any R&D costs. Microtech will assume the entire $40M R&D cost but ends up mitigating its highest development risks and also saves $10M (in present values) by not having to increase its own manufacturing competencies by hiring outside consultants and purchasing new equipment. The questions are: How much is this strategic path worth? Is the market research valuable? How much should Microtech share its net profits with the counterparty?

Strategy C is to purchase the start-up firm for $50M. However, by acquiring the firm, Microtech obtains additional options. Specifically, if the technology or market does not work out as expected, Microtech can sell the start-up (sell its intellectual property, patents, technology, assets, buildings, etc.) for an estimated salvage value of $25M within the first year. As the content of the start-up's intellectual property is expected to increase over time because of added development efforts, the salvage value is expected to increase by $1M each year. If the technology is successful within the next five years, other products can be created from this microdrive base platform technology. For instance, the microdrive is applicable for use not only in laptops; with an additional funding of $5M, the technology can be adapted into handheld global positioning system (GPS) map locators for cars and travel enthusiasts, personal pocket-size hard drives (where people can carry an entire computer on a key chain; all they have to do is plug it into a monitor and the virtual computer comes up), MP3 players, and a multitude of other products, which by Microtech's estimates, will increase the NPV of the microdrive by 35%. However, this expansion option exists only in Strategy C, as time to market is crucial for these new products and the start-up already has three-quarters of the technology completed, speeding Microtech's time to market tremendously. The questions are: How much is the start-up actually worth to Microtech? Is $50M too high a price to pay for the company? Figure 194.1 shows these three strategic paths and relevant information on each strategy branch.

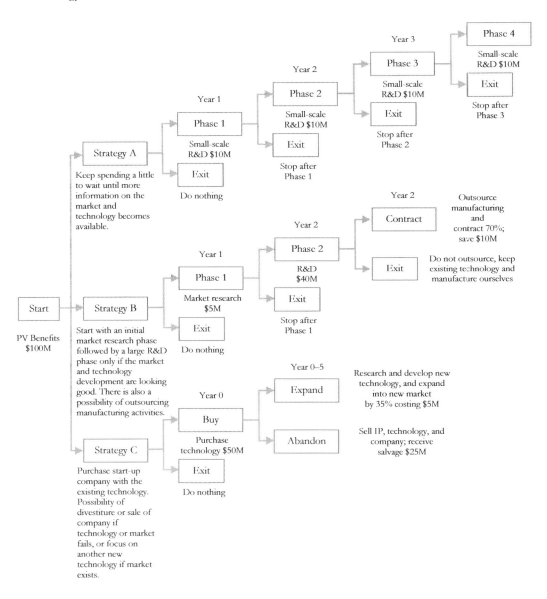

Figure 194.1: Strategy tree on build versus buy

Strategy A's total strategic value is worth $64.65M using the *Multiple Asset SLS* software with 100-step lattices as seen in Figure 194.2. The NPV is $60M, indicating that the option value is worth $4.65M. This means that there is definitely value in stage-gating the R&D initiative to hedge downside risks. To follow along, open the SLS file: *Strategic Cases – High-Tech Manufacturing's Strategy A*.

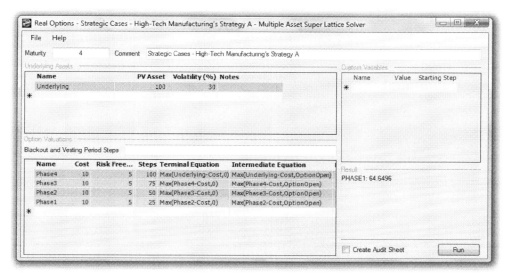

Figure 194.2 Value of Strategy A

When the annualized dividend rate exceeds 2.5%, the option value becomes zero and the total strategic value reverts to the NPV of $60M, as seen in Figure 194.3. This means that by spending more time and putting off development through a stage-gate process, as long as the maximum losses per year (lost market share and opportunity losses of net revenues from sales) do not exceed $2.5M (2.5% of $100M), then stage-gating is valuable. Otherwise, the financial leakage is too severe; the added risk is worth it and the $40M should be spent immediately on a large-scale development effort. Progressively modify each valuation phase's dividend rate from 0% to 2.5%.

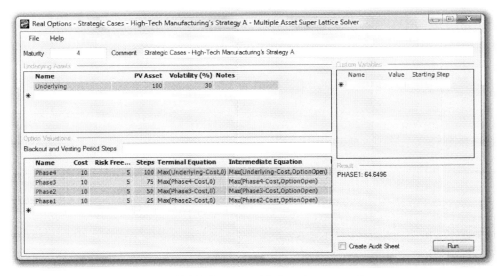

Figure 194.3: Strategy A's break-even point

Real Options Strategic Cases – High-Tech Manufacturing's Strategy B

The total strategic value of Strategy B is valued at $75.90 (rounded) as seen in Figure 194.4. The NPV is $55M (computed by taking $100M – $5M – $40M), which means that the options are valued at $20.90M. So, thus far, Strategy B is the better strategic path, with a value of $75.90M. In addition, Figure 194.5 shows the strategic value without the contraction option, worth $59.06M ($4.06M option value to stage-gate with market research and $55M NPV). Thus, the contraction option with the counterparty to hedge the downside technical risk is worth $16.84M. A further analysis can be performed by changing the contraction factor (how much is allocated to the counterparty) and the amount of savings, as seen in Figure 194.6.

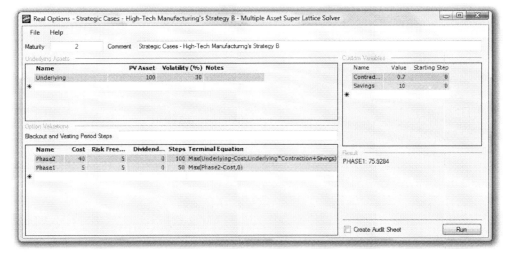

Figure 194.4: Value of Strategy B

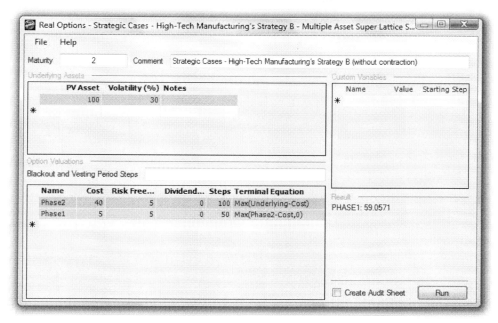

Figure 194.5: Strategy B without contraction

Strategic Option Value	Savings $0.00	Savings $5.00	Savings $10.00	Savings $15.00	Savings $20.00	Savings $25.00	Savings $30.00	Savings $35.00	Savings $40.00	Savings $45.00	Savings $50.00
Contraction Factor 0.05	$59.15	$59.27	$59.50	$59.86	$60.39	$61.11	$62.07	$63.25	$64.67	$66.41	$68.40
Contraction Factor 0.10	$59.19	$59.35	$59.64	$60.09	$60.74	$61.62	$62.73	$64.13	$65.83	$67.77	$69.94
Contraction Factor 0.15	$59.24	$59.47	$59.84	$60.40	$61.19	$62.26	$63.60	$65.24	$67.15	$69.31	$71.83
Contraction Factor 0.20	$59.32	$59.62	$60.11	$60.82	$61.80	$63.08	$64.66	$66.53	$68.68	$71.20	$73.97
Contraction Factor 0.25	$59.43	$59.82	$60.45	$61.36	$62.56	$64.07	$65.91	$68.06	$70.57	$73.36	$76.39
Contraction Factor 0.30	$59.60	$60.12	$60.91	$62.04	$63.50	$65.30	$67.43	$69.94	$72.76	$75.84	$79.15
Contraction Factor 0.35	$59.83	$60.53	$61.54	$62.92	$64.68	$66.80	$69.31	$72.15	$75.28	$78.67	$82.30
Contraction Factor 0.40	$60.16	$61.09	$62.38	$64.07	$66.18	$68.68	$71.54	$74.73	$78.19	$81.88	$85.80
Contraction Factor 0.45	$60.65	$61.86	$63.49	$65.55	$68.05	$70.94	$74.18	$77.72	$81.51	$85.48	$89.65
Contraction Factor 0.50	$61.35	$62.91	$64.93	$67.45	$70.38	$73.66	$77.26	$81.14	$85.22	$89.46	$93.83
Contraction Factor 0.55	$62.34	$64.32	$66.85	$69.82	$73.18	$76.87	$80.82	$84.98	$89.32	$93.77	$98.31
Contraction Factor 0.60	$63.70	$66.25	$69.26	$72.70	$76.49	$80.56	$84.83	$89.24	$93.76	$98.36	$103.01
Contraction Factor 0.65	$65.66	$68.71	$72.27	$76.18	$80.35	$84.72	$89.22	$93.81	$98.46	$103.15	$107.87
Contraction Factor 0.70	$68.24	$71.88	$75.90	$80.20	$84.68	$89.26	$93.92	$98.61	$103.34	$108.07	$112.82
Contraction Factor 0.75	$71.58	$75.72	$80.15	$84.72	$89.37	$94.08	$98.81	$103.55	$108.30	$113.05	$117.81
Contraction Factor 0.80	$75.65	$80.18	$84.83	$89.55	$94.28	$99.03	$103.78	$108.54	$113.29	$118.05	$122.81
Contraction Factor 0.85	$80.31	$85.02	$89.76	$94.51	$99.27	$104.02	$108.78	$113.54	$118.29	$123.05	$127.81
Contraction Factor 0.90	$85.25	$90.00	$94.76	$99.51	$104.27	$109.02	$113.78	$118.54	$123.29	$128.05	$132.81
Contraction Factor 0.90	$85.25	$90.00	$94.76	$99.51	$104.27	$109.02	$113.78	$118.54	$123.29	$128.05	$132.81

Figure 194.6: Decision table on savings and contraction factors

Real Options Strategic Cases – High-Tech Manufacturing's Strategy C

Finally, the total strategic value for Strategy C (Figure 194.7) is valued at $131.12 less $50 purchase price of the start-up company or a net strategic value of $81.12M. That is, Microtech should be willing to pay no more than $55.22M for the start-up (i.e., $50M + $81.12M – $75.90M), otherwise it is better off pursuing Strategy B and building the technology itself.

Thus, the optimal strategy is to purchase the start-up company, go to market quickly with the ability to abandon and sell the start-up should things fail, or to further invest an additional R&D sum later on to develop spin-off technologies. If real options analysis were not performed, Microtech would have chosen to develop the technology itself immediately and spend $40M. This strategy would yield the highest NPV if real options and risk mitigation options are not considered. Microtech would have made a serious decision blunder and taken unnecessary risks. By performing the real options analysis, additional spin-off products and opportunities surface, which prove to be highly valuable.

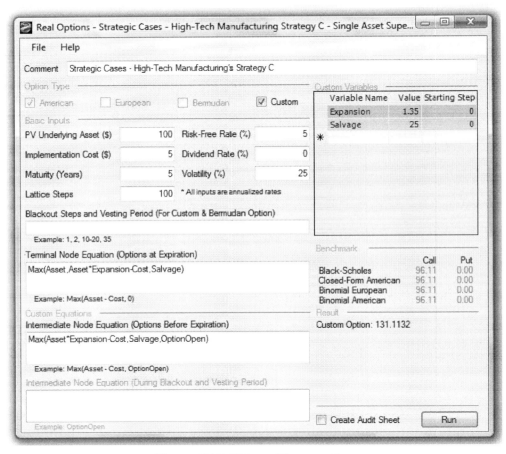

Figure 194.7: Value of Strategy C

195. Real Options Strategic Cases – Oil and Gas: Farmouts, Options to Defer, and Value of Information

File Names: Real Options Strategic Cases – Oil and Gas – Strategy A; Real Options Strategic Cases – Oil and Gas – Strategy B

Location: Modeling Toolkit | Real Options Models

Brief Description: Frames and solves a real options problem of choosing among various flexibilities of farmouts and outsourcing, deferring decisions, and the value of information, when the underlying project is filled with risk and uncertainty

Requirements: Modeling Toolkit, Real Options SLS

An oil and gas company, NewOil, is in the process of exploring a new field development. It intends to start drilling and exploring a region in Alaska for oil. Preliminary geologic and aerial surveys indicate that there is an optimal area for drilling. However, NewOil faces two major sources of uncertainties: market uncertainties (oil price volatility and economic conditions) and private uncertainties (geological area, porosity, oil pressure, reservoir size, etc.). Using comparable analysis and oil price forecasts, the development of this new oil field is expected to yield a sum PV of $200M, but drilling may cost up to $100M (in present values). The firm is trying to see if any strategic options exist to mitigate the market and private risks as well as to find the optimal strategic path.

Figure 195.1 represents the outcome of a strategic brainstorming activity at NewOil. Specifically, NewOil can simply take the risk and start drilling, shown as Strategy C. In this case, the NPV is found to be $100M, but there are tremendous amounts of risk in this strategy. To reduce the private risk, either a 3D-seismic can be implemented or a series of test wells can be drilled. The 3D-seismic studies will cost about $5M and take only 0.5 years to complete. The information obtained is fairly reliable but still contains significant amounts of uncertainty. In contrast, test wells can be drilled but will cost NewOil $10M and take 2 years to complete. However, test wells provide more solid and accurate information than seismic studies as the quality of the oil, the pressure, caps, porosity, and other geologic factors will become known over time as more test wells are drilled. Finally, to reduce the market risk, specifically the oil price reduction and volatility, NewOil has decided to execute a joint venture with LocalOil, a small second-tier oil and gas engineering company specializing in managing and running oil rigs. NewOil will provide LocalOil 49% of its gross profits from the oil field provided that LocalOil takes over the entire drilling operation at the request of NewOil. LocalOil benefits from a now fully developed oil field without any investments of its own, while NewOil benefits by pulling out its field personnel and saving $30M in total operating expenses during the remaining economic life of the oil rig, but it still captures a 51% share of the field's production. The question now is which strategic path in Figure 195.1 is optimal for NewOil? Should it take some risks and execute the seismic study or completely reduce the private risk through a series of test wells? Perhaps the risk is small enough such that the opportunity losses of putting off immediate development far surpass the risks taken and the oil field should be developed immediately.

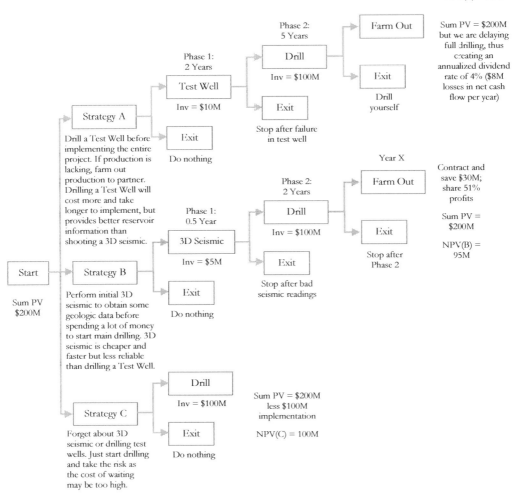

Figure 195.1: Strategy tree for oil and gas

Figure 195.2 shows the valuation of Strategy A. The NPV of Strategy A is $90M, which means that the option value is $33.74M ($123.74M – $90M). This means that putting off development by doing some test wells and farming out operations in the future when oil prices are not as high as NewOil expects is worth a lot. This total strategic value of $123.74 is now compared with the total strategic value of Strategy B valued at $129.58M (Figure 195.3). Clearly the cheaper and faster seismic study in Strategy B brings with it a higher volatility (Strategy B has a 35% volatility compared to 30% for Strategy A), and having the ability to farm out development of the field is worth more under such circumstances. In addition, the added dividend outflow in Strategy A reduces the option value of deferring and getting more valid information through drilling test wells. Thus, the higher the cost of waiting and holding on to this option, the lower the option value.

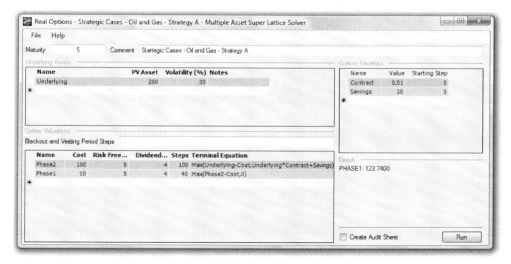

Figure 195.2: Value of Strategy A

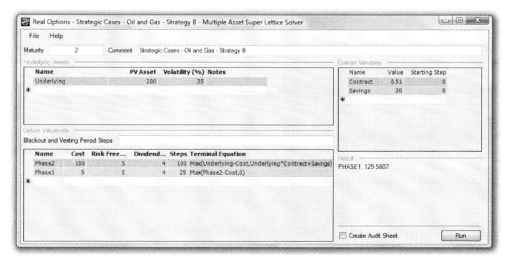

Figure 195.3: Value of Strategy B

196. Real Options Strategic Cases – Pharmaceutical Development: Value of Perfect Information and Optimal Trigger Values

File Names: Real Options – Strategic Cases – R&D Stage-Gate Process A; Real Options – Strategic Cases – R&D Stage-Gate Process B

Location: Modeling Toolkit | Real Options Models

Brief Description: Frames and values a real options application of performing stage-gate development processes versus fast-tracking a development, and the value of information, when the underlying project is filled with risk and uncertainty

Requirements: Modeling Toolkit, Real Options SLS

Suppose BioGen, a large multibillion dollar pharmaceutical firm is thinking of developing a new type of insulin that can be inhaled and the drug will be absorbed directly into the blood stream. This is indeed a novel and honorable idea. Imagine what this means to diabetics who will no longer need painful and frequent injections. The problem is, this new type of insulin requires a brand-new development effort. If the uncertainties of the market, competition, drug development, and Food and Drug Administration approval are high, perhaps a base insulin drug that can be ingested should first be developed. The ingestible version is a required precursor to the inhaled version. BioGen can decide to either take the risk and fast-track development into the inhaled version or buy an option to defer, to first wait and see if the ingestible version works. If this precursor works, then the firm has the option to expand into the inhaled version. How much should the firm be willing to spend on performing additional tests on the precursor and under what circumstances should the inhaled version be implemented directly?

Suppose that BioGen needs to spend $100M on developing the inhaled version. If successful, the expected NPV is $24M (i.e., $124M PV Asset less the $100M PV development cost). The probability of technical success, market prices, revenues, and operating expenses are all simulated in the discounted cash flow model. The resulting cash flow stream has a volatility of 22%. In contrast, if BioGen first develops the ingestible version, it will cost $10M and take an entire year to develop, forcing the later phase development of the inhaled version to start one year later. Because this inhaled version uses similar precursors, the development cost is only $95M, not $100M. However, by being one year late to market, the PV Asset of doing an ingestible version before attempting the inhaled version will be reduced to $120M. This means that the ingestible-inhaled strategy will yield an NPV of $15M. Figure 196.1 shows these two competing strategies.

Clearly, under an NPV analysis, the best approach is to pursue the inhaled version directly. However, when a real options analysis is performed by applying a two-phased sequential compound option, the total strategic value is found to be $27.24M, as seen in Figure 196.2. The strategic option value of being able to *defer* investments and to *wait and see* until more information becomes available and uncertainties become resolved is worth $12.24M because the NPV is worth $15M ($120M – $10M – $95M). In other words, the *Expected Value of Perfect Information* is worth $12.24M. This amount indicates that, for the intermediate phase of developing an ingestible precursor that can be used to obtain credible information to decide if further development is possible, the maximum the firm should be willing to spend in the ingestible intermediate phase is *on average no more than* $22.24M (i.e., $12.24M + $10M). If the cost to obtain the credible information exceeds this value, then it is optimal to take the risk and execute the entire project immediately at $100M, or Strategy B.

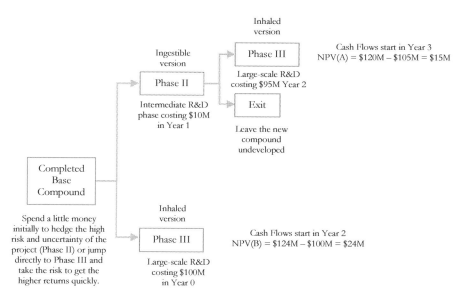

Figure 196.1: Real options strategy tree for pharmaceutical development

In contrast, if the volatility decreases (uncertainty and risk are lower), the strategic option value decreases. In addition, when the cost of waiting (as described by the *Dividend Rate* as a percentage of the *Asset Value*) increases, it is better not to defer and wait that long. Therefore, the higher the dividend rate, the lower the strategic option value. For instance, at a 17.20% dividend rate and 22% volatility, the resulting value reverts to the NPV of $15M (Figure 196.3), which means that the option value is zero, and that it is better to execute immediately as the cost of waiting far outstrips the value of being able to wait given the level of volatility (uncertainty and risk). Finally, if risks and uncertainty increase significantly even with a high cost of waiting (e.g., 17.20% dividend rate at 30% volatility), it is still valuable to wait.

This model provides the decision maker with a view into the optimal balancing between *waiting for more information* (Expected Value of Perfect Information) and the *cost of waiting*. You can analyze this balance by creating strategic *options to defer* investments through development stages where at every stage the project is reevaluated as to whether it is beneficial to proceed to the next phase. You can vary the volatility and dividend inputs to determine their interactions—specifically, where the break-even points are for different combinations of volatilities and dividends. Thus, using this information, firms can make better *go* or *no-go decisions* (for instance, break-even volatility points can be traced back into the DCF model to estimate the probability of crossing over and this ability to wait becomes valuable).

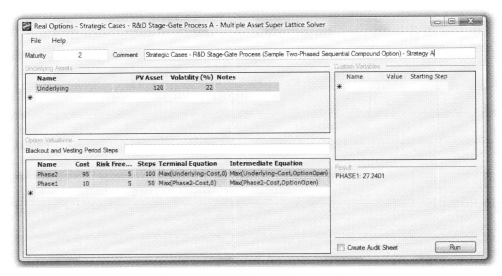

Figure 196.2: Value of Strategy A

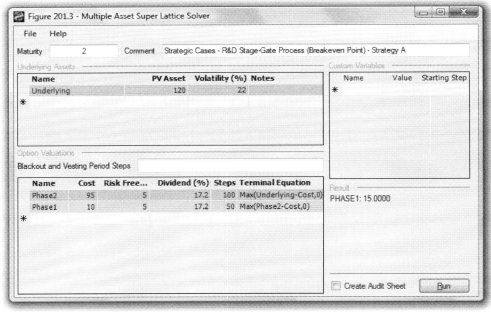

Figure 196.3: Sequential compound option's break-even point

197. Real Options Strategic Cases – Option to Switch Inputs

File Names: Real Options – Strategic Cases – Switching Option's Strategy A; Real Options – Strategic Cases – Switching Option's Strategy B

Location: Modeling Toolkit | Real Options Models

Brief Description: Frames and values a real options application of the ability to switch use when the underlying project is filled with risk and uncertainty

Requirements: Modeling Toolkit, Real Options SLS

This strategic case is a switching option (an electric generating plant can be retrofitted to take both coke and coal as inputs, as opposed to the current situation where only one type of input can be used) and can be summarized in the strategy tree shown in Figure 197.1.

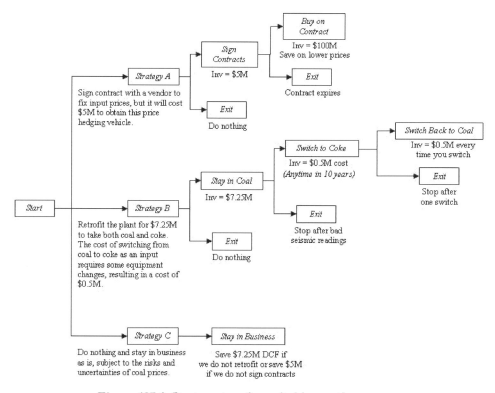

Figure 197.1: Strategy tree for switching options

In Strategy A, signing a contract where it comes into play only when prices hit a lower level is a Lower Down and In Barrier Call Option. The PV asset value is the current NPV staying on course, and the lower barrier is the NPV value that is obtained given the lower price level where the contract is executed. Signing the contract is worth more than Strategy B's ability to switch; hence, Strategy A should be executed. Besides, this is a lot less expensive than retrofitting the plant to take different inputs. The total strategic value is positive as the option value of this contract is $6.22M (Figure 197.2) but the cost of executing the contract to buy the option is $5M.

In Strategy B, the ability to switch back and forth has some value even if both input fuels are at the same price currently. In fact, the NPV shows that there is no value in the ability to switch. If using coal right now has an NPV of $10M and coke also has an NPV of $10M because their price levels are currently the same, then the act of switching incurs a $0.5M cost, and switching now yields an NPV of –$0.50M. Obviously, then, ability to switch is useless in an NPV paradigm. However, in a real options paradigm, having the ability to switch but not doing it right now is worth a lot. For instance, coal and coke have different volatilities in prices and may or may not be correlated (a negative correlation increases the switching option's value as the new input acts like a hedging vehicle). The price movements of both inputs are highly volatile and there is a chance that the first input's prices are higher than the second inputs such that switching becomes optimal. The strategic value yields $5.49M (regardless if it is switching from coal with 35% volatility to coke with 55%, or vice versa). However, the cost of getting this option (retrofitting the plant) is $7.25M, so the total strategic value is negative, making this strategy not optimal (Figure 197.3).

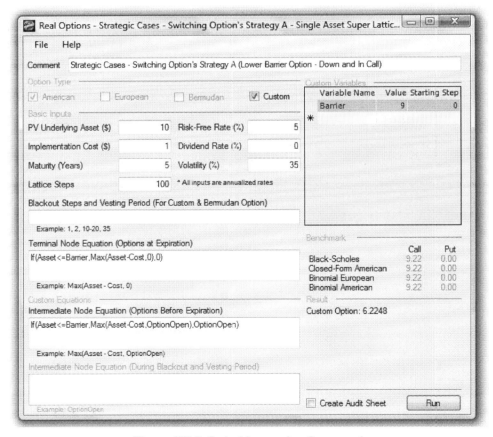

Figure 197.2: Switching option Strategy A

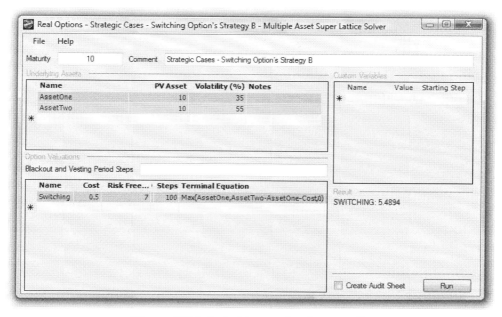

Figure 197.3: Switching option Strategy B

198. Valuation – Convertible Warrants with a Vesting Period and Put Protection

File Names: Valuation – Warrant – Combined Value; Valuation – Warrant – Put Only; Valuation – Warrant – Warrant Only

Location: Modeling Toolkit | Real Options Models

Brief Description: Frames and values issues of warrants and protective warrants with a put provision

Requirements: Modeling Toolkit, Real Options SLS

This case study provides a sample application of the Real Options SLS software on valuing a warrant (an instrument that can be converted into a stock, similar to a call option) that has a protective put option associated with it. The analysis herein also applies both a customized binomial lattice and a closed-form Black-Scholes model for comparison and benchmarking purposes.

The valuation analysis performed was based on an actual consulting project, but all proprietary information has been modified except for certain basic publicly available information. The accuracy of the results is dependent on this factual information at the time of valuation. This case details the input assumptions used as well as some benchmark due diligence to check the results. Certain technical details have been left out to simplify the case.

The client company very recently acquired a small IT firm. The acquisition consisted of both cash and some warrants, which are convertible into stocks. But because the client's stocks are fairly volatile, the acquired firm negotiated a protective put to hedge its downside risks. In return for providing this protective put, the client requested that the warrant be exercisable only if the target firm is solvent and its gross margins exceed 33% and are no less than $10 million.

Clearly, this problem cannot be solved using a Black-Scholes model because there exist dividends, a vesting period, a threshold price put protection at which the put can be exercised, and the fact that the put cannot be exercised unless the warrant is converted into a stock but only when the stock price is below $33.

To summarize, the following list shows the assumptions and requirements in this exotic warrant:

Stock price on grant date:	$30.12
Warrant strike price:	$15.00
Warrant maturity:	10.00 years (grant date)
Risk-free rate:	4.24% (grant date)
Volatility:	29.50%
Dividend rate:	0.51%
Put threshold price:	$33.00
Vesting for warrant:	3 years
Vesting for put option:	5 years

Further, these additional requirements were modeled:

- The protective put option can be exercised only if the warrant is exercised.

- The put option can be exercised only if the stock price is below $33.00 at the time of exercise.

- The warrant can be exercised only if the recipient's gross margin equals or exceeds 33% and is no less than $10 million. A simulation forecast puts an 85% to 90% uniform probability of occurrence for this event.

- The warrant can be exercised only if the recipient is solvent. Another simulation forecast puts a 90% to 95% uniform probability of occurrence for this event.

- The protective put payout is the maximum spread between the put threshold price less the client's common stock price or the warrant price.

The risk-free rate is based on the 10-year U.S. Treasury note. The volatility estimate is based on the client's historical weekly closing prices for the past one, two, and three years. The volatilities are estimated using the standard deviation of the natural logarithmic relative returns, annualized for a year, and then averaged. The dividend rate is assumed to be 0.51% based on available market data on client shares. The total probability of exceeding the gross margin threshold as well as solvency requirements is 80.9375% (calculated using the midpoint probability estimates of both independent events 87.50% times 92.50%, and were the results based on simulation forecasts using historical financial data). The only way to value such a protective put on a warrant is by using binomial lattices. However, a Black-Scholes model is used to benchmark the results.

Warrant Valuation

In order to solve the warrant part of the exotic vehicle, high-level analysis rules need to be created:

- If the period ≥ 3 years, then at maturity, the profit-maximizing decision is:

  Max (Exercise the warrant accounting for the probability the requirements are met; or let the warrant expire worthless otherwise).

- If the period ≥ 3 years, then prior to maturity, the profit maximizing decision is:

  Max (Exercise the warrant accounting for the probability the requirements are met; or keep the option open for future execution).

- If the period < 3 years, then hold on to the warrant as no execution is allowed.

Protective Put Option Valuation

The same is done for the protective put option:

- If the period ≥ 5 years, then at maturity, the profit maximizing decision is:

  Max (If the stock price is $< \$33$, then exercise the warrant and collect the protective put payout, after accounting for the probability the requirements are met; or let the warrant and put option expire worthless).

- If the period ≥ 5 years, then prior to maturity, the profit maximizing decision is:

  Max (If the stock price is < $33, then exercise the warrant and collect the protective put payout, after accounting for the probability the requirements are met; or keep the option open for future execution)

- If the period < 5 years, then hold on to the put option as no execution is allowed.

The binomial model used is a combination of a Bermudan vesting nested option, where all the requirements (vesting periods, threshold price, probability of solvency, probability of exceeding gross margin requirements) have to be met before the warrant can be executed, and the put option that can be executed only if the warrant is executed. However, the warrant can be executed even if the protective put is not executed.

Analytical Results

A summary of results follows. The results start with a decomposition of the Warrant call and the protective put valued independently. These results are then compared to benchmarks to ascertain their accuracy and model reliability. Then a combination of both instruments is valued in a mutually exclusive nested option model. The results of interest are the combined option model, but we can only obtain such a model by first decomposing the parts. The analysis was performed using the SLS software.

To follow along, you can start the Single Asset SLS software and load the relevant example files: *Valuation – Warrant – Combined Value; Valuation – Warrant – Put Only;* and *Valuation – Warrant – Warrant Only.*

A. Warrant at Grant Date

Naïve Black-Scholes (benchmark):	$19.71	
Adjusted Black-Scholes (benchmark):	$15.95	(prob.-adjusted benchmark)
Binomial lattice (100 steps):	$15.98	(using SLS)

As can be seen, the binomial lattice for the Warrant converges to the Black-Scholes results. The reason for this convergence is that the dividend rate is low, making it not optimal to exercise early, but still worth slightly more than a simple European option. See Figure 198.1 for the details.

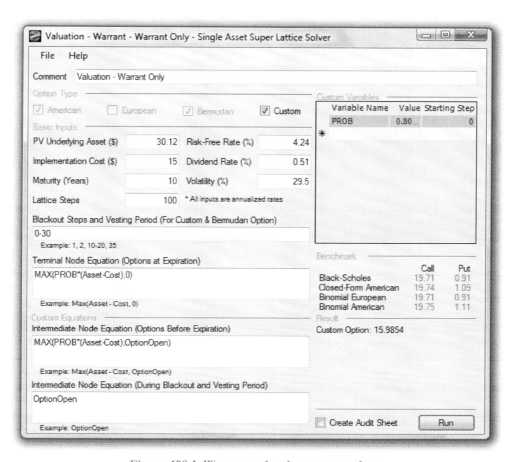

Figure 198.1: Warrant valuation at grant date

B. Protective Put Option at Grant Date

Static protection value (total):	$1.5 million	(100,000 warrants granted)
Static protection value (per warrant):	$15.00	(guaranteed minimum)
Adjusted static protection value:	$12.14	(prob.-adjusted benchmark)
Binomial lattice (100 steps):	$12.08	(using SLS)

The analysis can be seen in Figure 198.2.

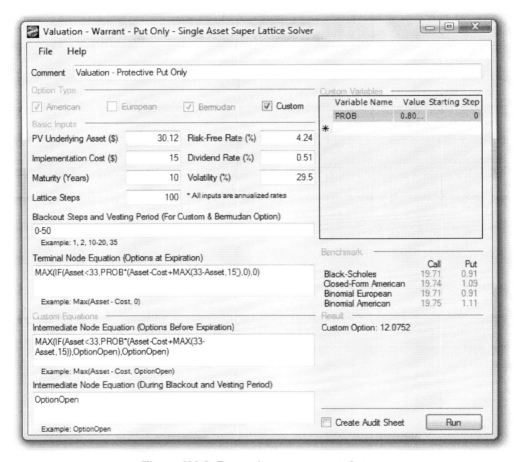

Figure 198.2: Protective put at grant date

The analysis up to this point decomposes the Warrant call and the protective put options, and their values are comparable to the static benchmarks, indicating that the models are specified correctly and the results are accurate. However, the warrant issues cannot be separated from the protective put because they are combined into one instrument. Separating them means that at certain points and conditions in time, the holder can both execute the call and execute the put option protection with another call. This constitutes double-counting. Thus, in such a mutually exclusive condition (either a call is executed or a protective put is executed with the call, not both), a combination valuation is performed. The results are shown next.

C. Combination of Warrant and Protective Put Option at Grant Date

Black-Scholes call option: $19.71   (benchmark)

Black-Scholes put option: $0.91   (benchmark)

Combination of both Black-Scholes: $20.62   (sum of both benchmarks)

Binomial lattice (100 steps): $22.37

Figure 198.3 illustrates the analysis performed.

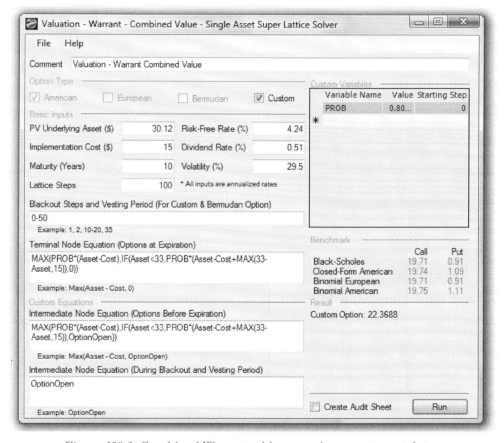

Figure 198.3: Combined Warrant with protective put at grant date

Using Black-Scholes call and put option models as benchmarks, we see that the sought-after result of $22.37 is valid, after considering that the decompositions of the model are also valid. Clearly the total combination value has to exceed the Black-Scholes as the Warrant-put is an American option (with vesting requirements). To summarize, the analysis cannot be completed without the use of the Single Asset SLS software. Even when solving such complicated instruments, using the software makes pricing relatively straightforward.

Appendix A: List of Models

Below is a list of the models included in the Modeling Toolkit software. As software programs are continually upgraded and improved, please check the user manual for the latest list of models available after this book's printing date.

The Modeling Toolkit is a set of mathematically sophisticated models written in C++ and linked into Excel spreadsheets. It comprises over 800 analytical models and functions (see Appendix B for the list of functions), with about 300 analytical model Excel/SLS templates and example spreadsheets (see the list below) covering the areas of risk analysis, simulation, forecasting, Basel II/III risk analysis, credit and default risk, statistical models, and much more.

Analytics

1. Central Limit Theorem
2. Central Limit Theorem (Lottery Numbers)
3. Flaw of Averages
4. Mathematical Integration
5. Parametric and Nonparametric Hypothesis Tests Dataset
6. Projectile Motion
7. Regression Diagnostics
8. Ships in the Night
9. Statistical Analysis
10. Weighting of Ratios

Banking Models

11. Audit of Construction Lending
12. Banker's Construction Budget
13. Classified Breakeven Loan Inventory
14. Classified Loan Borrowing Base
15. Classified Loan Cash Budget and Overdraft Facilities
16. Federal Reserve Camels Rating System
17. Firm in Financial Distress
18. Project Finance Risk Rating
19. Queuing Models
20. Reconciling Enron's Cash Flow
21. Risk Rating Model
22. Sample Cash Flow Model

Probability of Default

Project Management

Volatility

319. EWMA Model

320. GARCH Model

321. Implied Volatility

322. Log Asset Returns Approach

323. Log Cash Flow Returns Approach

324. Probability to Volatility

Yield Curve

325. CIR Model

326. Curve Interpolation BIM

327. Curve Interpolation NS

328. Forward Rates from Spot Rates

329. Spline Interpolation and Extrapolation

330. Term Structure of Volatility

331. US Treasury Risk Free Rate

332. Vasicek Model

Appendix B: List of Functions

Here is a comprehensive list of the functions in Modeling Toolkit that can be accessed either through the analytical DLL libraries or in Excel. Please keep checking back at the website for a more updated list. The software is continually evolving and newer applications and models are constantly added. Finally, the Risk Simulator tools applicable when using the Modeling Toolkit are also listed at the end.

1. MTAEPMarketValueAsset

    Market Value of Asset using the Asset-Equity Parity Model.

2. MTAEPMarketValueDebt

    Market Value of Debt using the Asset-Equity Parity Model.

3. MTAEPRequiredReturnDebt

    Required Return on Risky Debt using the Asset-Equity Parity Model.

4. MTAltDistributionCallOption

    Computes the European call option for an underlying asset returns distribution with skew and kurtosis, and is not perfectly normal. May return an error for unsolvable inputs.

5. MTAltDistributionPutOption

    Computes the European put option for an underlying asset returns distribution with skew and kurtosis, and is not perfectly normal. May return an error for unsolvable inputs.

6. MTAnnuityRate

    Returns the percentage equivalent of the required periodic payment on an annuity (e.g., mortgage payments, loan repayment). Returns the percentage of the total principal at initiation.

7. MTAsianCallwithArithmeticAverageRate

    An average rate option is a cash-settled option whose payoff is based on the difference between the arithmetic average value of the underlying during the life of the option and a fixed strike.

8. MTAsianCallwithGeometricAverageRate

    An average rate option is a cash-settled option whose payoff is based on the difference between the geometric average value of the underlying during the life of the option and a fixed strike.

9. MTAsianPutwithArithmeticAverageRate

    An average rate option is a cash-settled option whose payoff is based on the difference between a fixed strike and the arithmetic average value of the underlying during the life of the option.

10. MTAsianPutwithGeometricAverageRate

An average rate option is a cash-settled option whose payoff is based on the difference between a fixed strike and the geometric average value of the underlying during the life of the option.

11. MTAssetExchangeAmericanOption

Option holder has the right up to and including expiration to swap out Asset 2 and receive Asset 1, with predetermined quantities.

12. MTAssetExchangeEuropeanOption

Option holder has the right at expiration to swap out Asset 2 and receive Asset 1, with predetermined quantities.

13. MTAssetOrNothingCall

At expiration, if in the money, the option holder receives the stock or asset. For a call option, as long as the stock or asset price exceeds the strike at expiration, the stock is received.

14. MTAssetOrNothingPut

At expiration, if in the money, the option holder receives the stock or asset. For a put option, stock is received only if the stock or asset value falls below the strike price.

15. MTBarrierDoubleUpInDownInCall

Valuable or knocked in the money only if either barrier (upper or lower) is breached (i.e., asset value is above the upper or below the lower barriers), and the payout is in the form of a call option on the underlying asset.

16. MTBarrierDoubleUpInDownInPut

Valuable or knocked in the money only if either barrier (upper or lower) is breached (i.e., asset value is above the upper or below the lower barriers), and the payout is in the form of a put option on the underlying asset.

17. MTBarrierDoubleUpOutDownOutCall

Valuable or stays in the money only if either barrier (upper or lower barrier) is not breached, and the payout is in the form of a call option on the underlying asset.

18. MTBarrierDoubleUpOutDownOutPut

Valuable or stays in the money only if either barrier (upper or lower barrier) is not breached, and the payout is in the form of a put option on the underlying asset.

19. MTBarrierDownandInCall

Becomes valuable or knocked in the money if the lower barrier is breached, and the payout is the call option on the underlying asset. Sometimes cash is paid at maturity, assuming that the option has not been knocked in.

20. MTBarrierDownandInPut

Becomes valuable or knocked in the money if the lower barrier is breached, and the payout is the put option on the underlying asset. Sometimes cash is paid at maturity, assuming that the option has not been knocked in.

21. MTBarrierDownandOutCall

    Valuable or in the money only if the lower barrier is not breached, and the payout is the call option on the underlying asset. Sometimes cash is paid at maturity, assuming that the option has not been knocked out.

22. MTBarrierDownandOutPut

    Valuable or in the money only if the lower barrier is not breached, and the payout is the put option on the underlying asset. Sometimes cash is paid at maturity, assuming that the option has not been knocked out.

23. MTBarrierUpandInCall

    Becomes valuable or knocked in the money if the upper barrier is breached, and the payout is the call option on the underlying asset. Sometimes cash is paid at maturity, assuming that the option has not been knocked in.

24. MTBarrierUpandInPut

    Becomes valuable or knocked in the money if the upper barrier is breached, and the payout is the put option on the underlying asset. Sometimes cash is paid at maturity, assuming that the option has not been knocked in.

25. MTBarrierUpandOutCall

    Valuable or in the money only if the upper barrier is not breached, and the payout is the call option on the underlying asset. Sometimes cash is paid at maturity, assuming that the option has not been knocked out.

26. MTBarrierUpandOutPut

    Valuable or in the money only if the upper barrier is not breached, and the payout is the put option on the underlying asset. Sometimes cash is paid at maturity, assuming that the option has not been knocked out.

27. MTBDTAmericanCallonDebtLattice

    Computes the American call option on interest-based instruments and debt or bonds, and creates the entire pricing lattice.

28. MTBDTAmericanCallonDebtValue

    Computes the American call option value on interest-based instruments and debt or bonds, and returns only one value instead of the entire lattice.

29. MTBDTAmericanPutonDebtLattice

    Computes the American put option on interest-based instruments and debt or bonds, and creates the entire pricing lattice.

30. MTBDTAmericanPutonDebtValue

    Computes the American put option value on interest-based instruments and debt or bonds, and returns only one value instead of the entire lattice.

31. MTBDTCallableDebtPriceLattice

    Computes the revised price lattice of a callable debt such that the options-adjusted spread can be imputed. Allows for changing interest and interest volatilities over time.

32. MTBDTCallableDebtPriceValue

Computes the present value of a coupon bond/debt that is callable, to see the differences in value from a noncallable debt, and returns only one value instead of an entire lattice.

33. MTBDTCallableSpreadValue

Computes the option-adjusted spread (i.e., the additional premium that should be charged on the callable option provision).

34. MTBDTEuropeanCallonDebtLattice

Computes the European call option on interest-based instruments and debt or bonds, and creates the entire pricing lattice.

35. MTBDTEuropeanCallonDebtValue

Computes the European call option value on interest-based instruments and debt or bonds, and returns only one value instead of the entire lattice.

36. MTBDTEuropeanPutonDebtLattice

Computes the European put option on interest-based instruments and debt or bonds, and creates the entire pricing lattice.

37. MTBDTEuropeanPutonDebtValue

Computes the European put option value on interest-based instruments and debt or bonds, and returns only one value instead of the entire lattice.

38. MTBDTFloatingCouponPriceLattice

Value of the floater bond's lattice (coupon rate is floating and can be directly or inversely related to interest rates; e.g., rates drop, coupon increases, the bond appreciates in price, and the yield increases).

39. MTBDTFloatingCouponPriceValue

Value of the floater bond (coupon rate is floating and can be directly or inversely related to interest rates; e.g., rates drop, coupon increases, the bond appreciates in price, and the yield increases).

40. MTBDTNoncallableDebtPriceLattice

Computes the pricing lattice of a coupon bond/debt that is not callable, to see the differences in value from a callable debt.

41. MTBDTNoncallableDebtPriceValue

Computes the present value of a coupon bond/debt that is not callable, to see the differences in value from a callable debt.

42. MTBDTInterestRateLattice

Computes the short rate interest lattice based on a term structure of interest rates and changing interest volatilities, as a means to compute option values.

43. MTBDTNonCallableSpreadValue

Computes the straight spread on a bond that is noncallable in order to compare it with the option provision of an option-adjusted spread model.

44. MTBDTZeroPriceLattice

Computes the straight price lattice of zero bonds based on a term structure of interest rates and changing interest volatilities, as a means to compute interest-based option values.

45. MTBDTZeroPriceLattice2

Computes the straight price lattice of zero bonds based on a term structure of interest rates and changing interest volatilities, as a means to compute interest-based option values. Returns the same results as the MTBDTZeroPriceLattice function but requires interest rates and interest volatilities as inputs, rather than the entire interest rate lattice.

46. MTBDTZeroPriceValue

Computes the straight price of zero bonds at time zero, based on a term structure of interest rates and changing interest volatilities, as a means to compute interest-based option values.

47. MTBinaryDownAndInAssetAtExpirationOrNothing

Binary digital instrument receiving the asset at expiration, only if a corresponding asset hits a lower barrier or receives nothing otherwise. DT is monitoring steps: 1/12 monthly, 1/52 weekly, 1/250 daily, 0 continuously.

48. MTBinaryDownAndInAssetAtExpirationOrNothingCall

Binary digital call option receiving the asset at expiration if the asset hits a lower barrier or receives nothing otherwise. DT is monitoring steps: 1/12 monthly, 1/52 weekly, 1/250 daily, 0 continuously.

49. MTBinaryDownAndInAssetAtExpirationOrNothingPut

Binary digital put option receiving the asset at expiration if the asset hits a lower barrier or receives nothing otherwise. DT is monitoring steps: 1/12 monthly, 1/52 weekly, 1/250 daily, 0 continuously.

50. MTBinaryDownAndInAssetAtHitOrNothing

Binary digital instrument receiving the asset when it hits a lower barrier or receives nothing otherwise. DT is monitoring steps: 1/12 monthly, 1/52 weekly, 1/250 daily, 0 continuously.

51. MTBinaryDownAndInCashAtExpirationOrNothing

Binary digital instrument receiving a cash amount at expiration, only if a corresponding asset hits a lower barrier or receives nothing otherwise. DT is monitoring steps: 1/12 monthly, 1/52 weekly, 1/250 daily, 0 continuously.

52. MTBinaryDownAndInCashAtExpirationOrNothingCall

Binary digital call option receiving the cash at expiration if the asset hits a lower barrier or receives nothing otherwise. DT is monitoring steps: 1/12 monthly, 1/52 weekly, 1/250 daily, 0 continuously.

53. MTBinaryDownAndInCashAtExpirationOrNothingPut

Binary digital put option receiving the cash at expiration if the asset hits a lower barrier or receives nothing otherwise. DT is monitoring steps: 1/12 monthly, 1/52 weekly, 1/250 daily, 0 continuously.

54. MTBinaryDownAndInCashAtHitOrNothing

Binary digital instrument receiving a cash amount when a corresponding asset hits a lower barrier or receives nothing otherwise. DT is monitoring steps: 1/12 monthly, 1/52 weekly, 1/250 daily, 0 continuously.

55. MTBinaryDownAndOutAssetAtExpirationOrNothing

Binary digital instrument receiving the asset at expiration, only if a corresponding asset does not hit a lower barrier or receives nothing otherwise. DT is monitoring steps: 1/12 monthly, 1/52 weekly, 1/250 daily, 0 continuously.

56. MTBinaryDownAndOutAssetAtExpirationOrNothingCall

Binary digital call options receiving the asset at expiration, only if a corresponding asset does not hit a lower barrier or receives nothing otherwise. DT is monitoring steps: 1/12 monthly, 1/52 weekly, 1/250 daily, 0 continuously.

57. MTBinaryDownAndOutAssetAtExpirationOrNothingPut

Binary digital put options receiving the asset at expiration, only if a corresponding asset does not hit a lower barrier or receives nothing otherwise. DT is monitoring steps: 1/12 monthly, 1/52 weekly, 1/250 daily, 0 continuously.

58. MTBinaryDownAndOutCashAtExpirationOrNothing

Binary digital instrument receiving a cash amount at expiration, only if a corresponding asset does not hit a lower barrier or receives nothing otherwise. DT is monitoring steps: 1/12 monthly, 1/52 weekly, 1/250 daily, 0 continuously.

59. MTBinaryDownAndOutCashAtExpirationOrNothingCall

Binary digital call option receiving a cash amount at expiration, only if a corresponding asset does not hit a lower barrier or receives nothing otherwise. DT is monitoring steps: 1/12 monthly, 1/52 weekly, 1/250 daily, 0 continuously.

60. MTBinaryDownAndOutCashAtExpirationOrNothingPut

Binary digital put option receiving a cash amount at expiration, only if a corresponding asset does not hit a lower barrier or receives nothing otherwise. DT is monitoring steps: 1/12 monthly, 1/52 weekly, 1/250 daily, 0 continuously.

61. MTBinaryUpAndInAssetAtExpirationOrNothing

Binary digital instrument receiving the asset at expiration, only if a corresponding asset hits an upper barrier or receives nothing otherwise. DT is monitoring steps: 1/12 monthly, 1/52 weekly, 1/250 daily, 0 continuously.

62. MTBinaryUpAndInAssetAtExpirationOrNothingCall

Binary digital call option receiving the asset at expiration if the asset hits an upper barrier or receives nothing otherwise. DT is monitoring steps: 1/12 monthly, 1/52 weekly, 1/250 daily, 0 continuously.

63. MTBinaryUpAndInAssetAtExpirationOrNothingPut

Binary digital put option receiving the asset at expiration if the asset hits an upper barrier or receives nothing otherwise. DT is monitoring steps: 1/12 monthly, 1/52 weekly, 1/250 daily, 0 continuously.

64. MTBinaryUpAndInAssetAtHitOrNothing

Binary digital instrument receiving the asset when it hits an upper barrier or receives nothing otherwise. DT is monitoring steps: 1/12 monthly, 1/52 weekly, 1/250 daily, 0 continuously.

65. MTBinaryUpAndInCashAtExpirationOrNothing

Binary digital instrument receiving a cash amount at expiration, only if a corresponding asset hits an upper barrier or receives nothing otherwise. DT is monitoring steps: 1/12 monthly, 1/52 weekly, 1/250 daily, 0 continuously.

66. MTBinaryUpAndInCashAtExpirationOrNothingCall

Binary digital call option receiving the cash at expiration if the asset hits an upper barrier or receives nothing otherwise. DT is monitoring steps: 1/12 monthly, 1/52 weekly, 1/250 daily, 0 continuously.

67. MTBinaryUpAndInCashAtExpirationOrNothingPut

Binary digital put option receiving the cash at expiration if the asset hits an upper barrier or receives nothing otherwise. DT is monitoring steps: 1/12 monthly, 1/52 weekly, 1/250 daily, 0 continuously.

68. MTBinaryUpAndInCashAtHitOrNothing

Binary digital instrument receiving a cash amount when a corresponding asset hits an upper barrier or receives nothing otherwise. DT is monitoring steps: 1/12 monthly, 1/52 weekly, 1/250 daily, 0 continuously.

69. MTBinaryUpAndOutAssetAtExpirationOrNothing

Binary digital instrument receiving the asset at expiration, only if a corresponding asset does not hit an upper barrier or receives nothing otherwise. DT is monitoring steps: 1/12 monthly, 1/52 weekly, 1/250 daily, 0 continuously.

70. MTBinaryUpAndOutAssetAtExpirationOrNothingCall

Binary digital call options receiving the asset at expiration, only if a corresponding asset does not hit an upper barrier or receives nothing otherwise. DT is monitoring steps: 1/12 monthly, 1/52 weekly, 1/250 daily, 0 continuously.

71. MTBinaryUpAndOutAssetAtExpirationOrNothingPut

Binary digital put options receiving the asset at expiration, only if a corresponding asset does not hit an upper barrier or receives nothing otherwise. DT is monitoring steps: 1/12 monthly, 1/52 weekly, 1/250 daily, 0 continuously.

72. MTBinaryUpAndOutCashAtExpirationOrNothing

Binary digital instrument receiving a cash amount at expiration, only if a corresponding asset does not hit an upper barrier or receives nothing otherwise. DT is monitoring steps: 1/12 monthly, 1/52 weekly, 1/250 daily, 0 continuously.

73. MTBinaryUpAndOutCashAtExpirationOrNothingCall

    Binary digital call option receiving a cash amount at expiration, only if a corresponding asset does not hit an upper barrier or receives nothing otherwise. DT is monitoring steps: 1/12 monthly, 1/52 weekly, 1/250 daily, 0 continuously.

74. MTBinaryUpAndOutCashAtExpirationOrNothingPut

    Binary digital put option receiving a cash amount at expiration, only if a corresponding asset does not hit an upper barrier or receives nothing otherwise. DT is monitoring steps: 1/12 monthly, 1/52 weekly, 1/250 daily, 0 continuously.

75. MTBinomial3DAmericanDualStrikeCallOption

    Returns the American option with the payoff $[Max(Q_2S_2 - X_2, Q_1S_1 - X_1)]$ and valued using a 3D binomial lattice model.

76. MTBinomial3DAmericanDualStrikePutOption

    Returns the American option with the payoff $[Max(X_2 - Q_2S_2, X_1 - Q_1S_1)]$ and valued using a 3D binomial lattice model.

77. MTBinomial3DEuropeanDualStrikeCallOption

    Returns the European option with the payoff $[Max(Q_2S_2 - X_2, Q_1S_1 - X_1)]$ and valued using a 3D binomial lattice model.

78. MTBinomial3DEuropeanDualStrikePutOption

    Returns the European option with the payoff $[Max(X_2 - Q_2S_2, X_1 - Q_1S_1)]$ and valued using a 3D binomial lattice model.

79. MTBinomial3DAmericanExchangeOption

    Returns the American and European call and put option (same values exist for all types) with the payoff $(Q_2S_2 - Q_1S_1)$ and valued using a 3D binomial lattice model.

80. MTBinomial3DAmericanMaximumTwoAssetsCallOption

    Returns the American option with the payoff $[Max(Q_2S_2, Q_1S_1) - X]$ and valued using a 3D binomial lattice model.

81. MTBinomial3DAmericanMaximumTwoAssetsPutOption

    Returns the American option with the payoff $[X - Max(Q_2S_2, Q_1S_1)]$ and valued using a 3D binomial lattice model.

82. MTBinomial3DEuropeanMaximumTwoAssetsCallOption

    Returns the European option with the payoff $[Max(Q_2S_2, Q_1S_1) - X]$ and valued using a 3D binomial lattice model.

83. MTBinomial3DEuropeanMaximumTwoAssetsPutOption

    Returns the European option with the payoff $[X - Max(Q_2S_2, Q_1S_1)]$ and valued using a 3D binomial lattice model.

84. MTBinomial3DAmericanMinimumTwoAssetsCallOption

    Returns the American option with the payoff $[Min(Q_2S_2, Q_1S_1) - X]$ and valued using a 3D binomial lattice model.

85. MTBinomial3DAmericanMinimumTwoAssetsPutOption

Returns the American option with the payoff $[X - Min(Q_2S_2, Q_1S_1)]$ and valued using a 3D binomial lattice model.

86. MTBinomial3DEuropeanMinimumTwoAssetsCallOption

Returns the European option with the payoff $[Min(Q_2S_2, Q_1S_1) - X]$ and valued using a 3D binomial lattice model.

87. MTBinomial3DEuropeanMinimumTwoAssetsPutOption

Returns the European option with the payoff $[X - Min(Q_2S_2, Q_1S_1)]$ and valued using a 3D binomial lattice model.

88. MTBinomial3DAmericanPortfolioCallOption

Returns the American option with the payoff $(Q_2S_2 + Q_1S_1 - X)$ and valued using a 3D binomial lattice model.

89. MTBinomial3DAmericanPortfolioPutOption

Returns the American option with the payoff $(X - Q_2S_2 + Q_1S_1)$ and valued using a 3D binomial lattice model.

90. MTBinomial3DEuropeanPortfolioCallOption

Returns the European option with the payoff $(Q_2S_2 + Q_1S_1 - X)$ and valued using a 3D binomial lattice model.

91. MTBinomial3DEuropeanPortfolioPutOption

Returns the European option with the payoff $(X - Q_2S_2 + Q_1S_1)$ and valued using a 3D binomial lattice model.

92. MTBinomial3DAmericanReverseDualStrikeCallOption

Returns the American option with the payoff $[Max(X_2 - Q_2S_2, Q_1S1 - X_1)]$ and valued using a 3D binomial lattice model.

93. MTBinomial3DAmericanReverseDualStrikePutOption

Returns the American option with the payoff $[Max(Q_2S_2 - X_2, X_1 - Q_1S_1)]$ and valued using a 3D binomial lattice model.

94. MTBinomial3DEuropeanReverseDualStrikeCallOption

Returns the European option with the payoff $[Max(X_2 - Q_2S_2, Q_1S_1 - X_1)]$ and valued using a 3D binomial lattice model.

95. MTBinomial3DEuropeanReverseDualStrikePutOption

Returns the American option with the payoff $[Max(Q_2S_2 - X_2, X_1 - Q_1S_1)]$ and valued using a 3D binomial lattice model.

96. MTBinomial3DAmericanSpreadCallOption

Returns the American option with the payoff $(Q_1S_1 - Q_2S_2 - X)$ and valued using a 3D binomial lattice model.

97. MTBinomial3DAmericanSpreadPutOption

Returns the American option with the payoff $(X + Q_2S_2 - Q_1S_1)$ and valued using a 3D binomial lattice model.

98. MTBinomial3DEuropeanSpreadCallOption

Returns the European option with the payoff $(Q_1S_1 - Q_2S_2 - X)$ and valued using a 3D binomial lattice model.

99. MTBinomial3DEuropeanSpreadPutOption

Returns the European option with the payoff $(X + Q_2S_2 - Q_1S_1)$ and valued using a 3D binomial lattice model.

100. MTBinomialAdjustedBarrierSteps

Computes the correct binomial lattice steps to use for convergence and barrier matching when running a barrier option.

101. MTBinomialAmericanCall

Returns the American call option with a continuous dividend yield using a binomial lattice, where the option can be exercised at any time up to and including maturity.

102. MTBinomialAmericanPut

Returns the American put option with a continuous dividend yield using a binomial lattice, where the option can be exercised at any time up to and including maturity.

103. MTBinomialBermudanCall

Returns the American call option with a continuous dividend yield using a binomial lattice, where the option can be exercised at any time up to and including maturity except during the vesting period.

104. MTBinomialBermudanPut

Returns the American put option with a continuous dividend yield using a binomial lattice, where the option can be exercised at any time up to and including maturity except during the vesting period.

105. MTBinomialEuropeanCall

Returns the European call option with a continuous dividend yield using a binomial lattice, where the option can be exercised only at maturity.

106. MTBinomialEuropeanPut

Returns the European put option with a continuous dividend yield using a binomial lattice, where the option can be exercised only at maturity.

107. MTBlackCallOptionModel

Returns the Black model (modified Black-Scholes-Merton) for forward contracts and interest-based call options.

108. MTBlackPutOptionModel

Returns the Black model (modified Black-Scholes-Merton) for forward contracts and interest-based put options.

109. MTBlackFuturesCallOption

Computes the value of a commodities futures call option given the value of the futures contract.

110. MTBlackFuturesPutOption

Computes the value of a commodities futures put option given the value of the futures contract.

111. MTBlackScholesCall

European call option using the Black-Scholes-Merton model.

112. MTBlackScholesProbabilityAbove

Computes the expected probability the stock price will rise above the strike price under a Black-Scholes paradigm.

113. MTBlackScholesPut

European put option using the Black-Scholes-Merton model.

114. MTBondCIRBondDiscountFactor

Returns the discount factor on a bond or risky debt using the Cox-Ingersoll-Ross model, accounting for mean-reverting interest rates.

115. MTBondCIRBondPrice

Cox-Ross model on Zero Coupon Bond Pricing assuming no arbitrage and mean-reverting interest rates.

116. MTBondCIRBondYield

Cox-Ross model on Zero Coupon Bond Yield assuming no arbitrage and mean-reverting interest rates.

117. MTBondConvexityContinuous

Returns the debt's Convexity or second order sensitivity using a series of cash flows and current interest rate, with continuous discounting.

118. MTBondConvexityDiscrete

Returns the debt's Convexity or second order sensitivity using a series of cash flows and current interest rate, with discrete discounting.

119. MTBondConvexityYTMContinuous

Returns the debt's Convexity or second order sensitivity using an internal Yield to Maturity of the cash flows, with continuous discounting.

120. MTBondConvexityYTMDiscrete

Returns the debt's Convexity or second order sensitivity using an internal Yield to Maturity of the cash flows, with discrete discounting.

121. MTBondDurationContinuous

Returns the debt's first order sensitivity Duration measure using continuous discounting.

122. MTBondDurationDiscrete

Returns the debt's first order sensitivity Duration measure using discrete discounting.

123. MTBondHullWhiteBondCallOption

Values a European call option on a bond where the interest rates are stochastic and mean-reverting. Make sure Bond Maturity > Option Maturity.

124. MTBondHullWhiteBondPutOption

Values a European put option on a bond where the interest rates are stochastic and mean-reverting. Make sure Bond Maturity > Option Maturity.

125. MTBondMacaulayDuration

Returns the debt's first order sensitivity Macaulay Duration measure.

126. MTBondMertonBondPrice

Returns the bond price using Merton Stochastic Interest and Stochastic Asset Model.

127. MTBondModifiedDuration

Returns the debt's first order sensitivity Modified Duration measure.

128. MTBondPriceContinuous

Returns the bond price of a cash flow series given the time and discount rate, using continuous discounting.

129. MTBondPriceDiscrete

Returns the bond price of a cash flow series given the time and discount rate, using discrete discounting.

130. MTBondVasicekBondCallOption

Values a European call option on a bond where the interest rates are stochastic and mean-reverting to a long-term rate. Make sure Bond Maturity > Option Maturity.

131. MTBondVasicekBondPrice

Vasicek Zero Coupon Price assuming no arbitrage and mean-reverting interest rates.

132. MTBondVasicekBondPutOption

Values a European put option on a bond where the interest rates are stochastic and mean-reverting to a long-term rate. Make sure Bond Maturity > Option Maturity.

133. MTBondVasicekBondYield

Vasicek Zero Coupon Yield assuming no arbitrage and mean-reverting interest rates.

134. MTBondYTMContinuous

Returns bond's Yield to Maturity assuming continuous discounting.

135. MTBondYTMDiscrete

Returns bond's Yield to Maturity assuming discrete discounting.

136. MTCallDelta

Returns the option valuation sensitivity Delta (a call option value's sensitivity to changes in the asset value).

137. MTCallGamma

Returns the option valuation sensitivity Gamma (a call option value's sensitivity to changes in the Delta value).

138. MTCallOptionOnTheMax

The maximum values at expiration of both assets are used in option exercise, where the call option payoff at expiration is the maximum price between Asset 1 and Asset 2 against the strike price.

139. MTCallOptionOnTheMin

The minimum values at expiration of both assets are used in option exercise, where the call option payoff at expiration is the minimum price between Asset 1 and Asset 2 against the strike price.

140. MTCallRho

Returns the option valuation sensitivity Rho (a call option value's sensitivity to changes in the interest rate).

141. MTCallTheta

Returns the option valuation sensitivity Theta (a call option value's sensitivity to changes in the maturity).

142. MTCallVega

Returns the option valuation sensitivity Vega (a call option value's sensitivity to changes in the volatility).

143. MTCashOrNothingCall

At expiration, if the option is in the money, the option holder receives a pre-determined cash payment. For a call option, as long as the stock or asset price exceeds the strike at expiration, cash is received.

144. MTCashOrNothingPut

At expiration, if the option is in the money, the option holder receives a pre-determined cash payment. For a put option, cash is received only if the stock or asset value falls below the strike price.

145. MTChooserBasicOption

Holder chooses whether the option is a call or a put by the chooser time, with the same strike price and maturity. Typically cheaper than buying a call and a put together while providing the same level of hedge.

146. MTChooserComplexOption

Holder gets to choose whether the option is a call or a put within the Chooser Time, with different strike prices and maturities. Typically cheaper than buying a call and a put, while providing the same level of hedge.

147. MTClosedFormAmericanCall

Returns the American option approximation model with a continuous dividend yield call option.

148. MTClosedFormAmericanPut

Returns the American option approximation model with a continuous dividend yield put option.

149. MTCoefficientofVariationPopulation

Computes the population coefficient of variation (standard deviation of the sample divided by the mean), to obtain a relative measure of risk and dispersion.

150. MTCoefficientofVariationSample

Computes the sample coefficient of variation (standard deviation of the sample divided by the mean), to obtain a relative measure of risk and dispersion.

151. MTCommodityCallOptionModel

Computes the value of a commodity-based call option based on spot and futures market, and accounting for volatility of the forward rate.

152. MTCommodityPutOptionModel

Computes the value of a commodity-based put option based on spot and futures market, and accounting for volatility of the forward rate.

153. MTCompoundOptionsCallonCall

A compound option allowing the holder to buy (call) a call option with some maturity, in the future within the option maturity period, for a specified strike price on the option.

154. MTCompoundOptionsCallonPut

A compound option allowing the holder to buy (call) a put option with some maturity, in the future within the option maturity period, for a specified strike price on the option.

155. MTCompoundOptionsPutonCall

A compound option allowing the holder to sell (put) a call option with some maturity, in the future within the option maturity period, for a specified strike price on the option.

156. MTCompoundOptionsPutonPut

A compound option allowing the holder to sell (put) a put option with some maturity, in the future within the option maturity period, for a specified strike price on the option.

157. MTConvenienceYield

The convenience yield is simply the rate differential between a nonarbitrage futures and spot price and a real-life fair market value of the futures price.

158. MTConvertibleBondAmerican

Computes the value of an American convertible bond using binomial lattices, and accounting for the stock's volatility and dividend yield, as well as the bond's credit spread above risk-free.

159. MTConvertibleBondEuropean

Computes the value of a European convertible bond using binomial lattices, and accounting for the stock's volatility and dividend yield, as well as the bond's credit spread above risk-free.

160. MTCreditAcceptanceCost

Computes the risk-adjusted cost of accepting a new credit line with a probability of default.

161. MTCreditAssetSpreadCallOption

Provides protection from an increase in spread but ceases to exist if the underlying asset defaults and the option is based on the price of the asset.

162. MTCreditAssetSpreadPutOption

Provides protection from a decrease in spread but ceases to exist if the underlying asset defaults and the option is based on the price of the asset.

163. MTCreditDefaultSwapSpread

Returns the valuation of a credit default swap (CDS) spread, allowing the holder to sell a bond/debt at par value when a credit event occurs.

164. MTCreditDefaultSwapCorrelatedBondandSwapPrice

Computes the valuation of a bond with a credit default swap where both parties are correlated and each has a probability of default and possible recovery rates. At default, the holder receives the notional principal or par value of the bond.

165. MTCreditDefaultSwapCorrelatedBondPrice

Computes the valuation of a bond without any credit default swap where the bond or debt has a probability of default and possible recovery rate.

166. MTCreditDefaultSwapCorrelatedSwapPrice

Computes the price of a credit default swap where both parties are correlated and each has a probability of default and possible recovery rates. At default, the holder receives the notional principal or par value of the bond.

167. MTCreditRatingWidth

Computes the credit ratings width to generate the credit ratings table.

168. MTCreditRejectionCost

Computes the risk-adjusted cost of rejecting a new credit line with a probability of default.

169. MTCreditRiskShortfall

Returns the Credit Risk Shortfall given probability of default and recovery rates.

170. MTCreditSpreadCallOption

Provides protection from an increase in spread but ceases to exist if the underlying asset defaults. Only credit default swaps can cover default events. Credit spread options (CSOs) are sometimes combined with CDSs.

171. MTCreditSpreadPutOption

Provides protection from a decrease in spread but ceases to exist if the underlying asset defaults. Only credit default swaps can cover default events. Credit spread options (CSOs) are sometimes combined with CDSs.

172. MTCubicSpline

Interpolates and extrapolates (linear and nonlinear) the unknown Y values (based on the required X value) given some series of known X and Y values, and can be used to interpolate inside the data sample or extrapolate outside the known sample.

173. MTCurrencyCallOption

Option to exchange foreign currency into domestic currency by buying domestic currency (selling foreign currency) at a set exchange rate on a specified date. Exchange rate is foreign currency to domestic currency.

174. MTCurrencyForwardCallOption

Computes the value of a currency forward call option.

175. MTCurrencyForwardPutOption

Computes the value of a currency forward put option.

176. MTCurrencyPutOption

Option to exchange domestic currency into foreign currency by selling domestic currency (buying foreign currency) at a set exchange rate on a specified date. Exchange rate is foreign currency to domestic currency.

177. MTDeltaGammaHedgeCallBought

Computes the total amount of call values that has to be bought to perform a Delta-Gamma neutral hedge. Returns a negative value indicating cash outflow.

178. MTDeltaGammaHedgeCallSold

Computes the single unit of call value that has to be sold to perform a Delta-Gamma neutral hedge. Returns a positive value indicating cash inflow.

179. MTDeltaGammaHedgeMoneyBorrowed

Computes the amount of money that has to be borrowed to perform a Delta-Gamma neutral hedge. Returns a positive value indicating cash inflow.

180. MTDeltaGammaHedgeSharesBought

Computes the total value of stocks that have to be bought to perform a Delta-Gamma neutral hedge. Returns a negative value indicating cash outflow.

181. MTDeltaHedgeCallSold

Computes the single unit of call value that has to be sold to perform a Delta-neutral hedge. Returns a positive value indicating cash inflow.

182. MTDeltaHedgeMoneyBorrowed

Computes the amount of money that has to be borrowed to perform a Delta-neutral hedge. Returns a positive value indicating cash inflow.

183. MTDeltaHedgeSharesBought

Computes the total value of stocks that have to be bought to perform a Delta-neutral hedge. Returns a negative value indicating cash outflow.

184. MTDistributionBernoulliKurtosis

Returns the Bernoulli distribution's theoretical excess kurtosis (fourth moment), measuring the peakedness of the distribution and its extreme tail events. An excess kurtosis of 0 implies a normal tail.

185. MTDistributionBernoulliMean

Returns the Bernoulli distribution's theoretical mean or expected value (first moment), measuring the central tendency of the distribution.

186. MTDistributionBernoulliSkew

Returns the Bernoulli distribution's theoretical skew (third moment), measuring the direction of the distribution's tail. Positive skew means the average exceeds the median and the tail points to the right, whereas negative skew means the average is less than the median and the tail points to the left.

187. MTDistributionBernoulliStdev

Returns the Bernoulli distribution's theoretical standard deviation (second moment), measuring the width and average dispersion of all points around the mean.

188. MTDistributionBetaKurtosis

Returns the Beta distribution's theoretical excess kurtosis (fourth moment), measuring the peakedness of the distribution and its extreme tail events. An excess kurtosis of 0 implies a normal tail.

189. MTDistributionBetaMean

Returns the Beta distribution's theoretical mean or expected value (first moment), measuring the central tendency of the distribution.

190. MTDistributionBetaSkew

Returns the Beta distribution's theoretical skew (third moment), measuring the direction of the distribution's tail. Positive skew means the average exceeds the median and the tail points to the right, whereas negative skew means the average is less than the median and the tail points to the left.

191. MTDistributionBetaStdev

Returns the Beta distribution's theoretical standard deviation (second moment), measuring the width and average dispersion of all points around the mean.

192. MTDistributionBinomialKurtosis

Returns the Binomial distribution's theoretical excess kurtosis (fourth moment), measuring the peakedness of the distribution and its extreme tail events. An excess kurtosis of 0 implies a normal tail.

193. MTDistributionBinomialMean

Returns the Binomial distribution's theoretical mean or expected value (first moment), measuring the central tendency of the distribution.

194. MTDistributionBinomialSkew

Returns the Binomial distribution's theoretical skew (third moment), measuring the direction of the distribution's tail. Positive skew means the average exceeds the median and the tail points to the right, whereas negative skew means the average is less than the median and the tail points to the left.

195. MTDistributionBinomialStdev

Returns the Binomial distribution's theoretical standard deviation (second moment), measuring the width and average dispersion of all points around the mean.

196. MTDistributionCauchyKurtosis

Returns the Cauchy distribution's theoretical excess kurtosis (fourth moment), measuring the peakedness of the distribution and its extreme tail events. An excess kurtosis of 0 implies a normal tail.

197. MTDistributionCauchyMean

Returns the Cauchy distribution's theoretical mean or expected value (first moment), measuring the central tendency of the distribution.

198. MTDistributionCauchySkew

Returns the Cauchy distribution's theoretical skew (third moment), measuring the direction of the distribution's tail. Positive skew means the average exceeds the median and the tail points to the right, whereas negative skew means the average is less than the median and the tail points to left.

199. MTDistributionCauchyStdev

Returns the Cauchy distribution's theoretical standard deviation (second moment), measuring the width and average dispersion of all points around the mean.

200. MTDistributionChiSquareKurtosis

Returns the Chi-Square distribution's theoretical excess kurtosis (fourth moment), measuring the peakedness of the distribution and its extreme tail events. An excess kurtosis of 0 implies a normal tail.

201. MTDistributionChiSquareMean

Returns the Chi-Square distribution's theoretical mean or expected value (first moment), measuring the central tendency of the distribution.

202. MTDistributionChiSquareSkew

Returns the Chi-Square distribution's theoretical skew (third moment), measuring the direction of the distribution's tail. Positive skew means the average exceeds the median and the tail points to the right, whereas negative skew means the average is less than the median and the tail points to left.

203. MTDistributionChiSquareStdev

Returns the Chi-Square distribution's theoretical standard deviation (second moment), measuring the width and average dispersion of all points around the mean.

204. MTDistributionDiscreteUniformKurtosis

Returns the Discrete Uniform distribution's theoretical excess kurtosis (fourth moment), measuring the peakedness of the distribution and its extreme tail events. An excess kurtosis of 0 implies a normal tail.

205. MTDistributionDiscreteUniformMean

Returns the Discrete Uniform distribution's theoretical mean or expected value (first moment), measuring the central tendency of the distribution.

206. MTDistributionDiscreteUniformSkew

Returns the Discrete Uniform distribution's theoretical skew (third moment), measuring the direction of the distribution's tail. Positive skew means the average exceeds the median and the tail points to the right, whereas negative skew means the average is less than the median and the tail points to left.

207. MTDistributionDiscreteUniformStdev

Returns the Discrete Uniform distribution's theoretical standard deviation (second moment), measuring the width and average dispersion of all points around the mean.

208. MTDistributionExponentialKurtosis

Returns the Exponential distribution's theoretical excess kurtosis (fourth moment), measuring the peakedness of the distribution and its extreme tail events. An excess kurtosis of 0 implies a normal tail.

209. MTDistributionExponentialMean

Returns the Exponential distribution's theoretical mean or expected value (first moment), measuring the central tendency of the distribution.

210. MTDistributionExponentialSkew

Returns the Exponential distribution's theoretical skew (third moment), measuring the direction of the distribution's tail. Positive skew means the average exceeds the median and the tail points to the right, whereas negative skew means the average is less than the median and the tail points to left.

211. MTDistributionExponentialStdev

Returns the Exponential distribution's theoretical standard deviation (second moment), measuring the width and average dispersion of all points around the mean.

212. MTDistributionFKurtosis

Returns the F distribution's theoretical excess kurtosis (fourth moment), measuring the peakedness of the distribution and its extreme tail events. An excess kurtosis of 0 implies a normal tail.

213. MTDistributionFMean

Returns the F distribution's theoretical mean or expected value (first moment), measuring the central tendency of the distribution.

214. MTDistributionFSkew

Returns the F distribution's theoretical skew (third moment), measuring the direction of the distribution's tail. Positive skew means the average exceeds the median and the tail points to the right, whereas negative skew means the average is less than the median and the tail points to left.

215. MTDistributionFStdev

Returns the F distribution's theoretical standard deviation (second moment), measuring the width and average dispersion of all points around the mean.

216. MTDistributionGammaKurtosis

Returns the Gamma distribution's theoretical excess kurtosis (fourth moment), measuring the peakedness of the distribution and its extreme tail events. An excess kurtosis of 0 implies a normal tail.

217. MTDistributionGammaMean

Returns the Gamma distribution's theoretical mean or expected value (first moment), measuring the central tendency of the distribution.

218. MTDistributionGammaSkew

Returns the Gamma distribution's theoretical skew (third moment), measuring the direction of the distribution's tail. Positive skew means the average exceeds the median and the tail points to the right, whereas negative skew means the average is less than the median and the tail points to left.

219. MTDistributionGammaStdev

Returns the Gamma distribution's theoretical standard deviation (second moment), measuring the width and average dispersion of all points around the mean.

220. MTDistributionGeometricKurtosis

Returns the Geometric distribution's theoretical excess kurtosis (fourth moment), measuring the peakedness of the distribution and its extreme tail events. An excess kurtosis of 0 implies a normal tail.

221. MTDistributionGeometricMean

Returns the Geometric distribution's theoretical mean or expected value (first moment), measuring the central tendency of the distribution.

222. MTDistributionGeometricSkew

Returns the Geometric distribution's theoretical skew (third moment), measuring the direction of the distribution's tail. Positive (negative) skew means the average exceeds (is less than) the median and the tail points to the right (left).

223. MTDistributionGeometricStdev

Returns the Geometric distribution's theoretical standard deviation (second moment), measuring the width and average dispersion of all points around the mean.

224. MTDistributionGumbelMaxKurtosis

Returns the Gumbel Max distribution's theoretical excess kurtosis (fourth moment), measuring the peakedness of the distribution and its extreme tail events. An excess kurtosis of 0 implies a normal tail.

225. MTDistributionGumbelMaxMean

Returns the Gumbel Max distribution's theoretical mean or expected value (first moment), measuring the central tendency of the distribution.

226. MTDistributionGumbelMaxSkew

Returns the Gumbel Max distribution's theoretical skew (third moment), measuring the direction of the distribution's tail. Positive (negative) skew means the average exceeds (is less than) the median and the tail points to the right (left).

227. MTDistributionGumbelMaxStdev

Returns the Gumbel Max distribution's theoretical standard deviation (second moment), measuring the width and average dispersion of all points around the mean.

228. MTDistributionGumbelMinKurtosis

Returns the Gumbel Min distribution's theoretical excess kurtosis (fourth moment), measuring the peakedness of the distribution and its extreme tail events. An excess kurtosis of 0 implies a normal tail.

229. MTDistributionGumbelMinMean

Returns the Gumbel Min distribution's theoretical mean or expected value (first moment), measuring the central tendency of the distribution.

230. MTDistributionGumbelMinSkew

Returns the Gumbel Min distribution's theoretical skew (third moment), measuring the direction of the distribution's tail. Positive (negative) skew means the average exceeds (is less than) the median and the tail points to the right (left).

231. MTDistributionGumbelMinStdev

Returns the Gumbel Min distribution's theoretical standard deviation (second moment), measuring the width and average dispersion of all points around the mean.

232. MTDistributionHypergeometricKurtosis

Returns the Hypergeometric distribution's theoretical excess kurtosis (fourth moment), measuring the peakedness of the distribution and its extreme tail events. An excess kurtosis of 0 implies a normal tail.

233. MTDistributionHypergeometricMean

Returns the Hypergeometric distribution's theoretical mean or expected value (first moment), measuring the central tendency of the distribution.

234. MTDistributionHypergeometricSkew

Returns the Hypergeometric distribution's theoretical skew (third moment), measuring the direction of the distribution's tail. Positive (negative) skew means the average exceeds (is less than) the median and the tail points to the right (left).

235. MTDistributionHypergeometricStdev

Returns the Hypergeometric distribution's theoretical standard deviation (second moment), measuring the width and average dispersion of all points around the mean.

236. MTDistributionLogisticKurtosis

Returns the Logistic distribution's theoretical excess kurtosis (fourth moment), measuring the peakedness of the distribution and its extreme tail events. An excess kurtosis of 0 implies a normal tail.

237. MTDistributionLogisticMean

Returns the Logistic distribution's theoretical mean or expected value (first moment), measuring the central tendency of the distribution.

238. MTDistributionLogisticSkew

Returns the Logistic distribution's theoretical skew (third moment), measuring the direction of the distribution's tail. Positive (negative) skew means the average exceeds (is less than) the median and the tail points to the right (left).

239. MTDistributionLogisticStdev

Returns the Logistic distribution's theoretical standard deviation (second moment), measuring the width and average dispersion of all points around the mean.

240. MTDistributionLognormalKurtosis

Returns the Lognormal distribution's theoretical excess kurtosis (fourth moment), measuring the peakedness of the distribution and its extreme tail events. An excess kurtosis of 0 implies a normal tail.

241. MTDistributionLognormalMean

Returns the Lognormal distribution's theoretical mean or expected value (first moment), measuring the central tendency of the distribution.

242. MTDistributionLognormalSkew

Returns the Lognormal distribution's theoretical skew (third moment), measuring the direction of the distribution's tail. Positive (negative) skew means the average exceeds (is less than) the median and the tail points to the right (left).

243. MTDistributionLognormalStdev

Returns the Lognormal distribution's theoretical standard deviation (second moment), measuring the width and average dispersion of all points around the mean.

244. MTDistributionNegativeBinomialKurtosis

Returns the Negative Binomial distribution's theoretical excess kurtosis (fourth moment), measuring the peakedness of the distribution and its extreme tail events. An excess kurtosis of 0 implies a normal tail.

245. MTDistributionNegativeBinomialMean

Returns the Negative Binomial distribution's theoretical mean or expected value (first moment), measuring the central tendency of the distribution.

246. MTDistributionNegativeBinomialSkew

Returns the Negative Binomial distribution's theoretical skew (third moment), measuring the direction of the distribution's tail. Positive (negative) skew means the average exceeds (is less than) the median and the tail points to the right (left).

247. MTDistributionNegativeBinomialStdev

Returns the Negative Binomial distribution's theoretical standard deviation (second moment), measuring the width and average dispersion of all points around the mean.

248. MTDistributionNormalKurtosis

Returns the Normal distribution's theoretical excess kurtosis (fourth moment), measuring the peakedness of the distribution and its extreme tail events. An excess kurtosis of 0 implies a normal tail.

249. MTDistributionNormalMean

Returns the Normal distribution's theoretical mean or expected value (first moment), measuring the central tendency of the distribution.

250. MTDistributionNormalSkew

Returns the Normal distribution's theoretical skew (third moment), measuring the direction of the distribution's tail. Positive (negative) skew means the average exceeds (is less than) the median and the tail points to the right (left).

251. MTDistributionNormalStdev

Returns the Normal distribution's theoretical standard deviation (second moment), measuring the width and average dispersion of all points around the mean.

252. MTDistributionParetoKurtosis

Returns the Pareto distribution's theoretical excess kurtosis (fourth moment), measuring the peakedness of the distribution and its extreme tail events. An excess kurtosis of 0 implies a normal tail.

253. MTDistributionParetoMean

Returns the Pareto distribution's theoretical mean or expected value (first moment), measuring the central tendency of the distribution.

254. MTDistributionParetoSkew

Returns the Pareto distribution's theoretical skew (third moment), measuring the direction of the distribution's tail. Positive (negative) skew means the average exceeds (is less than) the median and the tail points to the right (left).

255. MTDistributionParetoStdev

Returns the Pareto distribution's theoretical standard deviation (second moment), measuring the width and average dispersion of all points around the mean.

256. MTDistributionPoissonKurtosis

Returns the Poisson distribution's theoretical excess kurtosis (fourth moment), measuring the peakedness of the distribution and its extreme tail events. An excess kurtosis of 0 implies a normal tail.

257. MTDistributionPoissonMean

Returns the Poisson distribution's theoretical mean or expected value (first moment), measuring the central tendency of the distribution.

258. MTDistributionPoissonSkew

Returns the Poisson distribution's theoretical skew (third moment), measuring the direction of the distribution's tail. Positive (negative) skew means the average exceeds (is less than) the median and the tail points to the right (left).

259. MTDistributionPoissonStdev

Returns the Poisson distribution's theoretical standard deviation (second moment), measuring the width and average dispersion of all points around the mean.

260. MTDistributionRayleighKurtosis

Returns the Rayleigh distribution's theoretical excess kurtosis (fourth moment), measuring the peakedness of the distribution and its extreme tail events. An excess kurtosis of 0 implies a normal tail.

261. MTDistributionRayleighMean

Returns the Rayleigh distribution's theoretical mean or expected value (first moment), measuring the central tendency of the distribution.

262. MTDistributionRayleighSkew

Returns the Rayleigh distribution's theoretical skew (third moment), measuring the direction of the distribution's tail. Positive (negative) skew means the average exceeds (is less than) the median and the tail points to the right (left).

263. MTDistributionRayleighStdev

Returns the Rayleigh distribution's theoretical standard deviation (second moment), measuring the width and average dispersion of all points around the mean.

264. MTDistributionTKurtosis

Returns the Student's T distribution's theoretical excess kurtosis (fourth moment), measuring the peakedness of the distribution and its extreme tail events. An excess kurtosis of 0 implies a normal tail.

265. MTDistributionTMean

Returns the Student's T distribution's theoretical mean or expected value (first moment), measuring the central tendency of the distribution.

266. MTDistributionTSkew

Returns the Student's T distribution's theoretical skew (third moment), measuring the direction of the distribution's tail. Positive (negative) skew means the average exceeds (is less than) the median and the tail points to the right (left).

267. MTDistributionTStdev

Returns the Student's T distribution's theoretical standard deviation (second moment), measuring the width and average dispersion of all points around the mean.

268. MTDistributionTriangularKurtosis

Returns the Triangular distribution's theoretical excess kurtosis (fourth moment), measuring the peakedness of the distribution and its extreme tail events. An excess kurtosis of 0 implies a normal tail.

269. MTDistributionTriangularMean

Returns the Triangular distribution's theoretical mean or expected value (first moment), measuring the central tendency of the distribution.

270. MTDistributionTriangularSkew

Returns the Triangular distribution's theoretical skew (third moment), measuring the direction of the distribution's tail. Positive (negative) skew means the average exceeds (is less than) the median and the tail points to the right (left).

271. MTDistributionTriangularStdev

Returns the Triangular distribution's theoretical standard deviation (second moment), measuring the width and average dispersion of all points around the mean.

272. MTDistributionUniformKurtosis

Returns the Uniform distribution's theoretical excess kurtosis (fourth moment), measuring the peakedness of the distribution and its extreme tail events. An excess kurtosis of 0 implies a normal tail.

273. MTDistributionUniformMean

Returns the Uniform distribution's theoretical mean or expected value (first moment), measuring the central tendency of the distribution.

274. MTDistributionUniformSkew

Returns the Uniform distribution's theoretical skew (third moment), measuring the direction of the distribution's tail. Positive (negative) skew means the average exceeds (is less than) the median and the tail points to the right (left).

275. MTDistributionUniformStdev

Returns the Uniform distribution's theoretical standard deviation (second moment), measuring the width and average dispersion of all points around the mean.

276. MTDistributionWeibullKurtosis

Returns the Weibull distribution's theoretical excess kurtosis (fourth moment), measuring the peakedness of the distribution and its extreme tail events. An excess kurtosis of 0 implies a normal tail.

277. MTDistributionWeibullMean

Returns the Weibull distribution's theoretical mean or expected value (first moment), measuring the central tendency of the distribution.

278. MTDistributionWeibullSkew

Returns the Weibull distribution's theoretical skew (third moment), measuring the direction of the distribution's tail. Positive (negative) skew means the average exceeds (is less than) the median and the tail points to the right (left).

279. MTDistributionWeibullStdev

Returns the Weibull distribution's theoretical standard deviation (second moment), measuring the width and average dispersion of all points around the mean.

280. MTDistributionCDFBernoulli

Computes the Bernoulli distribution's theoretical Cumulative Distribution Function (CDF)—that is, the cumulative probability of the distribution at all points less than or equal to X.

281. MTDistributionCDFBeta

Computes the Beta distribution's theoretical Cumulative Distribution Function (CDF)—that is, the cumulative probability of the distribution at all points less than or equal to X.

282. MTDistributionCDFBinomial

Computes the Binomial distribution's theoretical Cumulative Distribution Function (CDF)—that is, the cumulative probability of the distribution at all points less than or equal to X.

283. MTDistributionCDFChiSquare

Computes the Chi-Square distribution's theoretical Cumulative Distribution Function (CDF)—that is, the cumulative probability of the distribution at all points less than or equal to X.

284. MTDistributionCDFDiscreteUniform

Computes the Discrete Uniform distribution's theoretical Cumulative Distribution Function (CDF)—that is, the cumulative probability of the distribution at all points less than or equal to X.

285. MTDistributionCDFExponential

Computes the Exponential distribution's theoretical Cumulative Distribution Function (CDF)—that is, the cumulative probability of the distribution at all points less than or equal to X.

286. MTDistributionCDFFDist

Computes the F distribution's theoretical Cumulative Distribution Function (CDF)—that is, the cumulative probability of the distribution at all points less than or equal to X.

287. MTDistributionCDFGamma

Computes the Gamma distribution's theoretical Cumulative Distribution Function (CDF)—that is, the cumulative probability of the distribution at all points less than or equal to X.

288. MTDistributionCDFGeometric

Computes the Geometric distribution's theoretical Cumulative Distribution Function (CDF)—that is, the cumulative probability of the distribution at all points less than or equal to X.

289. MTDistributionCDFGumbelMax

Computes the Gumbel Max distribution's theoretical Cumulative Distribution Function (CDF)—that is, the cumulative probability of the distribution at all points less than or equal to X.

290. MTDistributionCDFGumbelMin

Computes the Gumbel Min distribution's theoretical Cumulative Distribution Function (CDF)—that is, the cumulative probability of the distribution at all points less than or equal to X.

291. MTDistributionCDFLogistic

Computes the Logistic distribution's theoretical Cumulative Distribution Function (CDF)—that is, the cumulative probability of the distribution at all points less than or equal to X.

292. MTDistributionCDFLognormal

Computes the Lognormal distribution's theoretical Cumulative Distribution Function (CDF)—that is, the cumulative probability of the distribution at all points less than or equal to X.

293. MTDistributionCDFNormal

Computes the Normal distribution's theoretical Cumulative Distribution Function (CDF)—that is, the cumulative probability of the distribution at all points less than or equal to X.

294. MTDistributionCDFPareto

Computes the Pareto distribution's theoretical Cumulative Distribution Function (CDF)—that is, the cumulative probability of the distribution at all points less than or equal to X.

295. MTDistributionCDFPoisson

Computes the Poisson distribution's theoretical Cumulative Distribution Function (CDF)—that is, the cumulative probability of the distribution at all points less than or equal to X.

296. MTDistributionCDFRayleigh

Computes the Rayleigh distribution's theoretical Cumulative Distribution Function (CDF)—that is, the cumulative probability of the distribution at all points less than or equal to X.

297. MTDistributionCDFStandardNormal

Computes the Standard Normal distribution's theoretical Cumulative Distribution Function (CDF)—that is, the cumulative probability of the distribution at all points less than or equal to X.

298. MTDistributionCDFTDist

Computes the Student's T distribution's theoretical Cumulative Distribution Function (CDF)—that is, the cumulative probability of the distribution at all points less than or equal to X.

299. MTDistributionCDFTriangular

Computes the Triangular distribution's theoretical Cumulative Distribution Function (CDF)—that is, the cumulative probability of the distribution at all points less than or equal to X.

300. MTDistributionCDFUniform

Computes the Uniform distribution's theoretical Cumulative Distribution Function (CDF)—that is, the cumulative probability of the distribution at all points less than or equal to X.

301. MTDistributionCDFWeibull

Computes the Weibull distribution's theoretical Cumulative Distribution Function (CDF)—that is, the cumulative probability of the distribution at all points less than or equal to X.

302. MTDistributionICDFBernoulli

Computes the Bernoulli distribution's theoretical Inverse Cumulative Distribution Function (ICDF); that is, given the cumulative probability between 0 and 1 and the distribution's parameters, the function returns the relevant X value.

303. MTDistributionICDFBeta

Computes the Beta distribution's theoretical Inverse Cumulative Distribution Function (ICDF); that is, given the cumulative probability between 0 and 1 and the distribution's parameters, the function returns the relevant X value.

304. MTDistributionICDFBinomial

Computes the Binomial distribution's theoretical Inverse Cumulative Distribution Function (ICDF); that is, given the cumulative probability between 0 and 1 and the distribution's parameters, the function returns the relevant X value.

305. MTDistributionICDFChiSquare

Computes the Chi-Square distribution's theoretical Inverse Cumulative Distribution Function (ICDF); that is, given the cumulative probability between 0 and 1 and the distribution's parameters, the function returns the relevant X value.

306. MTDistributionICDFDiscreteUniform

Computes the Discrete Uniform distribution's theoretical Inverse Cumulative Distribution Function (ICDF); that is, given the cumulative probability between 0 and 1 and the distribution's parameters, the function returns the relevant X value.

307. MTDistributionICDFExponential

Computes the Exponential distribution's theoretical Inverse Cumulative Distribution Function (ICDF); that is, given the cumulative probability between 0 and 1 and the distribution's parameters, the function returns the relevant X value.

308. MTDistributionICDFFDist

Computes the F distribution's theoretical Inverse Cumulative Distribution Function (ICDF); that is, given the cumulative probability between 0 and 1 and the distribution's parameters, the function returns the relevant X value.

309. MTDistributionICDFGamma

Computes the Gamma distribution's theoretical Inverse Cumulative Distribution Function (ICDF); that is, given the cumulative probability between 0 and 1 and the distribution's parameters, the function returns the relevant X value.

310. MTDistributionICDFGeometric

Computes the Geometric distribution's theoretical Inverse Cumulative Distribution Function (ICDF); that is, given the cumulative probability between 0 and 1 and the distribution's parameters, the function returns the relevant X value.

311. MTDistributionICDFGumbelMax

Computes the Gumbel Max distribution's theoretical Inverse Cumulative Distribution Function (ICDF); that is, given the cumulative probability between 0 and 1 and the distribution's parameters, the function returns the relevant X value.

312. MTDistributionICDFGumbelMin

Computes the Gumbel Min distribution's theoretical Inverse Cumulative Distribution Function (ICDF); that is, given the cumulative probability between 0 and 1 and the distribution's parameters, the function returns the relevant X value.

313. MTDistributionICDFLogistic

Computes the Logistic distribution's theoretical Inverse Cumulative Distribution Function (ICDF); that is, given the cumulative probability between 0 and 1 and the distribution's parameters, the function returns the relevant X value.

314. MTDistributionICDFLognormal

Computes the Lognormal distribution's theoretical Inverse Cumulative Distribution Function (ICDF); that is, given the cumulative probability between 0 and 1 and the distribution's parameters, the function returns the relevant X value.

315. MTDistributionICDFNormal

Computes the Normal distribution's theoretical Inverse Cumulative Distribution Function (ICDF); that is, given the cumulative probability between 0 and 1 and the distribution's parameters, the function returns the relevant X value.

316. MTDistributionICDFPareto

Computes the Pareto distribution's theoretical Inverse Cumulative Distribution Function (ICDF); that is, given the cumulative probability between 0 and 1 and the distribution's parameters, the function returns the relevant X value.

317. MTDistributionICDFPoisson

Computes the Poisson distribution's theoretical Inverse Cumulative Distribution Function (ICDF); that is, given the cumulative probability between 0 and 1 and the distribution's parameters, the function returns the relevant X value.

318. MTDistributionICDFRayleigh

Computes the Rayleigh distribution's theoretical Inverse Cumulative Distribution Function (ICDF); that is, given the cumulative probability between 0 and 1 and the distribution's parameters, the function returns the relevant X value.

319. MTDistributionICDFStandardNormal

Computes the Standard Normal distribution's theoretical Inverse Cumulative Distribution Function (ICDF); that is, given the cumulative probability between 0 and 1 and the distribution's parameters, the function returns the relevant X value.

320. MTDistributionICDFTDist

Computes the Student's T distribution's theoretical Inverse Cumulative Distribution Function (ICDF); that is, given the cumulative probability between 0 and 1 and the distribution's parameters, the function returns the relevant X value.

321. MTDistributionICDFTriangular

Computes the Triangular distribution's theoretical Inverse Cumulative Distribution Function (ICDF); that is, given the cumulative probability between 0 and 1 and the distribution's parameters, the function returns the relevant X value.

322. MTDistributionICDFUniform

Computes the Uniform distribution's theoretical Inverse Cumulative Distribution Function (ICDF); that is, given the cumulative probability between 0 and 1 and the distribution's parameters, the function returns the relevant X value.

323. MTDistributionICDFWeibull

Computes the Weibull distribution's theoretical Inverse Cumulative Distribution Function (ICDF); that is, given the cumulative probability between 0 and 1 and the distribution's parameters, the function returns the relevant X value.

324. MTDistributionPDFBernoulli

Computes the Bernoulli distribution's theoretical Probability Density Function (PDF). The PDF of a discrete distribution returns the exact probability mass function or probability of occurrence, but the PDFs of continuous distributions are only theoretical values and not exact probabilities.

325. MTDistributionPDFBeta

Computes the Beta distribution's theoretical Probability Density Function (PDF). The PDF of a discrete distribution returns the exact probability mass function or probability of occurrence, but the PDFs of continuous distributions are only theoretical values and not exact probabilities.

326. MTDistributionPDFBinomial

Computes the Binomial distribution's theoretical Probability Density Function (PDF). The PDF of a discrete distribution returns the exact probability mass function or probability of occurrence, but the PDFs of continuous distributions are only theoretical values and not exact probabilities.

327. MTDistributionPDFChiSquare

Computes the Chi-Square distribution's theoretical Probability Density Function (PDF). The PDF of a discrete distribution returns the exact probability mass function or probability of occurrence, but the PDFs of continuous distributions are only theoretical values and not exact probabilities.

328. MTDistributionPDFDiscreteUniform

Computes the Discrete Uniform distribution's theoretical Probability Density Function (PDF). The PDF of a discrete distribution returns the exact probability mass function or probability of occurrence, but the PDFs of continuous distributions are only theoretical values and not exact probabilities.

329. MTDistributionPDFExponential

Computes the Exponential distribution's theoretical Probability Density Function (PDF). The PDF of a discrete distribution returns the exact probability mass function or probability of occurrence, but the PDFs of continuous distributions are only theoretical values and not exact probabilities.

330. MTDistributionPDFFDist

Computes the F distribution's theoretical Probability Density Function (PDF). The PDF of a discrete distribution returns the exact probability mass function or probability of occurrence, but the PDFs of continuous distributions are only theoretical values and not exact probabilities.

331. MTDistributionPDFGamma

Computes the Gamma distribution's theoretical Probability Density Function (PDF). The PDF of a discrete distribution returns the exact probability mass function or probability of occurrence, but the PDFs of continuous distributions are only theoretical values and not exact probabilities.

332. MTDistributionPDFGeometric

Computes the Geometric distribution's theoretical Probability Density Function (PDF). The PDF of a discrete distribution returns the exact probability mass function or probability of occurrence, but the PDFs of continuous distributions are only theoretical values and not exact probabilities.

333. MTDistributionPDFGumbelMax

Computes the Gumbel Max distribution's theoretical Probability Density Function (PDF). The PDF of a discrete distribution returns the exact probability mass function or probability of occurrence, but the PDFs of continuous distributions are only theoretical values and not exact probabilities.

334. MTDistributionPDFGumbelMin

Computes the Gumbel Min distribution's theoretical Probability Density Function (PDF). The PDF of a discrete distribution returns the exact probability mass function or probability of occurrence, but the PDFs of continuous distributions are only theoretical values and not exact probabilities.

335. MTDistributionPDFLogistic

Computes the Logistic distribution's theoretical Probability Density Function (PDF). The PDF of a discrete distribution returns the exact probability mass function or probability of occurrence, but the PDFs of continuous distributions are only theoretical values and not exact probabilities.

336. MTDistributionPDFLognormal

Computes the Lognormal distribution's theoretical Probability Density Function (PDF). The PDF of a discrete distribution returns the exact probability mass function or probability of occurrence, but the PDFs of continuous distributions are only theoretical values and not exact probabilities.

337. MTDistributionPDFNormal

Computes the Normal distribution's theoretical Probability Density Function (PDF). The PDF of a discrete distribution returns the exact probability mass function or probability of occurrence, but the PDFs of continuous distributions are only theoretical values and not exact probabilities.

338. MTDistributionPDFPareto

Computes the Pareto distribution's theoretical Probability Density Function (PDF). The PDF of a discrete distribution returns the exact probability mass function or probability of occurrence, but the PDFs of continuous distributions are only theoretical values and not exact probabilities.

339. MTDistributionPDFPoisson

Computes the Poisson distribution's theoretical Probability Density Function (PDF). The PDF of a discrete distribution returns the exact probability mass function or probability of occurrence, but the PDFs of continuous distributions are only theoretical values and not exact probabilities.

340. MTDistributionPDFRayleigh

Computes the Rayleigh distribution's theoretical Probability Density Function (PDF). The PDF of a discrete distribution returns the exact probability mass function or probability of occurrence, but the PDFs of continuous distributions are only theoretical values and not exact probabilities.

341. MTDistributionPDFStandardNormal

Computes the Standard Normal distribution's theoretical Probability Density Function (PDF). The PDF of a discrete distribution returns the exact probability mass function or probability of occurrence, but the PDFs of continuous distributions are only theoretical values and not exact probabilities.

342. MTDistributionPDFTDist

Computes the Student's T distribution's theoretical Probability Density Function (PDF). The PDF of a discrete distribution returns the exact probability mass function or probability of occurrence, but the PDFs of continuous distributions are only theoretical values and not exact probabilities.

343. MTDistributionPDFTriangular

Computes the Triangular distribution's theoretical Probability Density Function (PDF). The PDF of a discrete distribution returns the exact probability mass function or probability of occurrence, but the PDFs of continuous distributions are only theoretical values and not exact probabilities.

344. MTDistributionPDFUniform

Computes the Uniform distribution's theoretical Probability Density Function (PDF). The PDF of a discrete distribution returns the exact probability mass function or probability of occurrence, but the PDFs of continuous distributions are only theoretical values and not exact probabilities.

345. MTDistributionPDFWeibull

Computes the Weibull distribution's theoretical Probability Density Function (PDF). The PDF of a discrete distribution returns the exact probability mass function or probability of occurrence, but the PDFs of continuous distributions are only theoretical values and not exact probabilities.

346. MTEquityLinkedFXCallOptionDomesticValue

Call options whose underlying asset is in a foreign equity market, and the fluctuations of the foreign exchange risk are hedged by having a strike price on the foreign exchange rate. Resulting valuation is in the domestic currency.

347. MTEquityLinkedFXPutOptionDomesticValue

Put options whose underlying asset is in a foreign equity market, and the fluctuations of the foreign exchange risk are hedged by having a strike price on the foreign exchange rate. Resulting valuation is in the domestic currency.

348. MTEWMAVolatilityForecastGivenPastPrices

Computes the annualized volatility forecast of the next period, given a series of historical prices and the corresponding weights placed on the previous volatility estimate.

349. MTEWMAVolatilityForecastGivenPastVolatility

Computes the annualized volatility forecast of the next period given the previous period's volatility and changes in stock returns in the previous period.

350. MTExtremeSpreadCallOption

Maturities are divided into two segments, and the call option pays the difference between the max assets of segment two and max of segment one.

351. MTExtremeSpreadPutOption

Maturities are divided into two segments, and the put option pays the difference between the min of segment two's asset value and the min of segment one's asset value.

352. MTExtremeSpreadReverseCallOption

Maturities are divided into two segments, and a reverse call pays the min from segment one less the min of segment two.

353. MTExtremeSpreadReversePutOption

Maturities are divided into two segments, and a reverse put pays the max of segment one less the max of the segment two.

354. MTFiniteDifferenceAmericanCall

Computes the American call option using finite differencing methods, as an alternative to simulation, closed-form approximation models, and lattices.

355. MTFiniteDifferenceAmericanPut

Computes the American put option using finite differencing methods, as an alternative to simulation, closed-form approximation models, and lattices.

356. MTFiniteDifferenceEuropeanCall

Computes the European call option using finite differencing methods, as an alternative to simulation, closed-form approximation models, and lattices.

357. MTFiniteDifferenceEuropeanPut

Computes the European put option using finite differencing methods, as an alternative to simulation, closed-form approximation models, and lattices.

358. MTFixedStrikeLookbackCall

Strike price is fixed, while at expiration the payoff is the difference between the maximum asset price and the strike price during the lifetime of the option.

359. MTFixedStrikeLookbackPut

Strike price is fixed, while at expiration the payoff is the maximum difference between the lowest observed asset price and the strike price during the lifetime of the option.

360. MTFixedStrikePartialLookbackCall

Strike price is fixed, while at expiration the payoff is the difference between the maximum asset price and the strike price during the starting period of the lookback to the maturity of the option.

361. MTFixedStrikePartialLookbackPut

Strike price is fixed, while at expiration the payoff is the maximum difference between the lowest observed asset price and the strike price during the starting period of the lookback to the maturity of the option.

362. MTFloatingStrikeLookbackCallonMin

Strike price is floating, while at expiration the payoff on the call option is being able to purchase the underlying asset at the minimum observed price during the life of the option.

363. MTFloatingStrikeLookbackPutonMax

Strike price is floating, while at expiration the payoff on the put option is being able to sell the underlying asset at the maximum observed asset price during the life of the option.

364. MTFloatingStrikePartialLookbackCallonMin

Strike price is floating, while at expiration the payoff on the call option is being able to purchase the underlying at the minimum observed asset price from inception to the end of the lookback time.

365. MTFloatingStrikePartialLookbackPutonMax

Strike price is floating, while at expiration the payoff on the put option is being able to sell the underlying at the maximum observed asset price from inception to the end of the lookback time.

366. MTForecastBrownianMotionSimulatedSeries

Computes the entire time series of Brownian motion stochastic process forecast values.

367. MTForecastDistributionValue

Computes the forecast price of an asset in the future, assuming the asset follows a Brownian motion random walk and returns the forecast price given the cumulative probability level.

368. MTForecastDistributionValuePercentile

Computes the cumulative probability or percentile of an asset in the future, assuming the asset follows a Brownian motion random walk and returns the forecast cumulative percentile given the future price.

369. MTForecastDistributionReturns

Computes the forecast return of an asset in the future, assuming the asset follows a Brownian motion random walk and returns the forecast percent return given the cumulative probability level.

370. MTForecastDistributionReturnsPercentile

Computes the cumulative probability or percentile of an asset's returns in the future, assuming the asset follows a Brownian motion random walk and returns the forecast cumulative percentile given the future returns.

371. MTForecastJumpDiffusionSimulatedSeries

Computes the entire time series of a jump-diffusion stochastic process forecast values.

372. MTForecastMeanReversionSimulatedSeries

Computes the entire time series of a mean-reverting stochastic process forecast values.

373. MTForecastIncrementalFinancialNeeds

Computes the incremental funds required to cover the projected organic sales growth of the company based on the projected year's financials.

374. MTForecastIncrementalPercentSalesGrowthFinancedExternally

Computes the incremental funds as a percent of sales growth that is required from external funding to cover the projected organic sales growth of the company.

375. MTForeignEquityDomesticCurrencyCall

Computes the value of a foreign-based equity call option struck in a domestic currency and accounting for the exchange rate volatility.

376. MTForeignEquityDomesticCurrencyPut

Computes the value of a foreign-based equity put option struck in a domestic currency and accounting for the exchange rate volatility.

377. MTForeignEquityFixedFXRateDomesticValueQuantoCall

Quanto call options are denominated in a currency other than the underlying asset, with expanding or contracting protection coverage of the foreign exchange rates.

378. MTForeignEquityFixedFXRateDomesticValueQuantoPut

Quanto put options are denominated in a currency other than the underlying asset, with expanding or contracting protection coverage of the foreign exchange rates.

379. MTForwardRate

Computes the Forward Interest Rate given two Spot Rates.

380. MTForwardStartCallOption

Starts proportionally in or out of the money in the future. Alpha < 1: call starts $(1 - A)$% in the money, put starts $(1 - A)$% out of the money. Alpha > 1: call $(A - 1)$% out of the money, put $(A - 1)$% in the money.

381. MTForwardStartPutOption

Starts proportionally in or out of the money in the future. Alpha < 1: call starts $(1 - A)$% in the money, put starts $(1 - A)$% out of the money. Alpha > 1: call $(A - 1)$% out of the money, put $(A - 1)$% in the money.

382. MTFuturesForwardsCallOption

Similar to a regular option but the underlying asset is a futures of a forward contract. A call option is the option to buy a futures contract, with the specified futures strike price at which the futures is traded if the option is exercised.

383. MTFuturesForwardsPutOption

Similar to a regular option but the underlying asset is a futures of a forward contract. A put option is the option to sell a futures contract, with the specified futures strike price at which the futures is traded if the option is exercised.

384. MTFuturesSpreadCall

The payoff of a spread option is the difference between the two futures' values at expiration. The spread is Futures 1 – Futures 2, and the call payoff is Spread – Strike.

385. MTFuturesSpreadPut

The payoff of a spread option is the difference between the two futures' values at expiration. The spread is Futures 1 – Futures 2, and the put payoff is Strike – Spread.

386. MTGARCH

Computes the forward-looking volatility forecast using the generalized autoregressive conditional heteroskedasticity (p, q) model where future volatilities are forecast based on historical price levels and information.

387. MTGapCallOption

The call option is knocked in if the asset exceeds the reference Strike 1, and the option payoff is the asset price less Strike 2 for the underlying.

388. MTGapPutOption

The put option is knocked in only if the underlying asset is less than the reference Strike 1, providing a payoff of Strike 2 less the underlying asset value.

389. MTGeneralizedBlackScholesCall

Returns the Black-Scholes model with a continuous dividend yield call option.

390. MTGeneralizedBlackScholesCallCashDividends

Modification of the Generalized Black-Scholes model to solve European call options, assuming a series of dividend cash flows that may be even or uneven. A series of dividend payments and time are required.

391. MTGeneralizedBlackScholesPut

Returns the Black-Scholes model with a continuous dividend yield put option.

392. MTGeneralizedBlackScholesPutCashDividends

Modification of the Generalized Black-Scholes model to solve European put options, assuming a series of dividend cash flows that may be even or uneven. A series of dividend payments and time are required.

393. MTGraduatedBarrierDownandInCall

Barriers are graduated ranges between lower and upper values. The option is knocked in the money proportionally depending on how low the asset value is in the range.

394. MTGraduatedBarrierDownandOutCall

Barriers are graduated ranges between lower and upper values. The option is knocked out of the money proportionally depending on how low the asset value is in the range.

395. MTGraduatedBarrierUpandInPut

Barriers are graduated ranges between lower and upper values. The option is knocked in the money proportionally depending on how high the asset value is in the range.

396. MTGraduatedBarrierUpandOutPut

Barriers are graduated ranges between lower and upper values. The option is knocked out of the money proportionally depending on how high the asset value is in the range.

397. MTImpliedVolatilityBestCase

Computes the implied volatility given an expected value of an asset, along with an alternative best-case scenario value and its corresponding percentile (must be above 50%).

398. MTImpliedVolatilityCall

Computes the implied volatility in a European call option given all the input parameters and the option value.

399. MTImpliedVolatilityPut

Computes the implied volatility in a European put option given all the input parameters and the option value.

400. MTImpliedVolatilityWorstCase

Computes the implied volatility given an expected value of an asset, along with an alternative worst-case scenario value and its corresponding percentile (must be below 50%).

401. MTInterestAnnualtoPeriodic

Computes the periodic compounding rate based on the annualized compounding interest rate per year.

402. MTInterestCaplet

Computes the interest rate caplet (sum all the caplets into the total value of the interest rate cap) and acts like an interest rate call option.

403. MTInterestContinuousToDiscrete

Returns the corresponding discrete compounding interest rate, given the continuous compounding rate.

404. MTInterestContinuousToPeriodic

Computes the periodic compounding interest rate based on a continuous compounding rate.

405. MTInterestDiscreteToContinuous

Returns the corresponding continuous compounding interest rate, given the discrete compounding rate.

406. MTInterestFloorlet

Computes the interest rate floorlet (sum all the floorlets into the total value of the interest rate floor) and acts like an interest rate put option.

407. MTInterestPeriodictoAnnual

Computes the annualized compounding interest rate per year based on a periodic compounding rate.

408. MTInterestPeriodictoContinuous

Computes the continuous compounding rate based on the periodic compounding interest rate.

409. MTInverseGammaCallOption

Computes the European call option assuming an inverse Gamma distribution, rather than a normal distribution, and is important for deep out-of-the-money options.

410. MTInverseGammaPutOption

Computes the European put option assuming an inverse Gamma distribution, rather than a normal distribution, and is important for deep out-of-the-money options.

411. MTIRRContinuous

Returns the continuously discounted Internal Rate of Return for a cash flow series with its respective cash flow times in years.

412. MTIRRDiscrete

Returns the discretely discounted Internal Rate of Return for a cash flow series with its respective cash flow times in years.

413. MTLinearInterpolation

Interpolates and fills in the missing values of a time series.

414. MTMarketPriceRisk

Computes the market price of risk used in a variety of options analyses, using market return, risk-free return, volatility of the market, and correlation between the market and the asset.

415. MTMathGammaLog

Returns the result from a Log Gamma function.

416. MTMathIncompleteBeta

Returns the result from an Incomplete Beta function.

417. MTMathIncompleteGammaP

Returns the result from an Incomplete Gamma P function.

418. MTMathIncompleteGammaQ

Returns the result from an Incomplete Gamma Q function.

419. MTMatrixMultiplyAxB

Multiplies two compatible matrices, such as $M \times N$ and $N \times M$, to create an $M \times M$ matrix. Copy and paste function to the entire matrix area and use Ctrl+Shift+Enter to obtain the matrix.

420. MTMatrixMultiplyAxTransposeB

Multiplies the first matrix with the transpose of the second matrix (multiplies $M \times N$ with $M \times N$ matrix by transposing the second matrix to $N \times M$, generating an $M \times M$ matrix). Copy and paste function to the entire matrix area and use Ctrl+Shift+Enter to obtain the matrix.

421. MTMatrixMultiplyTransposeAxB

Multiplies the transpose of the first matrix with the second matrix (multiplies $M \times N$ with $M \times N$ matrix by transposing the first matrix to $N \times M$, generating an $N \times N$ matrix). Copy and paste function to the entire matrix area and use Ctrl+Shift+Enter to obtain the matrix.

422. MTMatrixTranspose

Transposes a matrix from $M \times N$ to $N \times M$. Copy and paste function to the entire matrix area and use Ctrl+Shift+Enter to obtain the matrix.

423. MTMertonJumpDiffusionCall

Call value of an underlying whose asset returns are assumed to follow a Poisson Jump-Diffusion process; that is, prices jump several times a year, and cumulatively these jumps explain a percentage of the total asset volatility.

424. MTMertonJumpDiffusionPut

Put value of an underlying whose asset returns are assumed to follow a Poisson Jump-Diffusion process; that is, prices jump several times a year, and cumulatively these jumps explain a percentage of the total asset volatility.

425. MTNormalTransform

Converts values into a normalized distribution.

426. MTNPVContinuous

Returns the Net Present Value of a cash flow series given the time and discount rate, using continuous discounting.

427. MTNPVDiscrete

Returns the Net Present Value of a cash flow series given the time and discount rate, using discrete discounting.

428. MTOptionStrategyLongBearCreditSpread

Returns the matrix [stock price, buy put, sell put, profit] of a long bearish credit spread (buying a higher strike put with a high price and selling a lower strike put with a low price).

429. MTOptionStrategyLongBullCreditSpread

Returns the matrix [stock price, buy put, sell put, profit] of a bullish credit spread (buying a lower strike put at a low price and selling a higher strike put at a high price).

430. MTOptionStrategyLongBearDebitSpread

Returns the matrix [stock price, buy call, sell call, profit] of a long bearish debit spread (buying a higher strike call with a low price and selling a lower strike call with a high price).

431. MTOptionStrategyLongBullDebitSpread

Returns the matrix [stock price, buy call, sell call, profit] of a bullish debit spread (buying a lower strike call at a high price and selling a further out-of-the-money higher strike call at a low price).

432. MTOptionStrategyLongCoveredCall

Returns the matrix [stock price, buy stock, sell call, profit] of a long covered call position (buying the stock and selling a call of the same asset).

433. MTOptionStrategyLongProtectivePut

Returns the matrix [stock price, buy stock, buy put, profit] of a long protective put position (buying the stock and buying a put of the same asset).

434. MTOptionStrategyLongStraddle

Returns the matrix [stock price, buy call, buy put, profit] of a long straddle position (buying an equal number of puts and calls with identical strike price and expiration) to profit from high volatility.

435. MTOptionStrategyLongStrangle

Returns the matrix [stock price, buy call, buy put, profit] of a long strangle (buying a higher strike call at a low price and buying a lower strike put at a low price—close expirations) to profit from high volatility.

436. MTOptionStrategyWriteCoveredCall

Returns the matrix [stock price, sell stock, buy call, profit] of writing a covered call (selling the stock and buying a call of the same asset).

437. MTOptionStrategyWriteProtectivePut

Returns the matrix [stock price, sell stock, sell put, profit] of writing a protective put position (selling the stock and selling a put of the same asset).

438. MTOptionStrategyWriteStraddle

Returns the matrix [stock price, sell call, sell put, profit] of writing a straddle position (selling an equal number of puts and calls with identical strike price and expiration) to profit from low volatility.

439. MTOptionStrategyWriteStrangle

Returns the matrix [stock price, sell call, sell put, profit] of writing a strangle (sell a higher strike call at a low price and sell a lower strike put at a low price—close expirations) to profit from low volatility.

440. MTPayback

Computes the payback period given some initial investment and subsequent cash flows.

441. MTPerpetualCallOption

Computes the American perpetual call option. Note that it returns an error if dividend is 0% (this is because the American option reverts to European and a perpetual European has no value).

442. MTPerpetualPutOption

Computes the American perpetual put option. Note that it returns an error if dividend is 0% (this is because the American option reverts to European and a perpetual European has no value).

443. MTPortfolioReturns

Computes the portfolio weighted average expected returns given individual asset returns and allocations.

444. MTPortfolioRisk

Computes the portfolio risk given individual asset allocations and variance-covariance matrix.

445. MTPortfolioVariance

Computes the portfolio variance given individual asset allocations and variance-covariance matrix. Take the square root of the result to obtain the portfolio risk.

446. MTProbabilityDefaultAdjustedBondYield

Computes the required risk-adjusted yield (premium spread plus risk-free rate) to charge given the cumulative probability of default.

447. MTProbabilityDefaultAverageDefaults

Credit Risk Plus average number of credit defaults per period using total portfolio credit exposures, average cumulative probability of default, and percentile Value at Risk for the portfolio.

448. MTProbabilityDefaultCorrelation

Computes the correlations of default probabilities given the probabilities of default of each asset and the correlation between their equity prices. The result is typically much smaller than the equity correlation.

449. MTProbabilityDefaultCumulativeBondYieldApproach

Computes the cumulative probability of default from Year 0 to Maturity using a comparable zero bond yield versus a zero risk-free yield and accounting for a recovery rate.

450. MTProbabilityDefaultCumulativeSpreadApproach

Computes the cumulative probability of default from Year 0 to Maturity using a comparable risky debt's spread (premium) versus the risk-free rate and accounting for a recovery rate.

451. MTProbabilityDefaultHazardRate

Computes the hazard rate for a specific year (in survival analysis) using a comparable zero bond yield versus a zero risk-free yield and accounting for a recovery rate.

452. MTProbabilityDefaultMertonDefaultDistance

Distance to Default (does not require market returns and correlations but requires the internal growth rates).

453. MTProbabilityDefaultMertonI

Probability of Default (without regard to Equity Value or Equity Volatility, but requires asset, debt, and market values).

454. MTProbabilityDefaultMertonII

Probability of Default (does not require market returns and correlations but requires the internal asset value and asset volatility).

455. MTProbabilityDefaultMertonImputedAssetValue

Returns the imputed market value of asset given external equity value, equity volatility, and other option inputs. Used in the Merton probability of default model.

456. MTProbabilityDefaultMertonImputedAssetVolatility

Returns the imputed volatility of asset given external equity value, equity volatility, and other option inputs. Used in the Merton probability of default model.

457. MTProbabilityDefaultMertonMVDebt

Computes the market value of debt (for risky debt) in the Merton-based simultaneous options model.

458. MTProbabilityDefaultMertonRecoveryRate

Computes the rate of recovery in percent for risky debt in the Merton-based simultaneous options model.

459. MTProbabilityDefaultPercentileDefaults

Credit Risk Plus method to compute the percentile given some estimated average number of defaults per period.

460. MTPropertyDepreciation

Value of the periodic depreciation allowed on a commercial real estate project, given the percent of price going to improvement and the allowed recovery period.

461. MTPropertyEquityRequired

Value of the required equity down payment on a commercial real estate project, given the valuation of the project.

462. MTPropertyLoanAmount

Value of the required mortgage amount on a commercial real estate project, given the value of the project and the loan required (loan-to-value ratio or the percentage of the value that a loan represents is required).

463. MTPropertyValuation

Value of a commercial real estate property assuming Gross Rent, Vacancy, Operating Expenses, and the Cap Rate at Purchase Date (Net Operating Income/Sale Price).

464. MTPutCallParityCalltoPut

Computes the European put option value given the value of a corresponding European call option with identical input assumptions.

465. MTPutCallParityCalltoPutCurrencyOptions

Computes the European currency put option value given the value of a corresponding European currency call option on futures and forwards with identical input assumptions.

466. MTPutCallParityCalltoPutFutures

Computes the value of a European put option on futures and forwards given the value of a corresponding European call option on futures and forwards with identical input assumptions.

467. MTPutCallParityPuttoCall

Computes the European call option value given the value of a corresponding European put option with identical input assumptions.

468. MTPutCallParityPuttoCallCurrencyOptions

Computes the value of a European currency call option given the value of a corresponding European currency put option on futures and forwards with identical input assumptions.

469. MTPutCallParityPuttoCallFutures

Computes the value of a European call option on futures and forwards given the value of a corresponding European put option on futures and forwards with identical input assumptions.

470. MTPutDelta

Returns the option valuation sensitivity Delta (a put option value's sensitivity to changes in the asset value).

471. MTPutGamma

Returns the option valuation sensitivity Gamma (a put option value's sensitivity to changes in the Delta value).

472. MTPutOptionOnTheMax

The maximum values at expiration of both assets are used in option exercise, where the call option payoff at expiration is the strike price against the maximum price between Asset 1 and Asset 2.

473. MTPutOptionOnTheMin

The minimum values at expiration of both assets are used in option exercise, where the call option payoff at expiration is the strike price against the minimum price between Asset 1 and Asset 2.

474. MTPutRho

Returns the option valuation sensitivity Rho (a put option value's sensitivity to changes in the interest rate).

475. MTPutTheta

Returns the option valuation sensitivity Theta (a put option value's sensitivity to changes in the maturity).

476. MTPutVega

Returns the option valuation sensitivity Vega (a put option value's sensitivity to changes in the volatility).

477. MTQueuingMCAveCustomersinSystem

Average number of customers in the system, using a multiple-channel queuing model assuming a Poisson arrival rate with Exponential distribution of service times.

478. MTQueuingMCAveCustomersWaiting

Average number of customers in the waiting line, using a multiple-channel queuing model assuming a Poisson arrival rate with Exponential distribution of service times.

479. MTQueuingMCAveTimeinSystem

Average time a customer spends in the system, using a multiple-channel queuing model assuming a Poisson arrival rate with Exponential distribution of service times.

480. MTQueuingMCAveTimeWaiting

Average time a customer spends in the waiting line, using a multiple-channel queuing model assuming a Poisson arrival rate with Exponential distribution of service times.

481. MTQueuingMCProbHaveToWait

Probability an arriving customer has to wait, using a multiple-channel queuing model assuming a Poisson arrival rate with Exponential distribution of service times.

482. MTQueuingMCProbNoCustomer

Probability that no customers are in the system, using a multiple-channel queuing model assuming a Poisson arrival rate with Exponential distribution of service times.

483. MTQueuingMGKAveCustomersinSystem

Average number of customers in the system, using a multiple-channel queuing model assuming a Poisson arrival rate with unknown distribution of service times.

484. MTQueuingMGKCostPerPeriod

Total cost per time period, using a multiple-channel queuing model assuming a Poisson arrival rate with unknown distribution of service times.

485. MTQueuingMGKProbBusy

Probability a channel will be busy, using a multiple-channel queuing model assuming a Poisson arrival rate with unknown distribution of service times.

486. MTQueuingSCAAveCustomersinSystem

Average number of customers in the system, using an MG1 single-channel arbitrary queuing model assuming a Poisson arrival rate with unknown distribution of service times.

487. MTQueuingSCAAveCustomersWaiting

Average number of customers in the waiting line, using an MG1 single-channel arbitrary queuing model assuming a Poisson arrival rate with unknown distribution of service times.

488. MTQueuingSCAAveTimeinSystem

Average time a customer spends in the system, using an MG1 single-channel arbitrary queuing model assuming a Poisson arrival rate with unknown distribution of service times.

489. MTQueuingSCAAveTimeWaiting

Average time a customer spends in the waiting line, using an MG1 single-channel arbitrary queuing model assuming a Poisson arrival rate with unknown distribution of service times.

490. MTQueuingSCAProbHaveToWait

Probability an arriving customer has to wait, using an MG1 single-channel arbitrary queuing model assuming a Poisson arrival rate with unknown distribution of service times.

491. MTQueuingSCAProbNoCustomer

Probability that no customers are in the system, using an MG1 single-channel arbitrary queuing model assuming a Poisson arrival rate with unknown distribution of service times.

492. MTQueuingSCAveCustomersinSystem

Average number of customers in the system, using a single-channel queuing model.

493. MTQueuingSCAveCustomersWaiting

Average number of customers in the waiting line, using a single-channel queuing model.

494. MTQueuingSCAveTimeinSystem

Average time a customer spends in the system, using a single-channel queuing model.

495. MTQueuingSCAveTimeWaiting

Average time a customer spends in the waiting line, using a single-channel queuing model.

496. MTQueuingSCProbHaveToWait

Probability an arriving customer has to wait, using a single-channel queuing model.

497. MTQueuingSCProbNoCustomer

Probability that no customers are in the system, using a single-channel queuing model.

498. MTRatiosBasicEarningPower

Computes the basic earning power (BEP) by accounting for earnings before interest and taxes (EBIT) and the amount of total assets employed.

499. MTRatiosBetaLevered

Computes the levered beta from an unlevered beta level after accounting for the tax rate, total debt, and equity values.

500. MTRatiosBetaUnlevered

Computes the unlevered beta from a levered beta level after accounting for the tax rate, total debt, and equity values.

501. MTRatiosBookValuePerShare

Computes the book value per share (BV) by accounting for the total common equity amount and number of shares outstanding.

502. MTRatiosCapitalCharge

Computes the capital charge value (typically used to compute the economic profit of a project).

503. MTRatiosCAPM

Computes the capital asset pricing model's required rate of return in percent, given some benchmark market return, beta risk coefficient, and risk-free rate.

504. MTRatiosCashFlowtoEquityLeveredFirm

Cash flow to equity for a levered firm (accounting for operating expenses, taxes, depreciation, amortization, capital expenditures, change in working capital, preferred dividends, principal repaid, and new debt issues).

505. MTRatiosCashFlowtoEquityUnleveredFirm

Cash flow to equity for an unlevered firm (accounting for operating expenses, taxes, depreciation, amortization, capital expenditures, change in working capital, and taxes).

506. MTRatiosCashFlowtoFirm

Cash flow to the firm (accounting for earnings before interest and taxes [EBIT], tax rate, depreciation, capital expenditures, and change in working capital).

507. MTRatiosCashFlowtoFirm2

Cash flow to the firm (accounting for net operating profit after taxes [NOPAT], depreciation, capital expenditures, and change in working capital).

508. MTRatiosContinuingValue1

Computes the continuing value based on a constant growth rate of free cash flows to perpetuity using a Gordon Growth Model.

509. MTRatiosContinuingValue2

Computes the continuing value based on a constant growth rate of free cash flows to perpetuity using net operating profit after taxes (NOPAT), return on invested capital (ROIC), growth rate, and current free cash flow.

510. MTRatiosCostEquity

Computes the cost of equity (as used in a CAPM model) using the dividend rate, growth rate of dividends, and current equity price.

511. MTRatiosCurrentRatio

Computes the current ratio by accounting for the individual asset and liabilities.

512. MTRatiosDaysSalesOutstanding

Computes the days sales outstanding by looking at the accounts receivable value, total annual sales, and number of days per year.

513. MTRatiosDebtAssetRatio

Computes the debt-to-asset ratio by accounting for the total debt and total asset values.

514. MTRatiosDebtEquityRatio

Computes the debt-to-equity ratio by accounting for the total debt and total common equity levels.

515. MTRatiosDebtRatio1

Computes the debt ratio by accounting for the total debt and total asset values.

516. MTRatiosDebtRatio2

Computes the debt ratio by accounting for the total equity and total asset values.

517. MTRatiosDividendsPerShare

Computes the dividends per share (DPS) by accounting for the dividend payment amount and number of shares outstanding.

518. MTRatiosEarningsPerShare

Computes the earnings per share (EPS) by accounting for the net income amount and number of shares outstanding.

519. MTRatiosEconomicProfit1

Computes the economic profit using invested capital, return on invested capital (ROIC), and weighted average cost of capital (WACC).

520. MTRatiosEconomicProfit2

Computes the economic profit using net operating profit after taxes (NOPAT), return on invested capital (ROIC), and weighted average cost of capital (WACC).

521. MTRatiosEconomicProfit3

Computes the economic profit using net operating profit after taxes (NOPAT) and capital charge.

522. MTRatiosEconomicValueAdded

Computes the economic value added using earnings before interest and taxes (EBIT), total capital employed, tax rate, and weighted average cost of capital (WACC).

523. MTRatiosEquityMultiplier

Computes the equity multiplier (the ratio of total assets to total equity).

524. MTRatiosFixedAssetTurnover

Computes the fixed asset turnover by accounting for the annual sales levels and net fixed assets.

525. MTRatiosInventoryTurnover

Computes the inventory turnover using sales and inventory levels.

526. MTRatiosMarketBookRatio1

Computes the market to book value (BV) per share by accounting for the share price and the book value per share.

527. MTRatiosMarketBookRatio2

Computes the market to book value per share by accounting for the share price, total common equity value, and number of shares outstanding.

528. MTRatiosMarketValueAdded

Computes the market value added by accounting for the stock price, total common equity, and number of shares outstanding.

529. MTRatiosNominalCashFlow

Computes the nominal cash flow amount assuming some inflation rate, real cash flow, and the number of years in the future.

530. MTRatiosNominalDiscountRate

Computes the nominal discount rate assuming some inflation rate and real discount rate.

531. MTRatiosPERatio1

Computes the price-to-earnings (P/E) ratio using stock price and earnings per share (EPS).

532. MTRatiosPERatio2

Computes the price-to-earnings (P/E) ratio using stock price, net income, and number of shares outstanding.

533. MTRatiosPERatio3

Computes the price-to-earnings (P/E) ratio using growth rates, rate of return, and discount rate.

534. MTRatiosProfitMargin

Computes the profit margin by taking the ratio of net income to annual sales.

535. MTRatiosQuickRatio

Computes the quick ratio by accounting for the individual assets and liabilities.

536. MTRatiosRealCashFlow

Computes the real cash flow amount assuming some inflation rate, nominal cash flow (Nominal CF), and the number of years in the future.

537. MTRatiosRealDiscountRate

Computes the real discount rate assuming some inflation rate and nominal discount rate.

538. MTRatiosReturnonAsset1

Computes the return on assets using net income amount and total assets employed.

539. MTRatiosReturnonAsset2

Computes the return on assets using net profit margin percentage and total asset turnover ratio.

540. MTRatiosReturnonEquity1

Computes return on equity using net income and total common equity values.

541. MTRatiosReturnonEquity2

Computes return on equity using return on assets (ROA), total assets, and total equity values.

542. MTRatiosReturnonEquity3

Computes return on equity using net income, total sales, total assets, and total common equity values.

543. MTRatiosReturnonEquity4

Computes return on equity using net profit margin, total asset turnover, and equity multiplier values.

544. MTRatiosROIC

Computes the return on invested capital (typically used for computing economic profit) accounting for change in working capital; property, plant, and equipment (PPE); and other assets.

545. MTRatiosShareholderEquity

Computes the common shareholder's equity after accounting for total assets, total liabilities, and preferred stocks.

546. MTRatiosTimesInterestEarned

Computes the times interest earned ratio by accounting for earnings before interest and taxes (EBIT) and the amount of interest payment.

547. MTRatiosTotalAssetTurnover

Computes the total asset turnover by accounting for the annual sales levels and total assets.

548. MTRatiosWACC1

Computes the weighted average cost of capital (WACC) using market values of debt, preferred equity, and common equity, as well as their respective costs.

549. MTRatiosWACC2

Computes the weighted average cost of capital (WACC) using market values of debt and market values of common equity, as well as their respective costs.

550. MTROBinomialAmericanAbandonContract

Returns the American option to abandon and contract using a binomial lattice model.

551. MTROBinomialAmericanAbandonContractExpand

Returns the American option to abandon, contract, and expand using a binomial lattice model.

552. MTROBinomialAmericanAbandonExpand

Returns the American option to abandon and expand using a binomial lattice model.

553. MTROBinomialAmericanAbandonment

Returns the American option to abandon using a binomial lattice model.

554. MTROBinomialAmericanCall

Returns the American call option with dividends using a binomial lattice model.

555. MTROBinomialAmericanChangingRiskFree

Returns the American call option with dividends and assuming the risk-free rate changes over time, using a binomial lattice model.

556. MTROBinomialAmericanChangingVolatility

Returns the American call option with dividends and assuming the volatility changes over time, using a binomial lattice model. (Use small number of steps or it will take a long time to compute!)

557. MTROBinomialAmericanContractExpand

Returns the American option to contract and expand using a binomial lattice model.

558. MTROBinomialAmericanContraction

Returns the American option to contract using a binomial lattice model.

559. MTROBinomialAmericanCustomCall

Returns the American option call option with changing inputs, vesting periods, and suboptimal exercise multiple using a binomial lattice model.

560. MTROBinomialAmericanExpansion

Returns the American option to expand using a binomial lattice model.

561. MTROBinomialAmericanPut

Returns the American put option with dividends using a binomial lattice model.

562. MTROBinomialBermudanAbandonContract

Returns the Bermudan option to abandon and contract using a binomial lattice model, where there is a vesting/blackout period during which the option cannot be executed.

563. MTROBinomialBermudanAbandonContractExpand

Returns the Bermudan option to abandon, contract, and expand, using a binomial lattice model, where there is a vesting/blackout period during which the option cannot be executed.

564. MTROBinomialBermudanAbandonExpand

Returns the Bermudan option to abandon and expand using a binomial lattice model, where there is a vesting/blackout period during which the option cannot be executed.

565. MTROBinomialBermudanAbandonment

Returns the Bermudan option to abandon using a binomial lattice model, where there is a vesting/blackout period during which the option cannot be executed.

566. MTROBinomialBermudanCall

Returns the Bermudan call option with dividends, where there is a vesting/blackout period during which the option cannot be executed.

567. MTROBinomialBermudanContractExpand

Returns the Bermudan option to contract and expand, using a binomial lattice model, where there is a vesting/blackout period during which the option cannot be executed.

568. MTROBinomialBermudanContraction

Returns the Bermudan option to contract using a binomial lattice model, where there is a vesting/blackout period during which the option cannot be executed.

569. MTROBinomialBermudanExpansion

Returns the Bermudan option to expand using a binomial lattice model, where there is a vesting/blackout period during which the option cannot be executed.

570. MTROBinomialBermudanPut

Returns the Bermudan put option with dividends, where there is a vesting/blackout period during which the option cannot be executed.

571. MTROBinomialEuropeanAbandonContract

Returns the European option to abandon and contract, using a binomial lattice model, where the option can be executed only at expiration.

572. MTROBinomialEuropeanAbandonContractExpand

Returns the European option to abandon, contract, and expand, using a binomial lattice model, where the option can be executed only at expiration.

573. MTROBinomialEuropeanAbandonExpand

Returns the European option to abandon and expand, using a binomial lattice model, where the option can be executed only at expiration.

574. MTROBinomialEuropeanAbandonment

Returns the European option to abandon using a binomial lattice model, where the option can be executed only at expiration.

575. MTROBinomialEuropeanCall

Returns the European call option with dividends, where the option can be executed only at expiration.

576. MTROBinomialEuropeanContractExpand

Returns the European option to contract and expand, using a binomial lattice model, where the option can be executed only at expiration.

577. MTROBinomialEuropeanContraction

Returns the European option to contract using a binomial lattice model, where the option can be executed only at expiration.

578. MTROBinomialEuropeanExpansion

Returns the European option to expand using a binomial lattice model, where the option can be executed only at expiration.

579. MTROBinomialEuropeanPut

Returns the European put option with dividends, where the option can be executed only at expiration.

580. MTROJumpDiffusionCall

Returns the closed-form model for a European call option whose underlying asset follows a Poisson Jump-Diffusion process.

581. MTROJumpDiffusionPut

Returns the closed-form model for a European put option whose underlying asset follows a Poisson Jump-Diffusion process.

582. MTROMeanRevertingCall

Returns the closed-form model for a European call option whose underlying asset follows a mean-reversion process.

583. MTROMeanRevertingPut

Returns the closed-form model for a European put option whose underlying asset follows a mean-reversion process.

584. MTROPentanomialAmericanCall

Returns the Rainbow American call option with two underlying assets (these are typically price and quantity, and are multiplied together to form a new combinatorial pentanomial lattice).

585. MTROPentanomialAmericanPut

Returns the Rainbow American put option with two underlying assets (these are typically price and quantity, and are multiplied together to form a new combinatorial pentanomial lattice).

586. MTROPentanomialEuropeanCall

Returns the Rainbow European call option with two underlying assets (these are typically price and quantity, and are multiplied together to form a new combinatorial pentanomial lattice).

587. MTROPentanomialEuropeanPut

Returns the Rainbow European put option with two underlying assets (these are typically price and quantity, and are multiplied together to form a new combinatorial pentanomial lattice).

588. MTROQuadranomialJumpDiffusionAmericanCall

Returns the American call option whose underlying asset follows a Poisson Jump-Diffusion process, using a combinatorial quadranomial lattice.

589. MTROQuadranomialJumpDiffusionAmericanPut

Returns the American put option whose underlying asset follows a Poisson Jump-Diffusion process, using a combinatorial quadranomial lattice.

590. MTROQuadranomialJumpDiffusionEuropeanCall

Returns the European call option whose underlying asset follows a Poisson Jump-Diffusion process, using a combinatorial quadranomial lattice.

591. MTROQuadranomialJumpDiffusionEuropeanPut

Returns the European put option whose underlying asset follows a Poisson Jump-Diffusion process, using a combinatorial quadranomial lattice.

592. MTROStateAmericanCall

Returns the American call option using a state jump function, where the up and down states can be asymmetrical, solved in a lattice model.

593. MTROStateAmericanPut

Returns the American put option using a state jump function, where the up and down states can be asymmetrical, solved in a lattice model.

594. MTROStateBermudanCall

Returns the Bermudan call option using a state jump function, where the up and down states can be asymmetrical, solved in a lattice model, and where the option cannot be exercised during certain vesting/blackout periods.

595. MTROStateBermudanPut

Returns the Bermudan put option using a state jump function, where the up and down states can be asymmetrical, solved in a lattice model, and where the option cannot be exercised during certain vesting/blackout periods.

596. MTROStateEuropeanCall

Returns the European call option using a state jump function, where the up and down states can be asymmetrical, solved in a lattice model, and where the option can be exercised only at maturity.

597. MTROStateEuropeanPut

Returns the European put option using a state jump function, where the up and down states can be asymmetrical, solved in a lattice model, and where the option can be exercised only at maturity.

598. MTROTrinomialAmericanCall

Returns the American call option with dividend, solved using a trinomial lattice.

599. MTROTrinomialAmericanMeanRevertingCall

Returns the American call option with dividend, assuming the underlying asset is mean-reverting, and solved using a trinomial lattice.

600. MTROTrinomialAmericanMeanRevertingPut

Returns the American put option with dividend, assuming the underlying asset is mean-reverting, and solved using a trinomial lattice.

601. MTROTrinomialAmericanPut

Returns the American put option with dividend, solved using a trinomial lattice.

602. MTROTrinomialBermudanCall

Returns the Bermudan call option with dividend, solved using a trinomial lattice, where during certain vesting/blackout periods the option cannot be exercised.

603. MTROTrinomialBermudanPut

Returns the Bermudan put option with dividend, solved using a trinomial lattice, where during certain vesting/blackout periods the option cannot be exercised.

604. MTROTrinomialEuropeanCall

Returns the European call option with dividend, solved using a trinomial lattice, where the option can be exercised only at maturity.

605. MTROTrinomialEuropeanMeanRevertingCall

Returns the European call option with dividend, solved using a trinomial lattice, assuming the underlying asset is mean-reverting, and where the option can be exercised only at maturity.

606. MTROTrinomialEuropeanMeanRevertingPut

Returns the European put option with dividend, solved using a trinomial lattice, assuming the underlying asset is mean-reverting, and where the option can be exercised only at maturity.

607. MTROTrinomialEuropeanPut

Returns the European put option with dividend, solved using a trinomial lattice, where the option can be exercised only at maturity.

608. MTSCurveValue

Computes the S-Curve extrapolation's next forecast value based on previous value, growth rate, and maximum capacity levels.

609. MTSCurveValueSaturation

Computes the S-Curve extrapolation's saturation level based on previous value, growth rate, and maximum capacity levels.

610. MTSemiStandardDeviationPopulation

Computes the semi-standard deviation of the population; that is, only the values below the mean are used to compute an adjusted population standard deviation, a more appropriate measure of downside risk.

611. MTSemiStandardDeviationSample

Computes the semi-standard deviation of the sample; that is, only the values below the mean are used to compute an adjusted sample standard deviation, a more appropriate measure of downside risk.

612. MTSharpeRatio

Computes the Sharpe Ratio (returns-to-risk ratio) based on a series of stock prices of an asset and a market benchmark series of prices.

613. MTSimulateBernoulli

Returns simulated random numbers from the Bernoulli distribution. Type in RAND() as the random input parameter to generate volatile random values from this distribution.

614. MTSimulateBeta

Returns simulated random numbers from the Beta distribution. Type in RAND() as the random input parameter to generate volatile random values from this distribution.

615. MTSimulateBinomial

Returns simulated random numbers from the Binomial distribution. Type in RAND() as the random input parameter to generate volatile random values from this distribution.

616. MTSimulateChiSquare

Returns simulated random numbers from the Chi-Square distribution. Type in RAND() as the random input parameter to generate volatile random values from this distribution.

617. MTSimulatedEuropeanCall

Returns the Monte Carlo simulated European call option (only European options can be approximated well with simulation). This function is volatile.

618. MTSimulatedEuropeanPut

Returns the Monte Carlo simulated European put option (only European options can be approximated well with simulation). This function is volatile.

619. MTSimulateDiscreteUniform

Returns simulated random numbers from the Discrete Uniform distribution. Type in RAND() as the random input parameter to generate volatile random values from this distribution.

620. MTSimulateExponential

Returns simulated random numbers from the Exponential distribution. Type in RAND() as the random input parameter to generate volatile random values from this distribution.

621. MTSimulateFDist

Returns simulated random numbers from the F distribution. Type in RAND() as the random input parameter to generate volatile random values from this distribution.

622. MTSimulateGamma

Returns simulated random numbers from the Gamma distribution. Type in RAND() as the random input parameter to generate volatile random values from this distribution.

623. MTSimulateGeometric

Returns simulated random numbers from the Geometric distribution. Type in RAND() as the random input parameter to generate volatile random values from this distribution.

624. MTSimulateGumbelMax

Returns simulated random numbers from the Gumbel Max distribution. Type in RAND() as the random input parameter to generate volatile random values from this distribution.

625. MTSimulateGumbelMin

Returns simulated random numbers from the Gumbel Min distribution. Type in RAND() as the random input parameter to generate volatile random values from this distribution.

626. MTSimulateLogistic

Returns simulated random numbers from the Logistic distribution. Type in RAND() as the random input parameter to generate volatile random values from this distribution.

627. 627.MTSimulateLognormal

Returns simulated random numbers from the Lognormal distribution. Type in RAND() as the random input parameter to generate volatile random values from this distribution.

628. MTSimulateNormal

Returns simulated random numbers from the Normal distribution. Type in RAND() as the random input parameter to generate volatile random values from this distribution.

629. MTSimulatePareto

Returns simulated random numbers from the Pareto distribution. Type in RAND() as the random input parameter to generate volatile random values from this distribution.

630. MTSimulatePoisson

Returns simulated random numbers from the Poisson distribution. Type in RAND() as the random input parameter to generate volatile random values from this distribution.

631. MTSimulateRayleigh

Returns simulated random numbers from the Rayleigh distribution. Type in RAND() as the random input parameter to generate volatile random values from this distribution.

632. MTSimulateStandardNormal

Returns simulated random numbers from the Standard Normal distribution. Type in RAND() as the random input parameter to generate volatile random values from this distribution.

633. MTSimulateTDist

Returns simulated random numbers from the Student's T distribution. Type in RAND() as the random input parameter to generate volatile random values from this distribution.

634. MTSimulateTriangular

Returns simulated random numbers from the Triangular distribution. Type in RAND() as the random input parameter to generate volatile random values from this distribution.

635. MTSimulateUniform

Returns simulated random numbers from the Uniform distribution. Type in RAND() as the random input parameter to generate volatile random values from this distribution.

636. MTSimulateWeibull

Returns simulated random numbers from the Weibull distribution. Type in RAND() as the random input parameter to generate volatile random values from this distribution.

637. MTSixSigmaControlCChartCL

Computes the center line in a control C-chart. C-charts are applicable when only the number of defects is important.

638. MTSixSigmaControlCChartDown1Sigma

Computes the lower 1 sigma limit in a control C-chart. C-charts are applicable when only the number of defects is important.

639. MTSixSigmaControlCChartDown2Sigma

Computes the lower 2 sigma limit in a control C-chart. C-charts are applicable when only the number of defects is important.

640. MTSixSigmaControlCChartLCL

Computes the lower control limit in a control C-chart. C-charts are applicable when only the number of defects is important.

641. MTSixSigmaControlCChartUCL

Computes the upper control limit in a control C-chart. C-charts are applicable when only the number of defects is important.

642. MTSixSigmaControlCChartUp1Sigma

Computes the upper 1 sigma limit in a control C-chart. C-charts are applicable when only the number of defects is important.

643. MTSixSigmaControlCChartUp2Sigma

Computes the upper 2 sigma limit in a control C-chart. C-charts are applicable when only the number of defects is important.

644. MTSixSigmaControlNPChartCL

Computes the center line in a control NP-chart. NP-charts are applicable when proportions of defects are important, and where in each experimental subgroup the number of sample sizes is constant.

645. MTSixSigmaControlNPChartDown1Sigma

Computes the lower 1 sigma limit in a control NP-chart. NP-charts are applicable when proportions of defects are important, and where in each experimental subgroup the number of sample sizes is constant.

646. MTSixSigmaControlNPChartDown2Sigma

Computes the lower 2 sigma limit in a control NP-chart. NP-charts are applicable when proportions of defects are important, and where in each experimental subgroup the number of sample sizes is constant.

647. MTSixSigmaControlNPChartLCL

Computes the lower control limit in a control NP-chart. NP-charts are applicable when proportions of defects are important, and where in each experimental subgroup the number of sample sizes is constant.

648. MTSixSigmaControlNPChartUCL

Computes the upper control limit in a control NP-chart. NP-charts are applicable when proportions of defects are important, and where in each experimental subgroup the number of sample sizes is constant.

649. MTSixSigmaControlNPChartUp1Sigma

Computes the upper 1 sigma limit in a control NP-chart. NP-charts are applicable when proportions of defects are important, and where in each experimental subgroup the number of sample sizes is constant.

650. MTSixSigmaControlNPChartUp2Sigma

Computes the upper 2 sigma limit in a control NP-chart. NP-charts are applicable when proportions of defects are important, and where in each experimental subgroup the number of sample sizes is constant.

651. MTSixSigmaControlPChartCL

Computes the center line in a control P-chart. P-charts are applicable when proportions of defects are important, and where in each experimental subgroup the number of sample sizes might be different.

652. MTSixSigmaControlPChartDown1Sigma

Computes the lower 1 sigma limit in a control P-chart. P-charts are applicable when proportions of defects are important, and where in each experimental subgroup the number of sample sizes might be different.

653. MTSixSigmaControlPChartDown2Sigma

Computes the lower 2 sigma limit in a control P-chart. P-charts are applicable when proportions of defects are important, and where in each experimental subgroup the number of sample sizes might be different.

654. MTSixSigmaControlPChartLCL

Computes the lower control limit in a control P-chart. P-charts are applicable when proportions of defects are important, and where in each experimental subgroup the number of sample sizes might be different.

655. MTSixSigmaControlPChartUCL

Computes the upper control limit in a control P-chart. P-charts are applicable when proportions of defects are important, and where in each experimental subgroup the number of sample sizes might be different.

656. MTSixSigmaControlPChartUp1Sigma

Computes the upper 1 sigma limit in a control P-chart. P-charts are applicable when proportions of defects are important, and where in each experimental subgroup the number of sample sizes might be different.

657. MTSixSigmaControlPChartUp2Sigma

Computes the upper 2 sigma limit in a control P-chart. P-charts are applicable when proportions of defects are important, and where in each experimental subgroup the number of sample sizes might be different.

658. MTSixSigmaControlRChartCL

Computes the center line in a control R-chart. R-charts are used when the number of defects is important; in each subgroup experiment, multiple measurements are taken, and the range of the measurements is the variable plotted.

659. MTSixSigmaControlRChartLCL

Computes the lower control limit in a control R-chart. R-charts are used when the number of defects is important; in each subgroup experiment multiple measurements are taken, and the range of the measurements is the variable plotted.

660. MTSixSigmaControlRChartUCL

Computes the upper control limit in a control R-chart. R-charts are used when the number of defects is important; in each subgroup experiment multiple measurements are taken, and the range of the measurements is the variable plotted.

661. MTSixSigmaControlUChartCL

Computes the center line in a control U-chart. U-charts are applicable when the number of defects is important, and where in each experimental subgroup the number of sample sizes is the same.

662. MTSixSigmaControlUChartDown1Sigma

Computes the lower 1 sigma limit in a control U-chart. U-charts are applicable when the number of defects is important, and where in each experimental subgroup the number of sample sizes is the same.

663. MTSixSigmaControlUChartDown2Sigma

Computes the lower 2 sigma limit in a control U-chart. U-charts are applicable when the number of defects is important, and where in each experimental subgroup the number of sample sizes is the same.

664. MTSixSigmaControlUChartLCL

Computes the lower control limit in a control U-chart. U-charts are applicable when the number of defects is important, and where in each experimental subgroup the number of sample sizes is the same.

665. MTSixSigmaControlUChartUCL

Computes the upper control limit in a control U-chart. U-charts are applicable when the number of defects is important, and where in each experimental subgroup the number of sample sizes is the same.

666. MTSixSigmaControlUChartUp1Sigma

Computes the upper 1 sigma limit in a control U-chart. U-charts are applicable when the number of defects is important, and where in each experimental subgroup the number of sample sizes is the same.

667. MTSixSigmaControlUChartUp2Sigma

Computes the upper 2 sigma limit in a control U-chart. U-charts are applicable when the number of defects is important, and where in each experimental subgroup the number of sample sizes is the same.

668. MTSixSigmaControlXChartCL

Computes the center line in a control X-chart. X-charts are used when the number of defects is important; in each subgroup experiment, multiple measurements are taken; and the average of the measurements is the variable plotted.

669. MTSixSigmaControlXChartLCL

Computes the lower control limit in a control X-chart. X-charts are used when the number of defects is important; in each subgroup experiment multiple measurements are taken, and the average of the measurements is the variable plotted.

670. MTSixSigmaControlXChartUCL

Computes the upper control limit in a control X-chart. X-charts are used when the number of defects is important; in each subgroup experiment multiple measurements are taken, and the average of the measurements is the variable plotted.

671. MTSixSigmaControlXMRChartCL

Computes the center line in a control XmR-chart. XmR-charts are used when the number of defects is important; there is only a single measurement for each sample, and a time series of moving ranges is the variable plotted.

672. MTSixSigmaControlXMRChartLCL

Computes the lower control limit in a control XmR-chart. XmR-charts are used when the number of defects is important; there is only a single measurement for each sample, and a time series of moving ranges is the variable plotted.

673. MTSixSigmaControlXMRChartUCL

Computes the upper control limit in a control XmR-chart. XmR-charts are used when the number of defects is important; there is only a single measurement for each sample, and a time series of moving ranges is the variable plotted.

674. MTSixSigmaDeltaPrecision

Computes the error precision given specific levels of Type I and Type II errors, as well as the sample size and variance.

675. MTSixSigmaSampleSize

Computes the required minimum sample size given Type I and Type II errors, as well as the required precision of the mean and the error tolerances.

676. MTSixSigmaSampleSizeDPU

Computes the required minimum sample size given Type I and Type II errors, as well as the required precision of the defects per unit and the error tolerances.

677. MTSixSigmaSampleSizeProportion

Computes the required minimum sample size given Type I and Type II errors, as well as the required precision of the proportion of defects and the error tolerances.

678. MTSixSigmaSampleSizeStdev

Computes the required minimum sample size given Type I and Type II errors, as well as the required precision of the standard deviation and the error tolerances.

679. MTSixSigmaSampleSizeZeroCorrelTest

Computes the required minimum sample size to test whether a correlation is statistically significant at an alpha of 0.05 and beta of 0.10.

680. MTSixSigmaStatCP

Computes the potential process capability index Cp given the actual mean and sigma of the process, including the upper and lower specification limits.

681. MTSixSigmaStatCPK

Computes the process capability index Cpk given the actual mean and sigma of the process, including the upper and lower specification limits.

682. MTSixSigmaStatDPMO

Computes the defects per million opportunities (DPMO) given the actual mean and sigma of the process, including the upper and lower specification limits.

683. MTSixSigmaStatDPU

Computes the proportion of defects per unit (DPU) given the actual mean and sigma of the process, including the upper and lower specification limits.

684. MTSixSigmaStatProcessSigma

Computes the process sigma level given the actual mean and sigma of the process, including the upper and lower specification limits.

685. MTSixSigmaStatYield

Computes the nondefective parts or the yield of the process, given the actual mean and sigma of the process, including the upper and lower specification limits.

686. MTSixSigmaUnitCPK

Computes the process capability index Cpk given the actual counts of defective parts and the total opportunities in the population.

687. MTSixSigmaUnitDPMO

Computes the defects per million opportunities (DPMO) given the actual counts of defective parts and the total opportunities in the population.

688. MTSixSigmaUnitDPU

Computes the proportion of defects per unit (DPU) given the actual counts of defective parts and the total opportunities in the population.

689. MTSixSigmaUnitProcessSigma

Computes the process sigma level given the actual counts of defective parts and the total opportunities in the population.

690. MTSixSigmaUnitYield

Computes the nondefective parts or the yield of the process given the actual counts of defective parts and the total opportunities in the population.

691. MTStandardNormalBivariateCDF

Given the two Z-scores and correlation, returns the value of the bivariate standard normal (means of zero, variances of 1) cumulative distribution function.

692. MTStandardNormalCDF

Given the Z-score, returns the value of the standard normal (mean of zero, variance of 1) cumulative distribution function.

693. MTStandardNormalInverseCDF

Computes the inverse cumulative distribution function of a standard normal distribution (mean of zero, variance of 1).

694. MTStandardNormalPDF

Given the Z-score, returns the value of the standard normal (mean of zero, variance of 1) probability density function.

695. MTStockIndexCallOption

Similar to a regular call option but the underlying asset is a reference stock index such as the Standard & Poor's 500. The analysis can be solved using a Generalized Black-Scholes-Merton model as well.

696. MTStockIndexPutOption

Similar to a regular put option but the underlying asset is a reference stock index such as the Standard & Poor's 500. The analysis can be solved using a Generalized Black-Scholes-Merton model as well.

697. MTSuperShareOptions

The option has value only if the stock or asset price is between the upper and lower barriers, and at expiration provides a payoff equivalent to the stock or asset price divided by the lower strike price (S/X Lower).

698. MTSwaptionEuropeanPayer

European Call Interest Swaption, where the holder has the right to enter in a swap to pay fixed and receive floating interest payments.

699. MTSwaptionEuropeanReceiver

European Put Interest Swaption, where the holder has the right to enter in a swap to receive fixed and pay floating interest payments.

700. MTTakeoverFXOption

At a successful takeover (foreign firm value in foreign currency is less than the foreign currency units), option holder can purchase the foreign units at a predetermined strike price (in exchange rates of the domestic to foreign currency).

701. MTTimeSwitchOptionCall

Holder gets AccumAmount × TimeSteps each time asset > strike for a call. TimeSteps is the frequency at which the asset price is checked as to whether the strike is breached (e.g., for 252 trading days, set DT as 1/252).

702. MTTimeSwitchOptionPut

Holder gets AccumAmount × TimeSteps each time asset < strike for a put. TimeSteps is the frequency at which the asset price is checked as to whether the strike is breached (e.g., for 252 trading days, set DT as 1/252).

703. MTTradingDayAdjustedCall

Call option corrected for varying volatilities (higher on trading days than on nontrading days). Trading-Days Ratio is the number of trading days left until maturity divided by total trading days per year (between 250 and 252).

704. MTTradingDayAdjustedPut

Put option corrected for varying volatilities (higher on trading days than on nontrading days). Trading-Days Ratio is the number of trading days left until maturity divided by total trading days per year (between 250 and 252).

705. MTTrinomialImpliedArrowDebreuLattice

Computes the complete set of implied Arrow-Debreu prices in an implied trinomial lattice using actual observed data. Copy and paste the function and use Ctrl+Shift+Enter to obtain the matrix.

706. MTTrinomialImpliedArrowDebreuValue

Computes the single value of implied Arrow-Debreu price (for a specific step/column and up-down event/row) in an implied trinomial lattice using actual observed data.

707. MTTrinomialImpliedCallOptionValue

Computes the European call option using an implied trinomial lattice approach, taking into account actual observed inputs.

708. MTTrinomialImpliedDownProbabilityLattice

Computes the complete set of implied DOWN probabilities in an implied trinomial lattice using actual observed data. Copy and paste the function and use Ctrl+Shift+Enter to obtain the matrix.

709. MTTrinomialImpliedDownProbabilityValue

Computes the single value of implied DOWN probability (for a specific step/column and up-down event/row) in an implied trinomial lattice using actual observed data.

710. MTTrinomialImpliedLocalVolatilityLattice

Computes the complete set of implied local probabilities in an implied trinomial lattice using actual observed data. Copy and paste the function and use Ctrl+Shift+Enter to obtain the matrix.

711. MTTrinomialImpliedLocalVolatilityValue

Computes the single value of implied localized volatility (for a specific step/column and up-down event/row) in an implied trinomial lattice using actual observed data.

712. MTTrinomialImpliedUpProbabilityLattice

Computes the complete set of implied UP probabilities in an implied trinomial lattice using actual observed data. Copy and paste the function and use Ctrl+Shift+Enter to obtain the matrix.

713. MTTrinomialImpliedUpProbabilityValue

Computes the single value of implied UP probability (for a specific step/column and up-down event/row) in an implied trinomial lattice using actual observed data.

714. MTTrinomialImpliedPutOptionValue

Computes the European put option using an implied trinomial lattice approach, taking into account actual observed inputs.

715. MTTwoAssetBarrierDownandInCall

Valuable or knocked in the money only if the lower barrier is breached (reference Asset 2 goes below the barrier), and the payout is in the option on Asset 1 less the strike price.

716. MTTwoAssetBarrierDownandInPut

Valuable or knocked in the money only if the lower barrier is breached (reference Asset 2 goes below the barrier), and the payout is in the option on the strike price less the Asset 1 value.

717. MTTwoAssetBarrierDownandOutCall

Valuable or stays in the money only if the lower barrier is not breached (reference Asset 2 does not go below the barrier), and the payout is in the option on Asset 1 less the strike price.

718. MTTwoAssetBarrierDownandOutPut

Valuable or stays in the money only if the lower barrier is not breached (reference Asset 2 does not go below the barrier), and the payout is in the option on the strike price less the Asset 1 value.

719. MTTwoAssetBarrierUpandInCall

Valuable or knocked in the money only if the upper barrier is breached (reference Asset 2 goes above the barrier), and the payout is in the option on Asset 1 less the strike price.

720. MTTwoAssetBarrierUpandInPut

Valuable or knocked in the money only if the upper barrier is breached (reference Asset 2 goes above the barrier), and the payout is in the option on the strike price less the Asset 1 value.

721. MTTwoAssetBarrierUpandOutCall

Valuable or stays in the money only if the upper barrier is not breached (reference Asset 2 does not go above the barrier), and the payout is in the option on Asset 1 less the strike price.

722. MTTwoAssetBarrierUpandOutPut

Valuable or stays in the money only if the upper barrier is not breached (reference Asset 2 does not go above the barrier), and the payout is in the option on the strike price less the Asset 1 value.

723. MTTwoAssetCashOrNothingCall

Pays cash at expiration as long as both assets are in the money. For call options, both asset values must be above their respective strike prices.

724. MTTwoAssetCashOrNothingDownUp

Cash will be paid only if at expiration the first asset is below the first strike and the second asset is above the second strike.

725. MTTwoAssetCashOrNothingPut

Pays cash at expiration as long as both assets are in the money. For put options, both assets must be below their respective strike prices.

726. MTTwoAssetCashOrNothingUpDown

Cash will be paid only if the first asset is above the first strike price and the second asset is below the second strike price at maturity.

727. MTTwoAssetCorrelationCall

Asset 1 is the benchmark asset, whereby if at expiration Asset 1's value exceeds Strike 1's value, then the call option is knocked in the money, and the payoff on the option is Asset 2 – Strike 2; otherwise the option becomes worthless.

728. MTTwoAssetCorrelationPut

Asset 1 is the benchmark asset, whereby if at expiration Asset 1's value is below Strike 1's value, then the put option is knocked in the money, and the payoff on the option is Strike 2 – Asset 2; otherwise the option becomes worthless.

729. MTVaRCorrelationMethod

Computes the Value at Risk using the Variance-Covariance and Correlation method, accounting for a specific VaR percentile and holding period.

730. RMTVaROptions

Computes the Value at Risk of a portfolio of correlated options.

731. MTVolatility

Returns the Annualized Volatility of time-series cash flows. Enter in the number of periods in a cycle to annualize the volatility (1 = annual, 4 = quarterly, 12 = monthly data).

732. MTVolatilityImpliedforDefaultRisk

Used only when computing the implied volatility required for optimizing an option model to compute the probability of default.

733. MTWarrantsDilutedValue

Returns the value of a warrant (like an option) that is convertible to stock while accounting for dilution effects based on the number of shares and warrants outstanding.

734. MTWriterExtendibleCallOption

The call option is extended beyond the initial maturity to an extended date with a new extended strike if at maturity the option is out of the money, providing a safety net of time for the option holder.

735. MTWriterExtendiblePutOption

The put option is extended beyond the initial maturity to an extended date with a new extended strike if at maturity the option is out of the money, providing a safety net of time for the option holder.

736. MTYieldCurveBIM

Returns the Yield Curve at various points in time using the Bliss model.

737. MTYieldCurveNS

Returns the Yield Curve at various points in time using the Nelson-Siegel approach.

738. MTZEOB

Returns the Economic Order Batch or the optimal quantity to be manufactured on each production batch.

739. MTZEOBBatch

Returns the Economic Order Batch analysis's optimal number of batches to be manufactured per year.

740. MTZEOBHoldingCost

Returns the Economic Order Batch analysis's cost of holding excess units per year if manufactured at the optimal level.

741. MTZEOBProductionCost

Returns the Economic Order Batch analysis's total cost of setting up production per year if manufactured at the optimal level.

742. MTZEOBTotalCost

Returns the Economic Order Batch analysis's total cost of production and holding costs per year if manufactured at the optimal level.

743. MTZEOQ

Economic Order Quantity's order size on each order.

744. MTZEOQExcess

Economic Order Quantity's excess safety stock level.

745. MTZEOQOrders

Economic Order Quantity's number of orders per year.

746. MTZEOQProbability

Economic Order Quantity's probability of out of stock.

747. MTZEOQReorderPoint

Economic Order Quantity's reorder point.

Statistical and Analytical Tools in the Modeling Toolkit

748. Statistical Tool: Chi-Square Goodness of Fit Test

749. Statistical Tool: Chi-Square Independence Test

750. Statistical Tool: Chi-Square Population Variance Test

Risk Simulator Tools/Applications Used in the Modeling Toolkit

Real Options SLS Tools/Applications Used in the Modeling Toolkit

Glossary of Input Variables and Parameters in the ROV Modeling Toolkit Software

Each of the inputs used in the Modeling Toolkit functions is listed here. Typically, most inputs are single-point estimates, that is, a single value such as 10.50, with the exception of the input variables listed with "Series" in parenthesis.

A

This is the first input variable that determines the shape of the beta and gamma functions, and it is required to compute the Incomplete Beta and Incomplete Gamma values. The Incomplete Beta function is a generalization of the beta function that replaces the definite integral of the beta function with an indefinite integral, and is a mathematical expression used to compute a variety of probability distributions such as the gamma and beta distributions. The same can be said about the Incomplete Beta function. This input is used exclusively in the MTMathIncompleteBeta, MTMathIncompleteGammaP, and MTMathIncompleteGammaQ functions, and the parameter is a positive value.

Above Below

This input variable is used in the partial floating lookback options where the strike price is floating at the Above Below ratio, which has to be a positive value and is greater than or equal to 1 for a call, and less than or equal to 1 for a put.

Accruals

This is the amount in notes accruals, a subsection of current liabilities in the balance sheet. This variable is typically zero or a positive dollar or currency amount.

Additional Cost

This is the amount in additional operating cost used in the MTCreditAcceptanceCost function to determine if a specific credit should be accepted or rejected. This variable is typically a positive dollar or currency amount, and the amount can be zero or positive.

Alpha

Alpha is used in several places and has various definitions. In the first instance, alpha is the shape parameter in several distributions such as the beta, gamma, Gumbel, logistic, and Weibull distributions. It is also used in the Forward Call Option where if Alpha < 1, then a call option starts $(1 - \text{Alpha})\%$ in the money (a put option will be the same amount out of the money), or if Alpha > 1, then the call starts $(\text{Alpha} - 1)\%$ out of the money (a put option will be the same amount in the money). Finally, alpha is also used as the alpha error level, or Type I error, also known as the significance level in a hypothesis test. It measures the probability of not having the true population mean included in the confidence interval of the sample. That is, it computes the probability of rejecting a true hypothesis. $1 - \text{Alpha}$ is, of course, the confidence interval, or the probability that the true population mean resides in the sample confidence interval, and is used in several Six Sigma models. Regardless of use, this parameter has to be a positive value.

Amortization

This is the amount in amortization in the financial income statement of a firm, and is used to compute the cash flow to equity for both a levered and unlevered firm. This amount is typically zero or positive.

Amounts (Series)

This is a series of numbers (typically listed in a single column with multiple rows) indicating the dollar or currency amounts invested in a specific asset class, used to compute the total portfolio's Value at Risk and used only in the MTVaRCorrelationMethod function. These parameters have to be positive values and arranged in a column with multiple rows.

Arithmetic Mean

This is the simple average used in the lognormal distribution. We differentiate this from the geometric or harmonic means, as this arithmetic mean or simple average is the one used as an input parameter in the lognormal distribution. This parameter has to be a positive value, as the lognormal distribution takes on only positive values.

Arithmetic Standard Deviation

This is a simple population standard deviation that is used in the lognormal distribution. You can use Excel's STDEVP to compute this value from a series of data points. This parameter has to be a positive value.

Arrival Rate

This is the rate of arrival on average to a queue in a specific time period (e.g., the average number of people arriving at a restaurant per day or per hour), and typically follows a Poisson distribution. This parameter has to be a positive value.

Asset 1 and Asset 2

These are the first and second assets in a two-asset exotic option or exchange of asset options. Typically, the first asset (Asset 1) is the payoff asset, whereas the second asset (Asset 2) is some sort of benchmark asset. This is not to be confused with PVAsset, which is the present value of the asset used in a real options analysis. These parameters must be positive values.

Asset Allocation (Series)

These are a series of percentage allocations of assets in a portfolio and must sum to 100%, and this series is used to compute a portfolio's total risk and return levels. These parameters are arranged in a single column with multiple rows and can take on zero or positive values, but the sum of these values must equal 100%.

Asset Turnover

This is the total asset turnover financial ratio, or equivalent to annual total sales divided by total assets, used to compute return on equity or return on asset ratios. It has to be a positive value.

Asset Volatility

This is the internal asset volatility (not to be confused with regular volatility in an options model where we compute it using external equity values) used in determining probabilities of default and distance to default on risky debt (e.g., Merton models); it has to be a positive value. This value can only be determined through optimization either using Risk Simulator to solve for a multiple simultaneous equation function or using the function call: MTProbabilityDefaultMertonImputedAssetVolatility.

Average Lead

This is the average lead time in days required in order to receive an order that is placed. This parameter is typically a positive value, and is used in the economic order quantity models.

Average Measurement (Series)

This is a series of the average measurements per sample subgroup in a Six Sigma environment to determine the upper and lower control limits for a control chart (e.g., in an experiment, 5 measurements are taken of a production output, and the experiment is repeated 10 different times with 5 samples taken each time, and the 10 averages of the 5 samples are computed). These values are typically zero or positive, and are arranged in a single column with multiple rows.

Average Price

This is the average of historically observed stock prices during a specific lookback period, used to determine the value of Asian options. This parameter has to be positive.

B

This is the second input variable for the scale of the beta or gamma functions, and is required to compute the Incomplete Beta and Incomplete Gamma values. The Incomplete Beta function is a generalization of the Beta function that replaces the definite integral of the beta function with an indefinite integral, and is a mathematical expression used to compute a variety of probability distributions such as the gamma and beta distributions. The same can be said about the Incomplete Beta function. This input is used exclusively in the following functions: MTMathIncompleteBeta, MTMathIncompleteGammaP, and MTMathIncompleteGammaQ. This parameter is a positive value.

Barrier

This is the stock price barrier (it can be an upper or lower barrier) for certain exotic barrier and binary options where if the barrier is breached within the lifetime of the option, the option either comes into the money or goes out of the money, or an asset or cash is exchanged. This parameter is a positive value.

Base

This is the power value for determining and calibrating the width of the credit tables. Typically, it ranges between 1 and 4 and has to be a positive value.

Baseline DPU

This is the average number of defects per unit (DPU) in a Six Sigma process, and is used to determine the number of trials required to obtain a specific error boundary and significance level based on this average DPU. This parameter has to be a positive value.

Batch Cost

This is the total dollar or currency value of the cost to manufacture a batch of products each time the production line is run. This parameter is a positive value.

Benchmark Prices (Series)

This is a series of benchmark prices or levels arranged in a single column with multiple rows, such as the market Standard & Poor's 500, to be used as a benchmark against another equity price level in order to determine the Sharpe ratio.

Best Case

This is the best-case scenario value or dollar/currency, used in concert with the Expected Value and Percentile value, to determine the volatility of the process or project. This value is typically positive and has to exceed the expected value.

Beta

This parameter is used in several places and denotes different things. When used in the beta, gamma, Gumbel, logistic, and Weibull distributions, it is used to denote the scale of the distribution. When used in the capital asset pricing model (CAPM), it is used to denote the beta relative risk (covariance between a stock's returns and market returns divided by the variance of the market returns). Finally, beta is also used as the beta error or Type II error, measuring the probability of accepting a false hypothesis, or the probability of not being able to detect the standard deviation's changes. 1 − Beta is the power of the test, and this parameter is used in statistical sampling and sample size determination in the Six Sigma models. Regardless, this parameter has to be a positive value.

Beta 0, 1, and 2

These are mathematical parameters in a yield curve construction when applying the Bliss and Nelson-Siegel models for forecasting interest rates. The exact values of these parameters need to be calibrated with optimization, but are either zero or positive values.

Beta Levered

This is the relative risk beta level of a company that is levered or has debt, and can be used to determine the equivalent level of an unlevered company's beta. This parameter has to be a positive value.

Beta Unlevered

This is the relative risk beta level of a company that is unlevered or has zero debt, and can be used to determine the equivalent level of a levered company's beta with debt. This parameter has to be a positive value.

Bond Maturity

This is the maturity of a bond, measured in years, and has to be a positive value.

Bond Price

This is the market price of the bond in dollars or other currency units, and has to be a positive value.

Bond Yield

This is the bond's yield to maturity—that is, the internal rate of return on the bond when held to maturity—and has to be a positive value. These could be applied to corporate bonds or Treasury zero coupon bonds.

Buy Cap Rate

This is the capitalization rate computed by (net operating income/sale price) at the time of purchase of a property, and is typically a positive value, used in the valuation of real estate properties.

BV Asset

This is the book value (BV) of assets in a company, including all short-term and long-term assets.

BV Debt and BV Liabilities

This is the book value (BV) of debt or all liabilities in a company, including all short-term and long-term debt or liabilities, and has to be a positive value.

BV Per Share

This is the book value (BV) price of a share of stock, typically recorded at the initial public offering price available through the company's balance sheet, and has to be a positive value.

Calendar Ratio

This ratio is a positive value and is used in pricing an option with a Trading-Day Correction, which looks at a typical option and corrects it for the varying volatilities. Specifically, volatility tends to be higher on trading days than on nontrading days. The Trading-Days Ratio is simply the number of trading days left until maturity divided by the total number of trading days per year (typically between 250 and 252), and the Calendar Days Ratio is the number of calendar days left until maturity divided by the total number of days per year (365).

Callable Price

This is the amount that, when a bond is called, the bondholder will be paid, and is typically higher than the par value of the bond. This parameter requires a positive value.

Callable Step

This is the step number on a binomial lattice representing the time period when a bond can be called, and this parameter is a positive integer. For instance, in a 10-year bond when the bond is callable starting on the fifth anniversary, the callable step is 50 in a 100-step lattice model.

Call Maturity

This is the maturity of the call option in years, and is used in the complex chooser option (i.e., the exotic option where the holder can decide to make it a call or a put, and each option has its own maturity and strike values), and must be a positive value.

Call Strike

This is the strike price of the call option in dollars or currency, and is used in the complex chooser option (i.e., the exotic option where the holder can decide to make it a call or a put, and each option has its own maturity and strike values), and must be a positive value. Sometimes, this variable has different suffixes (e.g., Call Strike Sell Low, Call Strike Buy High, etc., whenever there might be more than one call option in the portfolio of option strategies, and these suffixes represent whether this particular call is bought or sold, and whether the strike price is higher or lower than the other call option).

Call Value

This is the value of a call option, and is used in the put-call parity model, whereby the value of a corresponding put can be determined given the price of the call with similar option parameters, and this parameter has to be a positive value. Sometimes, this variable has different suffixes (e.g., Call Value Sell Low, Call Value Buy High, etc., whenever there might be more than one call option in the portfolio of option strategies, and these suffixes represent whether this particular call is bought or sold, and whether the premium paid for the option or the option's value is higher or lower than the other call option).

Cap

This is the interest rate cap (ceiling) in an interest cap derivative, and has to be a positive value. The valuation of the cap is done through computing the value of each of its caplets and summing them up for the price of the derivative.

Capacity

This is the maximum capacity level, and is used in forecasting using the S-curve model (where the capacity is the maximum demand or load the market or environment can hold), and in the economic order quantity (batch production) model; it has to be a positive value.

Capital Charge

This is the amount of invested capital multiplied by the weighted average cost of capital or hurdle rate or required rate of return. This value is used to compute the economic profit of a project, and is a positive value.

Capital Expenditures

This is used to compute the cash flow to the firm and the cash flow to equity for a firm. Capital expenditures are deducted from the net cash flow to a firm as an expenditure, and this input parameter can be zero or a positive value.

Cash

This variable is used in several places. The first and most prominent is the amount of money that is paid when a binary or barrier option comes into the money; it is also used to denote the amount of cash available in a current asset on a balance sheet. This parameter is zero or positive.

Cash Dividend

This is the dividend rate or dividend yield, in percent, and is typically either zero or positive. This parameter is not to be confused with Cash Dividends series, which is a dollar or currency unit amount, and which can also be zero or positive. This variable is often used in exotic and real options models.

Cash Dividends (Series)

This is a series of cash dividends in dollars or currency units, which come as lump sum payments of dividends on the underlying stock of an option and can be zero or positive values. This input variable is used in the Generalized Black-Scholes model with cash dividends, and the timing of these cash dividends (Dividend Times) is also listed as a series in a single column with multiple rows.

Cash Flows (Series)

This is a series of cash flows used for a variety of models, including the computation of volatility (using the logarithmic cash flow returns approach) and bond models (bond pricing, convexity, and duration computations), and each cash flow value must be a positive number, arranged in a column with multiple rows.

Channels

This is the number of channels available in a queuing model—for instance, the number of customer service or point of sale cash registers available in a McDonald's fast-food restaurant, where patrons can obtain service. This parameter is a positive integer.

Channels Busy

This is the number of channels that are currently busy and serving customers at any given moment. This parameter can be zero or a positive integer.

Choose Time or Chooser Time

This is the time available for the holder of a complex chooser option whereby the option holder can choose to make the option a call or a put, with different maturities and strike prices. This parameter is a positive value.

Column

The column number in a lattice; for instance, if there is a 20-step lattice for 10 years, then the column number for the third year is the sixth step in the lattice and the column is set to 6, corresponding to the step in the lattice.

Columnwise

This variable is used in the changing risk-free and changing volatility option model, where the default is 1, indicating that the data (risk-free rates and volatilities) are arranged in a column. This parameter is either a 1 (values are listed in a column) or a 0 (values are listed in a row).

Common Equity

This is the total common equity listed in the balance sheet of a company, and is used in financial ratios analysis to determine the return on equity as well as other profitability and efficiency measures. This parameter is a positive value. This value is different than Total Equity, which also includes other forms such as preferred equity.

Compounding

This is the number of compounding periods per year for the European Swaptions (payer and receiver) and requires a positive integer (e.g., set it as 365 for daily compounding, 12 for monthly compounding, etc.).

Contract Factor

This is the contraction factor used in a real option to contract, and this value is computed as the after-contracting net present value divided by the existing base-case net present value (stated another way, this value is $1 - X$ where X is the fraction that is forgone if contraction occurs, or the portion that is shared with an alliance or joint venture partner or outsourcing outfit), and the parameter has to be between 0 and 1, noninclusive.

Conversion Date

This is the number of days in the future where the convertible bond can be converted into an equivalent value of equity.

Corporate Bond Yield

This is the yield of a risky debt or a risky corporate bond in percent, and is used to compute the implied probability of default of a risky debt given a comparable zero coupon risk-free bond with similar maturity. This input has to be a positive value.

Correlation

This variable is used in multiple places, including exotic options with multiple underlying assets (e.g., exchange of assets, two-asset options, foreign exchange, and futures or commodity options) and the bivariate normal distribution where we combine two correlated normal distributions.

Correlations (Series)

This is an $n \times n$ correlation matrix and is used to value the portfolio Value at Risk where the individual components of the portfolio are correlated with one another.

Cost, Cost 1, and Cost 2

This is a dollar or currency amount corresponding to the cost to execute a particular project or option, and has to be a positive value. This variable is used most frequently in real options models. When there are multiple costs (Cost 1 and Cost 2), this implies several underlying assets and their respective costs or strike prices.

Cost of Debt

This is the cost of debt before tax in percent, used to compute the weighted average cost of capital for a project or firm, and is typically a zero or positive value.

Cost of Equity

This is the cost of equity before tax in percent, used to compute the weighted average cost of capital for a project or firm, and is typically a zero or positive value.

Cost of Funds

This is the cost of obtaining additional funds, in percent, and used in determining credit acceptance levels, and this parameter can be zero or a positive value.

Cost of Losing a Unit

This is the monetary dollar or currency amount lost or forgone if one unit of sales is lost when there is an insufficient number of channels in the queuing models to determine the optimal number of channels to have available, and can be zero or a positive value.

Cost of Order

This is a dollar or currency amount of the cost of placing an order for additional inventory, used in the economic order quantity models to determine the optimal quantity of inventory to order and to have on hand.

Cost of Preferred Equity

This is the before-tax cost of preferred equity in percent, used to compute the cost of funds using the weighted average cost of capital model, and is either zero or a positive value.

Cost to Add Channel

This is the monetary dollar or currency amount required to add another channel in the queuing models, to determine the optimal number of channels to have available, and is a positive value.

Coupon and Coupons (Series)

This is the coupon payment in dollars or currency of a debt or callable debt, and is used in the options-adjusted spread model to determine the required spreads for a risky and callable bond. For Coupons, it is a time series of cash coupon payments at specific times.

Coupon Rate

This is the coupon payment per year, represented in percent, and is used in various debt-based options and credit options where the underlying is a coupon-paying bond or debt, and this value can be zero or positive.

Covariances (Series)

This is the $n \times n$ variance-covariance matrix required to compute the portfolio returns and risk levels given each individual asset's allocation (see Asset Allocation), and these values can be negative, zero, or positive values. The *Variance-Covariance Matrix* tool in the Modeling Toolkit can be used to compute this matrix given the raw data of each asset's historical values.

Credit Exposures

This is the number of credit or debt lines that exists in a portfolio, and it has to be a positive integer.

Credit Spread

This is the percentage spread difference between a risky debt or security and the risk-free rate with comparable maturity, and is typically a positive value.

Cum Amount

This is a dollar or currency amount, used in a Time Switch option, where the holder receives the Accumulated (Cum) Amount $\times$ Time Steps each time the asset price exceeds the strike price for a call option (or falls below the strike price for a put option).

Currency Units

This input parameter is a positive value and is used in a Foreign Takeover option with a foreign exchange element, which means that if a successful takeover ensues (if the value of the foreign firm denominated in foreign currency is less than the foreign currency units required), then the option holder has the right to purchase the number of foreign currency units at the predetermined strike price (denominated in exchange rates of the domestic currency to the foreign currency) at the expiration date of the option.

Current Asset

This is the sum of cash, accounts receivable, and inventories on a balance sheet, that is, the short-term liquid assets, and has to be a positive value.

Current Price

This is the price level of a variable at the current time. This known value has to be positive, and is used for forecasting future price levels.

Current Yield

This is the current spot interest rate or yield, used to price risky debt with callable and embedded option features, and has to be a positive value.

Custom Risk-free (Series)

This is a series of risk-free rates with the relevant times of occurrence—that is, where there are two columns with multiple rows and the first column is the time in years (positive values) and the second column lists the risk-free rates (each value has to be a positive percentage), and both columns have multiple rows. This variable is used in the custom option models where risk-free rates and volatilities are allowed to change over time.

Custom Volatility (Series)

This is a series of annualized volatilities with the relevant times of occurrence—that is, where there are two columns with multiple rows and the first column is the time in years (positive values) and the second column lists the volatilities (each value has to be a positive percentage), and both columns have multiple rows. This variable is used in the custom option models where risk-free rates and volatilities are allowed to change over time.

CY Reversion

This is the rate of mean reversion of the convenience yield (CY) of a futures and commodities contract, and has to be zero or a positive value. The convenience yield is simply the rate differential between a nonarbitrage futures and spot price and a real-life fair market value of the futures price, and can be computed using the MTConvenienceYield function. With the raw data or computed convenience yields, the mean reversion rate can be calibrated using Risk Simulator's *Statistical Analysis* tool.

CY Volatility

This is the annualized volatility of the convenience yield (CY) of a futures and commodities contract, and has to be a positive value. The convenience yield is simply the rate differential between a nonarbitrage futures and spot price and a real-life fair market value of the futures price, and can be computed using the MTConvenienceYield function. The volatility can be computed using the approaches discussed in the Volatility definition.

Daily Volatilities (Series)

This is a series of daily volatilities of various asset classes (arranged in a column with multiple rows), used in computing the portfolio Value at Risk, where each volatility is typically small but has to be a positive value. This can also be computed using annualized volatilities and dividing them by the square root of number of trading days per year.

Days Per Year

This is the number of days per year to compute days sales outstanding, and is typically set to 365 or 360. The parameter has to be a positive integer.

Debt Maturity

The maturity period measured in years for the debt, typically this is the maturity of a corporate bond, and is a positive value, used in the asset-equity parity models, to determine the market value of assets and market value of debt, based on the book value of debt and book value of assets as well as the equity volatility.

Default Probability

This is the probability of default, set between 0% and 100%, to compute the credit risk shortfall value, and can be computed using the Merton probability of default models, as well as other probability of default models in the Modeling Toolkit.

Defaults

This is the number of credit or debt defaults within some specified period, and can be zero or a positive integer.

Defective Units (Series)

These is the series of numbers of defective units in Six Sigma models, to compute the upper and lower control limits for quality control charts; the numbers are typically zero or positive integers, arranged in a column with multiple rows.

Defects

This is a single value indicative of the number of defects in a process for Six Sigma quality control, to determine items such as process capability (Cpk), defects per million opportunities (DPMO), and defects per unit (DPU). This parameter is either zero or a positive integer.

Delta

Delta is a precision measure used in Six Sigma models. Specifically, the Delta Precision is the accuracy or precision with which the standard deviation may be estimated. For instance, a 0.10% Delta with 5% Alpha for 2 tails means that the estimated mean is plus or minus 0.10%, at a 90% $(1 - 2 \times Alpha)$ confidence level.

Deltas (Series)

This is a series of delta measures, where the delta is defined here as a sensitivity measure of an option. Specifically, it is the instantaneous change of the option value with an instantaneous change in the stock price. You can use the MTCallDelta function to compute this input, which typically consists of positive values arranged in a column with multiple rows.

Demand

This is the level of demand for a particular manufactured product, used to determine the optimal economic order quantity or the optimal level of inventory to have on hand, and has to be a positive integer.

Depreciation

This is the level of depreciation, measured in dollars or currency levels, as a noncash expense add-back to obtain the cash flows available to equity and cash flows available to the firm.

DF

This is the degrees of freedom (DF) input used in the chi-square and t-distributions. The higher this value, the more closely these distributions approach the normal or Gaussian distribution. This input parameter is a positive integer, and is typically larger than 1. You can use Risk Simulator's distributional fitting tool to fit your existing data to obtain the best estimate of DF. Alternatively, the *Distribution Analysis* tool can also be used to see the effects of higher and lower DF values.

DF Denominator

This is the degrees of freedom (DF) of the denominator used in the F-distribution. This input parameter is a positive integer, and is typically larger than 1. You can use Risk Simulator's distributional fitting tool to fit your existing data to obtain the best estimate of DF. Alternatively, the *Distribution Analysis* tool can also be used to see the effects of higher and lower DF values.

DF Numerator

This is the degrees of freedom (DF) of the numerator used in the F-distribution. This input parameter is a positive integer, and is typically larger than 1. You can use Risk Simulator's distributional fitting tool to fit your existing data to obtain the best estimate of DF. Alternatively, the *Distribution Analysis* tool can also be used to see the effects of higher and lower DF values.

Discount Rate

This is the discount rate used to determine the price-to-earnings multiple by first using this input to value the future stock price. This parameter is a positive value, and in the case of the PE Ratio model it needs to be higher than the growth rate. Sometimes the weighted average cost of capital is used in its place for simplicity.

Dividend, Dividend Rate, Dividend 1 and 2

This is the dividend rate or dividend yield, in percent, and is typically either zero or positive. This parameter is not to be confused with Cash Dividend, which is a dollar or currency unit amount and can also be zero or positive. This variable is used many times in exotic and real options models. Dividend 1 and Dividend 2 are simply the dividend yields on the two underlying assets in a two-asset option.

Dividend Times (Series)

This is a series of times in years when the cash dividends in dollars or currency are paid on the underlying stock of an option, and can be zero or positive values. This input variable is used in the Generalized Black-Scholes model with cash dividends, and the timing of these cash dividends is listed as a series in a single column with multiple rows.

Domestic RF

This is the domestic risk-free (RF) rate used in foreign or takeover options that requires the inputs of a domestic and foreign RF rate, which in this case has to be a positive value.

Down

This is the down step size used in an asymmetrical state option pricing model, and needs to be a value between 0 and 1. This value should be carefully calibrated to the option's maturity and the number of lattice steps, to denote the down step size per lattice step.

DSO

This is days sales outstanding (DSO), or the average accounts receivables divided by the average sales per day, to be used to compute the profitability of issuing new credit to a corporation. This input variable can be computed using the MTRatiosDaysSalesOutstanding function, and the parameter has to be a positive value.

DT

This is the time between steps; that is, suppose a bond or an option has a maturity of 10 years and a 100-step lattice is used. DT is 0.1, or 0.1 years will elapse with every lattice step taken. This parameter has to be a positive value, and is used in the MTBDT lattice functions.

Duration

This variable is typically computed using some MTBondDuration function, but as an input it represents the conversion factor used in converting a spread or interest rate differential into a dollar currency amount, and is used in several debt-based options. This input has to be a positive value, and in some cases is set to 1 in order to determine the debt-based option's value in percentage terms.

EBIT

Earnings before interest and taxes (EBIT) is used in several financial ratios analysis models. EBIT is also sometimes called operating income, and can be a negative or positive value.

Ending Plot

This variable is used in the options trading strategies (e.g., straddles, strangles, bull spreads, etc.), representing the last value to plot for the terminal stock price (the x-axis on an option payoff chart); it has to be higher than the Starting Plot value, and is a positive input.

EPS

Earnings per share (EPS) is net income divided by the number of shares outstanding; EPS is used in several financial ratios analysis models, and can take on either negative or positive values.

Equity Correlation

This is the correlation coefficient between two equity stock prices (not returns), and can be between −1 and +1 (inclusive), including 0.

Equity Multiplier

Equity multiplier is the ratio of total assets to the total equity of the company, indicating the amount of increase in the ability of the existing equity to generate the available total assets, and has to be a positive value.

Equity Price or Share Price

This is the same as stock price per share, and has to be a positive value.

Equity Value or Total Equity

This is the same as total equity in a firm, computed by the number of shares outstanding times the market share price, and can be either zero or a positive value.

Equity Volatility

This is the volatility of stock prices, not to be confused with the volatility of internal assets. The term Volatility is used interchangeably with Equity Volatility, but this term is used in models that require both equity volatility and some other volatility (e.g., asset volatility or foreign exchange rate volatility), and this value is typically positive.

Exchange Rate

This is the foreign exchange rate from one currency to another, and is the spot rate for domestic currency to foreign currency; it has to be a positive value.

Exercise Multiple

This is the suboptimal exercise multiple ratio, computed as the historical average stock price at which an option with similar type and class, held by a similar group of people, was executed, divided by the strike price of the option. This multiple has to be greater than 1. This input variable is used in valuing employee stock options with suboptimal exercise behaviors.

Expand Factor

This is the expansion factor for real options models of options to expand, and has to be a positive value greater than 1.0, computed using the total expanded net present value (base case plus the expanded case) divided by the base case net present value.

Expected Value

This is the expected value or mean value of a project's net present value, used to determine the rough estimate of an annualized implied volatility of a project using the management approach (volatility to probability approach), and is typically a positive value.

Face Value

This is the face value of a bond, in dollars or currency, and has to be a positive value. This face value is the redeemable value at the maturity of the bond (typically, this value is $1,000 or $10,000).

First Period

This input variable is used in a spread option, where the maturity of a spread option is divided into two periods (from time zero to this first period, and from the first period to maturity) and the spread option pays the difference between the maximum values of these two periods. This input parameter has to be greater than zero and less than the maturity of the spread option.

First Variable

This is the first variable used in a pentanomial lattice model to value exotic or real options problems. In the pentanomial lattice, two binomial lattices (a binomial lattice models two outcomes, up or down, evolved through the entire lattice) are combined to create a single rainbow lattice with two underlying variables multiplied together, to create five possible outcomes (UP1 and UP2, UP1 and DOWN2, Unchanged 1 and Unchanged 2, DOWN1 and UP2, and DOWN2 and DOWN2). This input parameter has to be a positive value.

Fixed FX Rate

This input variable is used in valuing Quanto options that are traded on exchanges around the world (also known as foreign equity options). The options are denominated in a currency other than that of the underlying asset. The option has an expanding or contracting coverage of the foreign exchange value of the underlying asset, based on the fixed exchange rate (domestic currency to foreign currency), and has to be a positive value.

Floor

This is the interest rate floor and is an interest derivative; it has to be a positive value. The valuation of the floor is done through computing the value of each of its floorlets and summing them up to determine the price of the derivative.

Foreign Exchange Volatility or Forex Volatility

This is the annualized volatility of foreign exchange rates, typically computed using the annualized logarithmic relative returns (use the MTVolatility function to compute this volatility based on historical exchange rates), and has to be a positive value.

Foreign Rate or Foreign RF

This is the foreign risk-free (RF) rate, used in foreign exchange or foreign equity options and valuation models, and has to be a positive value.

Foreign Value

This is the value of a foreign firm denominated in foreign currency, used in valuing a takeover option, and this value has to be a positive number.

Forward CY Correlation

This variable is sometimes truncated to "ForCYCorrel." It is the linear correlation between forward rates and convenience yields (CYs), and is used in valuing commodity options. Correlations have to be between −1 and +1 (typically noninclusive).

Forward Days

This is the positive integer representing the number of days into the future where there is a corresponding forward rate that is applicable.

Forward Price

This is the prearranged price of a contract set today for delivery in the future. Sometimes also used interchangeably in terms of the future price of an asset or commodity that may not be prearranged but is known with certainty or is the expected price in the future.

Forward Rate

This is the forward rate in a commodity option, and has to be a positive value.

Forward Reversion Rate or For-Reversion

This input variable is used in valuing commodity options. It computes the values of commodity-based European call and put options, where the convenience yield and forward rates are assumed to be mean-reverting and each has its own volatilities and cross-correlations, creating a complex multifactor model with interrelationships among the variables. The forward reversion rate is the rate of mean reversion of the forward rate, and is typically a small positive value; it can be determined and calibrated using Risk Simulator's *Statistical Analysis* tool.

Forward Time

This is the time in the future when a Forward Start option begins to become active, and this input parameter has to be a positive value greater than zero and less than the maturity of the option.

Forward Volatility or For-Volatility

This input variable is used in valuing commodity options. It computes the values of commodity-based European call and put options, where the convenience yield and forward rates are assumed to be mean-reverting and each has its own volatilities and cross-correlations, creating a complex multifactor model with interrelationships among the variables. The forward volatility is the annualized volatility of forward rates and prices, and has to be a positive value, typically computed using the annualized logarithmic relative returns of historical forward prices (use the MTVolatility function to compute this volatility based on historical prices). It has to be a positive value.

Free Cash Flow

This is the free cash flow available to the firm, and can be computed as the net income generated by the firm with all the modifications of noncash expense add-backs as well as capital expenditure reductions, or it can be computed using the three MTRatiosCashFlow models.

Future Price

This is the price in the future of any variable that is either known in advance or forecasted. This value is not the price of a futures contract, and is typically a positive value.

Future Returns

This is the returns of any variable that is either known in advance or forecasted. This value is not the returns on a futures contract, and can be positive or negative in value.

Futures, Futures Price, and Futures 1 or Futures 2

This is the price of the futures contract (if there are two futures contracts, there will be a numerical value, as in the futures spread options computations); must be a positive value.

Futures Maturity

This is the maturity of the futures contract, measured in years; must be a positive value.

Granularities

This input parameter has to be a positive integer value and is used in the computation of finite differences in obtaining the value of an option. Great care has to be taken to calibrate this input, using alternate closed-form solutions.

Gross Rent

This is the dollar or currency amount of annualized gross rent, and can be zero or a positive value; it is used in property valuation models.

Growth Rate

This positive percentage value is used in various locations and signifies the annualized average growth of some variable. In the financial ratios analysis, this would be the growth rate of dividends (and this value must be less than the discount rate used in the model). In contrast, this parameter is the annualized growth rate of assets for the Merton probability of default models, and this variable is used as the growth of a population or market in the S-curve forecast computation on curve saturation rates.

Holding Cost

This is the zero or positive dollar or currency cost of holding on to an additional unit of inventory, used in the economic order quantity models to determine the optimal level of inventories to hold.

Horizon

This is a positive value representing some time period denominated in years, and is used in forecasting future values of some variable.

Horizon Days

This is a positive integer value representing the number of holding days to compute a Value at Risk for, which typically is between 1 and 10 days, and calibrated to how long it will take on average for the bank or company to liquidate its assets to cover any extreme and catastrophic losses or to move out of a loss portfolio.

Inflation

This is the annualized rate of inflation, measured as a percentage, and is typically a positive value, although zero and negative values may occur but are rare.

Interest Lattice

This refers to the lattice that is developed for the underlying interest rates modeled for a yield curve and its spot volatilities over time, and is used in pricing interest-sensitive derivatives.

Interest Paid

This is the dollar or currency amount of interest paid per year, and is either zero or a positive value.

Interest Rate

This is the percentage interest paid per year, and is typically zero or a positive value.

Interest Rates (Series)

This is a series of annualized interest rates or discount rates in percent, in a column with multiple rows, used in computing a project's net present value or the price of a bond (given a corresponding series of cash flows).

Interest Volatility

This is the annualized volatility of interest rates, in percent, and has to be a positive value. See the definition of Volatility in this Glossary for details on some of the techniques used in computing volatility.

Inventory

This is the amount of inventories in dollars or currency, and can be determined from a company's balance sheet; it is typically a positive number but can sometimes take on a zero value.

Invested Capital

This is the dollar or currency amount of invested capital, and is typically a positive value, used to compute capital charge and economic capital of a project or firm.

Investment

This is the initial lump sum investment dollar or currency amount, used to compute the internal rate of return (IRR) of a project, and this value is a positive number (although it is used as a negative value in the model, enter the value as positive).

Jump Rate

This variable is used in a Jump-Diffusion option, which is similar to a regular option with the exception that instead of assuming that the underlying asset follows a lognormal Brownian Motion process, the process here follows a Poisson Jump-Diffusion process, and is used in the MTROJumpDiffusion models. That is, stock or asset prices follow jumps, and these jumps occur several times per year (observed from history). Cumulatively, these jumps explain a certain percentage of the total volatility of the asset. The jump rate can be determined using historical data or using Risk Simulator's *Statistical Analysis* tool to calibrate the jump rate.

Jump Size

Similar to the Jump Rate, the Jump Size is used to determine the size of a jump in a Jump-Diffusion option model. Typically, this value is greater than 1, to indicate how much the jump is from the previous period, and is used on the MTROJumpDiffusion models.

Jumps Per Year

An alternative input to the Jump Size is the number of jumps per year, as it is easier to calibrate the total number of jumps per year based on expectations or historical data; this input is a positive integer used in the MTMertonJumpDiffusion models.

Known X and Known Y Values

These are the historical or comparable data available and observable, in order to use the cubic spline model (both interpolate missing values and extrapolate and forecast beyond the sample dataset), which is usually applied in yield curve and interest rate term structure construction.

Kurtosis

This is the fourth moment of a distribution, measuring the distribution's peakedness and extreme values. An excess kurtosis of 0 is a normal distribution with "normal" peaks and extreme values, and this parameter can take on positive, zero, or negative values.

Lambda, Lambda 1, and Lambda 2

Lambda is the mean or average value used in a Poisson (an event occurring on average during a specified time period or area) and an exponential (the average rate of occurrence) distribution, and is also used in calibrating the yield curve models. Regardless of the use, lambda has to be a positive value.

Last Return

This input is used in the exponentially weighted moving average (EWMA) volatility forecast, representing the last period's return; it can be periodic or annualized, and can take on positive or negative values. If entering a periodic return, make sure to set the Periodicity input in the EWMA function to 1 to obtain a periodic volatility forecast, or the correct periodicity value to obtain the annualized volatility forecast. Conversely, if entering an annualized return, set periodicity to be equal to 1 to obtain the annualized volatility forecast.

Last Volatility

This input is used in the EWMA volatility forecast, representing the last period's volatility; it can be periodic or annualized, and can take on only positive values. If entering a periodic volatility, make sure to set the Periodicity input in the EWMA function to 1 to obtain a periodic volatility forecast, or the correct periodicity value to obtain the annualized volatility forecast. Conversely, if entering an annualized volatility, set periodicity to be equal to 1 to obtain the annualized volatility forecast.

Likely

This is the most likely or mode value in a triangular distribution, and can take on any value, but has to be greater than or equal to the minimum and less than or equal to the maximum value inputs in the distribution.

Loan Value Ratio

This is a positive percentage ratio of the amount of loan required to purchase a real estate investment to the value of the real estate.

Location

This is the location parameter in the Pareto distribution, also used as the starting point or minimum of the distribution, and is sometimes also called the Beta parameter in the Pareto distribution; it can only take on a positive value.

Long Term Level

This is the long-term level to which the underlying variable will revert in the long run; it is used in mean-reverting option models, where the underlying variable is stochastically changing but reverts to some long-term mean rate, which has to be a positive value.

Long Term Rate

This is similar to the long-term level, but the parameter here is a percent interest rate, a long-term rate to which the underlying interest rate process reverts over time.

Lookback Length

This input variable is used in a floating strike partial lookback option, where at expiration the payoff on the call option is being able to purchase the underlying asset at the minimum observed price from inception to the end of the lookback time. Conversely, the put will allow the option holder to sell at the maximum observed asset price from inception to the end of the lookback time.

Lookback Start

This input variable is used in fixed strike lookback options, where the strike price is predetermined, such that at expiration, the payoff on the call option is the difference between the maximum observed asset price and the strike price during the time between the Lookback Start period to the maturity of the option. Conversely, the put will pay the maximum difference between the lowest observed asset price and the strike price during the time between the starting period of the lookback to the maturity of the option.

Lost Sales Cost

This is the dollar or currency amount of a lost sale, typically zero or a positive value, and is used in the economic order quantity models to determine the optimal levels of inventory to hold or levels of production to have.

Lower Barrier

This is the lower barrier stock price in a double barrier or graduated barrier option, where this barrier is typically lower than the existing stock price and lower than the upper barrier level; it must be a positive value.

Lower Delta

This is the instantaneous options delta (a Greek sensitivity measure that can be computed using the MTCallDelta or MTPutDelta functions) of the percentage change in option value given the instantaneous change in stock prices for the lower barrier stock price level. This value is typically set at zero or a positive value.

Lower Strike

This is the lower strike price (a positive value) in a Supershare option, which is traded or embedded in supershare funds and is related to a Down and Out, Up and Out double barrier option, where the option has value only if the stock or asset price is between the upper and lower barriers; at expiration, it provides a payoff equivalent to the stock or asset price divided by the lower strike price.

Lower Value

This input variable is used in the MTDT lattices for computing option-adjusted spreads in debt with convertible or callable options, and represents the value that is one cell adjacent to the right and directly below the current value in a lattice. All values in a lattice and this input must be positive.

LSL

This is the lower specification level (LSL) of a Six Sigma measured process—that is, the prespecified value that is the lowest obtainable or a value that the process should not be less than.

Marginal Cost

This is the additional dollar or currency cost to the bank or credit-granting institution of approving one extra credit application, and is used to determine if a credit should be approved; this parameter is typically a positive value.

Marginal Profit

This is the additional dollar or currency profit to the bank or credit-granting institution of approving one extra credit application, and is used to determine if a credit should be approved; this parameter is typically a positive value.

Market Price Risk

This input variable is used in mean-reverting option models as well as in the CIR, Merton, and Vasicek models of risky debt, where the underlying interest rate process is also assumed to be mean-reverting. The market price of risk is also synonymous with the Sharpe ratio, or bang for the buck—that is, the expected returns of a risky asset less the risk-free rate, all divided by the standard deviation of the excess returns.

Market Return

This is the positive percentage of the annualized expected rate of return on the market, where a typical index such as the Standard & Poor's 500 is used as a proxy for the market.

Market Volatility

This input variable is the annualized volatility of a market index, used to model the probability of default for both public and private companies using an index, a group of comparables, or the market, assuming that the company's asset and debt book values are known, as well as the asset's annualized volatility. Based on this volatility and the correlation of the company's assets to the market, we can determine the probability of default.

Matrix A and Matrix B (Series)

This is simply an $n \times m$ matrix where n and m can be any positive integer, and is used for matrix math and matrix manipulations.

Maturity

This is the period until a certain contract, project, or option matures, measured in years, and has to be a positive value.

Maturity Bought

This input variable is the maturity, measured in years (a positive value), of a call option that is bought in a Delta-Gamma hedge that provides a hedge against larger changes in the underlying stock or asset value. This is done by buying some equity shares and a call option, which are funded by borrowing some amount of money and selling a call option at a different strike price. The net amount is a zero sum game, making this hedge costless.

Maturity Extend

This is the maturity in years, for the writer extendible option of the extended maturity, and has to be a positive value.

Maturity Sold

This input variable is the maturity, measured in years, of a call option that is sold in a Delta-Gamma hedge that provides a hedge against larger changes in the underlying stock or asset value. This is done by buying some equity shares and a call option, which are funded by borrowing some amount of money and selling a call option at a different strike price. The net amount is a zero sum game, making this hedge costless.

Maximum or Max

This is the maximum value of a distribution (e.g., in a discrete uniform, triangular, or uniform distribution), indicating the highest attainable value, and can be both positive or negative values, as well as integer (used in discrete uniform, triangular, or uniform distributions) or continuous (used in triangular and uniform distributions).

Mean

This is the arithmetic mean used in distributions (e.g., logistic, lognormal, and normal distributions) as well as the average levels in a Six Sigma process. This value can be positive (e.g., logistic and lognormal distributions) or negative (e.g., normal distribution), and is typically positive when applied in Six Sigma.

Mean-Reverting Rate

This is the rate of reversion of an underlying variable (typically interest rates, inflation rates, or some other commodity prices) to a long-run level. This parameter is either zero or positive, and the higher the value, the faster the variable's value reverts to the long-run mean. Use Risk Simulator's *Statistical Analysis* tool to determine this rate based on historical data.

Measurement Range (Series)

In each sampling group in a Six Sigma process, several measurements are taken, and the range (maximum value less the minimum value) is determined. This experiment is replicated multiple times through various sampling groups. The measurement range is hence a series of values (one value for each statistical sampling or experiment subgroup) arranged in a column with multiple rows, where each row represents a group. The range has to be a positive value and is typically a positive integer, and the results are used to determine the central line, as well as upper and lower control limits for quality control charts in Six Sigma.

Minimum or Min

This is the minimum value of a distribution (e.g., in a discrete uniform, triangular, or uniform distribution), indicating the lowest attainable value, and can be both positive or negative values, as well as integer (used in discrete uniform, triangular, or uniform distributions) or continuous (used in triangular and uniform distributions).

MV Debt

This is the market value (MV) of risky debt, and can be priced using the Asset-Equity Parity models using book values of debt and equity, and applying the equity volatility in the market. Typically, this value is different from the book value of debt, depending on the market volatility and internal asset values, but is always zero or a positive value.

MV Equity

This is the total market value (MV) of equity, computed by multiplying the number of outstanding shares by the market price of a share of the company's stock; a positive value.

MV Preferred Equity

This is the total market value (MV) of preferred equity, computed by multiplying the number of outstanding shares by the market price of a share of the company's preferred stock, and is a positive value.

Net Fixed Asset

This is the total net fixed assets (gross fixed long-term assets less any accumulated depreciation levels), and is a positive value, obtained from a company's balance sheet.

Net Income

This is the net income after taxes, in dollar or currency amounts, and can be either positive or negative.

New Debt Issue

This is the amount of new debt issued to raise additional capital, and is either zero or positive.

Nominal CF

This is the nominal cash flow (CF) amounts, including inflation, and can be negative or positive. Nominal cash flow is the real cash flow levels plus inflation adjustments.

Nominal Rate

This is the quoted or nominal interest rate, which is equivalent to the real rate of interest plus the inflation rate, and as such is typically higher than either the real interest rate or the inflation rate, and must be a positive value.

Nonpayment Probability

This is the probability that a debt holder will be unable to make a payment and will default for one time. Sometimes the probability of default can be used, but in most cases the single nonpayment probability is higher than the complete default probability.

NOPAT

Net operating profits after taxes (NOPAT) is typically computed as net revenues less any operating expenses and less applicable taxes, making this value typically higher than net income, which accounts for other items such as depreciation and interest payments. This parameter can be positive or negative.

Notes or Notes Payable

The amount in dollars or currency for notes payable, a form of short-term current liability, it is typically zero or a positive value.

Notional

This is a positive dollar amount indicating the underlying contractual amount (e.g., in a swap).

Observed Max

This is the observed maximum stock price in the past for a lookback Asian option, and this parameter has to be a positive amount and larger than the observed minimum value.

Observed Min

This is the observed minimum stock price in the past for a lookback Asian option, and this parameter has to be a positive amount and smaller than the observed maximum value.

Old Value

This is the previous period's value or old value, used in computing the S-curve forecast, and must be a positive value.

Operating Expenses

The dollar or currency amount of total operating expenses (other than direct expenses or cost of goods sold, but including items like sales and general administrative expenses) has to be a positive value.

Option Maturity

This is the maturity of an option measured in years, and has to be a positive value; the longer the maturity, holding everything else constant, the higher the value of the option.

Option Strike

This is the contractual strike price of an option measured in dollars or currency levels, and has to be a positive value. Holding everything else constant, a higher strike price means a lower call option value and a higher put option value.

Option Value

This is the value of an option, and has to be either zero or a positive value. The option value is never negative, and can be computed through a variety of methods including closed-form models (e.g., Black-Scholes and American approximation models); lattices (binomial, trinomial, quadranomial, and pentanomial lattices); simulation; and analytical techniques (variance reduction, finite differences, and iterative processes).

Other Assets

The value of any short-term indirect or intangible assets is usually a zero or positive value.

Payables

The amount in dollars or currency values for accounts payable, a form of short-term current liability, is typically zero or a positive value.

Payment Probability

This is used to compute the cost of rejecting a good credit by accounting for the chances that payment will be received each time when it is due, and is a positive percentage value between 0% and 100%.

Percentile

This parameter has to be a positive value between 0% and 100%, and is used in Value at Risk computations and implied volatility computations. In VaR analysis, this value is typically 95%, 99%, or 99.9%, whereas it has to be lower than 50% for the worst-case scenario volatility model and higher than 50% for the best-case scenario volatility model.

Periodicity

Periodicity in the context of barrier options means how often during the life of the option the asset or stock value will be monitored to see if it breaches a barrier. As an example, entering 1 means annual monitoring, 12 implies monthly monitoring, 52 for weekly, 252 for daily trading, 365 for daily calendar, and 1,000,000 for continuous monitoring. In the application of GARCH volatility forecasts, if weekly stock price data is used, enter 52 for periodicity (250 for number of trading days per year if daily data is used, and 12 for monthly data). Regardless of the application, this parameter is a positive integer.

Periodic Rate

This is the interest rate per period, and is used to compute the implied rate of return on an annuity; this value has to be a positive percent.

Periods

This refers to a positive integer value representing the number of payment periods in an annuity, and is used to compute the equivalent annuity payment based on the periodic rate.

Population

This is used in the hypergeometric discrete distribution, indicating the population size. Clearly this positive integer value has to be larger than the population successes and is at least 2. The total number of items or elements or the population size is a fixed number, a finite population; the population size must be less than or equal to 1,750, the sample size (the number of trials) represents a portion of the population, and the known initial probability of success in the population changes after each trial.

Population Success or Pop Success

This is used in the hypergeometric discrete distribution, indicating the number of successes of a trait in a population. Clearly this positive integer value has to be smaller than the population size. The hypergeometric distribution is a distribution where the actual trials change the probability for each subsequent trial and are called *trials without replacement*. For example, suppose a box of manufactured parts is known to contain some defective parts. You choose a part from the box, find it is defective, and remove the part from the box. If you choose another part from the box, the probability that it is defective is somewhat lower than for the first part because you have removed a defective part. If you had replaced the defective part, the probabilities would have remained the same, and the process would have satisfied the conditions for a binomial distribution. The total number of items or elements (the population size) is a fixed number, a finite population; the population size must be less than or equal to 1,750, the sample size (the number of trials) represents a portion of the population, and the known initial probability of success in the population changes after each trial.

PPE

This is the dollar or currency value of plant, property, and equipment (PPE) values, and is either zero or positive.

Preferred Dividend

This is the dollar or currency amount of total dividends paid to preferred stocks (dividends per share multiplied by the number of outstanding shares), and is a positive value.

Preferred Stock

This is the price of a preferred stock per share multiplied by the number of preferred shares outstanding, and has to be a positive value.

Previous Value

This is the value of some variable in the previous period, used in forecasting time-series data. This has to be a positive value.

Price and CY Correlation

This is the correlation between bond price returns and convenience yields (CYs), used in the computation of commodity options, and can take on any value between –1 and +1, inclusive.

Price and Forward Correlation

This is the correlation between bond price returns and future price returns, used in the computation of commodity options, and can take on any value between –1 and +1, inclusive.

Price Improvement

This is a percentage value of the price of a real estate property that went to improvements, and is used to compute the depreciation on the property.

Price Lattice

This is the price lattice of an interest-based derivative (e.g., bond option) where the underlying is the term structure of interest rates with its own volatilities.

Principal Repaid

This is the dollar or currency amount indicating the value of principal of debt repaid, and is used to compute the adjusted cash flow to equity of a levered firm.

Probability

This is a probability value between 0% and 100% and used in the inverse cumulative distribution function (ICDF) of any distribution, where given a probability level and the relevant distributional parameters, it will return the X value of the distribution. For instance, in tossing a coin two times, using the binomial distribution (trials is set to 2 and the probability of success, in this case, obtaining heads in the coin toss, is set to 50%), the ICDF of a 25% probability parameter will return an X value of 0. That is, the probability of getting no heads (X of zero) is exactly 25%.

Profit Margin

This is the percentage of net income to total sales, and is typically a positive value, although zero and negative values are possible.

Proportion

This is the proportion of defects in a Six Sigma model to determine the requisite sample size to obtain in order to reach the desired Type I and Type II errors, and this value is between 0 and 1, inclusive.

Put Maturity

This is the maturity of the put option, measured in years, and this parameter is a positive value.

Put Strike

This is the contractual strike price for the put option, and has to be a positive value. Sometimes this variable has different suffixes (e.g., Put Strike Sell Low, Put Strike Buy High, and so forth, whenever there might be more than one put option in the portfolio of option strategies, and these suffixes represent whether this particular put is bought or sold, and whether the strike price is higher or lower than the other put option).

Put Value

This is the fair market value of the put option, and sometimes the theoretical price of a put option is used in its place when market information is unavailable. This parameter requires a positive input. Sometimes this variable has different suffixes (e.g., Put Value Sell Low, Put Value Buy High, and so forth, whenever there might be more than one put option in the portfolio of option strategies, and these suffixes represent whether this particular put is bought or sold, and whether the premium paid for this put option or the option value is higher or lower than the other put option).

PV Asset or Present Value of the Asset

This is the ubiquitous input in all real options models, and is the sum of the present values of all net benefits from a real options project or its underlying asset. Sometimes the net present value is used as a proxy, but typically the implementation cost is separated from the PV Asset value, such that PV Asset less any implementation cost, if executed immediately, equals the net present value of the project. The PV Asset input has to be a positive value.

Quantities (Series)

This is a series of positive integers indicating the number of a specific class of options in a portfolio in order to compute the Value at Risk of a portfolio of options, and these values are typically arranged in a column with multiple rows.

Quantity 1 and Quantity 2

These are positive integers indicating the amount of the first asset that is exchanged for the second asset in an asset exchange option with two correlated underlying assets.

Random

This value replaces the Probability value when used to obtain the inverse cumulative distribution function (ICDF) of a probability distribution for the purposes of running a simulation. This variable is between 0 and 1, inclusive, and is from a continuous uniform distribution. By choosing a random value between 0 and 1 with equal probability of any continuous value between these two numbers, we obtain a probability value between 0% and 100%, and when mapped against the ICDF of a specific distribution, it will return the relevant X value from that distribution. Then, when repeated multiple times, it will yield a simulation of multiple trials or outcomes from that specific distribution. You can use Excel's RAND() function for this input.

Rate of Return

This is the annualized percentage required rate of return on equity, used to compute the price to earnings ratio.

Real Cash Flow

This is the real cash flow level after adjusting and deducting inflation rates. Specifically, the real cash flow plus inflation is the nominal cash flow.

Real Rate

This is the real rate of return or real interest rate after inflation adjustments; in other words, the real rate of return plus the inflation rate is the nominal rate of return.

Receivables

The dollar or currency amount of accounts receivable, a short-term or current asset from the balance sheet, is usually a positive value or zero.

Recovery Period

This is the recovery period in determining the depreciation of real estate investments, in number of years.

Recovery Rate

This is the rate of recovery to determine the credit risk shortfall—that is, the percentage of credit that defaults and the proportion that is recoverable.

Remaining Time

This is the amount of time remaining in years in an Asian option model.

Return on Asset

This is the return on a project or an asset, computed by taking net income after taxes and dividing it by total assets, and this parameter value can be positive or negative.

Returns (Series)

These are the percentage returns on various assets in a portfolio, arranged in a column with multiple rows; they can be both negative and positive, and are used to compute the portfolio's weighted average returns.

Revenues

This is the dollar or currency amount of net revenues per year.

Risk-free Rate and Risk-free 0

This is the annualized risk-free rate of government securities comparable in maturity to the underlying asset under analysis (e.g., the risk-free rate with the same maturity as the option), and has to be positive. Risk-free 0 is the default variable for a changing risk-free rate option model, where if the risk-free series is left blank, this single rate is used throughout the maturity of the option.

ROIC

This is the return on invested capital (ROIC), and can be computed using the MTRatiosROIC function, using net operating profit after taxes, working capital, and assets used. This value can be negative or positive.

Row

This is the row number in a lattice, and starts from 0 at the top or first row.

Sales

This is the annual total sales of the company in dollar or currency values and is a positive number. Sales Growth is a related variable that looks at the difference of sales between two periods in percentage, versus Sales Increase, which is the difference in sales but denominated in currency amounts.

Salvage

This is the positive salvage value in dollars or currency value when an option is abandoned; the holder of the abandonment option will receive this amount.

Sample Size

This is the positive integer value of sample size in each subgroup used in the computation of a Six Sigma quality control chart and computation of control limits.

Savings

The positive dollar or currency value of savings when the option to contract is executed—that is, the amount of money saved.

Second Variable

This is the second underlying variable used in a pentanomial lattice, where the underlying asset lattice is the product of the first and second variables; this input parameter has to be positive.

Service Rate

This parameter measures the average rate of service per period (typically per day or per hour)—that is, on average, how many people will be serviced in a queue in a period (e.g., per hour or per day). This value has to be positive.

Shape

This is the second input assumption in the Pareto distribution, determining the shape of the distribution, and is a positive value.

Share Price or Equity Price

This is the current share or stock price per share at the time of valuation, used in a variety of options models, and has to be a positive dollar or currency value.

Shares

This is the number of outstanding shares of a stock, and is a positive integer.

Sigma

This is the variation or standard deviation measure of variation within a process and is used in Six Sigma quality control models. This parameter has to be a positive value.

Sigma Service Rate

This is the variation or standard deviation measure of variation within the service rate used in Six Sigma process and quality control models. This value has to be a positive value.

Single Interest

This is the interest rate used in computing a bond's convexity and duration models, the second- and first-level sensitivities, respectively. This input parameter has to be a positive value.

Single Period

This is the period in years or months that is used to interpolate the missing value within a range of values, applied in the MTLinerInterpolation model (used together with the Time Periods series and corresponding Values series).

Skewness

This is the third moment or measure of skew in a distribution. This input parameter is used in an Alternate Distribution option model, where the underlying distribution of the asset returns is assumed to be skewed and has some kurtosis. This value can be either positive or negative.

S Max

This is the observed maximum stock price in the past in an extreme spread option, where such options have their maturities divided into two segments, starting from time zero to the First Time Period (first segment) and from the First Time Period to Maturity (second segment). An extreme spread call option pays the difference between the maximum asset value from the second segment and the maximum value of the first segment. Conversely, the put pays the difference between the minimum of the second segment's asset value and the minimum of the first segment's asset value. A reverse call pays the minimum from the first segment less the minimum of the second segment, whereas a reverse put pays the maximum of the first segment less the maximum of the second segment. This variable is the observed maximum stock value in the observable past.

S Min

This is the observed minimum stock price in the past in an extreme spread option, similar to the S Max variable as described previously.

Spot FX Rate

This is the input in a currency option, which is the current or spot exchange rate, computed by the ratio of the domestic currency to the foreign currency; it has to be a positive value.

Spot Price

The spot price is the same as the existing or current stock price, and is a positive value. We use this definition to differentiate between the spot and average or future price levels, and this parameter has to be positive.

Spot Rate, Spot Rate 1, and Spot Rate 2

This is the input in an exotic currency forward option, which is the current or spot interest rate, and has to be a positive value.

Spot Volatility

This is the commodity option's spot price return's annualized volatility, as measured by the zero bond price level, and this value has to be positive.

Spread

Certain types of debt come with an option-embedded provision; for instance, a bond might be callable if the market price exceeds a certain value (when prevailing interest rates drop, making it more profitable for the issuing company to call the debt and reissue new bonds at the lower rate) or prepayment allowance of mortgages or lines of credit and debt. This input is the option-adjusted spread (i.e., the additional premium that should be charged on the option provision). This value is computed using an optimization or internal search algorithm.

Standard Deviation

The standard deviation or sigma is the second moment of a distribution, and can be defined as the average dispersion of all values about the central mean; it is an input into the normal distribution. The higher the sigma level, the wider the spread and the higher the risk or uncertainty. When applying it as a normal distribution's parameter, it is the standard deviation of the population and has to be a positive value (there is no point in using a normal distribution with a sigma of zero, which is nothing but a single-point estimate, where all points in the distribution fall exactly at the mean, generating a vertical line).

Standard Deviation of Demand

This is the measure of the variability of demand as used in the determination of economic order quantity, and this value is either zero or positive.

Standard Deviation of Lead Time

This is the measure of the variability of lead time it takes to obtain the inventory or product after it is ordered, as used in the determination of economic order quantity, and this value is either zero or positive.

Starting Plot

This variable is used in the options trading strategies (e.g., straddles, strangles, bull spreads, and so forth), representing the first value to plot for the terminal stock price (the x-axis on an option payoff chart); it has to be lower than the Ending Plot value, and is a positive input.

Steps

This is a positive integer value (typically at least 5, and between 100 and 1000) denoting the total number of steps in a lattice, where the higher the number of steps, the higher the level of precision but the longer the computational time.

Stock

This is the current stock price per share at the time of valuation, used in a variety of options models, and has to be a positive dollar or currency value.

Stock Index

This is the stock index level, and must be a positive value, measured at the time of valuation; it is used in index options computations.

Stock Prices (Series)

This is a list of stock prices over time in a series as used in the GARCH volatility model (MTGARCH) or computation of the Sharpe ratio (MTSharpeRatio), listed in chronological order (e.g., Jan, Feb, Mar, and so forth) in a single column with multiple rows, versus stock prices at valuation dates for various options in a portfolio, when used to compute the portfolio's Value at Risk (MTVarOptions).

Stock Volatility

This is the same as Equity Volatility or simply Volatility described in this Glossary (and used interchangeably), but this definition is used when multiple volatilities are required in the model, in order to reduce any confusion.

Strike, Strike 1, and Strike 2

The strike price in an option is the contractually prespecified price in advance at which the underlying asset (typically a stock) can be bought (call) or sold (put). Holding everything else constant, a higher (lower) strike price means a lower (higher) call option value and a higher (lower) put option value. This input parameter has to be a positive value, and in some rare cases it can be set to very close to zero for a costless strike option. Strike 1 and Strike 2 are used when referring to exotic option inputs with two underlying assets (e.g., exchange options or a 3D binomial model).

Strike Bought

This is the positive dollar or currency strike price of an option (usually a call) purchased in a Delta-Gamma hedge that provides a hedge against larger changes in the underlying stock or asset value. This is done by buying some equity shares and a call option, which are funded by borrowing some amount of money and selling a call option at a different strike price.

Strike Extend

This is the positive value of the new strike price in a writer extendible option, which is an insurance policy in case the option becomes worthless at maturity. Specifically, the call or put option can be automatically extended beyond the initial maturity date to an extended date with a new extended strike price, assuming that at maturity the option is out of the money and worthless. This extendibility provides a safety net of time for the option holder.

Strike FX Rate

This is the positive dollar or currency value of the contractual strike price denominated in exchange rates (domestic currency to foreign currency) for a foreign exchange option.

Strike Rate

This is the positive percentage value of the contractual strike price in a swaption (option to swap) or a futures option.

Strike Sold

This is the positive dollar or currency strike price of an option (usually a call) sold in a Delta-Gamma hedge that provides a hedge against larger changes in the underlying stock or asset value. This is done by buying some equity shares and a call option, which are funded by borrowing some amount of money and selling a call option at a different strike price.

Successes

This is the number of successes in the negative binomial distribution, which is useful for modeling the distribution of the number of additional trials required on top of the number of successful occurrences required. For instance, in order to close a total of 10 sales opportunities, how many extra sales calls would you need to make above 10 calls, given some probability of success in each call? The x-axis of the distribution shows the number of additional calls required or the number of failed calls. The number of trials is not fixed; the trials continue until the required number of successes, and the probability of success is the same from trial to trial. The successes input parameter has to be a positive integer less than 8,000.

Success Probability

This is a probability percent, between 0% and 100%, inclusive, for the probability of an event occurring, and is used in various discrete probability distributions such as the binomial distribution.

Tails

This is the number of tails in a distribution for hypothesis testing as applied in Six Sigma models to determine the adequate sample size for specific Type I and Type II errors. This parameter can only be either 1 or 2.

Tax Rate

This is the corporate tax rate in percent and has to be a positive value.

Tenure

This is the maturity of a swaption (option to swap).

This Category

This is the category index number (a positive integer—1, 2, 3, etc.), to compute the relative width of the credit rating table.

Time, Time 1, and Time 2

The Time variable is in years (positive value) to indicate the specific time period to forecast the interest rate level using various yield curve models, whereas Time 1 and Time 2 are the years for different spot rates, in order to impute the forward rate between these two periods.

Time Interval or DT

This is the positive time step input used in a time switch option, where the holder of the option receives the Accumulated Amount × Time Steps each time the asset price exceeds the strike price for a call option (or falls below the strike price for a put option). The time step is how often the asset price is checked as to whether the strike threshold has been breached (typically, for a one-year option with 252 trading days, set DT as 1/252).

Time Periods (Series)

This is a series of positive time periods in years, arranged in a column with multiple rows, concurrent with another column of values, so that any missing values within the range of the time periods can be interpolated using the MTLinearInterpolation and MTCubicSpline models. The time periods do not have to be linearly and sequentially increasing.

Timing (Series)

This is a series of positive time periods in years, arranged in a column with multiple rows, concurrent with another column of cash flows, so that the present value or price of the bond or some other present value computations can be done. Typically, the timing in years is linearly increasing.

Total Asset

This is the total assets in a company, including all short-term and long-term assets, and can be determined from the company's balance sheets. Typically, this parameter is a positive value, and is used in financial ratios analysis.

Total Capital

This is the total dollar or currency amount of capital invested in order to compute the economic value added in a project.

Total Category

This is a positive integer value in determining the number of credit rating categories required (e.g., AAA, AA, A, etc.). Typically, this value is between 3 and 12.

Total Debt

This is the total debt in a company, including all short-term and long-term debt, and can be determined from the company's balance sheets. Typically, this parameter is zero or a positive value, and is used in financial ratios analysis.

Total Equity or Equity Value

This is the total common equity in a company, and can be determined from the company's balance sheets. Typically, this parameter is zero or a positive value.

Total Liability

This is the total liabilities in a company, including all short-term and long-term liabilities, and can be determined from the company's balance sheets. Typically, this parameter is zero or a positive value, and is used in financial ratios analysis.

Trading Ratio

This is the number of trading days left until maturity divided by the number of trading days in a year (typically around 250 days), and is used to compute the plain vanilla option value after adjusting for the number of trading days left; it is typically a positive value.

Trials

This value is used in several places. For a probability distribution, it denotes the number of trials or events (e.g., in a binomial distribution where a coin is tossed 10 times, the number of trials in this case is 10) or denotes the number of simulation trials and iterations to complete in order to compute the value of an option using the simulation approach. Regardless, this parameter has to be a positive integer.

Units

This is the positive integer value denoting the number of units sampled in a Six Sigma quality control study, to determine the number of defects and proportion of defects.

Units Fulfilled

This zero or positive integer input variable is used in the Time Switch option model, where in such an option, the holder receives the Accumulated Amount × Time Steps each time the asset price exceeds the strike price for a call option within the maturity period (or falls below the strike price for a put option). Sometimes the option has already accumulated past amounts (or as agreed to in the option as a minimum guaranteed payment) as measured by the number of time units fulfilled (which is typically set at zero).

Unlevered Cost of Equity

This is the cost of equity in an unlevered firm with no debt, and has to be a positive value, used to compute the weighted average cost of capital for a company.

Up

This is the up step size used in an asymmetrical state option pricing model, and needs to be a value greater than 1. This value should be carefully calibrated to the option's maturity and the number of lattice steps, to denote the up step size per lattice step.

Upper Barrier

This is the upper barrier stock price in a double barrier or graduated barrier option, where this barrier is typically higher than the existing stock price and higher than the lower barrier level; it must be a positive value.

Upper Delta

This is the instantaneous options delta (a Greek sensitivity measure that can be computed using the MTCallDelta or MTPutDelta functions) of the percentage change in option value given the instantaneous change in stock prices, for the upper barrier stock price level. This value is typically set at zero or a positive value.

Upper Strike

This is the upper strike price (a positive value) in a Supershare option, which is traded or embedded in supershare funds, and is related to a Down and Out, Up and Out double barrier option, where the option has value only if the stock or asset price is between the upper and lower barriers, and at expiration provides a payoff equivalent to the stock or asset price divided by the lower strike price.

Upper Value

This input variable is used in the MTDT lattices for computing option-adjusted spreads in debt with convertible or callable options, and represents the value that is one cell adjacent to the right and directly above the current value in a lattice. All values in a lattice and this input must be positive.

USL

This is the upper specification level (USL) of a Six Sigma measured process—that is, the prespecified value that is the highest obtainable value or a value that the process should not exceed.

Vacancy Factor and Collection Factor

This is the percentage (between 0% and 100%) where the ratio of vacancies or noncollectable rent occurs as a percentage of 100% occupancy, and is used in the valuation of real estate properties.

Values (Series)

This is a series of values or numbers, either negative of positive values, arranged in a column with multiple rows, to be used in concert with the Time Period variable, where any missing values can be interpolated and internally fitted to a linear model. As an example, suppose the following series of time periods and values exist (Time 1 = 10, Time 2 = 20, Time 5 = 50); we can then use the MTLinearInterpolation and MTCubicSpline models to determine the missing value(s).

Vesting Year

This is the number of years or partial years in which the option is still in the vesting period and cannot be executed. This vesting year period can range from zero to the maturity of the option (the latter being a no-vesting American option, whereas the latter reverts to a European option), and if the value is somewhere in between, it becomes a Bermudan option with blackout and vesting periods.

Volatilities (Series)

This is a series of annualized volatilities (see the definition of Volatilities for more details) arranged in a row with multiple columns going across, for use in the valuation of risky debt and callable bonds or bond spreads. Each value in the series must be positive.

Volatility

This is the annualized volatility of equity or stock prices; it has to be a positive value, and can be computed in various ways—for example, exponentially weighted moving average (EWMA), generalized autoregressive conditional heteroskedasticity (GARCH), logarithmic relative returns, and so forth. Review the volatility examples and models in the Modeling Toolkit to obtain details on these methodologies.

Volatility 0, 1, 2

These volatility variables are computed exactly as discussed in the Volatility definition, but the difference is that for Volatility 0, this is the default volatility used in a customized option model with changing volatilities (i.e., if the changing volatilities input is left empty, this Volatility 0 will be used as the single repeated volatility in the model), whereas Volatility 1 and 2 are the volatilities for the first underlying asset and the second underlying asset in a multiple asset option model. These values have to be positive values.

Volatility FX or Volatility Foreign Exchange Rate

This is the annualized volatility of foreign exchange rates (see the Volatility definition for the various methods applicable in valuing this parameter), and this value has to be positive.

Volatility Ratio

This variable is used in the Merton Jump-Diffusion models, where this ratio is the percentage of volatility that can be explained by the jumps, and is typically a positive value not exceeding 1.

WACC

The weighted average cost of capital (WACC) is the average cost of capital from common equity, debt (after tax), and preferred equity, all weighted by the amount obtained from each source. It has to be a positive value, and when used in perpetual firm continuity values with growth rates, WACC has to be greater than the growth rate parameter.

Warrants

This is the positive integer number indicative of the total number of warrants issued by the company.

Working Capital

This is also known as the net working capital of a company and can be determined using the company's balance sheet, and is typically a positive dollar or currency value (while zero is a rare but possible occurrence).

Worst Case

This is the worst-case scenario's dollar or currency value of a project or asset within a one-year time frame, and is used in the implied volatility (volatility to probability) estimation. When used together with the Best Case and Expected Value input parameters, this worst case value has to be less than these two latter inputs.

X

This is the ubiquitous random variable X, and is used in multiple locations. When used in probability distributions, it denotes the X value on the x-axis of the probability distribution or the specific outcome of a distribution (e.g., in tossing a coin 10 times, where the probability of getting heads is 50%, we can compute the exact probability of getting exactly four heads, and in this case, $X = 4$). X is typically a positive value (continuous values in continuous distributions, and discrete positive values, including zero, for discrete probability distributions).

Z1 and Z2

These are the standard normal z-scores used in a bivariate normal distribution. These values can be either negative or positive.

Zero Bond Price

This is the price of a zero coupon bond, used in the valuation of callable and risky debt and for pricing commodity options, and this parameter has to be a positive value.

Zero Yields

This is the yield of a zero coupon bond, used in the valuation of callable and risky debt, and this parameter has to be a positive value.

INDEX

BOOKS BY DR. JOHNATHAN MUN

See: www.amazon.com/author/johnathanmun

Real Options Analysis: Tools and Techniques for Valuing Strategic Investments & Decisions, 3rd Edition
680 Pages (2016)
ISBN: 978-1530075114
Thomson–Shore

Certified Quantitative Risk Management (CQRM): Readings
736 Pages (2015)
ISBN: 978-1515114406
ROV Press

Modeling Risk: Applying Monte Carlo Risk Simulation, Strategic Real Options Analysis, Stochastic Forecasting, and Portfolio Optimization, 3rd Edition
1112 Pages (2015)
ISBN: 978-0470592212
Thomson–Shore

Certified Quantitative Risk Management (CQRM): Case Studies
352 Pages (2015)
ISBN: 978-1515125549
ROV Press

Advanced Analytical Models in ROV Modeling Toolkit: Over 800 Models and 300 Applications from the Basel Accords to Wall Street and Beyond
760 Pages (2016)
ISBN: 978-1533649515
Thomson–Shore

Risk Simulator Guide
216 Pages (2015)
ISBN: 978-1515273639
ROV Press

Credit Engineering for Bankers (with Morton Glantz)
529 Pages (2010)
ISBN: 978-0123785855
Elsevier Academic Press

PEAT: Project Economics Analysis Tool
348 Pages (2015)
ISBN: 978-1515273530
ROV Press

The Banker's Handbook on Credit Risk
(with Morton Glantz)
420 Pages (2008)
ISBN: 978-0123736666
Elsevier Science

Real Options SLS Guide
152 Pages (2015)
ISBN: 978-1515273677
ROV Press

CQRM Training
250 Pages (2015)
ISBN: Restricted
ROV Press

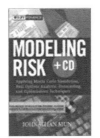

Modeling Risk Applying
Monte Carlo Simulation, Real
Options Analysis, Stochastic
Forecasting, and Optimization
610 Pages (2006)
ISBN: 0-471-78900-3
Wiley Finance

Modeling Risk: Applying Monte
Carlo Risk Simulation, Strategic
Real Options, Stochastic
Forecasting, Portfolio
Optimization, 2nd Ed.
1112 Pages (2005)
ISBN: 978-1943290000
Wiley Finance

Applied Risk Analysis:
Moving Beyond
Uncertainty
460 Pages (2003)
ISBN: 0-471-47885-7
Wiley Finance

Real Options Analysis: Tools and
Techniques for Valuing Strategic
Investments & Decisions, 2nd
Edition
670 Pages (2005)
ISBN: 978-0471747483
Wiley Finance

Real Options Analysis Course:
Business Cases and Software
Applications
360 Pages (2003)
ISBN: 0-471-43001-3
Wiley Finance

Advanced Analytical Models:
Over 800 Models and 300
Applications from the Basel
Accords to Wall Street and
Beyond
1002 Pages (2008)
ISBN: 978-0470179215
Wiley Finance

Real Options Analysis: Tools and
Techniques for Valuing Strategic
Investments & Decisions
416 Pages (2002)
ISBN: 0-471-25696-X
Wiley Finance

Valuing Employee Stock Options:
Under 2004 FAS 123
320 Pages (2004)
ISBN: 0-471-70512-8
Wiley Finance

Managing Your
Finances God's Way
128 Pages (2015)
ISBN: 978-1515212362
ROV Press

Printed in Great Britain
by Amazon